Wall Art

ARTISTRY IN FIBER VOL. 1

Wall Art

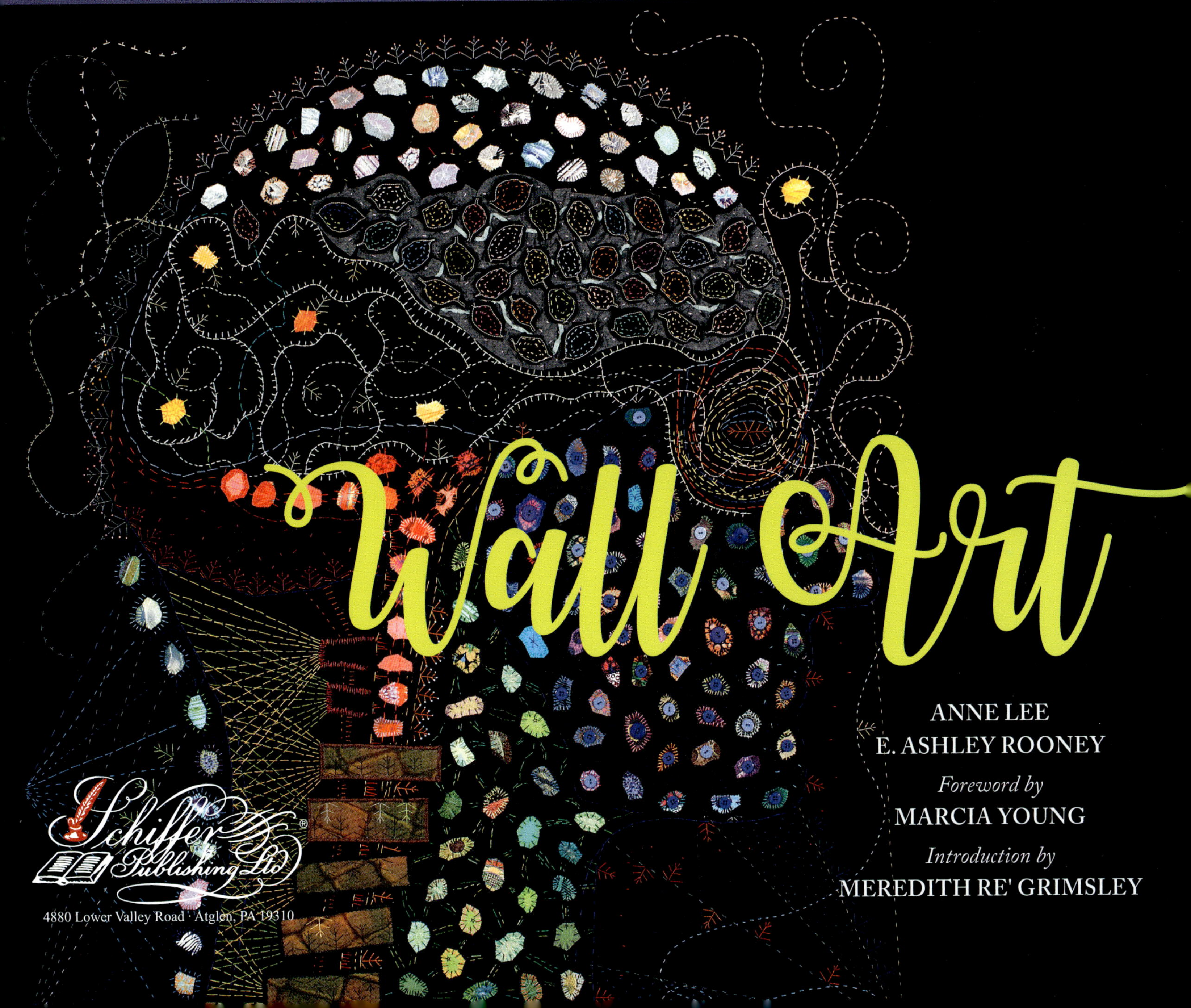

ANNE LEE

E. ASHLEY ROONEY

Foreword by

MARCIA YOUNG

Introduction by

MEREDITH RE' GRIMSLEY

Schiffer Publishing Ltd

4880 Lower Valley Road · Atglen, PA 19310

Other Schiffer Books by the Authors:

Artistry in Fiber, Vol. 2: Sculpture, Anne Lee and E. Ashley Rooney, foreword by Lois Russell, introduction by Adrienne Sloane, ISBN 978-0-7643-5342-0

Encaustic Art in the Twenty-First Century, Anne Lee and E. Ashley Rooney, foreword by Kim Bernard, afterword by Ellen Koment, ISBN 978-0-7643-5023-8

The Contemporary Art of Nature: Mammals, E. Ashley Rooney, foreword by Donna Dodson, introduction by Carel P. Brest van Kempen, ISBN 978-0-7643-4786-3

Other Schiffer Books on Related Subjects:

Contemporary International Tapestry, Carol K. Russell, ISBN 978-0-7643-4869-3

Studio Craft as Career: A Guide to Achieving Excellence in Art-Making, Paul J. Stankard, ISBN 978-0-7643-5252-2

Weave Leno: In-Depth Instructions for All Levels, with 7 Projects, Martha Reeves, ISBN 978-0-7643-5101-3

Library of Congress Control Number: 2017934254

Designed by Brenda McCallum

Type set in NewsGothic/Adobe Caslon Pro

Front cover image: Ann Harwell *(Dick Cicone)*. Back cover images, clockwise from left: Elena Stokes, Sue Hotchkis (*Pool,* detail. Felt, silk, scrim, and velvet. 57" × 22" × 3". 2014), Michael Radyk. Front endsheet: Rowen Schussheim-Anderson *(Ogy Blazevic)*. Title page: Diane Siebels *(Scott Smith)*. Pages 3–4: Jennifer Davies *(Christopher Gardner)*. Page 9: Alex Friedman, Jim Arendt *(Stacey Evans)*, Glenda Richardson *(John Woo)*. Page 10: Jessica Wohl, George-Ann Bowers *(Dana M. Davis)*, Chiachio & Giannone (*Ciudad Frondosa* [Leafy City]. Cotton threads, wool, and embroidery floss on fabric. 9.18' × 17.7'. 2011–2012) *(Daniel Kiblisky)*. Page 12: Susan Hersey *(Robert H. Hersey)*. Page 13: Helen Cowans. Page 214: Gaye S. Lasher *(Wes Magyar)*. Page 223: Ida-Lovisa Rudolfsson *(Hendrik Zeitler)*. Back endsheet: Jette Clover *(Pol Leemans)*.

ISBN: 978-0-7643-5304-8
Printed in China

Published by Schiffer Publishing, Ltd.
4880 Lower Valley Road
Atglen, PA 19310
Phone: (610) 593-1777; Fax: (610) 593-2002
E-mail: Info@schifferbooks.com
Web: www.schifferbooks.com

For our complete selection of fine books on this and related subjects, please visit our website at www.schifferbooks.com. You may also write for a free catalog.

Schiffer Publishing's titles are available at special discounts for bulk purchases for sales promotions or premiums. Special editions, including personalized covers, corporate imprints, and excerpts, can be created in large quantities for special needs. For more information, contact the publisher.

We are always looking for people to write books on new and related subjects. If you have an idea for a book, please contact us at proposals@schifferbooks.com.

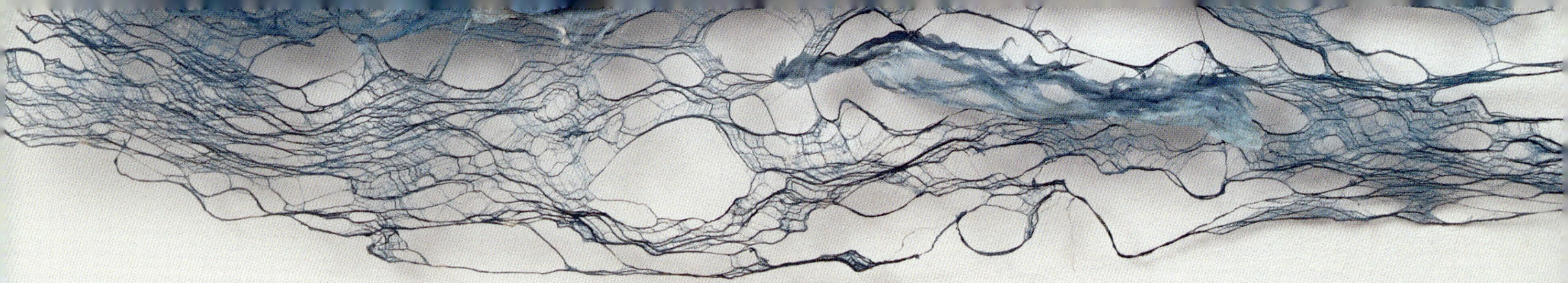

CONTENTS

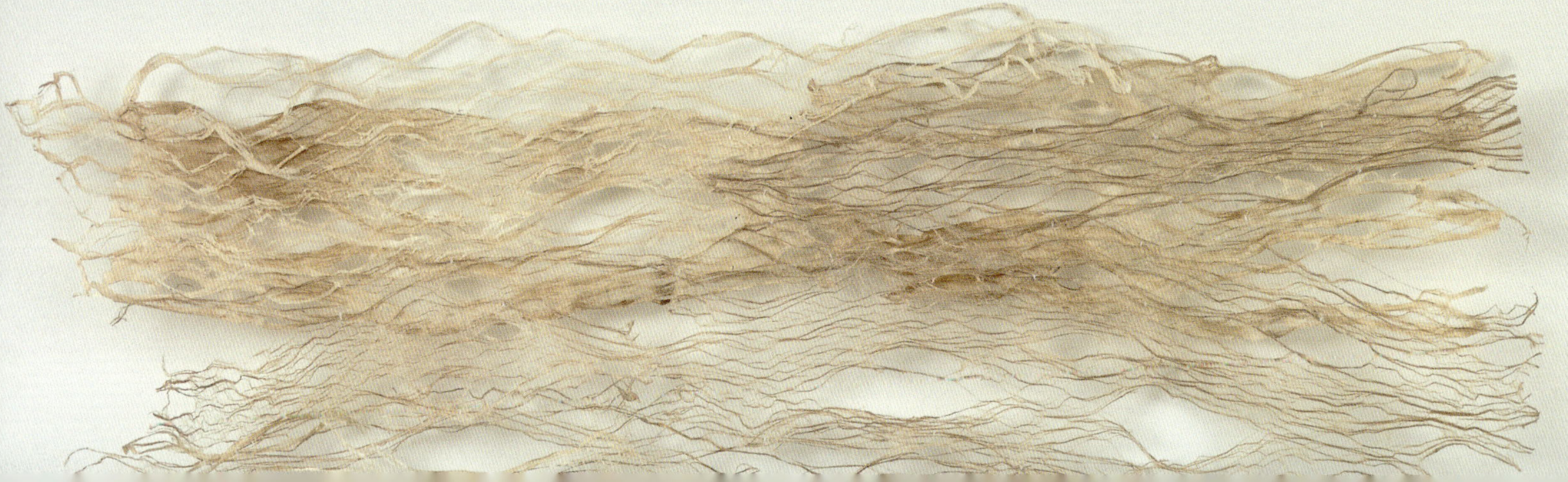

FOREWORD

The Humanizing Force of Fiber Art *Marcia Young*

As editor-in-chief of *Fiber Art Now* magazine, I have immersed myself in fiber art for years, interviewing, writing about, and learning from countless artists over time. Even so, I still occasionally find myself at an art museum, standing in front of what I know empirically is an important work, but unable to make a connection to it. Has this ever happened to you? Perhaps by virtue of the political statement of its time, the techniques it employed, the watershed moment in history that it captures, or maybe its status as a recent "discovery" from what used to be considered the exotic and unknown, it is clearly "important." And yet, how we experience the work feels like an academic exercise in Socratic monologue.

On a recent museum day, I had such an experience: As I stared at the work, asking and answering myself questions to draw out ideas and underlying presumptions, it occurred to me how far I felt from the artist's work. I was ready for the pilgrimage, but was keenly aware of the work being separate from the viewer, requiring me to make those connections and find the intended meaning—at least *my* meaning.

With any visual art experience, it is up to us to inquire and answer these questions for ourselves as we make our way through the galleries. I may peer into some galleries and can tell from afar that I'm not attracted to the work; I anticipate the actual "work" I will be doing to make my own sense of it. Still, my curiosity forces me to attempt understanding, pushing me beyond my initial response. I study it, absorb it, parse its elements, and, finally, as I exit the gallery, I may be relieved that I have made some sense of the work.

On one such day, it occurred to me how I might have felt differently if the work had been fiber-based. Fiber art is unique in that it's refreshingly free of pretension and doesn't rely on expectations of the viewers' ken. Although fiber art is often criticized for being preoccupied with materiality and technique, I find that those very qualities provide viewers with a gateway to the work. Fiber viewers are highly engaged because the materiality gives us an initial connection, before the inner Socratic monologue has a chance to begin.

If, as Howard Risatti noted in *A Theory of Craft: Function and Aesthetic Expression*, "the purpose of art is to try to communicate,"[1] then fiber arts have an advantage over many other mediums. Although the best work in fiber, like any art, has observations, themes, or concepts at its core, the chosen materials and techniques give us a lifeline to that meaning. As Emily Zilber, curator of Contemporary Decorative Arts at the Museum of Fine Arts, Boston, states, "Many craft-based artists actively investigate ways in which we as viewers can be immersed in an object rather than adjacent to or presiding over it."[2]

E. Ashley Rooney and Anne Lee have joined their extensive experience sets together in creating the first of this unique series, researching and assembling a diverse group of fiber artists and their work. Rooney, the editor of over fifty books specializing in contemporary art and architecture, and Lee, with her broad experience in researching, curating, and writing about exhibitions, are poised to bring us an approachable and humanizing experience with fiber art. I encourage you to let yourself get lost in these pages.

Fiber art impacts us, doesn't require anything of us, and yet it gives generously. It is a humanizing force in the art world, and for that I am deeply grateful. *Artistry in Fiber, Volume 1: Wall Art* will provide a bridge to inspiration and new understanding as you absorb the images and artist sentiments, gathering them up to take along on your own journey.

Notes

1. Risatti, Howard. *A Theory of Craft: Function and Aesthetic Expression*. Chapel Hill: University of North Carolina Press, 2007.
2. Zilber, Emily. *Crafted: Objects in Flux*. Boston: MFA Publications, 2015.

PREFACE

For centuries, artists have explored, explained, and enhanced our world. While that concept has not altered, today's artists are more apt to break with tradition, reject classic notions of beauty, and express their inner world. Many old definitions of art have become obsolete. Traditional methods, processes, and materials are evolving in fascinating and sometimes perplexing directions. Contemporary art is fluid, dynamic, challenging, and open to multiple interpretations. The resurgence of fiber art beautifully illustrates these trends. Through much of its history, fiber came exclusively from plants and animals and was crafted—mostly by women—into domestic and utilitarian functions. The Feminist movement appropriated fiber art in the 1970s, recognizing its versatility as well as its ability to yield a vast range of expression.

Artists today expand their use of natural materials, such as cowhide and plant stalks, and explore unexpected synthetics—strands of acrylic paint, artificial hair, plastic, fiberglass, tape, and wire. They combine different fiber techniques together in a single piece, braiding, tacking, weaving, and knitting in seemingly endless variations. They push technical processes, whether knitting with glass or felting with silk. They cross-pollinate mediums, incorporating photographs, paint, metal, and all manner of found or repurposed objects. They explore social, political, economic, and environmental issues, as well as tell their own personal stories. They turn inward, they look back, they look to the future.

The language of textiles is rich in metaphors, many of which allude to connection and conversation. Just by picking up a strand, whether it is a knotted strand of cotton fiber or a shiny strand of copper wire, fiber artists begin to make a physical mark to tell their story. For us, the artists of today not only tell the stories of today but also create the excitement for tomorrow. Like today's authors, they are delineating our stories for future generations. They differ from state to state, country to country. To find them, we talked to gallery owners, museum curators, and the artists themselves; read fiber magazines and books; researched textile societies and organizations; read bios, searched awards, perused exhibitions. We explored the work of literally hundreds of artists.

Our intention in undertaking a three-volume series exploring contemporary fiber art was to offer a fresh look at the thought-provoking and insightful ways in which today's fiber artists have interpreted life in this century. We wanted those who would bring strength, excitement, passion, and variety to this series. We believe we have found them.

Join us, and discover an endlessly fascinating and evolving medium that has always been part of our history and will be part of our future.

ACKNOWLEDGMENTS

When we decided to compile a book on contemporary fiber art, we quickly realized what an enormous and potentially daunting project we had taken on. One book could not begin to adequately showcase the amazing creative energy of fiber artists and the fascinating directions they are pushing the medium. With three books planned—Wall Art, Sculpture, and Wearable Art—our year-long journey began.

We discovered an artistic community that is close-knit and supportive—perhaps because of the warm and tactile nature of the medium itself. Artists were eager to laud and to share the work of others, offer suggestions for avenues to explore, and check in on our progress. Our foreword and introduction writers, Marcia Young and Meredith Re′ Grimsley, each offered valuable insights into the ever-evolving world of fiber art, and we thank them for rising to the challenge.

INTRODUCTION

The Matter of Fiber *Meredith Re' Grimsley*

Hello, explorer of fiber art. I am Meredith, a forty-year-old with a wonderful husband, two children, and a dog; I am a professor of fabric design and a fiber artist. I have been professionally addicted to textiles / fiber art / fabric design / surface design for twenty years, but it all began much further back before I knew what I was doing was called art.

Artists, I have looked at your work and have deep respect and admiration for all of you. Thank you for your art and your words. What a beautiful tribe we occupy!

Reader, you may be asking yourself, what is fiber art? The organization Friends of Fiber Art International defines fiber art as contemporary art that cultivates "one-of-a-kind works . . . constructed of flexible materials using textile techniques."[1] I would add to this definition that contemporary fiber art is conceptually driven and committed to the materials, processes, and craftsmanship associated with traditional craft.

How do we actually explore contemporary fiber art? What does it mean? For those of us featured in these pages and for fiber-engaged readers, delving into this book is a nuanced experience informed by years of practice and familiarity with the materials and/or processes of fiber. Others of you may be pioneering into this new world with what you think is inexperience, a lack of knowledge, perhaps fear, or the assumption that this medium is inferior in some way. Let me remind you of an amazing fact: fabric and thread are essential to human life and are the most familiar material known to human kind. Mildred Constantine and Laurel Reuter, in their book *The Whole Cloth,* say this about fabric and fiber art:

> Cloth. What an elegant substance it is, at play with the breeze, in combat with the wind, protecting and wrapping and shielding and comforting. Like a seductive woman, sometimes it is bold and sometimes it is barely there. Cloth is the stuff of mystery for making costumes and stage sets, wedding veils and death shrouds. Even children use lengths of cloth when they first begin to play dress-up. Cloth, that old silent companion of the human race . . .[2]

The processes represented by this book have accompanied us through thousands of years. From the day we are born to the day we die, we are wrapped in fiber. It has been a second skin: ushered us into this world; kept us warm; made us fashionable; embraced us in fear, love, memory, and nostalgia; adorned us in ceremony; ornamented the spaces we occupy; been passed down through families in heirloom and practice; and will usher us out when we pass from this world. Our interaction with textiles is the longest sustained physical relationship we have in our lives. Other than our own body, it is the only material that will always accompany us through life, ranging from disposable to sacred. Further, fiber art is made from materials that are perceived to be delicate or fragile. Yet, when a fiber art work is made, the materials can withstand incredible physical manipulation, harsh chemical environments, and extreme temperatures; the fiber is beaten, stomped, tied, knotted, tangled, pierced with needles, and still remains strong or becomes stronger. This is simply awesome. I am moved by the metaphorical capabilities of fiber as an artistic medium and as a conduit to the subconscious.

So now what? I have a diverse group of artists from varied backgrounds about whom to write. They work in numerous disciplines with different approaches, resulting in wide-ranging solutions under the umbrella of fiber art. My approach came to this: I read every single artist statement within this book and let the common themes rise to the surface. Thus, the most intrinsic qualities of contemporary fiber art are revealed. The amazing part is that we are all connected by thoughts that are uniquely highlighted by fiber art and its processes. Instead of looking at and interpreting the images that follow, I dug deeply into the words. I have gathered some of them together to bring to light what I see as the common trends among this group of artists and, frankly, all fiber artists past and present: Touch; Tradition and the Love of Craft; Contemplation/Memory; Time and Place; and Language.

Touch

By nature, fiber art is a contact sport. All the artists in this book have the connection to touch. Each of us, no matter what the final presentation or driving idea, has a physical relationship with the materials we have chosen to utilize. Alex Friedman reflects that fiber art "is a slow art that allows time for meditation and focus. It also satisfies four of [the] five senses." Fiber art calls upon the viewer to engage with direct or perceived touch. Whether texture is actual or visual, fiber processes summon tactile curiosity for artist and viewer. Leisa Rich describes that she seeks "to re-communicate with [her] audience in reaction to our disconnected society. Creating art that invites play empowers viewers." Touch through materiality can be significant conceptually, as in Jim Arendt's work: "My materials purposely reflect the lives and struggles of the people I come from." Others have described the supple movement and sensual qualities of fiber, like Luisa F. Gil Fandino, whose work "captivates and encourages curiosity and tactile seduction." We all comment, directly or ambiguously, about the corporeal experiences as one of the more valuable aspects of making and encountering fiber art.

Tradition and the Love of Craft

Fiber artists seem to approach the idea of tradition in extremes—with reverence, amendment, or subversion. Indeed, the traditions set before us as fiber artists have accompanied the human race for as long as recorded history and before. What a beautiful connection to our ancestry! Some artists, like Carolina Yrarrázaval, revive tradition so that it will not be lost in an ever-technologically-evolving world. Yrarrázaval says that she has "devoted [herself] to investigating traditional textile techniques from diverse cultures, especially pre-Columbian techniques . . . [She seeks] ways to speak of the beauty and dignity that we have lost through the decades."

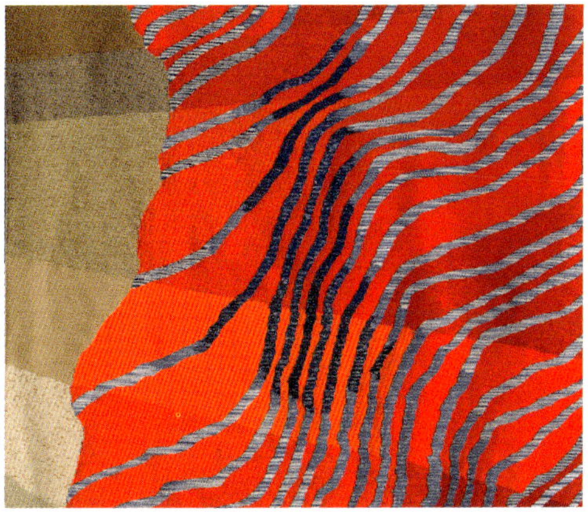

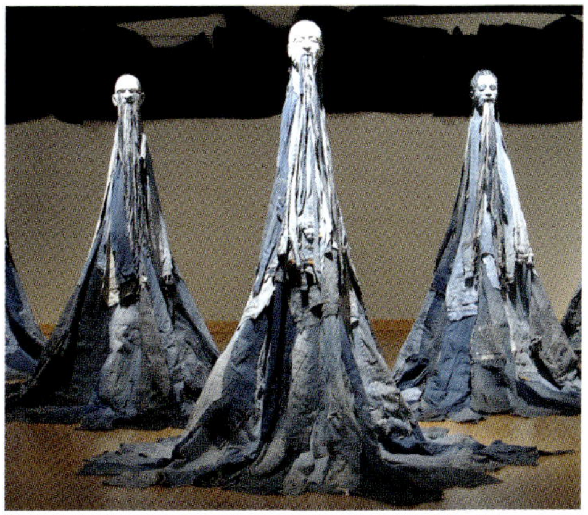

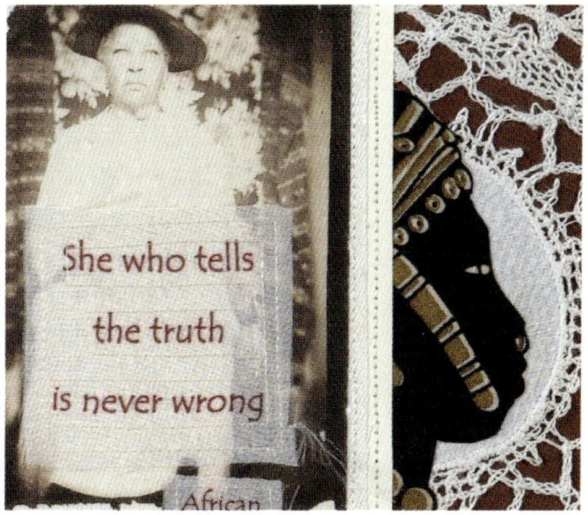

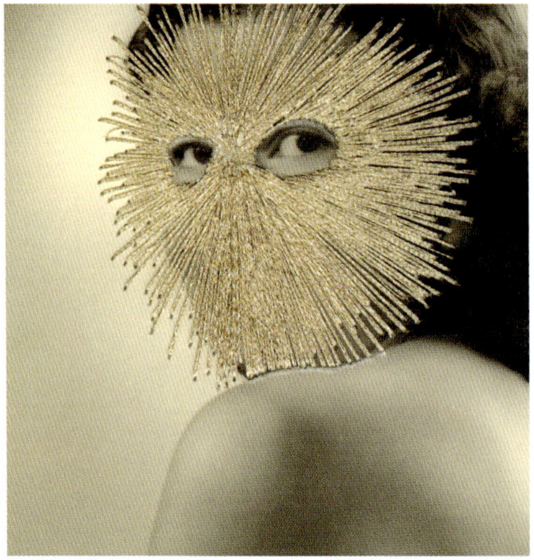 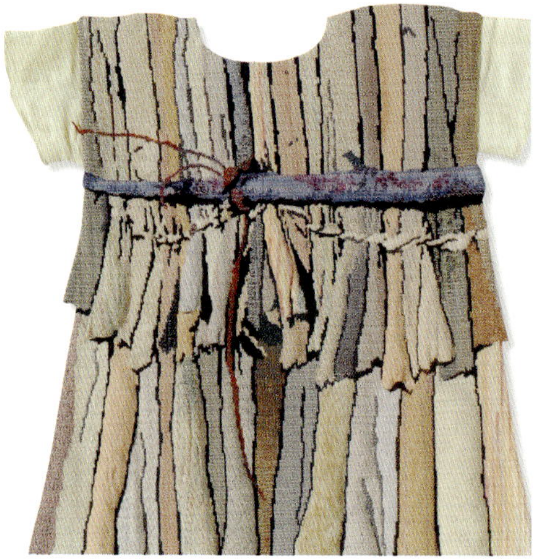 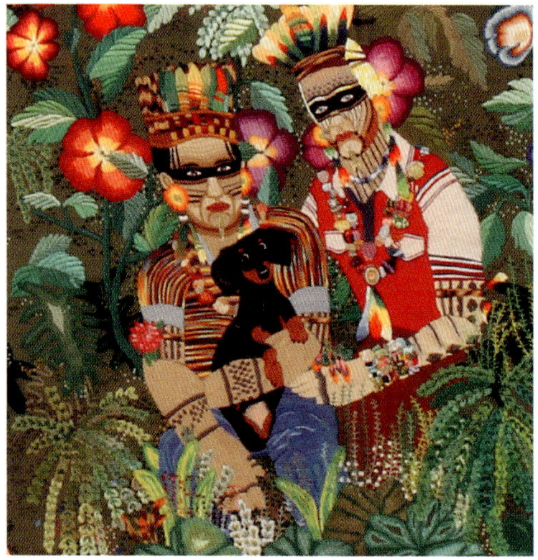

Others of us learn all the rules and quickly seek to break them. We love our fiber roots but crave invention, innovation, and rebellion. Michelle Browne puts it well when she proclaims, "I am very interested in experimenting, pushing myself, and my work, in new directions untethered by tradition." Further, many fiber artists confront the long-held notion of domesticity through a contemporary feminist lens. Artist Jessica Wohl uses "processes such as quilting and embroidery to subvert the notions of comfort and familiarity we often experience with domestic materials." No matter if the artist is celebrating, breaking beyond, or constructing a critical argument against tradition and craft, rest assured that these artists are all aware of where they stand on the issue.

Contemplation/Memory

Of all the areas I explored, I found that nearly all of the artists in this book allude to contemplation as one of the most vital aspects of implementing fiber art practices. Fiber art evokes memories. It tells stories. It holds historical residue. Terry Jarrard-Dimond describes her work as "evidence . . . every moment as we live our lives . . . creates a pathway for connection, knowledge, understanding, and memory." By busying their hands, artists are able to be more mindful of their interior. Through elements that are both structurally and metaphorically, as Jennifer Davies puts it, "revealed and obscured," many fiber artists recognize that the unique somatic qualities of fiber allow for meditation on spiritual and emotional levels. Other artists connect with fiber as a material that helps them to repair and recover from an overwhelming heartbreak. Pinky/MM Bass reveals that she has engaged in "handwork all [her] life and the comfort of working that way . . . helped [her] through a very long grieving period." Because fiber exercises the sense of touch and familiarity most viscerally of all mediums, it provides an incomparable platform for coping with grief, loss, or lost memory. Diane Siebels expresses that she stitches "with both hands so it becomes very rhythmic and meditative." Bilateral movement indicative of fiber art techniques helps us to relax, release anxiety, and connect to ourselves in the moment.

Time and Place

From what I've read here and what I know of my peers, fiber artists are deeply rooted to time and place. They may love nature, a city, a foreign land or culture, and home. George-Ann Bowers says, "My work is, in a way, a journal of places I have visited, where I see weaving patterns . . . [it] celebrates the infinite intricacies of the natural world." Or, fiber artists are activists who comment on the state of humanity through social/environmental concerns and/or identity. Margaret Scott describes that "As a visual artist, my work is created from the particularity of who I am: a black woman, a feminist, a daughter, a mother, an activist, and a British textile artist." Chiachio & Giannone "transform a handcraft art . . . traditionally known and associated with women . . . into the dual work of a male couple," which "[demonstrates] that two men could access this world with absolute freedom." Often the two concepts of time and place are inextricably linked. Merill Comeau brings together "incongruous fibers redolent of past lives . . . These cast-offs reflect memories of lives lived, social constructs of identity and class, our speeded up consumer cycle, and global issues of sustainability." Lastly, fiber artists are keenly aware of the ephemeral. We understand our own place in time. Our life span—birth, death, decay—all informs our exploration of fiber art.

Language

As Susan Klebanoff says, "Fiber is the universal language of all cultures." Fiber laws hold steady: no matter what it is made of, a weft is a weft, a stitch is a stitch, a technique is . . . you get the idea. Not that there is only one way for fiber processes to exist, but rather that a common knowledge transcends words, gesture, and experience. Susan T. Avila tells us that there is a "historical precedent for reading a textile; before written communication, the semiotic patterns and colors of textiles provided pivotal information about culture and social beliefs." Fundamental elements and principles of fiber are constant: patterns are read, interpreted, and entwined with technique and material, resulting in forms which we can all recognize, read, and comprehend. Sara Impey tells us that she likes "to experiment with the visual, textural, and structural properties of fabric and thread to play with language, often commenting on social or personal issues, sometimes with a dash of humor."

Another vital undercurrent of the language of fiber art is the artist's connection to the matriarch. How many of us first learned of fiber techniques from our grandmothers or mothers? Techniques have been passed down through family tradition, cultural heritage, or as practical survival skills, if not creative ones. Anna Hergert "was exposed to fiber art at an early age . . . [her] maternal grandmother gently guided [her] in embroidery at age four." If we did not learn of these techniques from an important person in our life, many associate these processes with particular relationships. Fiber art, because of its shared language, forges new communities at an intrinsic, profound level: what I earlier called our tribe.

Conclusion

Fiber artists are great organizers. We are not generally confronted by a "blank canvas" to figure out our next idea. We often end up looking at a collection of pieces, swatches, yarns, or materials—salvaged or created—which we have handled in some interesting way. Then, we rearrange them into beautiful stories. As Melissa Sobotka states, "Fiber adds a texture and richness to my work that I did not find in other mediums."

Fiber art currently exists in a paradoxical duality: fiber makers love their identity within the medium as separate but equal from contemporary art, but they also feel an urgency to be recognized/legitimized/homogenized into contemporary art, thus breaking down old barriers of art and craft. Our tribe loves that we can slip in and out of both art and craft realms like a wisp of silk. Whether seen as a means capable of communicating what we feel we have lost, what we strive to overcome, or simply as a process from the past, fiber art will survive and evolve. Glenda Richardson's fiber work tells "a personal story whose themes have universal meaning [including] physical and spiritual healing, family and cultural heritage, memorializing loved ones, rites of passage as they relate to women, and the spiritual aspects of love and sensuality." If we assume that the human race will continue to crave touch, tradition, rebellion, contemplation, communication, and companionship, fiber art and its myriad of manifestations will thrive and be explored for many more lifetimes to come.

Notes

1. www.friendsoffiberart.org/what.php
2. Constantine, Mildred, and Laurel Reuter. *The Whole Cloth.* New York: Monacelli Press, 1997, 9.

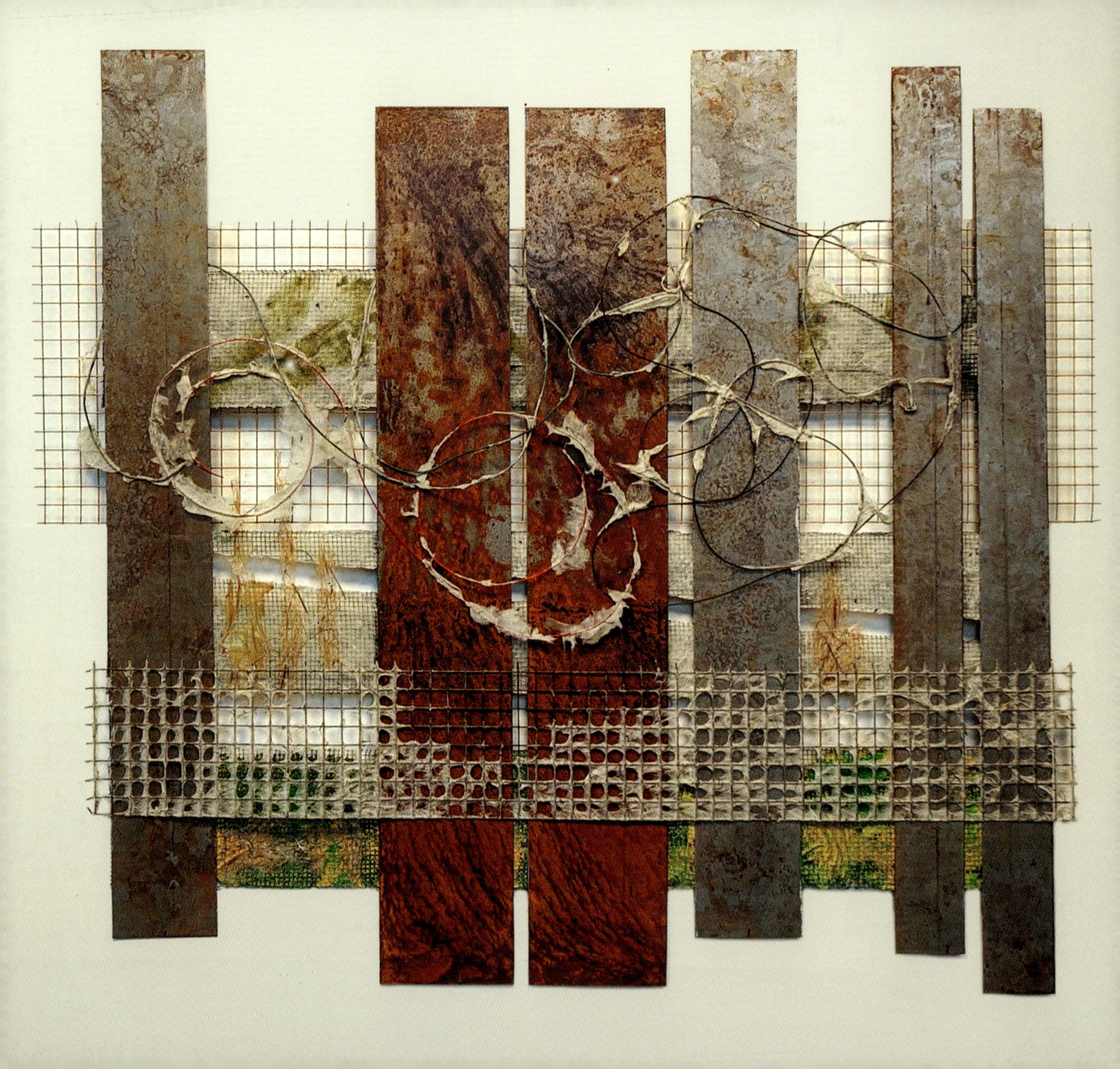

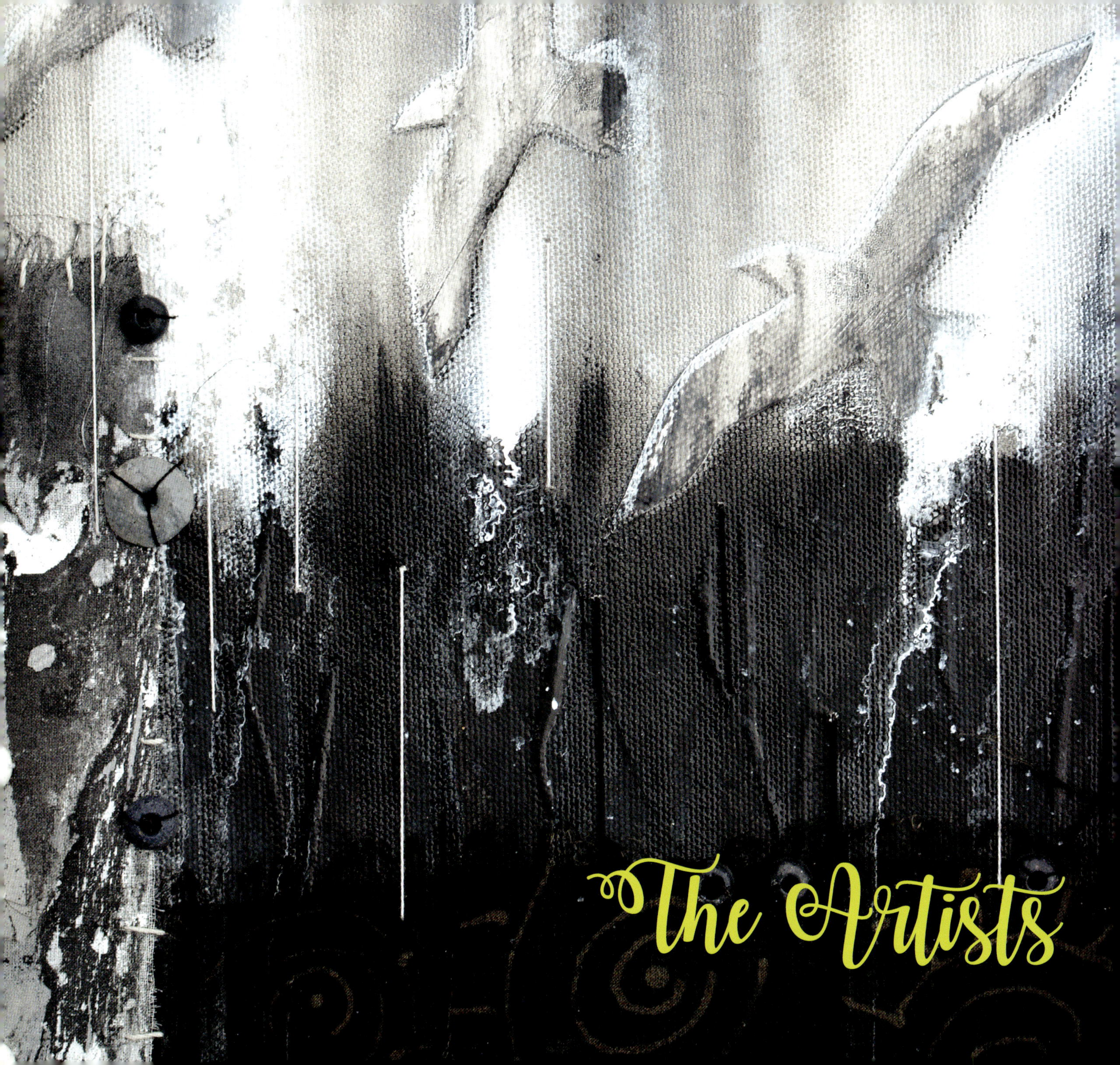

The Artists

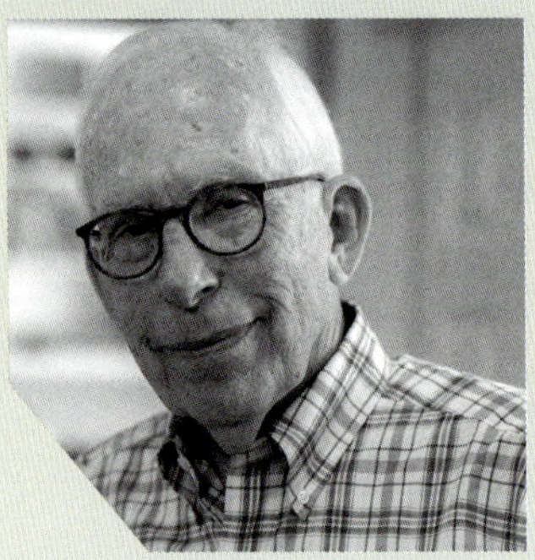

Klaus Anselm

Keswick, Virginia

I started weaving in 1999, about the time I retired from practicing medicine. Always interested in textiles, I found a workshop on weaving techniques at a local art center in Colorado and was soon drawn to the art of tapestry weaving as an expression of my imagination.

My tapestries, woven in wool on cotton warp, reflect inspirations from travel, nature, and contemporary designs. In particular, images of the Southwest with the stunningly simple compositions of sky, country, and architecture influenced my work. Lasting impressions from rafting trips through the Grand Canyon have also found their way into several of my tapestries. Most of all, I owe much of what I do to the teaching, mentoring, and friendship of James Koehler, who is missed by many.

Weaving tapestries is my passion; it means everything to me; it changed me as a person and allows me to see the world from a different perspective.

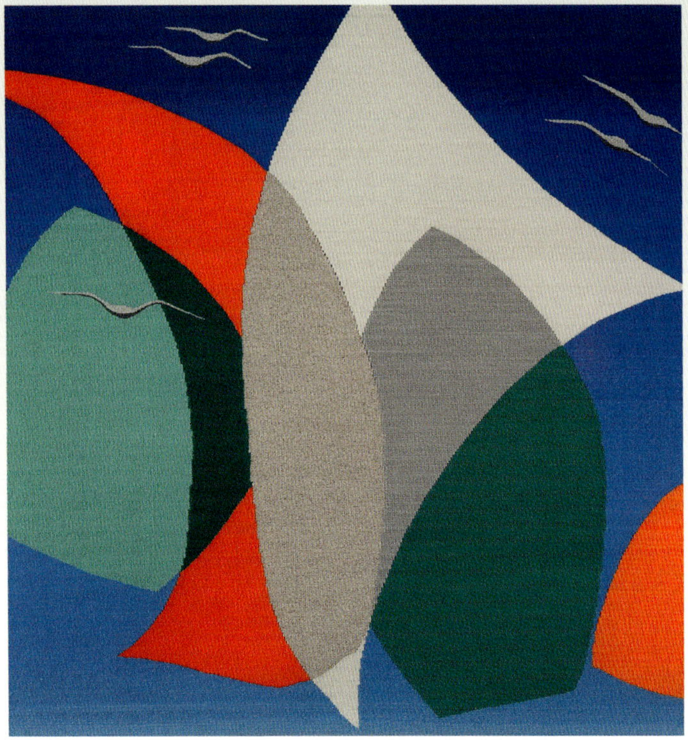

Sunday Morning. Wool on cotton. 58" × 31". 2004.

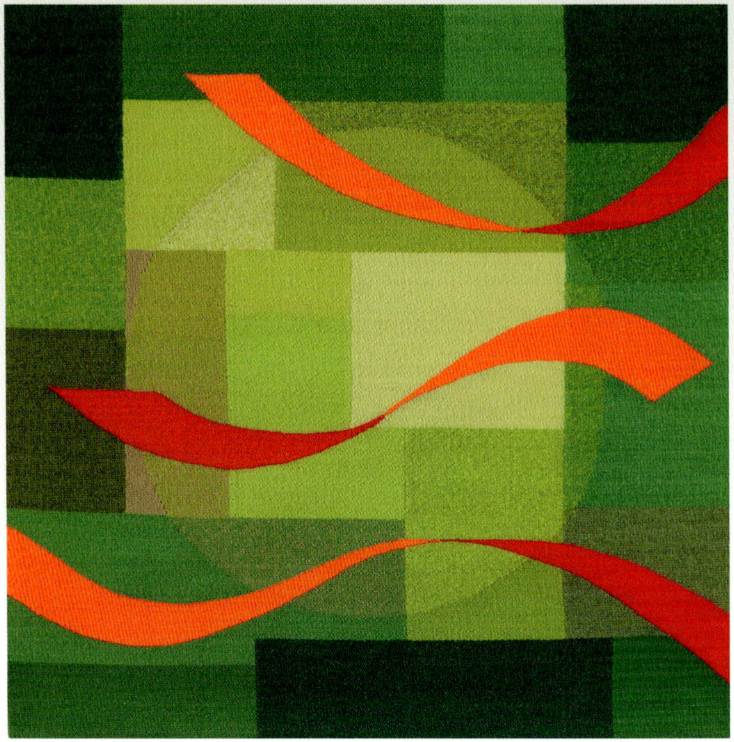

Music in Space. Wool on cotton. 31" × 31". 2012.

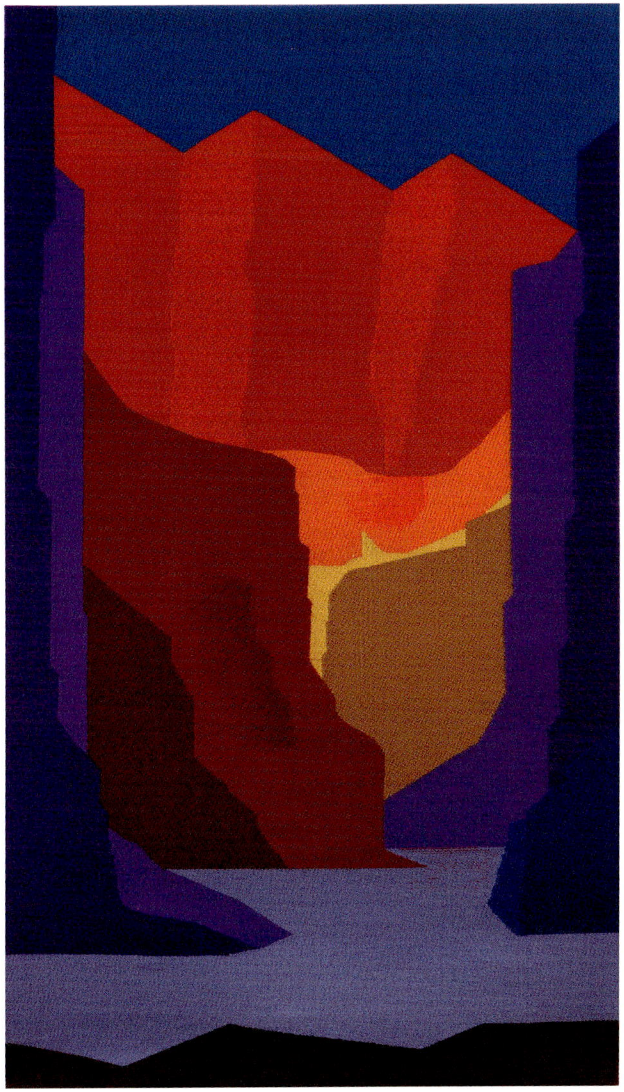

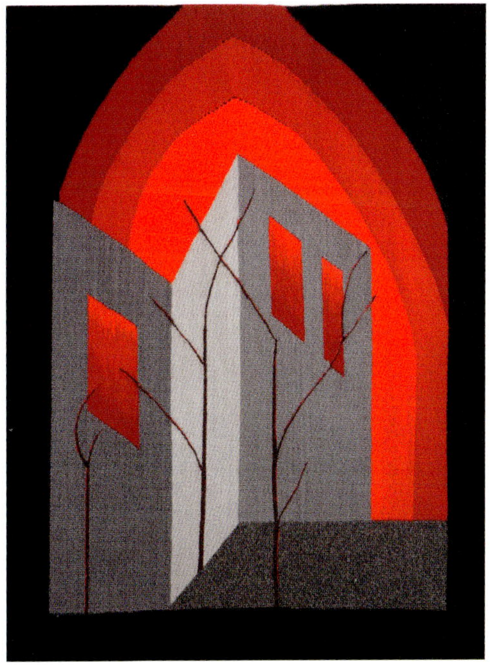

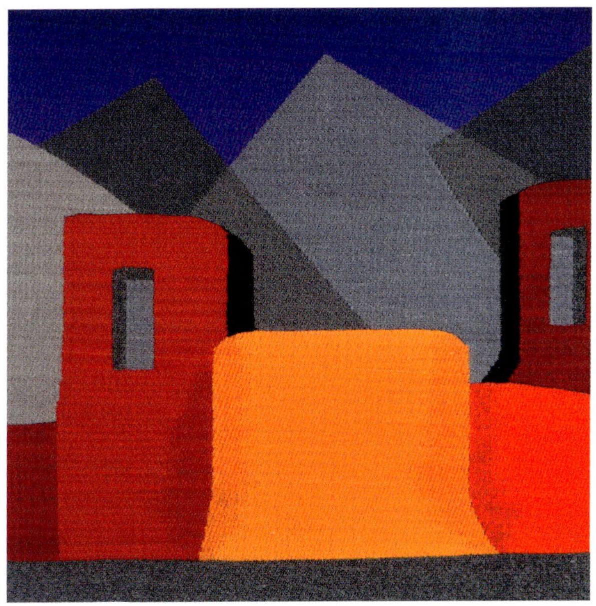

▲ *Camp 50 Miles.* Wool on cotton. 60" × 36". 2011.

◂ *Firestorm.* Wool on cotton. 35" × 29". 2013.

➤ *Look to the West.* Wool on cotton. 24" × 24". 2015.

All images courtesy of Stacey Evans.

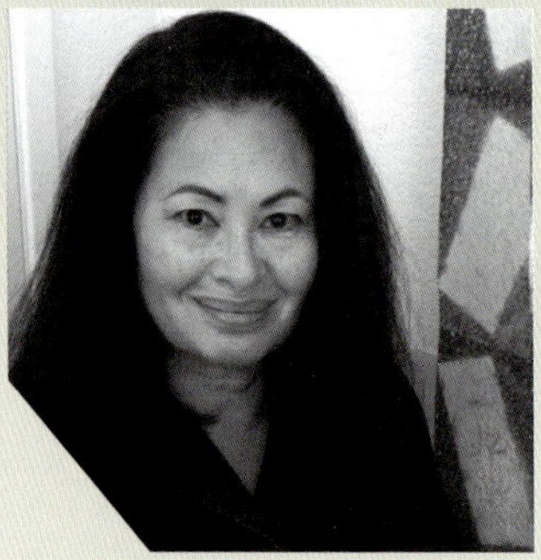

Photo: Bill Abramson.

Lucy Arai

Oakley, California &
Washington, DC

Through each stitch my fingers sew, I feel a deep reverence for the connection between all that was and all that can be. *Sashiko*, a utilitarian stitching used for reinforcing and quilting fabric, and *temari*, geometrically embroidered handballs dating from the Heian Period (794 to 1185 CE), are Japanese textile arts transmitted to me by my late Tokyo uncle and Japanese mother. These traditions give form and voice to those things for which I have no words to express.

My work with needle and thread embodies the dualism of my Japanese and European-American self into dynamic objects of art. They connect me to the stitching traditions of cultures around the world and throughout history, many of which are now at risk for survival.

Innovations transform my work with spontaneous alterations; over time, fluency and refinements emerge through practice. Today, the integrity of the *sashiko* and *temari* are retained with continuity and respect for relationships and the traditions that have been transmitted to me; the forms, however, are non-traditional.

It is my belief that the strength of a stitch to quilt and reinforce material is like the interdependent and resilient nature of life. For this reason, I stitch and reach out into the world to share my work with the humble needle and thread. I believe that the intimate nature of a stitch builds relationships that nurture compassion and understanding, which have the strength to both preserve traditions and make them relevant.

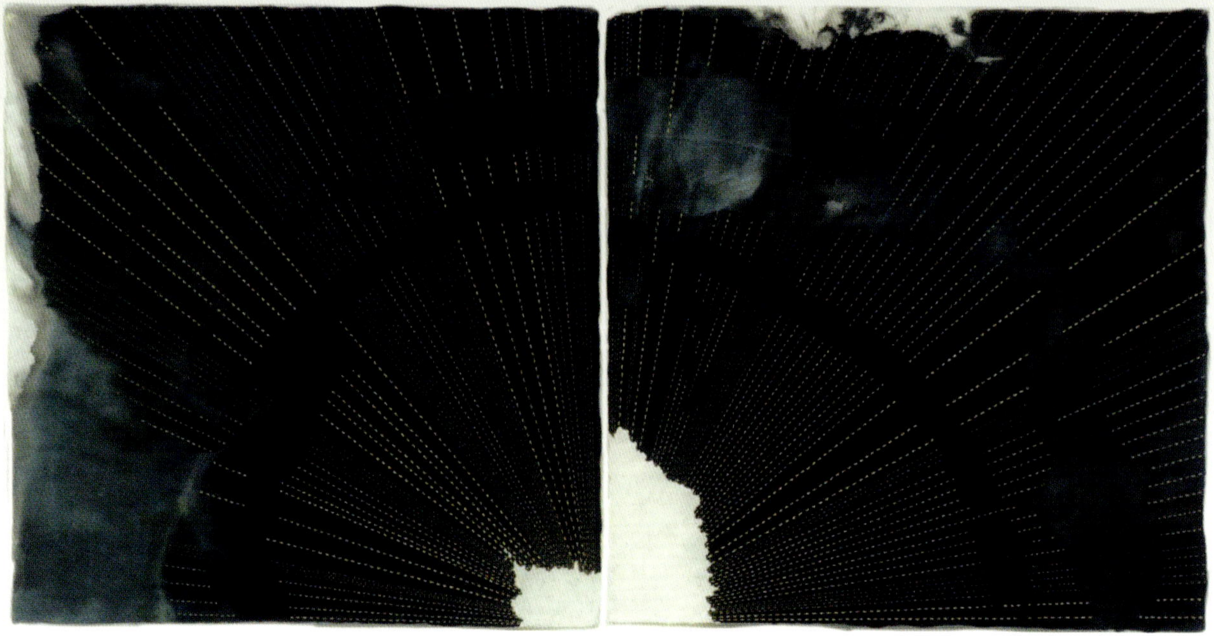

2001.15: Diptych. Japanese handmade mulberry paper, indigo dye, sumi ink, and metallic thread. 39" × 78" (each panel 39" × 39"). 2001. Photo: Bill Abramson.

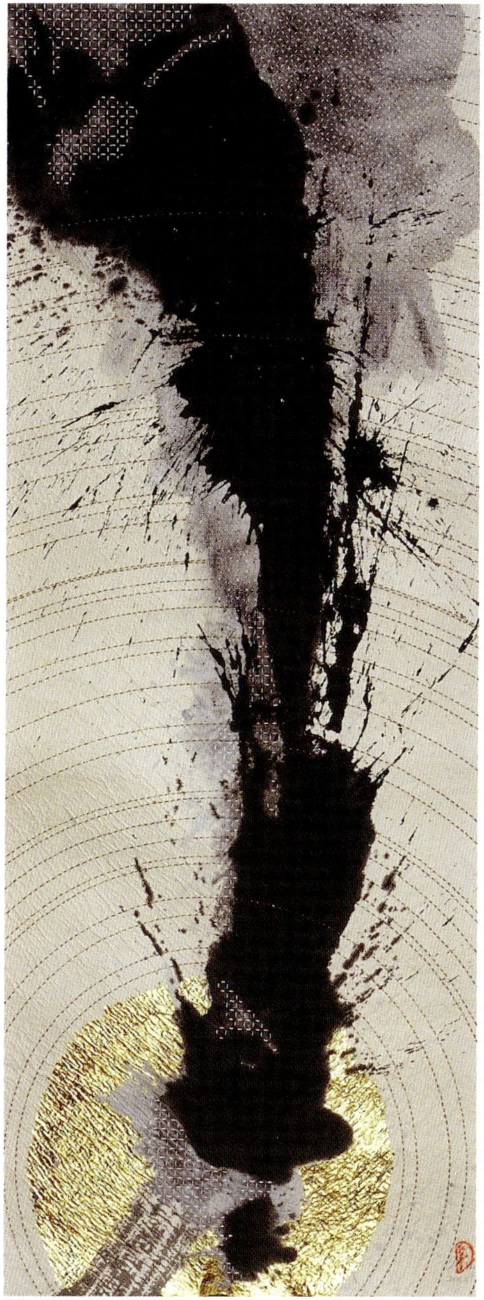

◄ *2005.05: Radiating and Cultivating Compassion.* Abaca handmade paper, sumi ink, indigo pigment, thread, and 18 karat gold gilding. 71.5" × 27". Photo: Richard Sargent.

► *1996.21: Triptych.* Abaca handmade paper, sumi ink, and cotton. 120" × 120". 1996.

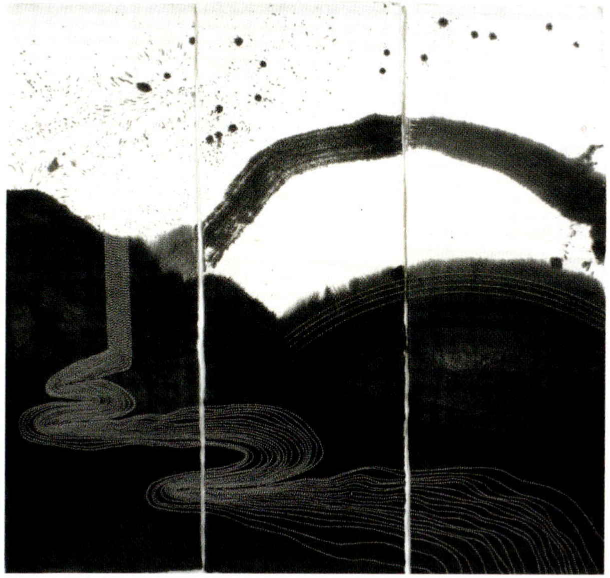

▼ *2006.01: Diptych.* Abaca handmade paper, sumi ink, indigo pigment, cotton, and 18 karat gold gilding. 28" × 45". 2006. Photo: Richard Sargent.

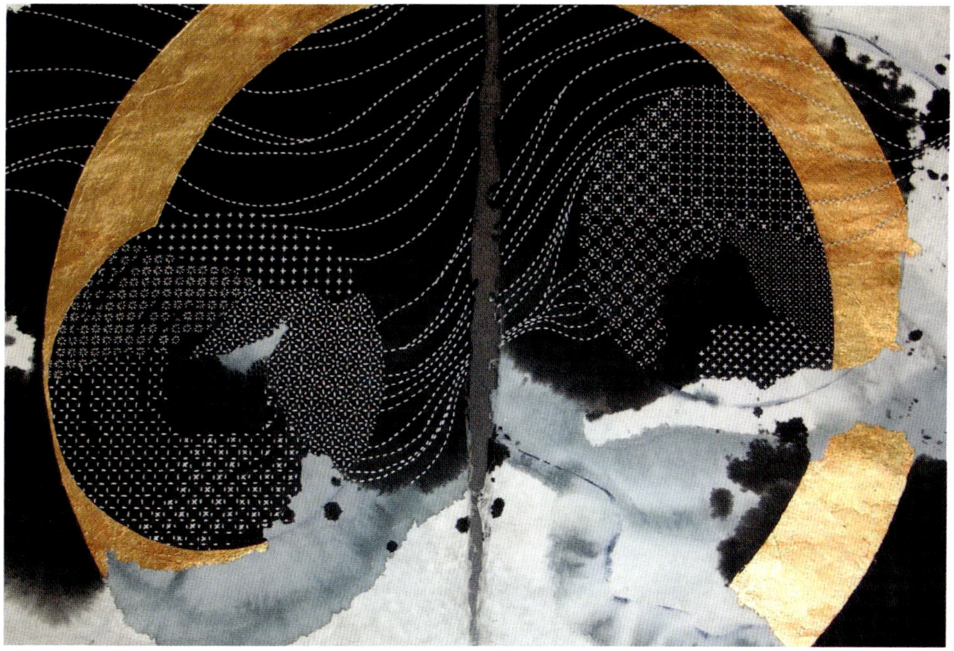

Courtesy of Bill Edwards.

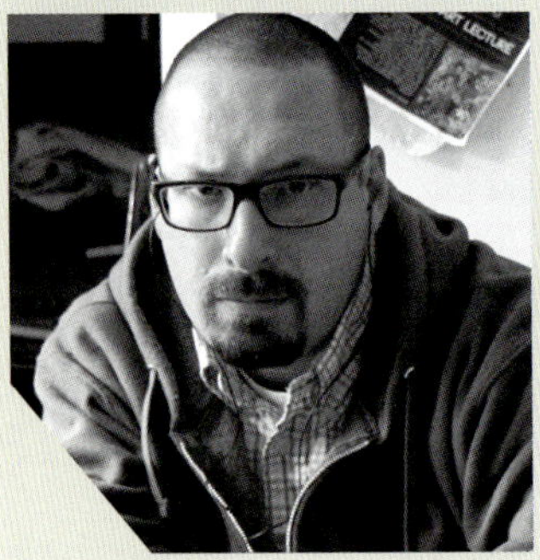

Jim Arendt

Conway, South Carolina

I use art as a way to investigate how labor and industry affect individual lives. Influenced by the radical reshaping of the rural and industrial landscapes I grew up in, I continue to examine how individuals are affected by transitions in economic structures. My early engagement with work as a whole and undivided process has left me with a persistent feeling that our present economic configuration has alienated most of us from the finest use of our skills.

Casting the people I know best into the center of my work, I explore how the changing landscape of labor has shaped them. My materials purposely reflect the lives and struggles of the people I come from. Denim seems created to be abused, stained, and burnt through but with the right pair of boots can still go to the ball. I like that. Still, it's hard to make pictures out of it. I guess I like that, too.

My award-winning work has been exhibited internationally in numerous group and solo shows. I was awarded the top prize at *ArtFields* and Best in Show during Fantastic Fibers at Yeiser Art Center, Paducah, Kentucky; exhibited in Fiberarts International in 2013 and 2016; and included in the 2013 Museum Rijswijk Textile Biennial, the Netherlands.

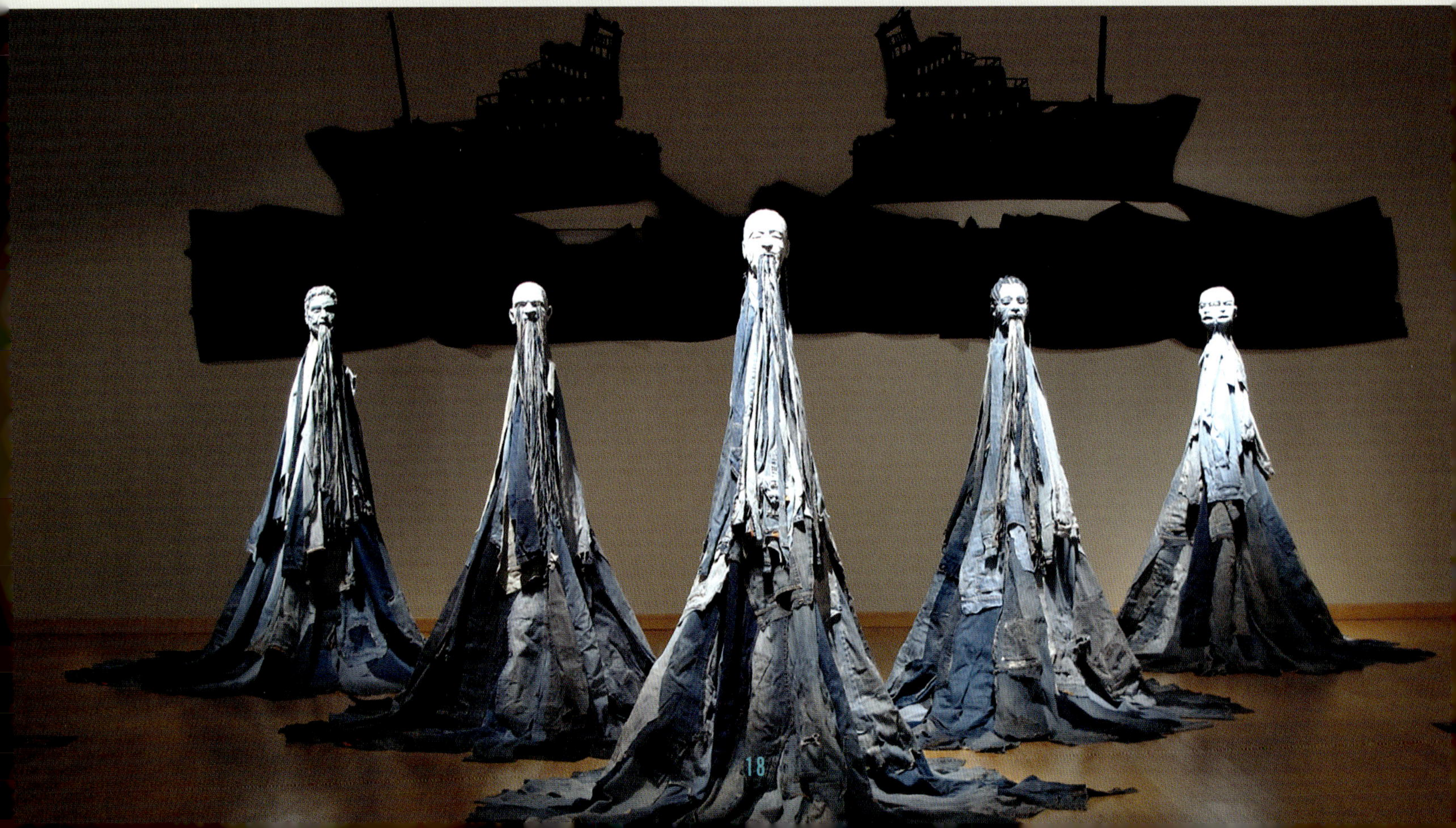

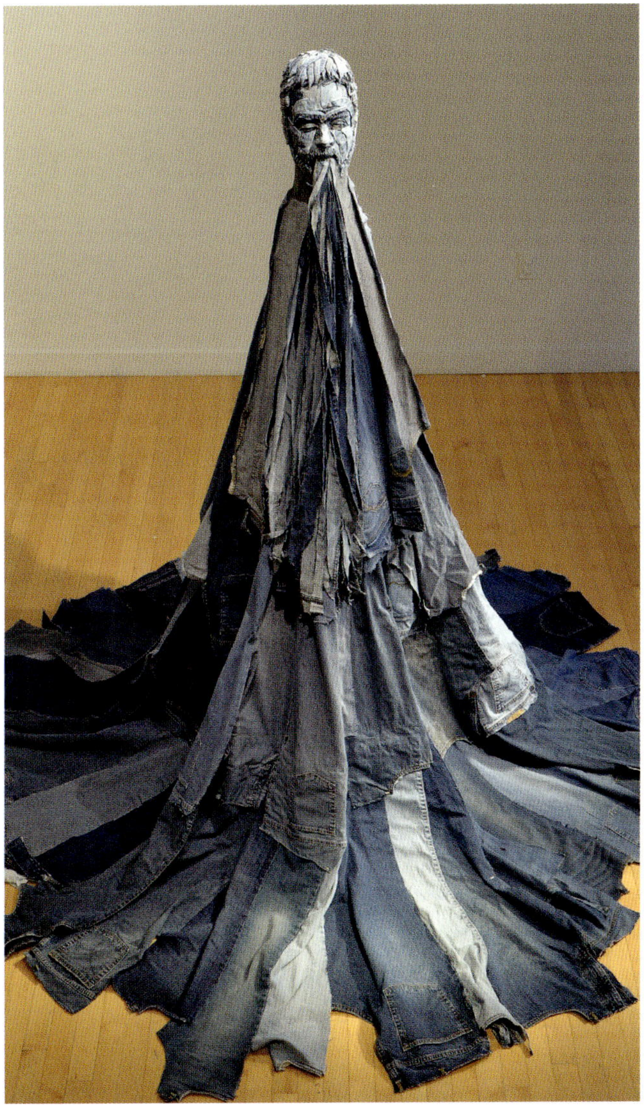

▲ *Logan (Totemic Figures).*
Denim, wood, and polystyrene. 78" × 48" × 48". 2014.

OPPOSITE
Totemic Figures. Denim, wood, and polystyrene.
78" × 48" × 48". 2014.

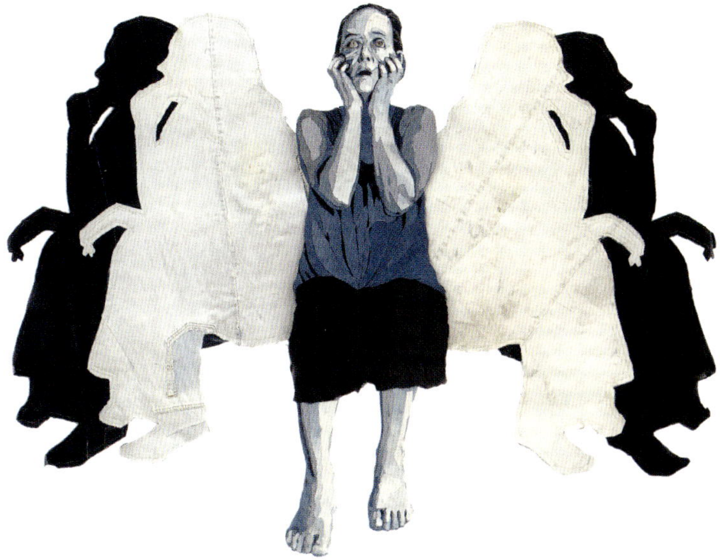

Catherine. Denim. 50" × 75". 2014.

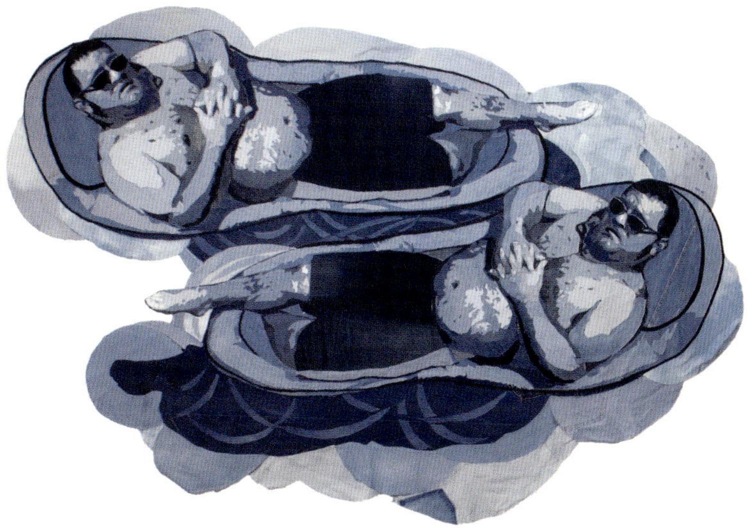

Robs: Permanent Vacation. Denim. 60" × 90". 2015.

All art images courtesy of Stacey Evans.

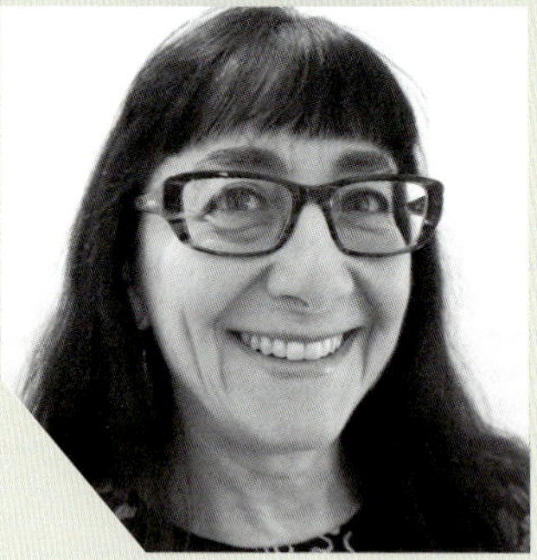

Courtesy of Lee Weisz.

Susan T. Avila

Emeryville, California

There is a long-standing tradition of textiles as text. Etymologically, textiles and text share the same stem of the Latin word *texere,* which means to weave. Metaphorically, textile words are often used to describe language: a tale is woven, ideas are strung together, stories follow a connecting thread. There is also a historical precedent for reading a textile; before written communication, the semiotic patterns and colors of textiles provided pivotal information about culture and social beliefs.

My wall pieces are embedded with words, symbols, and numbers to help give the viewer a point of departure, providing a built-in context to enhance the conceptual meaning of the work and stimulate a thought-provoking conversation.

Garden of Delights uses Photoshopped images I took at a chrysanthemum festival in China to illustrate words that promise dream fulfillment, wealth, and life enhancement. The other pieces shown here take as inspiration the mysterious information cloud that seems to permeate everyday life, such as all the identification numbers, passwords, and codes in *Information Overload.* From my series on health and well-being, *Matters of Dis-Ease,* I've included work that is sardonically punctuated with healthy messages, reminding all of us to become more aware and proactive in maintaining our own health.

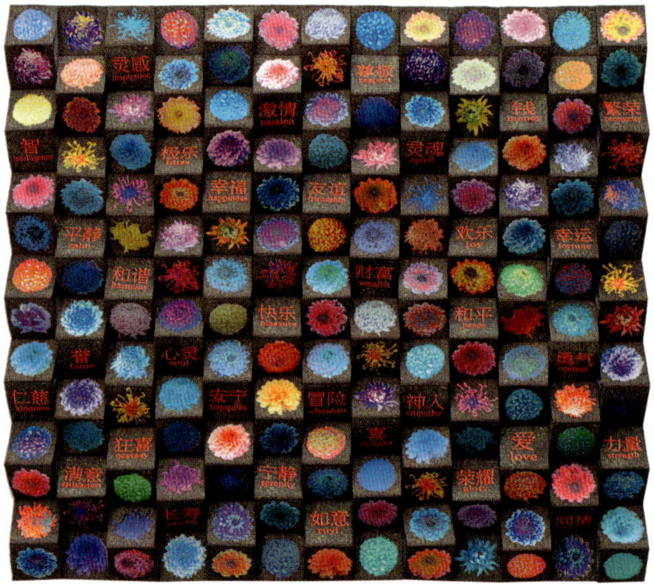

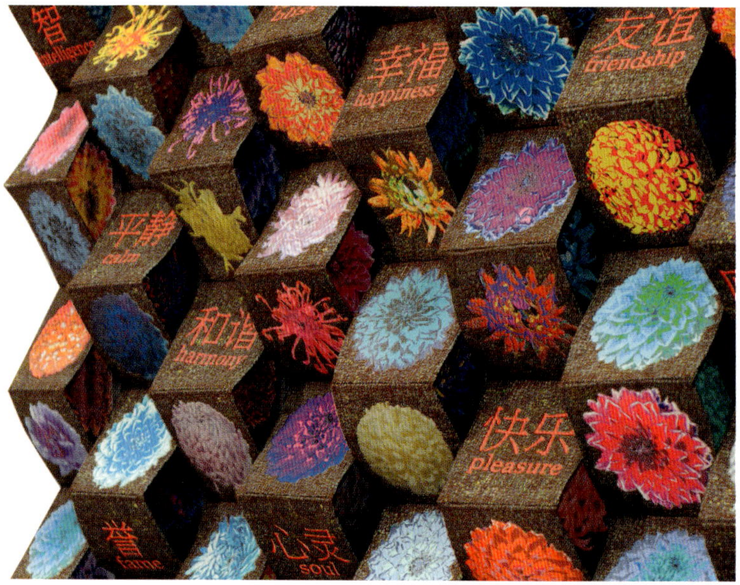

Garden of Delights. Digitally printed silk, industrial felt, and recycled muslin. 70" × 78" × 3.5". 2012. Photo: John Bagley. | Detail

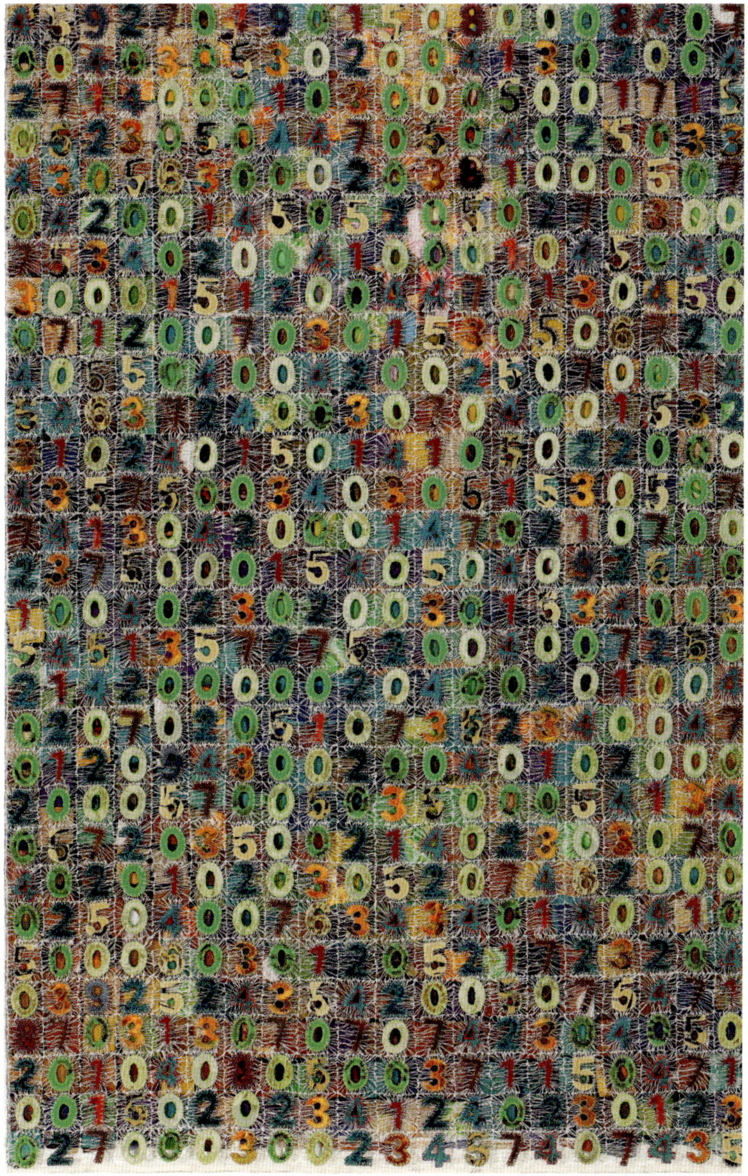

Information Overload. Thread, hand dyed fabric remnants, and industrial felt. 73" × 46" × 0.5". 2008. Photo: Lee Fatherree.

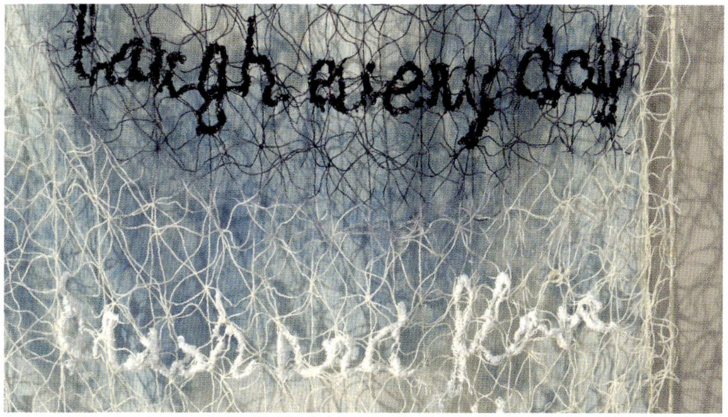

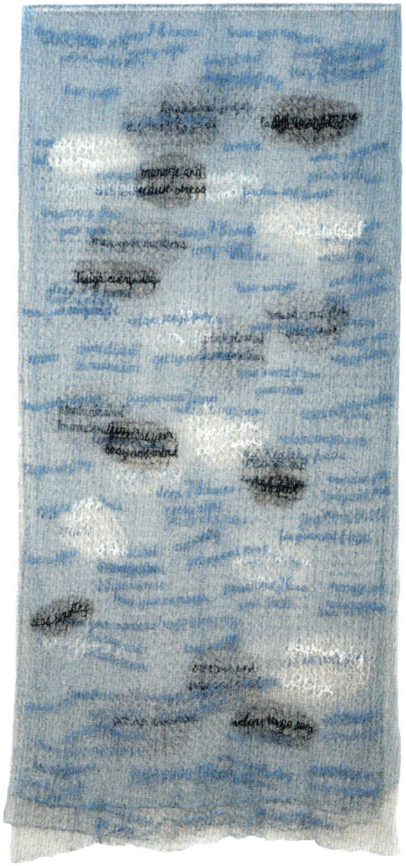

▲ *Tag Cloud.* Thread. 102" × 50" × 1". 2015. Photo: John Bagley.

◄ *Information Cloud v. 1.1.* Thread and cotton voile. 102" × 50". 2015. Photo: John Bagley.

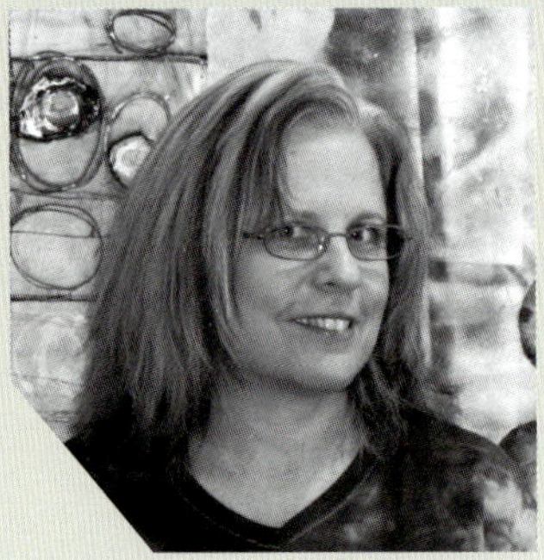

Shelley Brenner Baird

Columbus, Ohio

An archivist by instinct, I collect and create images to construct a visual vocabulary. I make non-literal narratives, finding connections and catalysts that tell a story in time and place with people, objects, marks, and layers. Marks may be balanced or reckless, austere or angry, surgical or ragged, literal or obscure. Images are superimposed on cloth by screen printing, painting, and drawing with dyes, paints, and bleaching agents. These processes are both directed and serendipitous, as the reaction with the fabric is instantaneous and slightly out of my control. The exact result is revealed when the dye residue is washed from the fabric, much like seeing a photograph develop in the darkroom. Finally, I add intense stitching to create lines, structure, and texture.

My formal education took place at Ohio State (MA in photography) and Indiana University (BFA in printmaking). My working habits and processes originate in printmaking, painting/drawing, and photography. I work "whole cloth," thinking about the fabric just as I would a canvas or piece of paper.

Instead of a sketchbook, I keep an idea book of words, concepts, titles, and newspaper headlines. I never sketch or plan extensively. I prefer spontaneity and don't mind being taken in a totally unexpected direction.

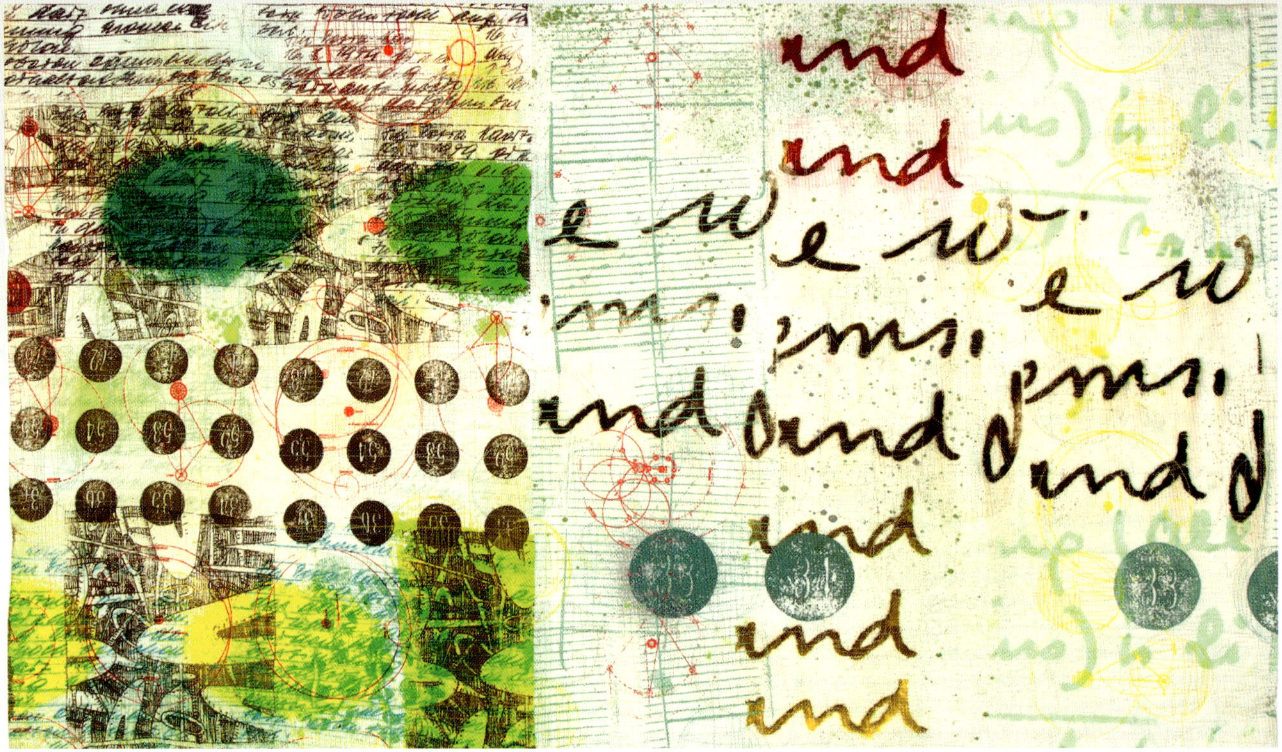

Subtext.
Screen-printed, painted, and stitched textile.
22" × 38".
2014.

➤ *Cambrian Explosion.* Screen-printed, painted, and stitched textile. 43" × 77". 2014.

▼ *Nonconforming Parts.* Screen-printed, painted, and stitched textile. 34" × 42". 2010.

◄ *Plot.* Screen-printed, painted, and stitched textile. 42" × 60". 2010.

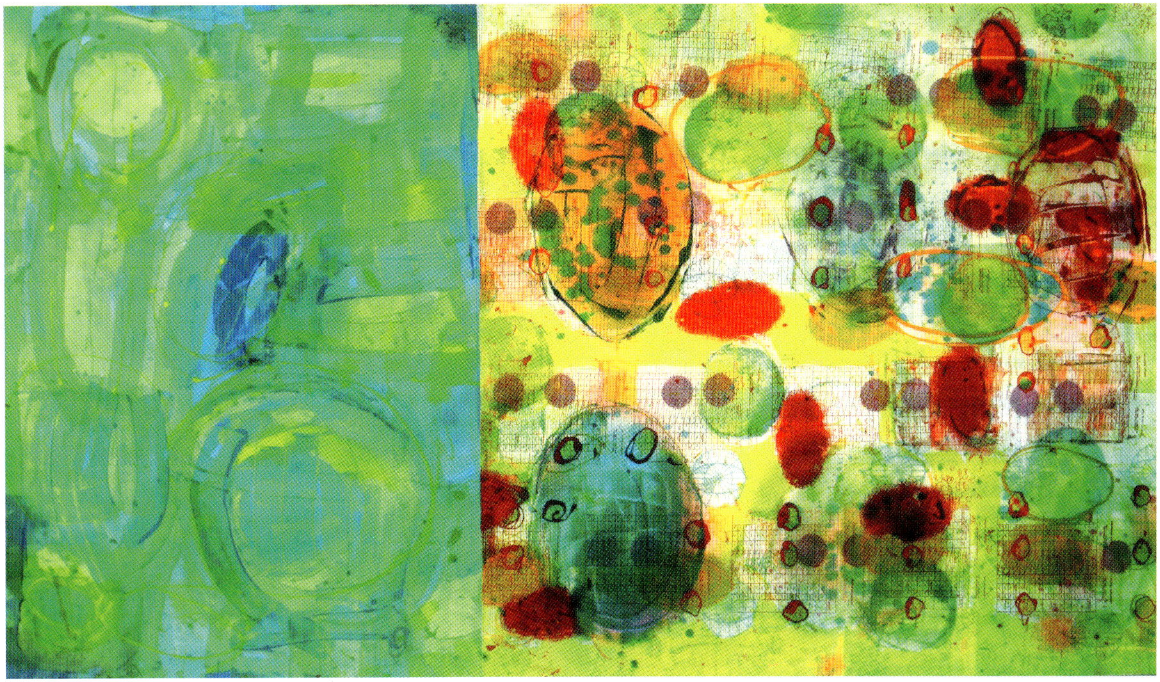

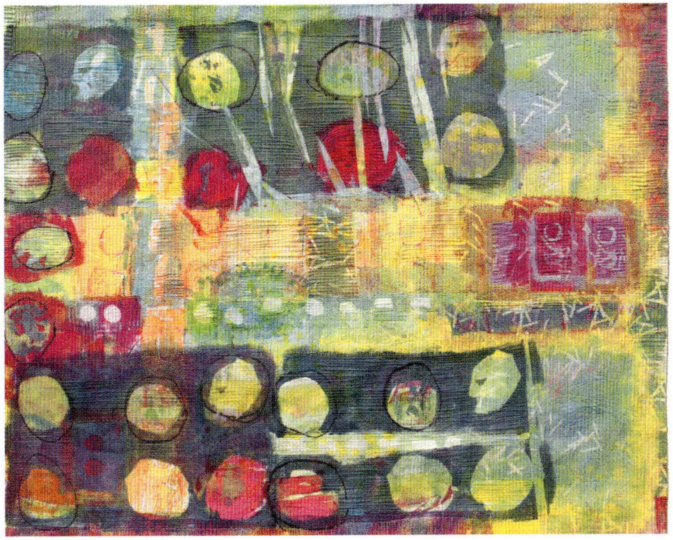

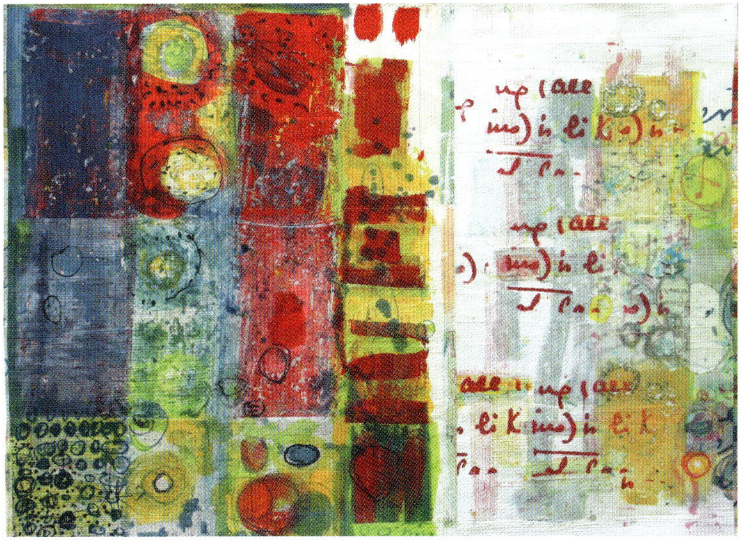

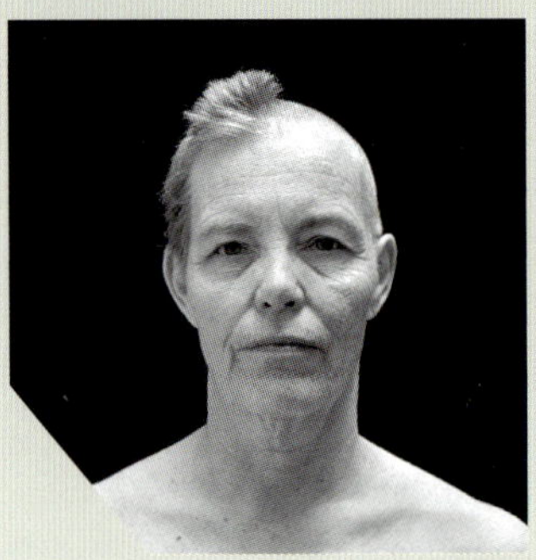

Courtesy of Carolyn DeMeritt.

Pinky/MM Bass
Fairhope, Alabama

As a photographer, I always aimed to explore the threads of the mystery of life: incarnation, regeneration, aging, and death. My stitchery work began during my sister's battle with cancer. I became obsessed with what was going on inside her body and began a series of internal organs sewn onto photographs of the human figure. In addition, my eldest son, both my parents, and two close artist/collaborators died over a period of just a few years. I have done handwork all my life, and the comfort of working that way on my photo images helped me through a very long grieving period.

Recently, my work has moved to the cellular level of the human body. I was greatly moved by the book *The Immortal Life of Henrietta Lacks* by Rebecca Skloot, about a young woman in the 1950s whose cancer cells were harvested without her knowledge or consent, and used to create an immortal cell line for scientific experimentation—the so-called HeLa cells. Using the Tenerife Lace process, I explore and enhance fluorescent microscopic cell images—including the HeLa cell itself.

At age fifty-two, I went back to school, received my MFA in photography, and returned to live in Fairhope, Alabama. I worked as an Artist in Education, assisted by several grants and an Alabama Artist Fellowship. I am thrilled to have my work in various collections, including the Philadelphia Museum and the High Museum of Art in Atlanta, as well as in publications such as *Aperture*, the *Pinhole Journal*, the *Polaroid Book,* and Christopher James' *Book of Alternative Processes.*

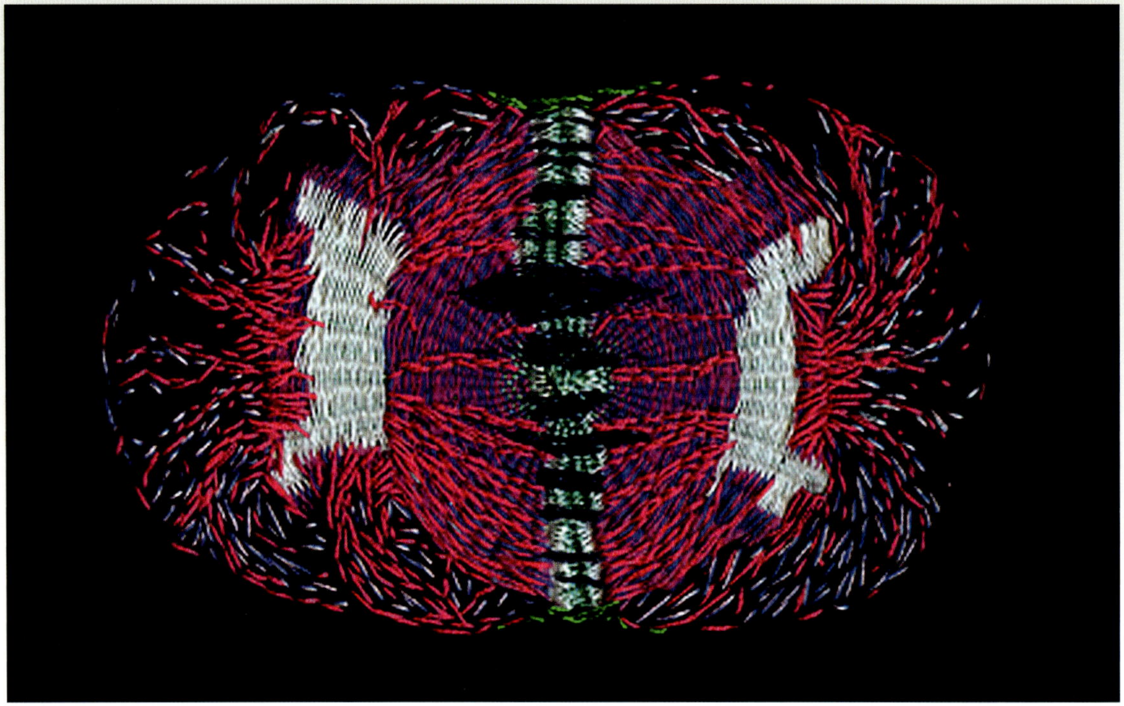

HeLa Cell Dividing (from *The Immortal Life of Henrietta Lacks*). Tenerife lace weaving, embroidery hoop, yarn, and thread. 5.5" × 9.5". 2011.

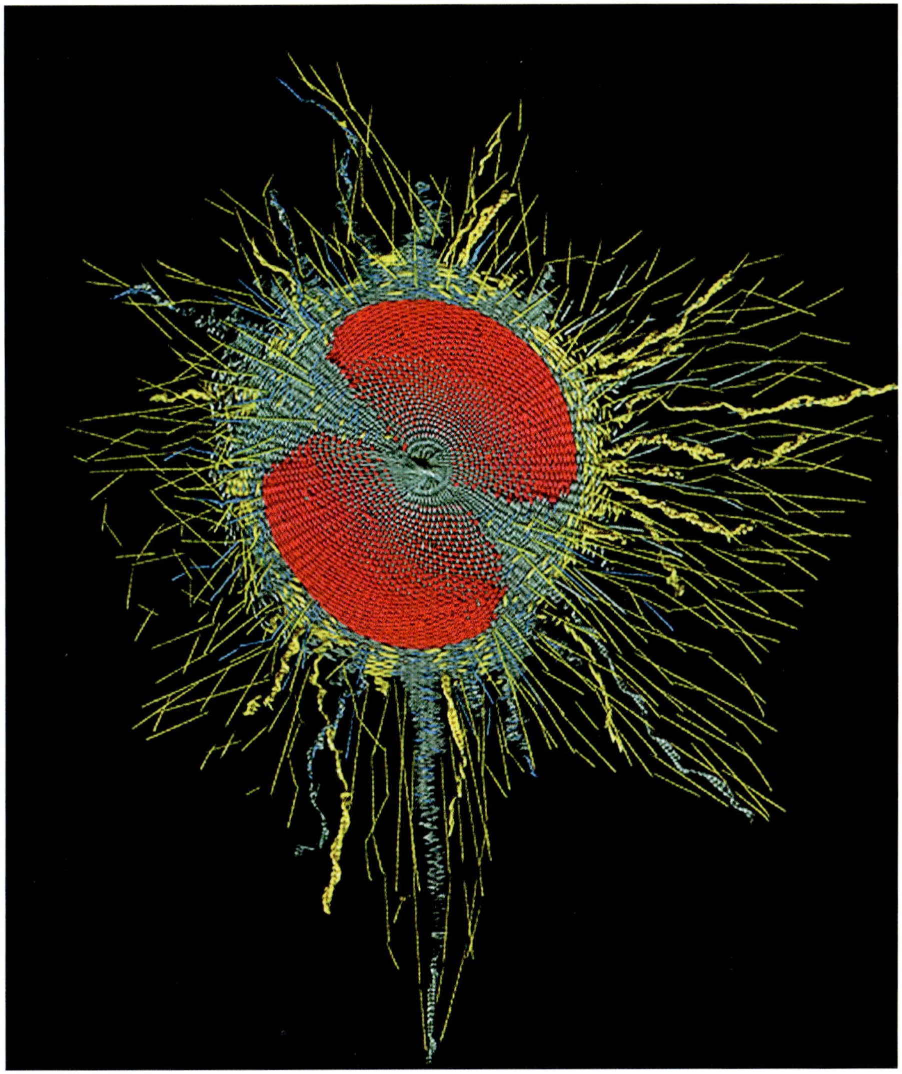

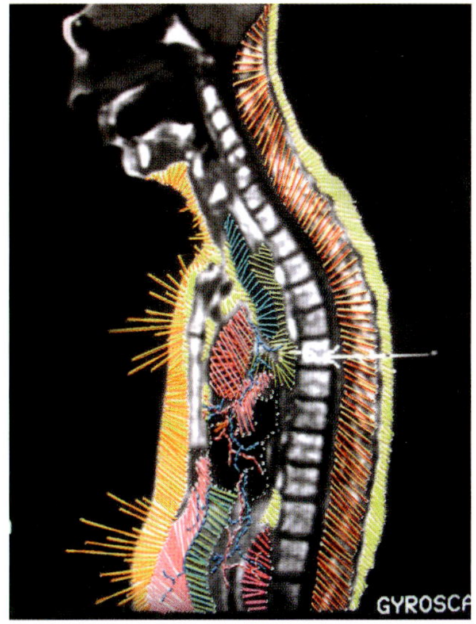

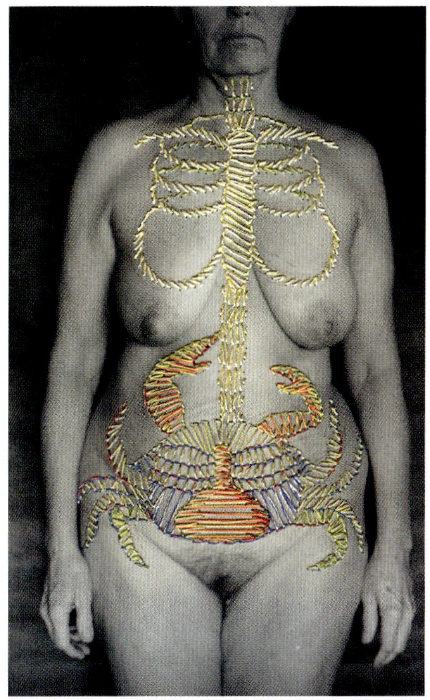

▲ *Human Cervical Adenocarcinoma Cells (HeLa Line).* Tenerife lace weaving, embroidery hoop, yarn, and thread. 8.5" × 8.5". 2011.

◀ *Fran's X-ray.* Silver gelatin print with embroidery thread. 10" × 8". 2007.

➤ *Skeletal Alternative.* Silver gelatin print with embroidery thread. 11" × 9". 2012.

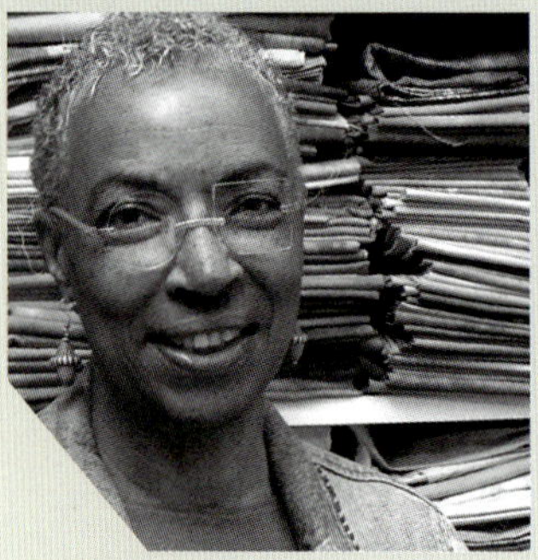

Alice Beasley

Oakland, California

I am a self-taught artist who began making portraits of people and objects in 1988. As a portrait artist working in fiber, I utilize the basic techniques of quilting; that is, I take small pieces of many different fabrics and sew them together to make a composition. But what elevates my work to the unexpected is that I incorporate, within the boundaries of this familiar tactile medium, the same qualities of light, shadow, and realistic perspective found in a painting but with a palette limited to fabric and thread—in other words, without using paints, dyes, or other surface treatments.

More important than the medium, however, are the subject matters explored in my body of work and the manner in which I express my feelings about the world I see. My focus is primarily on the human figure and the intricate web that plays out as we bob and weave in community with each other. The result is sometimes playful, often deadly serious. Regardless of subject matter, everything is done with the same goal: to put a little piece of my soul on the wall so that you might see what my mind sees.

My work has been exhibited in many venues throughout the United States, including the American Folk Art Museum in New York City and the Smithsonian Anacostia Museum in Washington, DC, as well as abroad in Spain, France, Namibia, and Japan.

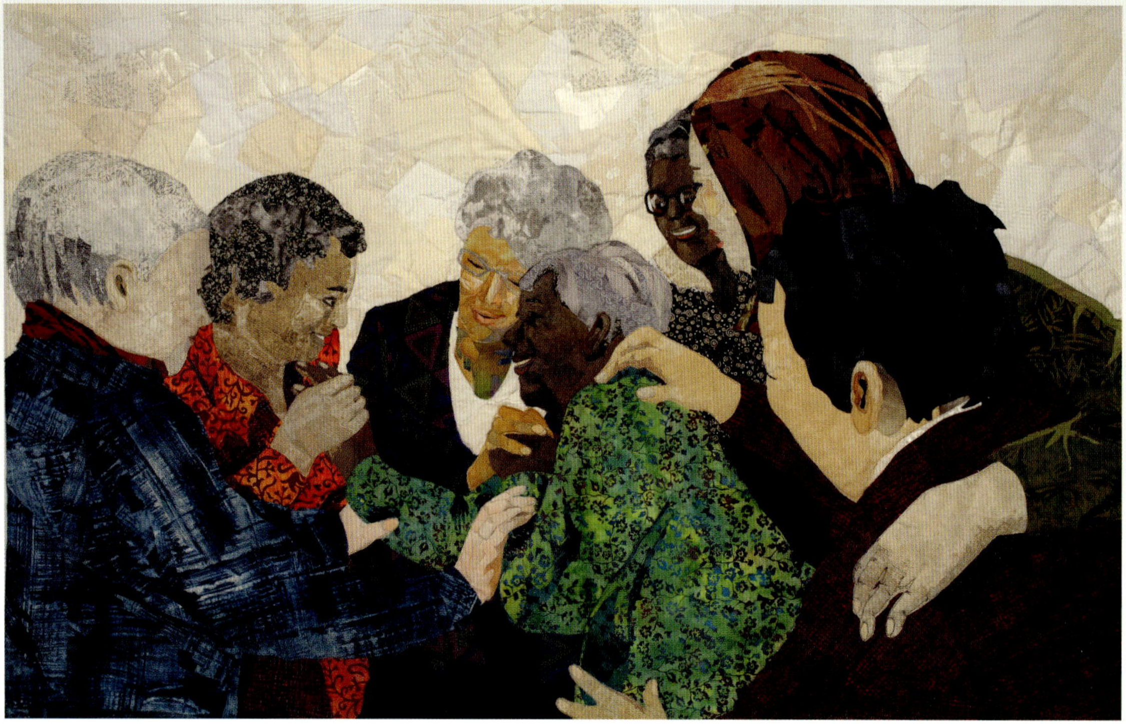

Circle of Friends.
Cotton. 33" × 53". 2012.

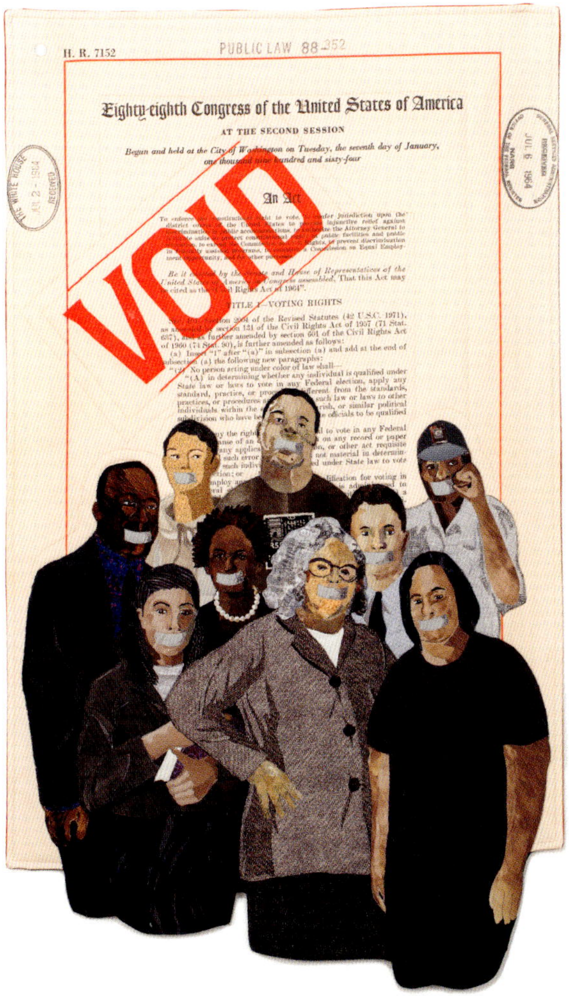

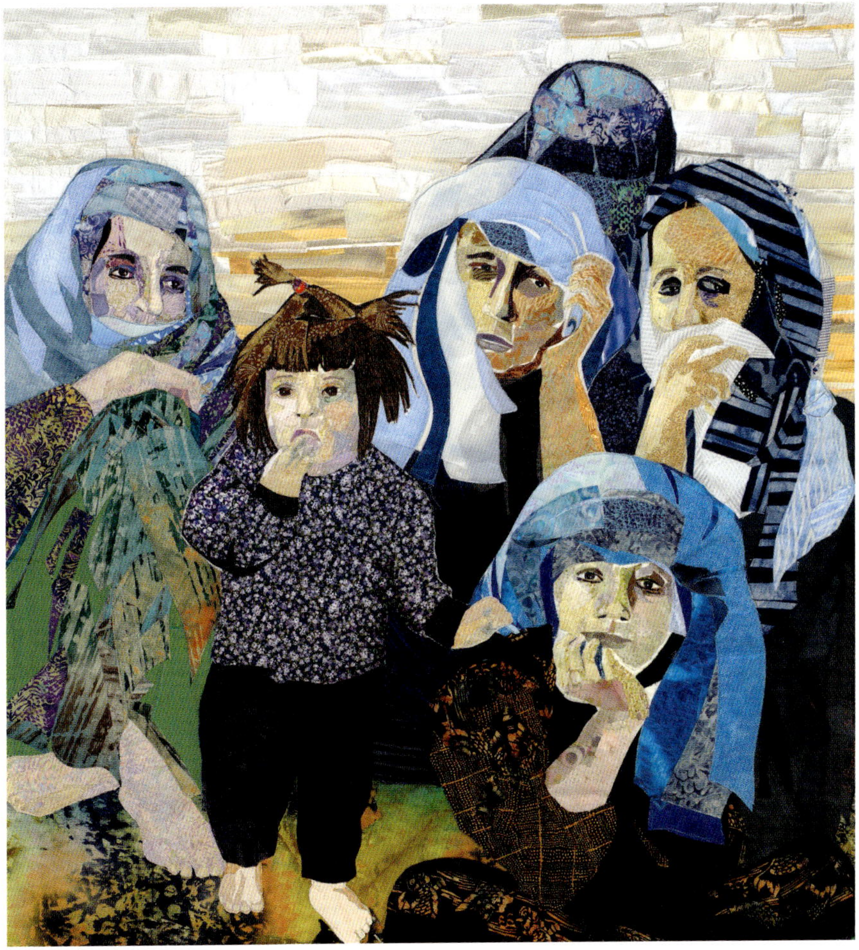

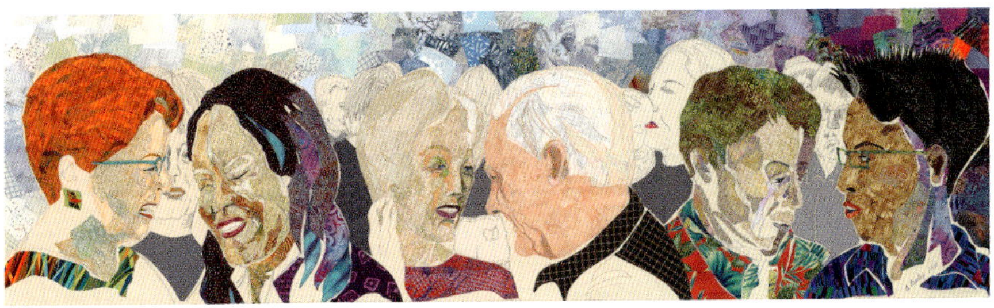

▲ *No Vote, No Voice*. Cotton and silk fabrics and printed text. 60" × 36". 2014.

◄ *Blue Burqas*. Cotton and silk fabrics. 44" × 41". 2011.

► *Entre Nous*. Cotton fabrics. 26" × 89". 2010.

All art images by Sibila Savage Photography.

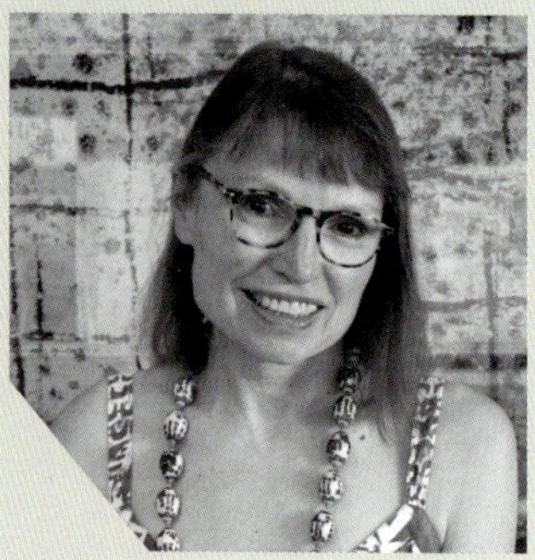

Sue Benner

Dallas, Texas

I grew up in Wisconsin. My mother sewed creatively for our home and made most of our clothes. My father was a businessman with the heart of an artist; he was always sketching and painting. I spent time as a young girl making Barbie Doll clothes and later tailored Pendleton wool suits on a human scale; of course, the plaids had to be matched perfectly!

During college, while majoring in molecular biology, I learned to batik and dye fabric, first from a friend and then more formally in a University of Wisconsin fabric design class. I pursued more art classes, often using science as subject matter and inspiration. These experiments with fabric led to my first art quilt: a batiked plant cell complete with nucleus and organelles!

Today, my work is created primarily with silk and cotton that I have dyed and painted, incorporating estate sale and thrift store fabrics. I compose the surface of the quilt with layers of textile collage and paint. I work on five to ten quilts at a time, often in two different series. Ideas naturally overlap and play off one another to push my creative process forward.

My recent body of work conveys my love of plaids and grids. Metal mesh and chain link fences are something I photograph all the time, including the world beyond. The fences form a scrim for the scene behind: instant units, instant analysis . . . an instant quilt.

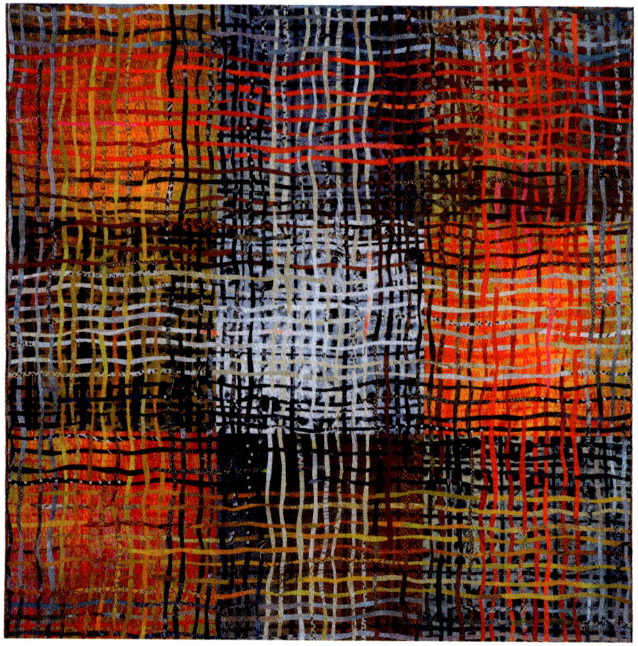

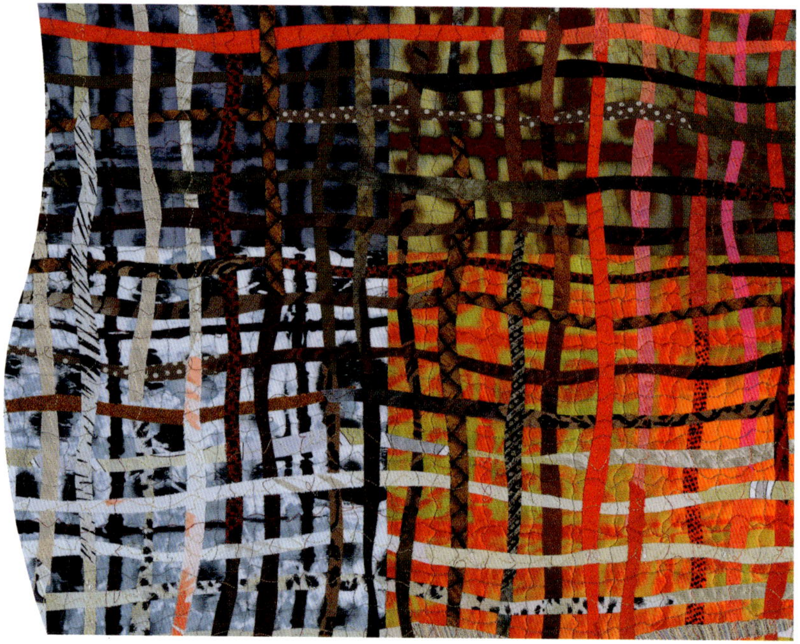

Spotted Plaid 2. Dye and paint on silk, cotton, and found fabrics. 51.5" × 51.5". 2015. | Detail

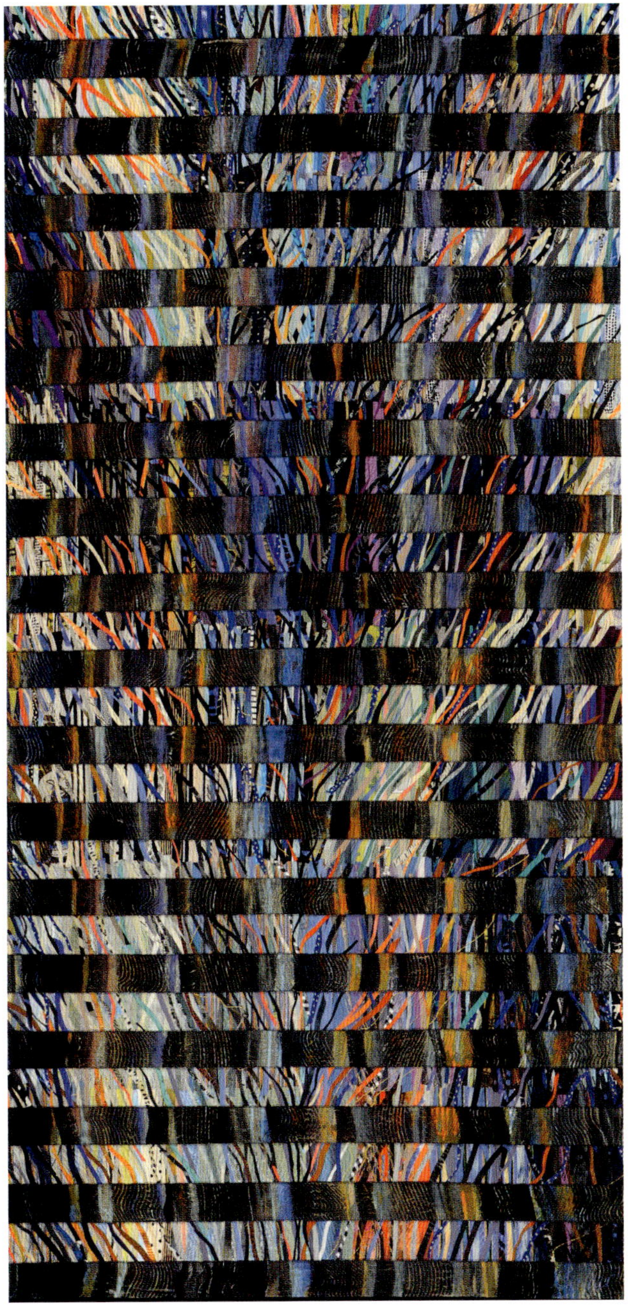

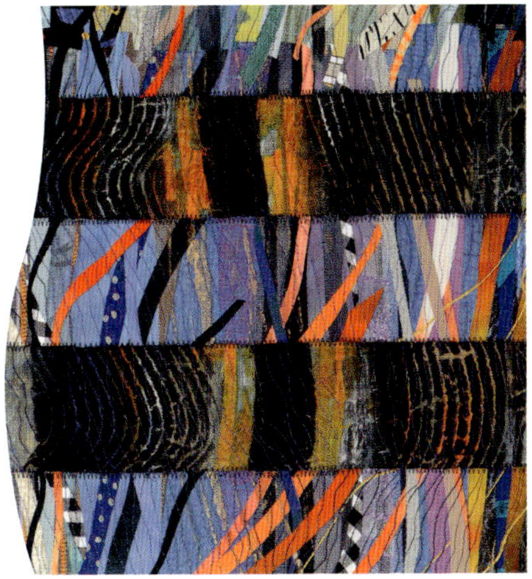

◄ *Tallgrass II.* Dye and paint on silk, cotton, and found fabrics. 2.5" × 41". 2015. | Detail

▼ *Wearing Plaid 3.* Gingham; dye and paint on silk, cotton, and found fabrics. 43.5" × 43.5". 2014.

All images courtesy of Eric Neilsen Photography.

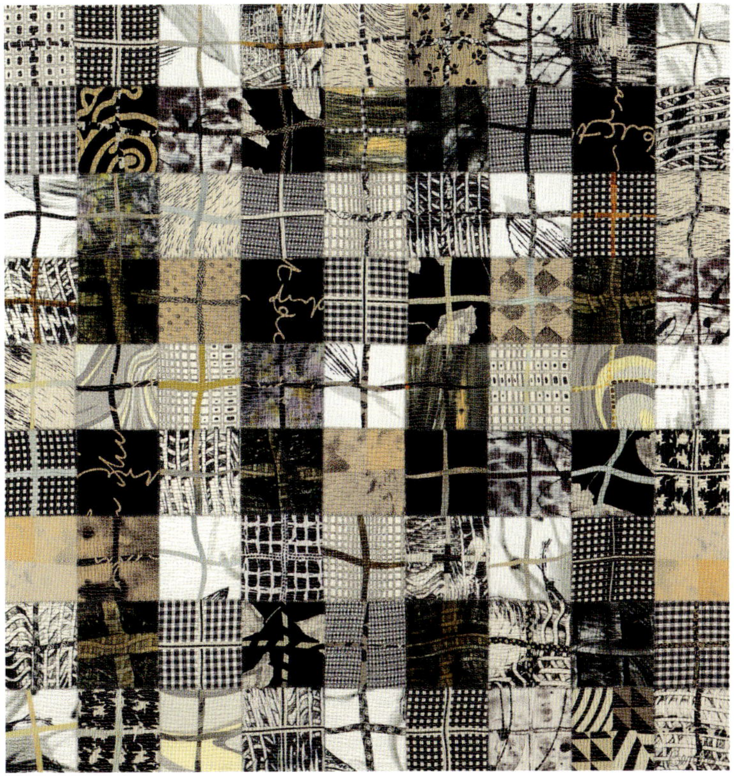

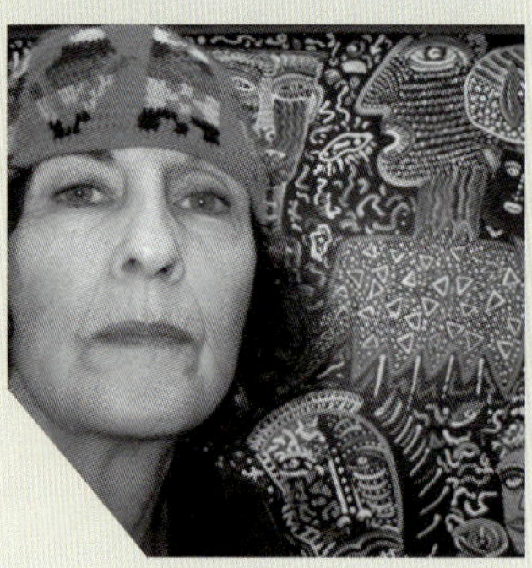

In my artistic career, I feel like I won the artist's lottery two different times when my peers rewarded me twice with National Endowment Fellowships! The first time was in 1987 when I was working nights at the IRS checking individual tax forms, while spending my days dreaming of being an artist. I had already been denied entry into graduate school because I didn't know how to speak the language, and my undergraduate degree was not in art. The second fellowship was awarded to me after a serious health issue, allowing me to pick myself back up and continue creating again. Thus, my journey began, and thus it continues. It takes hard work and a lot of luck.

Mary Bero

Madison, Wisconsin

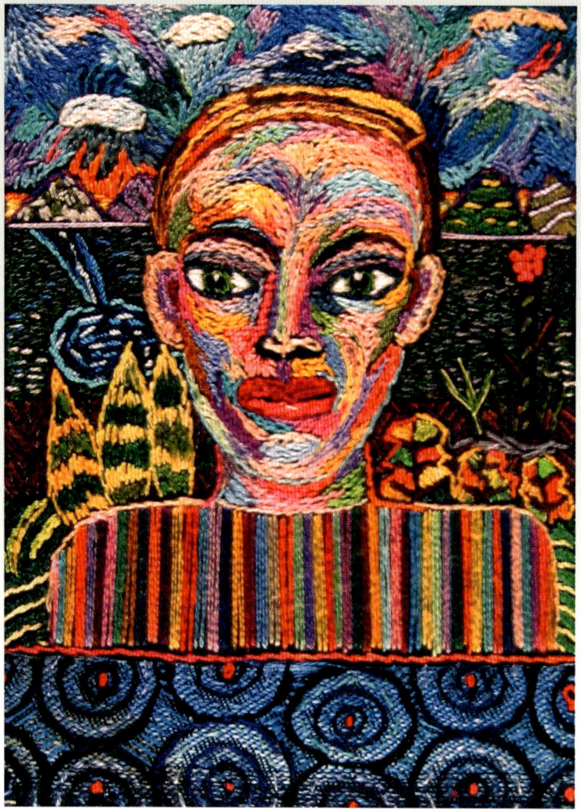

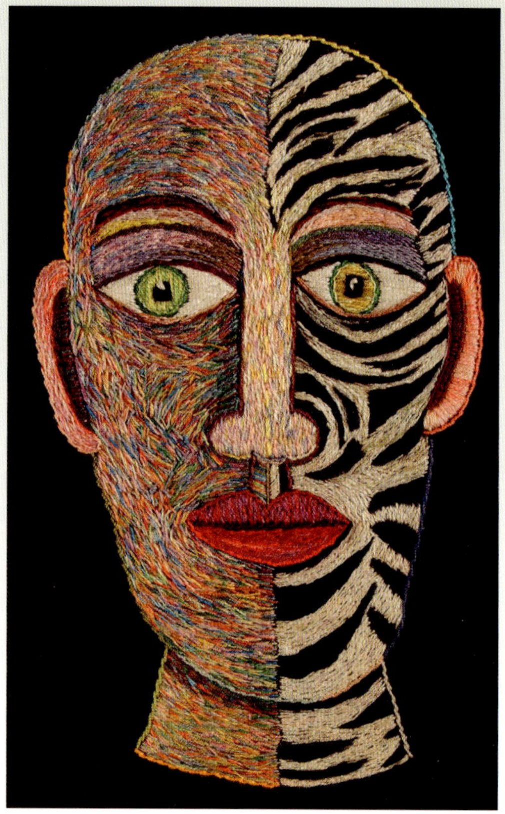

Changing Seasons.
Cotton, silk, and rayon.
5" × 3.75".

➤ *Stuffed Head: Anima.*
Cotton fabric, silk and cotton thread, and Poly-Fil® stuffing.
7" × 4.25".

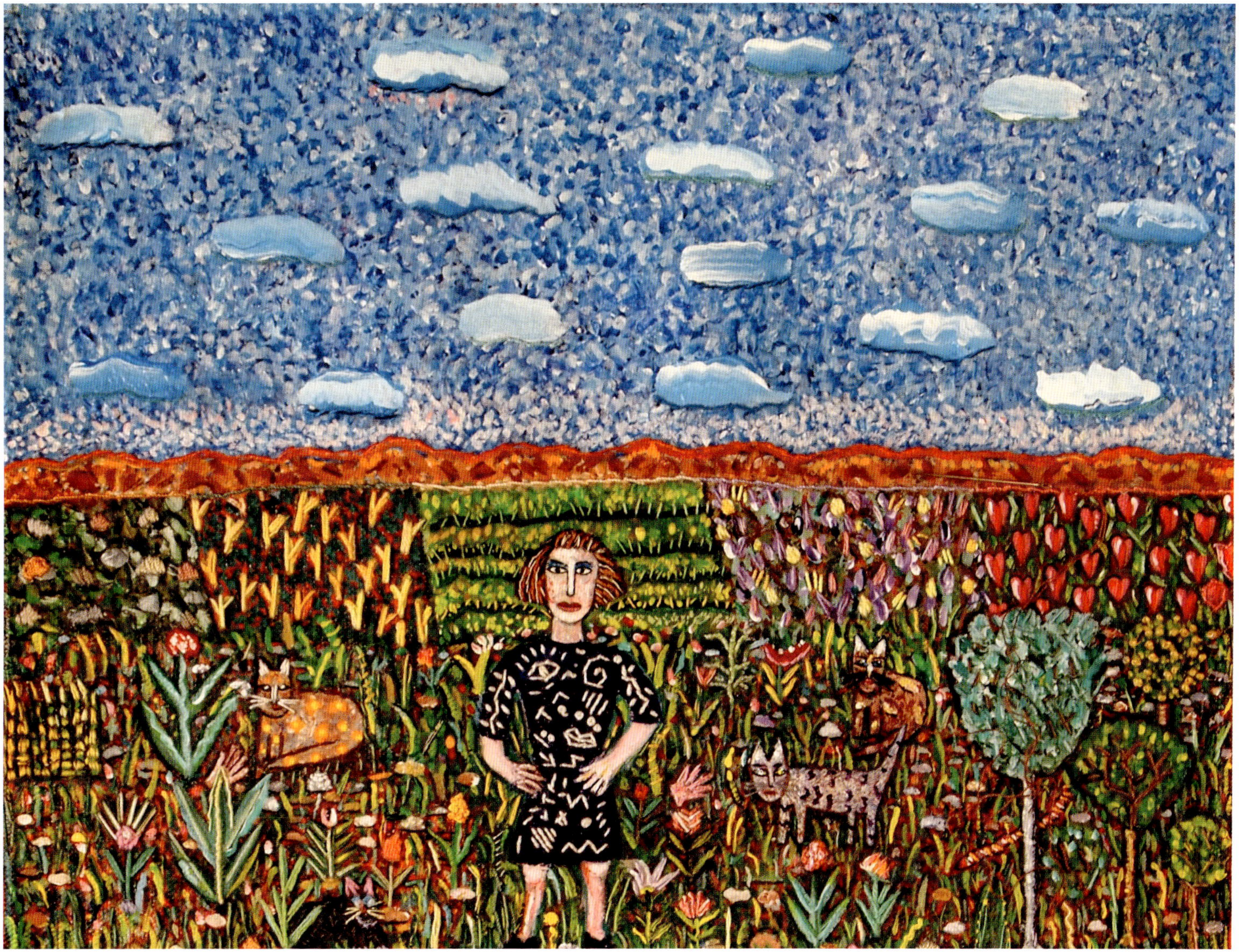

Stepping Out. Canvas, acrylic paint, cotton and silk thread. 9" × 12".

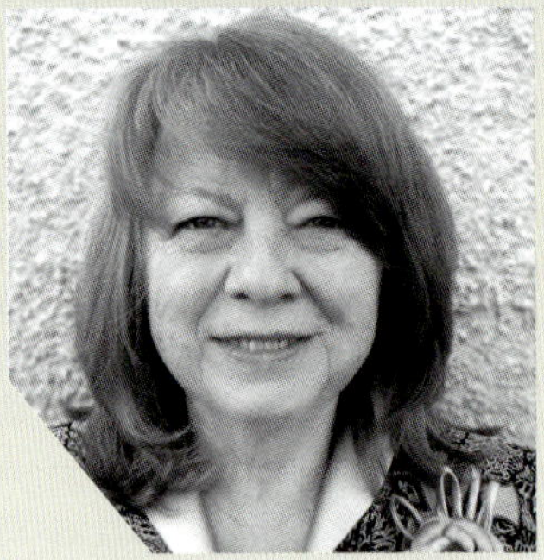

Chris Berry

Glasgow, Scotland

My work is inspired by Venice, its architecture, and its canals. Venetian Renaissance architectural decoration, with its emphasis on symmetry and proportion, is formal and static, enclosed and imprisoned by water. Yet it is this very element that reveals this same architecture at its most fluid, in beautiful fleeting reflections, glimpses of transient eddies in the ebb and flow of the canals. Linking these two disparate ideas has led me to experiment with linear stencils capturing the static Gothic quatrefoils within a wave-like undulating mesh. I see future work continuing to explore three-dimensional shapes with the option of expressing ideas in virtual pieces that can be "investigated from within."

As chairman of the Embroiderers' Guild, I was Chair of the Selectors for the biennial International Exhibition *Art of the Stitch* from 1999 to 2009. I am a contributing author to the Textile Study Group publication *Embroidery Studio,* in which textile artists take inspiration from historic or foreign textiles from the Embroiderers' Guild Collection and produce a contemporary work of art based on their study. I am a regular contributor to *Stitch* and *Embroidery* magazines, both published by the Embroiderers' Guild.

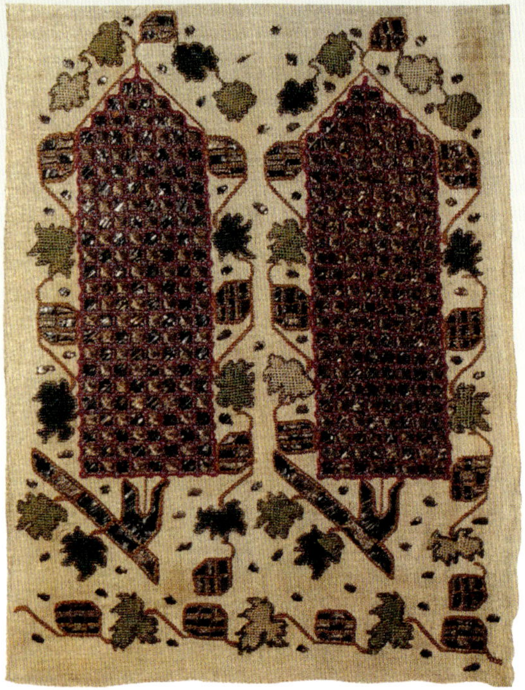

Turkish inspiration: A 19th century Turkish sash. Hand stitchery using cotton and metal threads. 12.6" × 8.7".

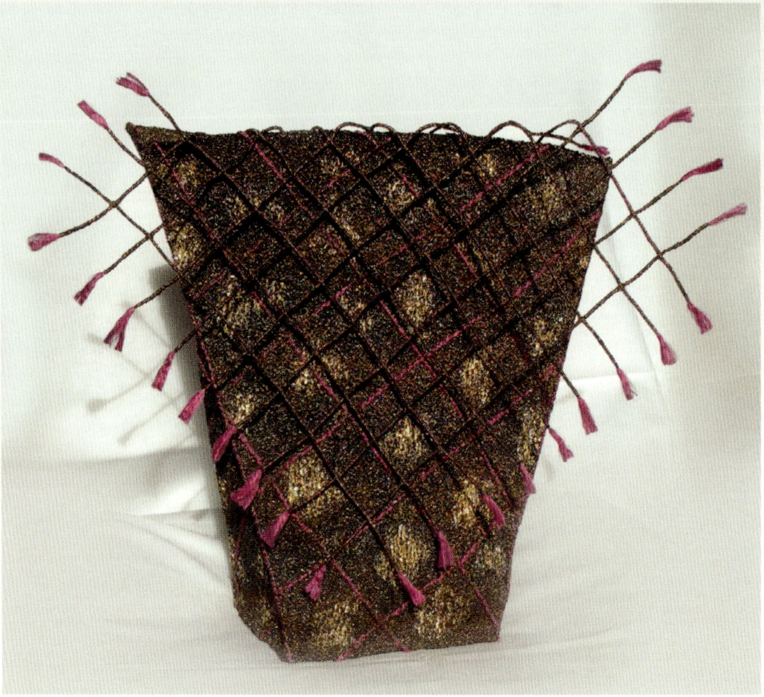

20th century artwork. Machine embroidery using felt, machine embroidery threads, and sweet papers. 11.8" × 5.5" × 5.5". 1993.

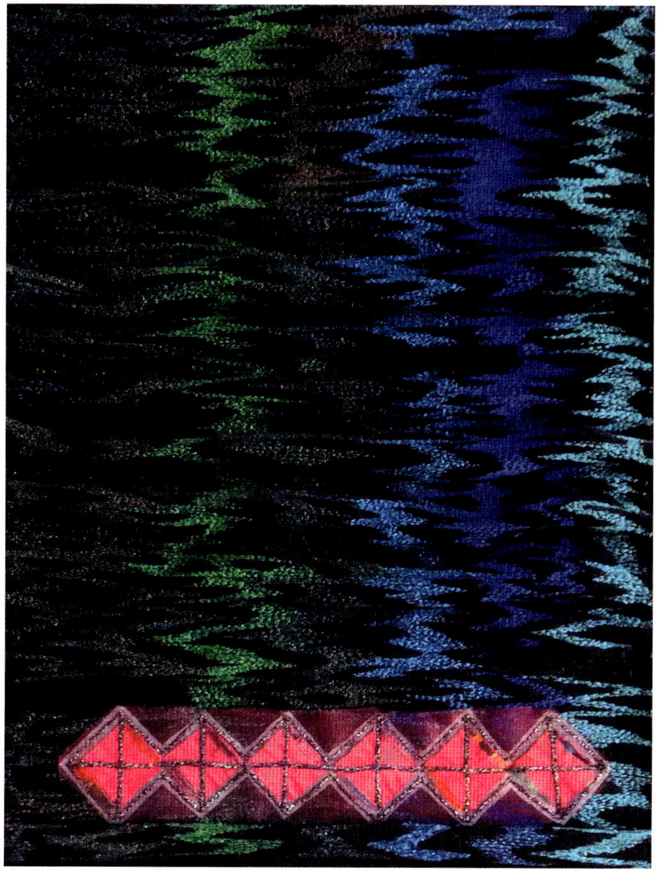

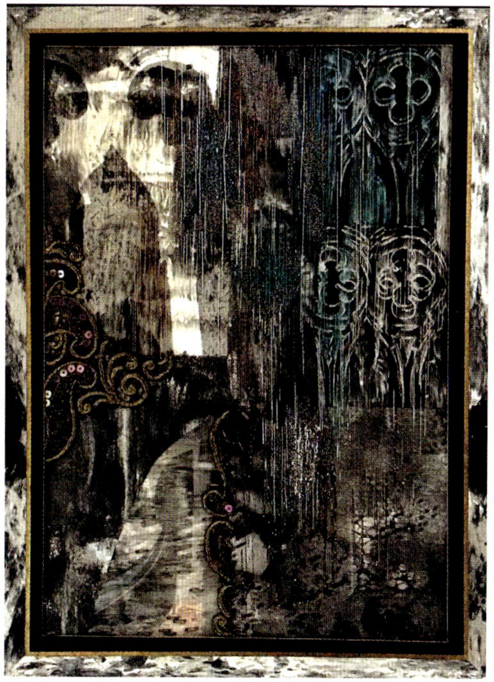

▲ *Acqua molto alta.* Felt, Thai silk, transparent fabrics, and machine embroidery threads. 14.96" × 10.6" × 1.18". 2013.

◄ *Venetian Reflections 1*. Bead and metal thread hand decoration on opaque and transparent fabrics, machine embroidery threads, lace, metal threads, and beads.
18.1" × 13.4". 1996.

► *Ancora acqua alta.* Transparent fabrics, paper, and machine embroidery thread. 13.4" × 32.5" × 1.96". 2006.

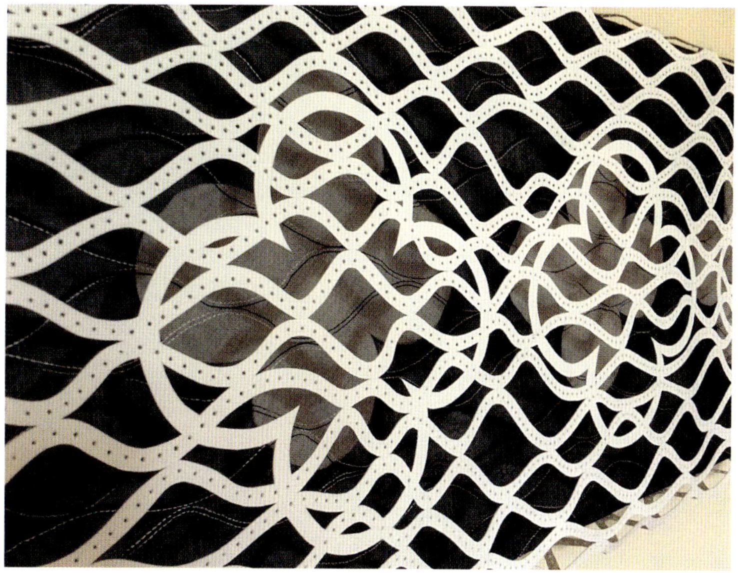

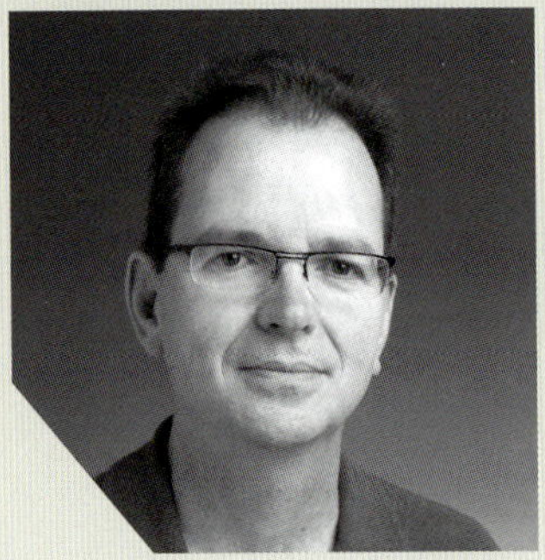

Courtesy of Tom Van Eynde.

Jerry Bleem

Joliet, Illinois

My art practice starts with paying attention to my immediate environment and selecting materials that trigger memories while suggesting contemporary issues. In the studio, these collected objects are cut into lines and re-configured using traditional fiber processes.

These wall works are from my *Oil Products* and *Nationalism* series. The *Oil Products* series uses common disposable/recyclable plastic shopping bags. By selecting this specific plastic product, I wanted to focus attention on something so familiar that we rarely question its presence in our lives. Our unconscious acceptance allows this oil product to inhabit our homes, our landfills, and our environment. Perhaps re-presenting them will encourage more thoughtful use.

Nationalism, which uses American flags, was inspired by the way the wars in Iraq and Afghanistan were reported as either disimpassioned stories of national policy or heart-wrenching accounts of individual soldiers' disrupted lives. I wasn't concerned with taking an ideological stance; instead, I wanted to consider how to bridge the divide that existed between the public life of the nation and the individual lives of her citizens. These pieces document the time I spent both making the work and thinking about the relationship between these two very different versions of war.

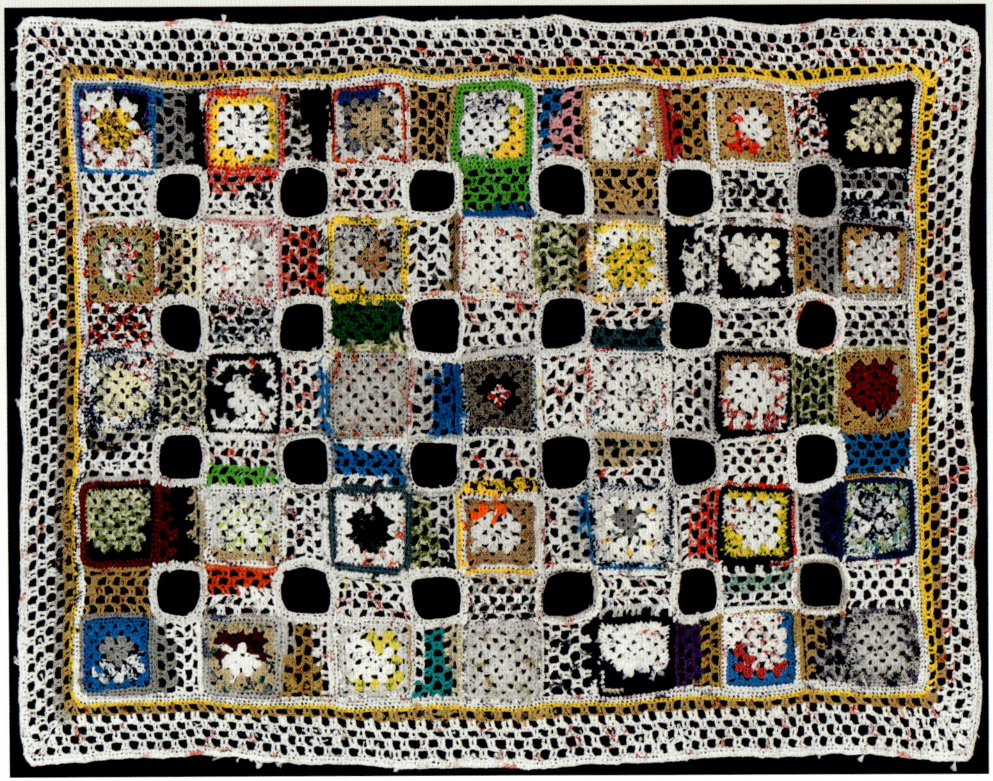

Remind me again why we're depleting the earth's resources and burying them in landfills. Crocheted wall hanging using postconsumer plastic bags. 62" × 83.5". 2008. Courtesy of Tom Van Eynde.

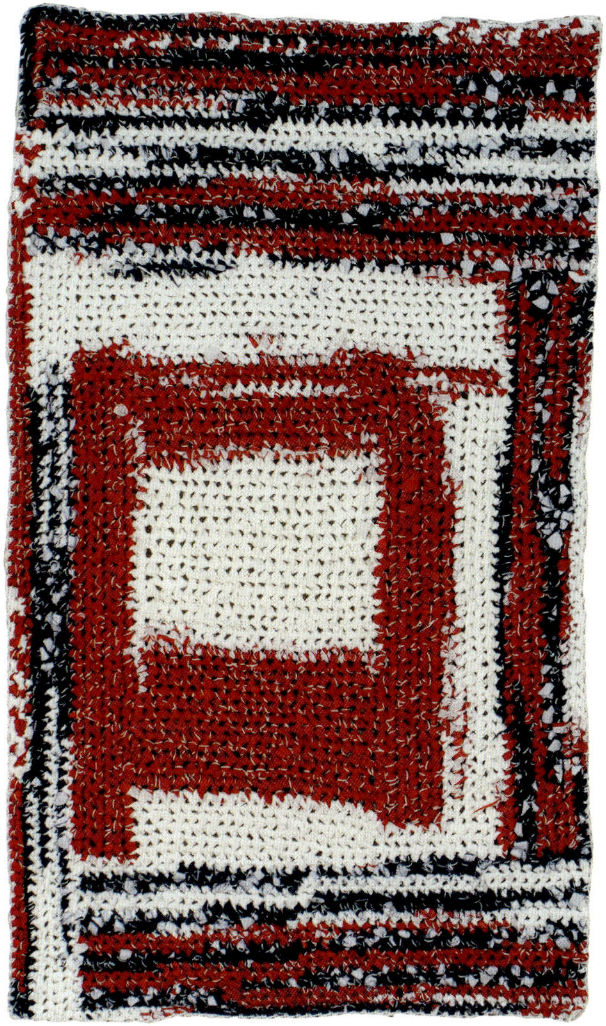

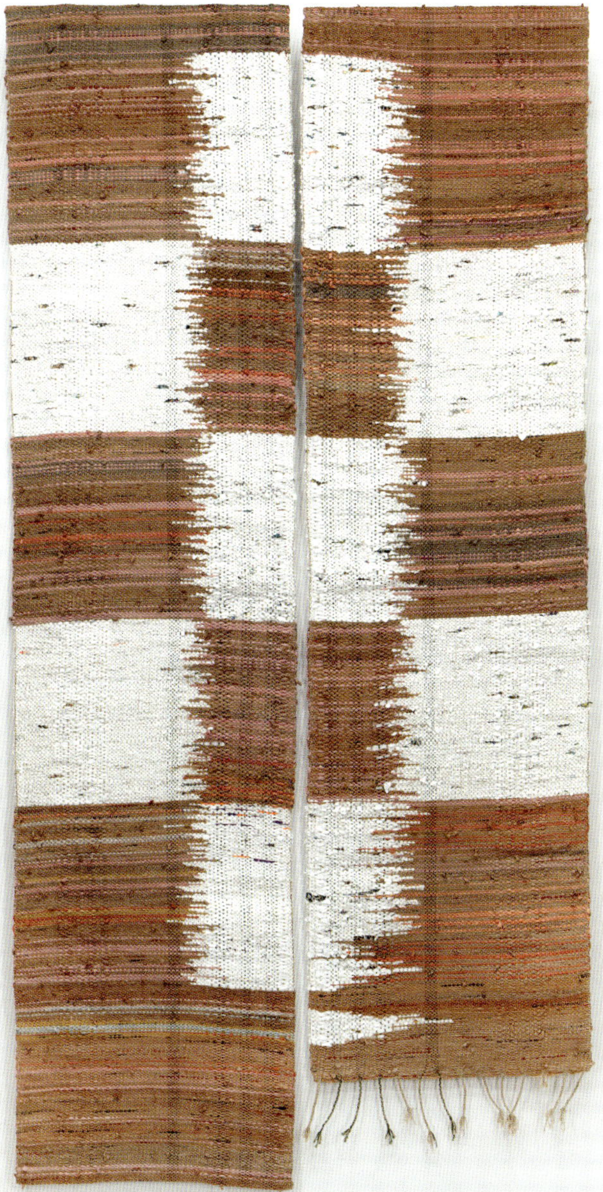

▲ *Nationalism as an intellectual exercise: its complexities and assumptions, its hazards and domestic implications.* Crocheted wall hanging using US flag and nylon cord. 69" × 41". 2008. Courtesy of Tom Van Eynde.

➤ *Oil Ikat (homage to Virginia Davis).* Woven wall hanging using postconsumer plastic bags and found warp. 88" × 45". 2012.

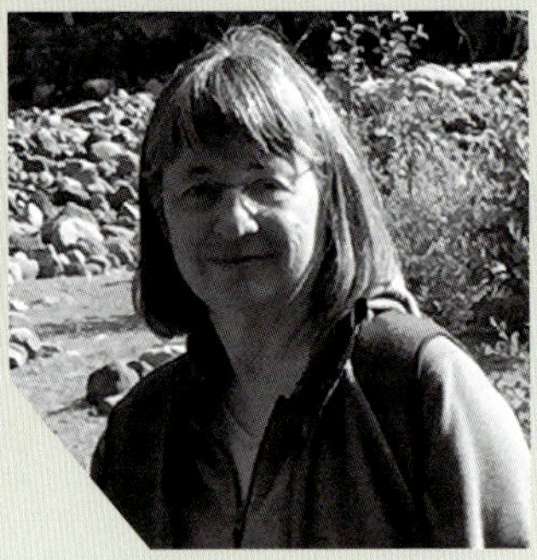

Courtesy of Richard Tomaselli.

George-Ann Bowers

Berkeley, California

My work celebrates the infinite intricacies of the natural world. I am intrigued by the patterns and structure of trees, seedpods, or rock formations, for example, and in another life might have become a botanist or geologist. My work is, in a way, a journal of places I have visited, where I see weaving patterns in a stream-eroded canyon wall or find exciting the myriad colors of rocks washed down over time from a far mountain range. I thrill to the fine detail of lichens on tree bark or the shapes and shadows formed by the bark itself. I choose small vignettes from these observations of nature to translate into textile form, aiming for a sense of movement and interplay of elements as I create works that reflect fleeting moments in a dynamic and continuous cycle of creation, growth, destruction, and change.

Color, contrast, and texture are important elements in my work, as is dimensionality, whether implied through visual illusion or in actual form. For woven pieces, I weave in multiple layers with a variety of yarn fibers to achieve a richness of color and form. I work with eccentric shaping and sculptural form, often using clothing shapes as a framework for nature imagery. In non-woven work, I explore different types of fiber materials and techniques to create shapes inspired by the natural world.

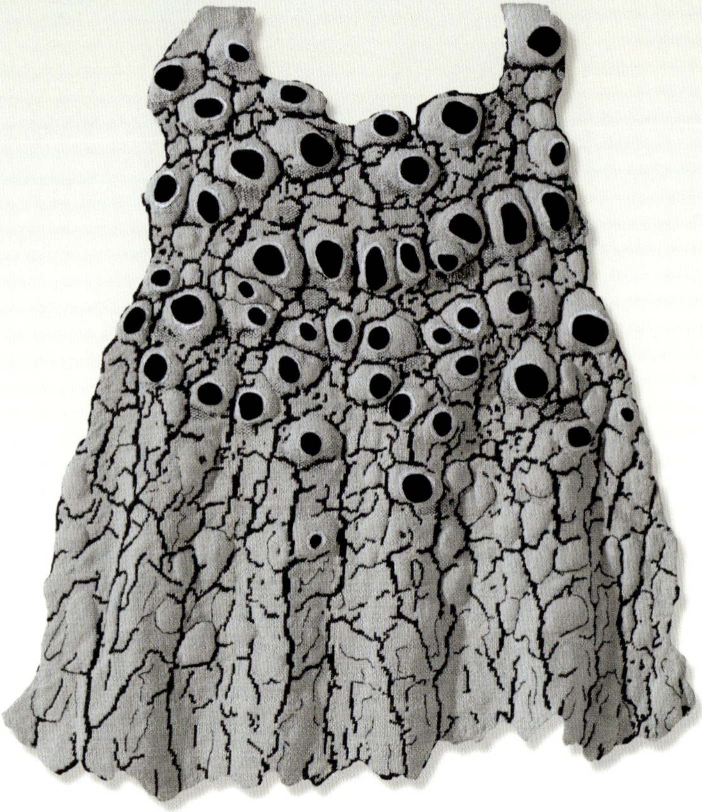

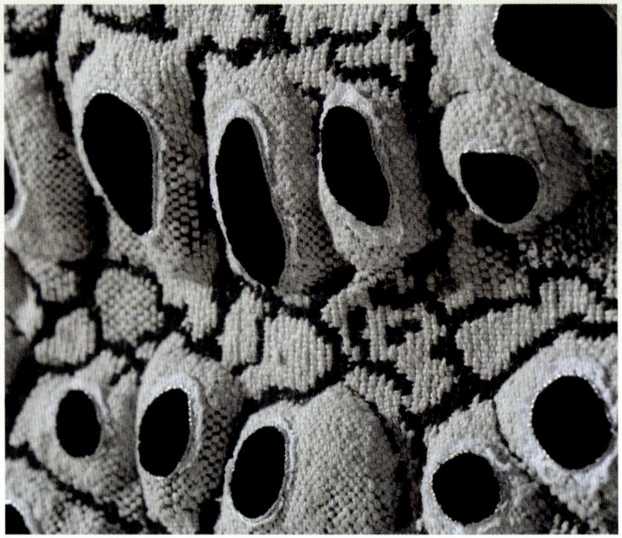

Lichen Party Frock. Cotton, silk and linen yarns, leather, cotton sewing thread, and metallic cord. 34" × 30" × 3". 2014. | Detail

All art images courtesy of Dana M. Davis.

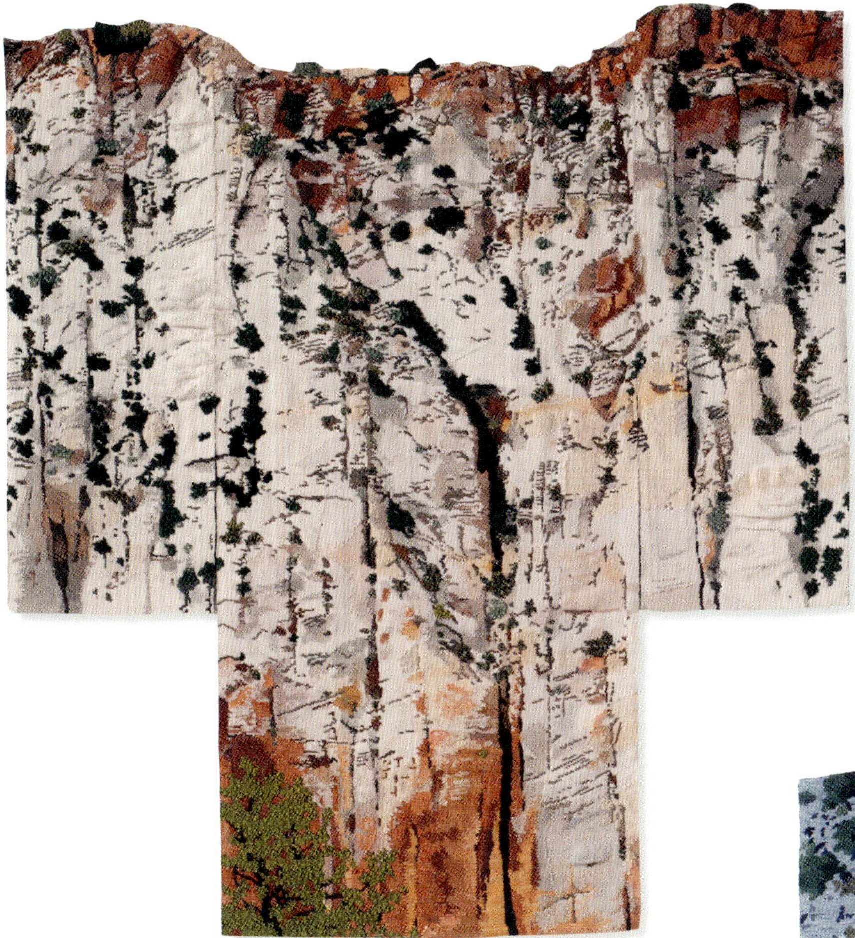

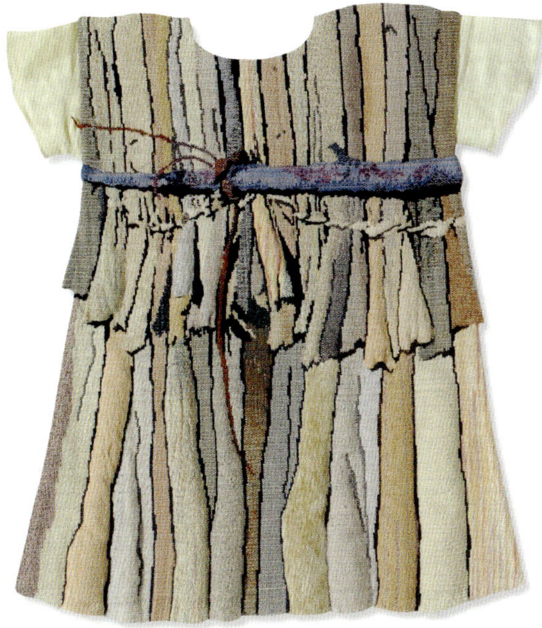

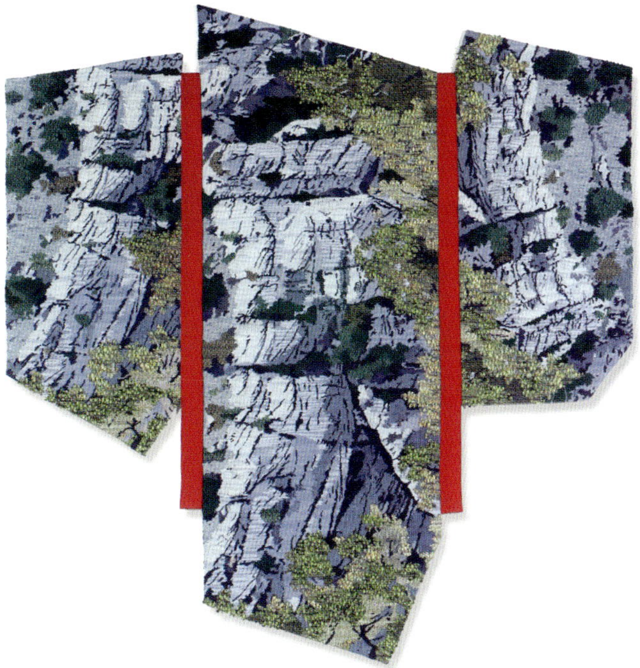

▲ *Over the Edge.* Hand woven cotton, wool, rayon, and silk yarns. 56" × 53". 2012.

◄ *Ohlone Housecoat*. Hand woven cotton, wool, rayon, silk yarns, and fabric. 36" × 33" × 1.5". 2009.

► *Canyon Kimono*. Hand woven cotton wool, rayon, and silk yarns. 59" × 58". 2006.

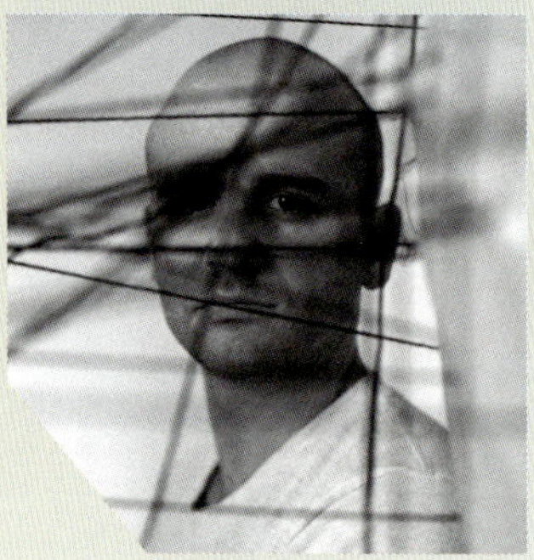

In my current body of visual art, I use line, pattern, and fiber to explore lost memories and personal histories through abstract images. I digitize the delicate hand-drawn line works and run them through an embroidery formatting software that attempts to translate the simple two-dimensional pencil lines into a complex, thread-based object. The results are beautiful, impromptu abstractions that are systematically made when the line drawings are mistranslated through a logic-based machine. I am essentially trying to teach my sewing machine to think and react like a painter!

Most recently, I earned the Eben Demarest Trust Award from the Pittsburgh Foundation—a prize shared with Jackson Pollock. I was named Best in Show at the Three Rivers Arts Festival, featured at Aqua Art Miami @ Art Basel, and accepted in the Smithsonian Institution's Contemporary Craft Show.

Terry M. Boyd

Pittsburgh, Pennsylvania

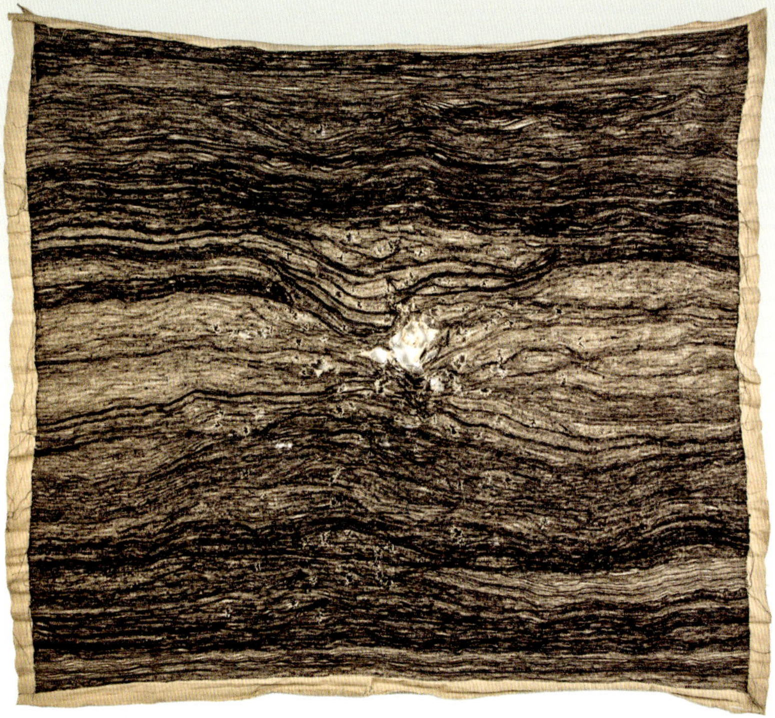

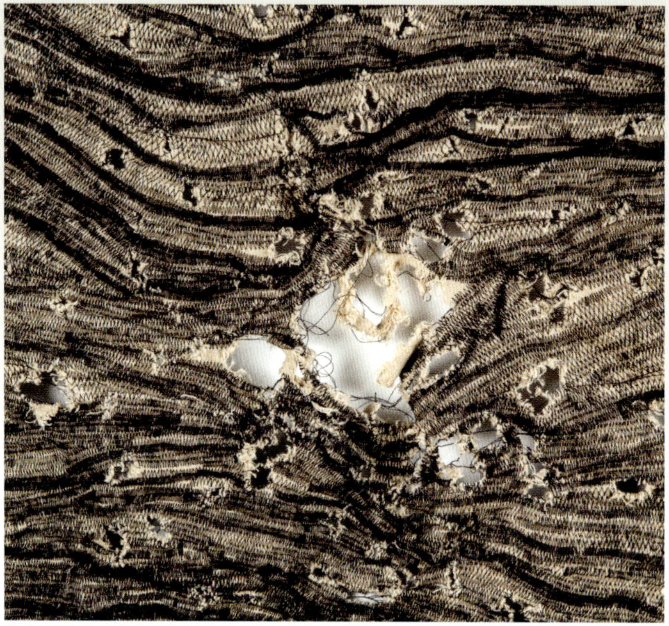

Perhaps She Is Frightened at Being Dead. 9.2 miles of thread on linen. 72" × 72". 2014. Courtesy of Adam Milliron. | Detail

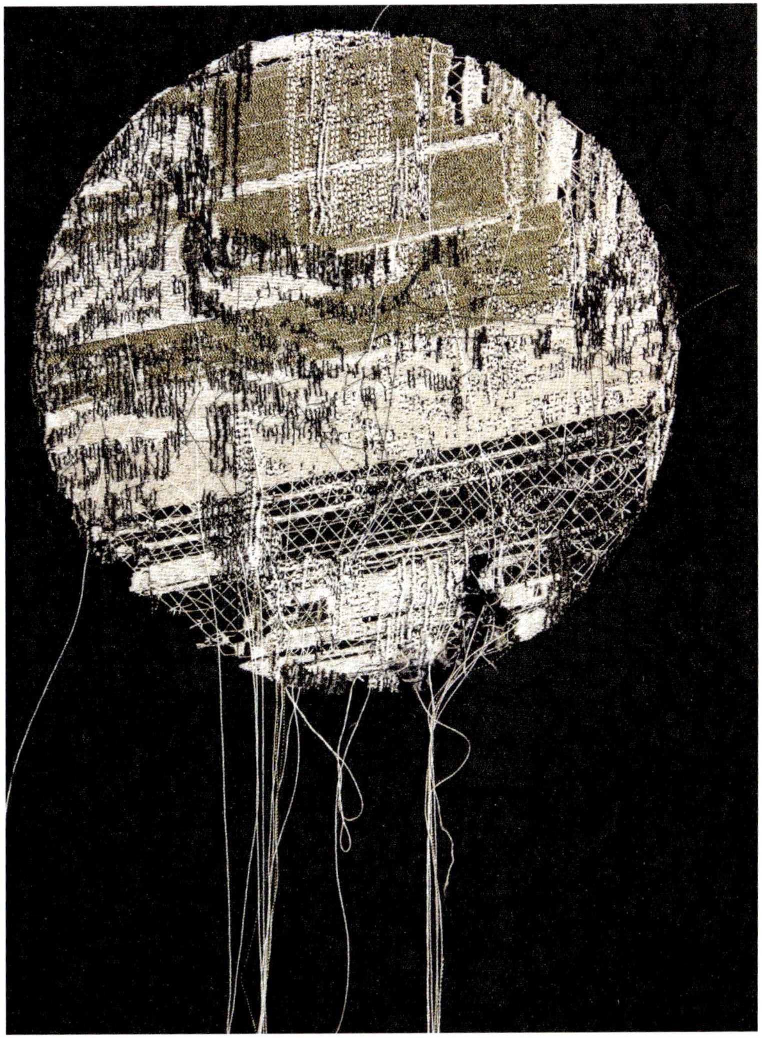

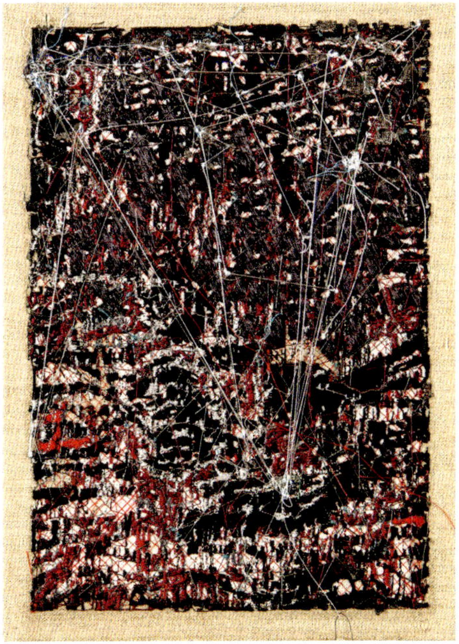

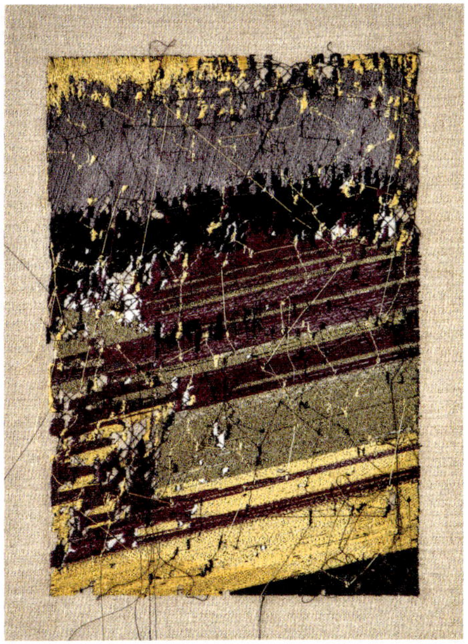

▲ *Infinity Plus One (WR 42e).* Rayon thread on fabric. 12" × 9". 2015.

◄ *Insufficient Data For Meaningful Answer (NGC 4889).* Rayon thread on linen. 12" × 9". 2014. Courtesy of Adam Milliron.

► *Insufficient Data For Meaningful Answer (RX J1532.9+3021).* Rayon thread on linen. 12" × 9". 2014. Courtesy of Adam Milliron.

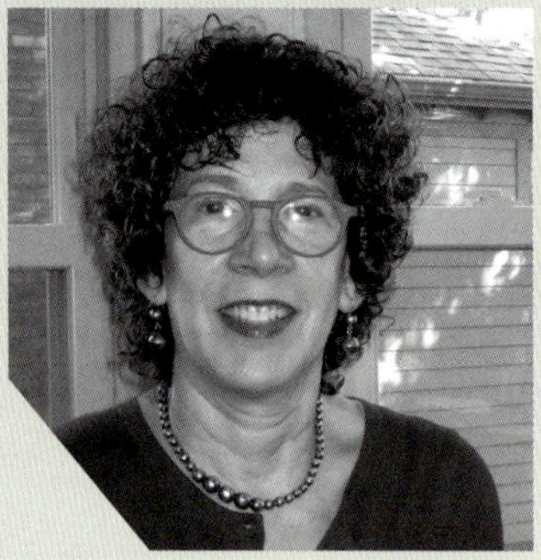

Schooled as a painter and printmaker, I love the immediacy of drawing and painting, but am also drawn to fiber. In working with fiber, I have employed a number of printmaking techniques, including silkscreen and block printing. My favorite is paper matrix lithography, which I studied in Italy and have adapted for fabric. When my drawings are printed on cotton batting with this technique, they retain the luscious quality of a rich charcoal drawing.

To enhance my imagery, I often use surface design techniques, such as rusting, needle felting, dyeing, painting, or stitching, and unusual printmaking techniques, such as Chine-collé. I am very interested in experimenting, pushing both my work and myself in new directions untethered by tradition.

Michelle Browne

Pittsburgh, Pennsylvania

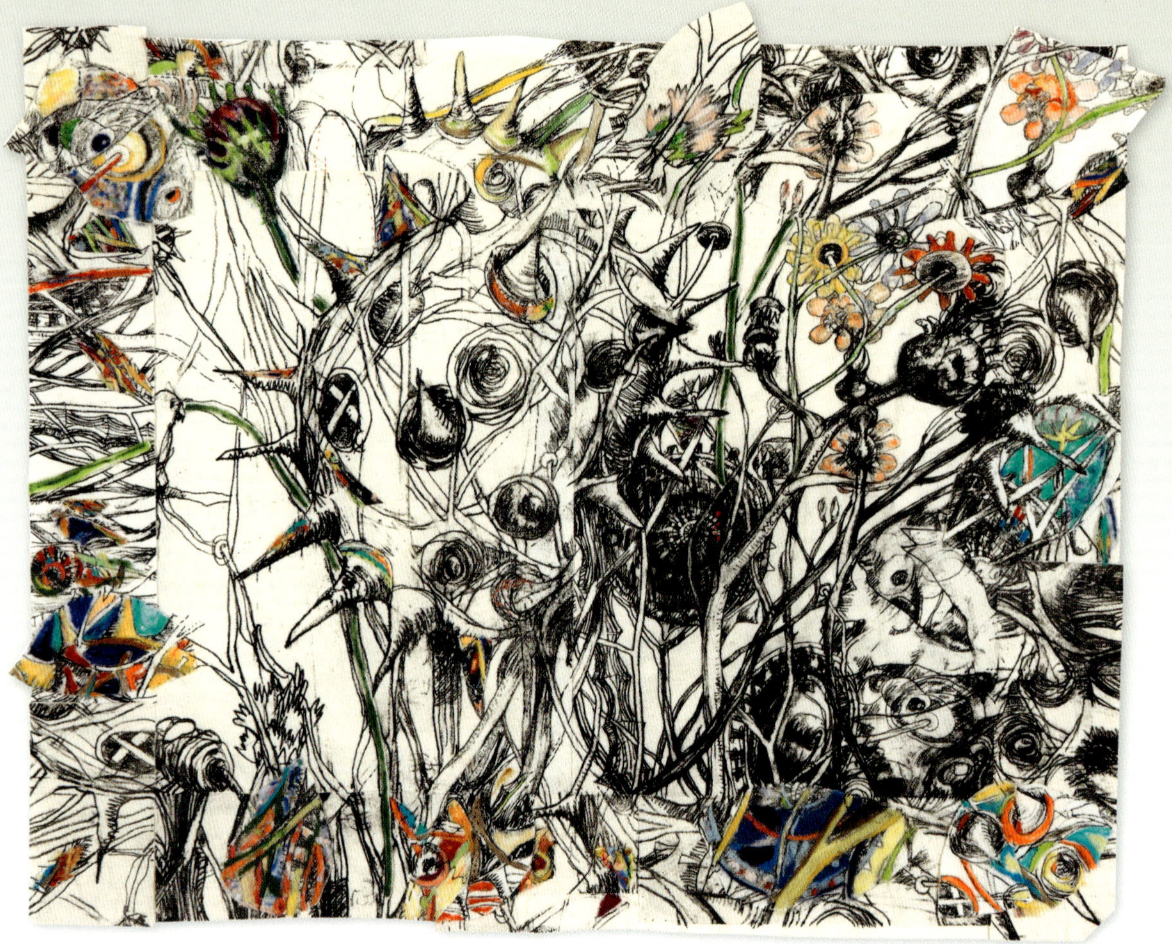

Floradora Grande.
Oil base etching ink on cotton batting, hand dyed wool, and silk roving. 43" × 53". 2015.

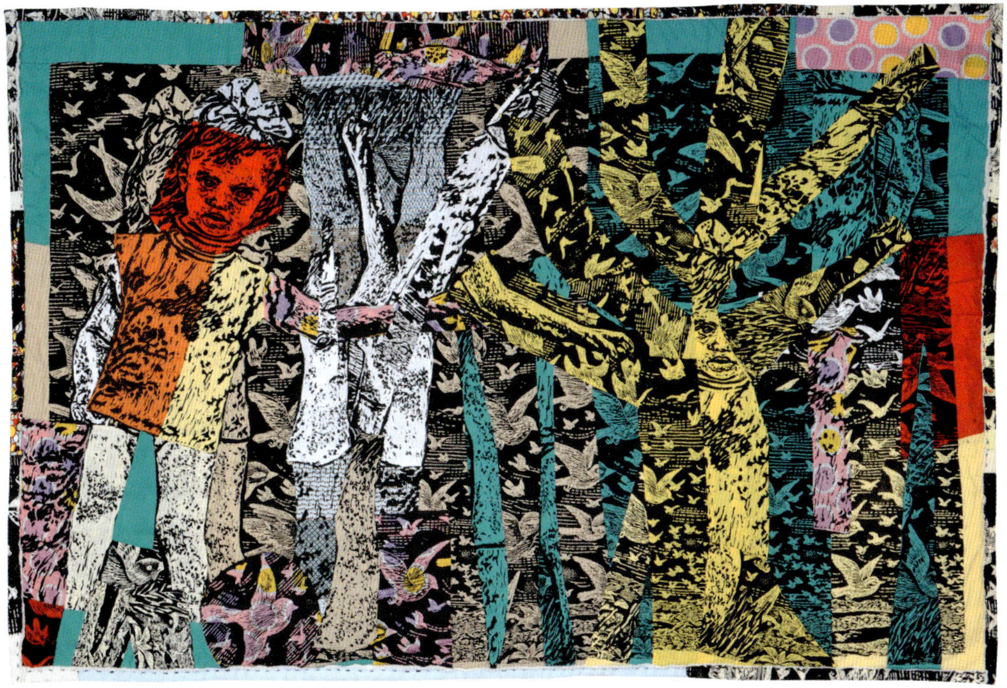

◄ *Betsy in the Forest*. Commercial cotton fabrics and silkscreen ink. Collaboration with Leslie Golomb and quilted by Louise Silk. 45" × 68". 2009.

► *Life on Europa*. Heavily rusted silk noil, gesso, acrylic paint, India ink, and vintage lace. 48" × 49". 2015.

▼ *Red Thicket*. Cotton batting, silk organza, embroidery floss, and oil base etching ink. 34" × 52". 2015.

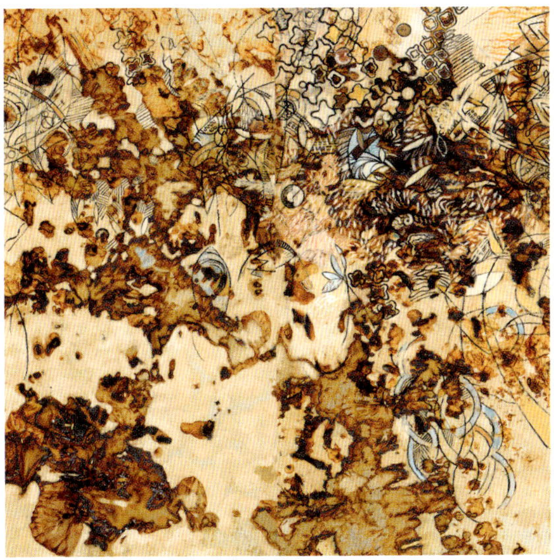

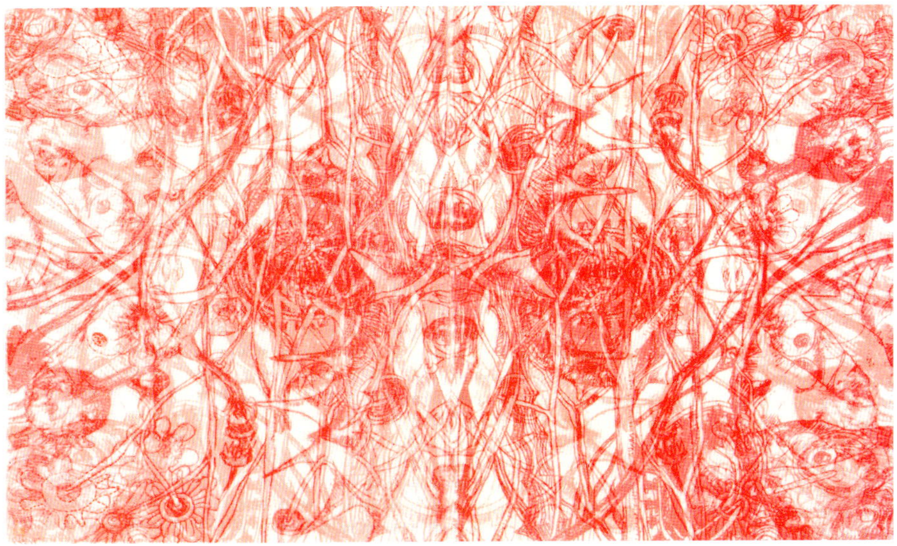

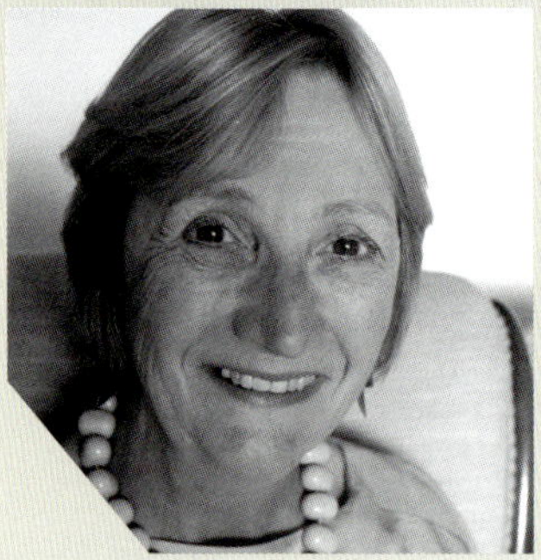

Rosemary Campbell

Edinburgh, Scotland

I was born and brought up on the banks of the Tay in the east of Scotland, and for a long time this river landscape with its reflections, beautiful light, and family connections was the inspiration for my work. Recently, however, a visit to Rome captured my imagination, allowing me to change from the rural to an urban landscape. I felt as though I was in the here and now—and that I was also in the "there and then." The pattern of the mosaics, the color and textures of the ancient buildings, the art and imagery found in the churches all conveyed a sense of perpetuity.

I love to use traditional techniques in a contemporary way. I draw, paint, photograph, and collage, incorporating found objects and emphasizing them using couched gold thread and reverse appliqué, and a variety of hand-dyed fabrics ranging from silk to felt.

I trained at Duncan of Jordanstone College of Art in Dundee, specializing in screen printing and embroidery. Throughout my career, I developed these techniques more into mixed media while maintaining stitch as an important element.

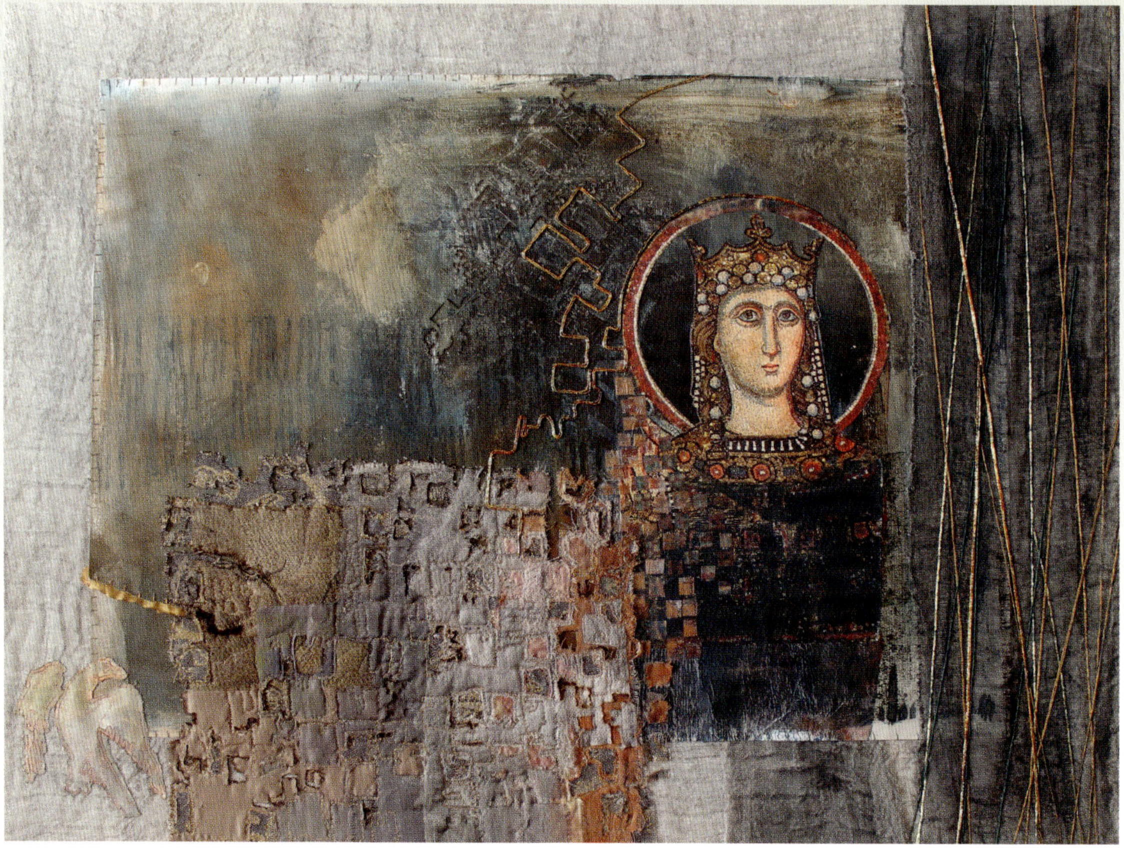

Sanctity. Paper, paint, hand dyed fabric, hand stitch and couched metal thread. 23.6" × 31.5". 2015.

All art images courtesy of Heather Jack.

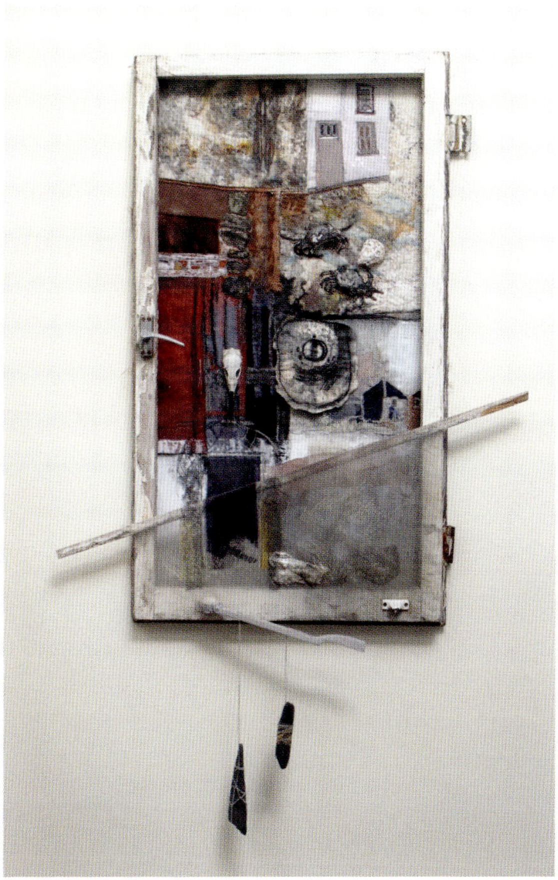

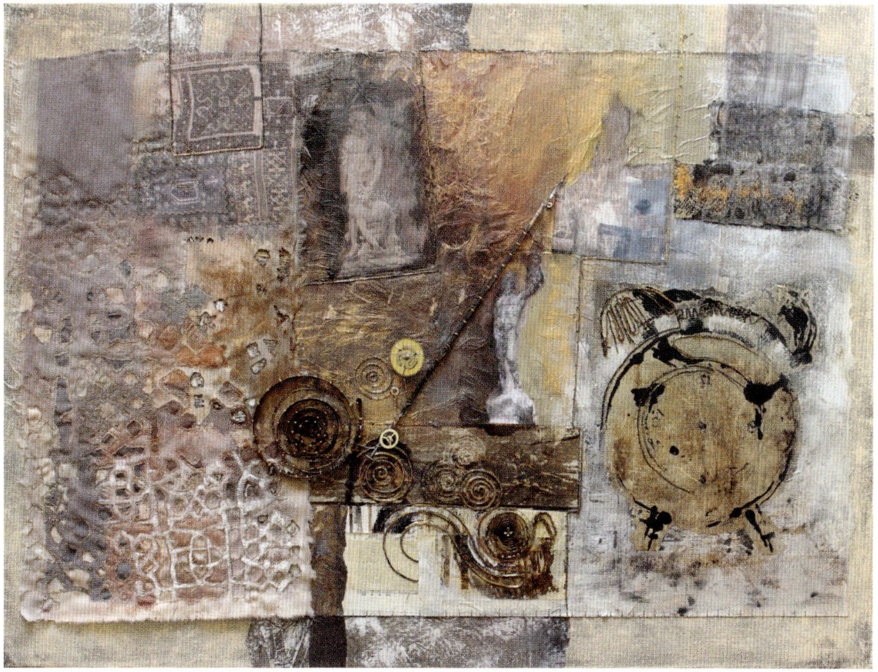

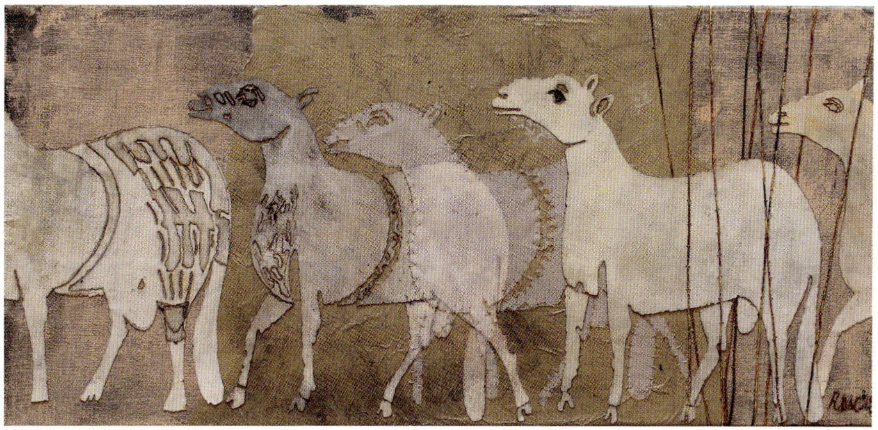

▲ *Window of Opportunity.* Paper, paint, organza, felt, found objects, machine and hand stitch. 51.2" × 23.6". 2008.

◄ *There and Then.* Paper, paint, hand dyed fabric, hand stitch and couched metal thread. 23.6" × 31.5". 2015.

► *Follow Me.* Paper, paint, organza, and couched metal thread. 7.9" × 19.7". 2015.

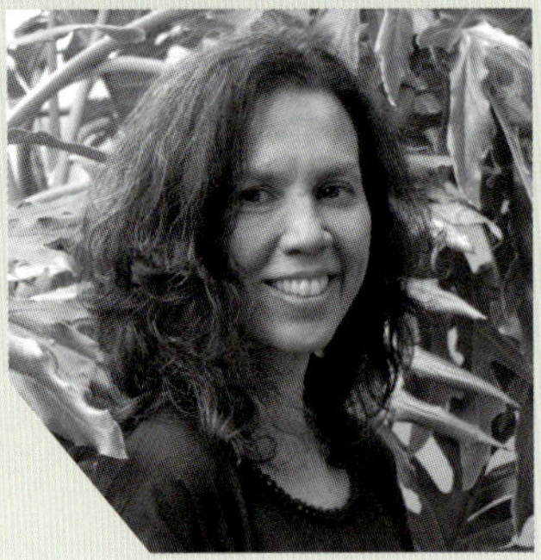

Courtesy of Zoltan Kovacs.

Ying Chew

Sydney, Australia

I draw my influences from the history of art, other cultural traditions, folk art, and iconography, focusing on textiles and embellishment. I am also interested in the relationship between women and needlework; the making of textiles ranges from being representative of domestic constraint and drudgery to being a means of creativity and self, social, and political expression.

In using textiles as a medium, I am trying to challenge the distinction between art and craft. But also, by combining the innocent form of needlework with macabre or even sinister subject matter, I hope to trick the viewer into thinking about aspects of the human condition such as the impermanence of life. It seems appropriate that a medium embodying a conceptual idea should not be everlasting, which makes textiles particularly suitable.

Today, textiles are products of technology, which means that there is little opportunity to instill them with individual and spiritual values. I am interested in combining the technological with the handmade. Specifically, I use digital technology as a tool to produce a pattern, which is then hand-embroidered, employing techniques that have been used for centuries. In this way I hope to imbue humble raw materials with a uniqueness, visual richness, and excitement.

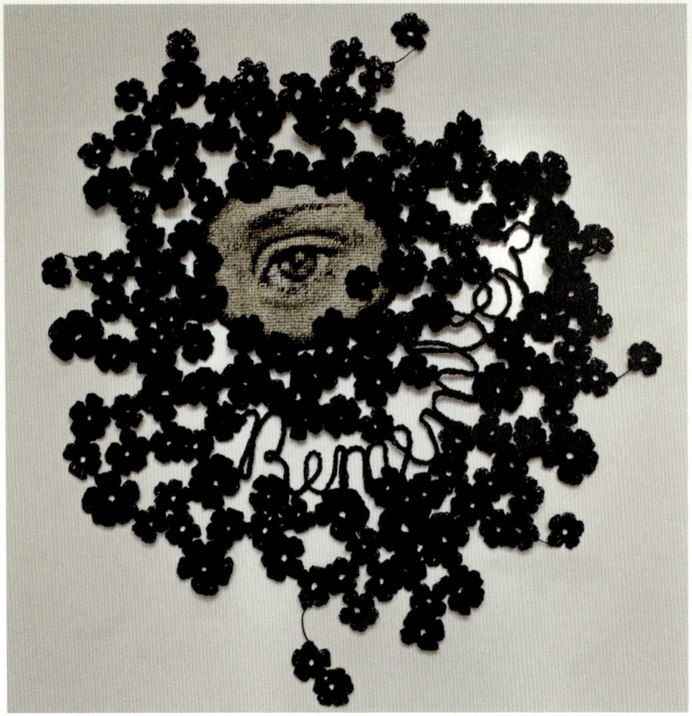

Remember 3. Linen. 8" × 8". 2014.

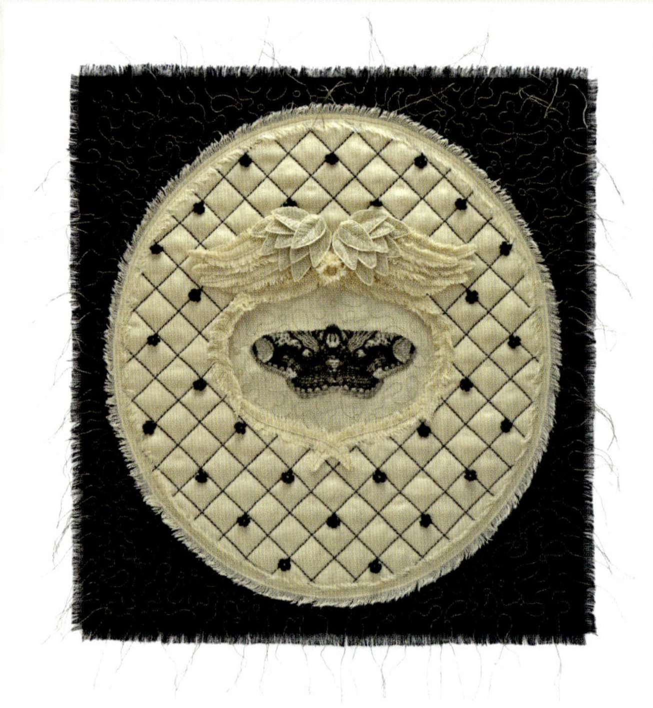

Memento Mori 4. Linen. 18" × 16" × 1". 2012.

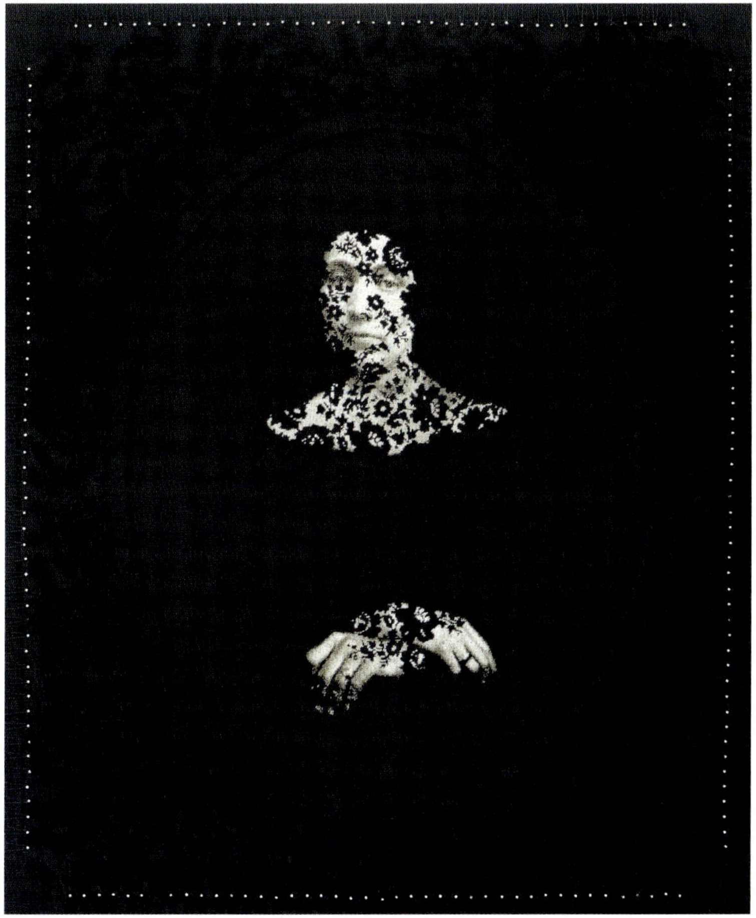

Unidentified Woman 5. Linen. 24" × 20" × 2". 2015.

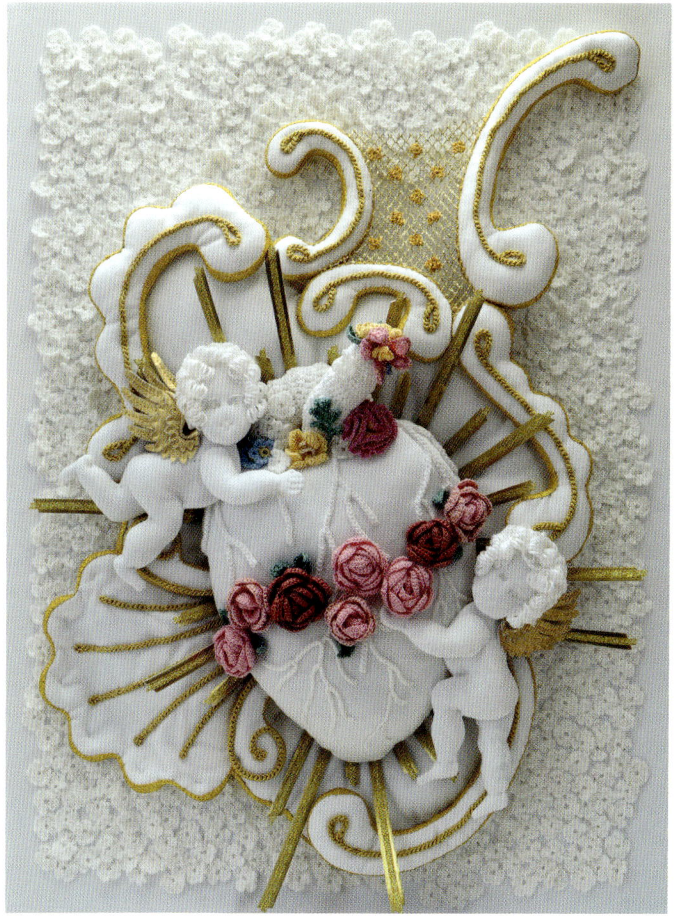

Cor Immaculatum. Mixed textiles. 20" × 14". 2013.

Photo: Pompi Gutnisky.

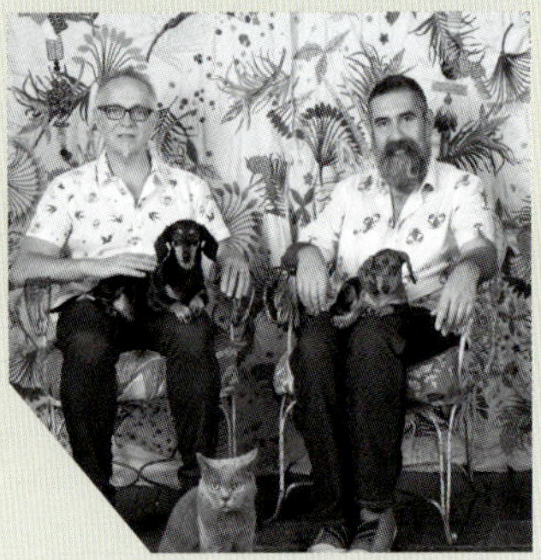

Chiachio & Giannone

Buenos Aires, Argentina

We have been devoting ourselves to embroidery since 2003. We consider ourselves one artist with four hands and two heads and believe that this collaborative process-based method can expand the boundaries of our art. As we experiment with embroidery, traditionally known and associated with women, we transform a handicraft art form into the dual work of a male couple; it also demonstrates that two men can access this world with absolute freedom. Two men playing as children . . .

We are also interested in working with the simple and most common materials such as ones found in school—glitter, colored pencils—or in domestic usage—sewing thread, embroiders, embellished buttons.

In all of our works, our self-portraits remain as the main characters. In our portraits, where we are the unique players, the image of Piolin (our dachshund), our pet-son, began to appear. The scenes in which we situate ourselves arise from the research we do on legends and myths of different cultures.

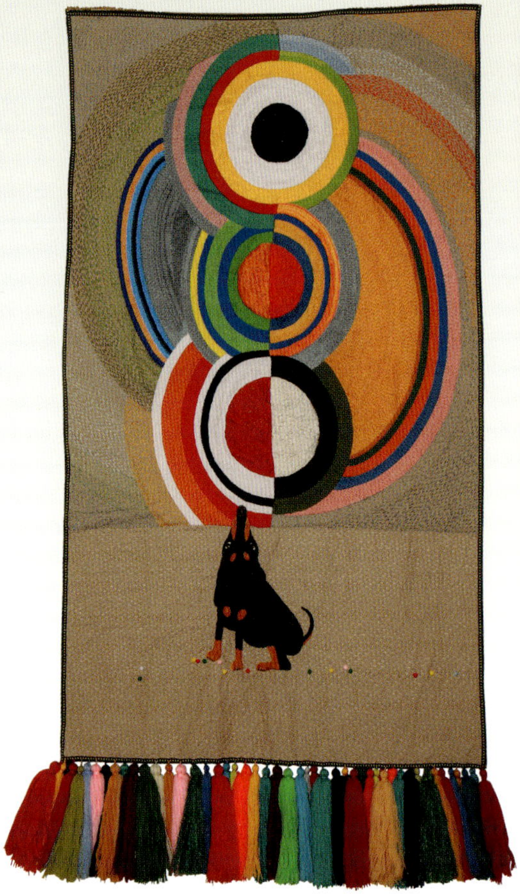

Payé en el Pompidou.
Cotton thread and embroidery floss on Hermès linen towel. 51.1" × 31.2". 2014. Photo: Gabriel Cano.

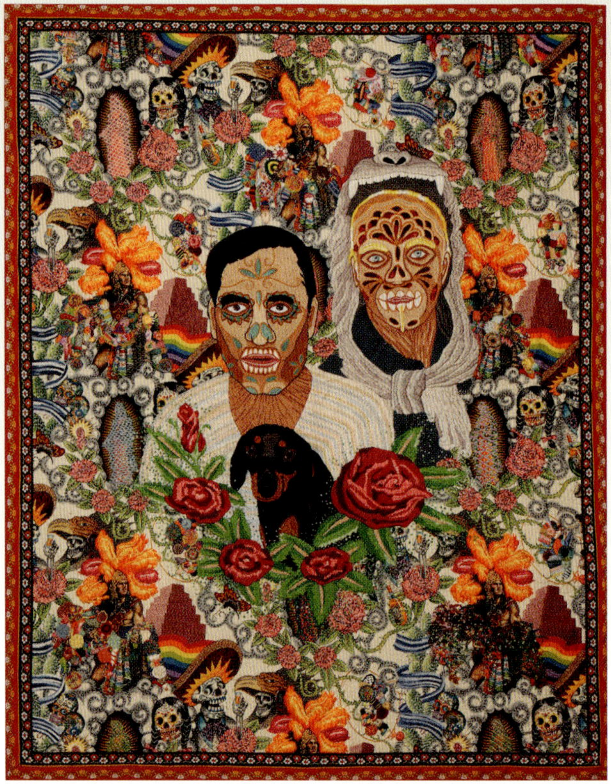

➤ *Calaverita* (Skull). Cotton thread and embroidery floss on Alexander Henry© fabric. 43.2" × 55". 2014. Photo: Gabriel Cano.

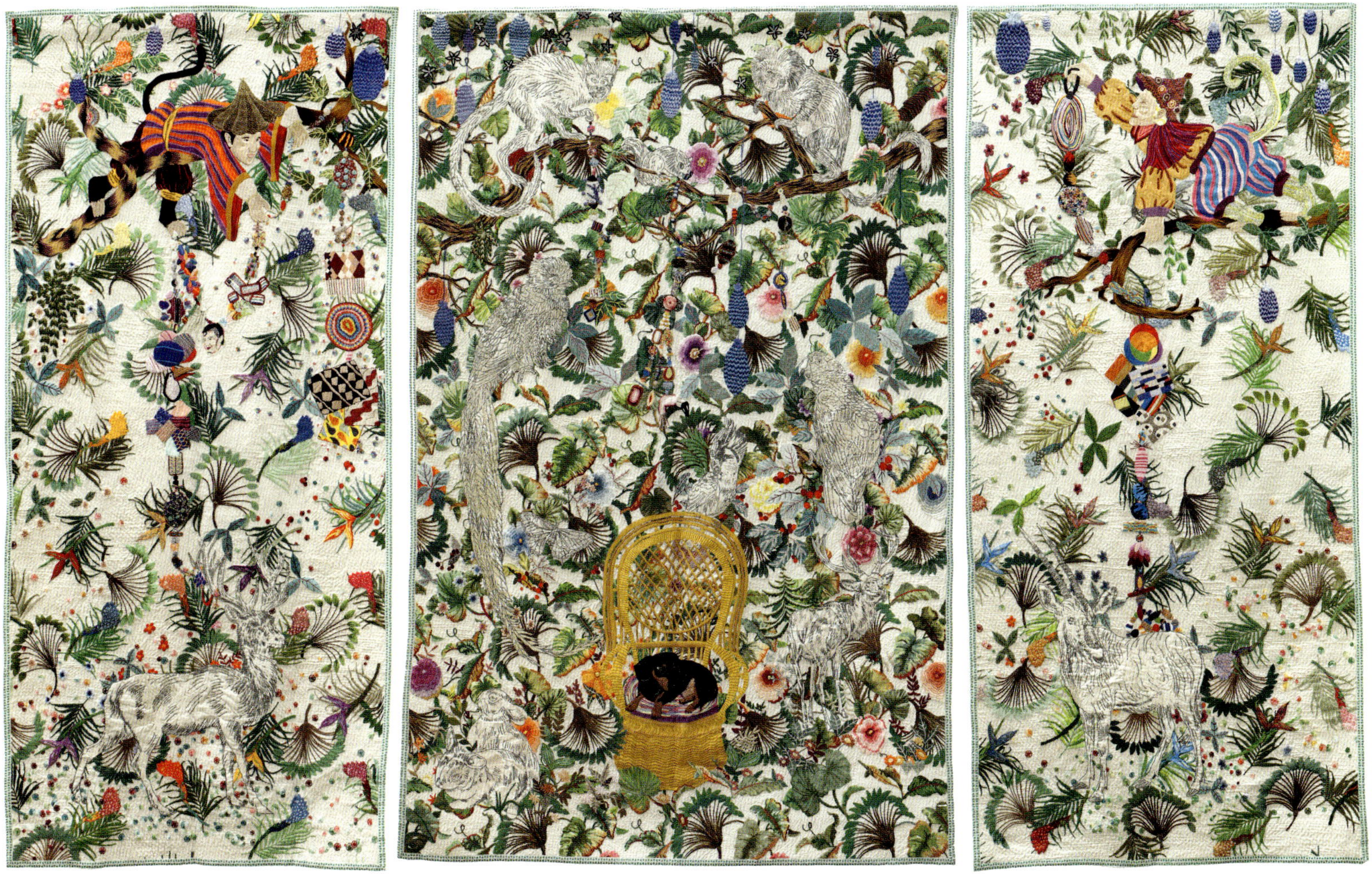

Selva Blanca (White Jungle). Cotton thread, wool, and embroidery floss on fabric. 110.2" × 181.1". 2014–2015. Photo: Nacho Iasparra.

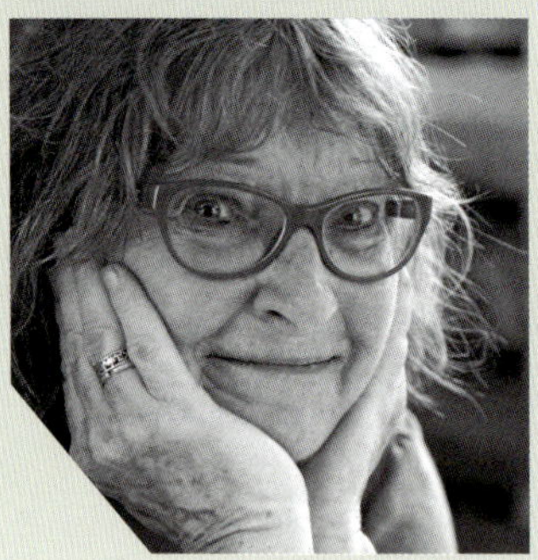

Jette Clover

Antwerp, Belgium

I love living in the city with its arbitrary layers of communication. I am especially inspired by the walls with posters, advertisements, messages about lost pets, and scrawling graffiti. Almost all of my work refers to writing. I was a journalist before I became an artist, and language and communication continue to be my main source of inspiration—from printed book pages to handwritten notes and letters, from crude graffiti to overlapping advertisements in the streets. The text on my pieces is meant to be seen rather than to be read and symbolizes our human need to communicate.

I construct my quilts like a collage with many layers of cotton, linen, cheese cloth, and paper, which I have painted, printed, screened, rusted, and bleached. I am fond of subtle colors and of hand-quilting with big stitches. For the last five years, I have been focusing on the color white and on handwriting.

I was born and raised in Denmark, but I have lived and worked for many years in the United States and the Netherlands. Since 2005, I have lived in the beautiful old city of Antwerp. I have a degree in art history, and for more than ten years I curated exhibitions for the Dutch Textile Museum. Besides being a maker, I also teach workshops and masters classes internationally.

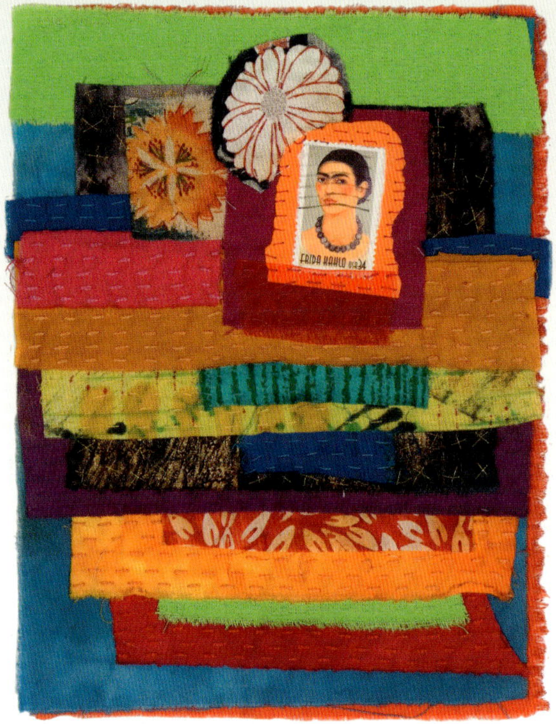

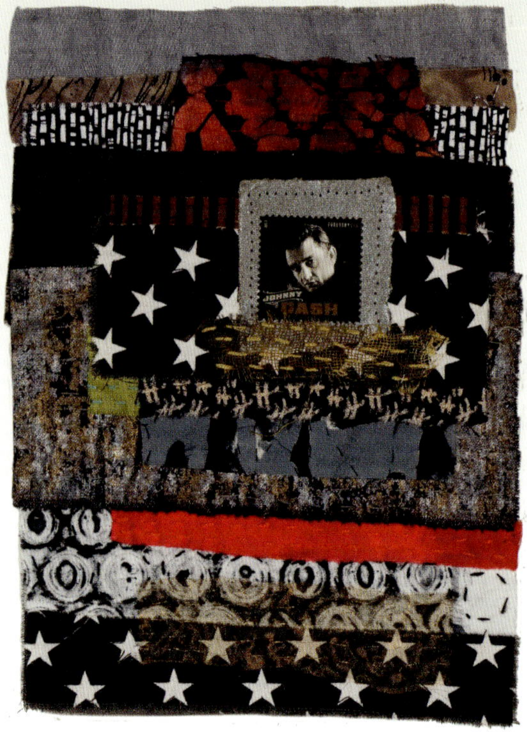

Small Note #243, Frida Kahlo. Scrap metal and postage stamp. 8" × 6". 2012.

➤ *Small Note #303, Johnny Cash.* Scrap metal and postage stamp. 8" × 6". 2014.

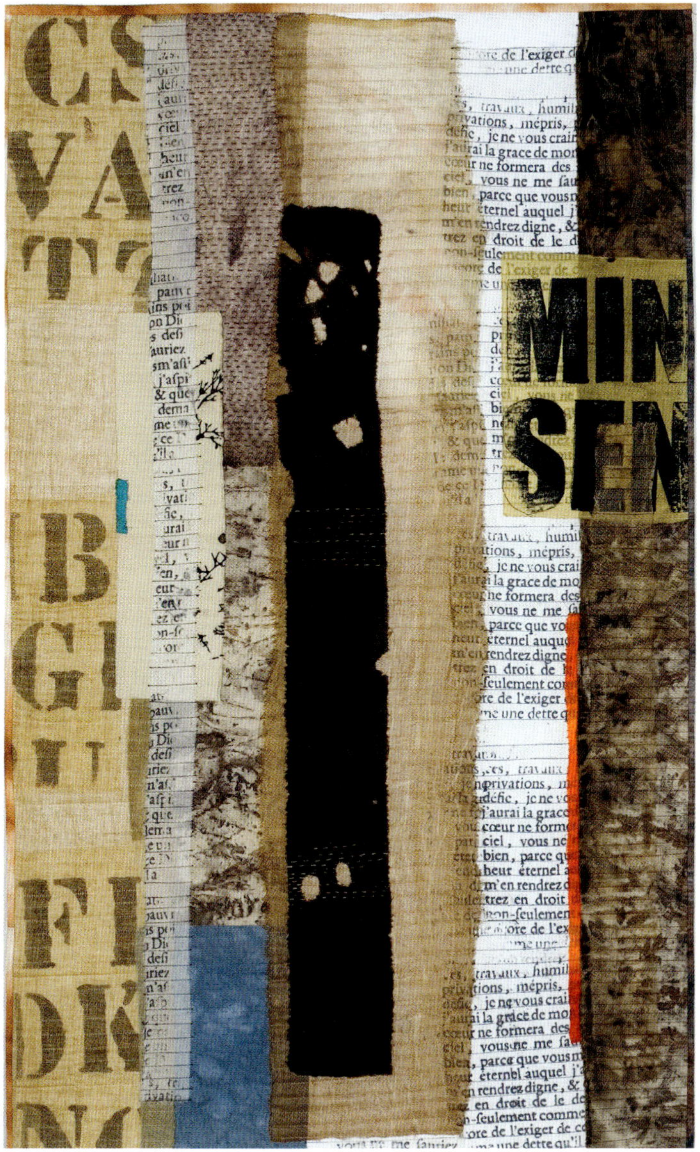

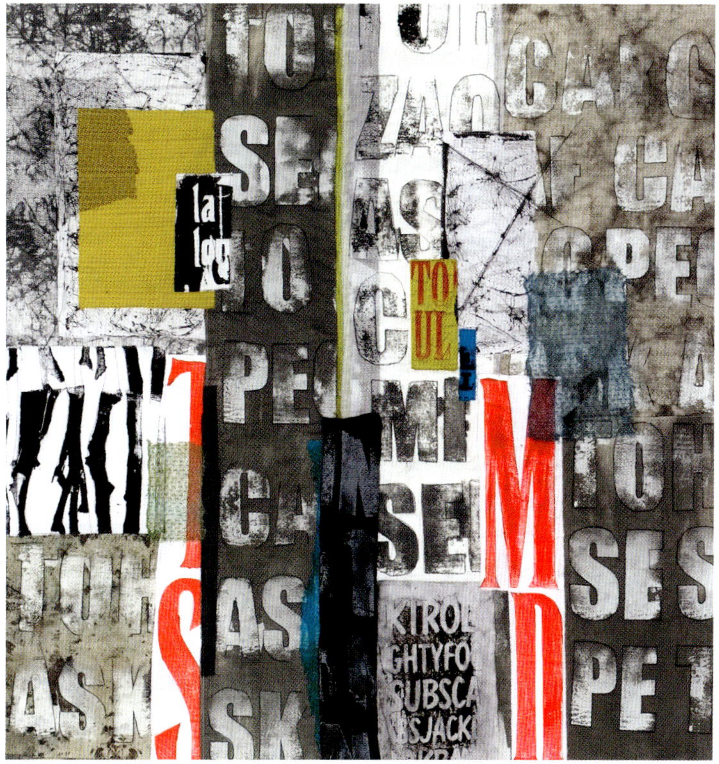

◄ *Conversation with B.* Cotton, linen, silk, and cheesecloth. 59" × 31". 2014.

▲ *Metropolis 6.* Cotton, linen, and cheesecloth. 41" × 40". 2015.

All images courtesy of Pol Leemans.

Courtesy of Daniel Mathieu - Devezon LLC.

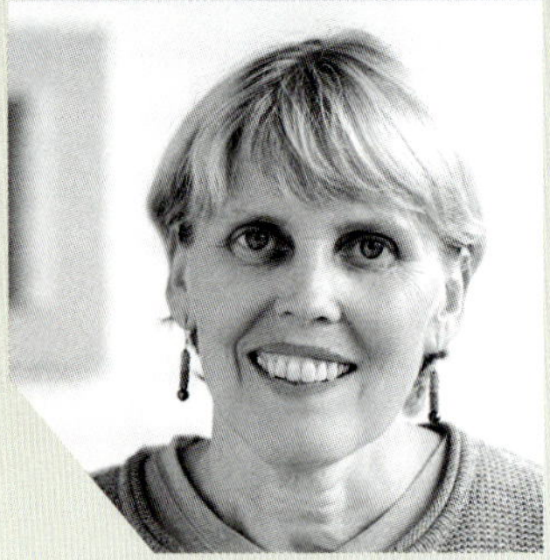

Tarja Cockell

North Andover, Massachusetts

My fiber art explores traditional textile techniques with a contemporary twist. As a native of Finland, my work reflects the Scandinavian sense of simplicity in design. My desire to be creative with my hands led me to pursue a degree in weaving and design. I have worked as a weaving teacher and as an independent artist and designer.

I enjoy the process of weaving and the unique textures it creates. My motifs vary from abstract to representational images and are often merely suggestive, hinting at shapes and forms. I strive to expand the boundaries of traditional weaving by achieving a more painterly sensibility that weaving alone does not offer.

To express my artistic intention fully, I incorporate several different techniques, such as dyes, paint, appliqué, and stitching, to create a layered, three-dimensional effect. The viewer is encouraged to look closely and explore the depths within the different fiber layers and to try and understand the mystery behind the subtle effects. The effects of the layers change when viewed from varying perspectives, creating a dynamic relationship between the viewer and the work. My current direction is towards the interplay of these textural and three-dimensional qualities using contour, light, and shadow.

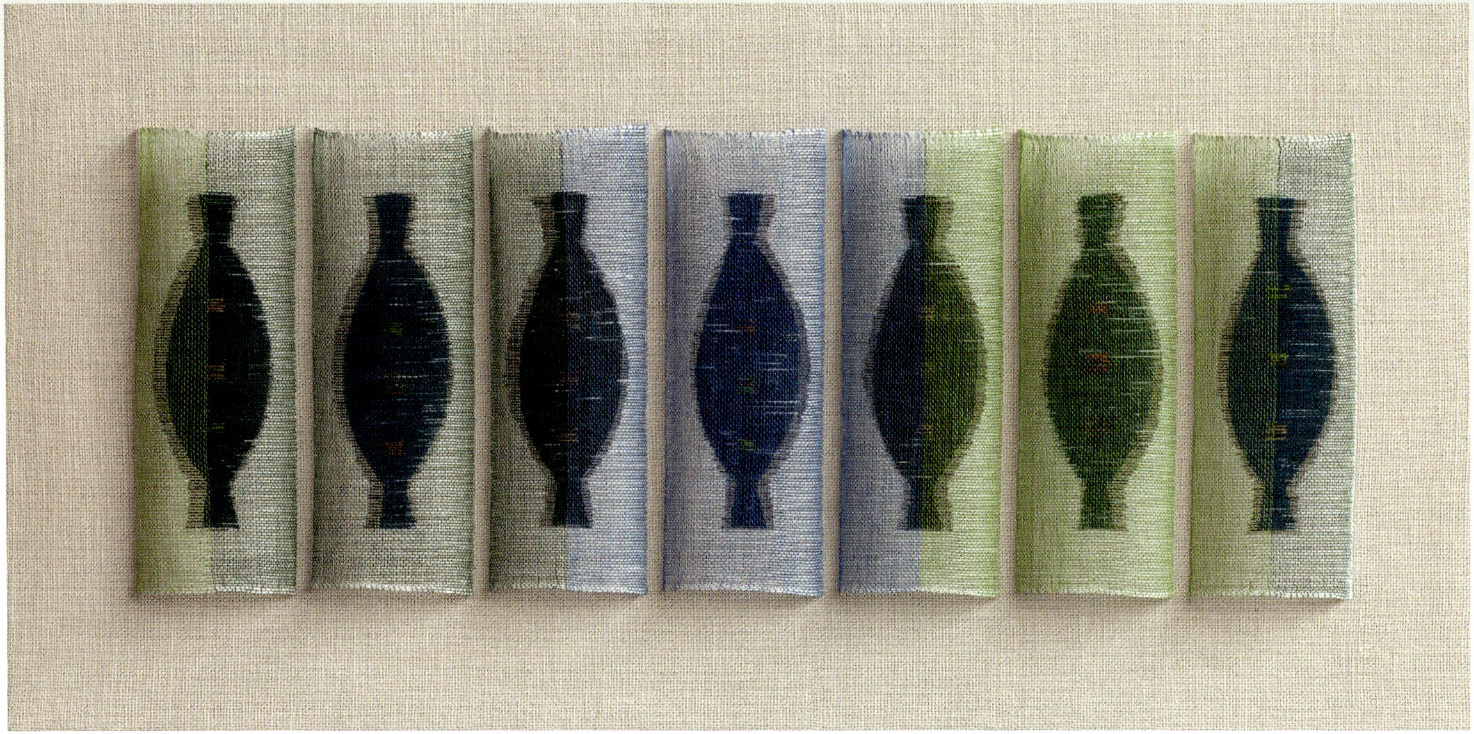

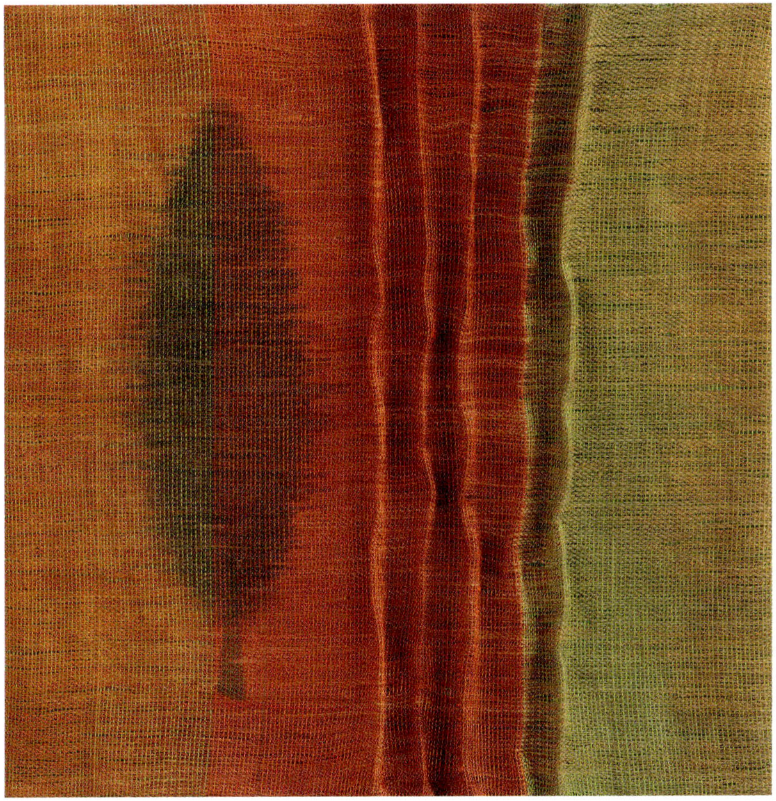

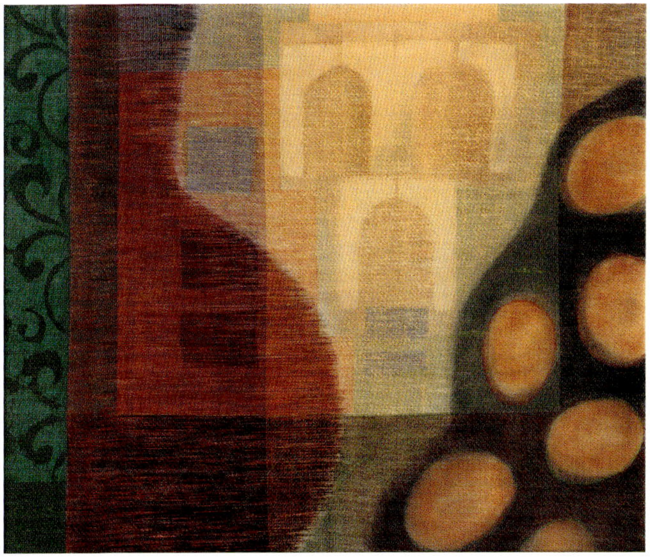

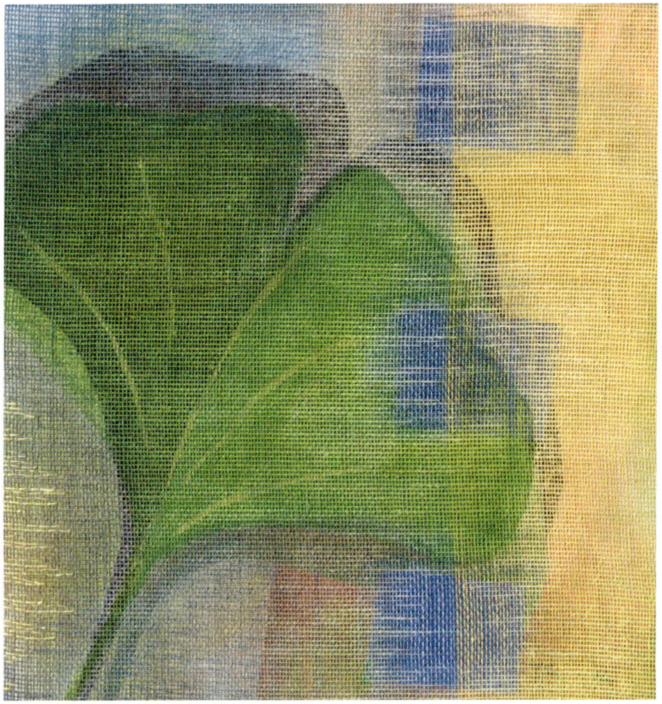

OPPOSITE
Vessels. Linen, cotton, and paper yarn, hand woven and painted with acrylic. 19" × 39". 2014. Courtesy of Daniel Mathieu – Devezon LLC.

▲ *Greener on the Other Side.* Linen, coated copper, hand woven and warp painted with acrylic. 12" × 12". 2015.
Courtesy of Daniel Mathieu – Devezon LLC.

◄ *The Window.* Top layer: hand woven linen, stitching, and acrylic. Under layer: cotton, appliqué, and stitching. 28" × 34". 2013.
Courtesy of Daniel Mathieu – Devezon LLC.

► *Ginkgo.* Top layer: hand woven linen, stitching, and acrylic. Under layer: cotton, appliqué, and stitching. 12" × 12". 2014. Courtesy of Jeffrey Engel.

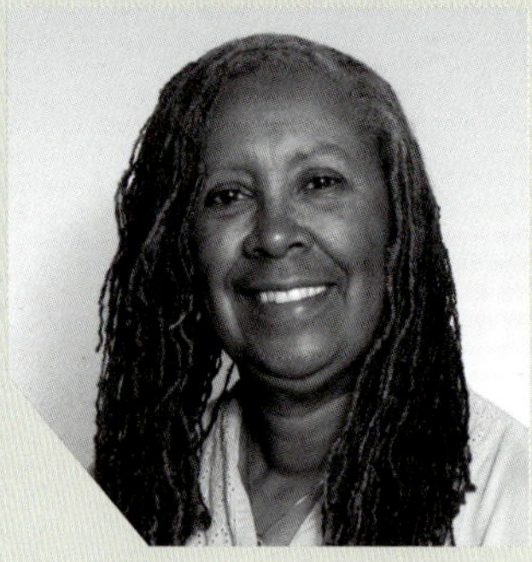

Marion Coleman

Castro Valley, California

For over a decade, I have been making art that is inspired by people, history, and social/cultural events and their impact on our individual and community relationships. These works explore traditional and contemporary techniques related to quilting and fiber collage with a focus on narrative projects, and use technology combined with vintage and found materials. My art has been exhibited in galleries, museums, and a variety of private, educational, and public spaces both nationally and internationally.

I have completed public art projects in several California communities. I have exhibited by invitation in the US Consulate in Jerusalem; Quilt Week Yokohama, Japan; and Kaunas Biennial, Lithuania; and have shown in juried exhibitions in South Africa, Costa Rica, England, France, and Finland.

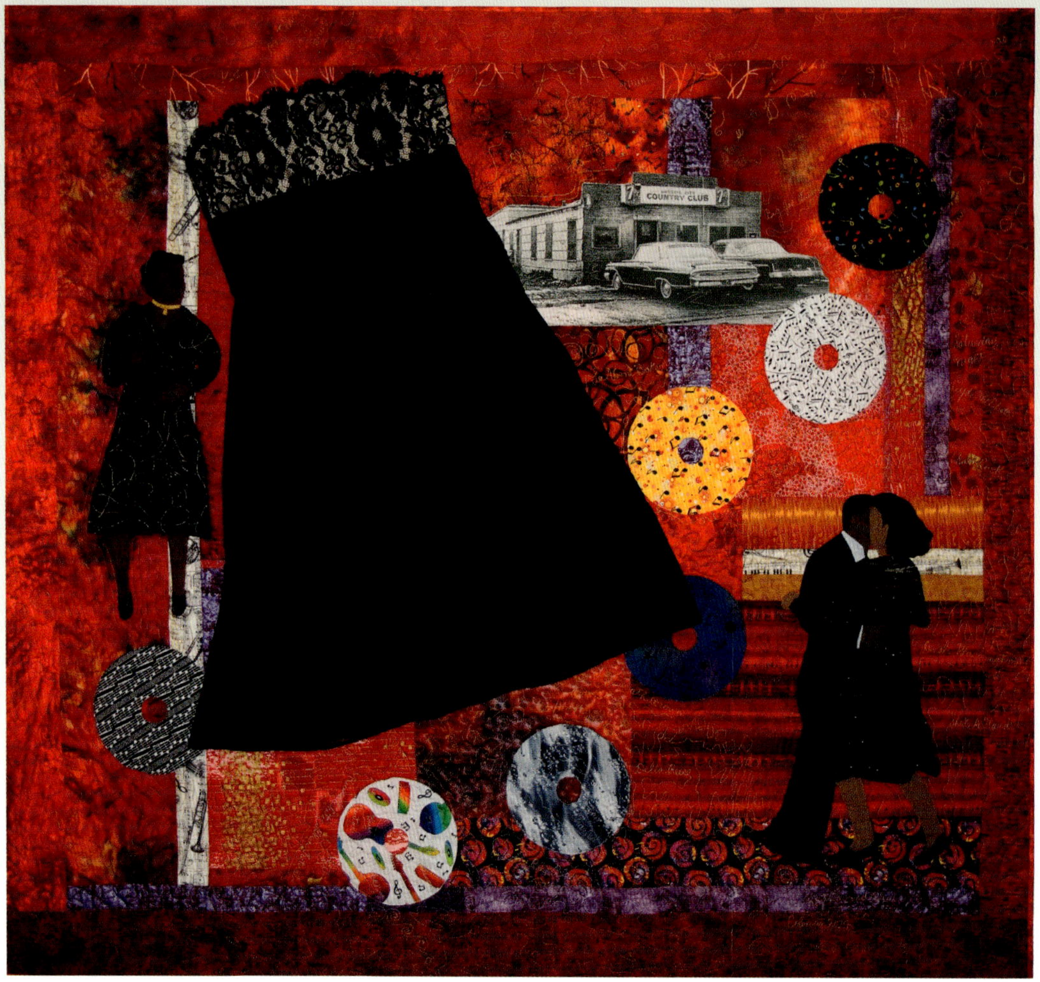

Country Club Nights. Cotton, polyester, and found garment. 52.5" × 57.5". 2014.

All art images courtesy of Eric Murphy.

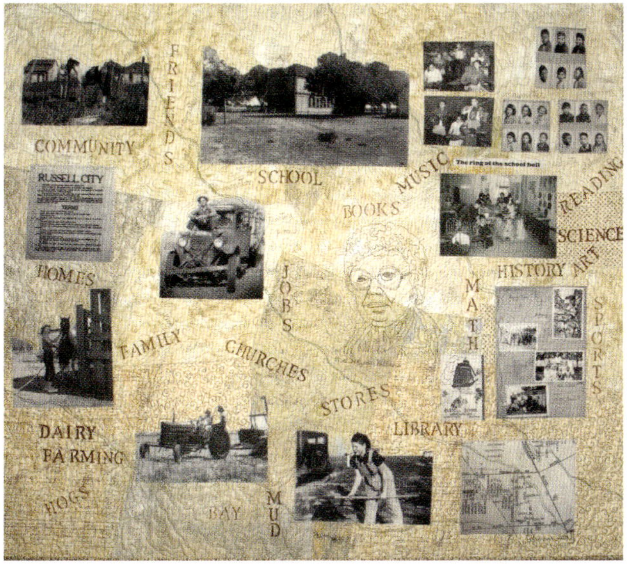

◄ *Close Ties.*
Cotton. 49.5" × 43.5". 2014.

► *We Are Family.*
Cotton. 50" × 52". 2015.

▼ *Old Glory.*
Cotton. 50" × 51.5". 2015.

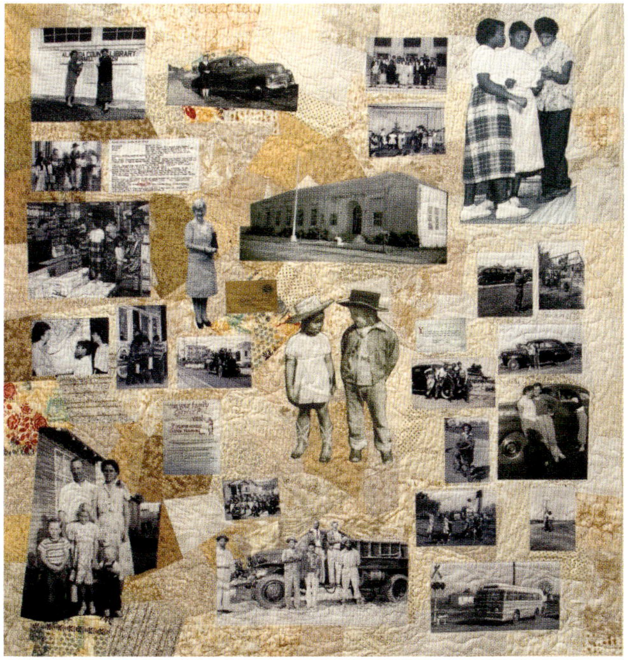

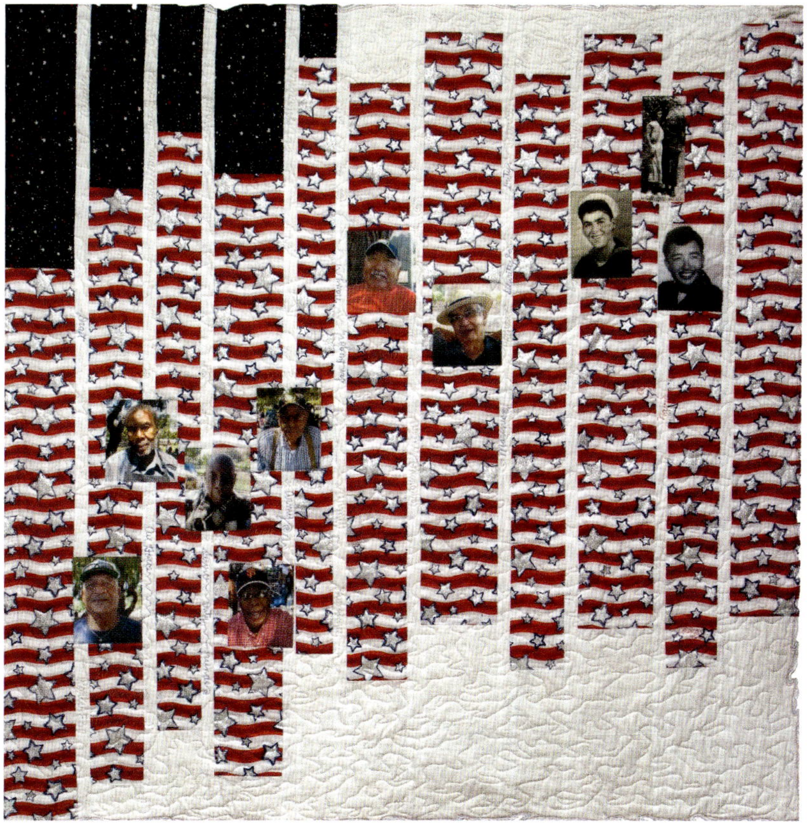

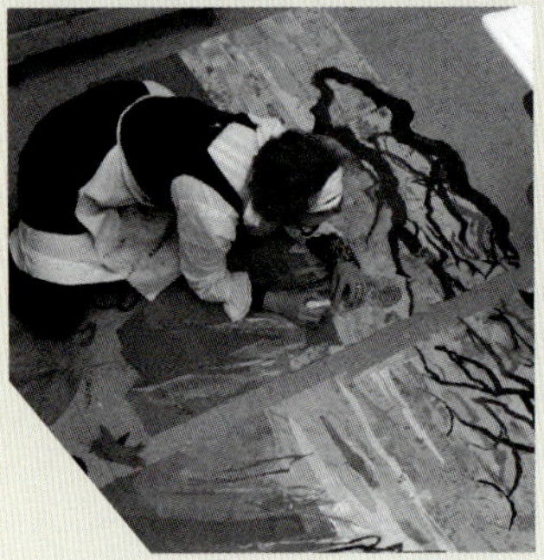

Courtesy of Rick Eifler.

Merill Comeau

Concord, Massachusetts

I am a mixed media artist creating large, wall-hung murals exploring decline, regeneration, and bloom. I bring together incongruous fibers redolent of past lives: antique silk bodices; my mother-in-law's blouses; worn blue jeans; plastic mesh vegetable bags; vintage linens; paper cups; and cardboard boxes. These cast-offs reflect memories of lives lived, social constructs of identity and class, our speeded up consumer cycle, and global issues of sustainability.

I apply traditional fabric manipulation and sewing construction methods to convey contemporary issues of loss, grief, and repair. Sometimes I use scraps in their original form respecting the source of the debris; other times I deconstruct and alter materials with paint and print; and often I use thread to draw line. I collage these snippets into a unified whole representing our shared human experience of coping with a complex world where we are bombarded with information and beset with challenges. My pieces are informally constructed and presented: glued, taped, hand- and machine-stitched, and pinned to the wall with map pins.

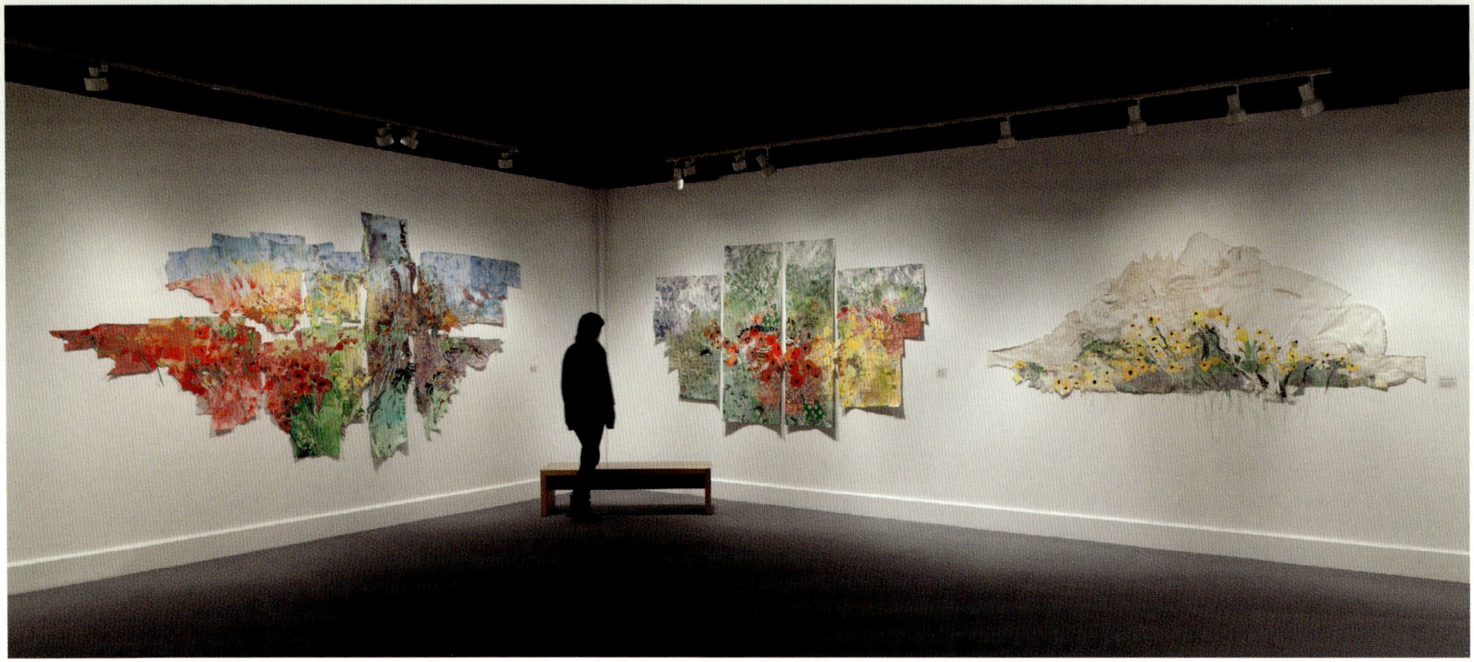

Installation view of solo exhibition, Danforth Museum of Art, Framingham, Massachusetts. 2014.
Will Howcroft Photography.

➤ *Remains of the Day*. Painted and printed discarded cardboard, Coke® cups, vegetable net bags, printed materials, saplings, and hand stitching. Size varies with installation. 2014. Will Howcroft Photography.

▼ *Alice's Garden*. Deconstructed dresses, painted and printed deconstructed repurposed clothing and linens, commercial fabrics, and machine stitching. 60" × 78". 2012. Susan Byrne Photography.

◄ *Edge of Darkness III: Remember Me*. Painted and printed vintage linens and artist's clothing, deconstructed vintage clothing, hand and machine stitching. 72" × 144". 2013. Susan Byrne Photography.

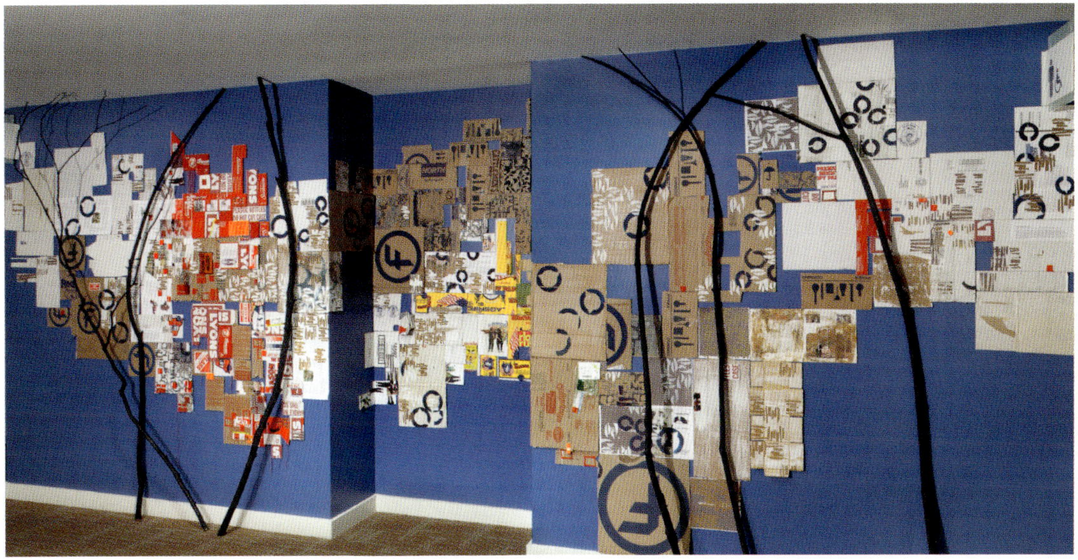

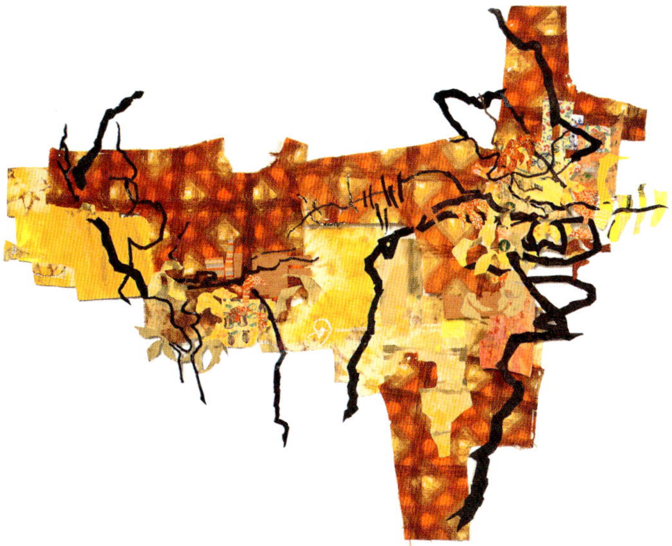

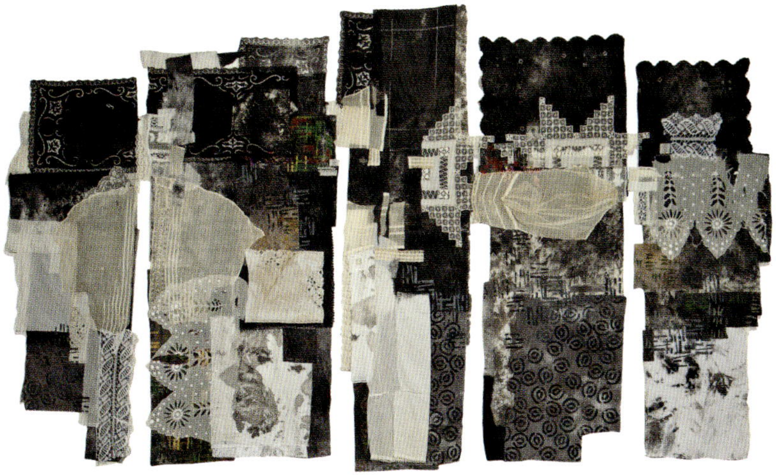

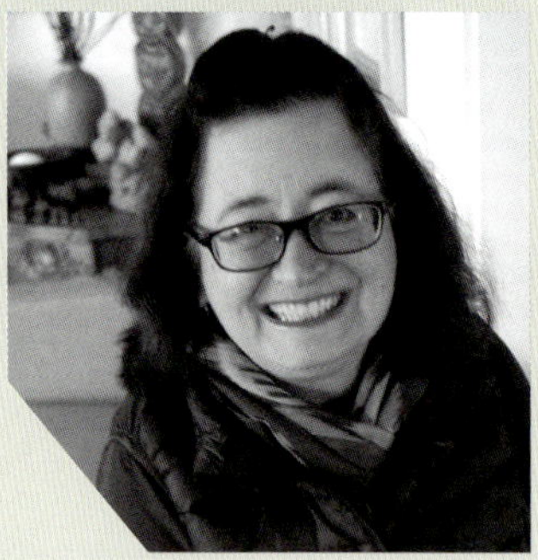

Deborah Corsini

Pacifica, California

My art is woven. I use the elements of dynamic line, expressive color, and graphic shapes to compose my tapestries. I weave with an eccentric weaving technique—wedge weave—and design my pieces while in the weaving process on the loom. In wedge weave, the weft (or weaving yarn) is woven at an angle to the warp. This causes the parallel warp threads to deflect, creating the undulating scalloped edges, an additional and wonderful byproduct of the technique. I love the rhythmic flow of weaving the bands across the warp and the spontaneity and adventure of designing the piece as I weave it.

My tapestries are abstract and depict, for me, symbolic representations of a frame of mind, an imagined environment, or an abstracted architectural form. The lines and forms are a part of a personal calligraphy and convey a suggestion of layers and depth, things hidden and behind, kinetic movement and space, and impermanence. The juxtaposition of positive and negative space combines to create vibrant fields of movement and energy.

My work has been exhibited nationally and internationally in the 7th International Fiber Art Biennale in Nantong, China. It is included in the collection of US embassies in Bulgaria, Georgia, and Kazakhstan, as well as in private and corporate collections.

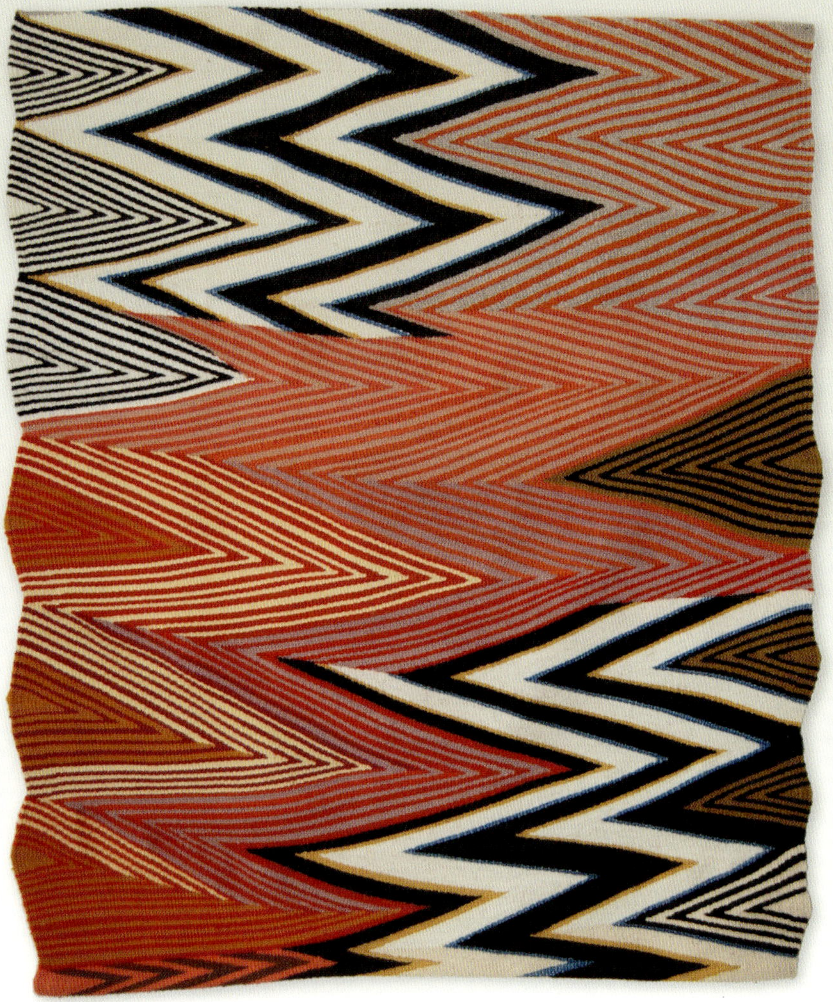

Disconnect. Wool with cotton warp and natural dyes. 44.5" × 38". 2013.

All art images photographed by Bruno Corsini.

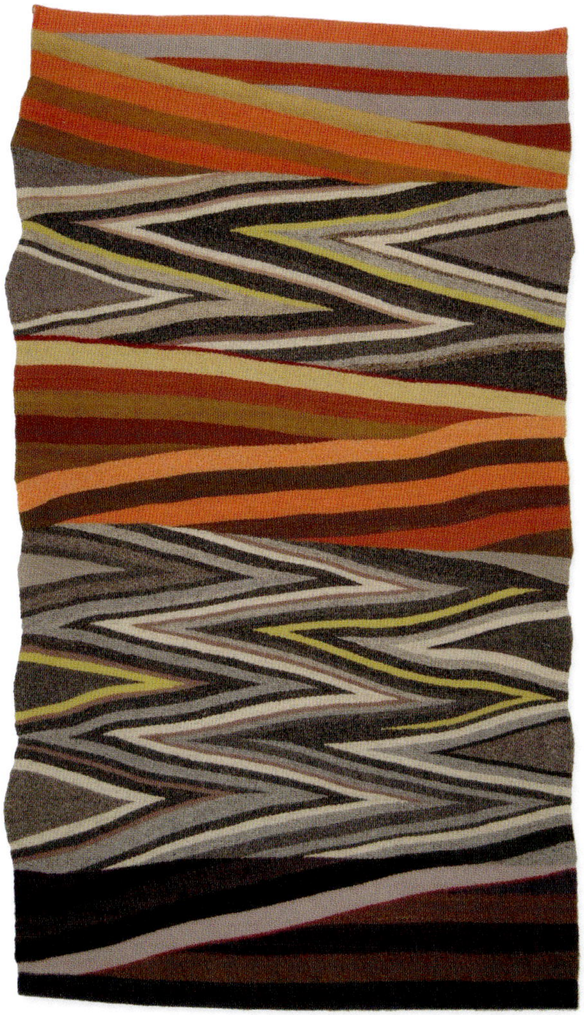

Storm Watch. Wool with cotton warp and natural dyes. 59" × 39". 2015.

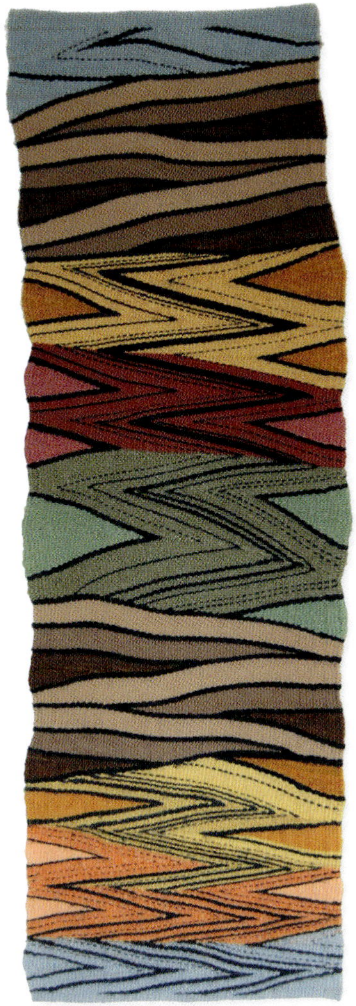

Borders. Wool with cotton warp. 48" × 16". 2015.

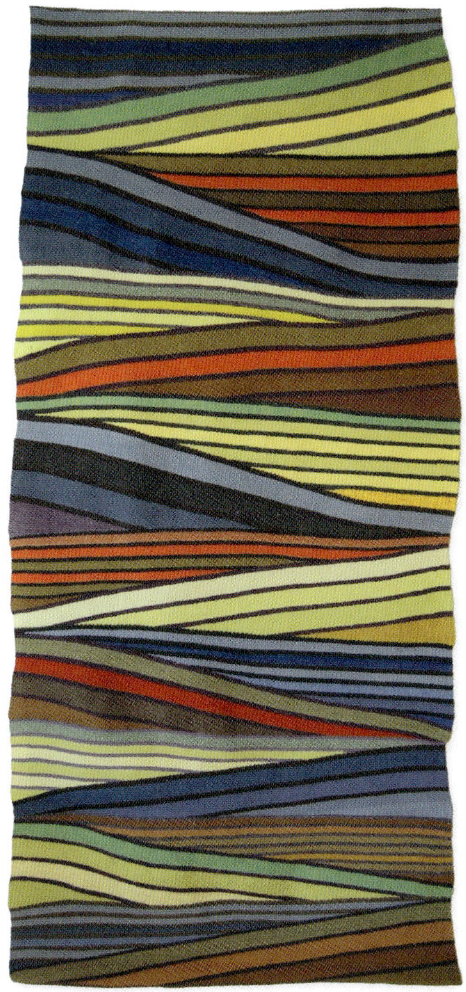

Troubled Water. Wool with cotton warp. 71" × 34". 2010.

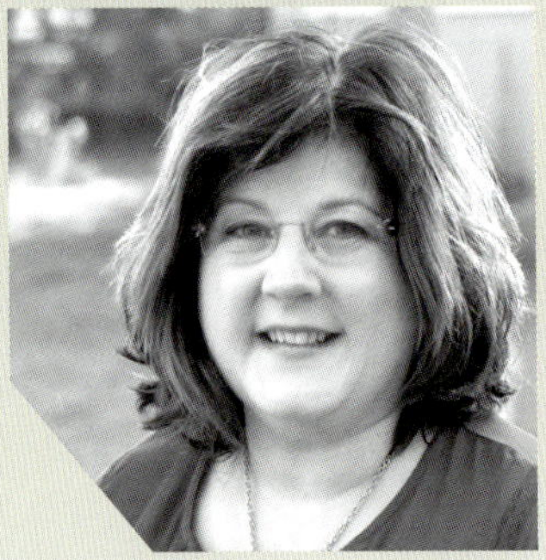

Helen Cowans

Wooler, Northumberland, England

I am an award-winning, qualified tutor and lecturer with a passion and love of textiles and Northumberland. I've taught embroidery courses for the skills-development organization City & Guilds; now I work freelance as a tutor and lecturer, and occasionally write for magazines. I've organized several solo and joint exhibitions. In a past life, I worked in a laboratory as a molecular biologist. I prefer stitching.

I'm presently investigating the landscape and history of Northumberland: a land of battles, castles, and hidden rocks, the "Land of the Far Horizons," where vistas are simply stunning. I'm researching archaeological and historical knowledge and geography, and looking at old abandoned homesteads and ancient carved rocks. I've been thinking about the women who lived in these hills, and who lived through battles, cattle raids, and long, hard winters.

I'm exploring natural dyeing and weathering methods, so the fabric is "of the land." I'm looking at the animal and plants that live here, especially the wild flowers, hares, and curlews (the symbol of the Northumberland National Park). I also have a passion for Eastern patterns and colors. So I'm quite a contrast. I've learned not to fight it, but to go with it and enjoy it all. It's now becoming a fusion of styles.

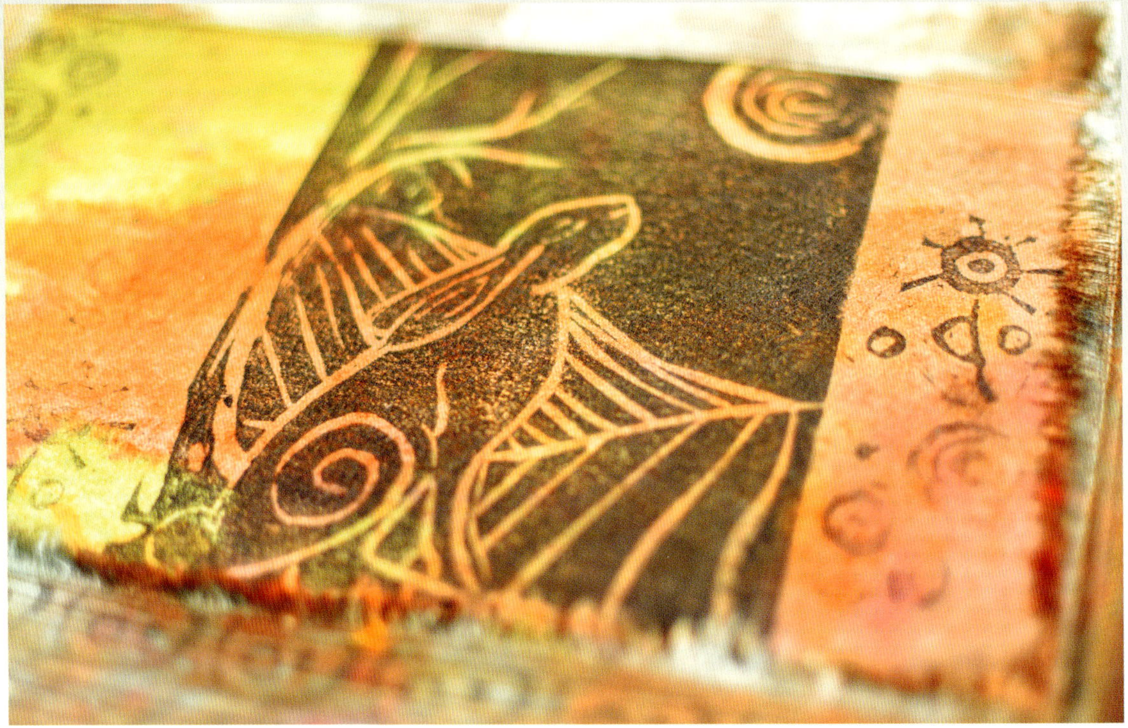

Moon Gazing Hare (detail). Silks, cottons, procion dye, lino printing ink, and rayon thread. 10" × 8". 2013.

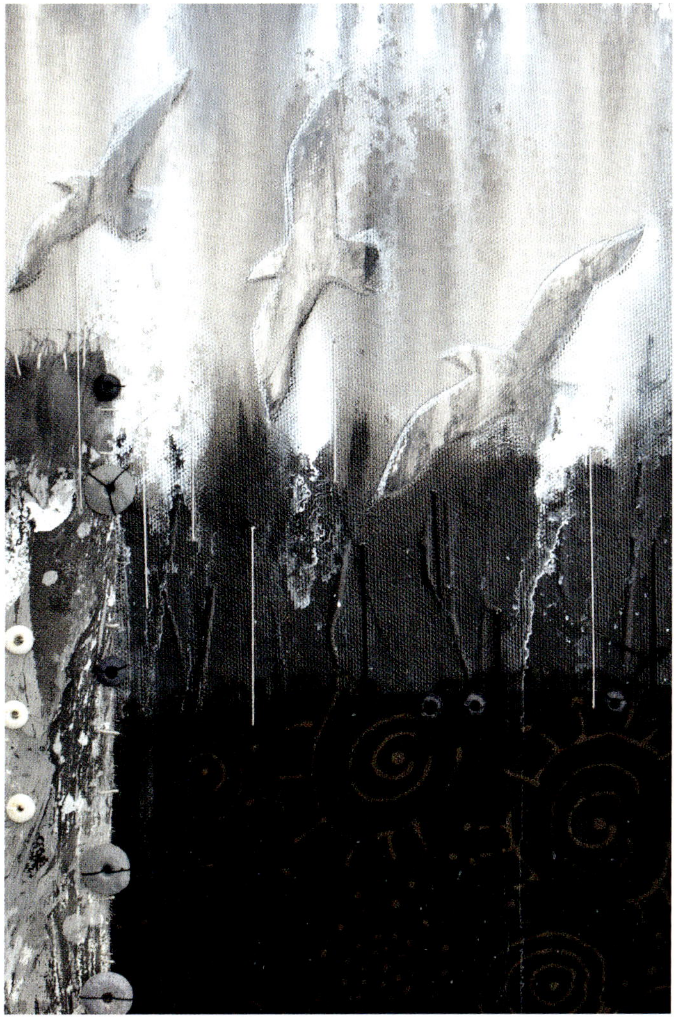

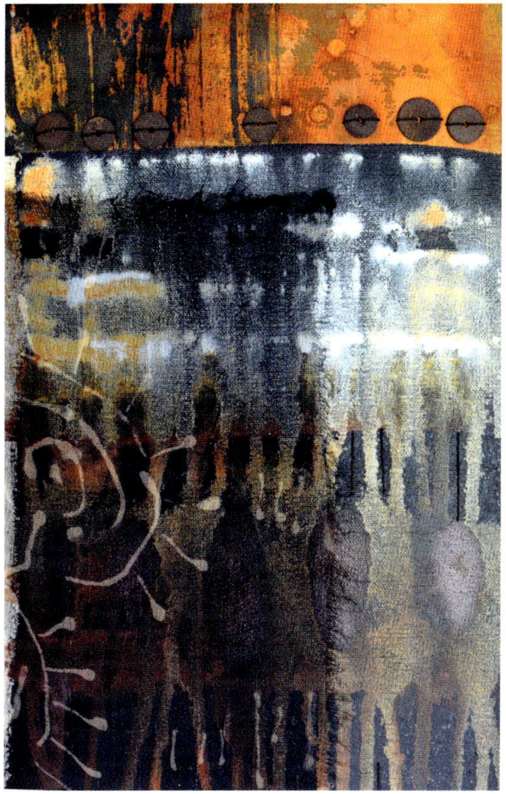

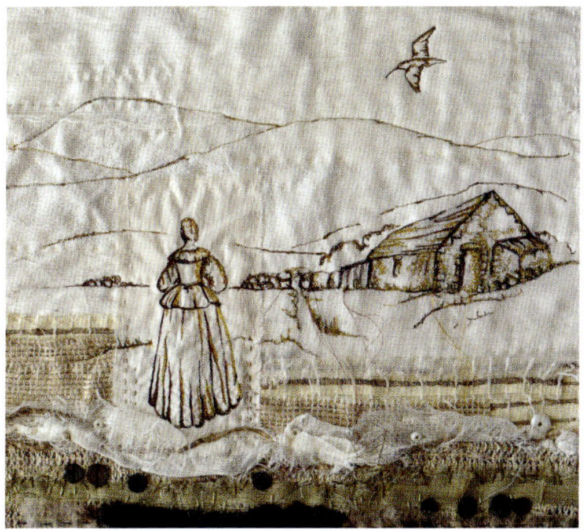

▲ *Land to Sea.* Canvas, acrylic paint, charcoal, ink, silk, wax, silk thread, and beads. 12" × 9". 2015.

◄ *Under the Earth.* Canvas, acrylic paints, silks, wax, silk thread, and buttons. 12" × 10". 2015.

► *House on the Moor.* Cottons, silks, scrims, silk and rayon thread, and bone buttons. 24" × 30". 2014.

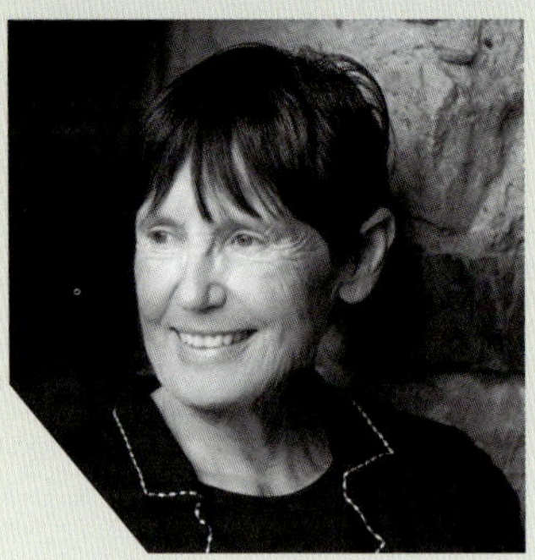

Candace Crockett

San Francisco, California

I was first drawn to textiles as a means of artistic expression because of their tactile quality and their historic connection to all peoples and to all cultures. I have come to realize that through textiles I bring balance and perspective to my life. In particular, the discipline and labor-intensive activity of weaving are both a joy and an anchor.

I began exploring loom weaving in the early 1960s; in the late '60s, I learned about an ancient weaving technique that used multiple cards for producing patterned bands. Card weaving, also called tablet weaving, is an ancient craft with roots in Asia, Africa, Europe, and Scandinavia. I've written books on it, taught the process to hundreds of students, and continue to use it along with loom weaving and dyeing as my means for artistic expression. As I look back over the textiles I have created, I see that all my woven and dyed works are concerned with building a visually satisfying whole through a complex interlacing of color, pattern, and structure.

I taught in the art department at San Francisco State University for thirty-five years. I am now retired and split my time between San Francisco and a small mountain town in Italy, maintaining studios in both countries.

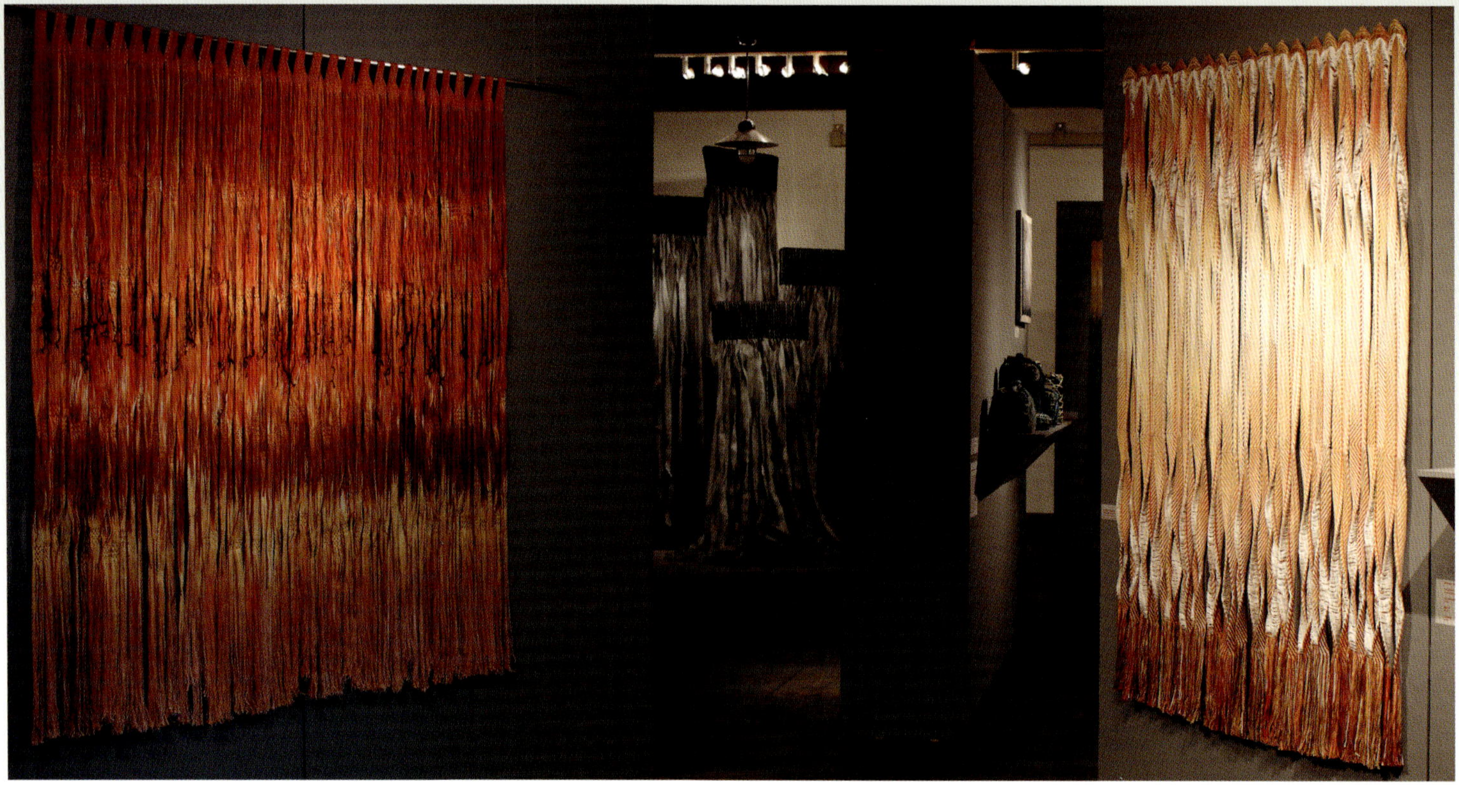

OPPOSITE
The City: Past—Present—Future. Hand dyed and commercial quilting cottons, acrylic paint, and polyester sheers. 60" × 108" × 2". 2008-2014.

▼ *Icebergs and Cool Breezes.* Hand dyed cotton, polyester sheer, and overlay glass beads. 43" × 35". 2010.

➤ *Prairie Springtime Ritual—Return of the Blue Heron.* Hand painted silk and polyester sheer overlay. 42" × 32". 2015.

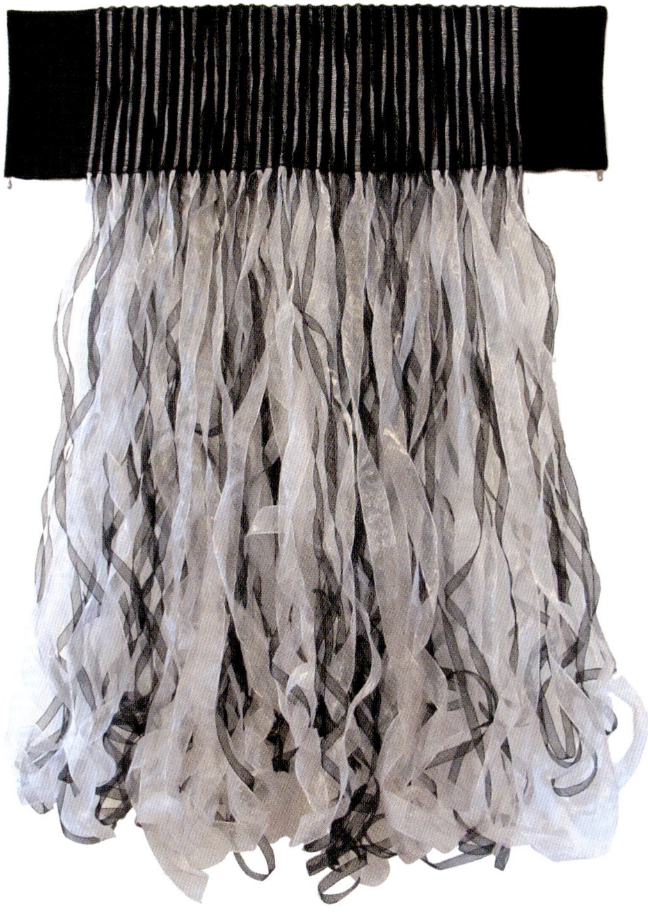

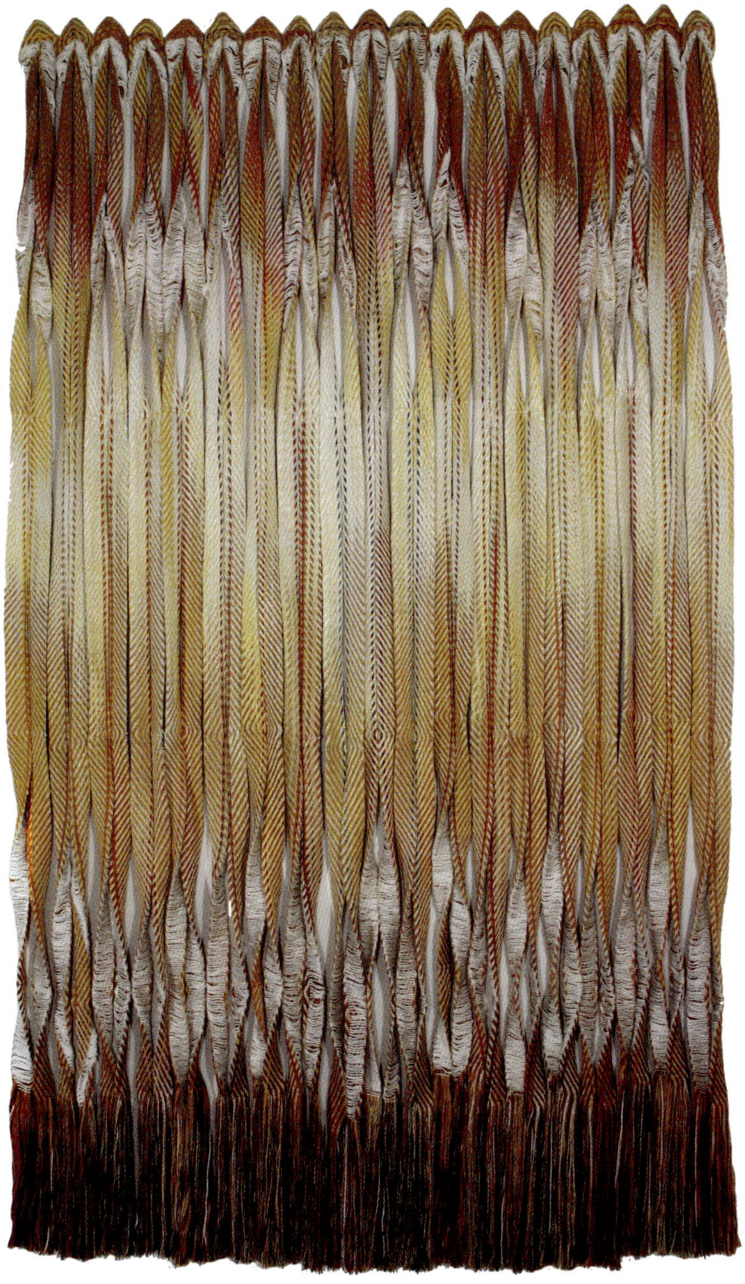

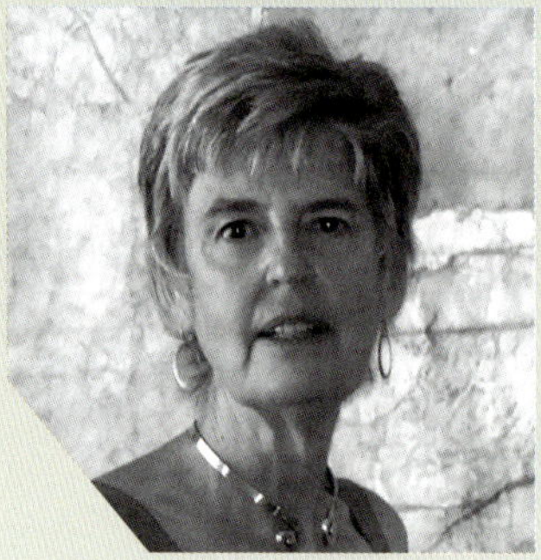

Courtesy of Kathy Kane.

Jennifer Davies

Branford, Connecticut

I suspect many humans carry a gene for loving lace. If so, I have more than my share. I love patterns with holes, from perfect tatting to hastily repaired spider webs. There is magic in seeing through to a background simultaneously revealed and obscured.

To make my webs, I combine weaving and handmade paper. I make Asian paper (*kozo)* myself—cooking, cleaning, and beating mulberry stalks until they yield a feathery pulp. I then wrap simple looms with string and dip them into the slurry of paper and water. I sew the resulting lacy webs together and often embroider or paint the top layers. I find the careful stitching meditative and feel this slow process imbues the work with the mark of the hand.

The central message of my work is its materiality. After a lifetime of painting, fiber offers me richer textures and greater physical presence. I like to surprise myself. Therefore, in the give and take of creating, my collaborators are the unplanned and the "*Wow!* How did that happen?" Color, surface, and composition are principles of fine art that I apply to my work in crafts. My aim is to make work that draws one in with its warmth of texture and the evident pleasure of its creation.

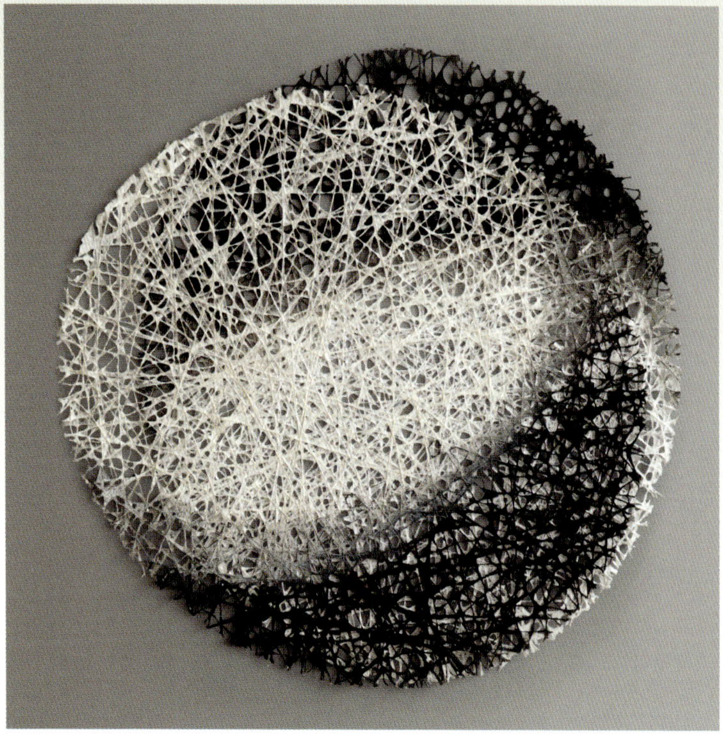

Snowmoon. String and handmade paper. 52" diameter. 2014.

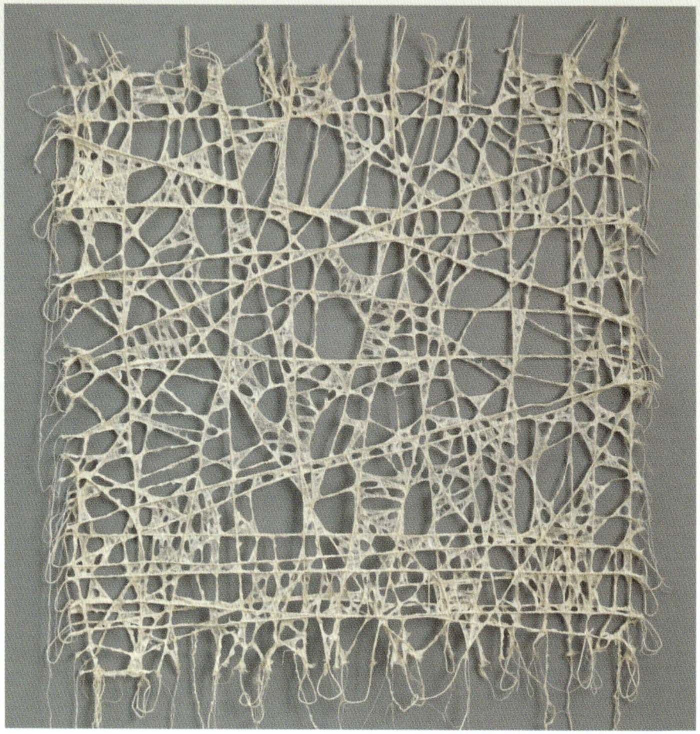

Float. String and handmade paper. 44" × 37". 2015.

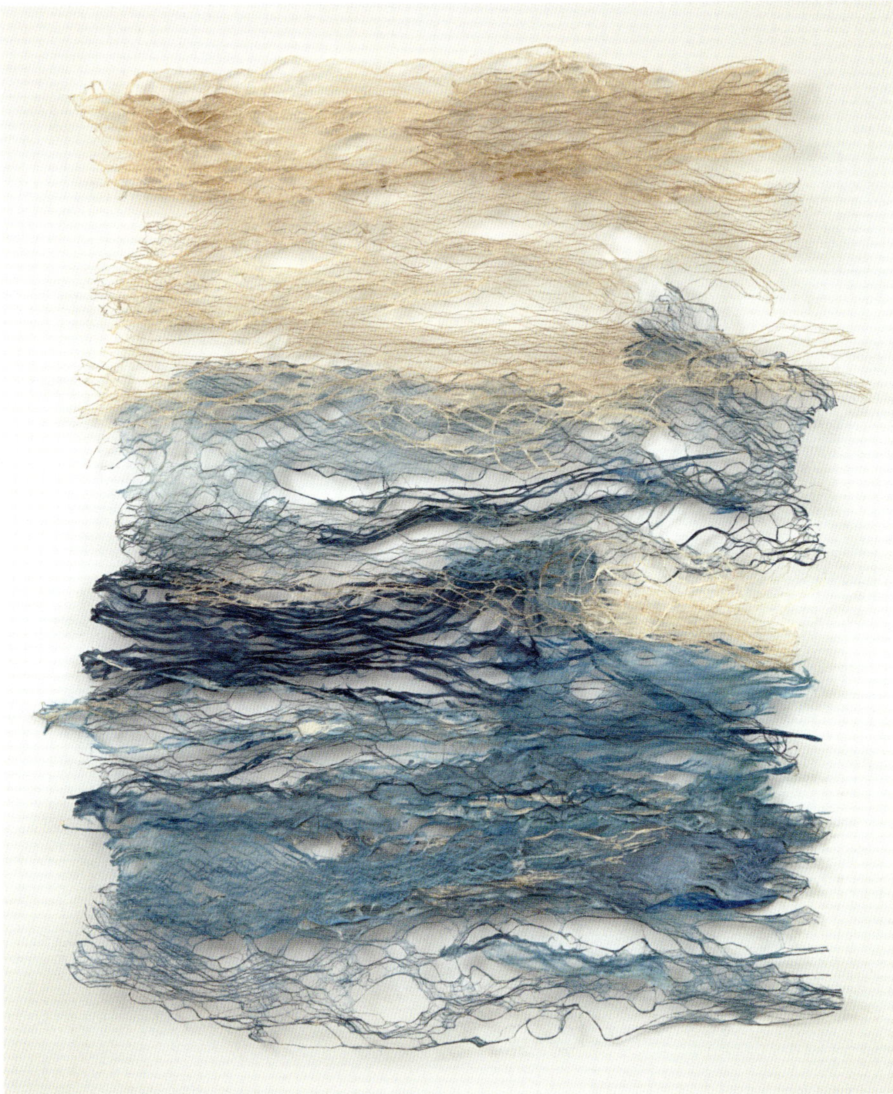

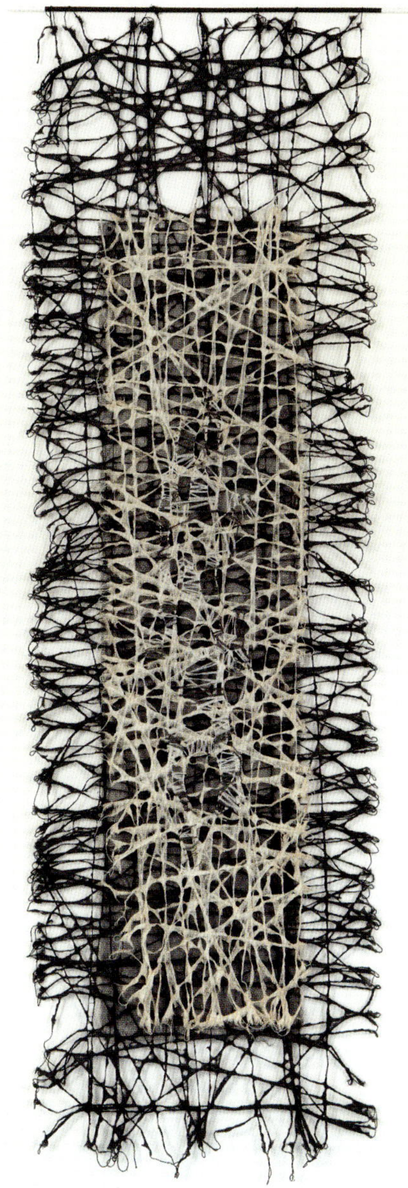

▲ *Shimmer.* Pigmented dried kozo stalks and thread. 60" × 52". 2015.

➤ *Background Voices.* String and handmade paper. 58" × 23". 2012.

All art images courtesy of Christopher Gardner.

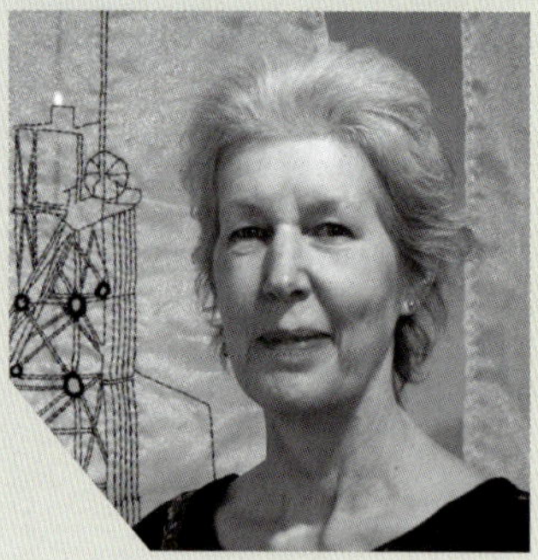

Courtesy of Lanny Bergner.

Eve Deisher

Anacortes, Washington

Drawing is my foundation. Exploring the combining of paper, fabric, and sewing in my work, I move between two dimensional to relief and three-dimensional formats. I equally love the mark or line of charcoal and thread. I like to combine the effects of shadows, translucency, and layering.

I live in the Pacific Northwest with my husband, sculptor Lanny Bergner. This rural environment of density, darkness, mist, and mystery fuels my exploration of these landscapes. Chaos and order exist in a visual web of imagery within the work. Often my mixed media artworks refer to the duality of humans and nature within a psychological landscape.

Eve passed away on January 30, 2017, as this book went to press.

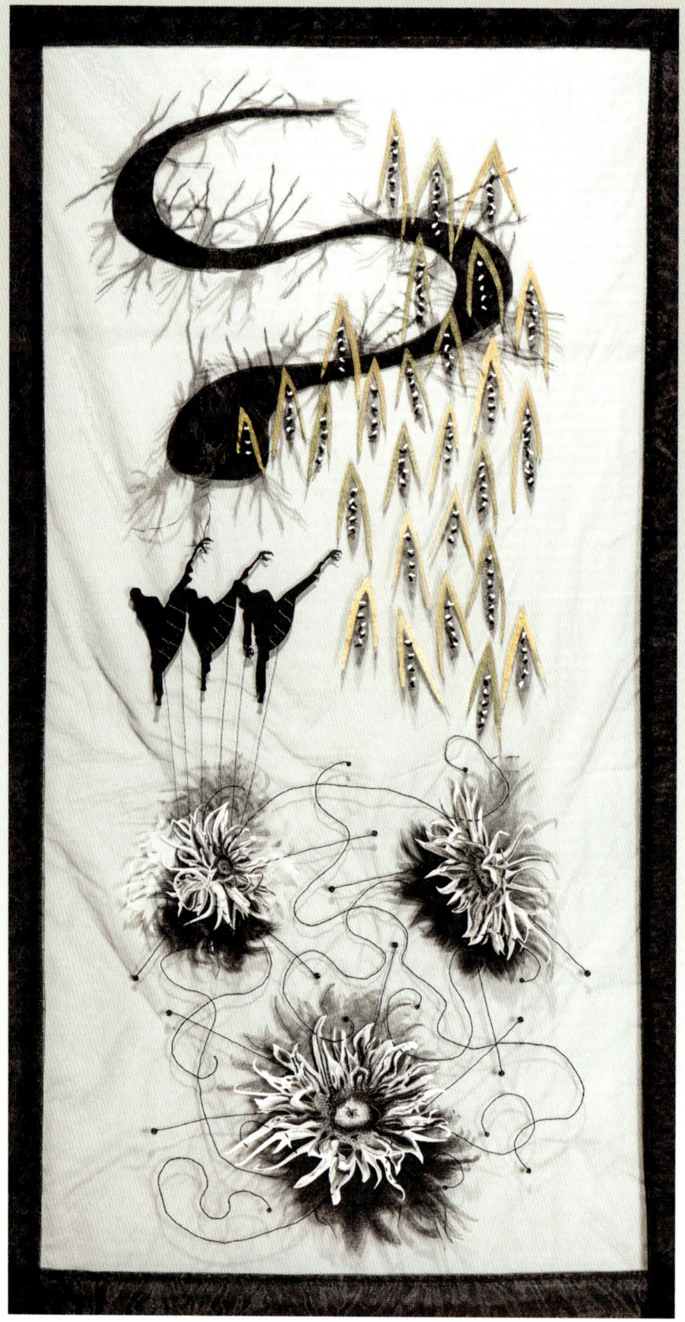

Skyward. Mixed media charcoal drawing on paper and translucent organza fabric, hand stitched embroidery, and snaps. 63" × 33". 2012. Courtesy of kp studios.com.

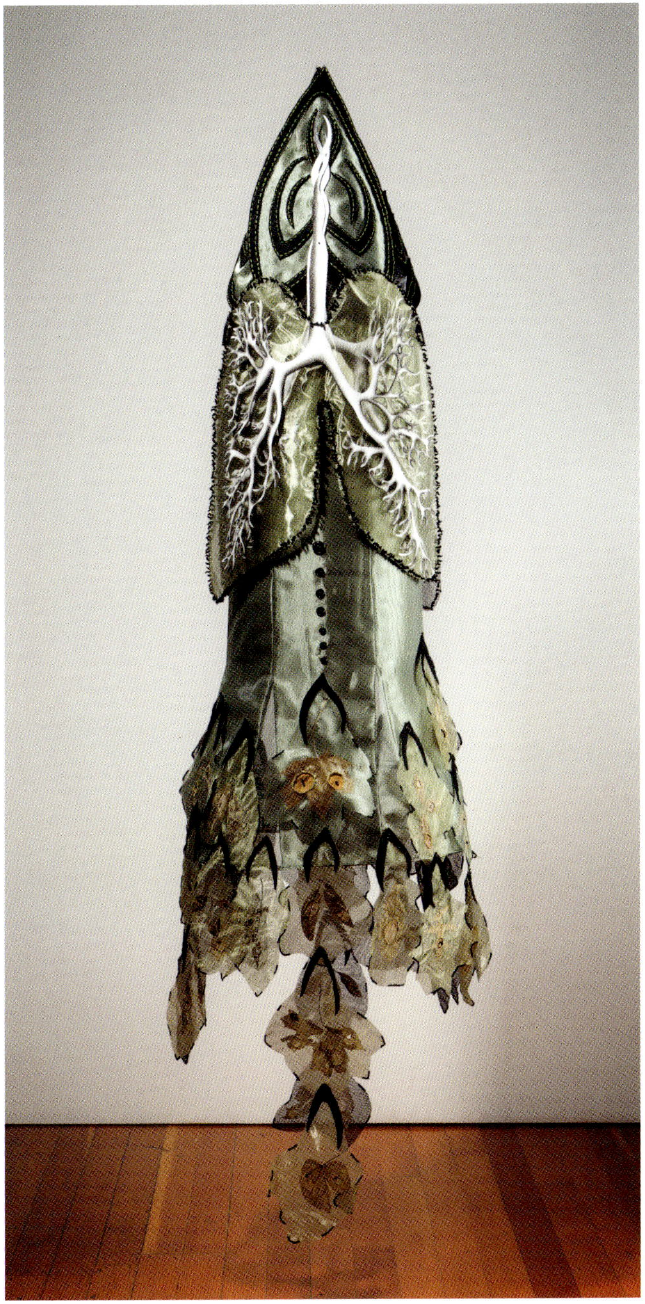

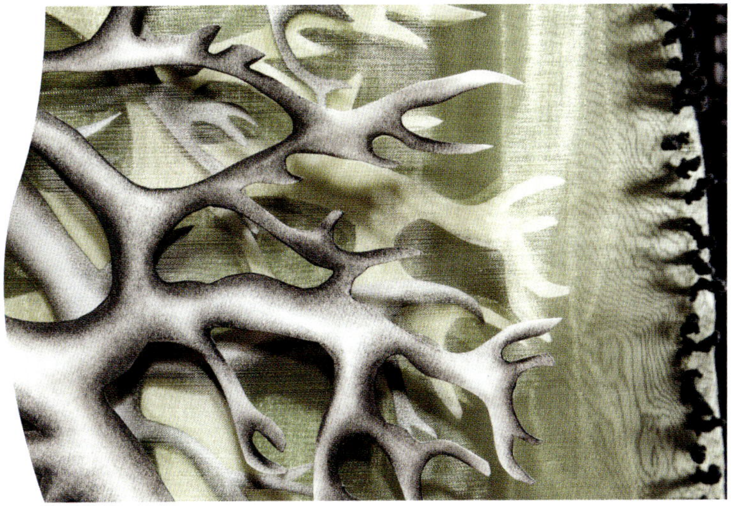

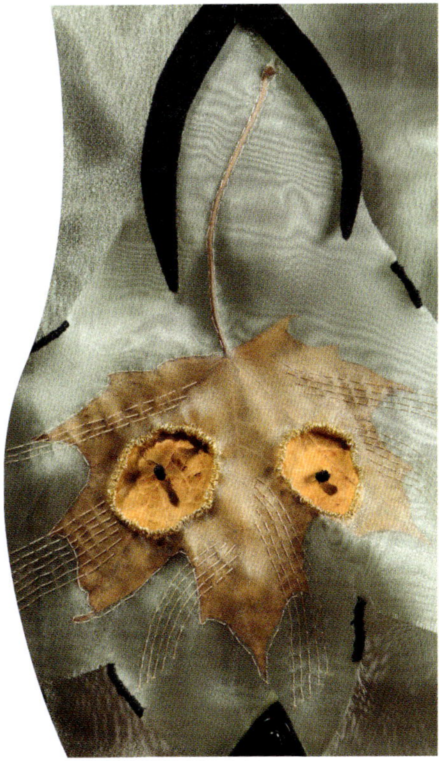

Breathe (green side). Mixed media charcoal drawing on paper and translucent organza fabric, hand stitched embroidery, leaves, snaps, and felt. 72" × 20" × 20". 2012. | Details. Courtesy of kpstudios.com.

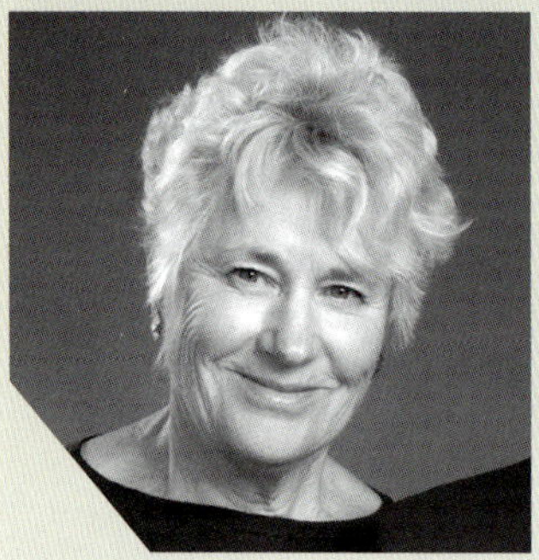

Susan Kathleen Doyle

San Geronimo, California

Materials inspire me—a discarded encyclopedia (thrown away by my husband who *never* throws away a book), old *National Geographic* magazines in an attic, scraps of beautiful silk . . . I enjoy taking these materials and using them to explore particular ideas or compositions from a variety of perspectives. My art is inspired by color and relationships, both personal, political, and in nature. I use techniques traditionally used in fiber art in non-traditional ways—weaving pages from a book, making a dress that has more meaning than just a fashion statement.

I have always had a drive to experiment and make unique things with my hands. Art is one of my languages for expression.

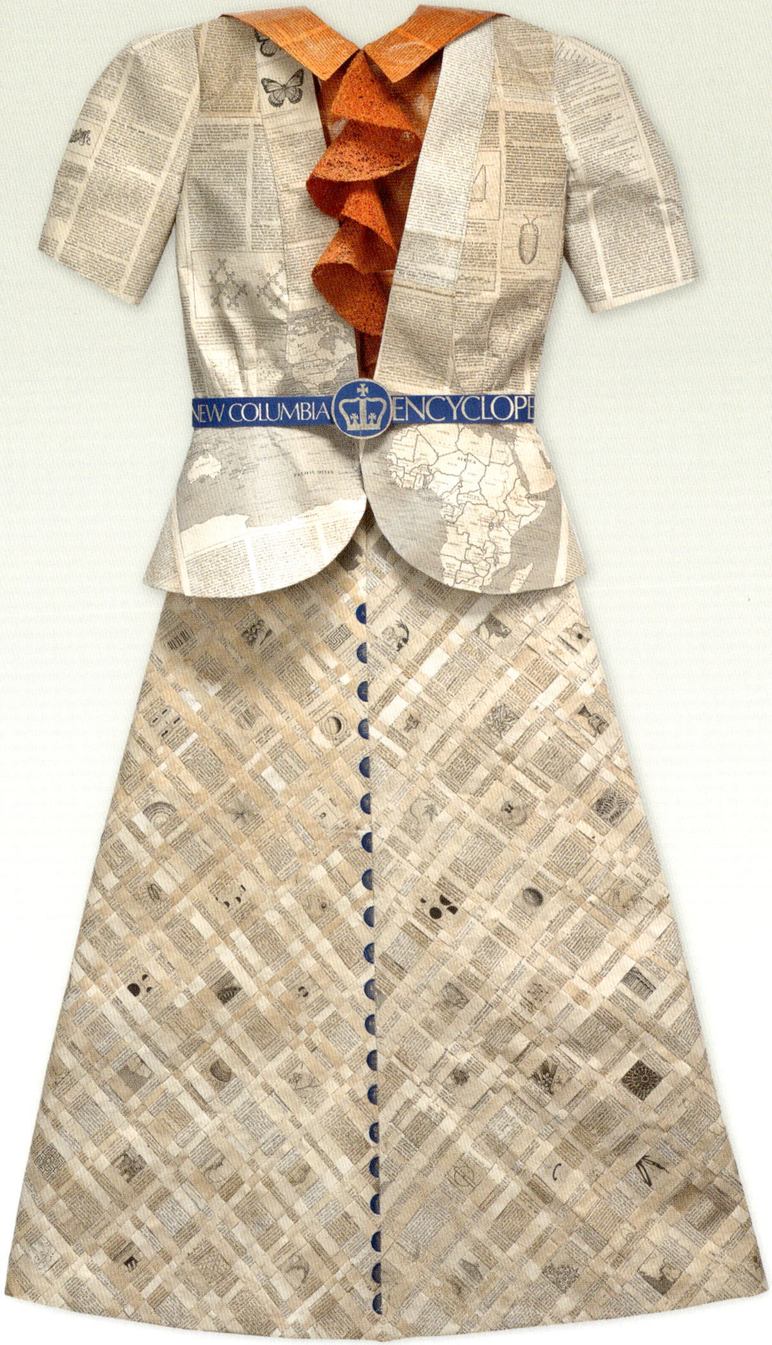

Columbia. Encyclopedia pages and cover, thread. 47" × 28" × 2". 2014.
Courtesy of Jay Daniels, Black Cat Studio.

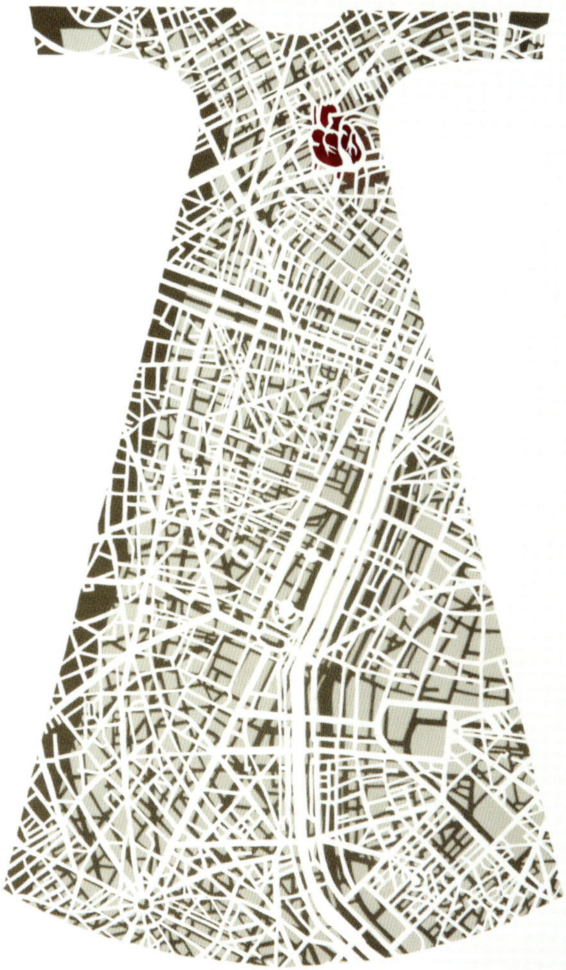

Rue Nicolas Appert. Paper and rubylith. 30" × 20". 2014. Courtesy of Dana Davis.

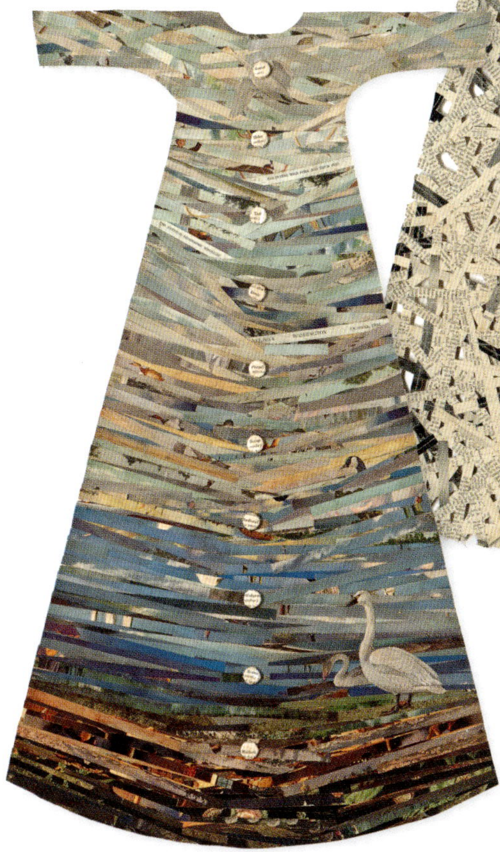

Far Flying Fowl. National Geographic magazine and buttons. 28" × 18" × 0.5". 2014. Courtesy of Jay Daniels, Black Cat Studio.

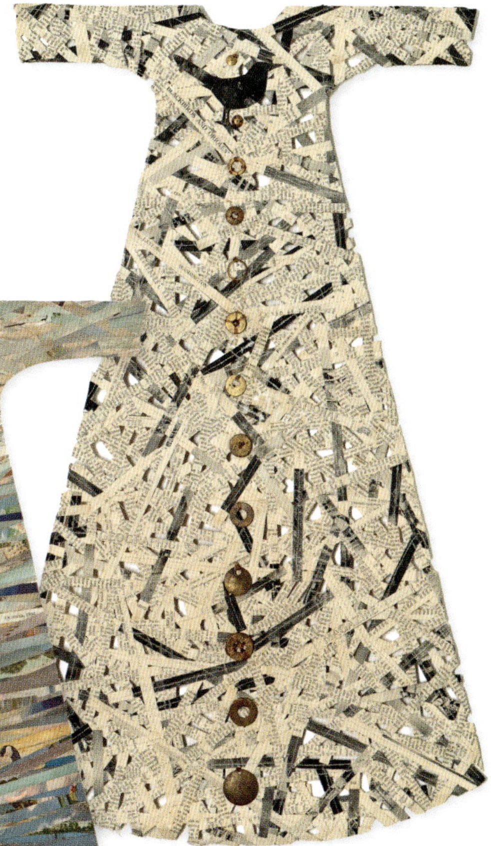

Blackbirds and Orioles. National Geographic magazine, thread, and metal. 20" × 18" × 0.5". 2014. Courtesy of Jay Daniels, Black Cat Studio.

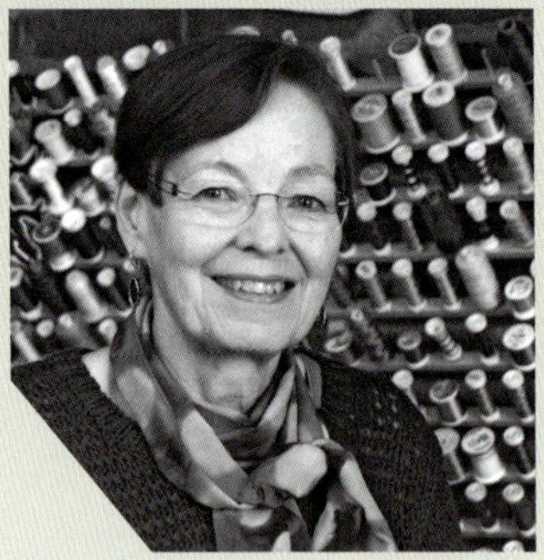

Candace Edgerley

Alexandria, Virginia

As both an artist and educator, my work is driven by technique, which then dictates its form. My focus continues to be traditional Japanese shibori combined with a contemporary color sense. Tiny pleats and folds in sheer fabric create patterns. Small segments of shibori-dyed silk organza, joined by tiny French seams, form wall pieces that stir with the slightest breeze. My work illustrates a history similar to strata within canyon walls, mapping ancient life and tectonics.

I currently teach surface design classes at The Art League School in Alexandria, Virginia. My work has been exhibited in China, France, Germany, Japan, Korea, and Spain; at the Corcoran Gallery of Art, Washington, DC; and in other national venues.

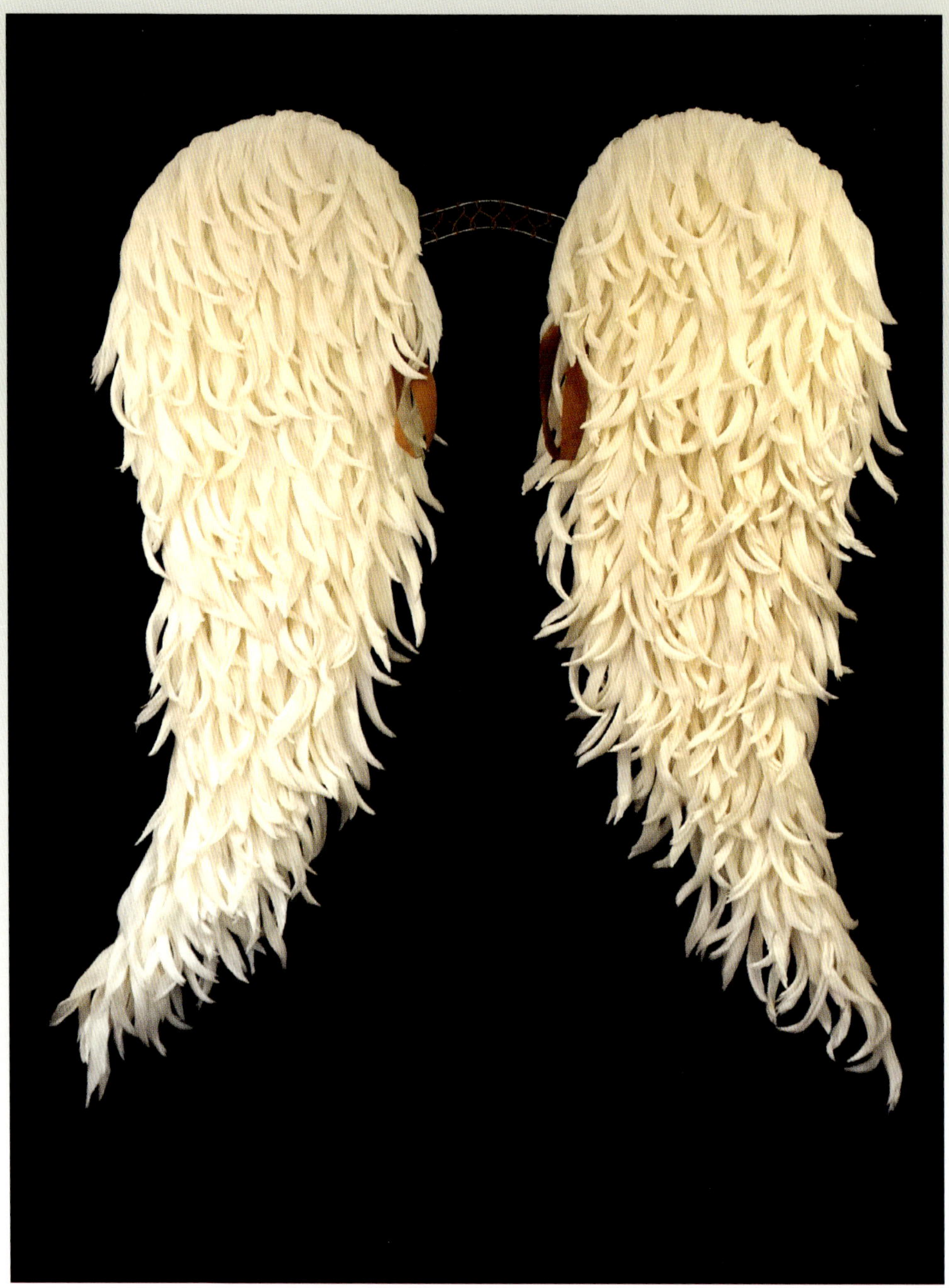

Winged Flight. Silk organza and Arashi shibori on welded steel frame. 60" × 45". 2013.

All images courtesy of Gregory Staley.

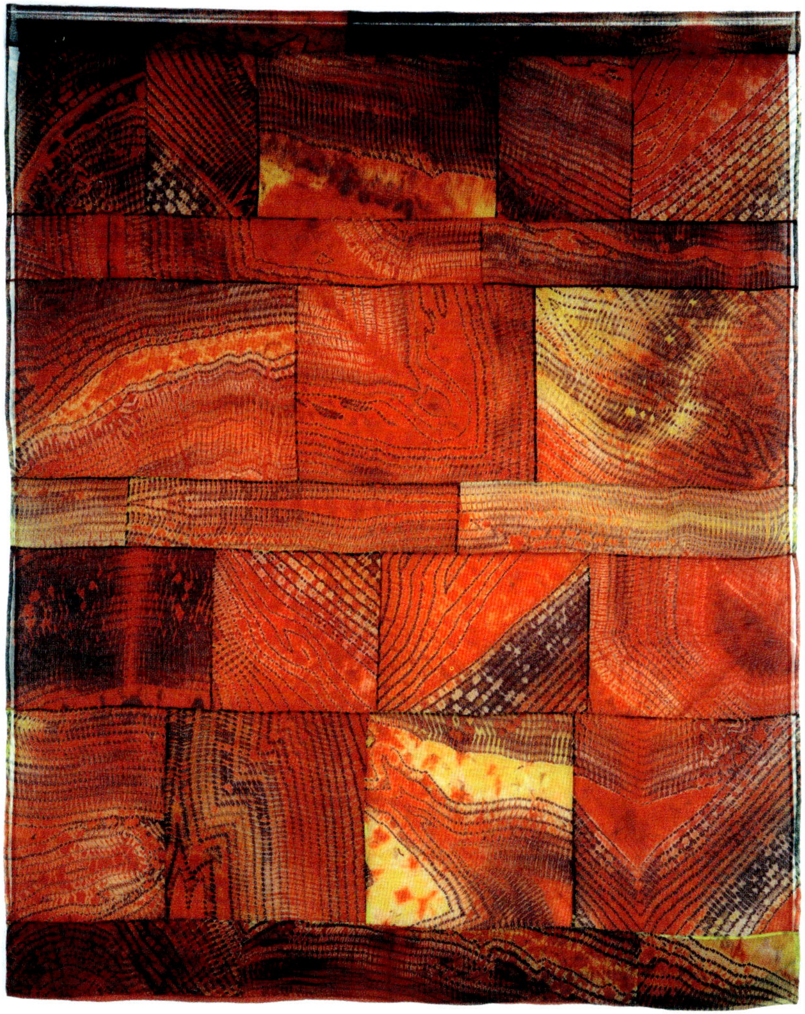

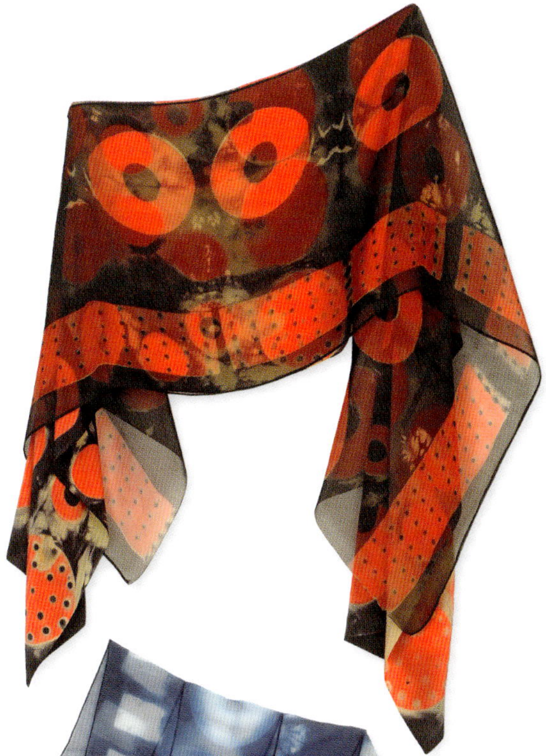

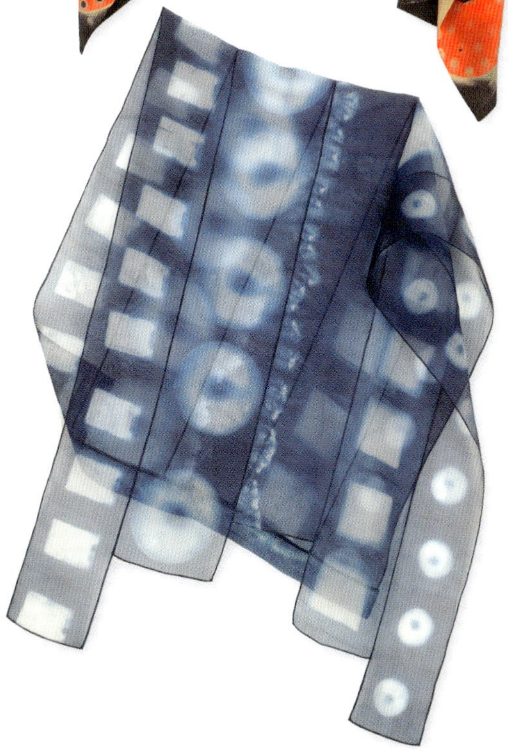

▲ *Sidewinder Dawn*. Shibori-dyed silk organza, pieced. 47" × 39". 2005

◀ *Seeing Red.* Shibori-dyed silk, pieced. 35" × 28". 2014.

➤ *Blue Work*. Shibori-dyed silk organza, pieced. 35" × 25". 2014.

Photo by Ron Gentry.

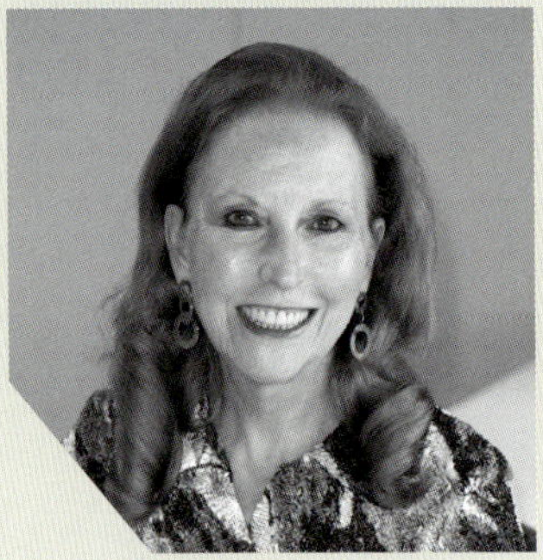

Caryl Bryer Fallert-Gentry

Port Townsend, Washington

For as long as I can remember, I have expressed myself through art. My formal training was in design, drawing, and studio painting. Later I discovered that fabric, used as a fine art medium, best expressed my personal vision. Since 1983, I have made more than five hundred art quilts, which have appeared in hundreds of national and international exhibitions and publications and won numerous awards.

All of my quilts are made with fabric I created, usually by dyeing and painting to create a palette of colors and visual texture. The commercial fabrics I use are all from various collections I have designed for Benartex Fabrics, based on my hand painted originals.

The focus of my work is on the qualities of color, line, and texture that engage the spirit and emotions of the viewer, evoking a sense of mystery, excitement, or joy. Textures, created by layering, embroidering, and quilting, invite the viewer to touch, as well as to look. Illusions of movement, depth, and luminosity are also common to most of my work. Although some of my quilts include pictorial images, my work is most often about seeing, experiencing, and imagining, rather than pictorial representation of any specific object or species. My intention is to focus on positive energy and depict that in my work, lifting the spirits and delighting the eyes of those who see them.

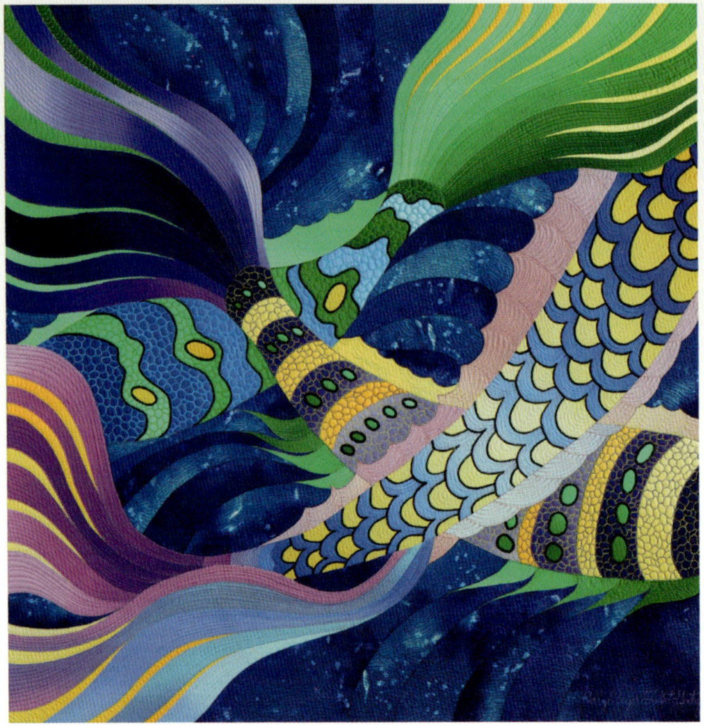

Aquarium 2. Cotton and cotton/bamboo batting. 30" × 30". 2014.

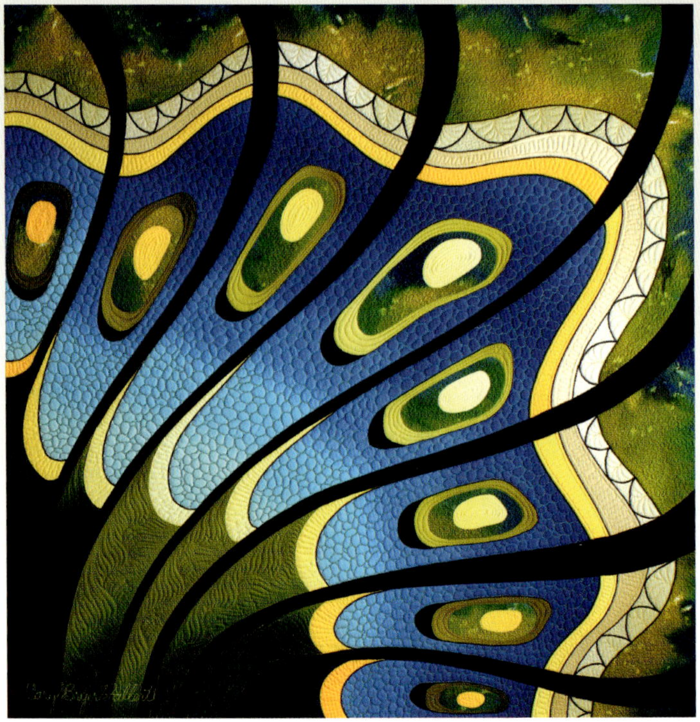

Lepidopteran 3. Cotton and cotton/bamboo batting. 30" × 30". 2012.

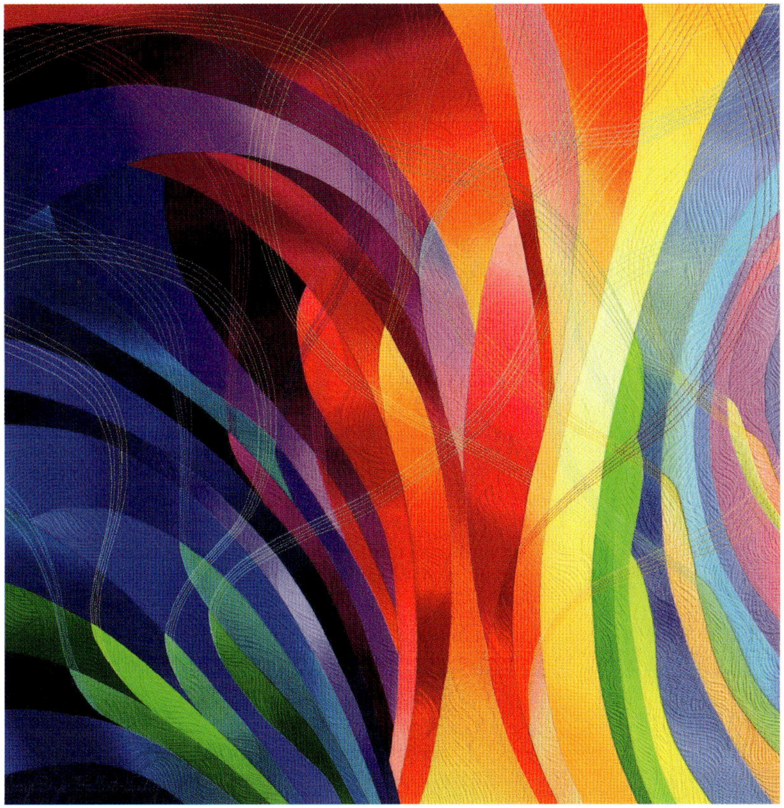

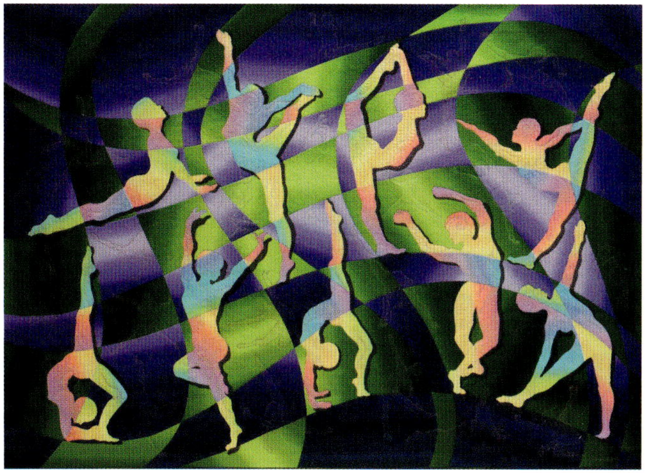

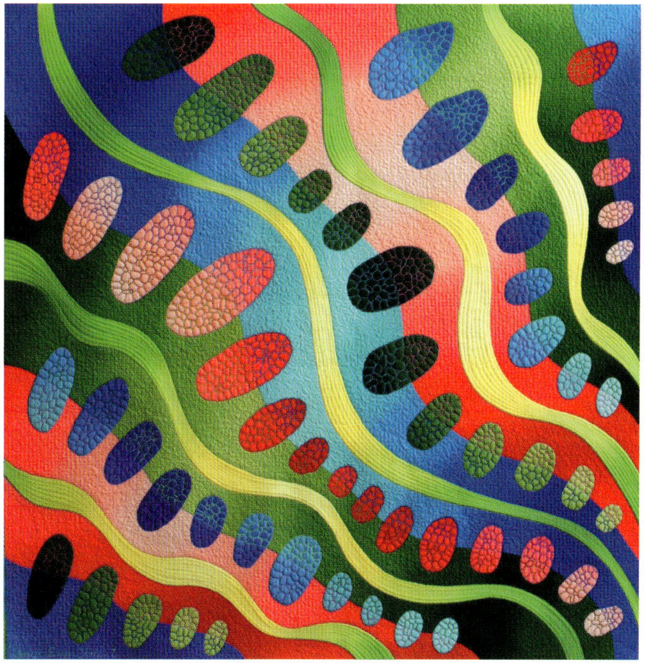

▲ *Celebration*. Cotton and cotton/bamboo batting. 30" × 30". 2014.

◀ *Checks & Balances.* Cotton and cotton/bamboo batting. 65" × 93". 2010.

➤ *Spirogyra 4.* Cotton and cotton/bamboo batting. 30" × 30". 2012.

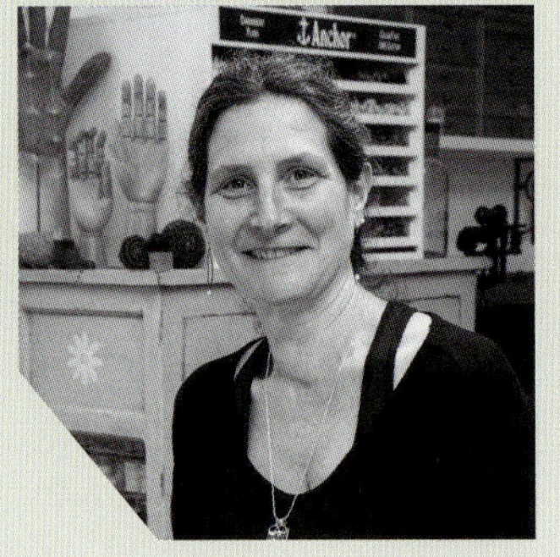

Liz Alpert Fay

Sandy Hook, Connecticut

I have always been inspired by the beauty and simplicity found in nature. An unexpected splash of color or the unusual twist of a branch have the ability to catch my eye and stay with me until these elements come together in my mind and become a visual language. My love of color and of telling stories also plays an important role in each piece that I create. I love the richness of hand dyed colors and the varied textures of recycled fabrics.

Working in an improvisational style, I challenge myself to create a feeling of spontaneity while engaged in labor-intensive practices. I enjoy working in traditional textile techniques, using them in new ways, to create a lively and contemporary feel.

Most of my hand-hooked rugs can be used on the floor as well as hung on the wall. I aim to challenge conventional ideas of what a rug is and how it functions. I create pieces with unusual shapes or irregular edges and sometimes cut into the body of the piece itself to expose the floor beneath. Experimenting with unusual or unexpected materials is also something that I enjoy.

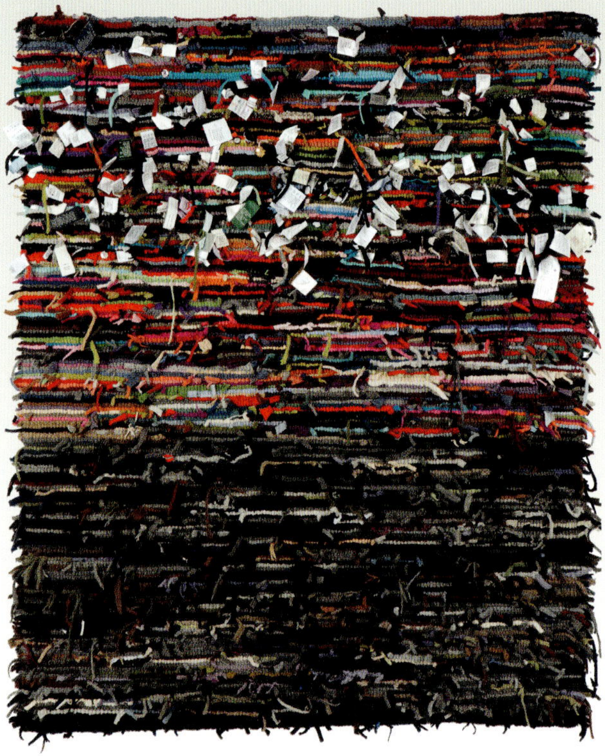

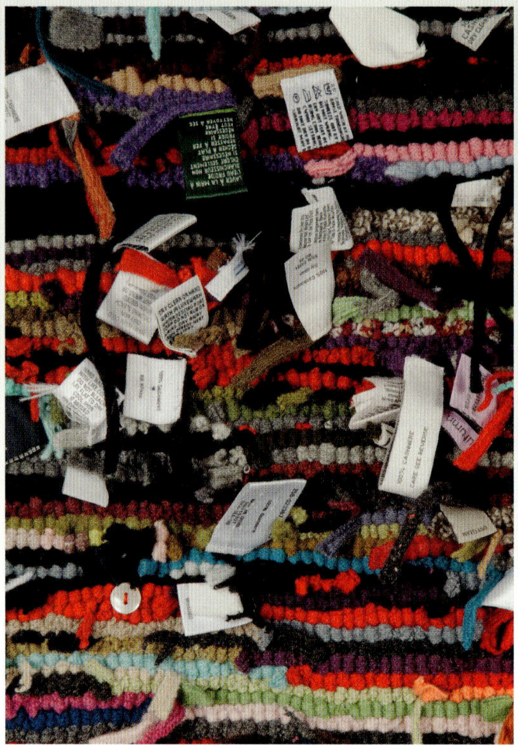

It's Not What It Seams.
Seams from recycled cashmere sweaters, care tags and extra buttons still attached.
48" × 40". 2011. | Detail

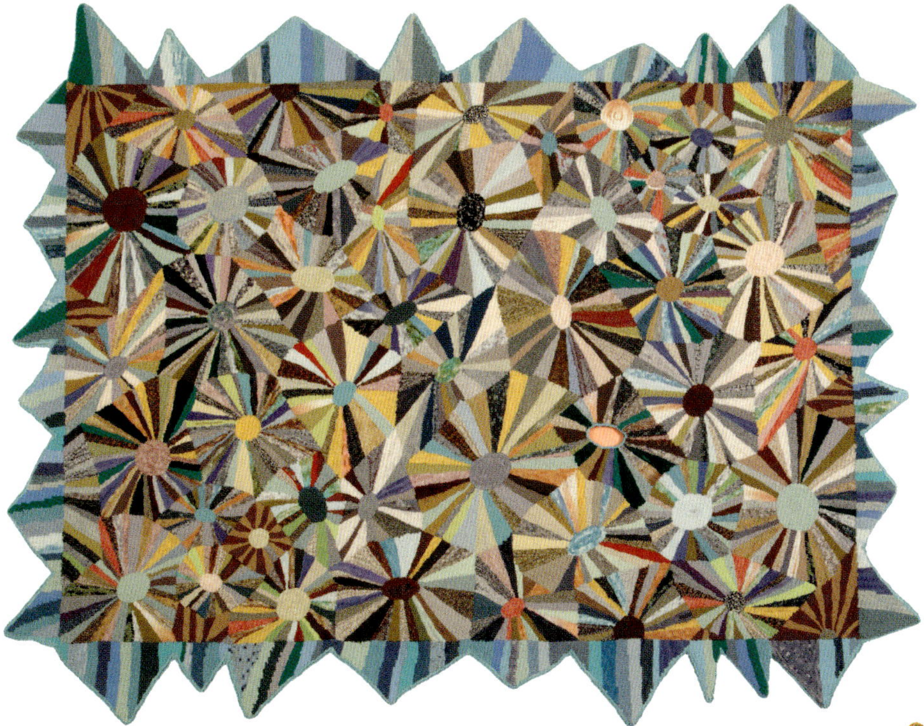

◄ *Petoskey Stone: Memories of Michigan*. Hand dyed and recycled wool on linen and silk organza. 56" × 73". 2010.

► *Ripple: Lake Water*. Hand dyed, recycled, and commercial wool on linen. Approximately 76" × 47". 2011.

▼ *Autumn Garden*. Hand dyed and recycled wool on linen. 48" × 53". 2009.

All images courtesy of Brad Stanton Photography.

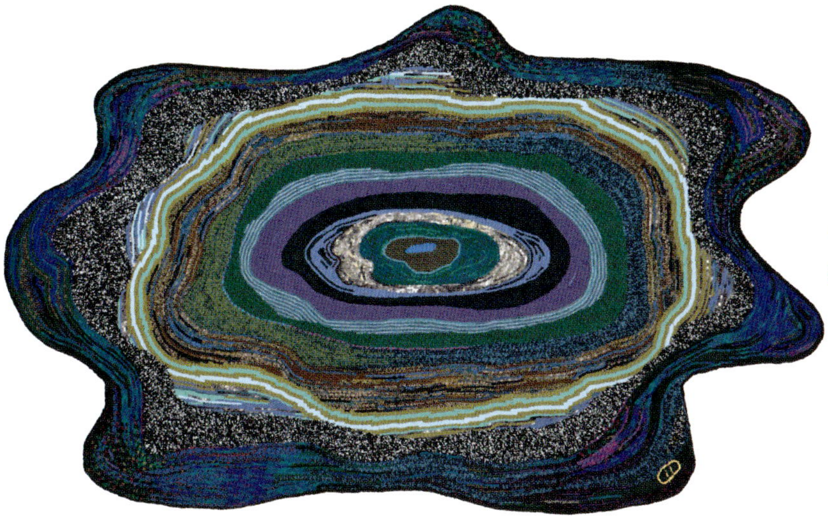

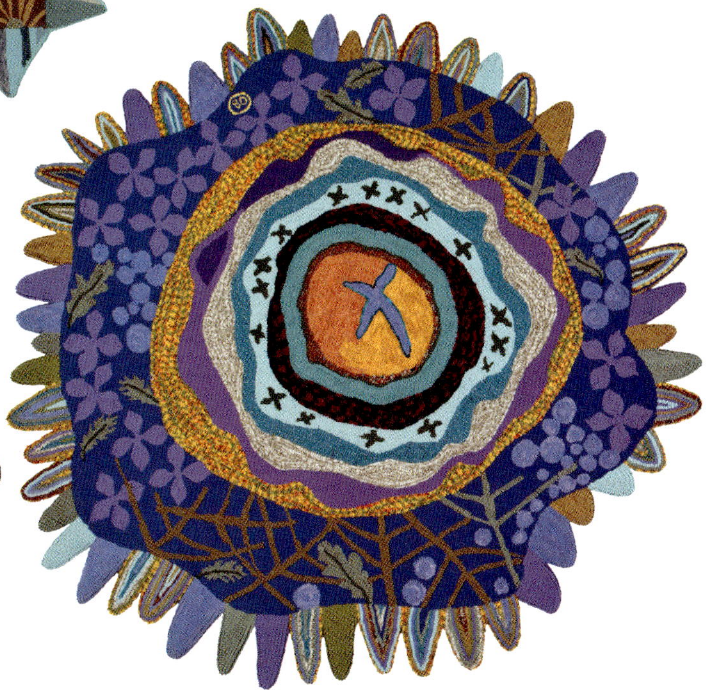

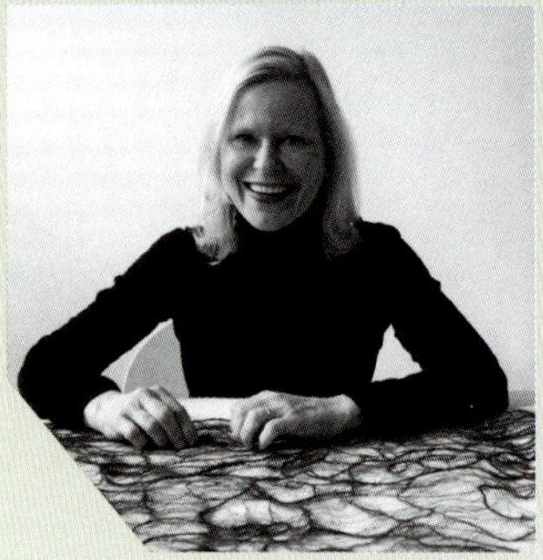

Carson Fox

Brooklyn, New York

My work relies heavily on the imprint that individual experience has on the artist, and centers on producing sculpture, installation, and printmaking.

My series of filigree fiber sculptures was originally inspired by Victorian hair sculpture and jewelry. Historically, these objects were crafted out of the hair of a deceased loved one and acted as a memento of the departed. My own works are laboriously crafted tapestries of delicate, hair-thin wire that bring to mind lace on a large scale. Often these objects are installed with the intent of allowing the object and shadow to act in concert, suggesting the ineffable qualities of both life and death. These works began at a point in my life when my mother, father, and mother-in-law all died in quick succession.

My work can be found in the permanent collections of the Museum of Arts and Design in New York City; the Noyes Museum of Art, Newark Public Library, Jersey City Museum, and New Jersey State Museum, all in New Jersey; the Pennsylvania Academy of the Fine Arts Museum; and The Royal Museum of Belgium, among others.

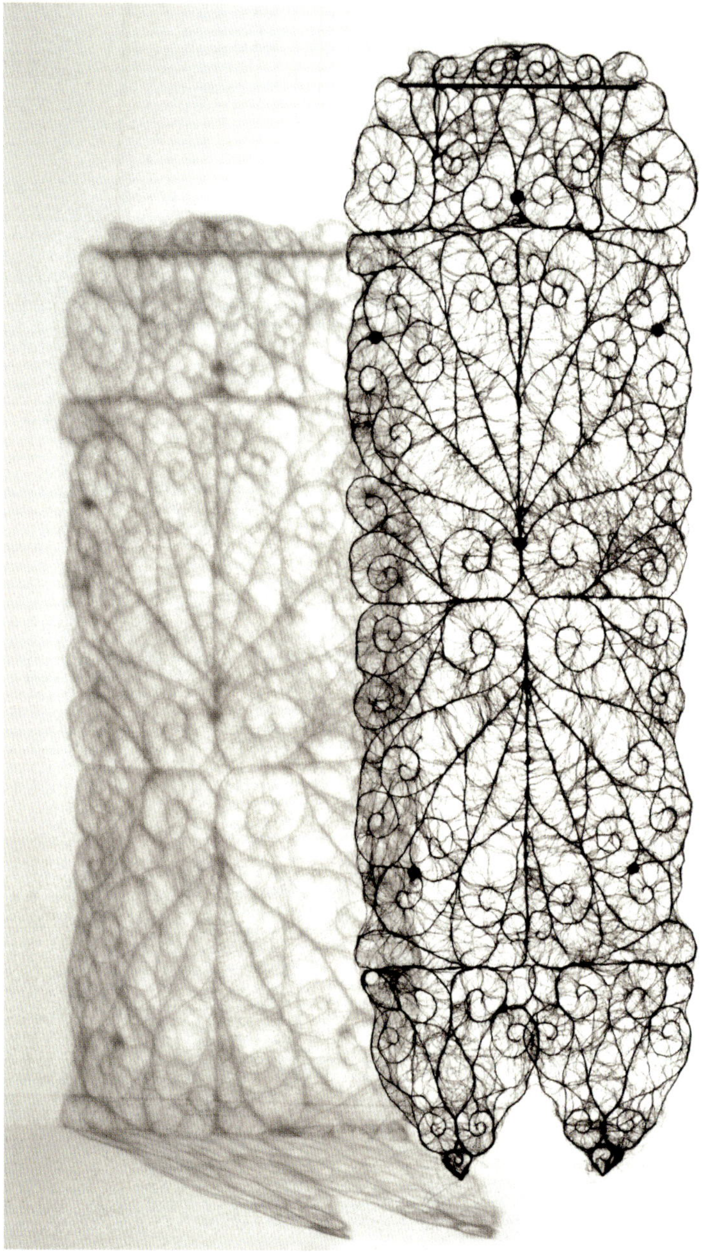

Filigree #5. Hanging sculpture, wire, and artificial hair. 84" × 30". 2004.

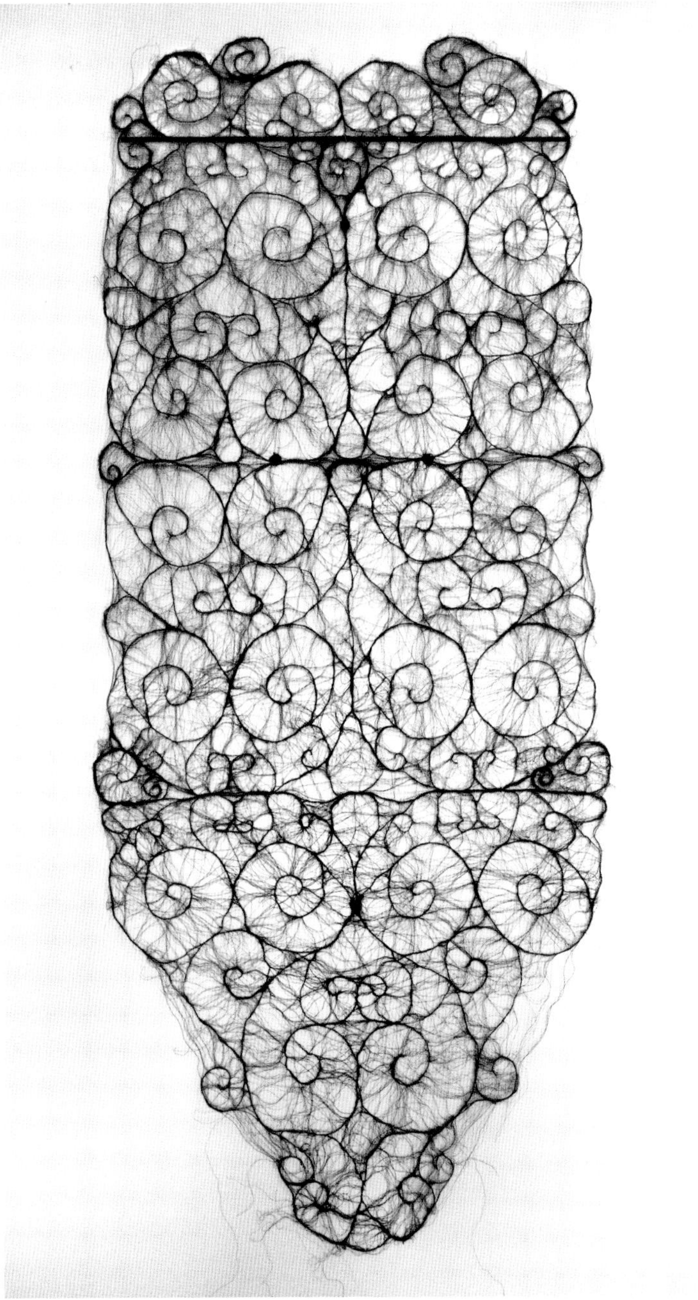

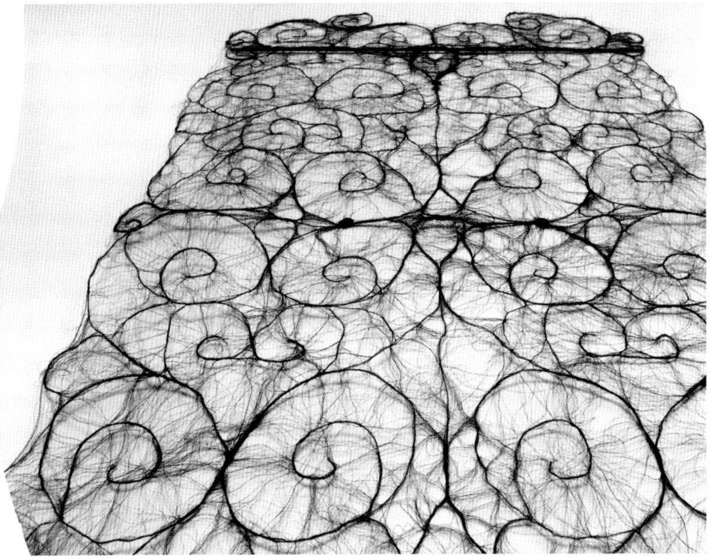

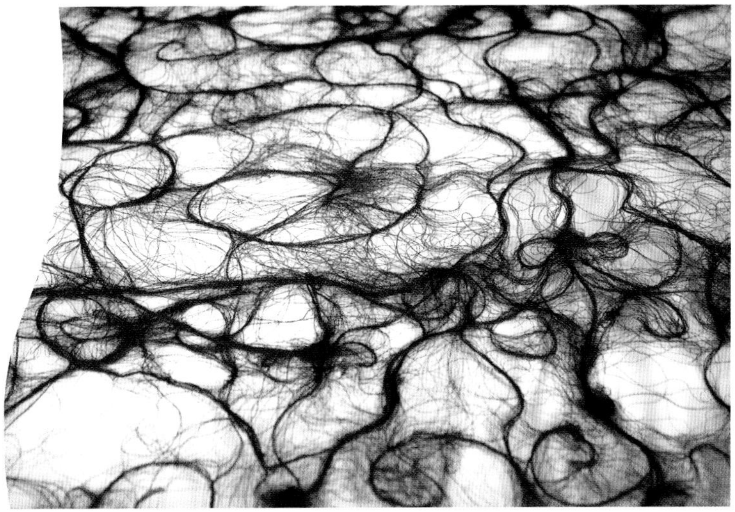

Filigree #7. Hanging sculpture, wire, and artificial hair.
84" × 50". 2004. | Details

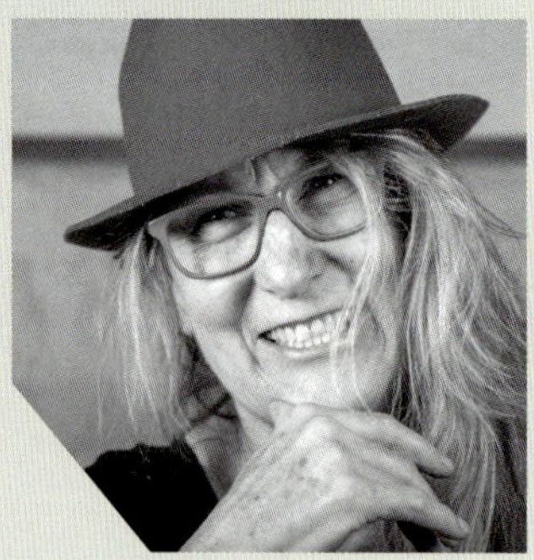

Kathryn Harmer Fox

East London, Eastern Cape, South Africa

I draw and paint with thread and fabric. I have always been able to describe what I see using a pencil, and though my mom taught me to sew when I was a little girl, I only began marrying the one to the other in my early forties.

Being both an impatient personality and an artist who appreciates the slow art of embroidery, I had to find my own way. And I did! I began to describe what I saw using my sewing machine as a tool, with the thread being the line and the fabric the paint.

I experience great nostalgia when I snip up a packet of old silk ties while remembering all those old men, now gone, or when I stitch shredded twists of fabric together, creating a whole new surface. I delight in the shadows created with a bit of netting, the cracks and creases of a rhino hide made from satins and brocades, the hair of a wild dog, or the feather of a bird made from thread.

This is the joy, the excitement, the wonder that fiber art holds for me; it is the medium, the very stuff from which it is made, which carries an undeniable promise and an intention to describe something other than itself. My passion for this medium is translated not only into my artwork but also into a workshop, "Using Your Sewing Machine as a Creative Tool," that I developed and teach.

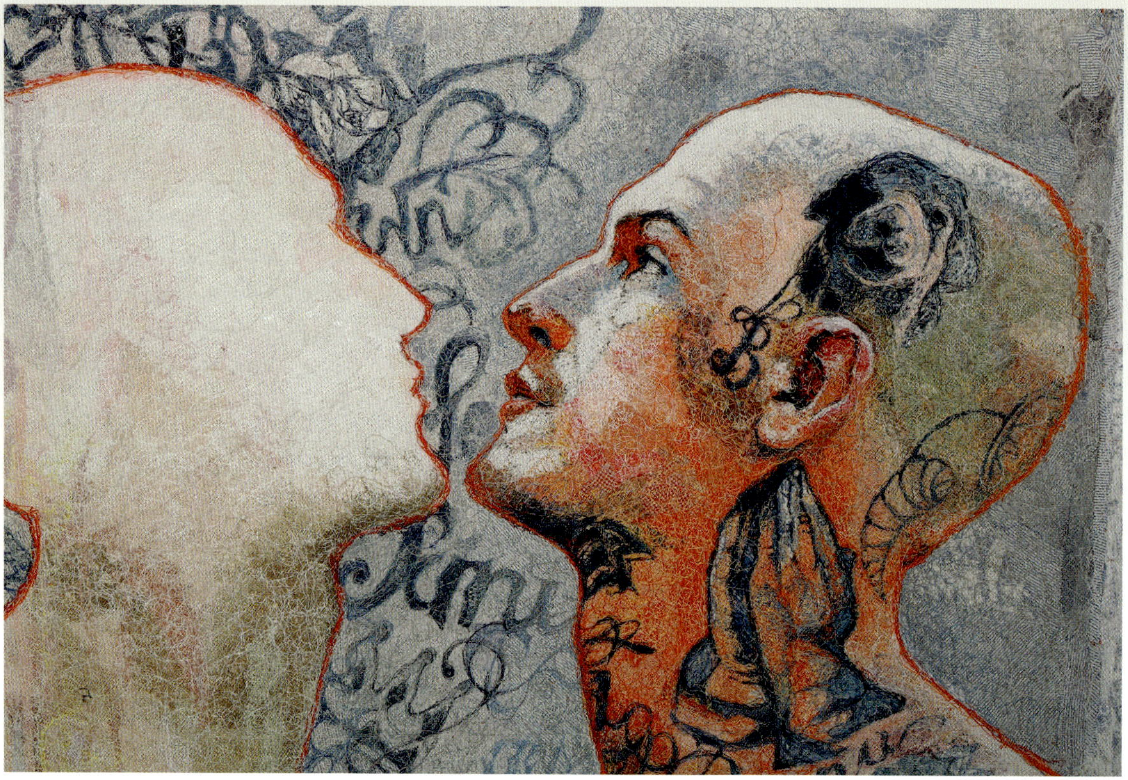

A Life Lived in Ink (detail). Assorted dress fabrics and various sewing threads. 51" × 29.7". 2015.

OPPOSITE
Full image. Photographer: PhotoQuip SA.

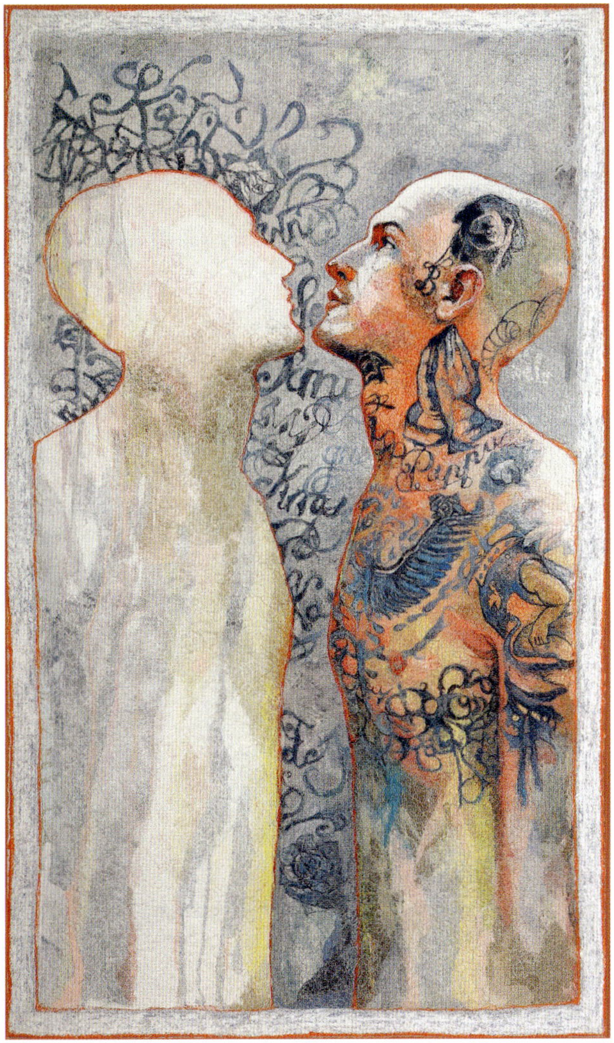

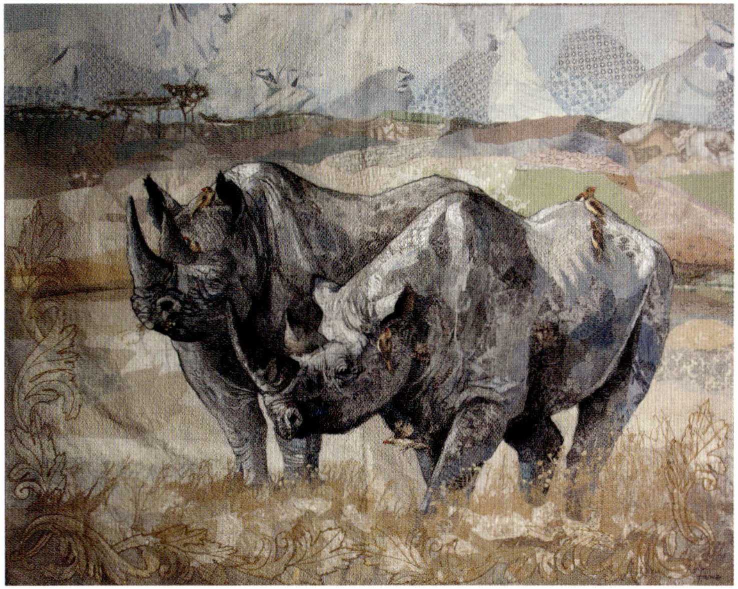

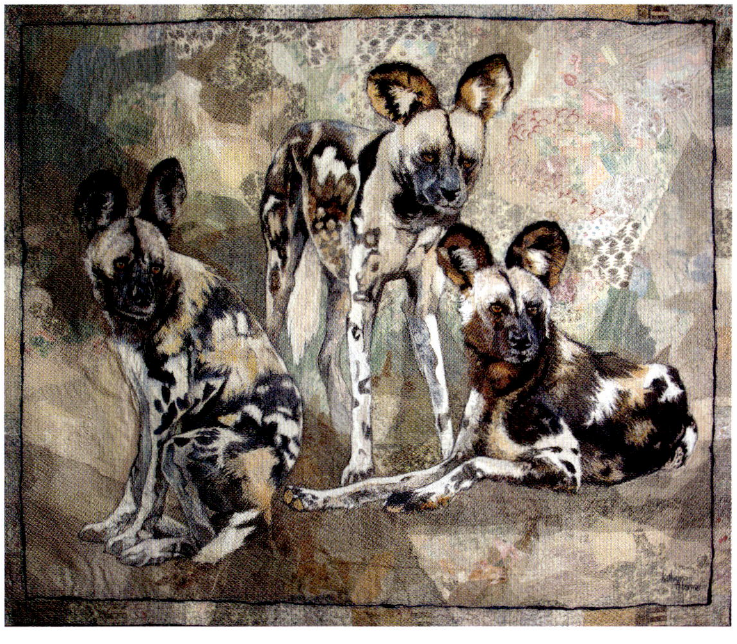

➤ *Once There Were...* Assorted dress and upholstery fabrics and various sewing threads. 55" × 71.5". 2014. Photographer: Leigh Skinner Tebbit.

➤ *The Three Watchers.* Assorted dress and upholstery fabrics and various sewing threads. 56" × 72.5". 2014. Photographer: Leigh Skinner Tebbit.

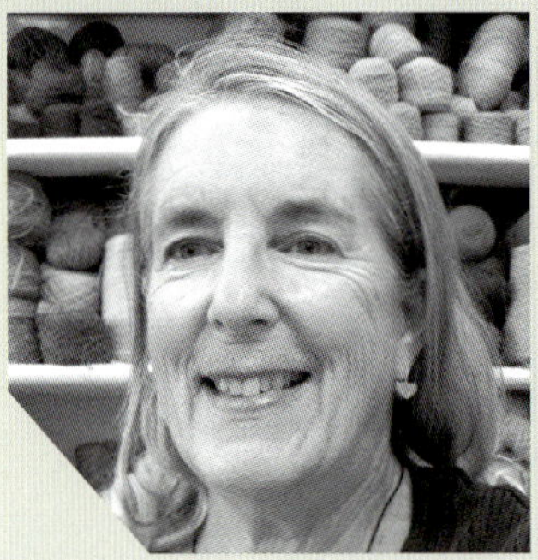

Alex Friedman

Sausalito, California

My tapestry career began with a commission to make tapestries for a fleet of jumbo jets. From those early days, I have been weaving tapestries of my own design and evolving a unique style that includes dimensional elements in a traditionally flat medium. The construction of a tapestry allows it to become more sculptural depending on how it is woven. It is these possibilities as well as the color and texture that have provided me inspiration over the years. I have notebooks of sketches, which is another source of design ideas. Tapestry is a slow art that allows time for meditation and focus. It also satisfies four of my five senses.

My tapestries have been exhibited both nationally and abroad. I have won numerous awards, including a prestigious Fellowship Award for the Visual Arts from the New England Foundation for the Arts. My commissions are installed in corporate, medical, and liturgical venues, and I have been fortunate to have many private collectors across the country. I have served as a co-director of the internationally known American Tapestry Alliance, and been an active member of many other fiber guilds as well. To further promote tapestry, I have given workshops and lectures that celebrate this exciting art form.

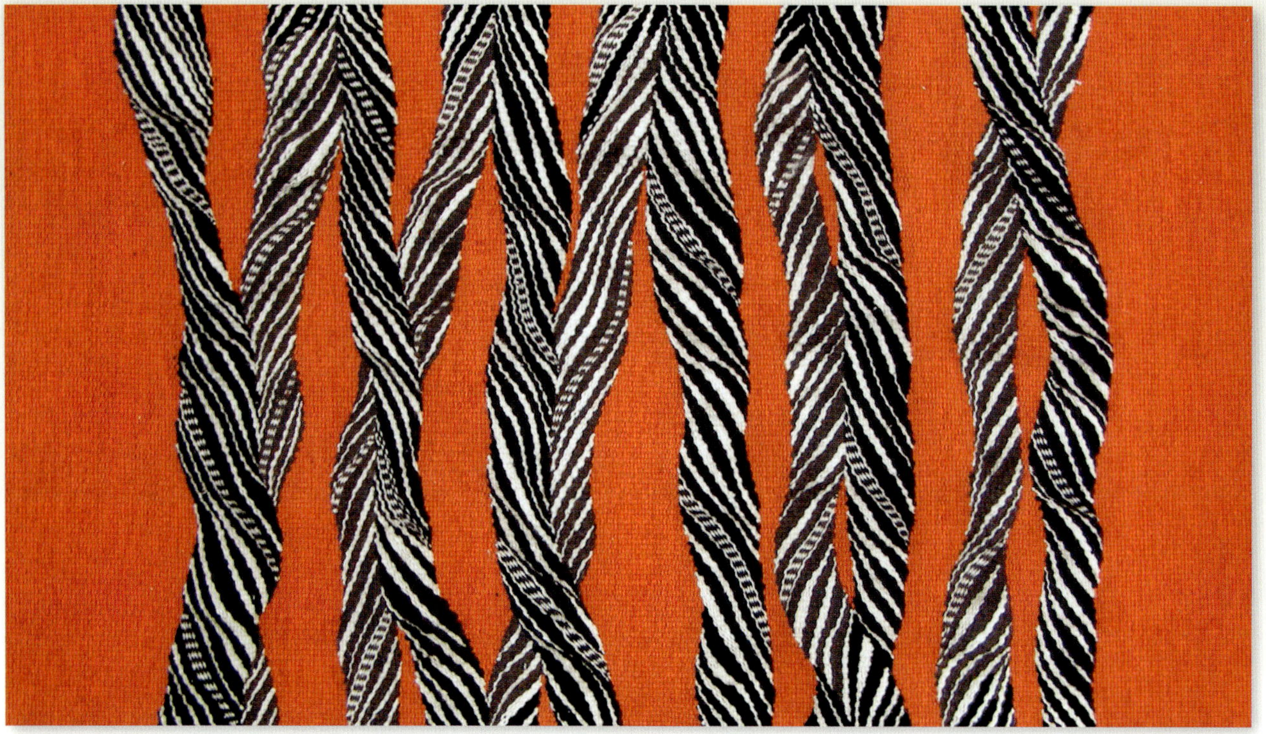

Dynamic Flow.
Wool and cotton.
19" × 33". 2010.

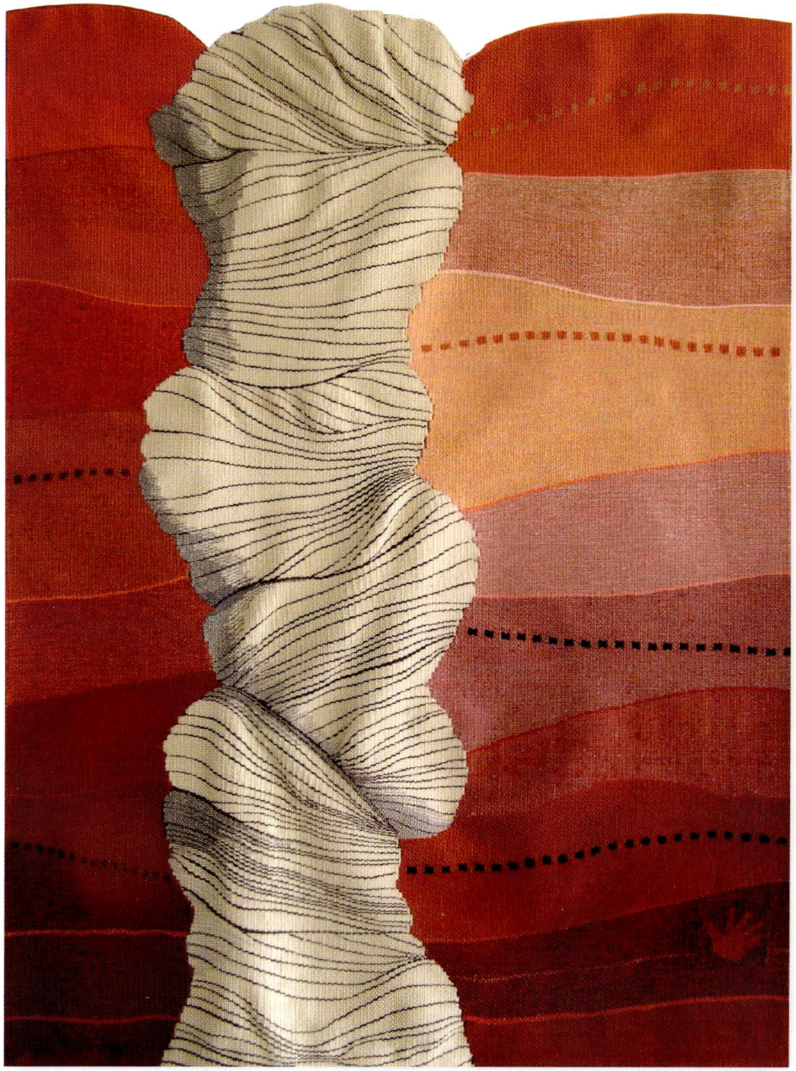

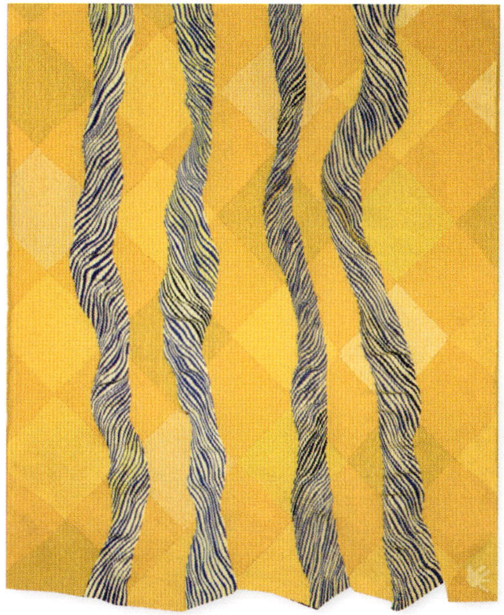

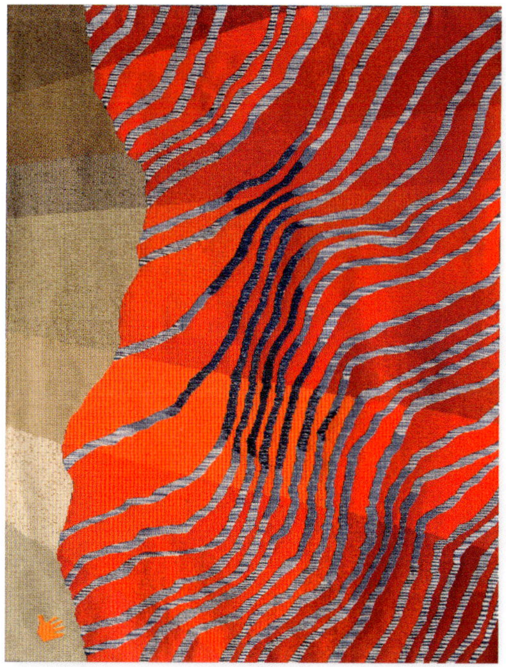

▲ *Bound.* Wool, cotton, and embroidery floss. 45" × 35". 2007.

◄ *Flow 3.* Wool and cotton. 50" × 43". 2007.

► *Here Today.* Wool and cotton. 72" × 54". 2013.

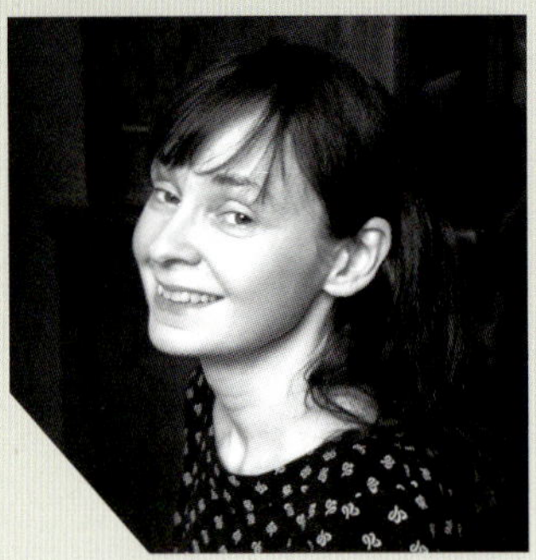

My work consists in appropriating and manipulating old photographs (using embroidery, collage, or digitally) to give them a new lease of life. I create photo-embroideries by embroidering over found photographs. In this way, I add another layer of meaning to these pictures, which already contain their own (hi)story, while at the same time hiding some parts of the original image behind the colored thread.

I play on the ambiguity between recognition (above all, one must recognize a friend or family member in a snapshot, little matter if the photograph itself is "bad") and anonymity (the photographs I find and use are anonymous, abandoned, long forgotten). Often centered on the face or head, my interventions render these images unrecognizable or unlike, make the familiar unfamiliar, and reveal how they are inherently uncanny.

Flore Gardner

Edinburgh, Scotland &
Avignon, France

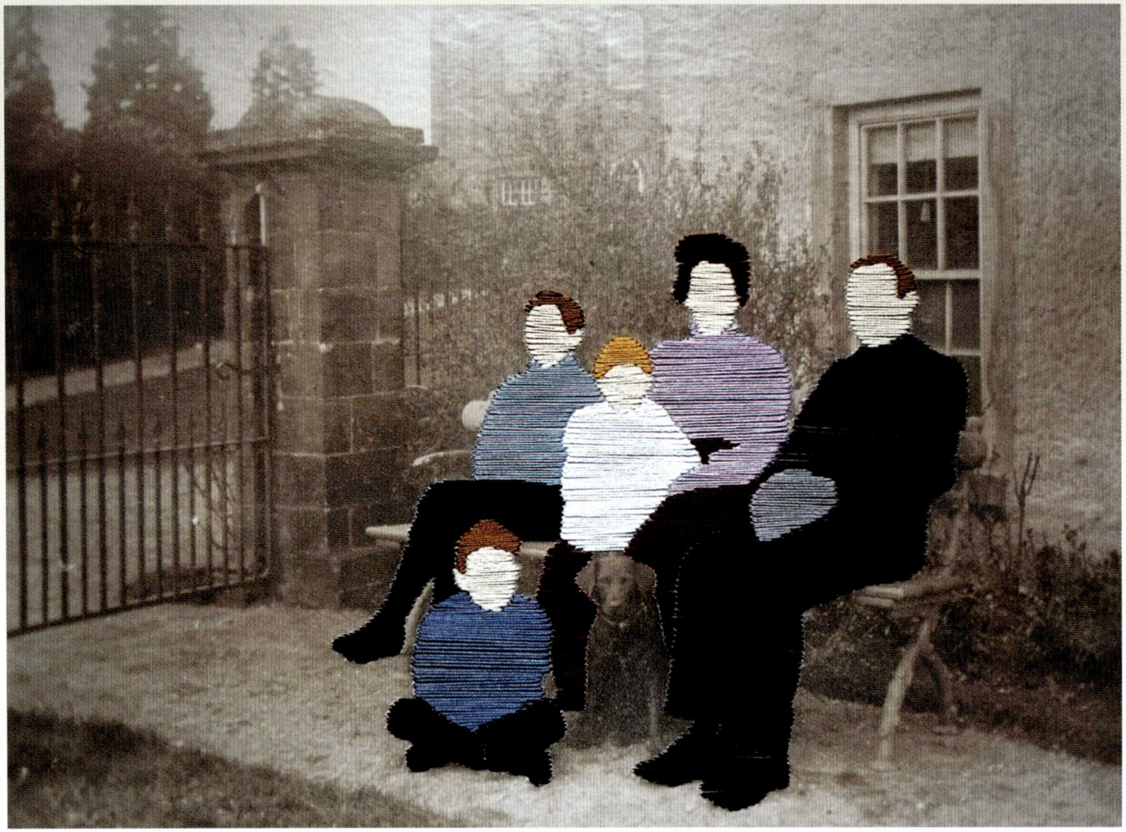

Ghosts. Embroidered found photograph. 7.9" × 11.8". 2014.

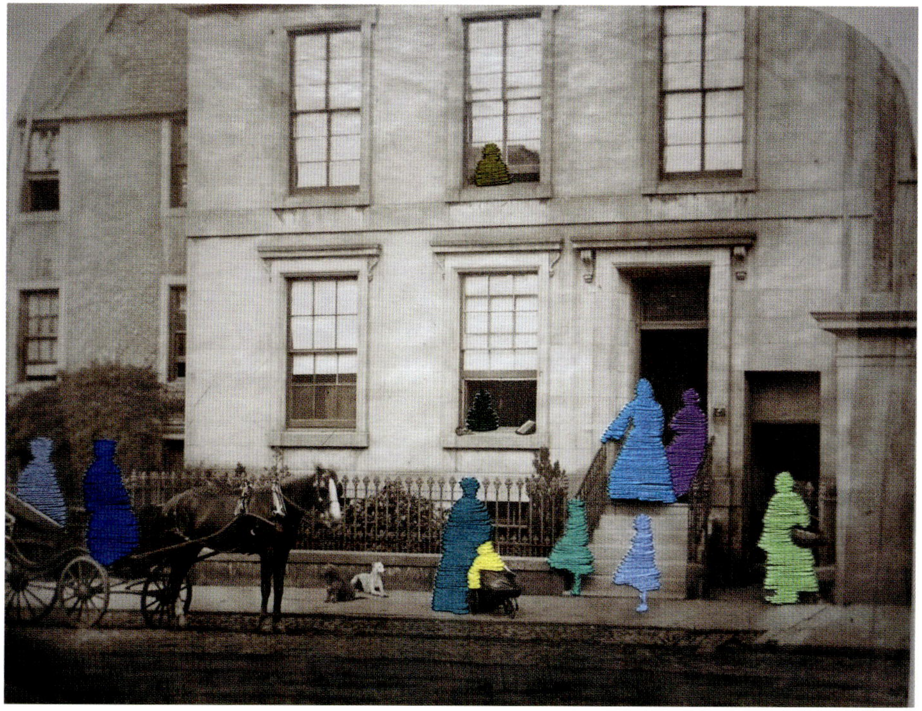

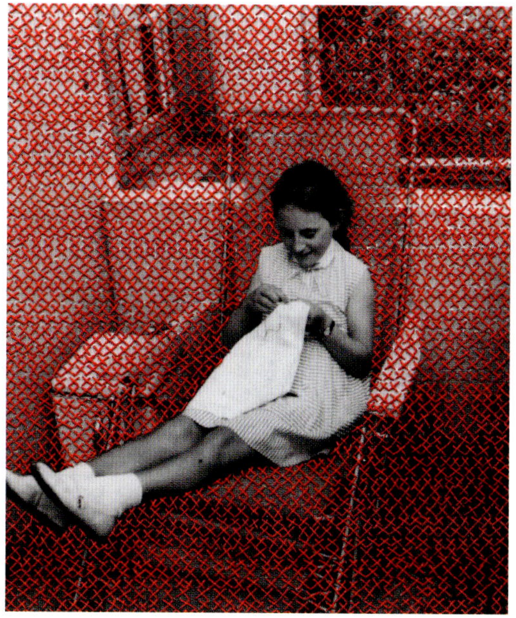

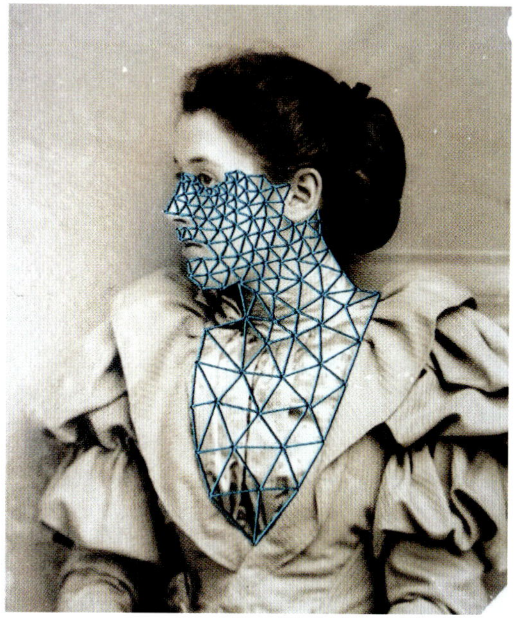

▲ *Ghosts*. Embroidered found photograph. 9" × 11.8". 2014.

➤ *Chiasmus*. Embroidered found photograph. 7.9" × 7.9". 2013.

➤ *Rhizome*. Embroidered found photograph. 8.26" × 5.9". 2014.

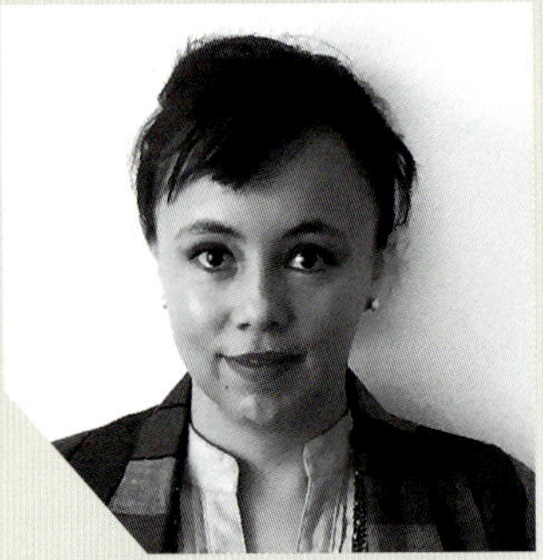

Luisa F. Gil Fandino

Austin, Texas

My work explores repetition in nature through the implementation of industrial processes and computer-generated algorithms, translating it into fiber media that captivates and encourages curiosity and tactile seduction.

Ever since I graduated, and began my journey into textiles, I have been fascinated by the marriage between technology and art. What starts out as a simple yarn, a flat fabric or surface, soon becomes manipulated into an organic yet organized entropic tessellation, leaving a sense of space and volume that invites interaction—a passion I like to share with my interior and fashion design students.

I have exhibited in New York City, London, and Paris and currently reside in Texas, where I teach textiles at different institutions.

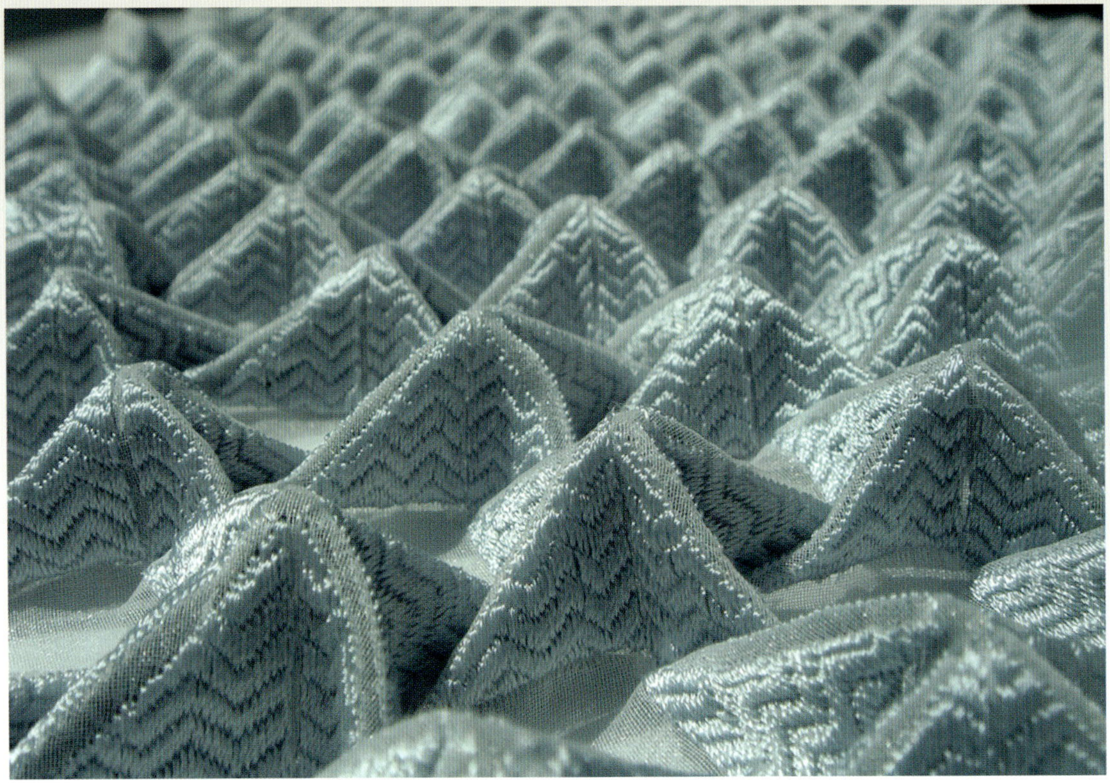

Pyramids. Cotton organza and poly thread. 36" × 12". 2012.

➤ *Waves.* Wool, cotton, and Lycra®. 52" × 10". 2012.

▼ *Surimi.* Wool, cotton, and Lycra®. 52" × 10". 2012.

➤ *Crooked Squares.* Cotton organza, and polyester thread. 10" × 50".

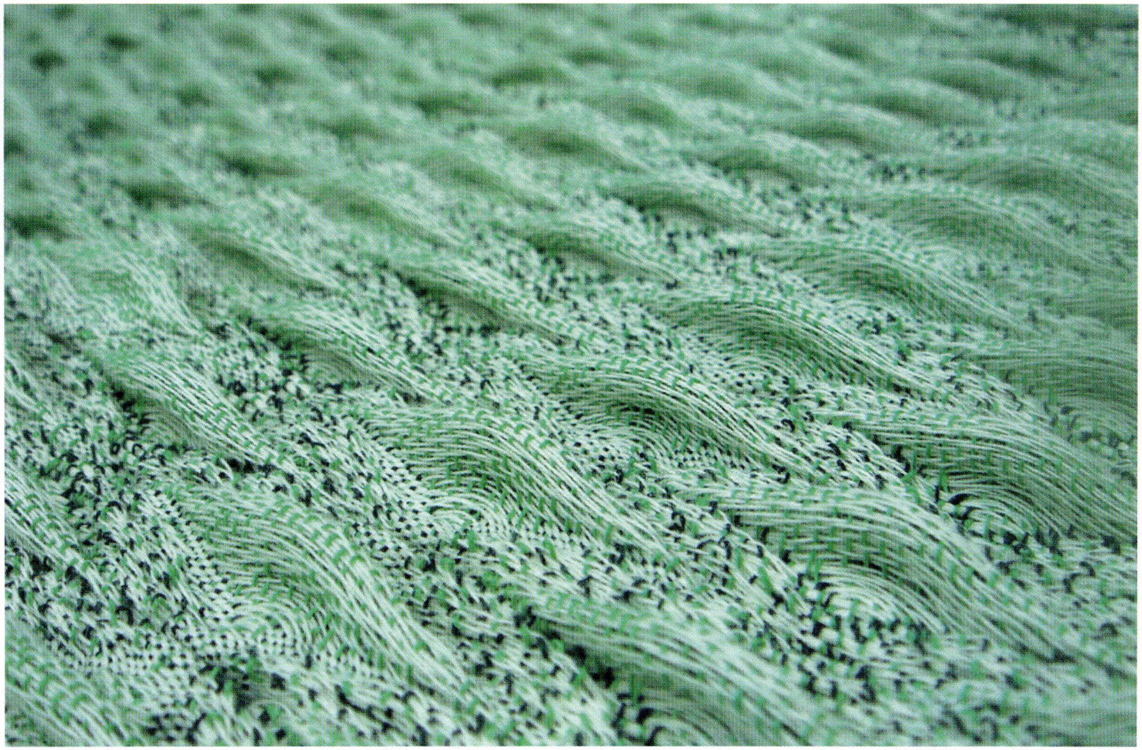

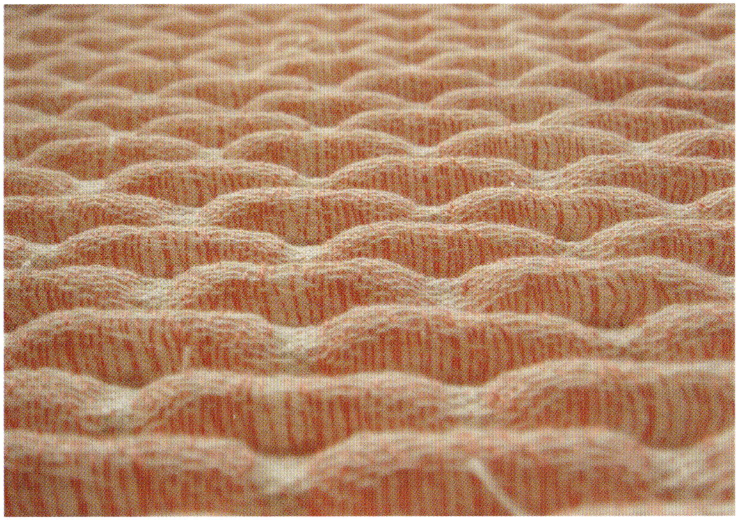

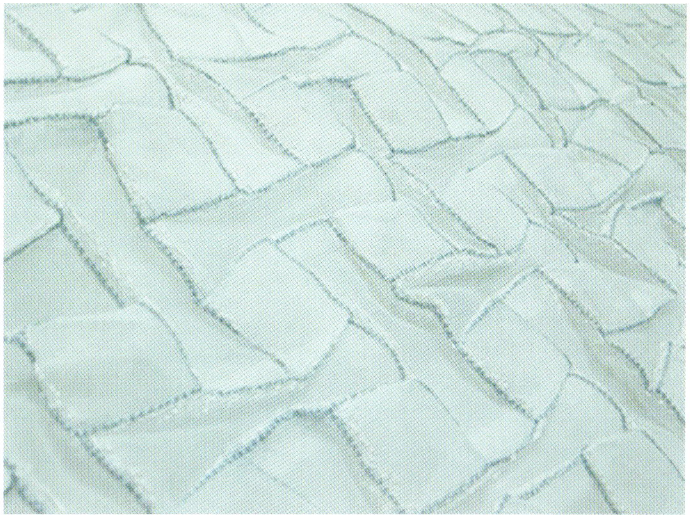

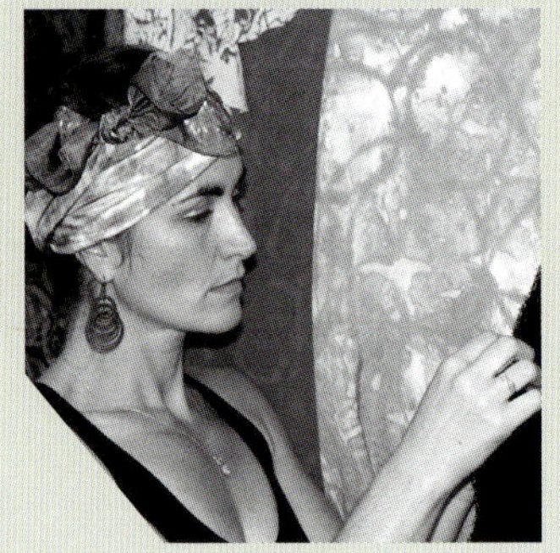

Meredith Re' Grimsley

Bloomsburg, Pennsylvania

In Zora Neale Hurston's novel *Their Eyes Were Watching God*, she describes the altered state of a woman seeking resolution and solace in prayer:

"There is a basin in the mind where words float around a thought and thought on sound and sight. Then there is a depth of thought untouched by words and deeper still a gulf of formless feelings untouched by thought."

Acknowledging a sense of loss and gratitude in daily life, I construct pieces that reflect moments of meditation and a longing for grace. In pursuit of truth, my spiritual identity emerges. My soul's yearning for a connection fuels my imagination. To my audience, I whisper about my search with the physical, indelible mark of the stitch.

Recently, I have begun to contemplate pivotal experiences that permanently alter a person's life and path. Correlating the nature of dysfunctional family legacies through both unsettling and alluring imagery, I reveal the psychological impact of patterns of behavior that each generation inherits. Significant events, words, and behaviors occur within families and are absorbed into our daily routine without examination. Some happen in a breath while others linger endlessly, either corroding or correcting our core. Our minds and bodies are formed. We either languish with our habits or are reborn with a new perspective. My work describes a balance between beauty and distortion and the endurance of the human spirit no matter what physiological, emotional, psychological, or spiritual residue is imbedded by both constructive and destructive family models.

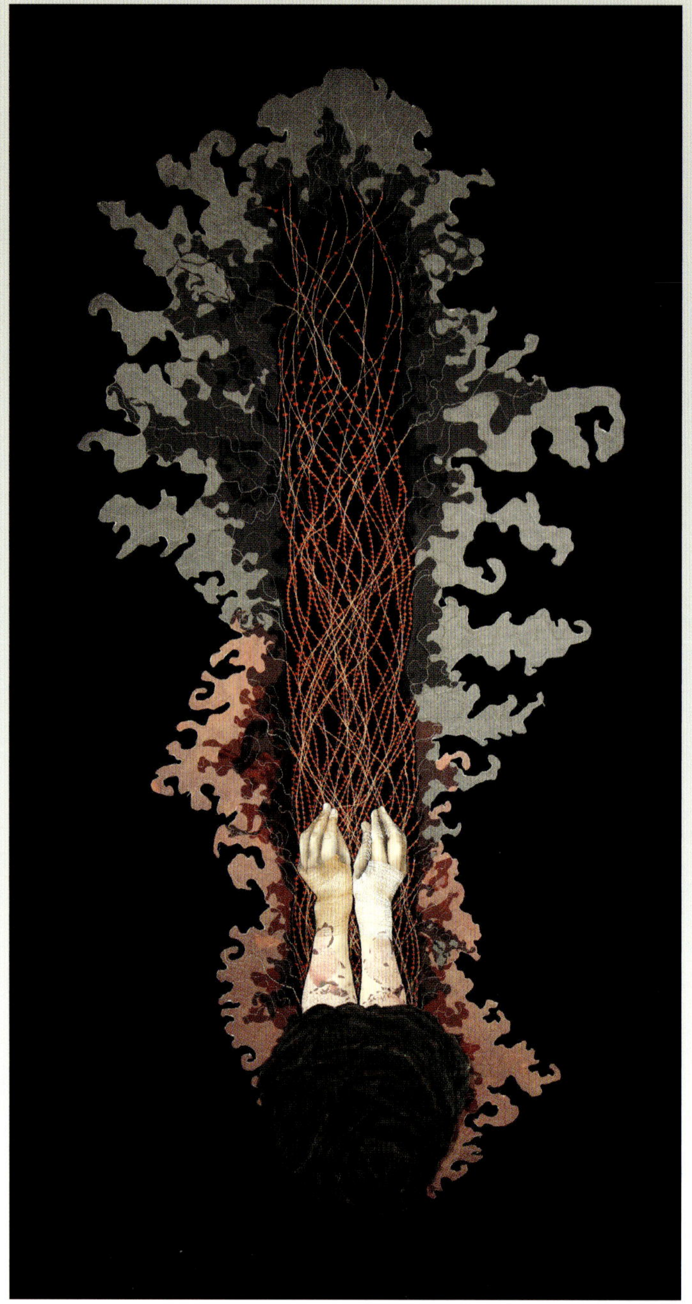

Foundress. Rayon, silk organza, muslin, handmade abaca paper, and acrylic paint. 71" × 35". 2014.

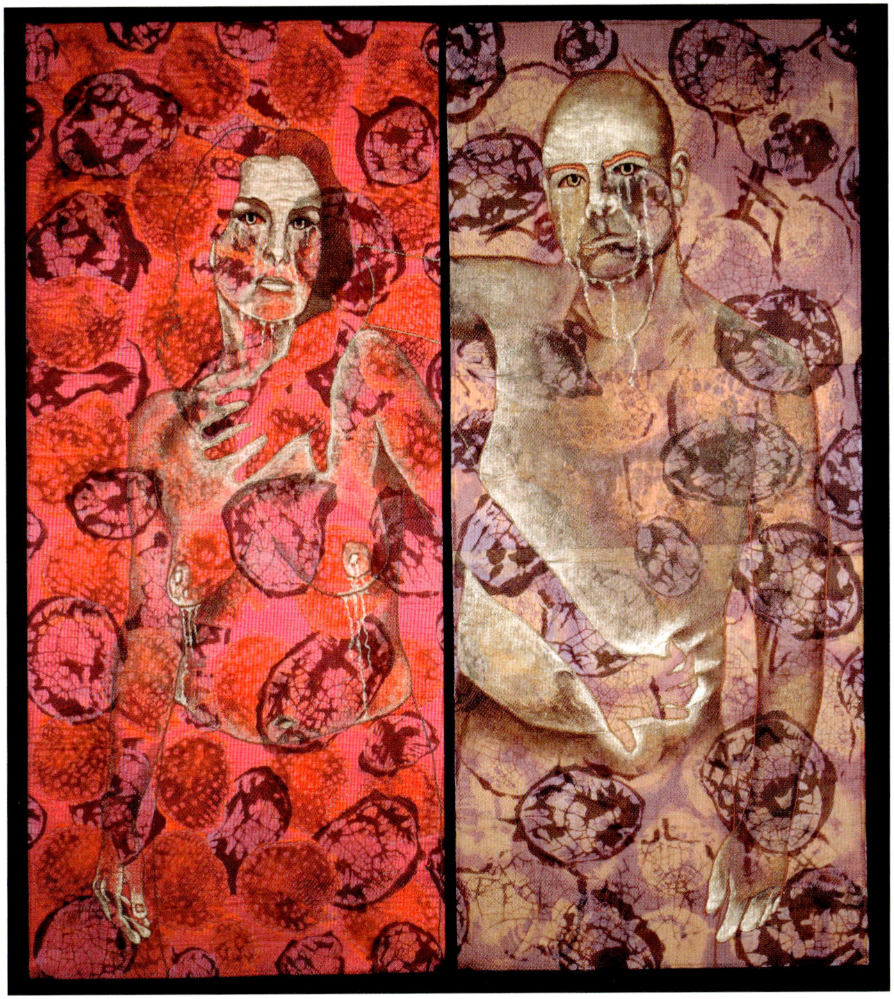

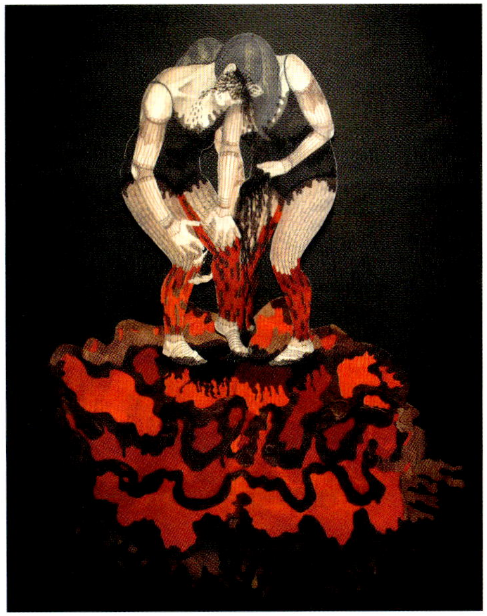

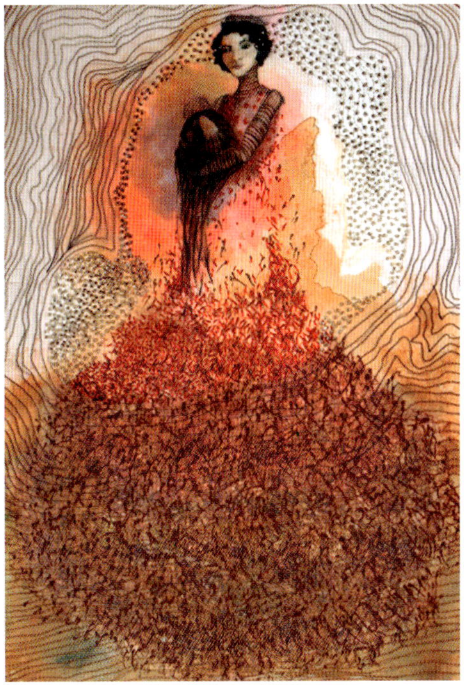

▲ *Same Old Wounds: A Marriage.* Muslin, thread, silk organza, silk habotai, MX® fiber reactive dye, potato dextrin, and textile pigment. 31" × 31". 2015.

◄ *Deep Horizon*. Muslin, silk satin, fiber reactive dye, digital print, fusible web, and batting. 64" × 43". 2015.

► *Pterygium.* Muslin, recycled bed sheets, thread, beads, MX® fiber reactive dye, metallic pigment, digital print, machine and hand embroidery. 18" × 12". 2013.

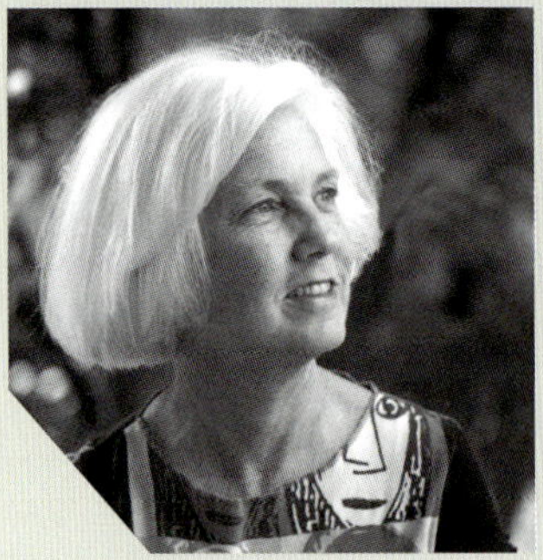

Louise Halsey

Little Rock, Arkansas

Weaving, for me, is a meditative practice. The required steps—for example, winding the warp or threading the heddles—have a rhythm I cherish. Vibrant colors and bold designs, traits seen in my childhood crayon drawings, continue to be important elements in my work.

My weaving explores concerns about environmental and social issues, most recently through a series of house tapestries that reflect on the nature of home. This iconic image represents safety, as well as the possibility of loss, through unsettling forces such as earthquakes, fracking, rising waters caused by global warming, or gentrification. *High Fiber: Women to Watch in the Arts 2012*, at the National Museum of Women in the Arts in Washington, DC, exhibited four of my works from the house series. The houses express both the wonder and the sorrow I have, while weaving from a place of great beauty in the Ozarks, as I experience the threatened destruction of the planet.

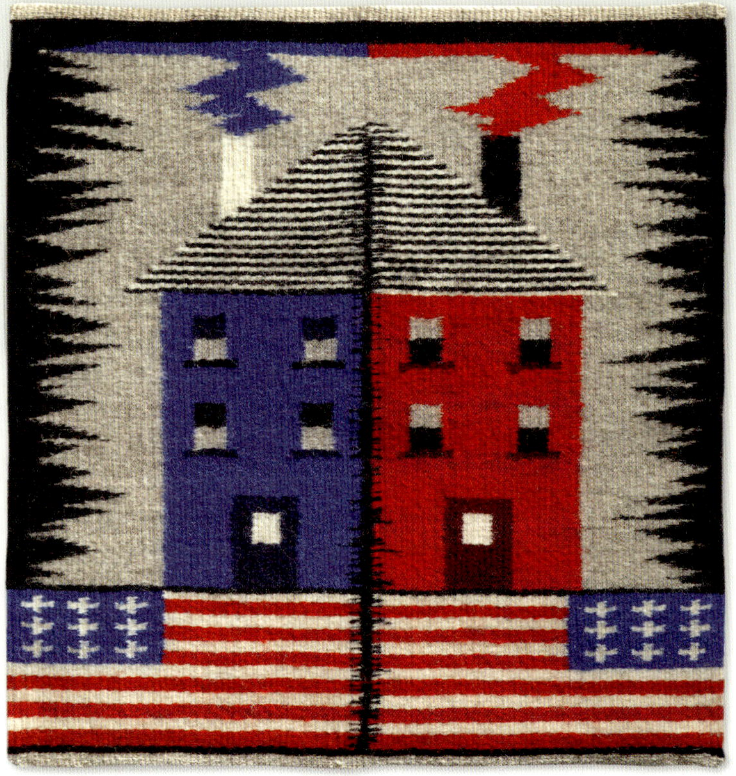

Stitching the Union Together. Wool on linen warp. 15" × 14.5" × 0.25".

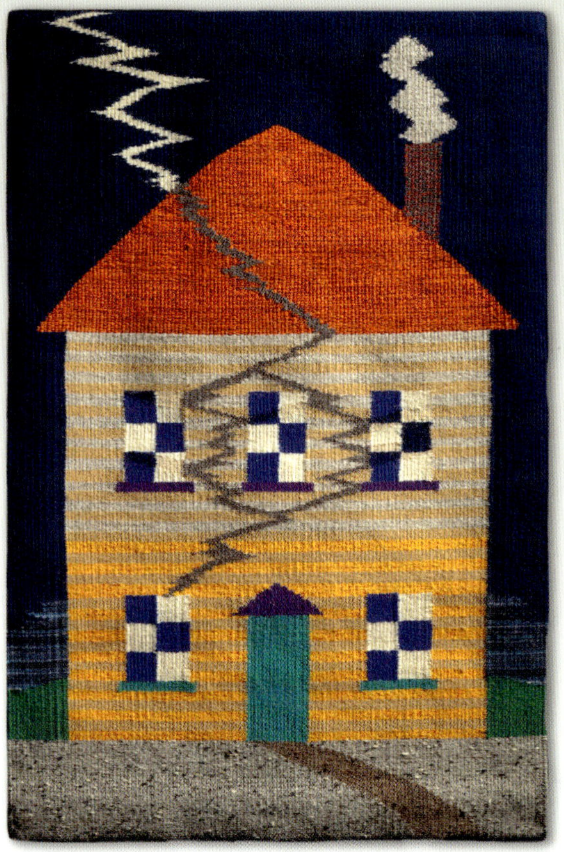

House and Lightning. Wool, mixed fibers, and linen. 26" × 17". 2012.

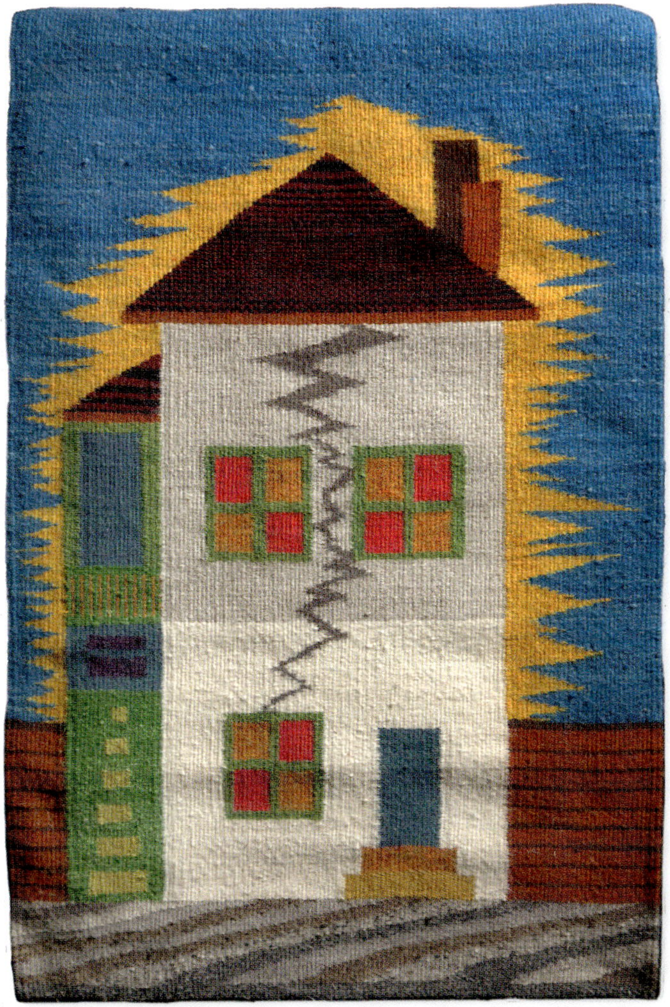

Crackhouse. Wool and linen. 25.5" × 17.5". 2008.

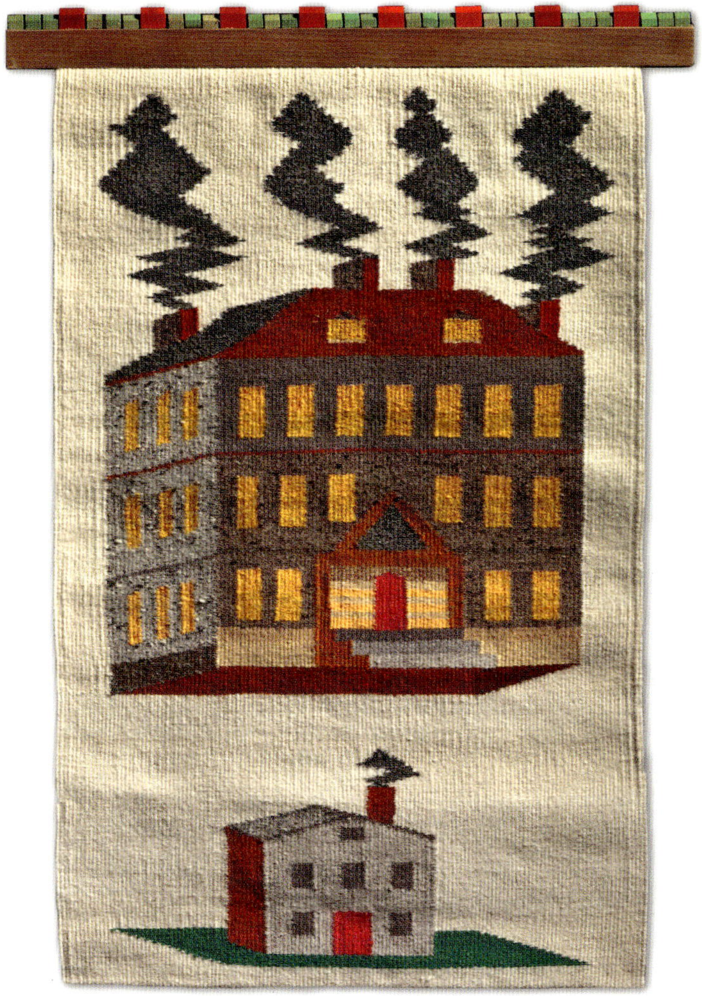

Supersize My House. Wool, linen, and wooden hanger with Monopoly houses. 27.5" × 17.25". 2011.

All images courtesy of George Chambers.

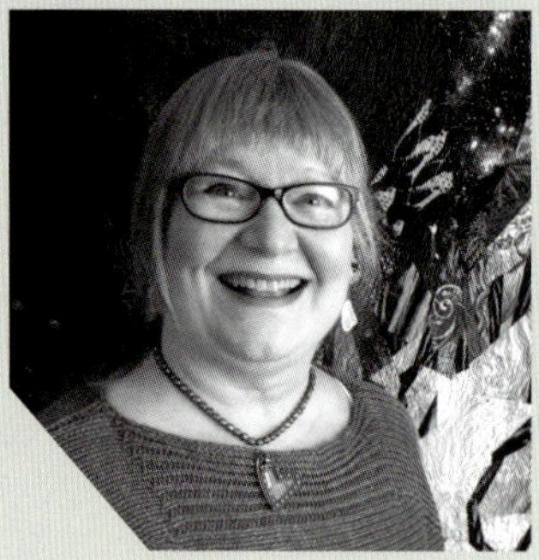

Courtesy of Shelly Heesacker.

Ann Harwell

Wendell, North Carolina

Sewing has been a part of my life since age five when I received a child's Singer sewing machine. I worked at a fabric store during high school. After college I managed the alterations department in several stores and did custom dressmaking from my home. When my first son was born in 1977, I made him a baby quilt and have not stopped quilting. In 1999, quilting became an occupation instead of an avocation, and I rented a studio in downtown Raleigh, North Carolina.

My work is constructed like a fine garment, with great attention to detail: seams are strong and straight, corners are sharp, and points are precise. I precision-cut each piece of cotton fabric, sew it together with my 1945 Singer Featherweight, and quilt it with a hand-guided Juki home sewing machine.

In the sixteen years I have been a professional artist, my work has been juried into over fifty shows both nationally and internationally, winning numerous awards.

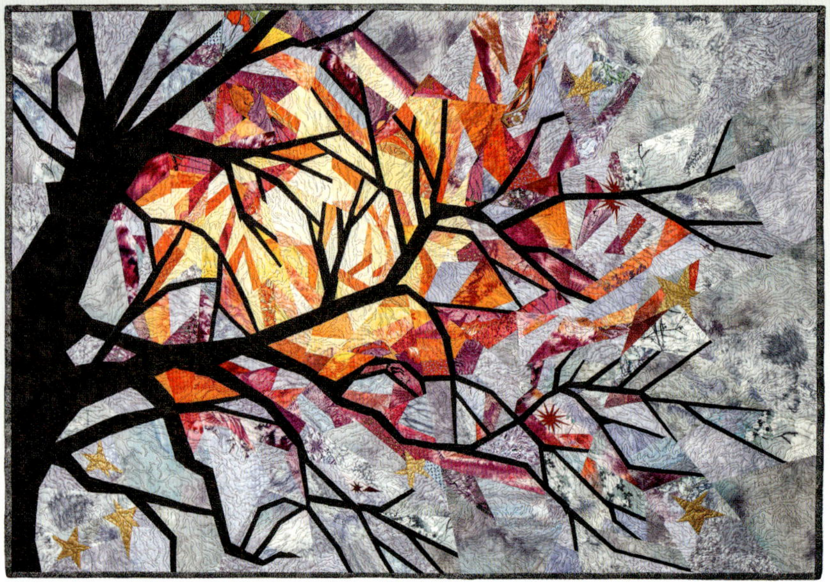

Overreaching for the Stars. Cotton fabric, batting, and backing, and Polyneon thread. 39" × 56". Courtesy of Dick Cicone.

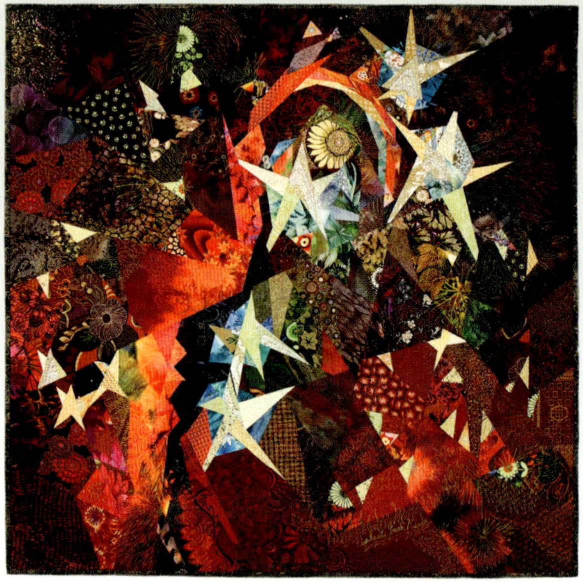

Elephants Trunk Nebula. Cotton fabric, batting, and backing, and Polyneon thread. 52" × 50". 2009. Courtesy of Dick Cicone.

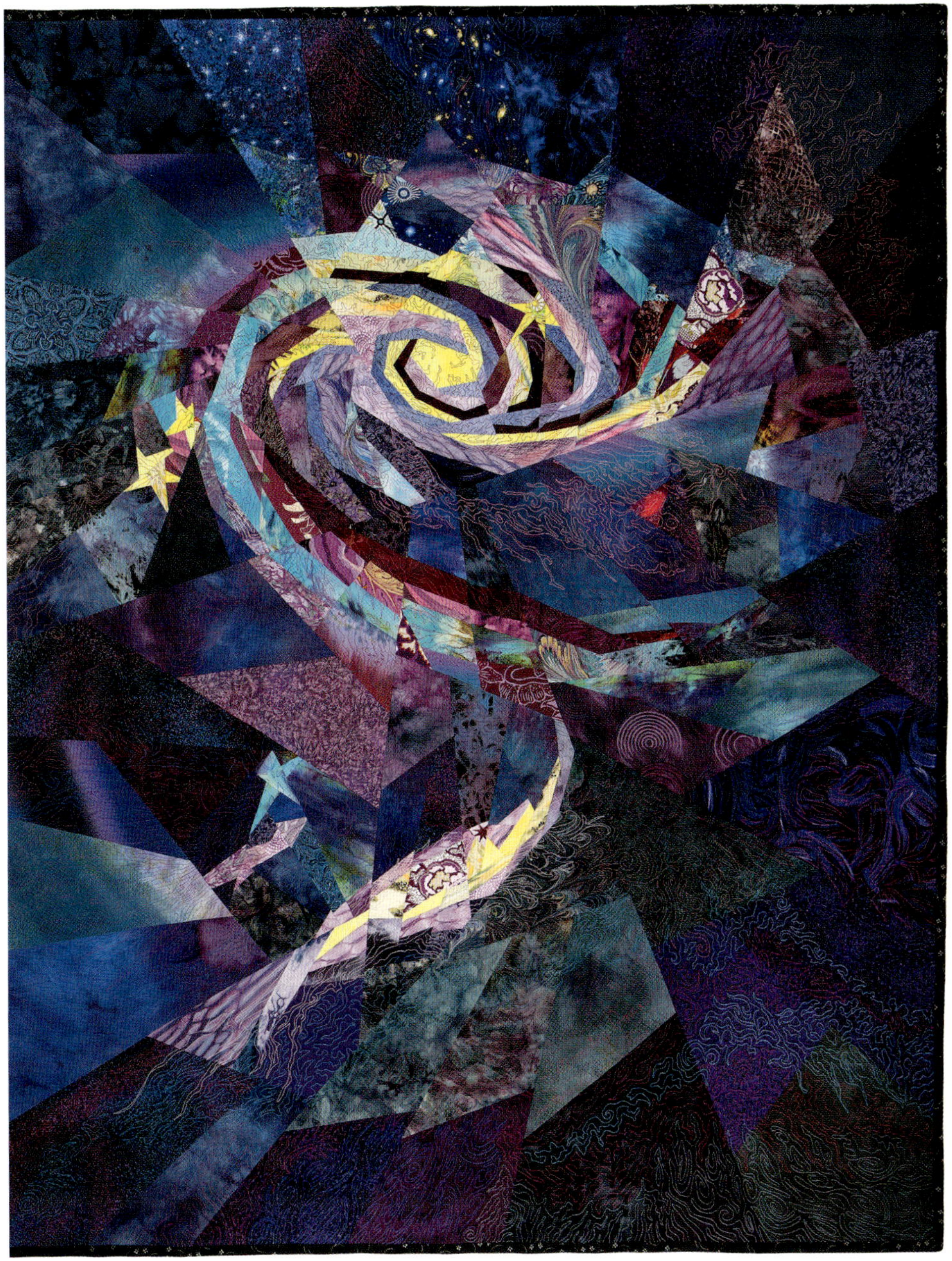

◄ *Interacting Galaxies.* Cotton fabric, batting, and backing, and Polyneon thread. 56" × 44". 2015. Courtesy of Dick Cicone.

▼ *Eagle Nebula.* Cotton fabric, batting, and backing, and Polyneon thread. 79" × 37". 2005. Courtesy of Lynn Ruck.

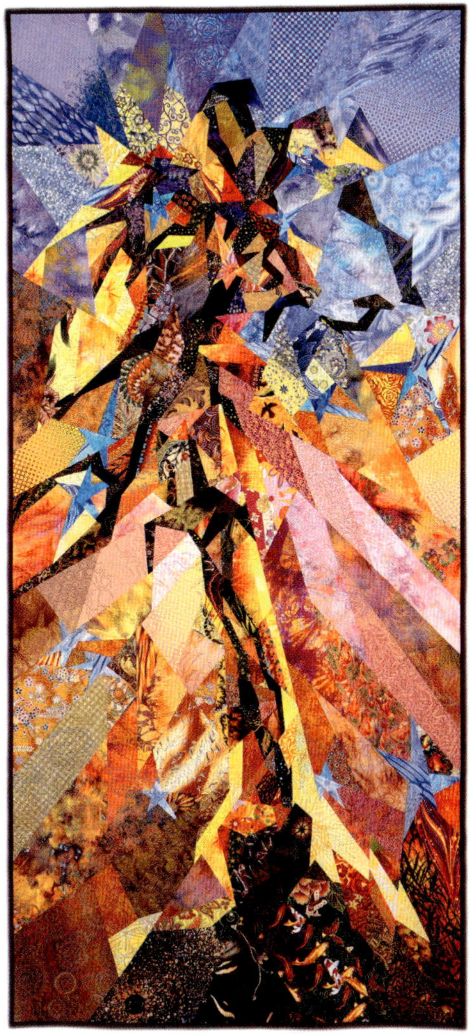

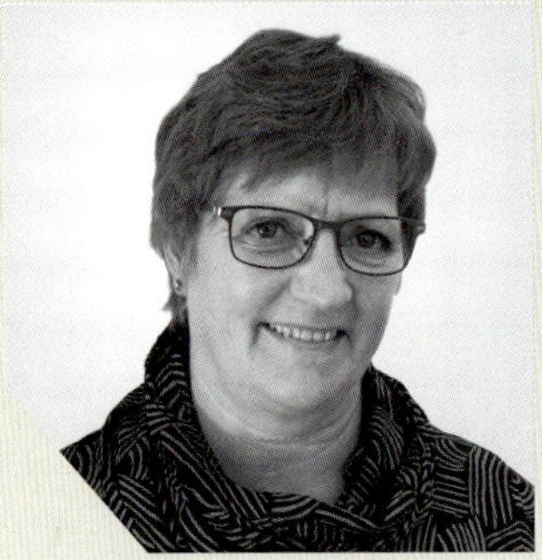

Ulla Hein

Rønne, Denmark

For as long as I can remember, I have made things with my hands. Mostly, these were objects in needlework such as knitting, crocheting, sewing, or bobbin lace—crafts I learned from my mother and grandmother. Fiber and the variety of techniques it encompasses has always fascinated me. It can be used for the cutest knitted baby sock, a macramé trawl for a fishing boat, or a bobbin lace dress for a Victorian queen.

For me, glass lace is a melding of tradition, craft, technique, fantasy, and challenge. When I started to work with glass and combined it with the bobbin lace technique, a whole new world of possibilities opened up. Suddenly, I was not constrained by the limitations of the thread and the bobbin lace technique. Lace in glass increases what is possible with shape and pattern.

Progression shows the development from the simplest pattern to a more advanced lace technique. My *Variation* focuses on the individual knots and how their variety results in five different patterns—even though each knot is made with the same amount of threads, the same thickness of threads, and the same pricking.

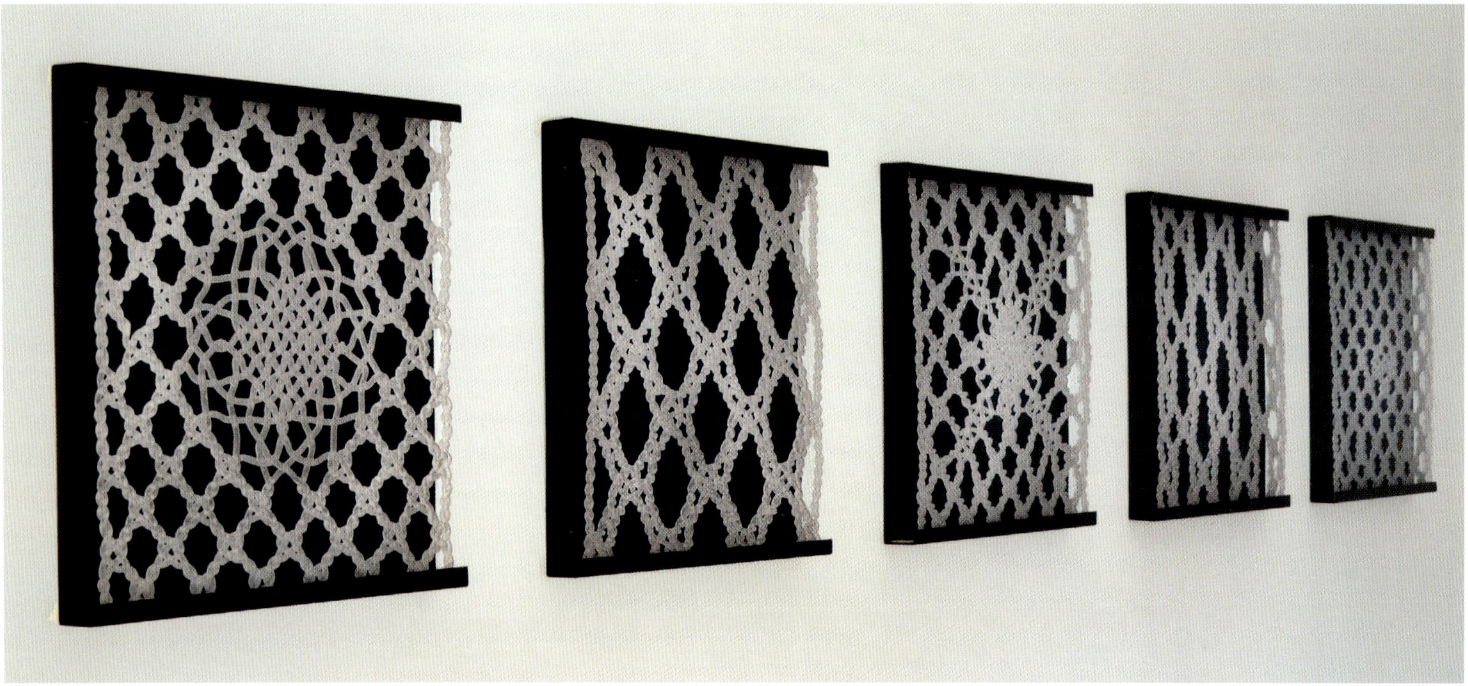

Variation. Lost wax. Glass and metal. 13" × 13.5" each. 2015.

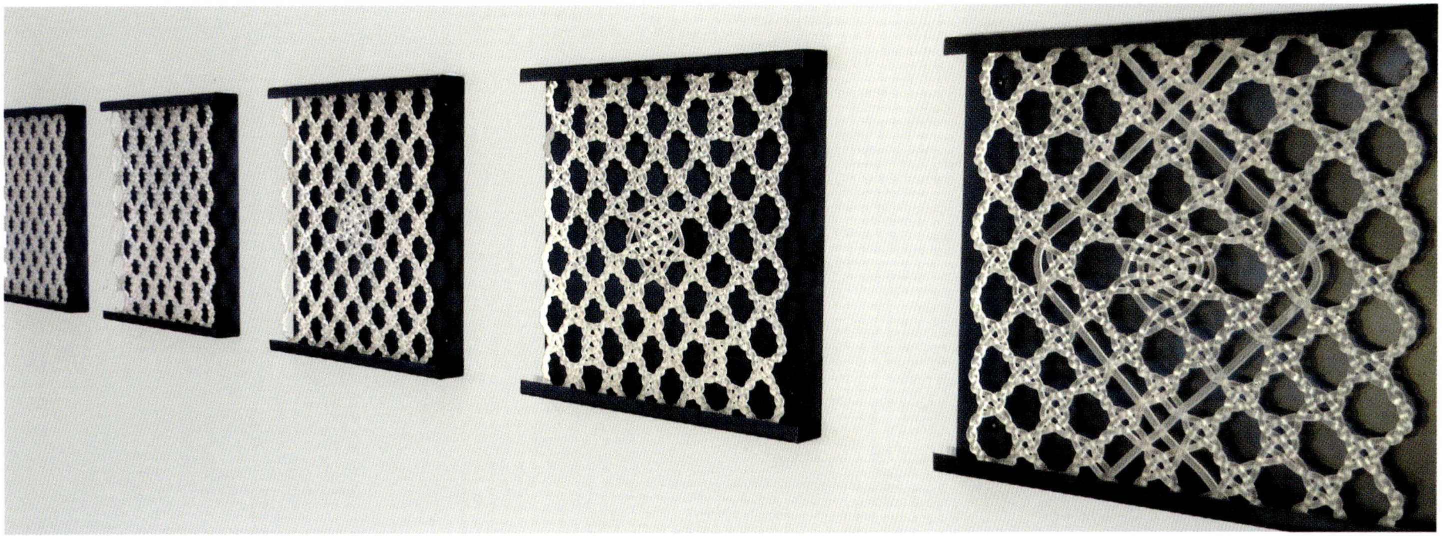

Progression. Lost wax. Glass and metal.
13" × 13" each. 2015. | Detail

Courtesy of Soren Lauridsen, Mathilde Foto.

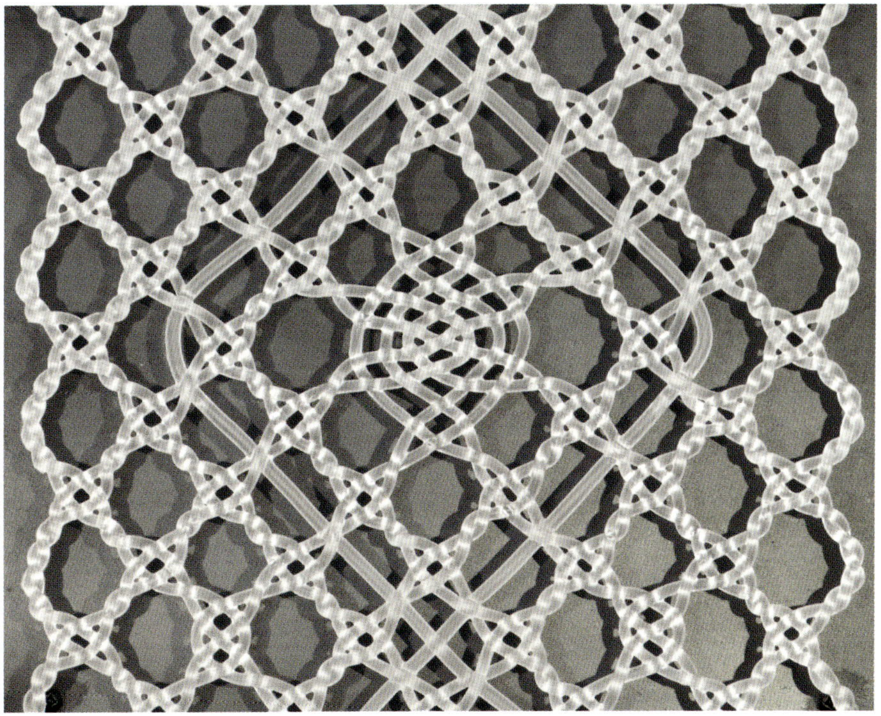

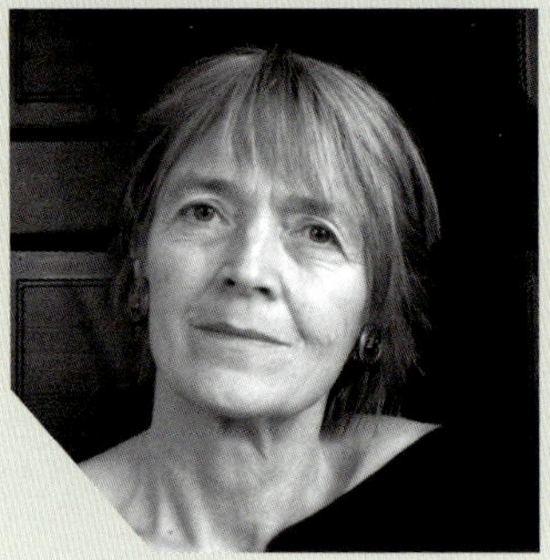

My pictures are, in a sense, like my skin—an expression of something vulnerable. I try to contain the world around me and transform it to fit my reality—to a new kind of internal logic, a stillness. Searching with a mixture of doubt and conviction, I am confused and contradictory, which is perhaps why I need to try to create silence.

With emotion-bearing threads, I want to form a space and the possibility of escape. I do not try to distract the viewers' attention, but to call them to attention and perhaps awaken them to wonder. I would like to sound quiet tones, whilst seeking to understand my world. I dream of embracing the world, not of convincing it. After a trip to Iceland, where nature bubbles, puffs, and explodes, I have played with the uncertainty in the identifiable: is it the body or is it the planet that groans?

Ane Henriksen

Copenhagen, Denmark

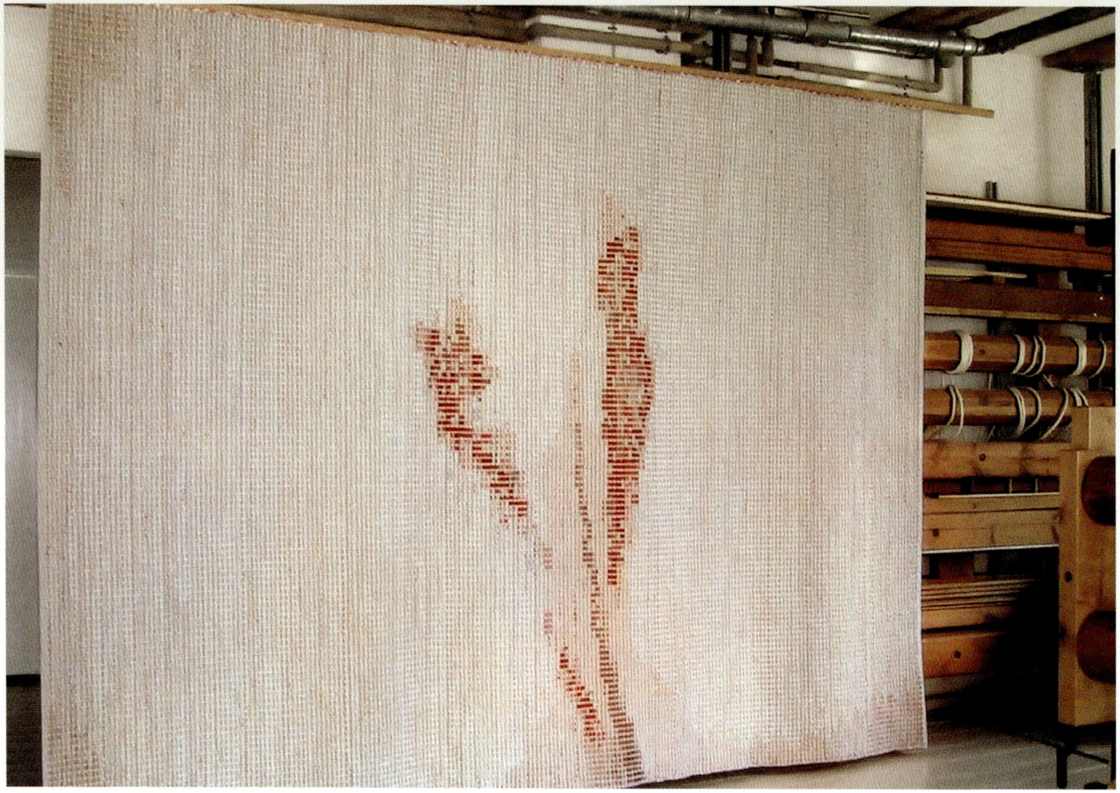

My Icelandic Flower.
Silk warp and bed cloth weft.
94.5" × 126". 2003.

➤ *A Condition*. Silk warp and bed cloth weft and jersey dots. 93.7" × 100.8". 2012. Photographer: Ole Akhøj.

▼ *Trembling 3*. Silk warp and bed cloth weft. 94.5" × 126". 2005. Photography by anders sune berg.

➤ *Trembling* (detail). Silk warp and bed cloth weft. Photographer: Ole Akhøj.

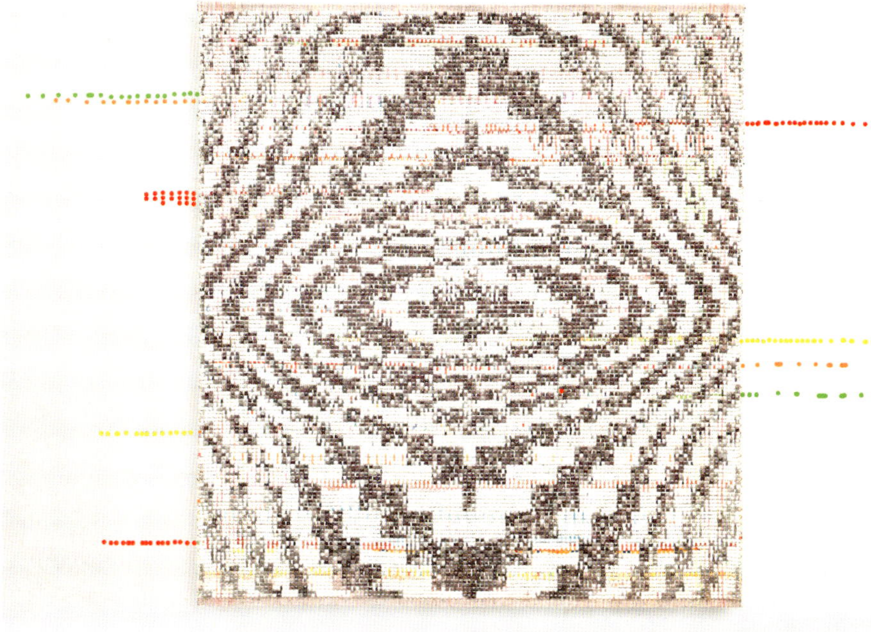

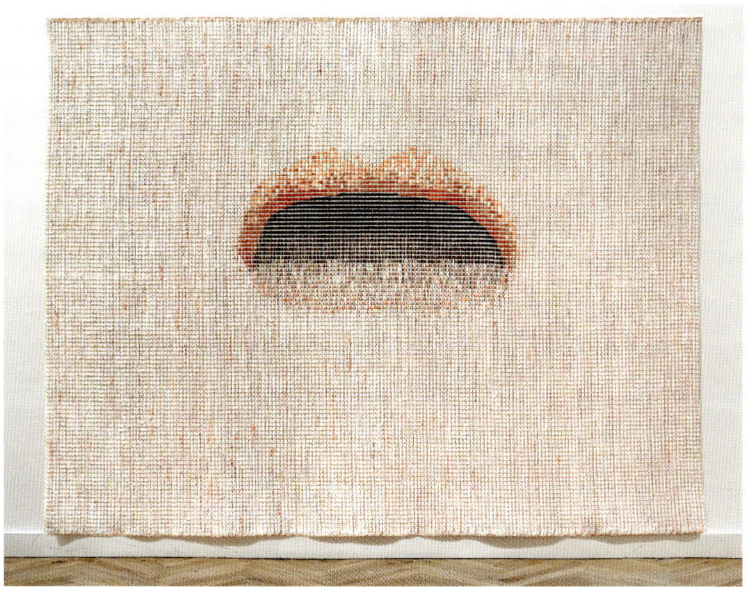

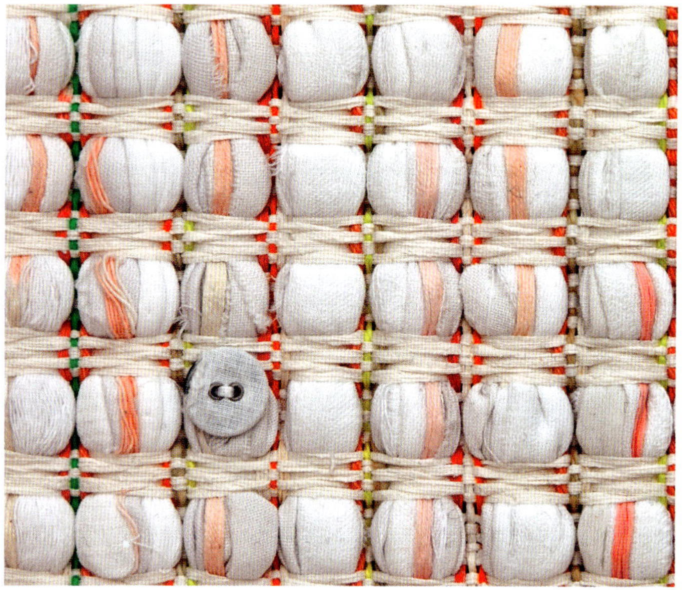

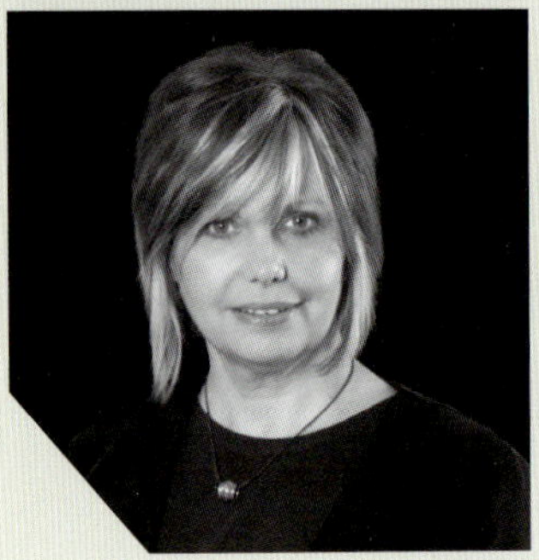

Anna Hergert

Moosejaw, Saskatchewan, Canada

Born and educated in Germany, I was exposed to fiber art at an early age. After my maternal grandmother gently guided me in embroidery at age four, I was introduced to formal handiwork sessions at school. This passion for art and textiles has become a lifelong pursuit and led to my obtaining diplomas in art, design, and contemporary embroidery, as well as in patchwork and quilting from City & Guilds of London Institute.

I consider myself a passionate artist, teacher, lecturer, and writer. In 2001, I committed to a career as a full-time professional artist and began exhibiting two years later; venues include Korea, the United States, Canada, Germany, and Austria. Teaching design and special techniques to fiber artists is a vital part of my life. I have received the Canadian Quilters Association's Teacher of the Year Award, and have received various awards for my art work. I am a regular contributor to the *Canadian Quilter Magazine* and have authored a book on kantha quilting.

My work is about the visual and formal: line, shape, color, texture, negative and positive space, and how these design elements communicate with each other and with the onlooker. I translate these elements into fabric because I recognize its infinite possibilities. Fabric is sensual and can be made to have weight, mass, and texture. It creates atmosphere by reflecting and changing its appearance in light. For me, the result is a material with the potential for infinite expression and form.

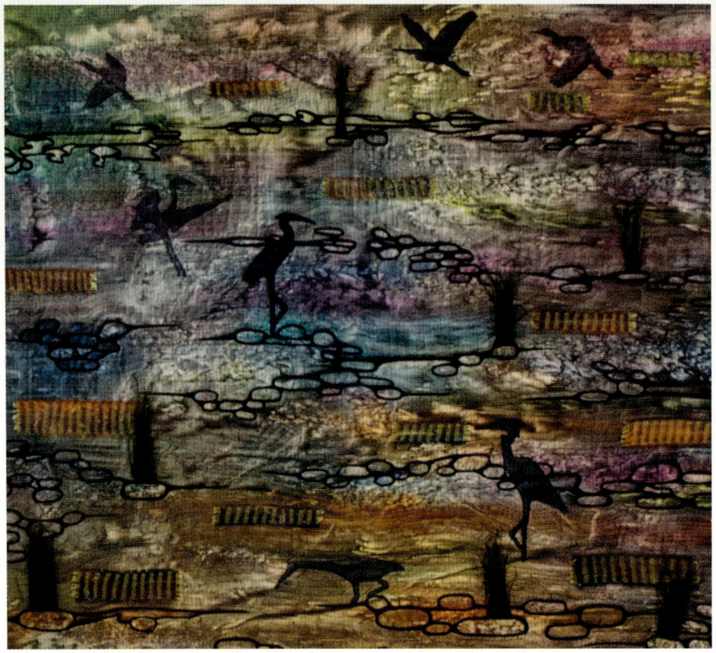

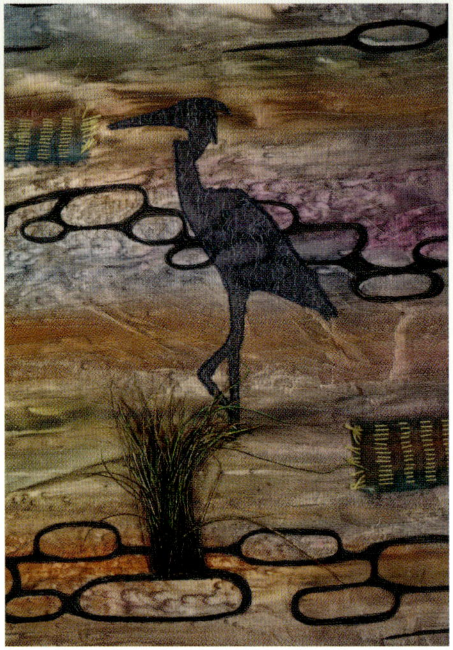

Prairie Springtime Ritual—Return of the Blue Heron. Hand painted silk and polyester sheer overlay. 42" × 32". 2015. | Detail

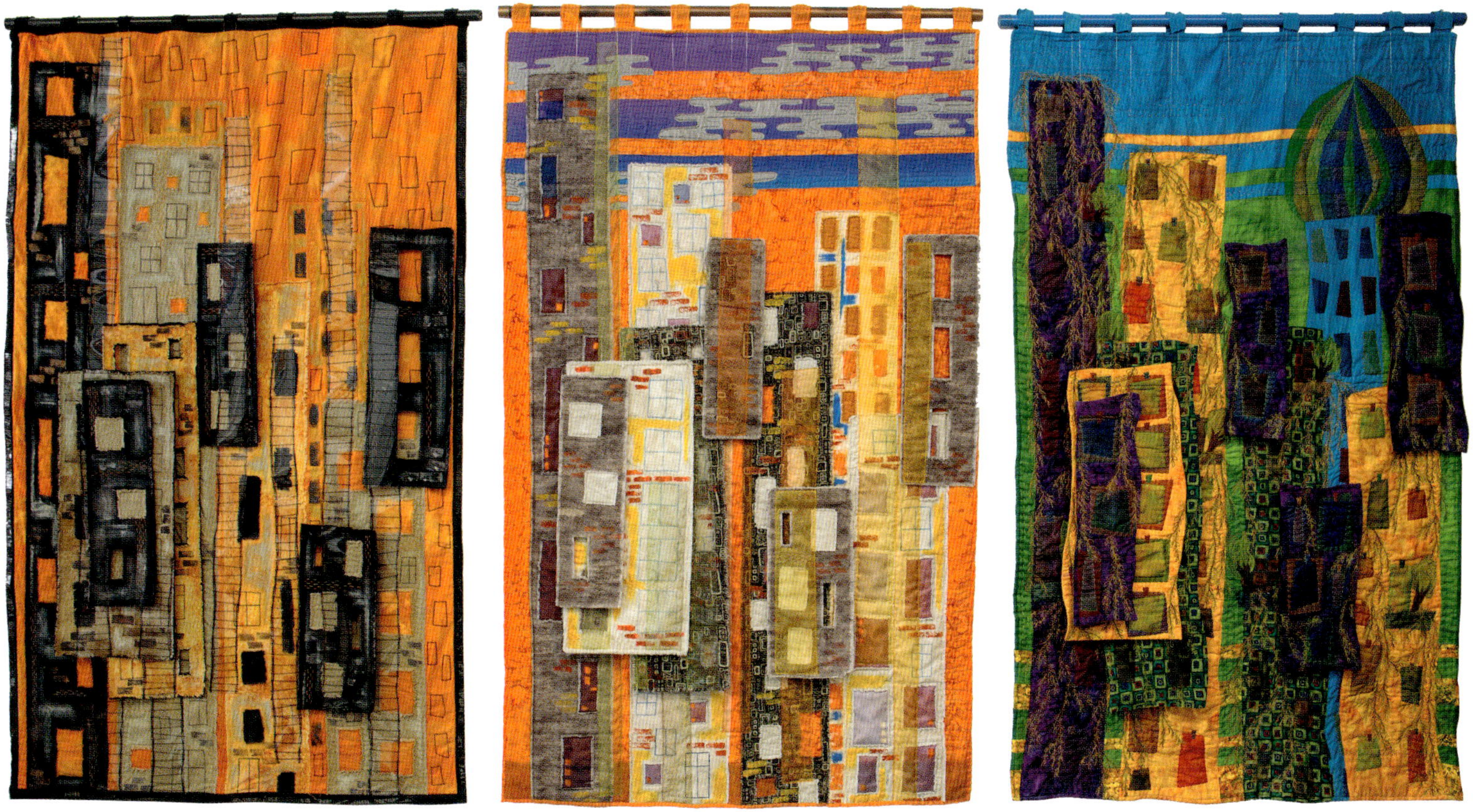

The City: Past—Present—Future. Hand dyed and commercial quilting cottons, acrylic paint, and polyester sheers. 60" × 108" × 2". 2008-2014.

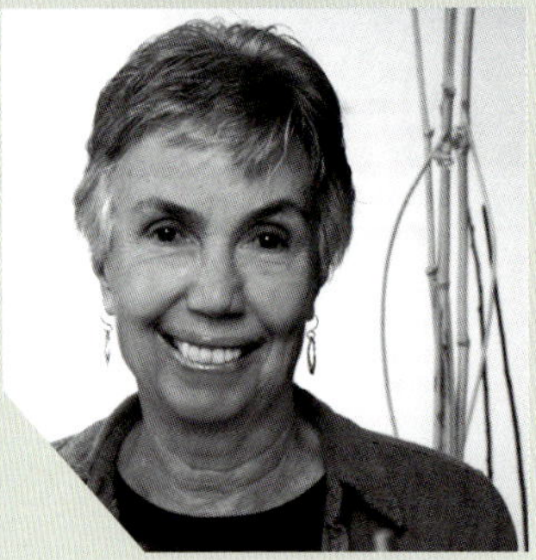

I have been an artist all my life. I began as a painter, responding directly to my physical environment, seeking to express the colors and patterns that I observed in nature. From painting on canvas, I found my way to papermaking in the late 1970s. As a medium, paper pulp offers endless opportunities for innovation in technique as well as the certainty of being surprised by the unexpected.

The summer of 1985 was a watershed year for me. I had the good fortune to spend a month at the Djerassi Resident Artists Program in Woodside, California, where I was able to further explore the potential of this medium to the point where my materials and methods as well as my vision changed.

Change continues as I embark on new paths. The current work I am doing with paper, fibers, and steel is a reflection of where I live, looking out our tall windows onto extraordinary scenes of contrast in the natural world. My work reflects my sense of continuity and transition in the flow of creative life.

Susan Hersey

Petaluma, California

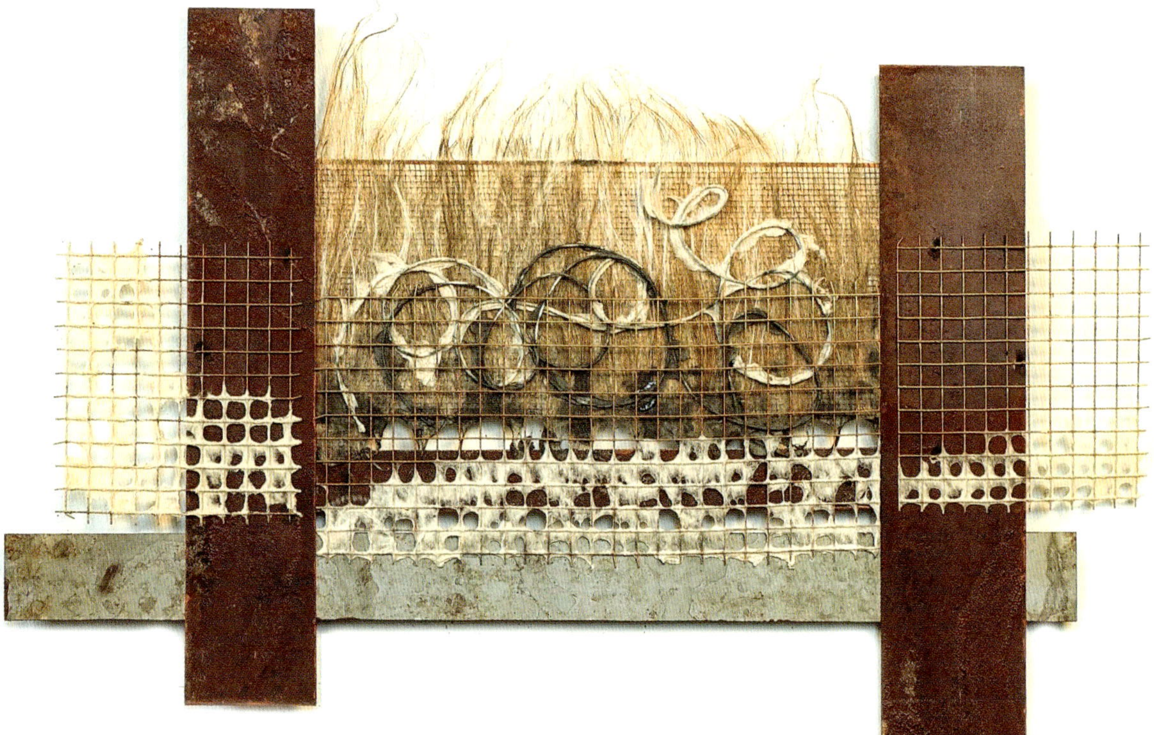

Fences III. Rusted steel, hardware cloth, electric wire, flax fibers, and paper pulp. 15" × 26". 2015.

All images courtesy of Robert H. Hersey.

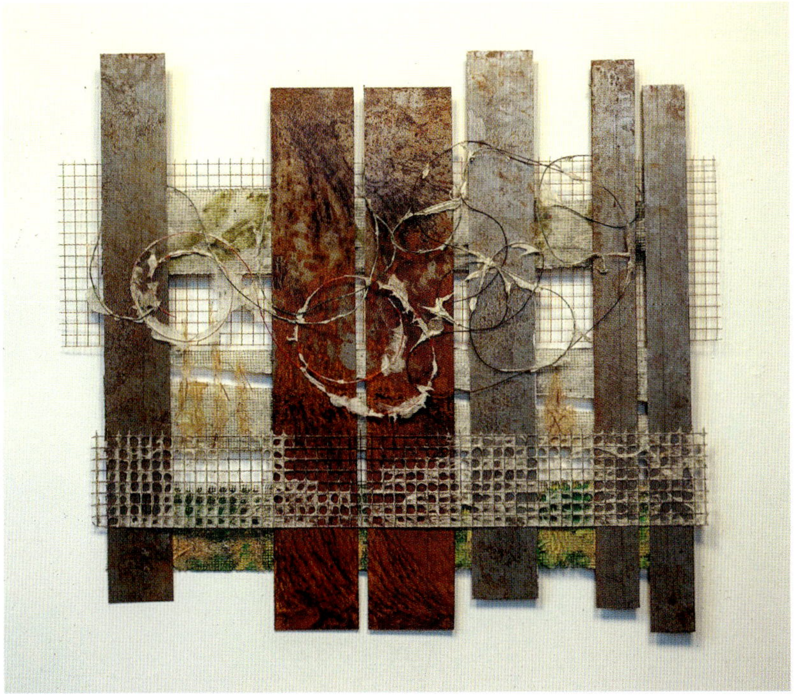

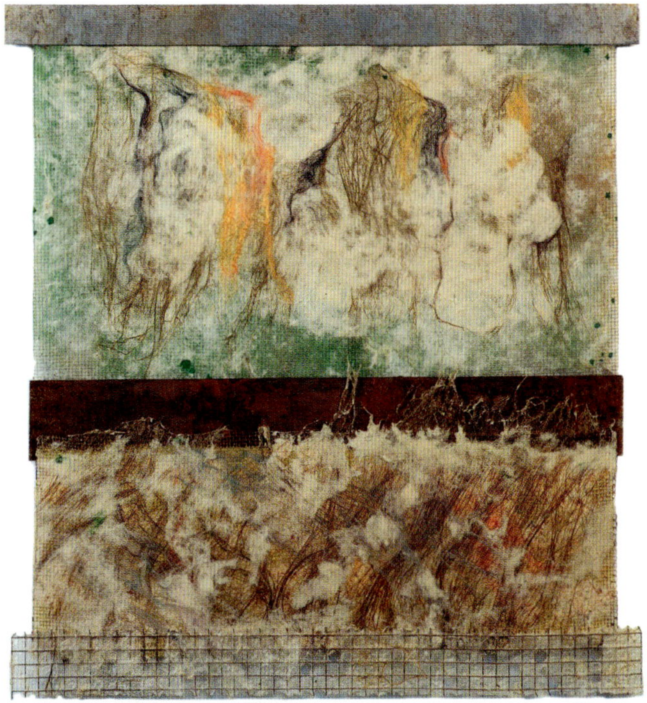

▲ *Fences I.* Rusted steel strips, hardware cloth, electric wire, and paper pulp. 26" × 30". 2014.

➚ *Contrasts I.* Steel bars, hardware cloth, silk and flax fibers, and paper pulp. 25" × 24". 2015.

➘ *Forest Series II.* Bronze screen, paper pulp, silk fibers, copper bars, and acrylic. 31" × 24". 2008.

➤ *Forest Series VII.* Bronze screen, paper pulp, silk fibers, copper bars, and acrylic. 48" × 36". 2010.

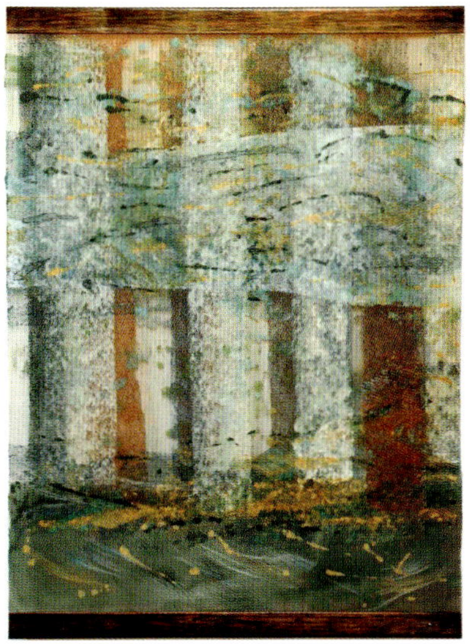

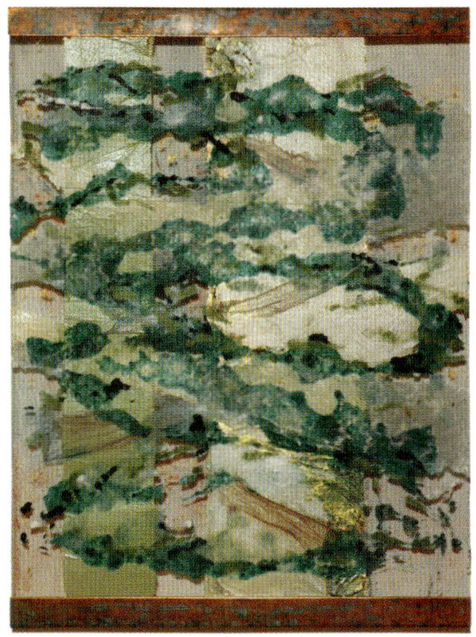

Courtesy of Frank Vitale.

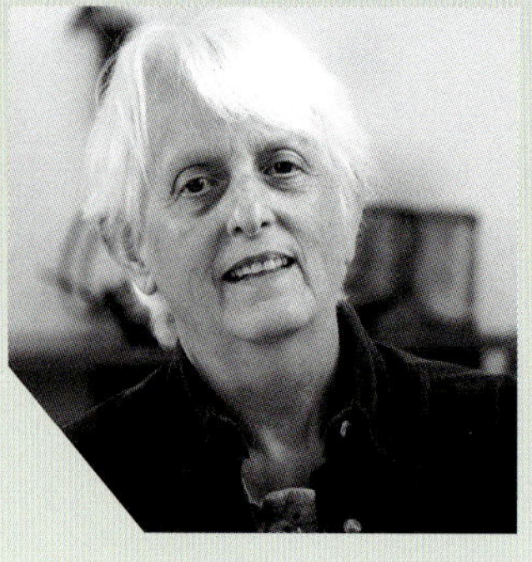

Pat Hickman

Haverstraw, New York

When I first came upon a gut parka made by native people in Alaska, I saw how an inner membrane could be used as an outer, protective skin. I began my exploration with a similar inner animal membrane that became my signature material.

I find recurring themes: the passage of time; the inevitability of change; cycles and seasons; memory and loss; aging and mortality. I bring to these themes elements and images of the natural world of which I am a tiny part.

I make use of river teeth, so named by sailors who found them in water and imagined they came from some unknown creature. Rather, they are the last piece of the tree to decay. Combining them with hog casing, I make visual metaphors, continuing my obsession with impermanence. Tooth and skin, object and shadow: my hands take these ordinary but mostly unseen materials and make something visible and new.

My commission, *Nets of Makali'i—Nets of the Pleiades*, stands as monumental entrance gates for the Maui Arts and Cultural Center.

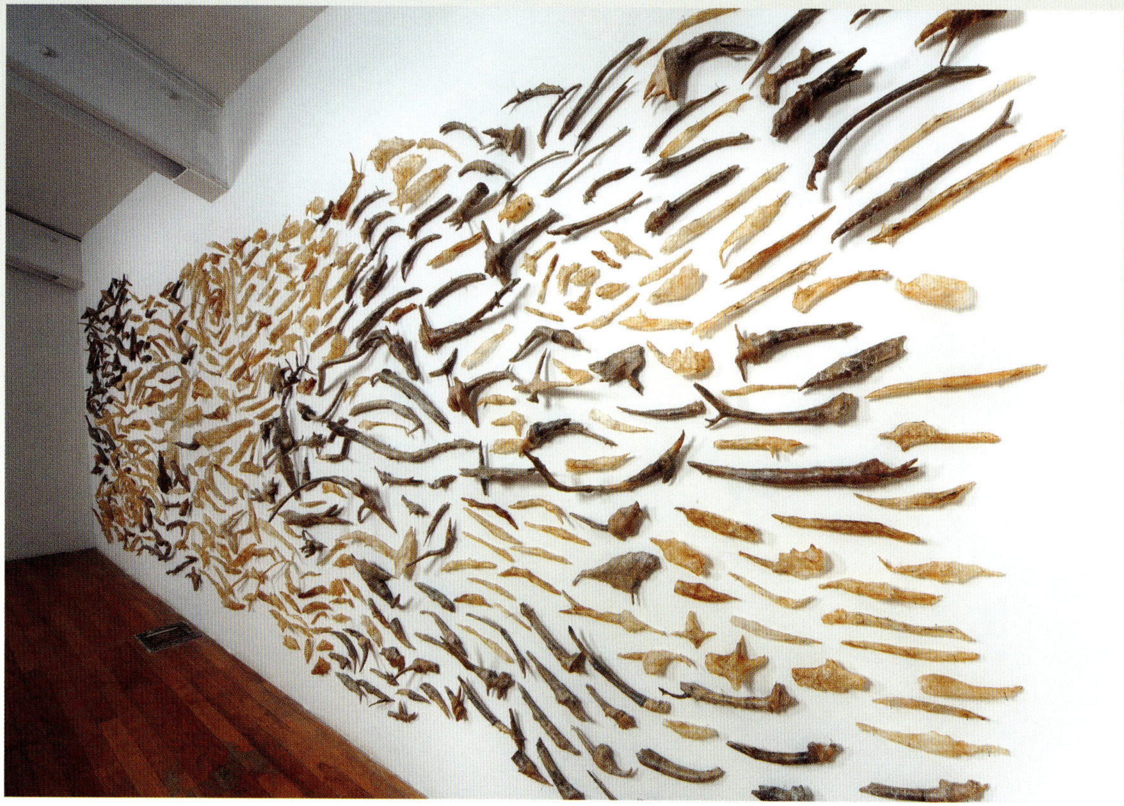

River That Flows Both Ways. River teeth (wood), animal membrane, and insect mounting pins. 72" × 228" × 6". 2015.

All art images courtesy of George Potanovic, Jr.

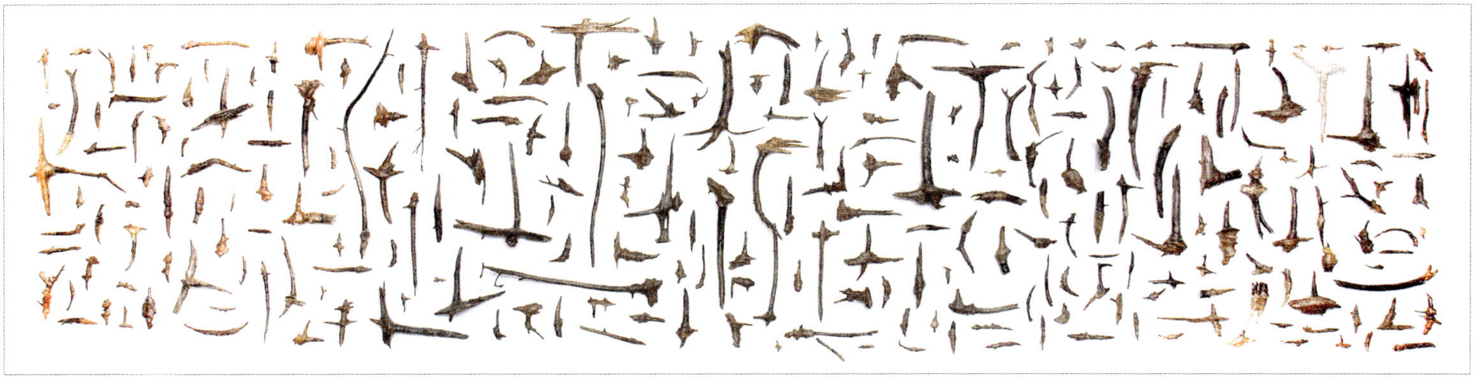

▲ *River Teeth.* River teeth (wood), animal membrane, and insect mounting pins. 48" × 7". 2011.

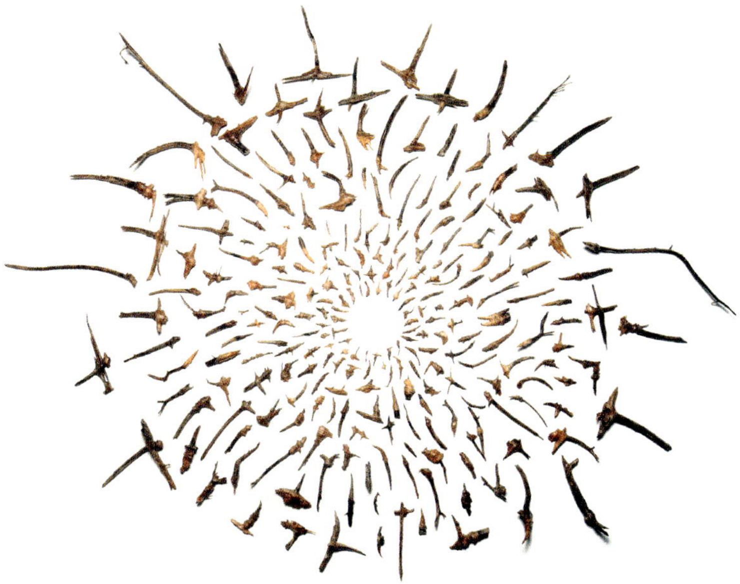

▲ *And in the Whirling.* River teeth (wood), animal membrane, and insect mounting pins. 128" diameter. 2011.

➤ *Count.* Animal membrane and rusty nails. Dimensions variable. 2011.

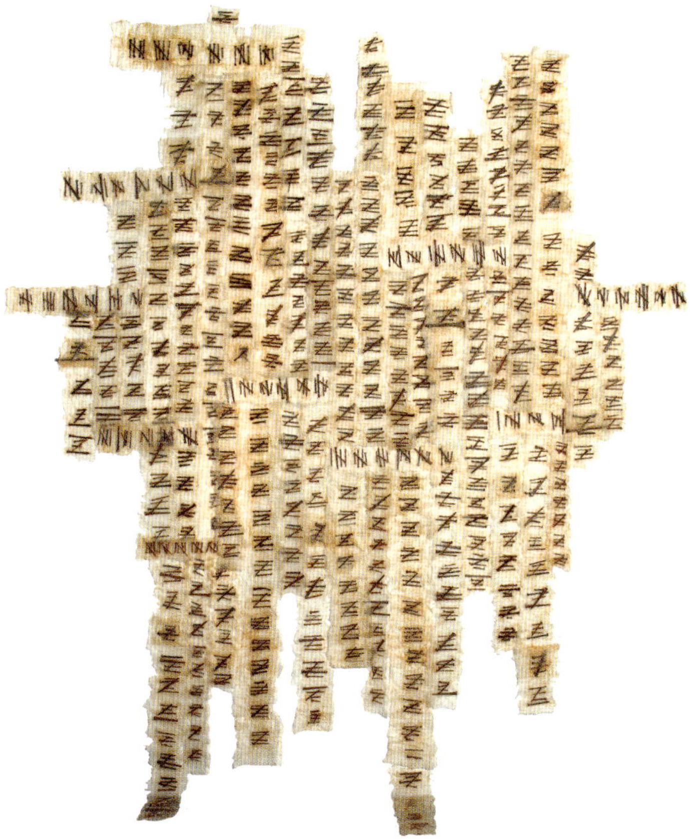

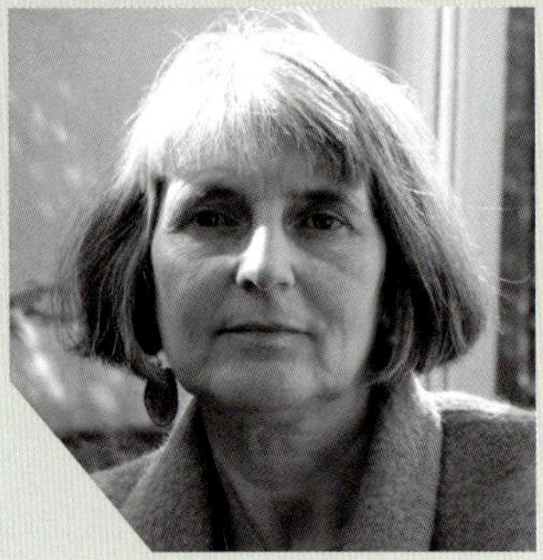

Cas Holmes

Maidstone, Kent, England

I work between the disciplines of painting, drawing, and textiles. Salvaged materials are torn, cut, and re-assembled to create mixed media pieces which draw their inspiration from hidden or overlooked observations of daily life. My work processes are reflected in my publications, the most recent being *Stitch Stories*.

I make reference to the views from our windows: field edges, roadsides, and the places where our gardens meet the greater landscape. This relationship between urban and nature has been informed by stories of my Romany grandmother, by old and forgotten textiles, and by the natural cycle of growth, decay, and renewal. Working with stitch sketching, I seek to capture a moment before it is gone.

I produce award-winning artworks for public and private spaces and am represented in major collections, including Arts Council England, Embroiderers' Guild UK, and the Museum of Art and Design, New York. Working on collaborations with galleries and the community is an important part of my practice, and I was recently commissioned to create a piece entitled *Gardens and War* in collaboration with the Garden Museum, London.

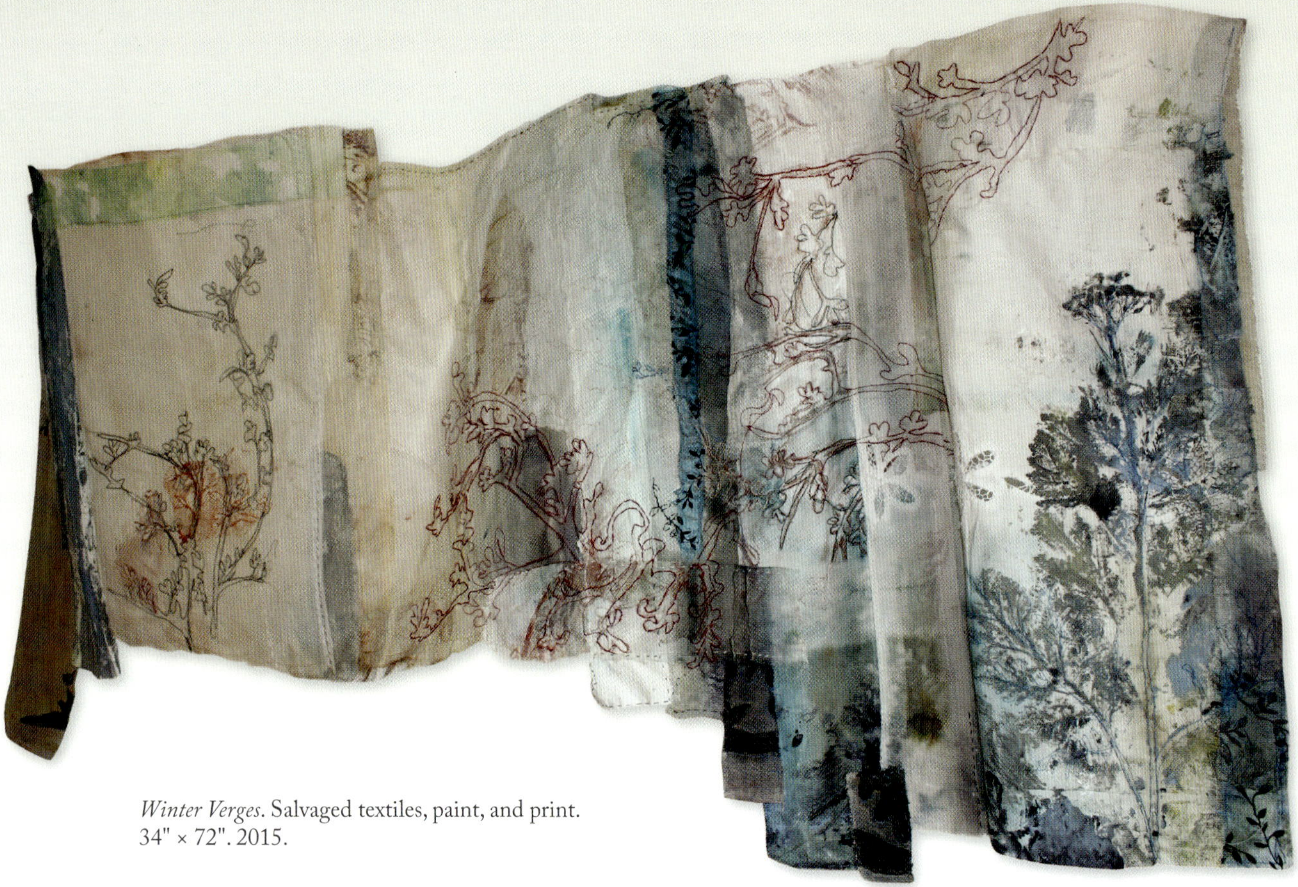

Winter Verges. Salvaged textiles, paint, and print. 34" × 72". 2015.

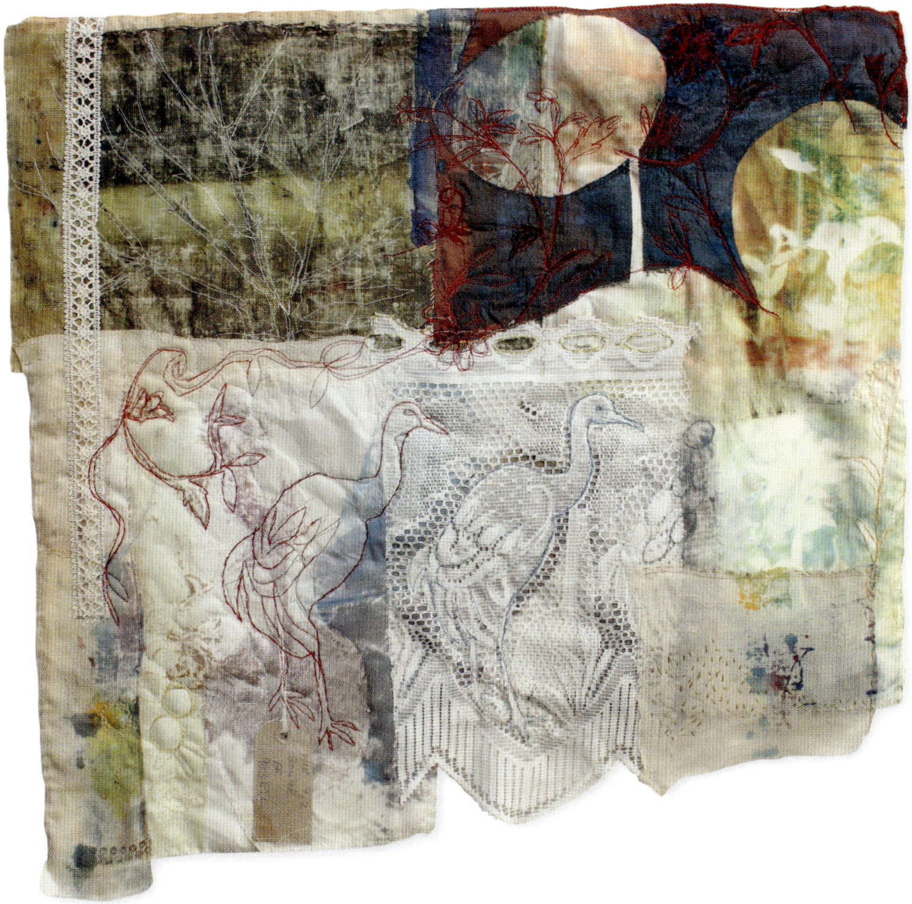

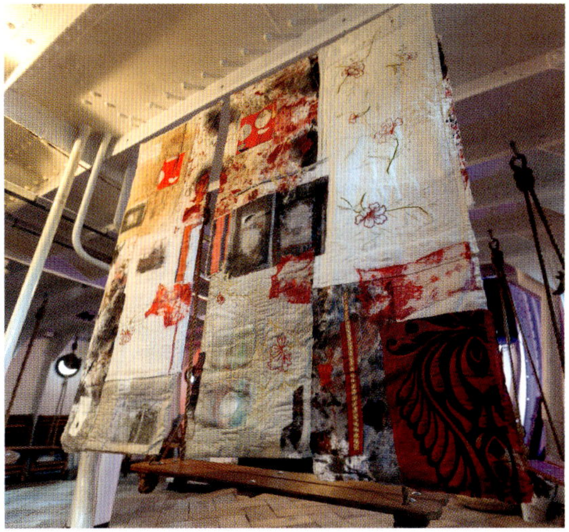

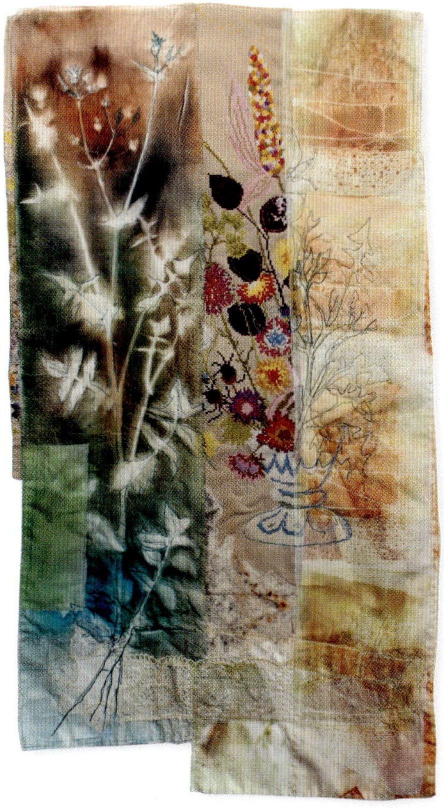

▲ *40 Yards, Cranes*. Salvaged textiles, paint, and print. 25" × 35". 2015.

◄ *LV21*. Salvaged textiles, paint, and print. 55" × 70". 2013. Courtesy Gary Weston.

► *Common Place, Marsh Sowthistle*. Salvaged textiles, paint, and print. 56" × 32". 2015.

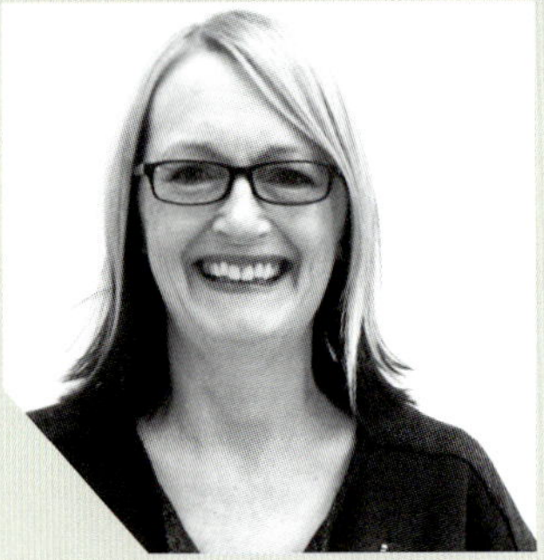

Sue Hotchkis

Vale, Guernsey

I am an artist with a passion for texture, surface, and space. I construct abstract forms in fragments, highlighting the beauty found in the inherent processes of aging and decay. The core theme of my work is texture and surface, strongly influenced by the Japanese aesthetic of wabi-sabi. I therefore seek out imperfection in the insignificant and the overlooked. Using a camera to freeze a moment in time, I record marks and surfaces that are in the process of breaking down, ephemeral, in a state of flux. Working intuitively with print and stitch, I exaggerate marks, textures, and colors to highlight the detail and complexity within the images.

The work evolves organically, built up with layers into three-dimensional abstract forms that hover between object and image to create a unique visual and tactile landscape of form and texture.

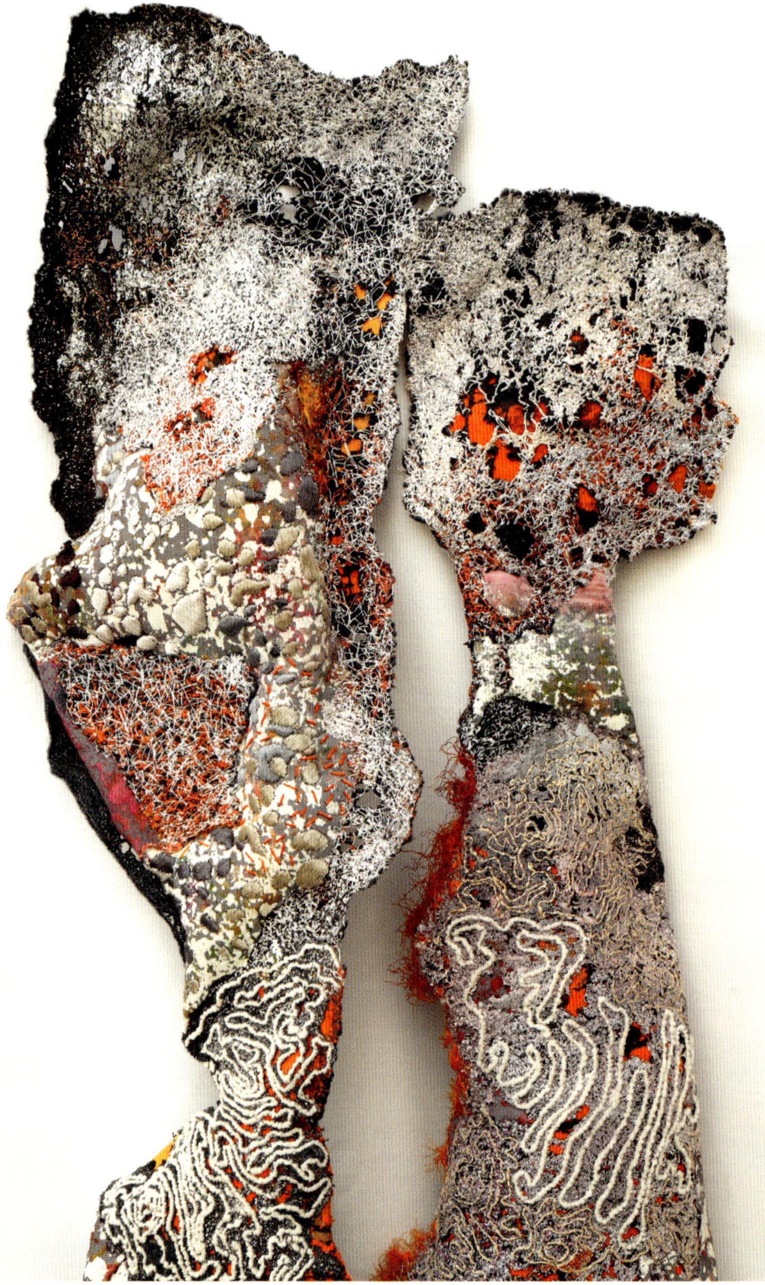

Embrace (detail). Felt, cotton, polyester wadding, and machine threads. 64" × 20" × 4". 2015.

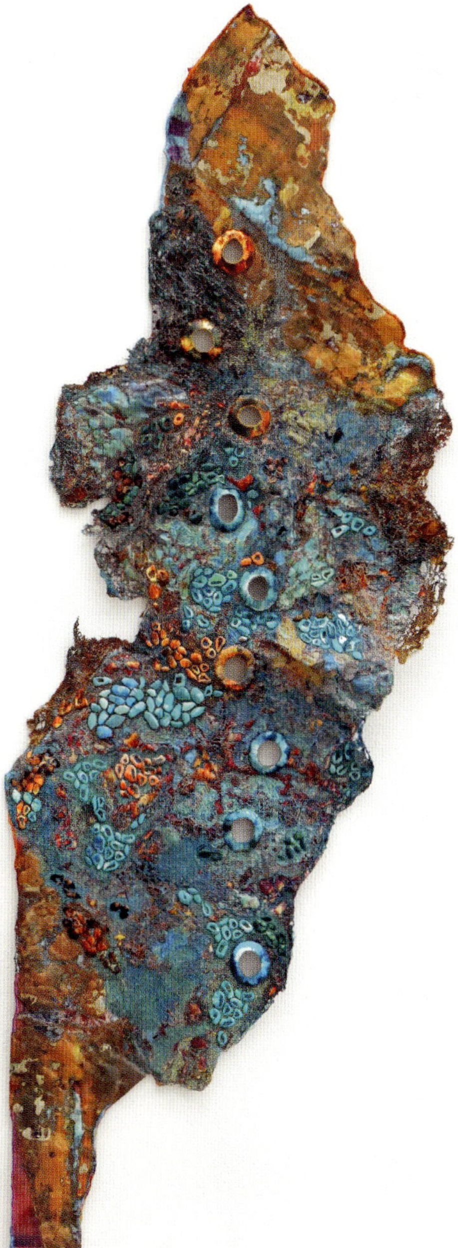

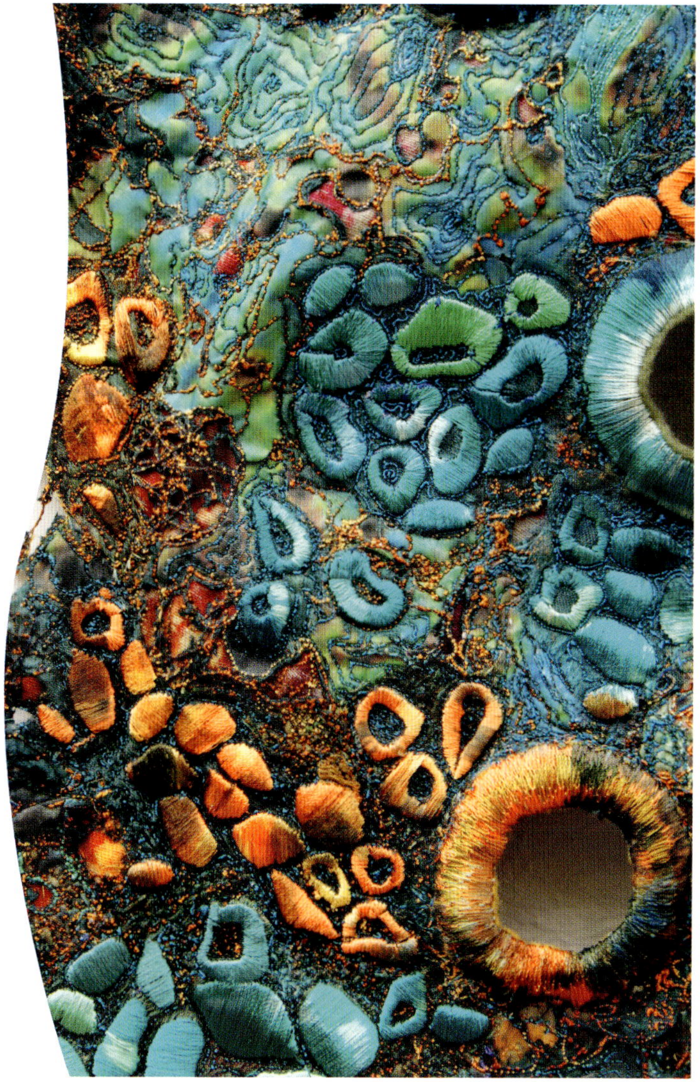

Verdigris. Voile, paper, cotton fabric, and threads.
57" × 19". 2014. | Detail

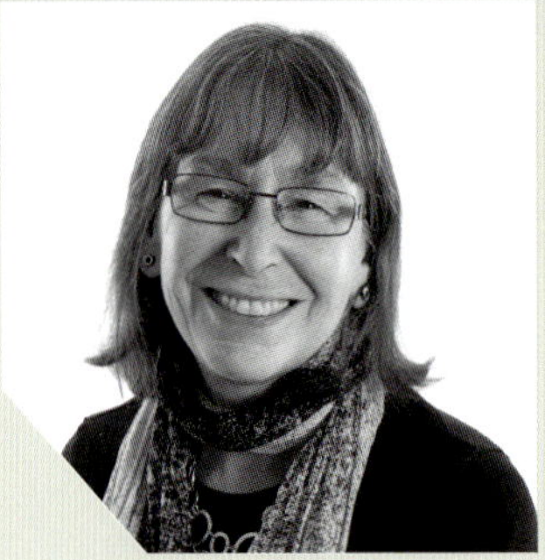

Courtesy of www.pauladayphotography.co.uk.

Sara Impey

Colchester, Essex, England

I am a British fiber artist from a farming family, and I live in a small town about seventy miles northeast of London. With a background in both journalism and quilt-making, it is perhaps not surprising that I was attracted to the idea of exploring the expressive potential of the stitched word. I like to experiment with the visual, textural, and structural properties of fabric and thread and play with language, often commenting on social or personal issues, sometimes with a dash of humor. The lettering is stitched using free-machine embroidery, and I write my own material.

My work has been exhibited nationally and internationally and is in several public and private collections. I belong to the European exhibiting group Quilt Art and the British groups Anglia Textile Works and Blackwater Polytechnic. I am an honorary member of the Quilters' Guild in Britain. I lecture and write on contemporary quilt-making, and in 2013 published *Text in Textile Art.*

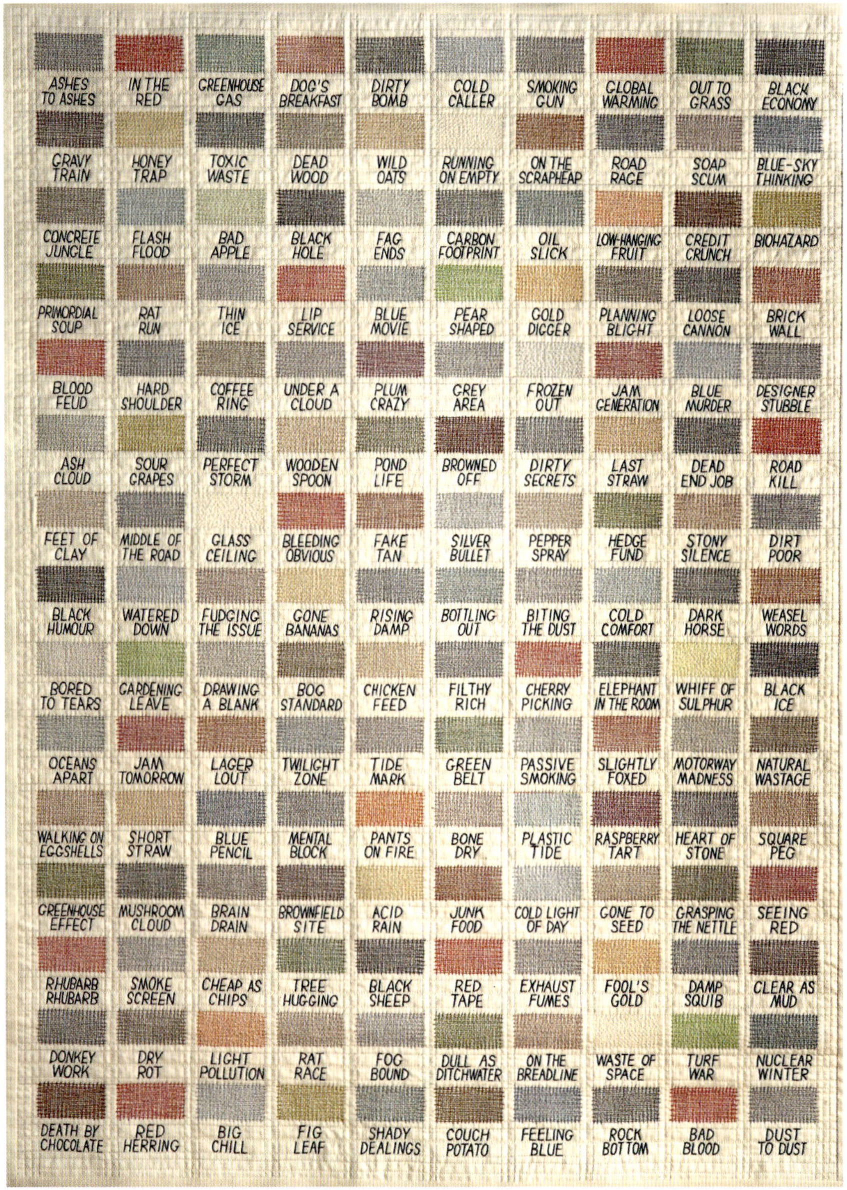

Spoiled for Choice. Cotton and wholecloth quilt. 43" × 32". 2012.

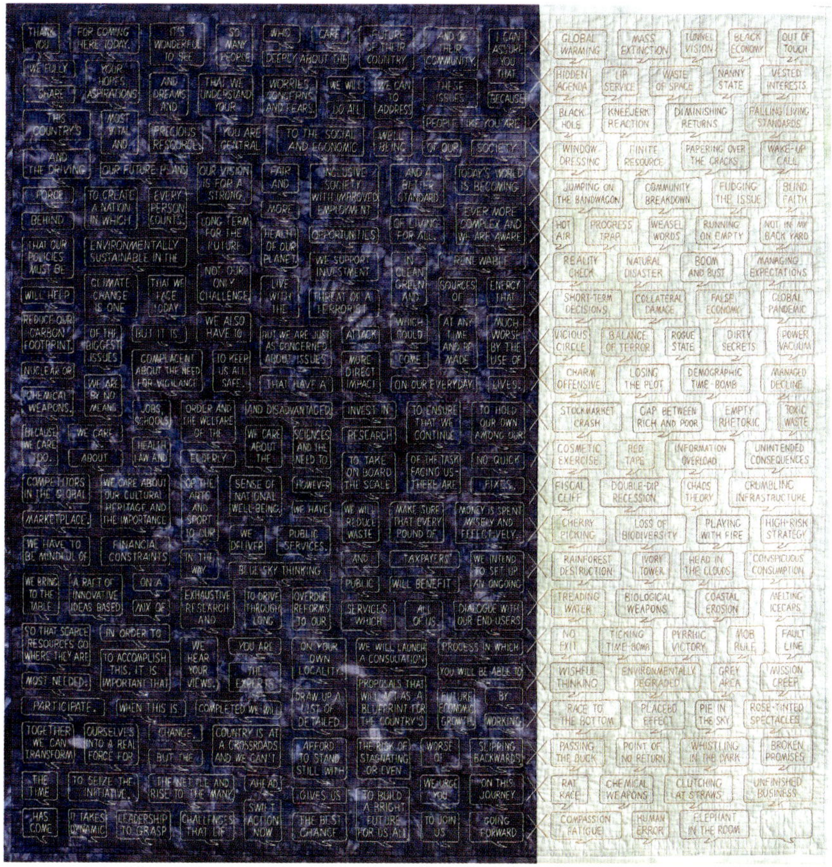

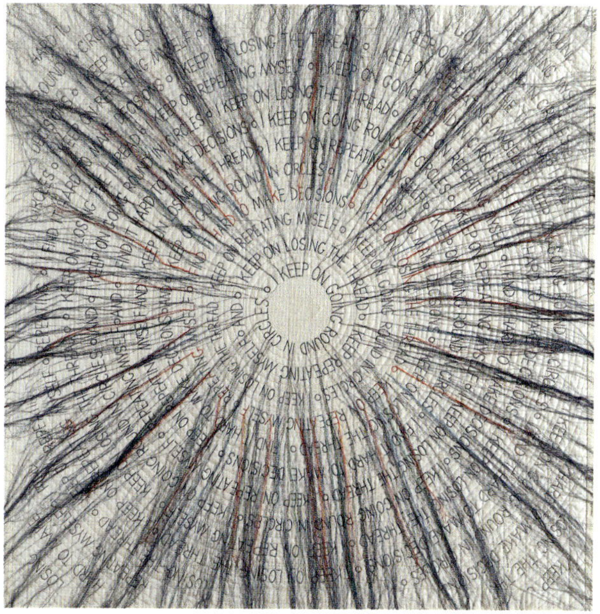

▲ *Hustings*. Cottons. 51" × 51". 2013

◄ *Losing the Plot.* Cotton and wholecloth quilt. 34" × 34". 2013.

► *Meeting Point.* Silk and wholecloth quilt. 35" × 35". 2007.

All art images courtesy of Art Van Go.

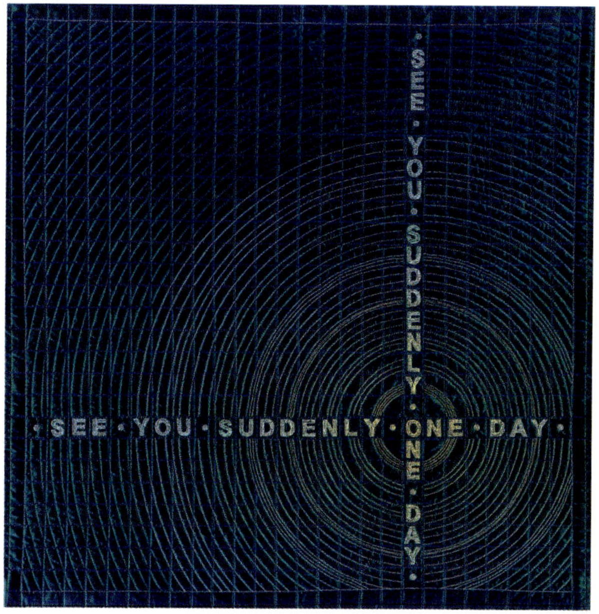

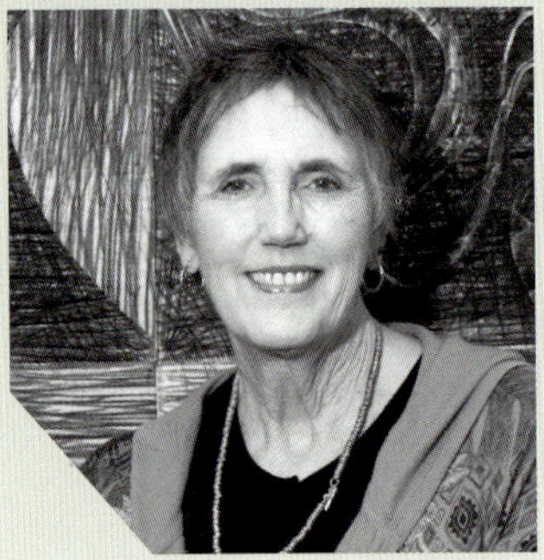

Terry Jarrard-Dimond

Seneca, South Carolina

For many years, my work has been focused on recording my experiences in the studio. Most often my art develops through the act of "working," or allowing the subject to emerge through process and having a dialogue with my materials. I sort. I pin things up. I doodle. I sit and look at things I've done previously. I think about how to start, then when the time is right, I begin. I want viewers to connect with my work emotionally and intellectually and have their own unique experiences.

My current work is about the evidence we leave behind every day and every moment as we live our lives. All elements of the natural world leave evidence of being or having been on this earth. Think of your day and the trail you leave behind. This evidence can be in the form of scratches, stains, smudges, notes, and scraps of this or that. I could make a very long list. These items, markings, or objects can be discovered, interpreted, saved, loved, valued, or tossed. If we are lucky, someone will value something we leave behind. This evidence creates a pathway for connection, knowledge, understanding, and memory.

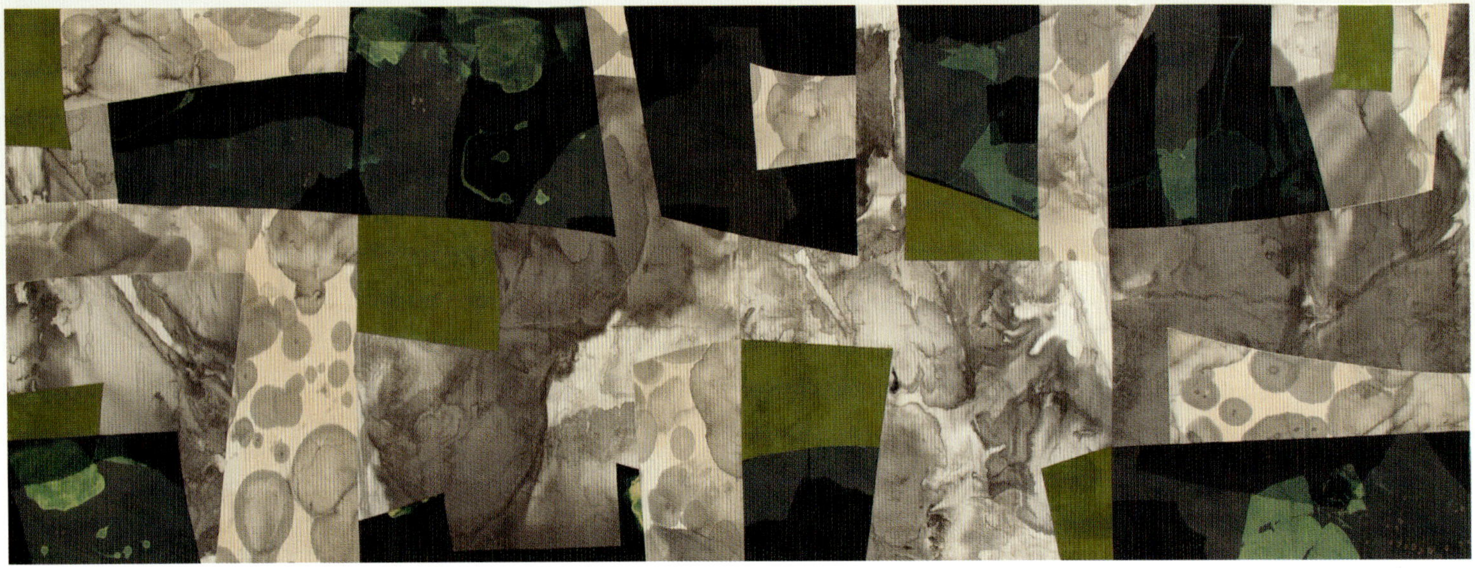

Aurora. Cotton muslin, walnut ink, India ink, dye, and color remover. 31" × 84.5". 2012.

All photographs courtesy of Tom Dimond.

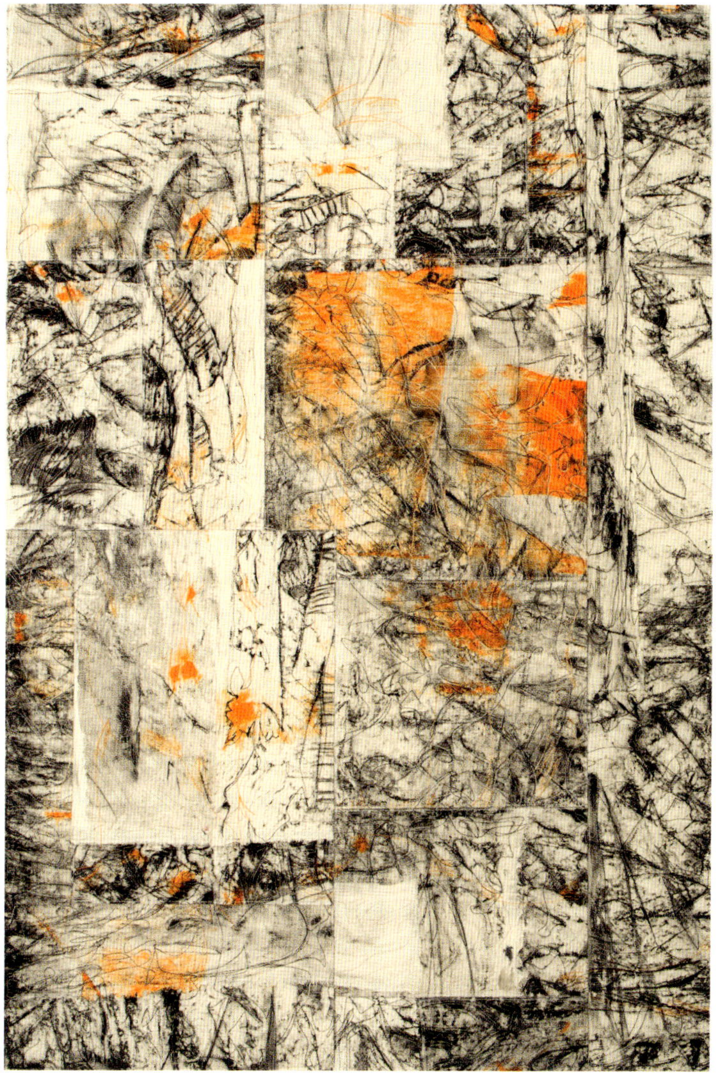

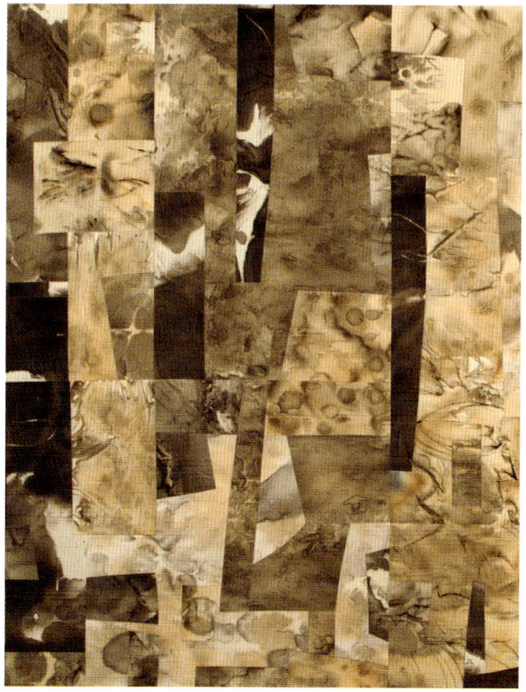

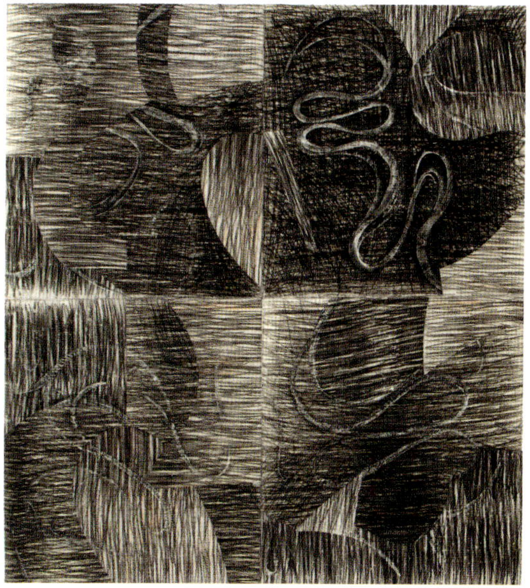

▲ *Windfall*. Charcoal, textile ink, and textile medium. 50.25" × 34". 2015.

◀ *Selena.* Cotton muslin, walnut ink, India ink, colored ink, and tea. 78" × 61". 2012.

➤ *See and Hide.* Cotton muslin, charcoal, graphite, and textile medium. 45.25" × 41.5". 2015.

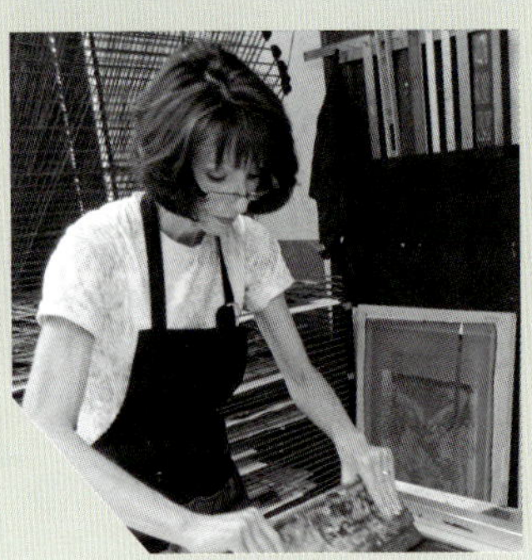

Patricia Kennedy-Zafred

Murrysville, Pennsylvania

As a storyteller, my goal is to create thought-provoking narratives using fabric, dyes, silkscreens, and ink to develop a visual dialogue with the viewer. I conceive the interpretation of each piece through the lens of individual experiences, memories, or perspectives. My quilts marry a lifelong fascination with photography, history, and stitch, often reflecting faces of pride and dignity, sometimes captured under challenging circumstances. My intent is that the technical and physical demand creating them is lost on audiences, as they focus entirely on the nuance or intrigue of the story, transported to another time or place.

The stories expressed in my work are an essential part of our diverse American fabric, which I hope will touch viewers, remind them of someone or something they may have forgotten, or compel them to linger just a moment longer.

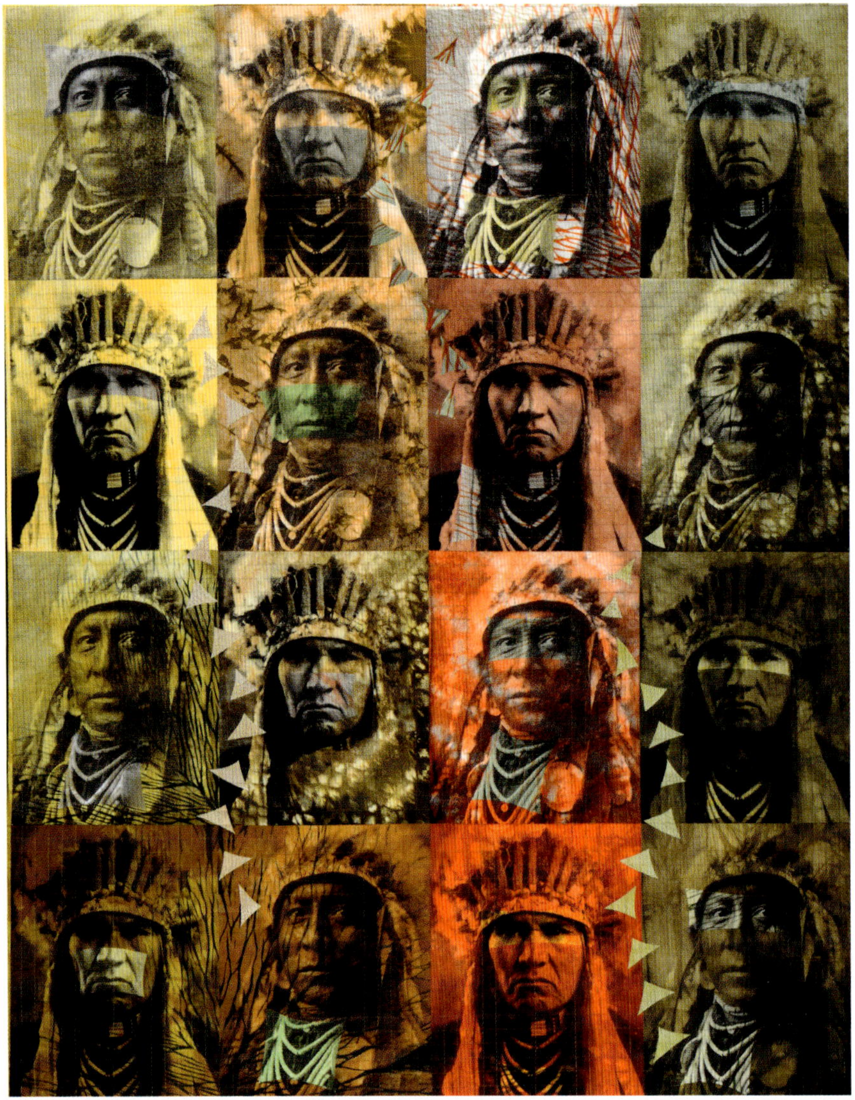

Shared Destiny. Cotton fabric, Procion® dyes, textile inks, fusible web, cotton batting, cotton and rayon threads. Original images courtesy Library of Congress. 80" × 64". 2013. Courtesy of Larry Berman.

➤ *Street Hustle: The Newsies.* Cotton fabric, Procion® dyes, textile inks, image transfer materials, discharge paste, fusible web, cotton batting, cotton and rayon threads. 42" × 60". 2014. Original images courtesy Library of Congress. Courtesy of Larry Berman.

▼ *Tagged.* Cotton fabric, Procion® dyes, textile inks, image transfer materials, fusible web, cotton batting, cotton and rayon threads. 45" × 84". 2015. Original images courtesy Library of Congress and Bancroft Collection, University of California, Berkeley, with permission.
Courtesy of Larry Berman.

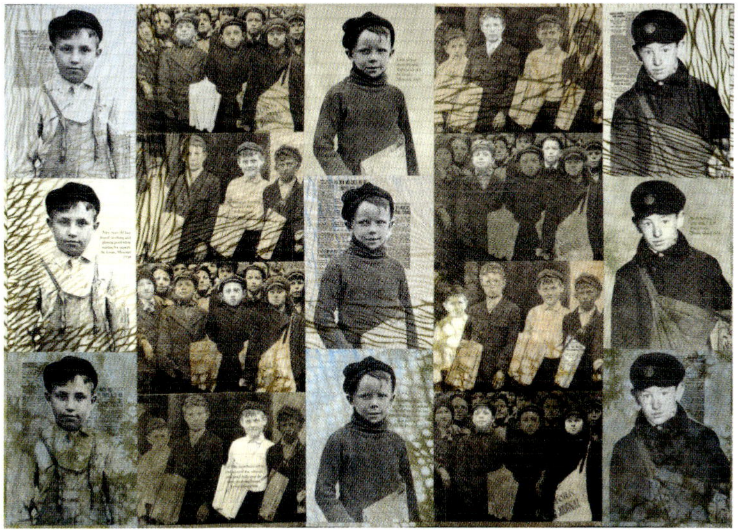

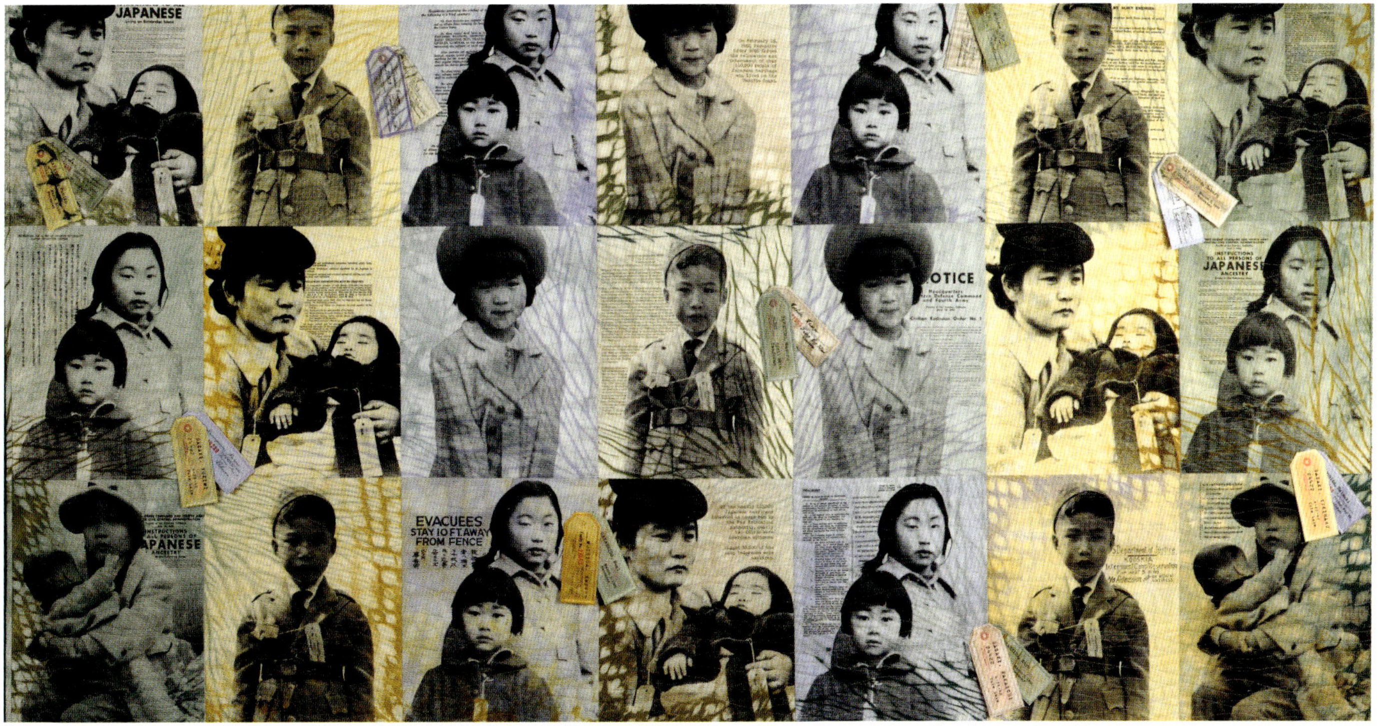

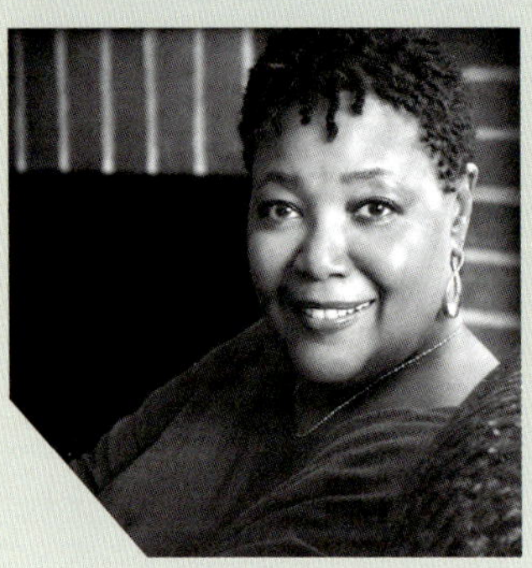

Toni Kersey

Springfield, Pennsylvania

I am fascinated by color, pattern, shape, and visual rhythm. I am drawn to the juxtaposing and mixing of materials. Works by diverse artists such as Romare Bearden, Sam Maitin, Betye Saar, and Mickalene Thomas inspire and inform my work. As a child I began to sew under the tutelage of my mother, and by working with fiber, I pay homage to and maintain a deep connection to her.

My work is noted for its use of color, shape, and texture. I was always attracted to pattern and how mixing unrelated patterns and textures created an interesting visual story. My work, for which I have won awards and grants, represents a conduit through which I channel my experience as a member of the African Diaspora and as a woman in the world.

Improvisation guides my inspiration through mixed media on textiles. I meld hand-painted and commercial fabrics with buttons, beads, and sometimes text to create abstract art that explores color, shape relationships, pattern, and rhythm, while also expressing a sense of community.

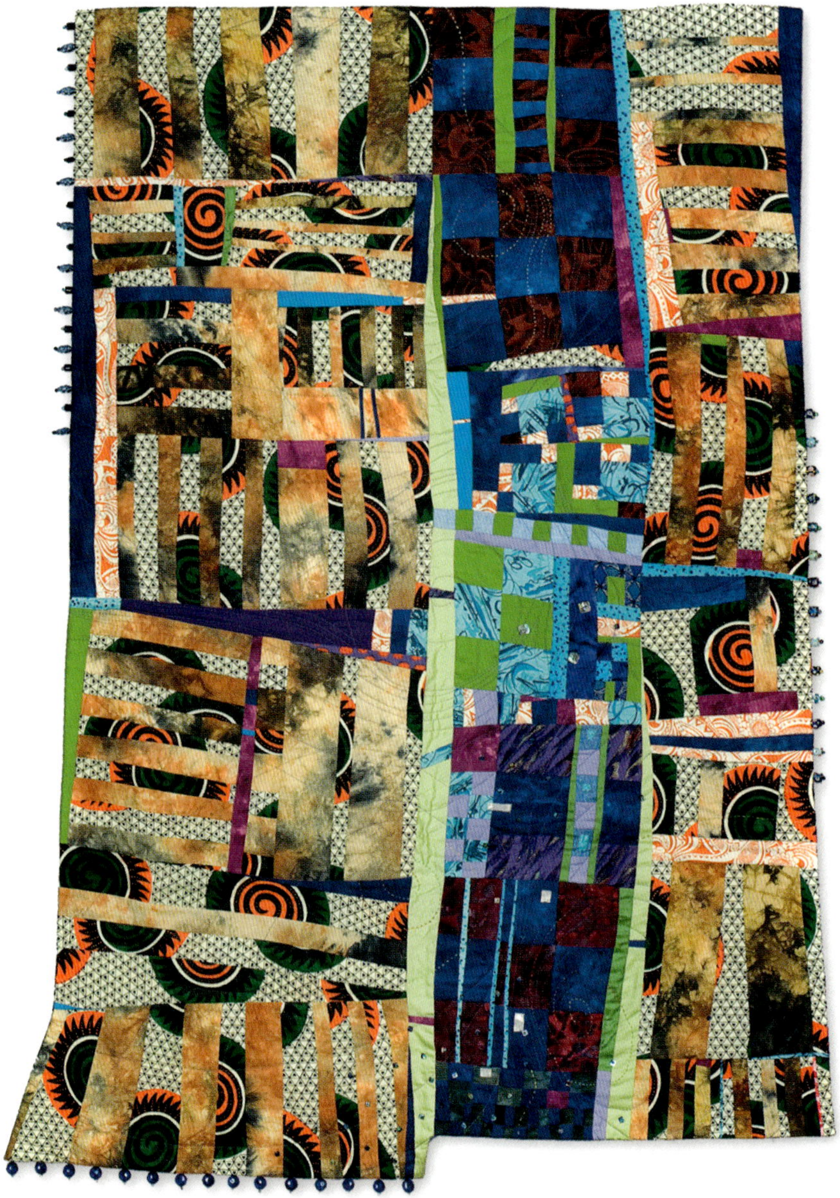

Dancing in the River of Yemenya. Commercial and hand dyed fabrics, embroidery, buttons, beads, and raw-edged and reverse appliqué. 53" × 38". 2010.

All art images courtesy of Moskow Photography.

➤ *Urban VooDoo 2*. Commercial fabrics, text, buttons, and raw-edged appliqué. 43" × 42". 2008.

➤ *Untitled.* Embroidery, raw edged appliqué, lace, and buttons. 45" × 41". 2015.

➤ *Heatwave #5*. Beads, embroidery, reverse and raw-edged appliqué, batik, hand dyed, commercial, and silk-screened fabric (Gilbraith & Paul). 35" × 38". 2014.

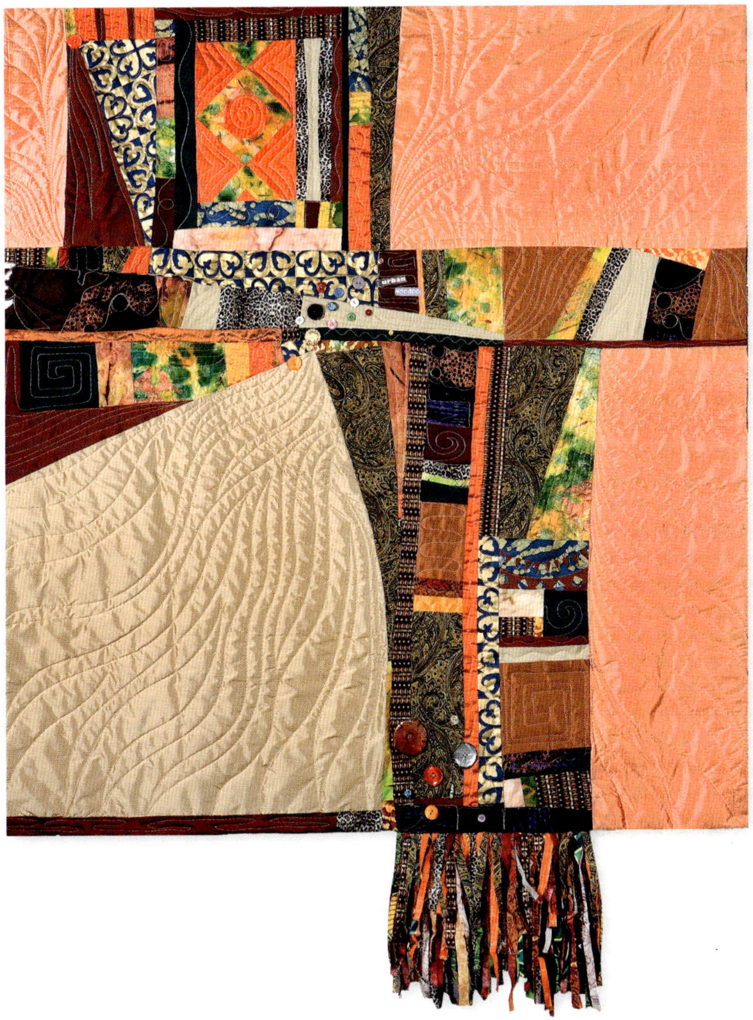

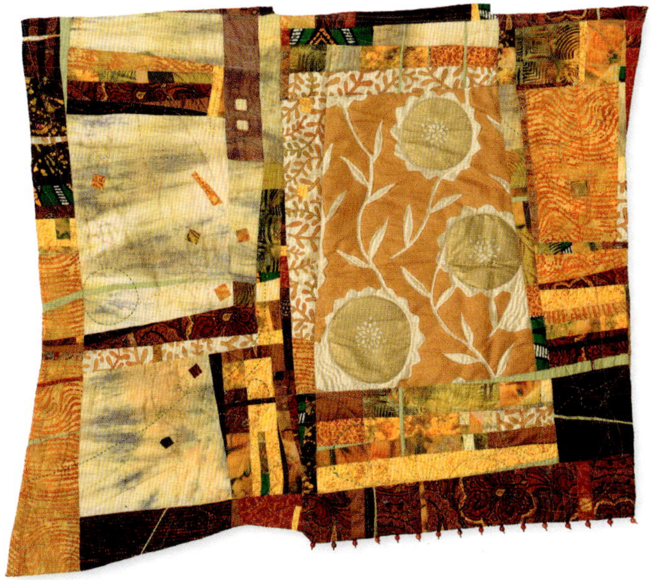

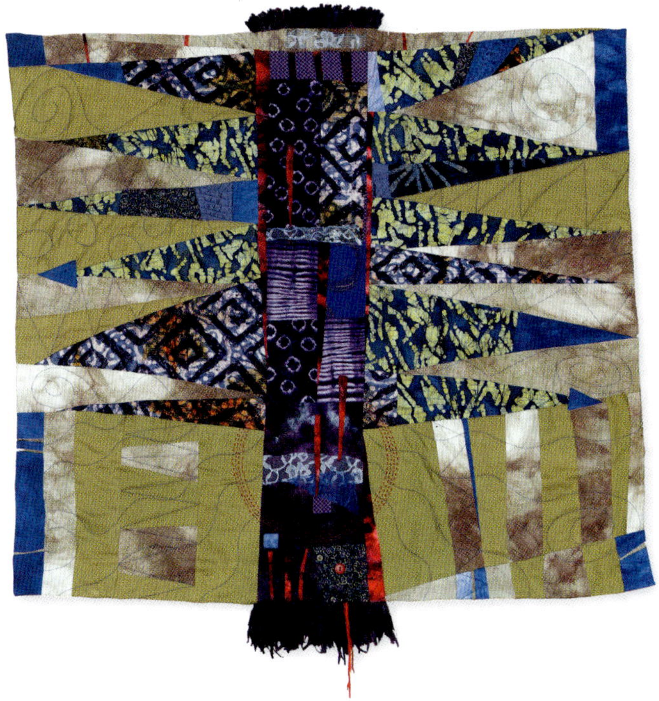

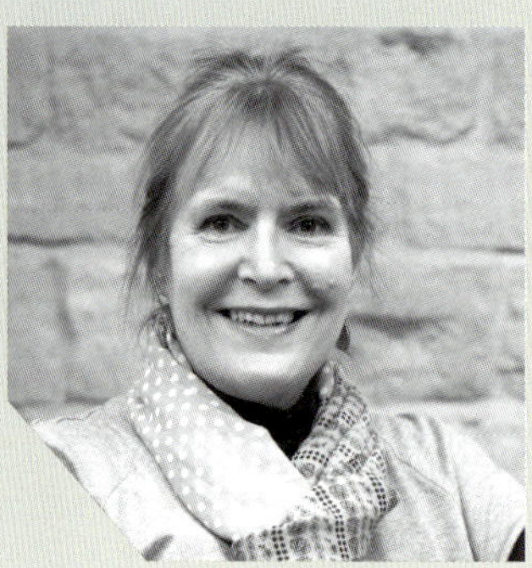

Alison King
Edinburgh, Scotland

When I moved to Scotland from London, it was a life-changing experience. Suddenly, all this beautiful, atmospheric landscape of mountains, moors, and rivers surrounded me. Most of my work has been in response to this. I was trained as a painter at Edinburgh College of Art, but deep down I think there has always been a textile artist trying to get out! I discovered the joys of fabric and thread while teaching, and over many years I have blended embroidery with painting in my wall hangings. I use a variety of techniques in my work, including hand-made felt, paint, and machine embroidery and embellishment.

I spend much of my time in rural Aberdeenshire in an almost deserted glen amongst the heather and abandoned settlements that tell of a lost way of life. It is these wild places and the impact of man on the land that excite me. Vanishing skills, like peat cutting and heather burning, all leave their distinctive marks on the hillsides. Viewed under an ever-changing light, the patterns they make have been a constant source of inspiration. In recent work, I have included references to old maps and have experimented with hangings that, like real maps, can be folded up and stored in boxes. With passing years, my interest in my roots grows, and my latest panel is a tribute to my husband's grandfather and his role in World War I.

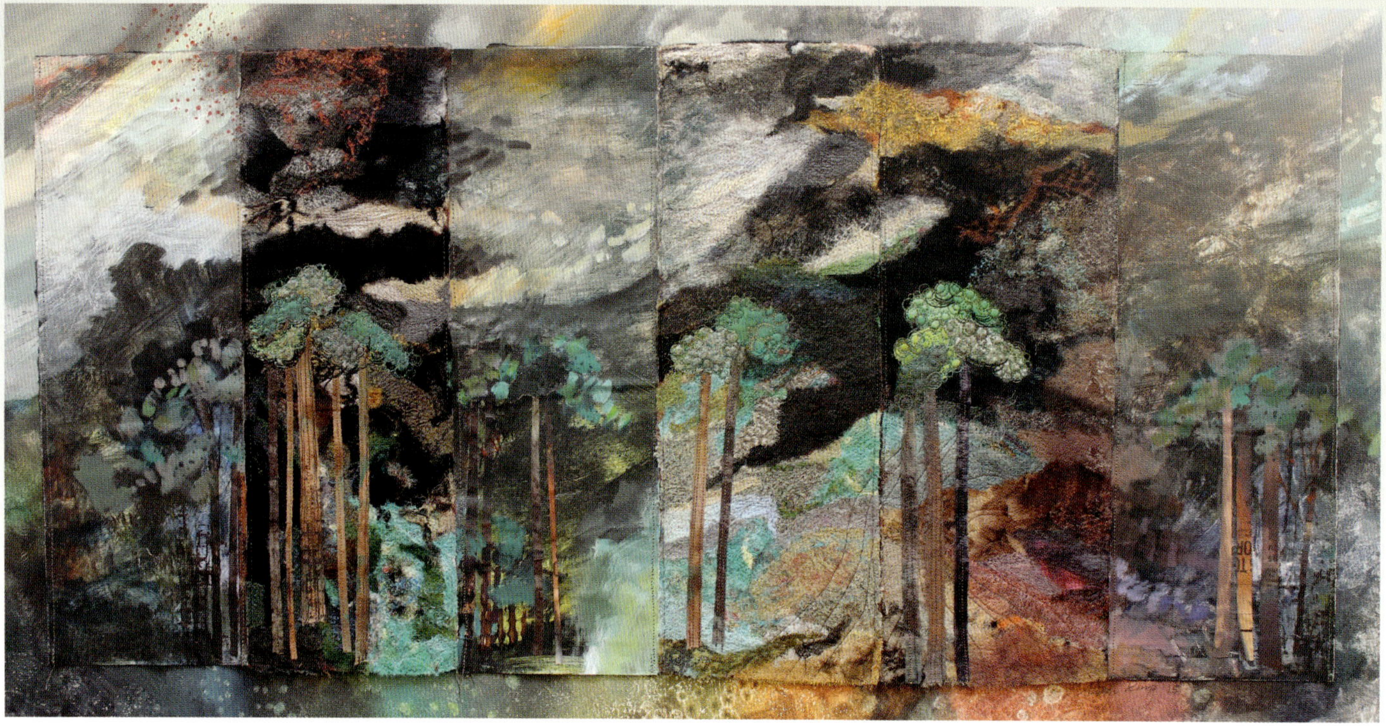

Witch Light. Paint, fabric, and paper with machine stitch and embellishment. 60" × 80.3". 2015. Courtesy of Heather Jack.

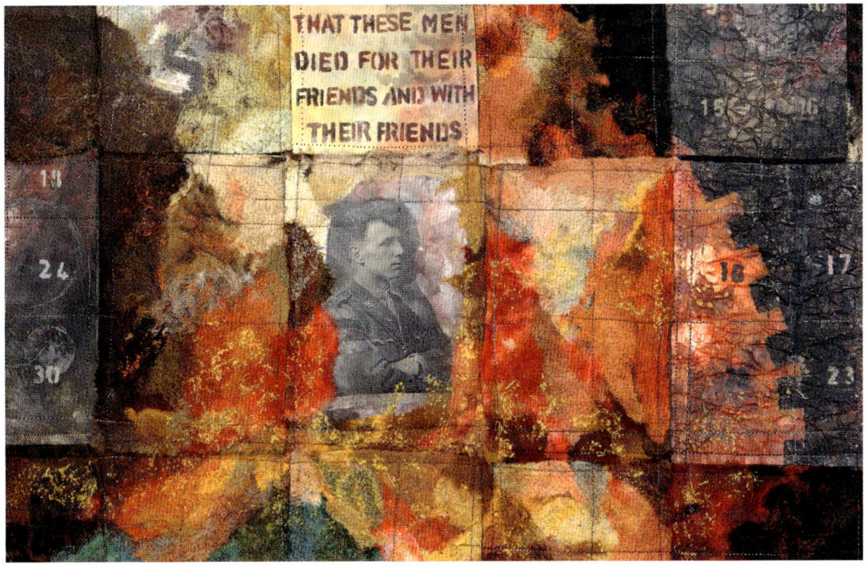

◄ *Where Is the Consolation?* (detail). Paint, fabric, and paper with machine stitch and embellishment. 19.7" × 39.4". 2015.

▼ *Beyond the River the Heather Burns.* Dyed fabrics, handmade felt, and machine embroidery. 30" × 31". 2012. | Detail Courtesy of Kevin Mead of Art Van Go.

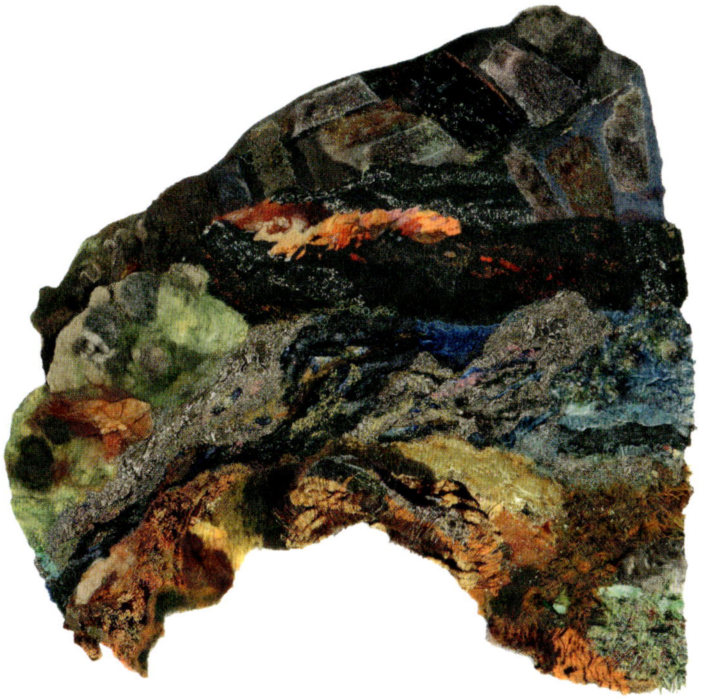

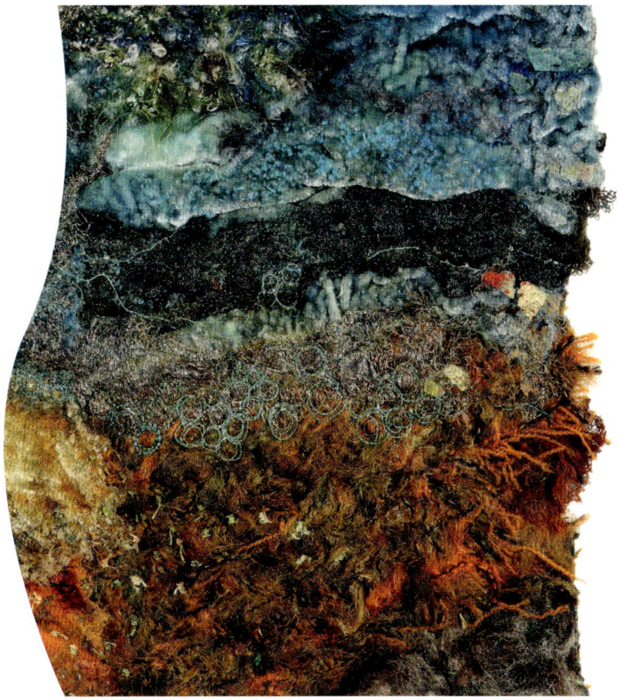

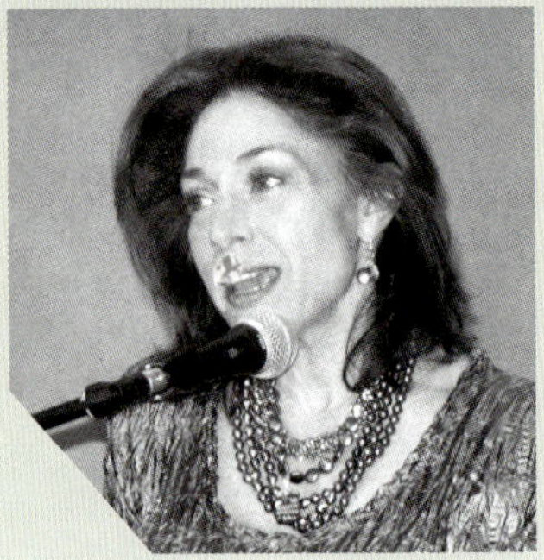

Susan Klebanoff

Albuquerque, New Mexico

Fiber is the universal language of all cultures. My works, multilayer tapestries, speak this language. They play with the viewer's perception of what is background and what is shadow. Only the human eye can detect the difference.

The loom is the predecessor to the computer and remains a relevant tool for artists today. It can be used for various expressive applications such as ones that are painterly, sculptural, conceptual, and even mathematical.

I have been blessed with a wide acceptance of my artwork, being in such notable collections as the Smithsonian Institution in Washington, DC, and the Museum of Modern Art in Nagoya, Japan. I have lectured in many countries including Japan, Thailand, Russia, Finland, and Korea. The New Mexico State Committee of the National Museum for Women in the Arts named me "Woman of the Year," and I have received numerous commission awards.

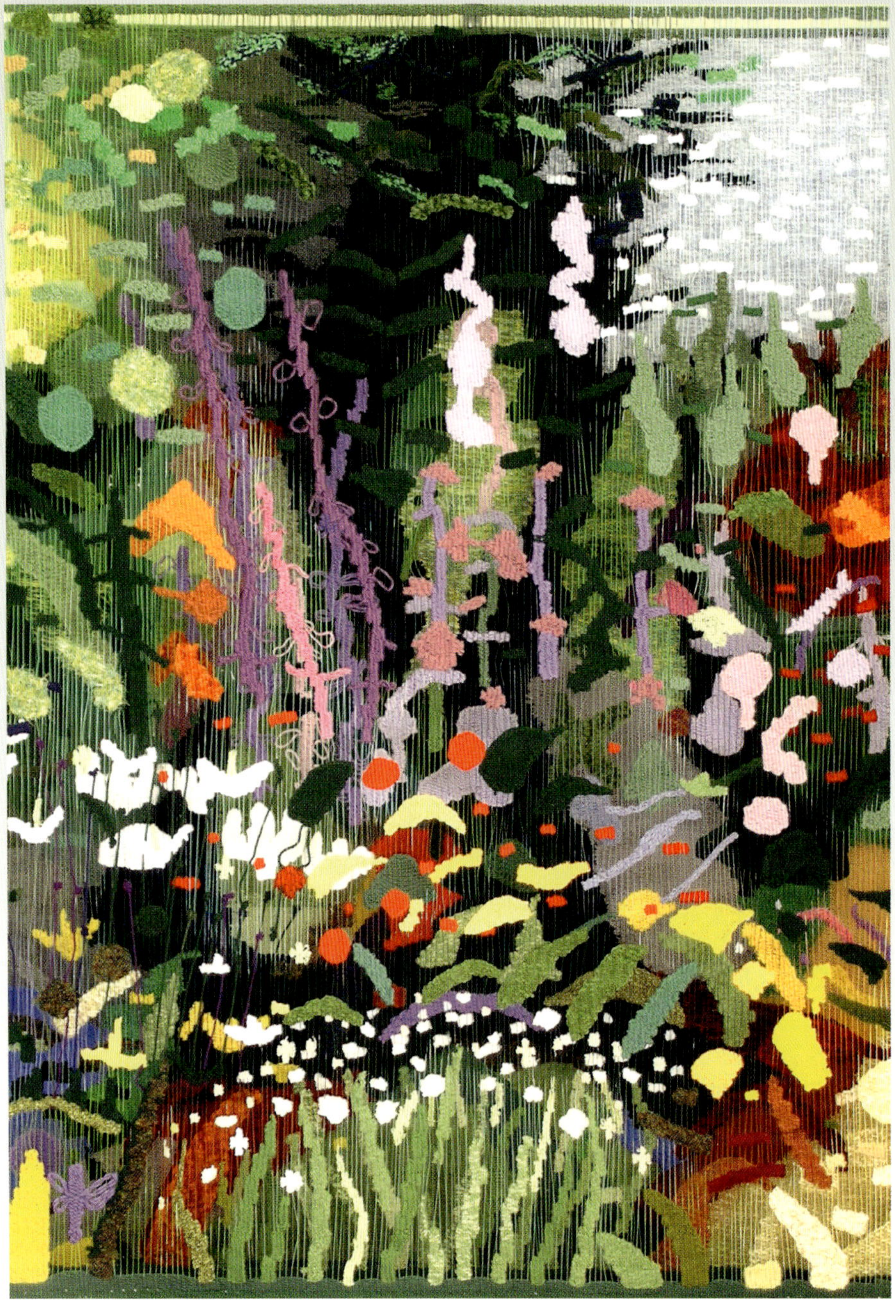

Improvisational Garden. Multilayer tapestry in cottons, wools, and synthetics. 57" × 53" × 8". 2010.

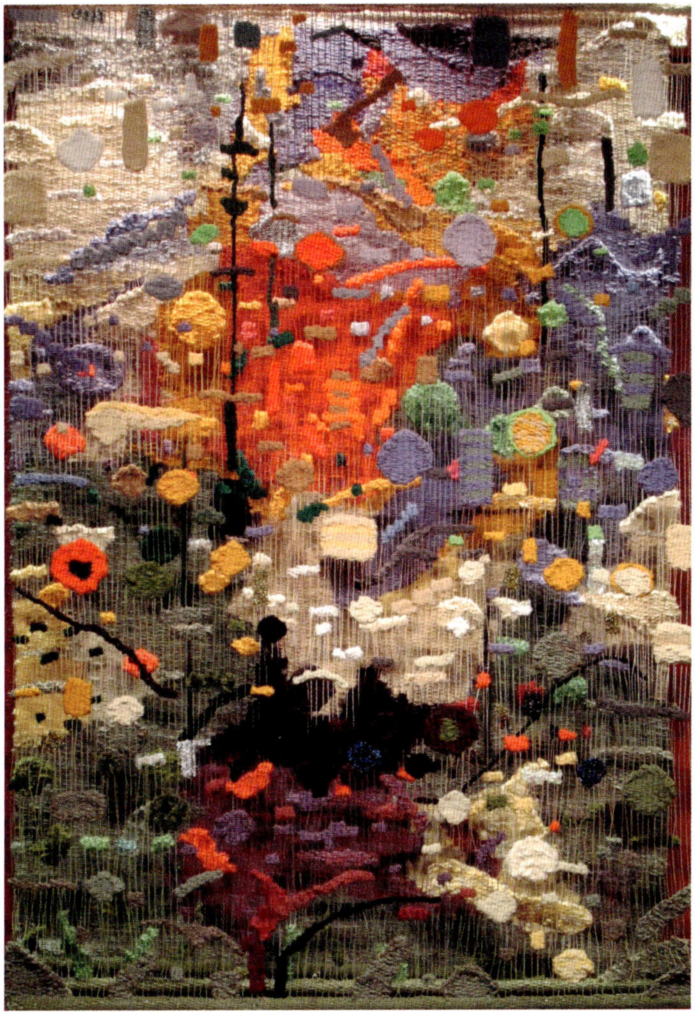

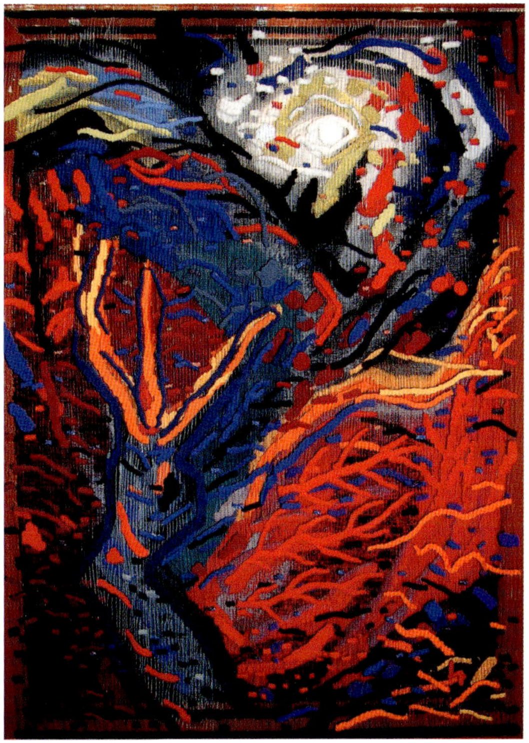

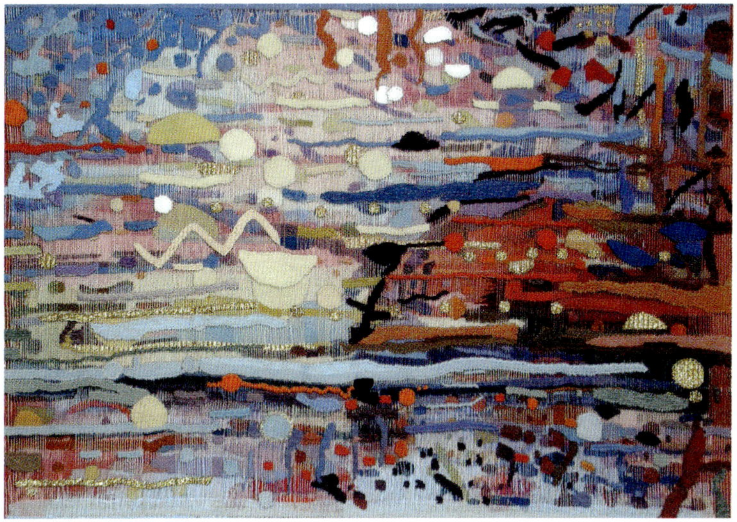

▲ *Springs Energy.* Multilayer tapestry in cottons, wools, synthetics, and metallic. 49" × 36" × 3". 2013.

◄ *Phoenix.* Multilayer tapestry in cottons, wools, and synthetics. 72" × 48" × 9". 2009.

► *Virginia Beach.* Multilayer tapestry in cottons, wools, synthetics, and metallic. 4' × 5' × 8". 2008.

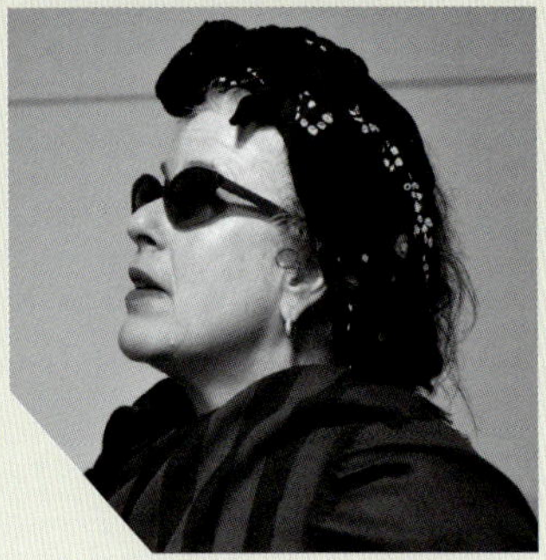

Sheila Klein

Edison, Washington

The world is my studio.

I want to dress the world.

I am the artist, architect, engineer, and dreamer.

I am making intimate things monumental and monumental things human.

Trying to make the connection between all things.

I am building the world as I see it one bit at a time. Catapulting the domestic into the architectural. Much of my work includes interaction; it's about being in the work as well as seeing it. Getting inside it, opening it, hugging it, swinging in it, stepping on it, and wearing it. My work is meant to be seen while driving, walking, landing, and waiting. I perform with materials.

I started making things as a child, interspersed with performing and thinking/unthinking. I made my first piece in grade one. It was the beginning of my interest in material and performance. The teacher was mean and wouldn't allow erasers. I figured out that I could erase the paper with my rubber soled gym shoes. I got caught.

unravel the skein
you see something
you make something
you let it happen
see what you think
think, see some more
See, Think, Make!

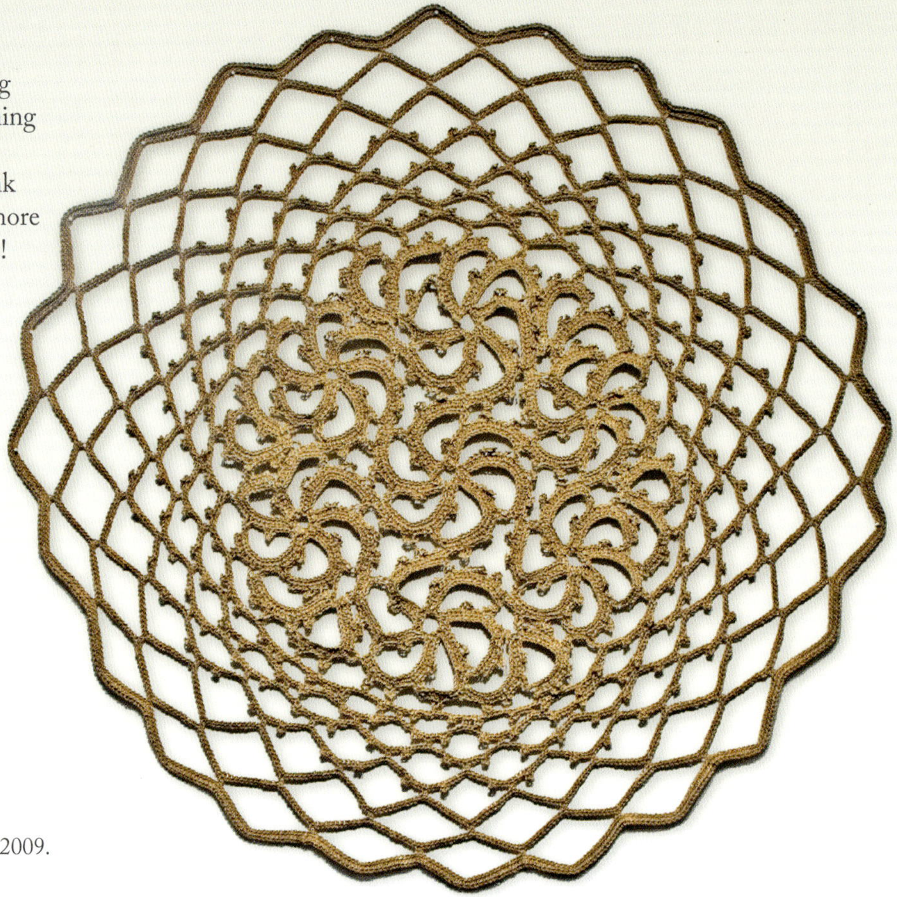

Dome. Cotton. 34" × 34". 2009.

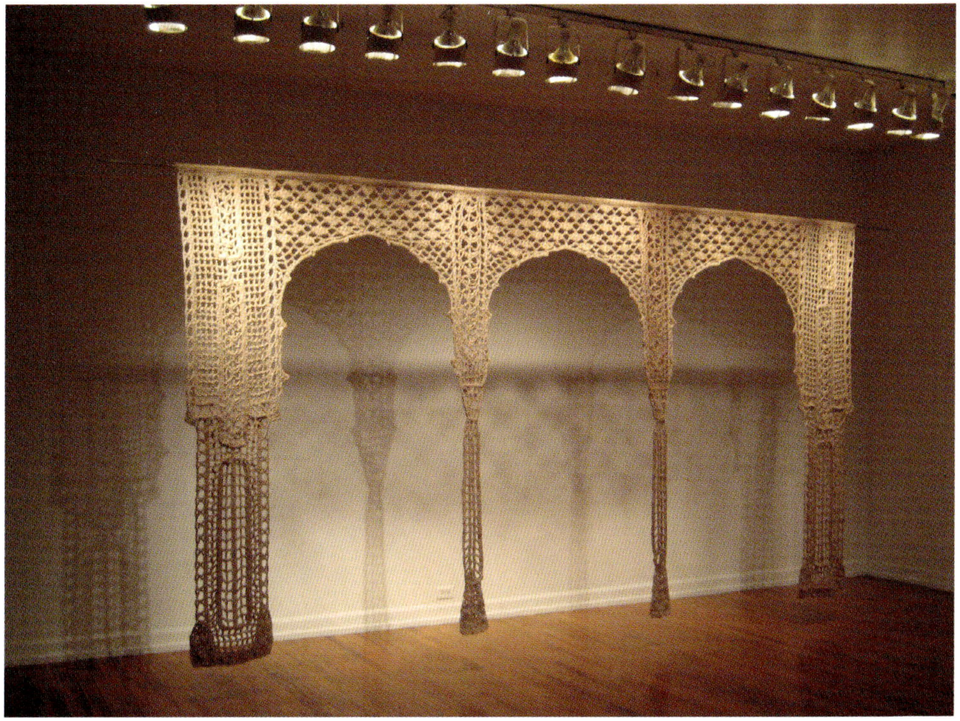

◄ *Textile Wallah.* Crocheted tea dyed cotton. 88" × 153" × 0.25". 2009.

▼ *Sarkhej Rosa.* Tea dyed cotton. 82" × 79". 2015. | Details

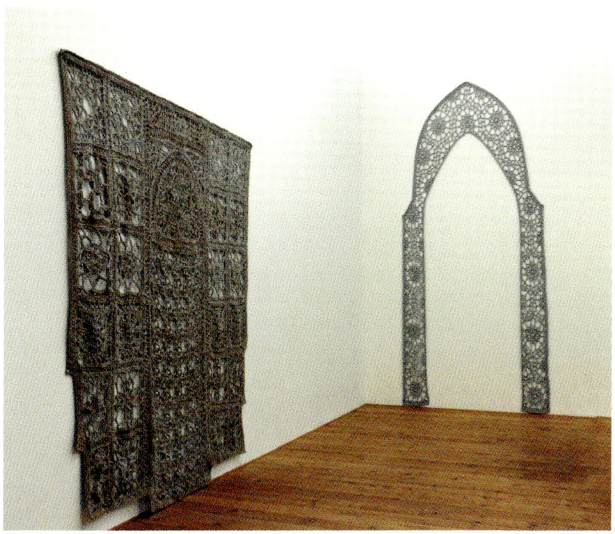

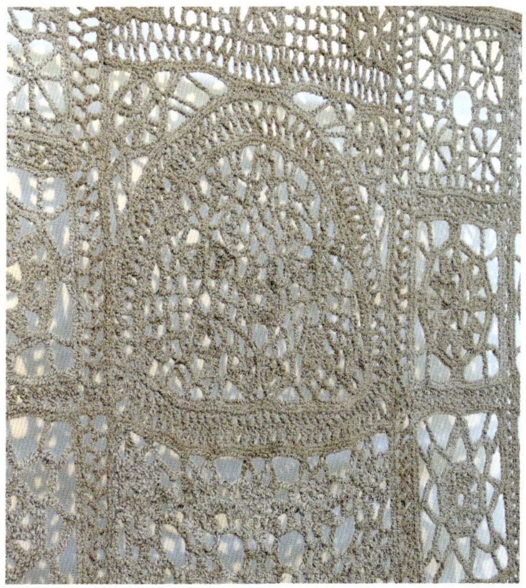

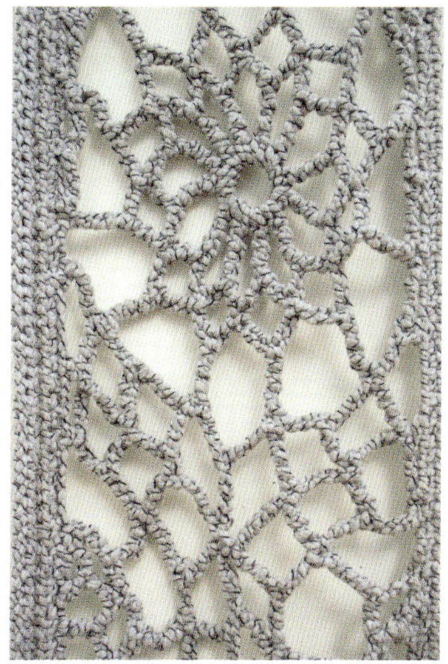

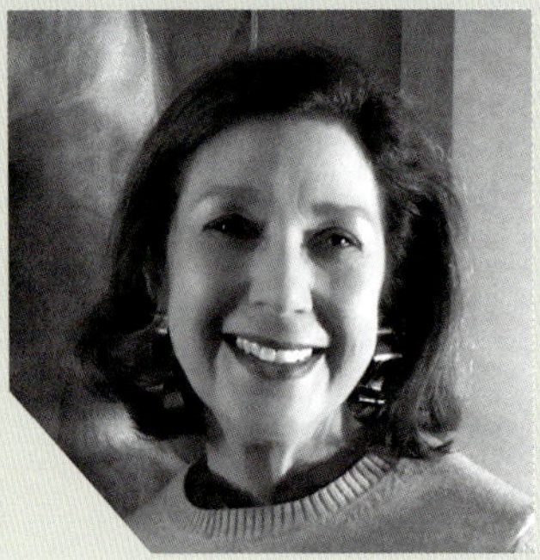

Courtesy of Cookie Tager.

Joan Konkel

Washington, DC

My wall hangings in three dimensions unchain color from a canvas and free it to cross dimensions and form new hues. When color, light, and space interact with layers of mesh and metal, an amorphous labyrinth of color arises. This is a dimension where forces are in opposition: the absorption of light is juxtaposed with the refraction of light. Sometimes a shimmering luminescence occurs. Within this realm, optical illusions and physics play with one's perception, challenging notions of depth. Metal might appear ethereal, and layers of overlapping color can become different hues or fracture into bi- and tri-colored moiré patterns.

What drives me is a fascination with the naturally occurring phenomena that arise in my work. I seek ways to harness as well as enhance these effects. Patterns are manipulated, space is altered, colors layered, and the door left open for the materials and ambient light to perform their magic. It is important to me that the work is not static. I delight in watching someone discover that movement sets in motion the dance of color, space, patterns, and light.

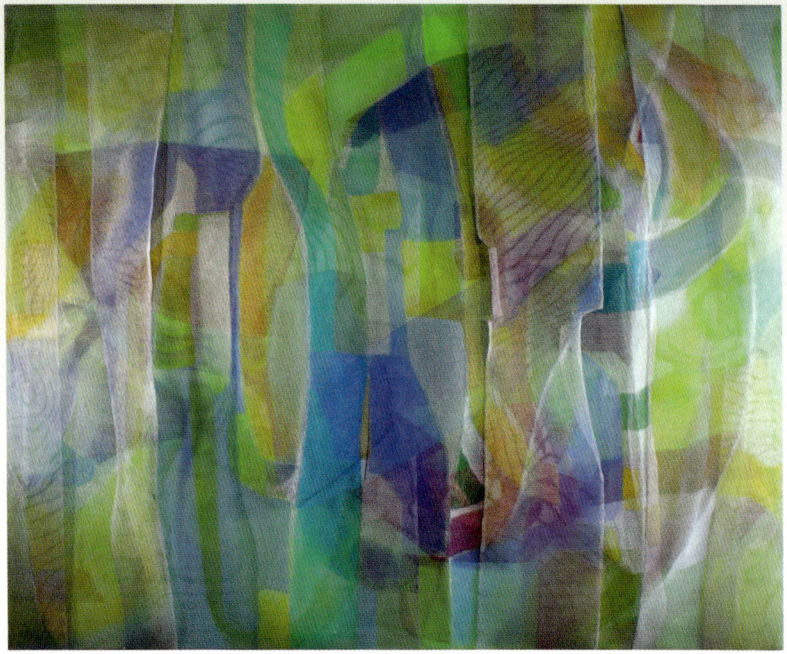

Morning of the Magician. Finely woven mesh and acrylic on canvas. 49" × 60" × 5". 2015.

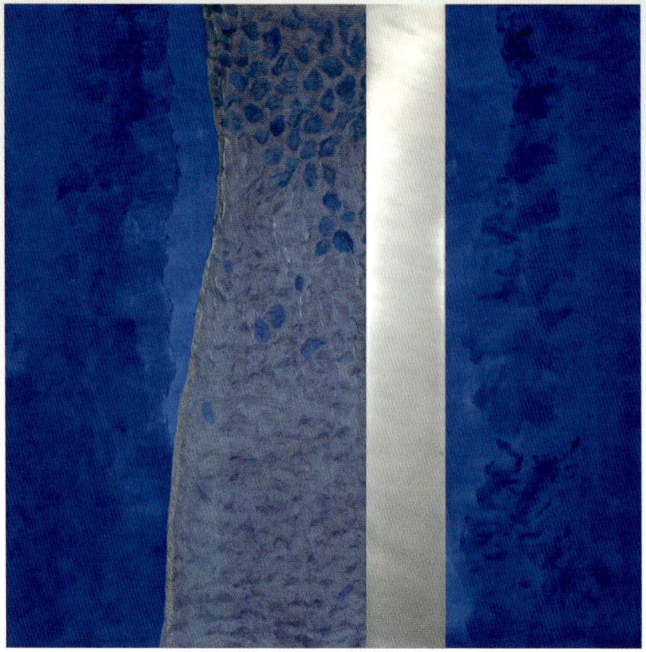

Visiting Salicia's Garden. Finely woven aluminum wire, acrylic, aluminum, and thread on canvas. 48" × 48" × 5". 2014.

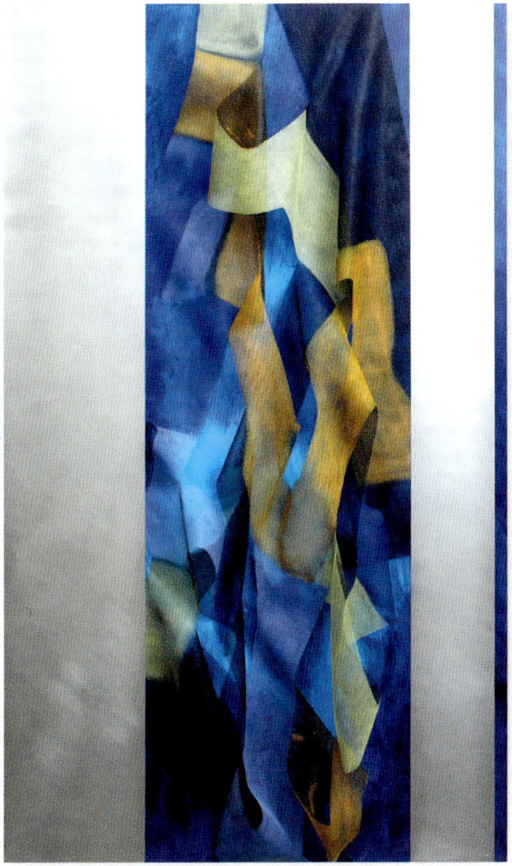

Calling the Shots. Finely woven aluminum wire, aluminum, and acrylic on canvas. 60" × 36" × 9". 2014.

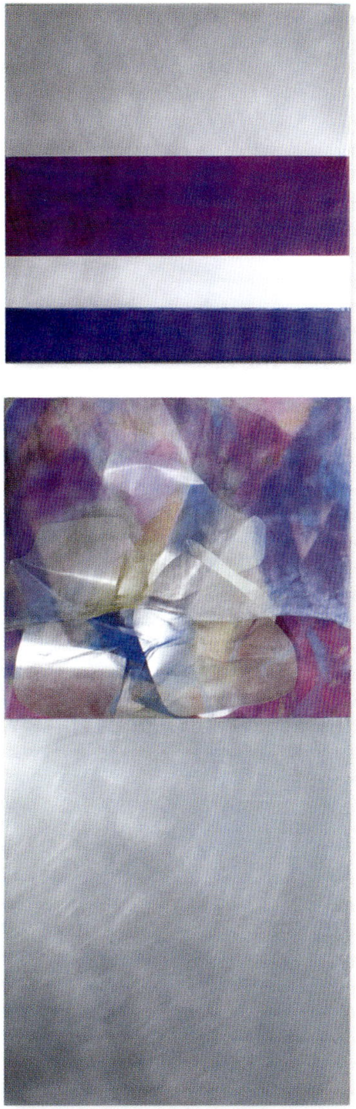

Cloudy with a Chance of Rain. Finely woven aluminum wire, aluminum, and acrylic on canvas. Diptych: 24" × 24" × 2" and 48" × 24" × 5". 2015.

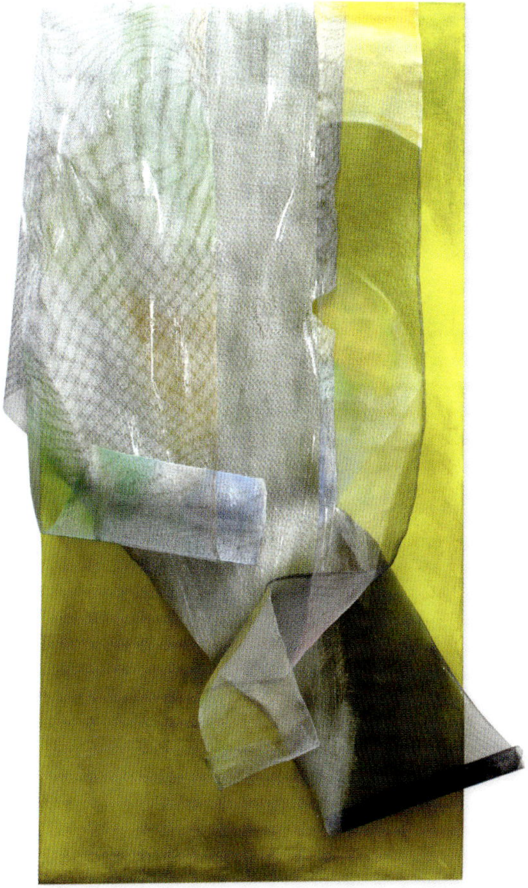

Mojito. Finely woven aluminum wire, acrylic, and thread on canvas. 48" × 29" × 7". 2014.

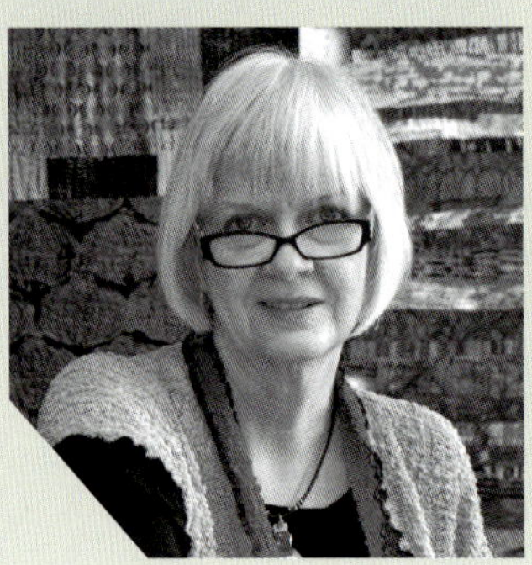

Carol Larson

Petaluma, California

I design textile art for the wall, integrating commercial fabrics with cloth of my own design. My tools are dye, wax, paint, and stitch. I use a variety of fabrics in my work, including African and Indonesian batiks, silks, vintage kimono, ethnic cloth, and vintage linens. No tea towel, hand-woven sampler, or family heirloom is too precious for my dye pot! After the dyeing process, I then undertake a complex layering of color and imagery on the fabric surface.

The imagery is original and created from photos of my travels. I take photos everywhere; where others see landscape, history, or structure, I see pattern, texture, and inspiration. A path of oval rocks from a Japanese garden, a jute window covering, ancient cave dwellings, and a kelp forest have all become screens through which I have pulled paint and dye. Layers of stitching and often more paint complete each piece.

My award-winning work is in several corporate art collections in California, including the James Irvine Foundation in San Francisco, Kaiser Permanente Hospital in Santa Rosa, and John Muir Hospital in Walnut Creek.

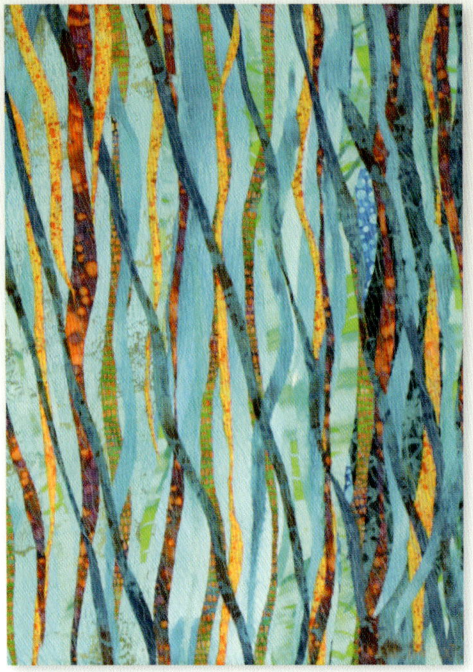

Currents 8. Cotton, rayon, and screen-printed batik. 30" × 30". 2009.

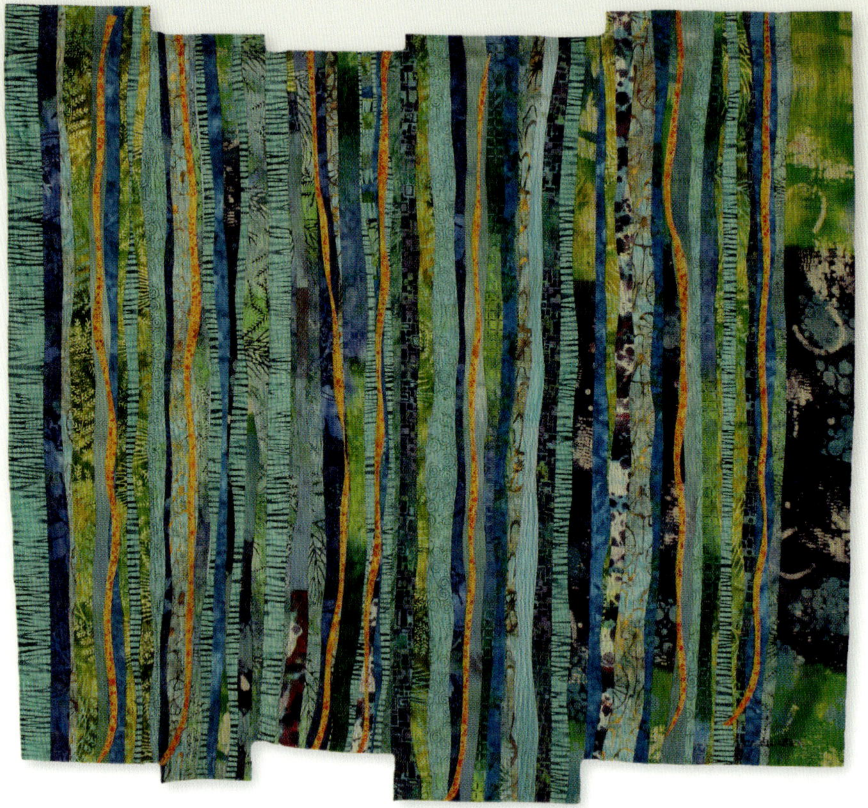

Upheaval 10. Cotton batik tablecloth. 40" × 44". 2011.

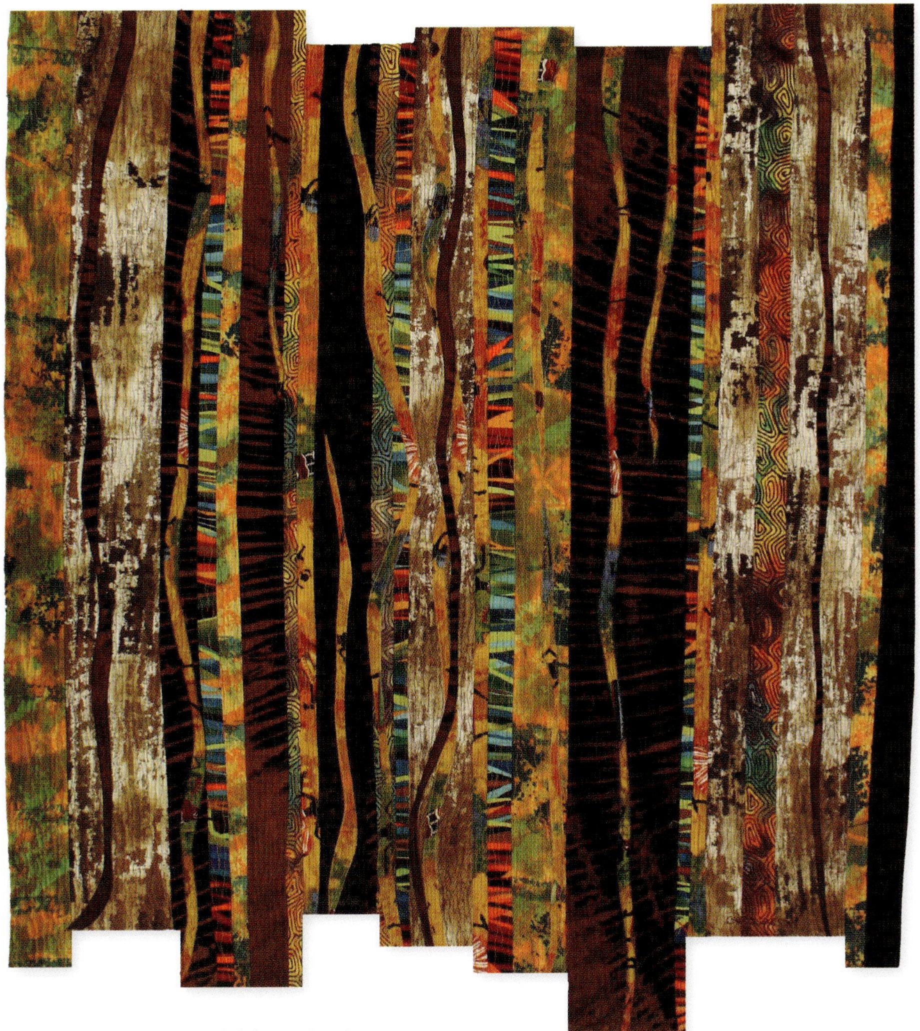

Upheaval 7. Cotton and African batiks.
44" × 41". 2010.

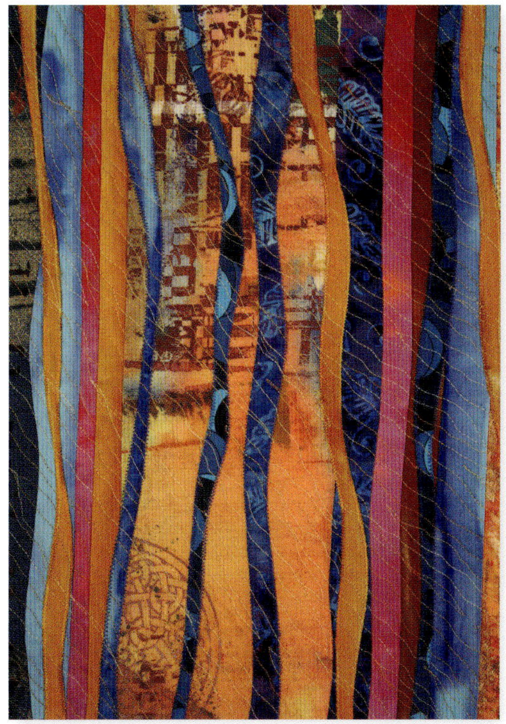

Currents 13 (detail). Cotton and screen-printed batik. 40" × 35". 2011.

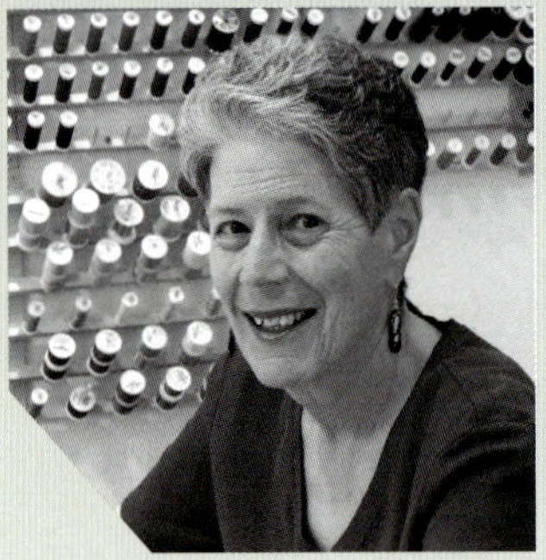

Courtesy of Robert S. Lasher.

Gaye S. Lasher

Denver, Colorado

Where do artists get their ideas? Sometimes it's from circumstances of everyday life. Most of us contend with traffic on a daily basis. However, when the Great Recession eased, Denver experienced an explosion of construction projects that had been on hold, together with a sprouting of signs saying "No Left Turn," "Road Work 500 Feet," and "Detour." Sitting in traffic, taking unaccustomed routes, and never being sure about how to get to the same place twice inspired my current series, *Playing In Traffic*. As I worked on the visual compositions, I found myself liking the idea of using traffic signs as titles. Strong saturated colors and chaotic shapes express my frustration and impatience with the complexities of modern life.

My work derives from computer-altered abstractions and transformations of my own photographs. Starting with a digital photograph, I alter the appearance of the photo's contents with a combination of Photoshop filters and push the color saturation to the limit. Then, selecting a small area of the altered photo, I greatly enlarge that area and print the image in sixteen-inch wide panels on paper-backed cotton fabric. The panels are sewn together, sandwiched with batting and backing, and densely stitched. The body of work represented in this portfolio displays a concern with formal elements such as color, shape, repetition, texture, and movement.

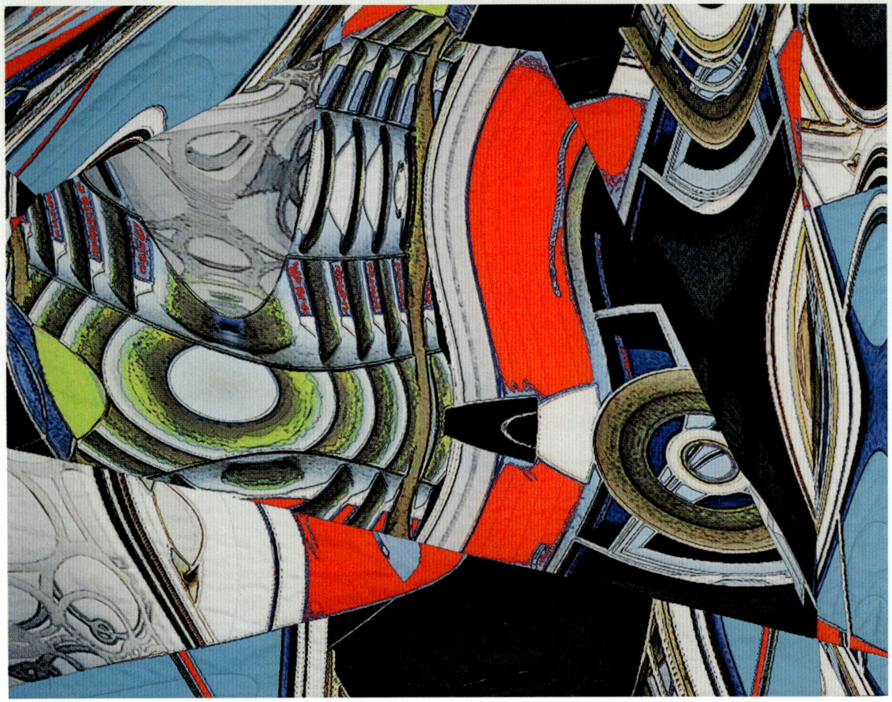

No Turn On Red. Cotton and polyester fabrics, cotton, rayon and polyester threads, batting, and Epson UltraChrome inks. 31" × 41". 2014.

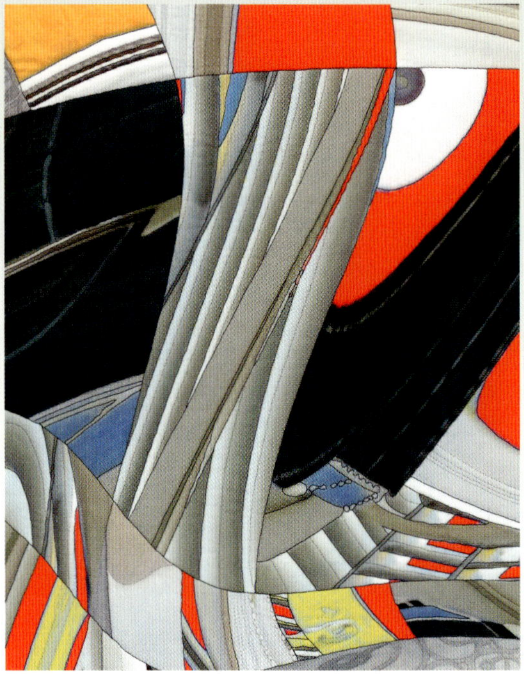

Detour #1. Cotton and polyester fabrics, cotton, rayon and polyester threads, batting, and Epson UltraChrome inks. 20" × 16". 2015.

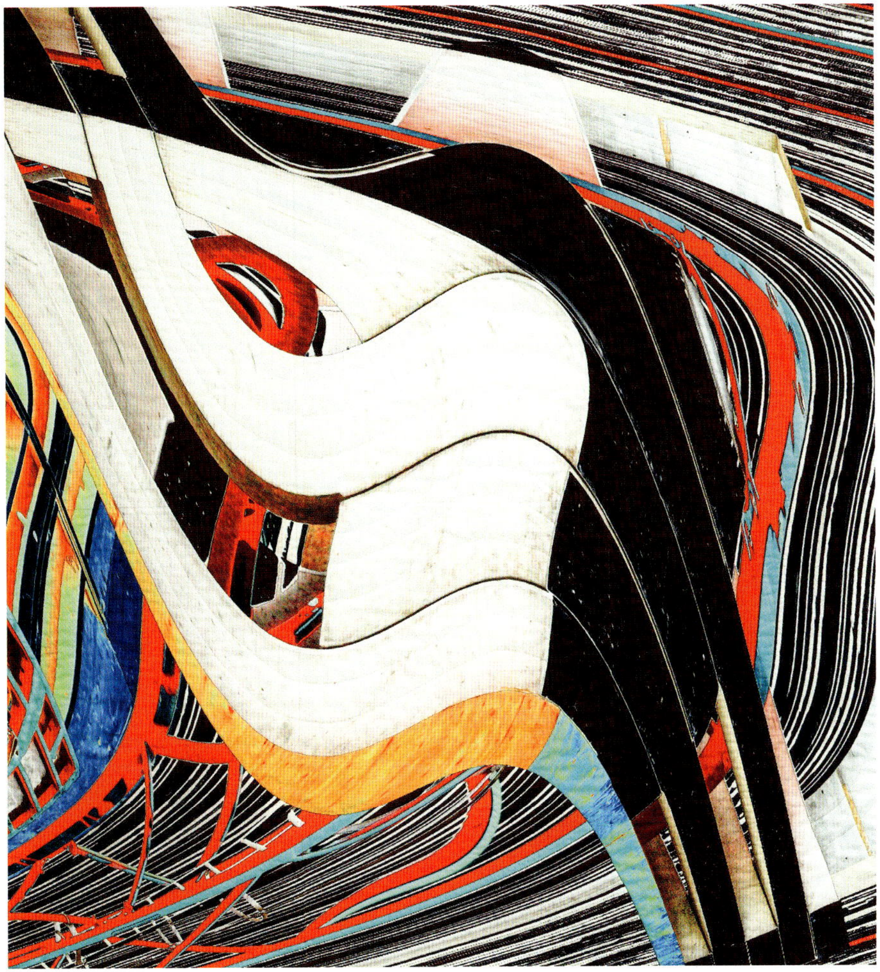

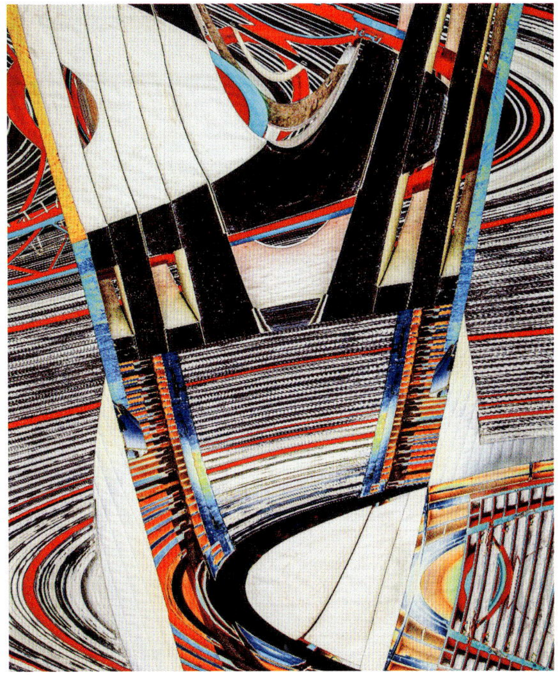

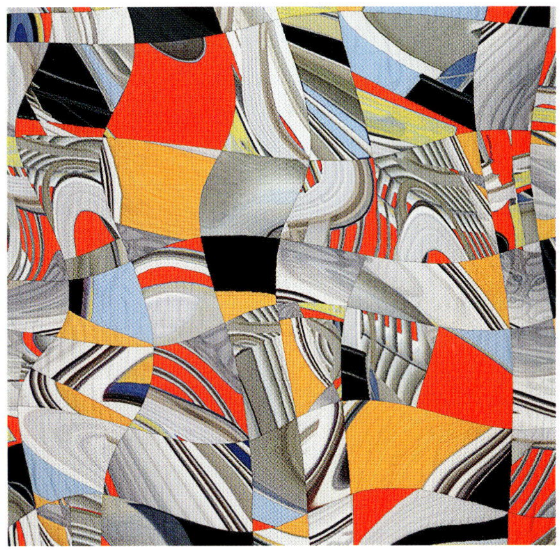

▲ *Dangerous Curves.* Cotton and polyester fabrics, cotton, rayon and polyester threads, batting, Epson UltraChrome inks, and acrylic paint. 48" × 45". 2014.

◄ *No Exit.* Cotton and polyester fabrics, cotton, rayon and polyester threads, batting, and Epson UltraChrome inks. 50" × 42". 2014.

► *Grid Lock.* Cotton and polyester fabrics, cotton, rayon and polyester threads, batting, and Epson UltraChrome inks, acrylic inks. 47.5" × 45.5". 2015.

All art images courtesy of Wes Magyar.

Courtesy of Ulrich Levi-Goerlich.

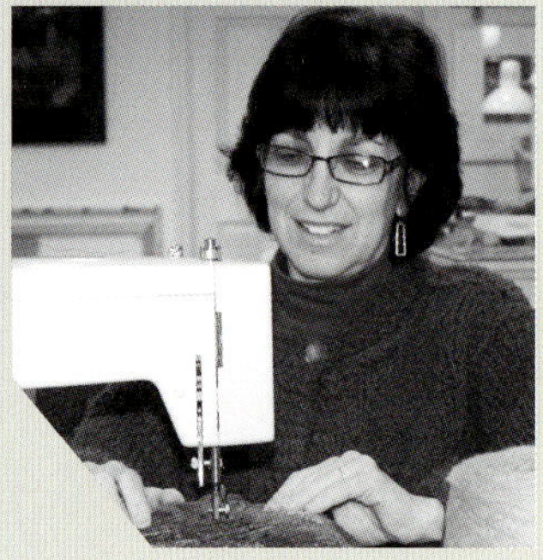

Susan Levi-Goerlich

Columbia, Maryland

My fiber work combines my passion for gardening and garden imagery with free-motion machine embroidery, needle-felting, and painted silk. I create painterly effects through thousands of stitches and achieve rich textures by fluidly and continually shifting the fabric under the rapidly moving needle of my forty-year-old (non-computerized) sewing machine. The imagery is inspired by landscapes and gardens encountered during my travels and by favorite photographs.

My fascination with layers includes layering fabrics, threads, and yarns to create depth, rich color, and texture. Movement and flow of color play an important role in my work, as do shadows and reflections.

I show and sell my work at national and regional art shows and have exhibited nationally and internationally. In addition, I teach workshops and classes.

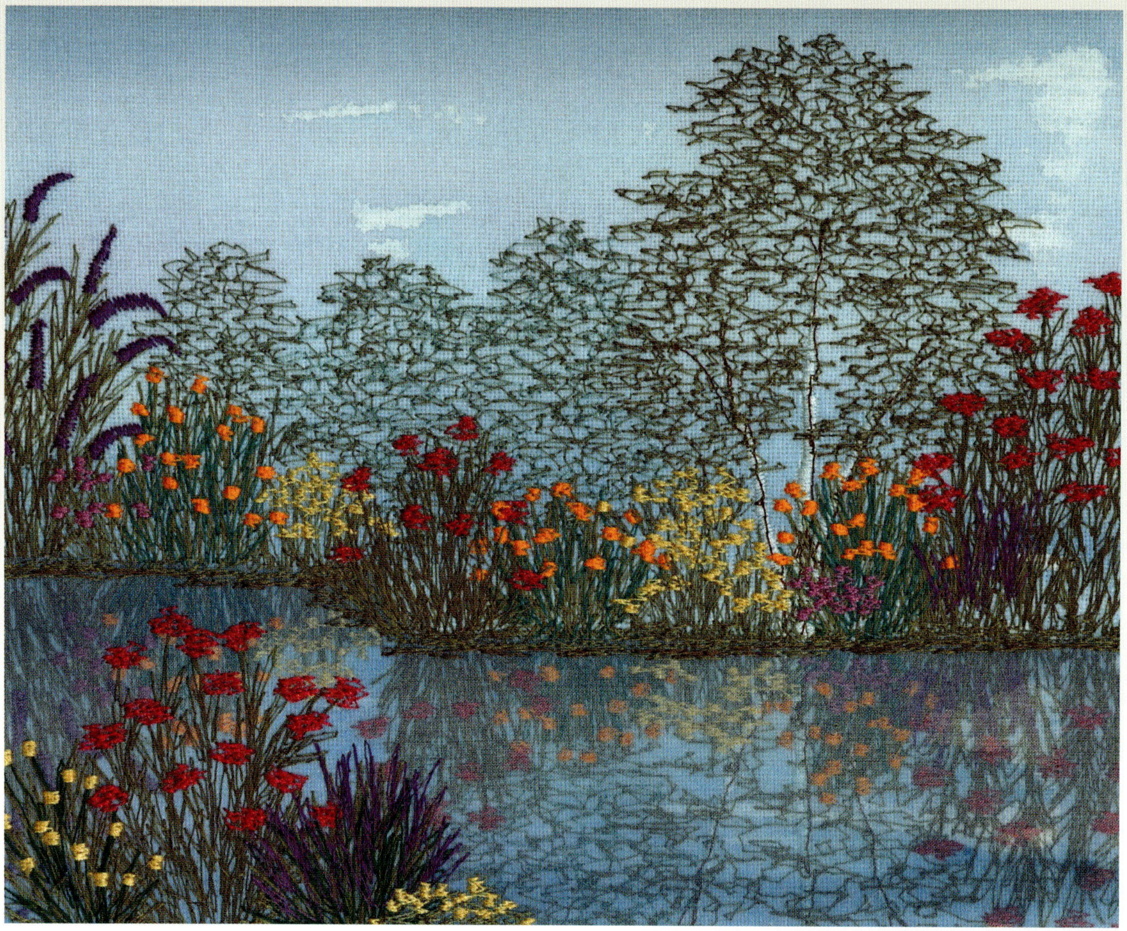

Birch with Reflections.
Silk and threads. 8" × 10". 2011.

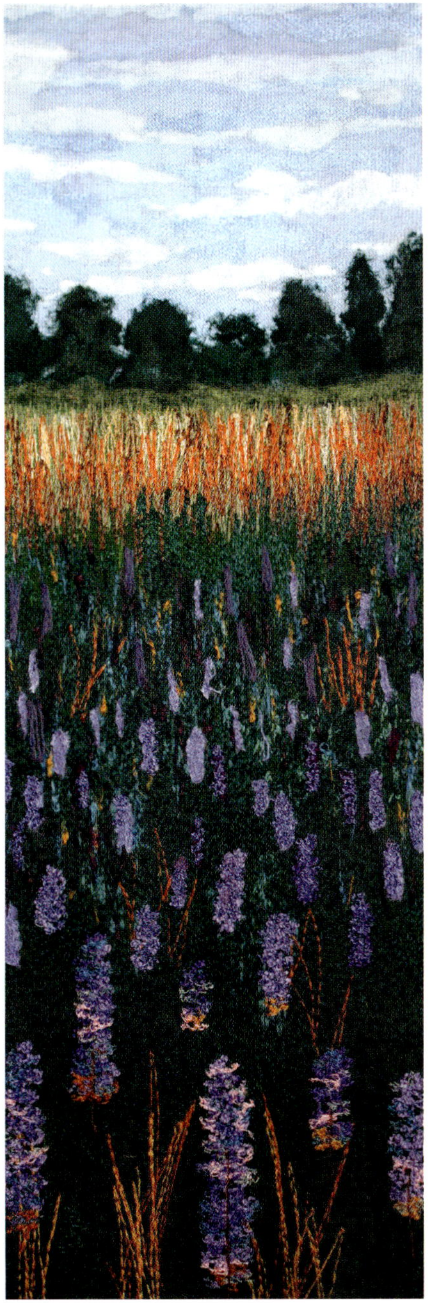

➤ *Larkspur.*
Silk, threads, and yarns. 32" × 10". 2010.

➤ *Yellow Vineyards.*
Silk, threads, and yarns. 16" × 18". 2013.

▼ *Dolly Sods.*
Silk and threads. 8" × 10". 2015.

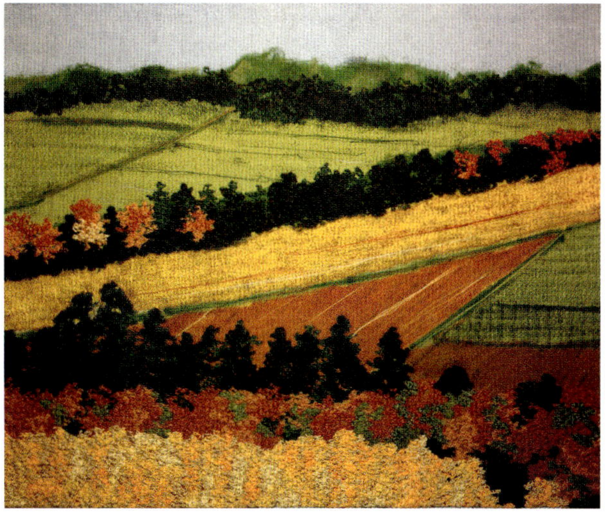

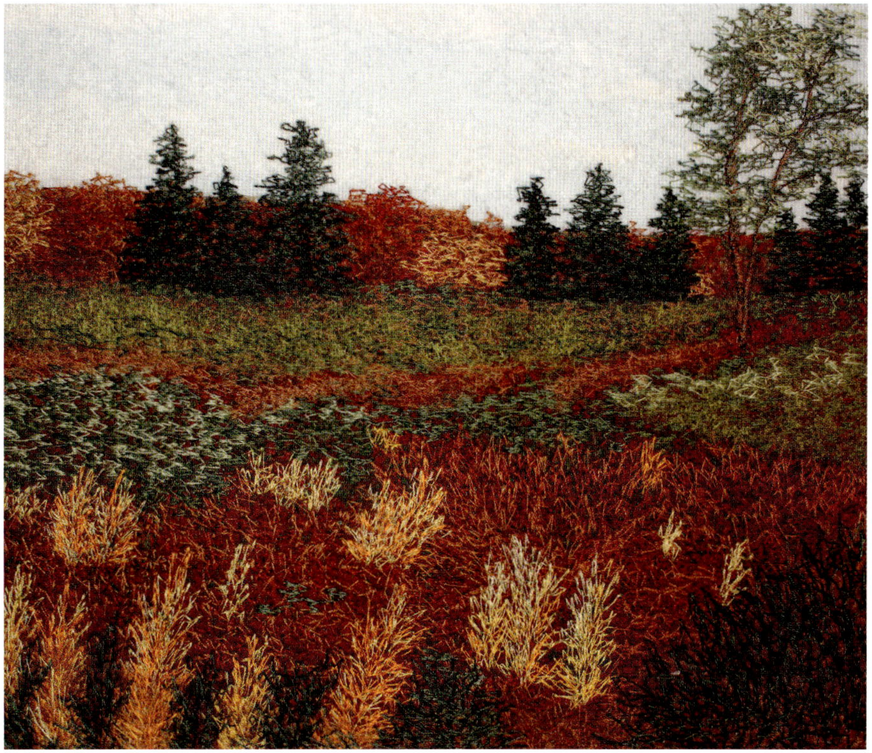

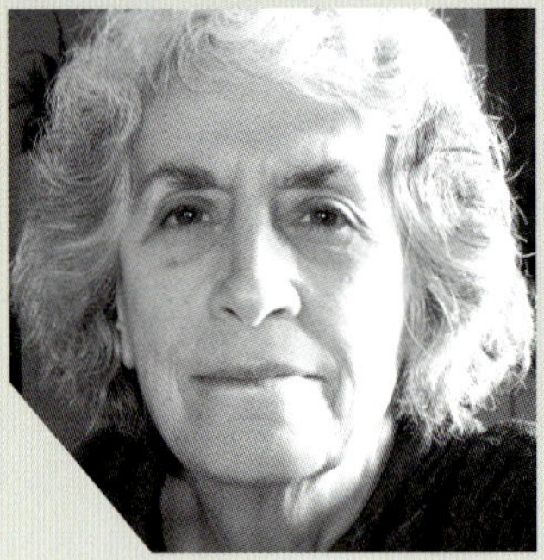

Susan Martin Maffei

New Baltimore, New York

Development of early relationships with the males of my immediate family centered on sports. I accompanied Grandpa regularly to horse races and pool halls. My father and I shared a passion for watching baseball even though we rooted for different teams. My kid brother was a great sailor, and some of my fondest memories are of the time we shared on board his sailboat. We all searched for and found common ground in sports.

As I look for visions that fit with my preferred medium of woven tapestry, I am again and again drawn to the patterns of sports that are so textile-related. The use of decorative cuttings of grass that adorn the fields of football, baseball, soccer, and golf, the rhythm of the waves on the sea, and the patterns of fans in the colors of their teams all shouted to me and became an integral part of my work.

I have been weaving professionally since 1985. I teach, lecture, and exhibit in North America and abroad and have work in both public and private collections.

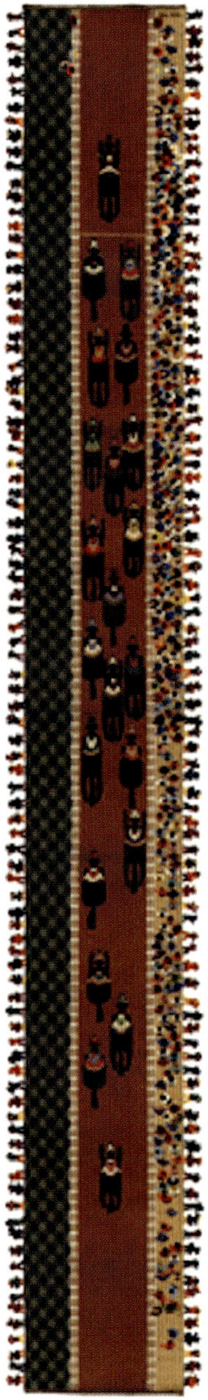

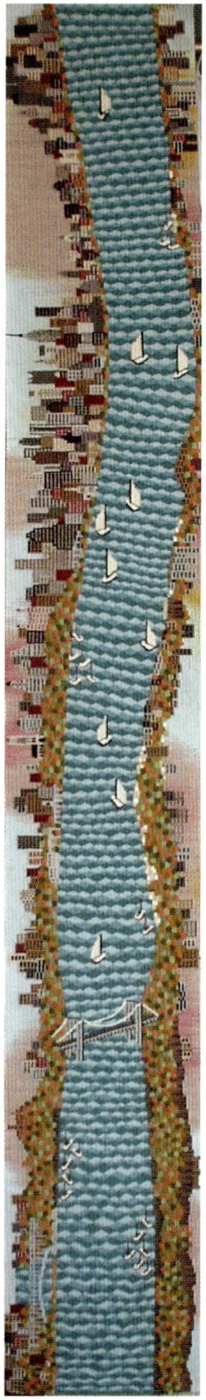

Sport Series

Day at the Races. Wool, cotton, silk, and linen. 79" × 12". 2010.

➤ *Sailing down the Hudson.* Wool, cotton, silk, and linen. 72" × 8". 2007.

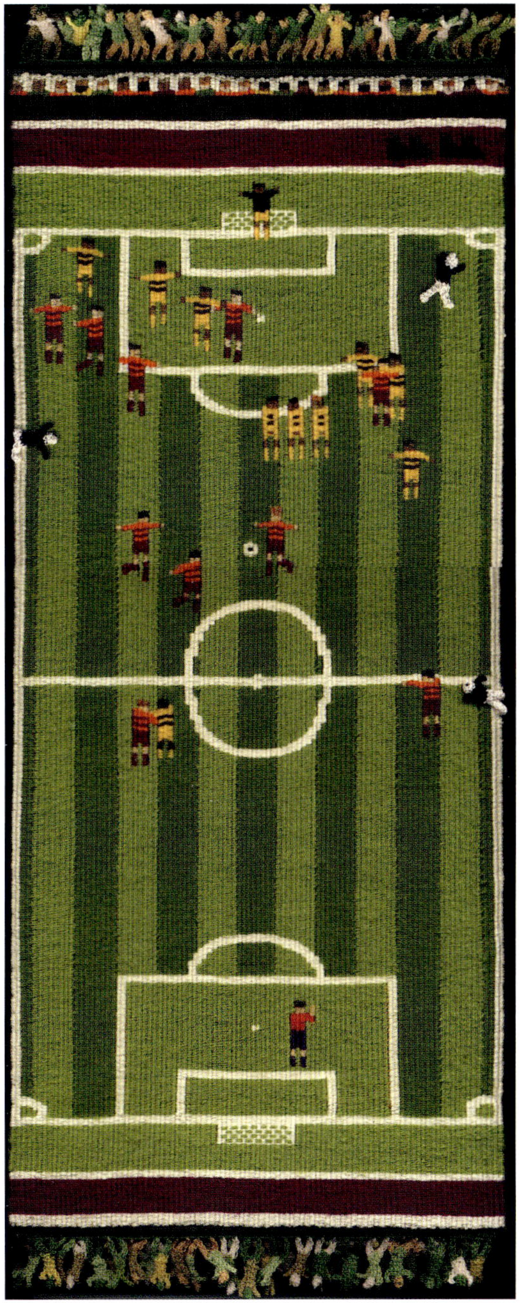

➤ *Soccer.* Wool, cotton, silk, and linen. 18" × 8". 2010.

➤ *Pool Table.* Wool, cotton, silk, and linen. 6" × 8". 2012.

▼ *Who's Not on 2nd?* Linen, cotton, wool, and silk fibers with official miniature shirts. 37" × 28". 2007.

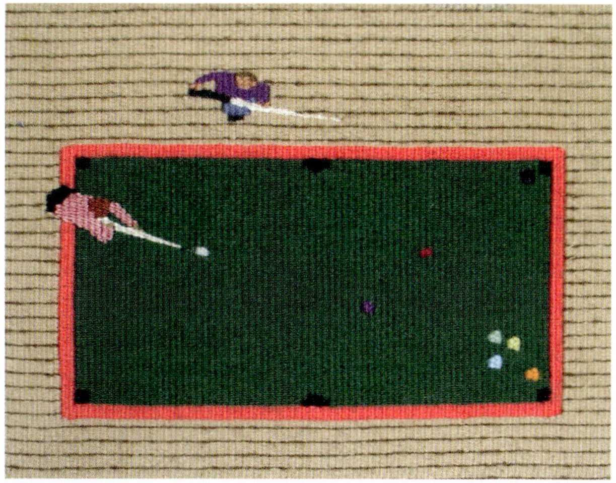

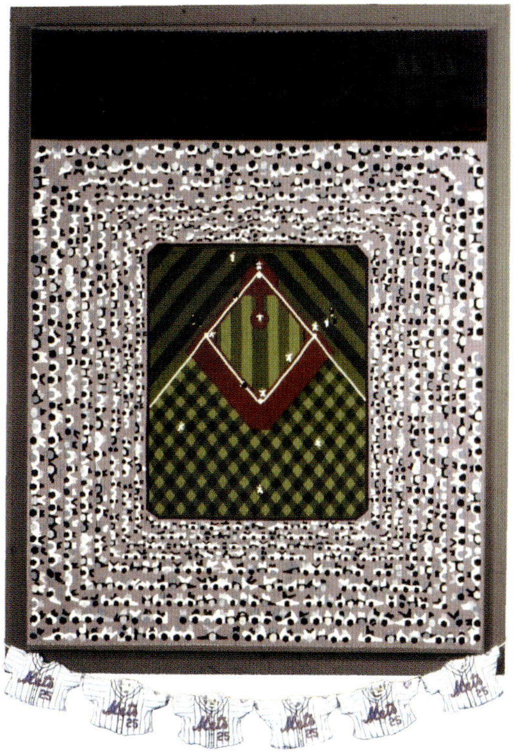

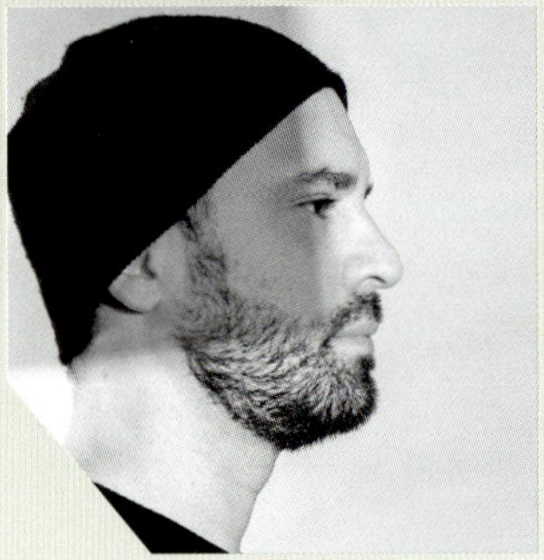

Ruben Marroquin

Bridgeport, Connecticut and New York, New York

I embraced textiles early on, through embroidery and patchwork, originally because paints and canvases weren't available to me. I believe that a big part of why I work with textiles is my Guatemalan/Venezuelan heritage. I gravitate towards the sculptural quality in textiles, often expanding this aspect by incorporating bamboo poles as an inner armature. I am interested in this experimental combination of materials, the spontaneity intrinsic to the assembly process, and the physical act of wrapping, knotting, and weaving all these elements together.

In my weaving studio, I embroider photographs, postcards, and posters; I also paint and, later, embroider over the painted areas. In one series, I may limit my yarn additions to accents that give a pop of color to the structure of a building. In another, I may stitch more drastically, filling in, or "line drawing," over topographic regions with parallel threads.

I received a scholarship from the Carla Bruni Sarkozy foundation to study weaving in Paris at Les Ateliers-Paris Design Institute. I have conducted weaving demonstrations at the Metropolitan Museum of Art as part of textile exhibitions and Hispanic Heritage month.

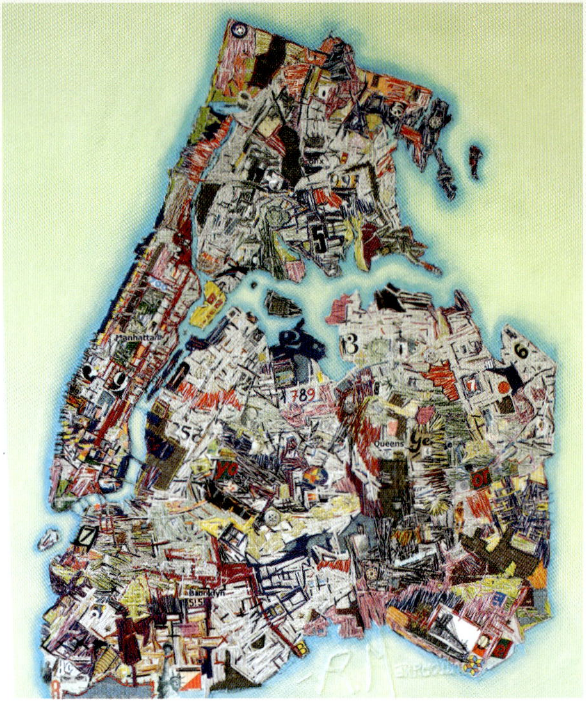

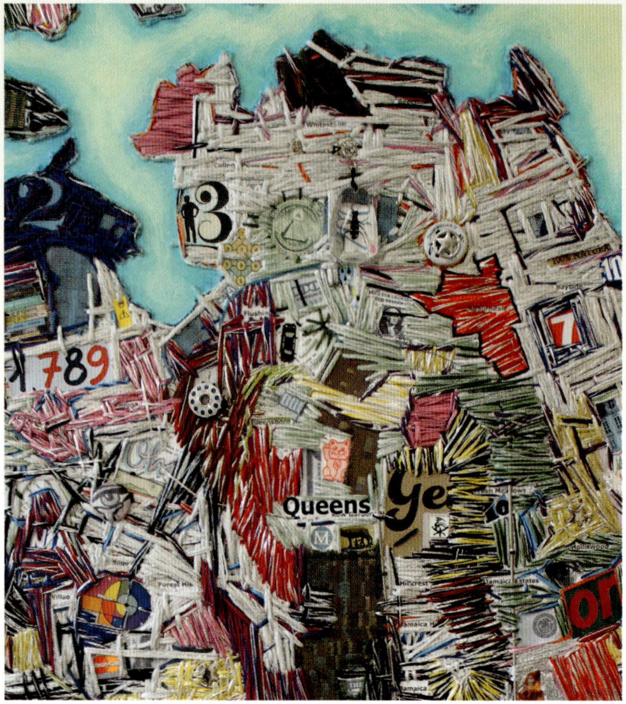

New York City Map. Fabric, paper, yarns, metallic wires, needles, and found objects. 50" × 40". 2014. | Detail Courtesy of Frank Foster Post.

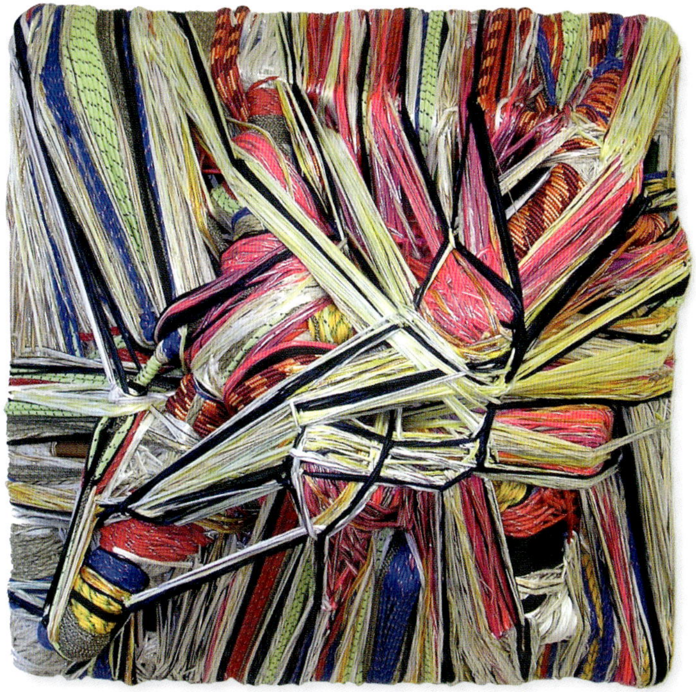

◄ *Habitat*. Layered yarns, mason twine, paracords, and metallic threads over bamboo armature. 36" × 36" × 12". 2014.

► *U.S.A. Map, Red and Blue States*. Paper, maps of the US, and thread. 32" × 50". 2014.

◄ *Tikal*. Natural and metallic yarns, bamboo, wood, bottles, and found objects. 22" × 36" × 30". 2013.

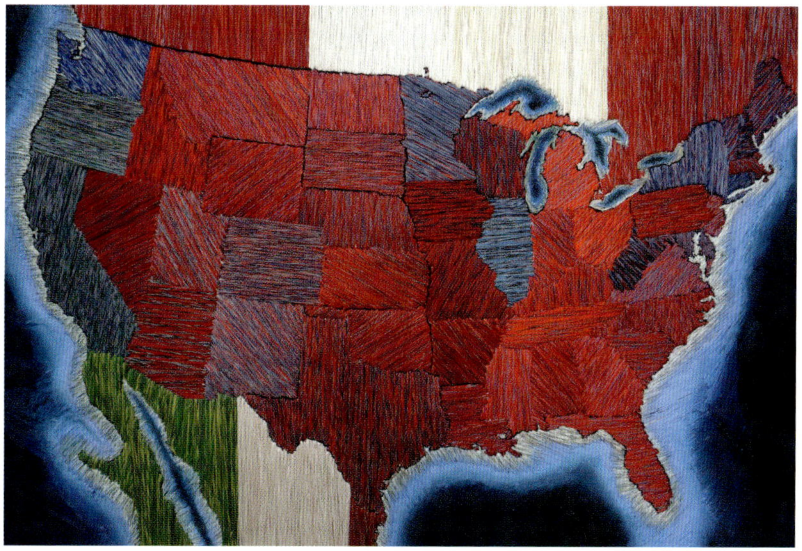

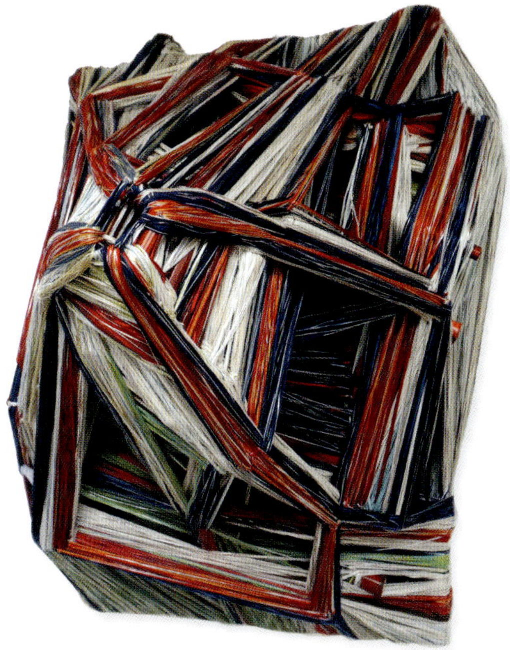

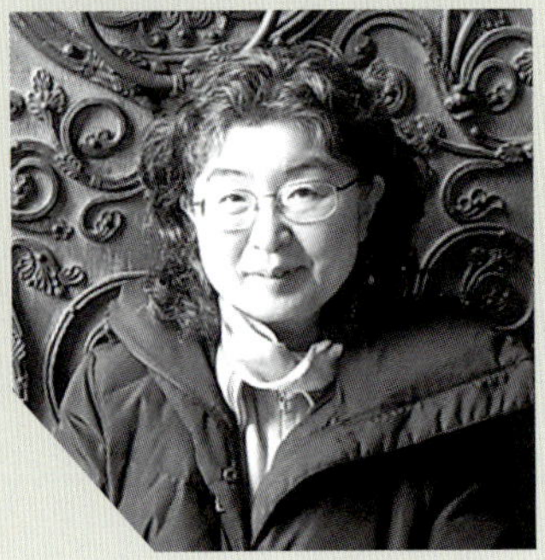

Courtesy of Camilla Canlan Photography.

Fuyuko Matsubara

Indiana, Pennsylvania

The process of weaving matches the concept of my imagery. Through the consecutive actions of painting, deconstruction, and reconstruction, I observe the image disintegrate and transform.

In the Earth consists of twelve panels. Each panel contains an image that is compositionally complete and may be viewed as an independent piece. When the twelve panels are viewed together, they create a single composition called *In the Earth*. The concept behind these arrangements reflects my view of the elements of the world, dealt with individually or as groupings.

In my recent series of work, *A Phase of Light*, light represents an energy source from a spiritual view. The overlapping, growing circles of luminous light emphasize the positive quality of the energy. The numerous lights suggest their endless and infinite numbers. The light exists like air for us. It is so common that we forget its quality as an essential and vital energy source.

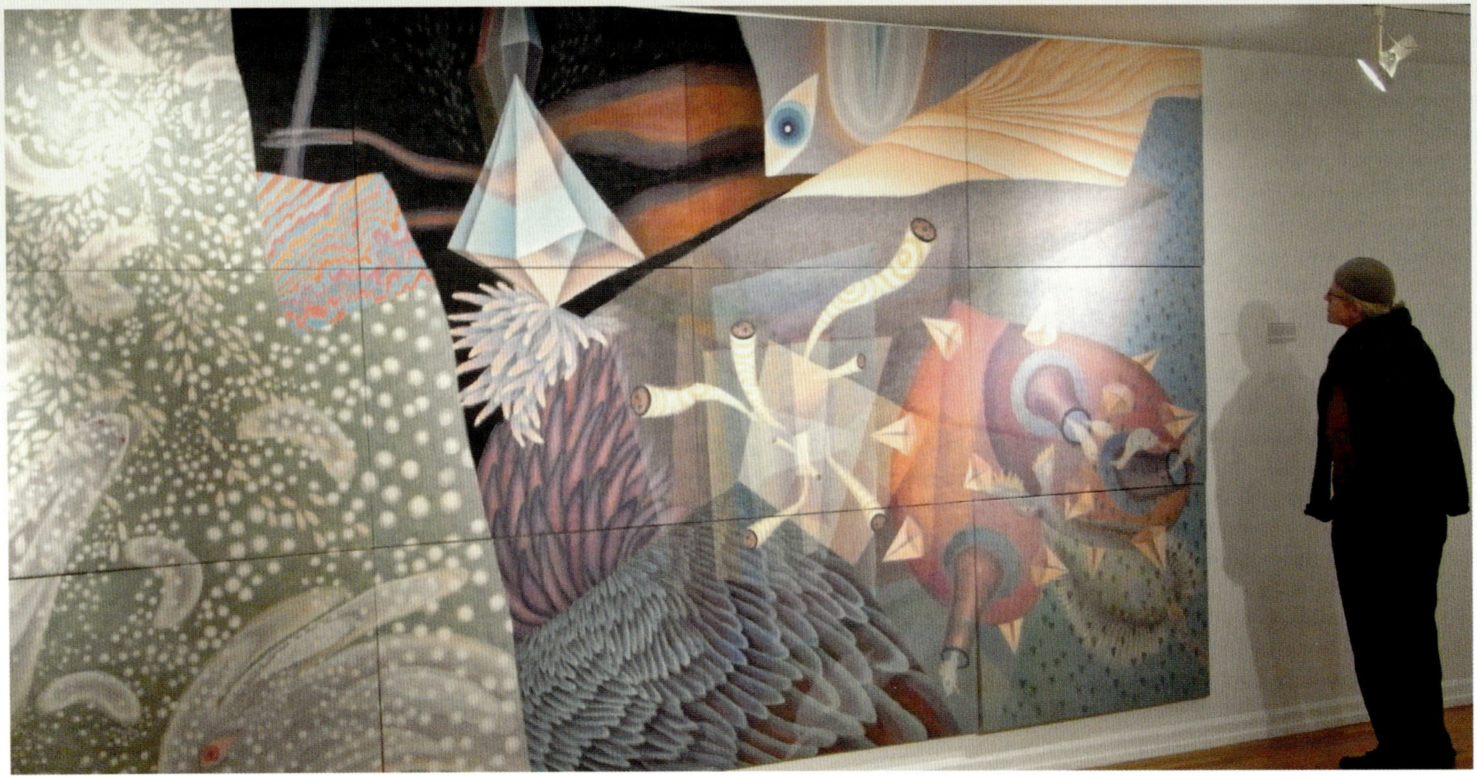

In the Earth 2. Installation at Pittsburgh Center for the Arts. 93" × 168". 1985–2004.

➤ *A Phase of Light: Unfold 2*. Hand plied yarn: linen, cotton, rayon, and silk. 39" × 49". 2009.

➤ *Phase of Light: Recovery 1*. Hand plied yarn: linen, cotton, rayon, and silk. 20.5" × 20.5". 2006.

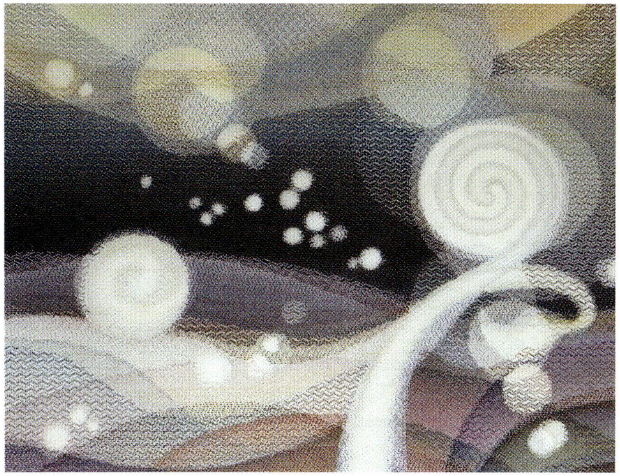

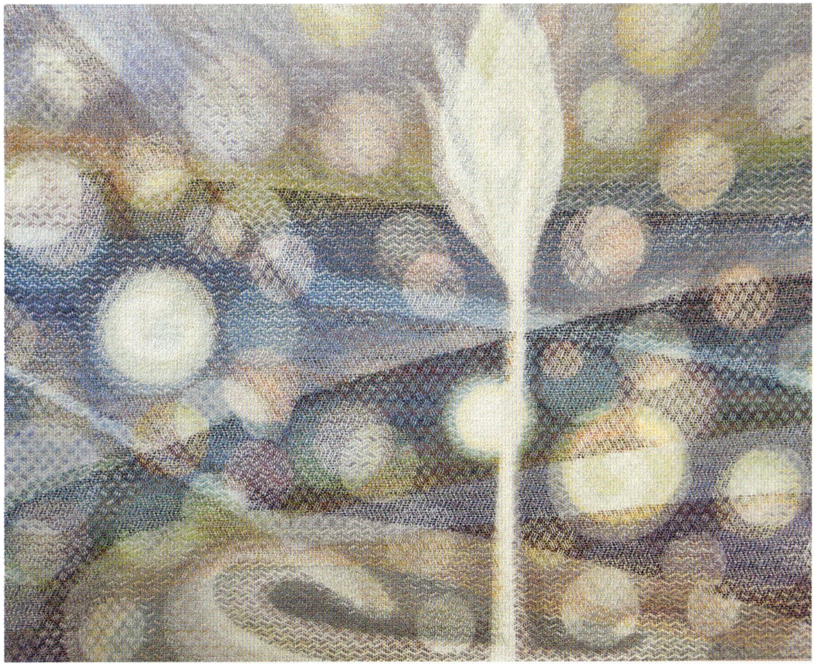

▲ *A Phase of Light: Sprout 2*. Hand plied yarn: linen, cotton, rayon, and silk. 30.5" × 41". 2008.

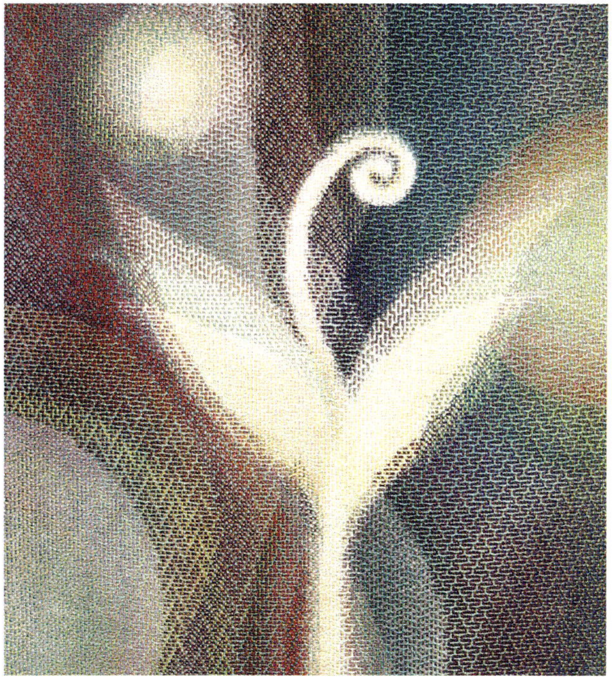

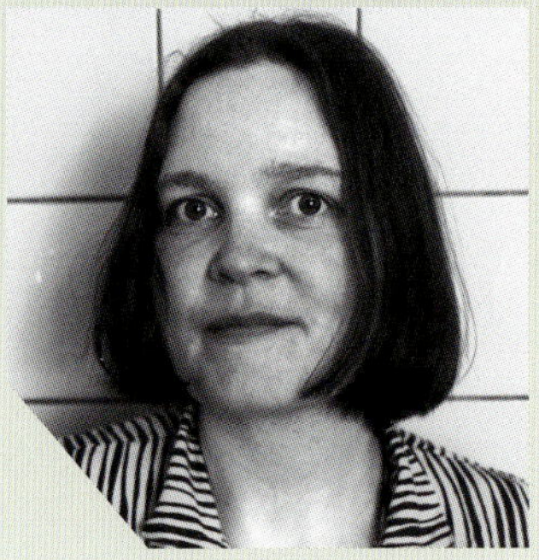

Jennie McMillen

Uppsala, Sweden

Since 2010, I have been working on a narrative embroidery, *In the Borderland*, building a city and surroundings where a conflict between civilization and nature is taking place. I see my work as a way of seeing the world, dismantling it, and building it up again. In my pictures, civilization overcomes areas of nature with flags, vehicles, and domestic animals, and nature takes over areas of civilization with water, fire, and predatory animals. I work slowly with black sewing thread on white cotton fabric, and I see time as an important aspect in my work. I see my work as something akin to how I played as a child, letting the work control me at the same time as I control the work.

After attending Gotland Art School, I studied weaving at Sätergläntan, a traditional craft school. I got my master's degree in textile art at HDK (School of Design and Crafts) in Gothenburg, Sweden. I also studied theoretical subjects for three years at Uppsala University and Umeå University.

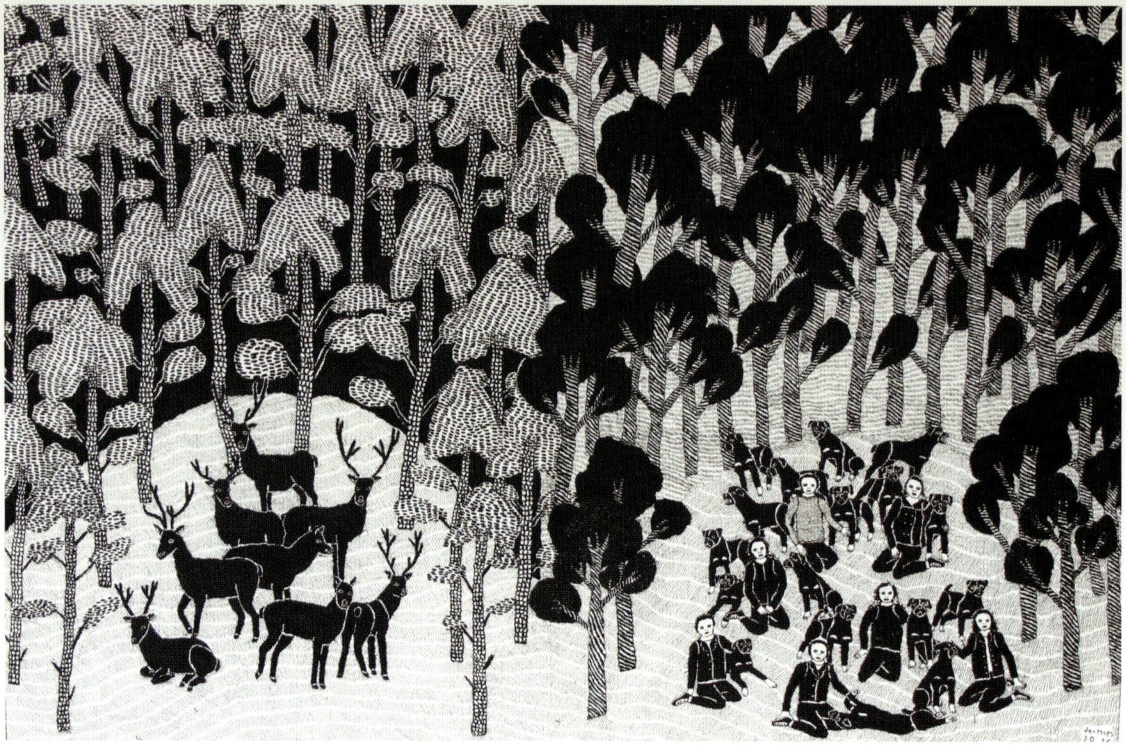

In the Forest. Cotton fabric and cotton sewing thread. 28" × 42.9". 2016.

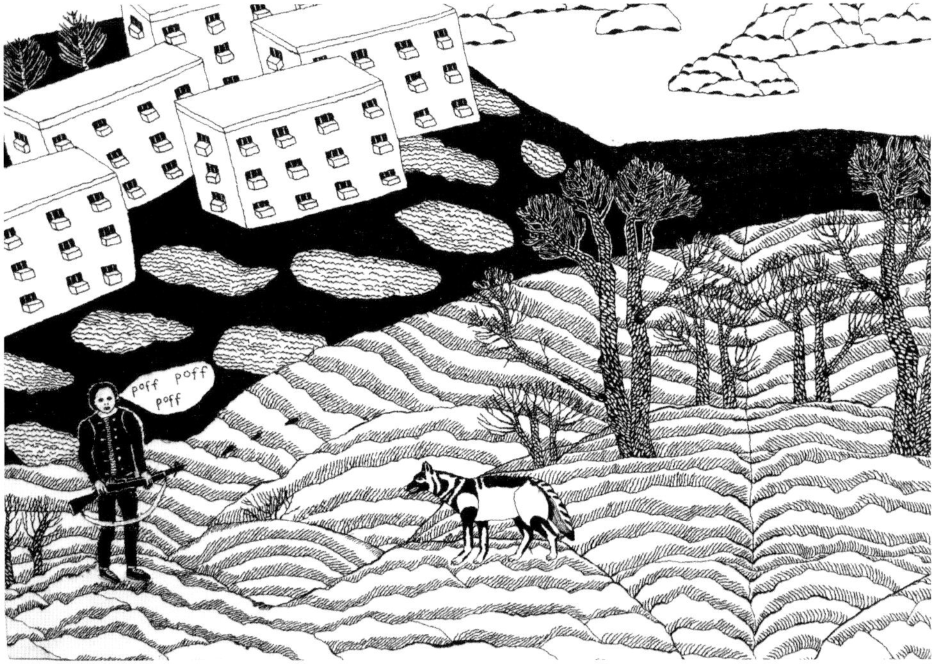

◄ *Poff Poff Poff*. Cotton fabric and cotton sewing thread. 47.2" × 31.5". 2011–2014.

► *Rain above House*. Cotton fabric and cotton sewing thread. 15.7" × 13.4". 2012–2014.

▼ *The Island*. Cotton fabric and cotton sewing thread. 18.9" x 30.7". 2013.

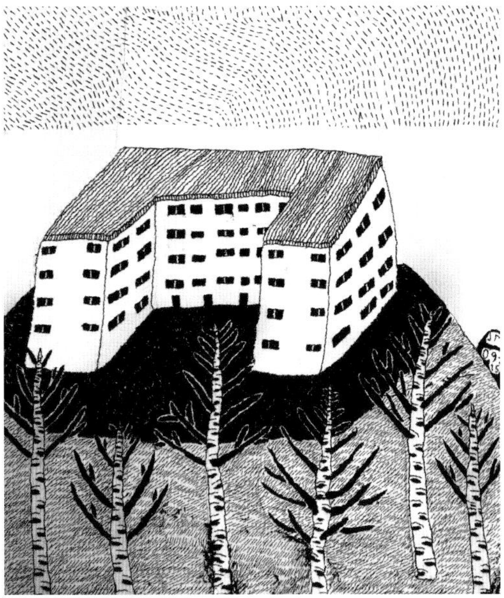

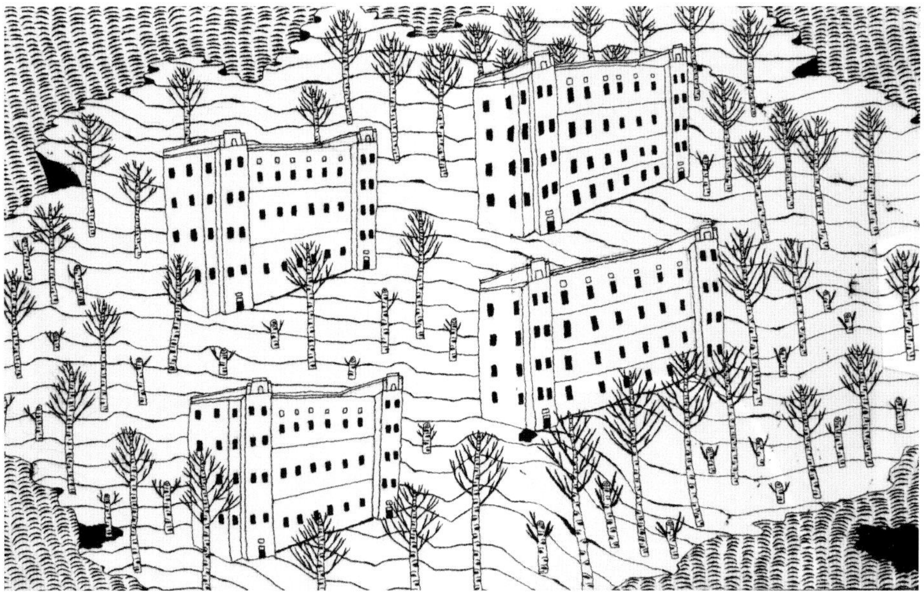

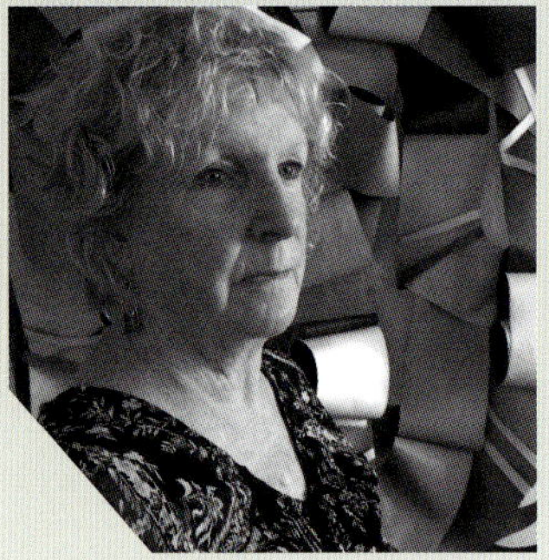

Kathy Miller

San Diego, California

As a child, I spent many hours observing my father, a draftsman, and grandfather, a carpenter, and learned at an early age how things were designed and constructed. My formal education includes studies in graphic arts and architecture.

I'm inspired and intrigued by the simplicity of form and the beauty of humble things found in the traditional crafts of Japan. *How to Wrap Five Eggs,* a book about Japanese packaging, influenced my approach to art.

My work takes its initial inspiration from line and may resolve in a profusion of ways: rhythmic threads of hand twisted text, the contours in a piece of fabric, the directional fall of horse hair, or the outline of a curved piece of metal. Working intuitively, I often twist, wrap, and weave to build on these principles. I strive to structure these elements as a poet arranges words, and to capture an ethereal and serenely quiet aesthetic—one that questions and challenges the viewer in ways of seeing and thinking.

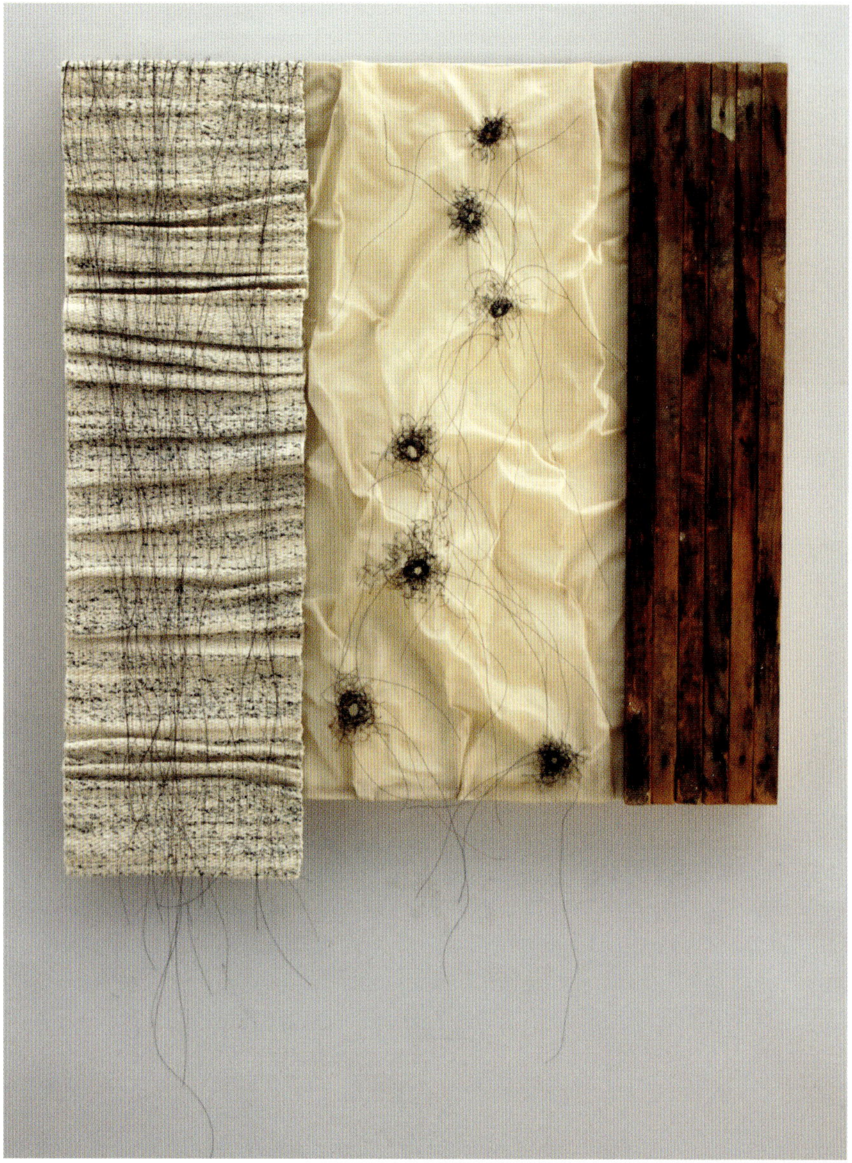

Words I Should Have Said. Handspun Japanese text woven into shifu, encaustic, organza, beeswax, and wood on panel. 20" × 18" × 2.4". 2012.

All art images courtesy of Gary Miller.

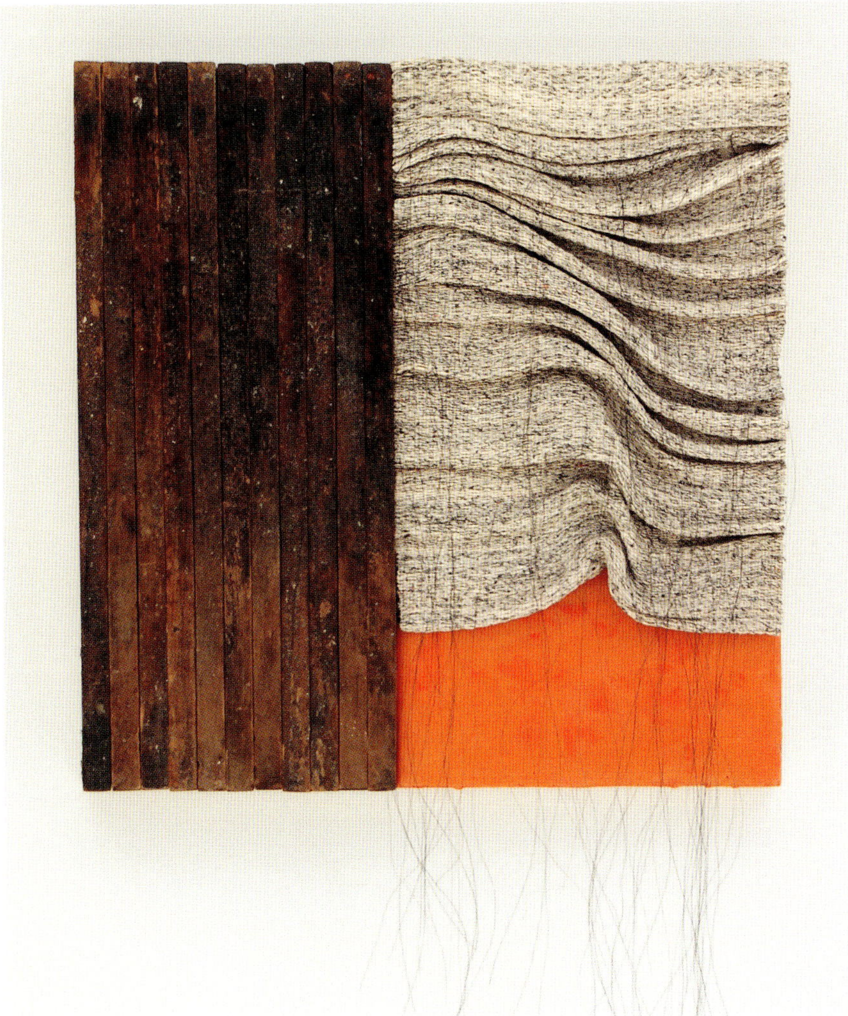

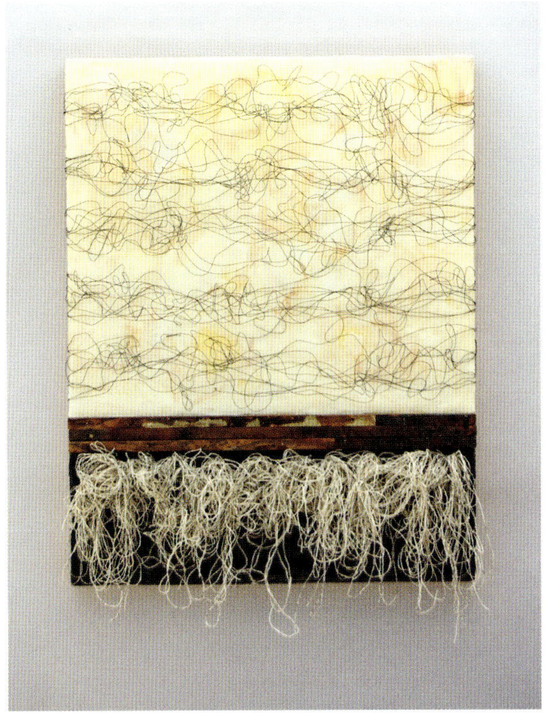

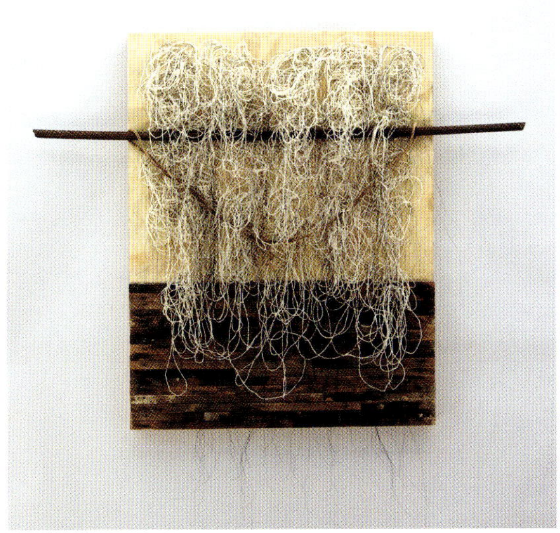

▲ *Contours.* Handspun Japanese text woven into shifu, encaustic, and wood on panel. 16" × 16" × 23". 2011.

◀ *Duality.* Handspun Japanese text, wire, paper, and found wood on panel. 30" × 24" × 3". 2011.

➤ *Stress Load.* Handspun Japanese text, encaustic, wire, and rubber on panel. 30" × 24" × 3". 2012.

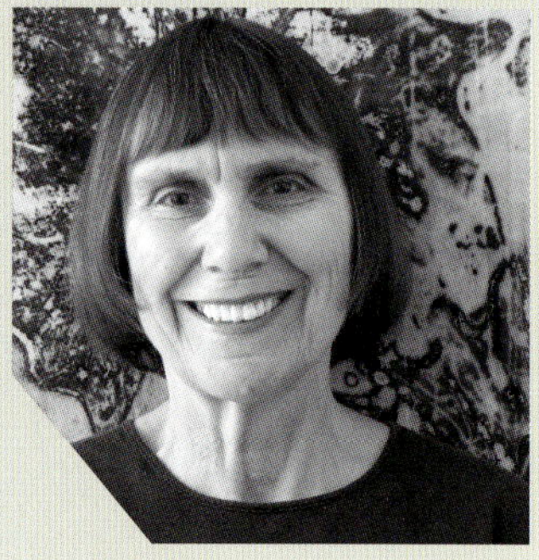

Dominie Nash

Bethesda, Maryland

I work in a collage-like manner, whether a particular piece is representational or abstract in nature. Of particular concern to me are the layers that result from overlapping forms, lines, and fabrics, creating a sense of mystery and depth. I hope that the viewer will want to return and will see more and different things at each viewing. The coloring and patterning of the fabric are essential elements in my attempt to achieve this goal; the uneven and serendipitous results contribute to the spontaneity and expressiveness of the work, even though the composition may be planned in advance.

I am a full-time fiber artist working in Washington, DC. My work is included in the collection of the Renwick Gallery of the Smithsonian Museum, International Monetary Fund, Braintree District Museum (England), Kaiser Permanente, and DC Art Bank. I have also received numerous awards in juried exhibits and have exhibited widely in solo and group exhibits, nationally and in Europe and Japan.

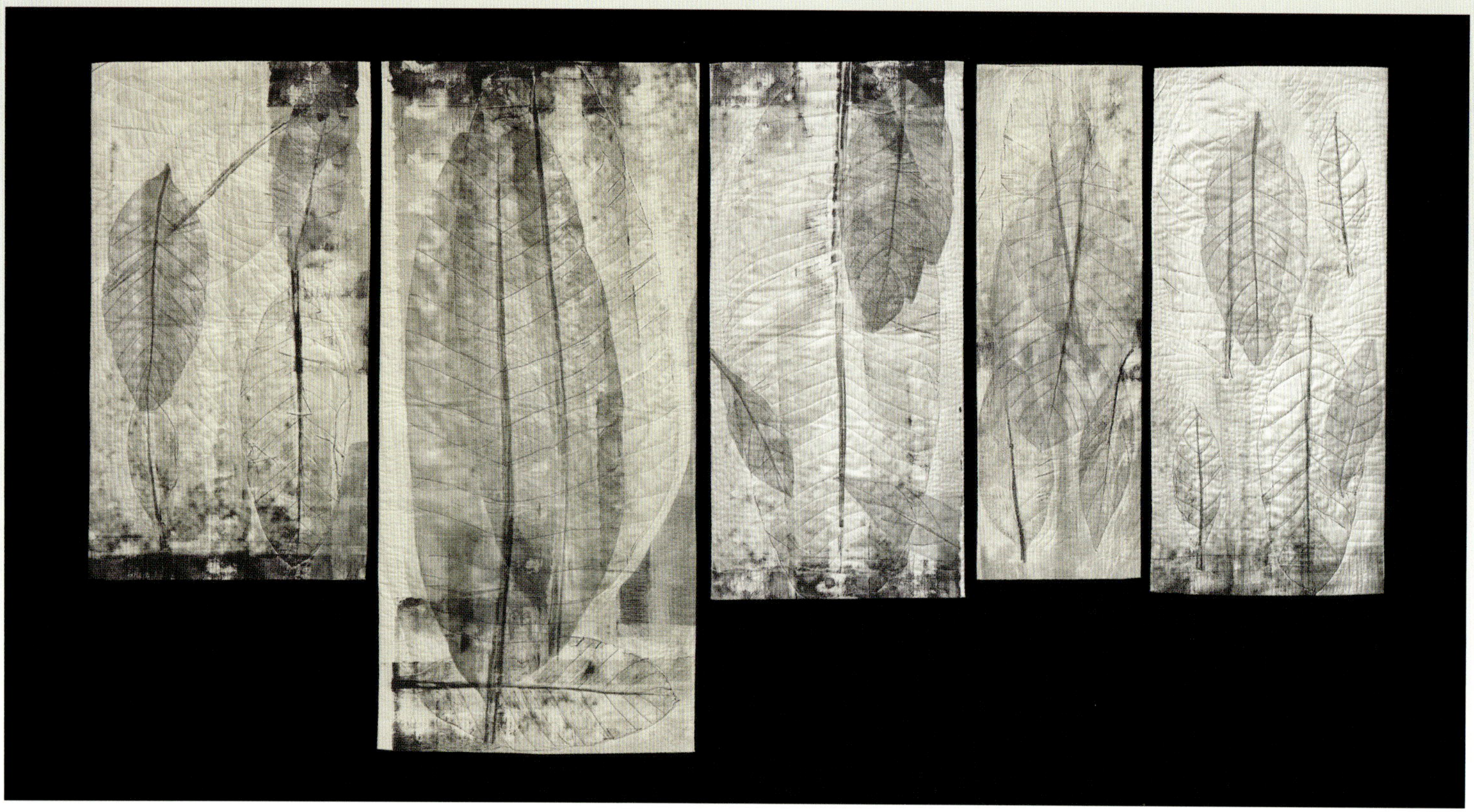

Big Leaf 38. Cotton and silk organza. 54" × 100". 2015.

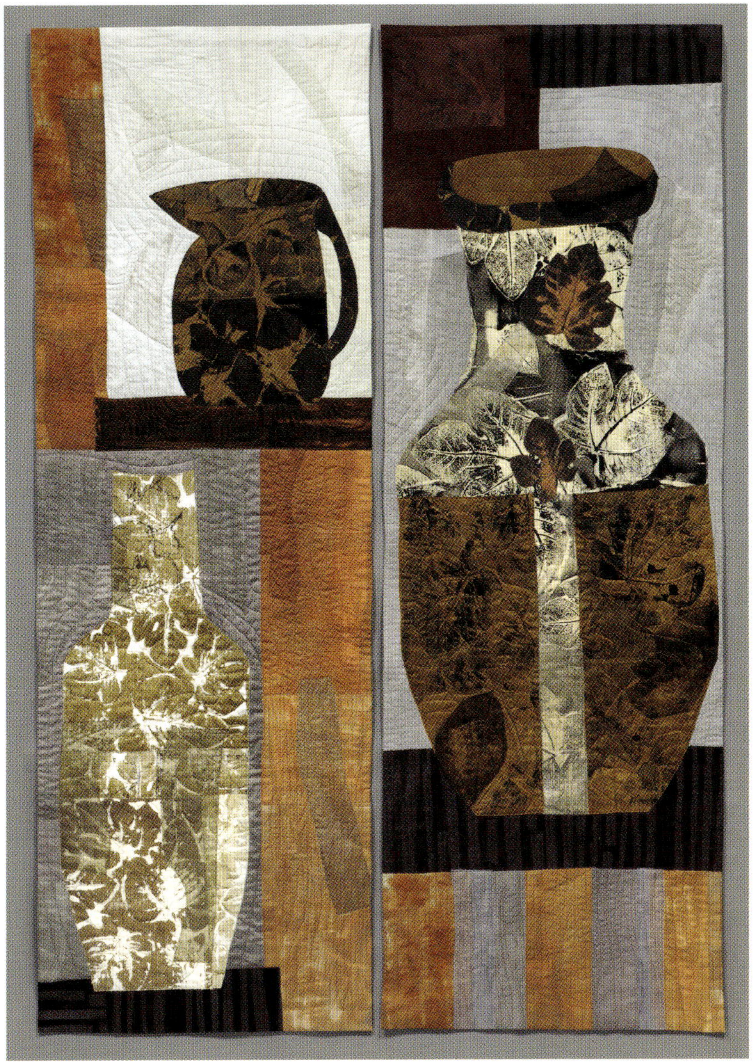

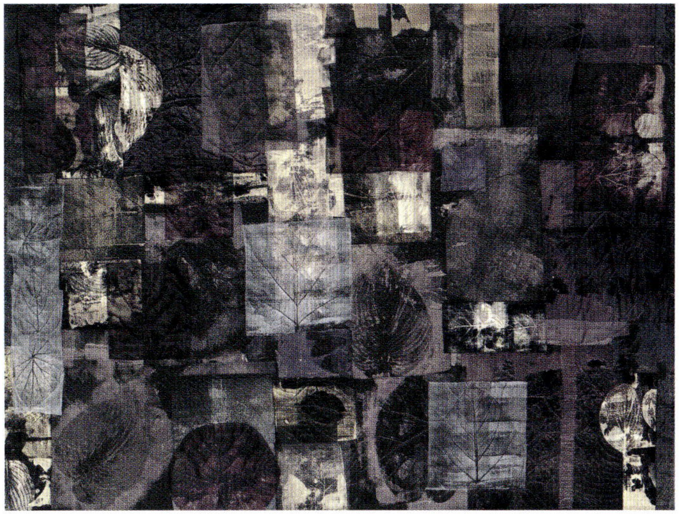

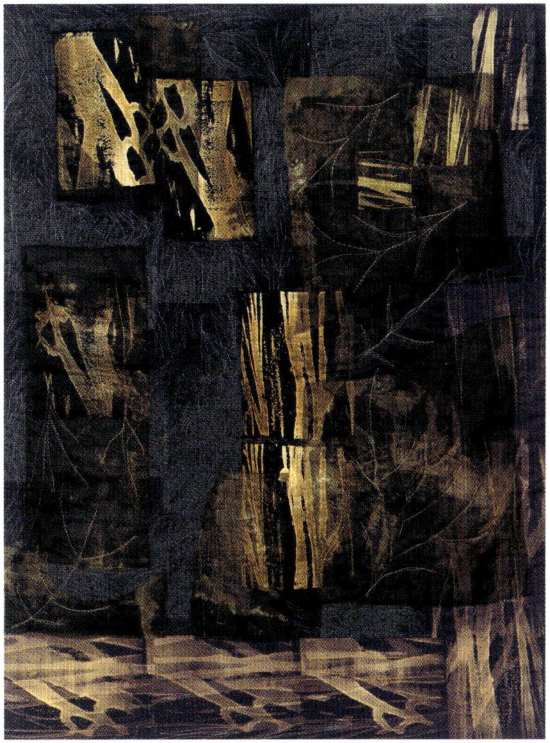

▲ *Stills from a Life 42.* Cotton and silk organza. 71" × 49". 2011.

➶ *Big Leaf 33.* Cotton and silk organza. 58" × 79". 2013.

➤ *Big Leaf 37.* Cotton and silk organza. 43" × 33". 2015.

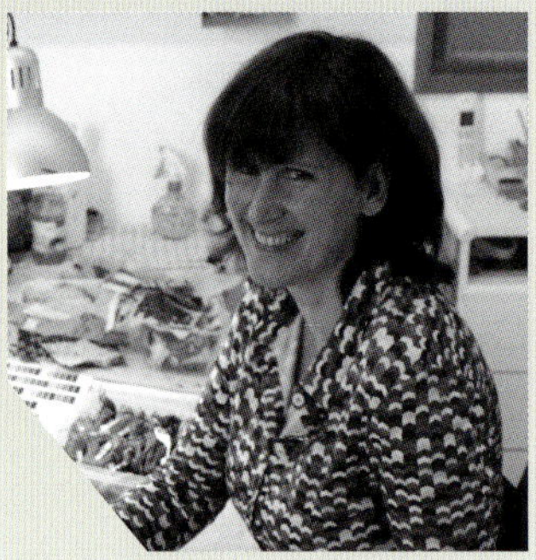

Pauline MM Nijenhuis

Zutphen, The Netherlands

I believe that the speed of our daily actions will increase only more in the future. The quality of life will change. We are forced to live faster and make decisions faster. I ask myself: Is this a good development?

As an artist, I want to investigate the price of this increasing speed. I am especially interested in the changing landscape, so I look for images where speed is shown—for example, the highway. I start my work from a moving car and take pictures of the highway landscape. The result will be different depending on the speed of the car. The images get more abstract the faster the car drives. The distortions in the picture give a different, new truth. It is not important if it is the correct visualization of the reality. I represent the risk of living in our fast time using the time-consuming technique of embroidery. Perhaps unconsciously I want to slow down the speed!

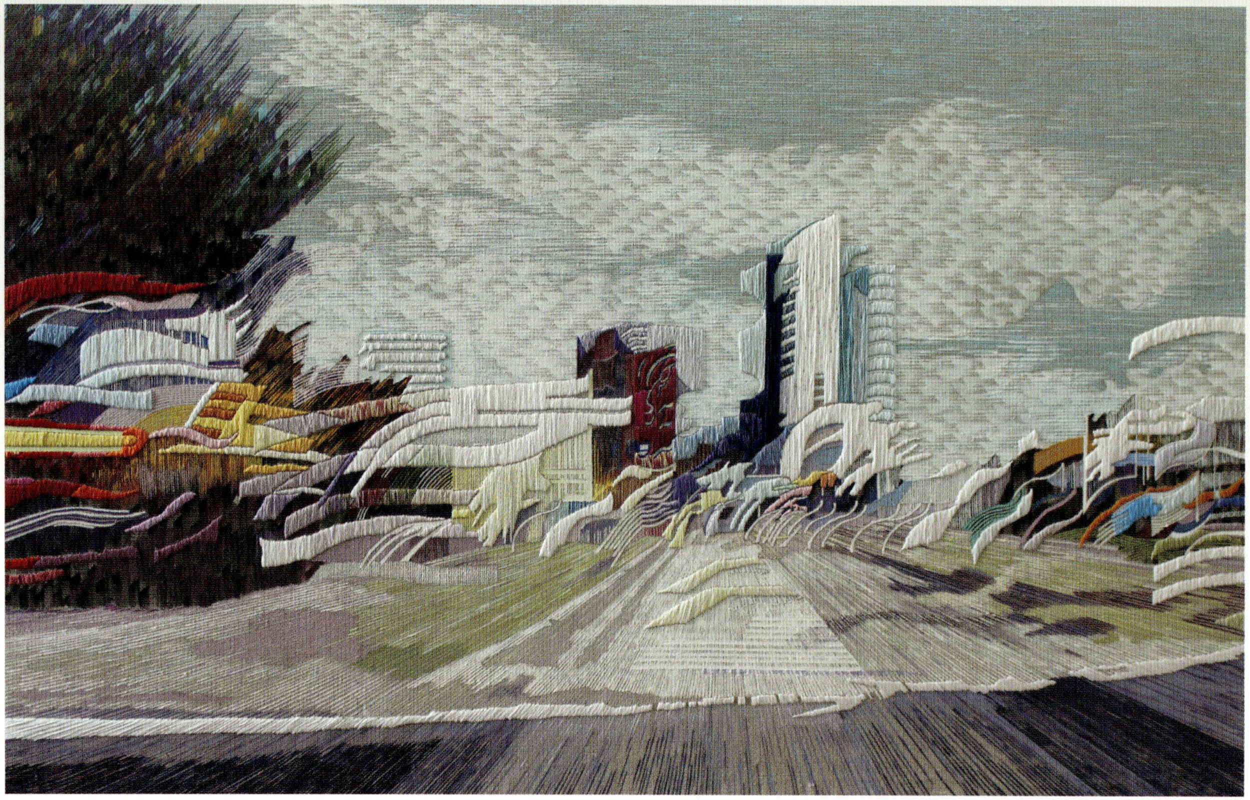

Suncity Fast Landscape. Acrylic and thread on untreated canvas. 27.6 " × 43.4". 2015.

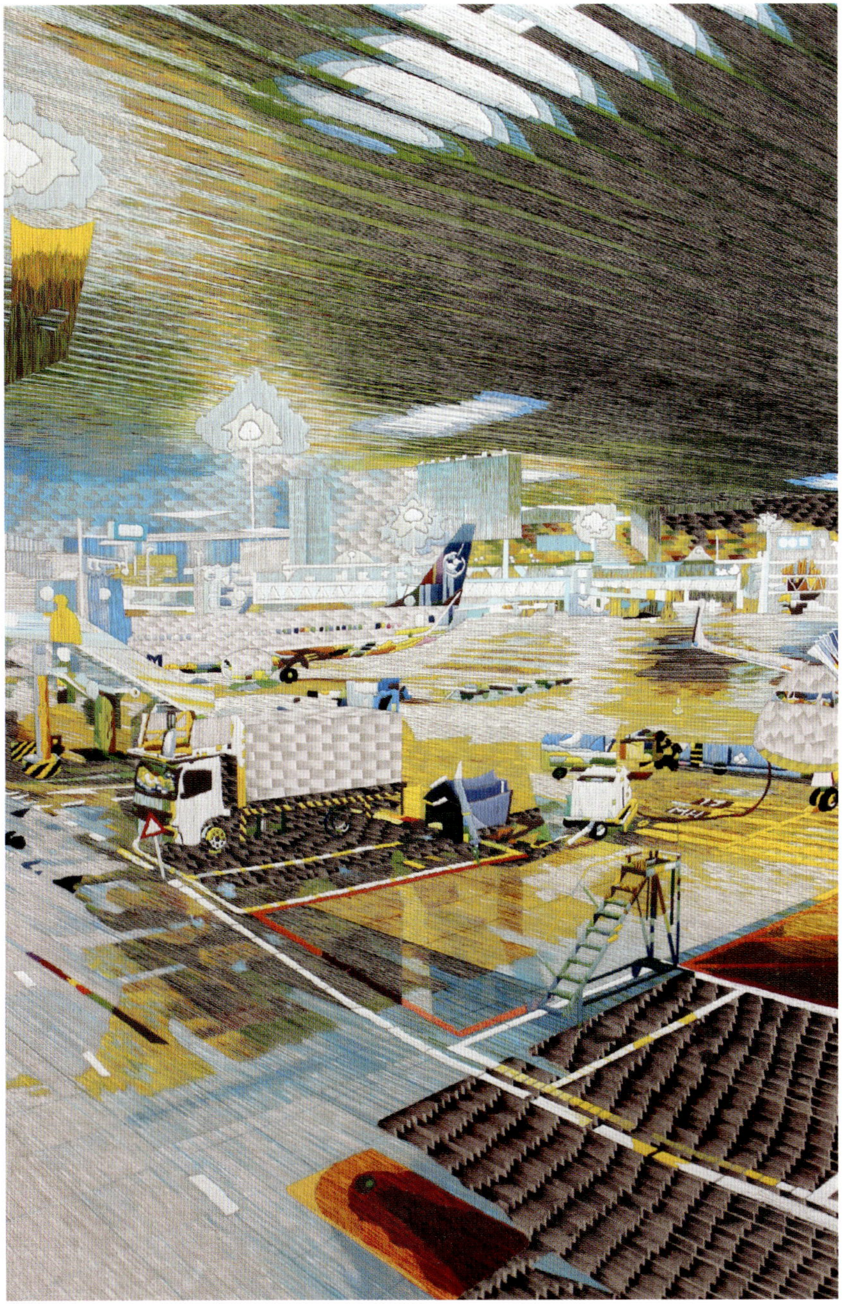

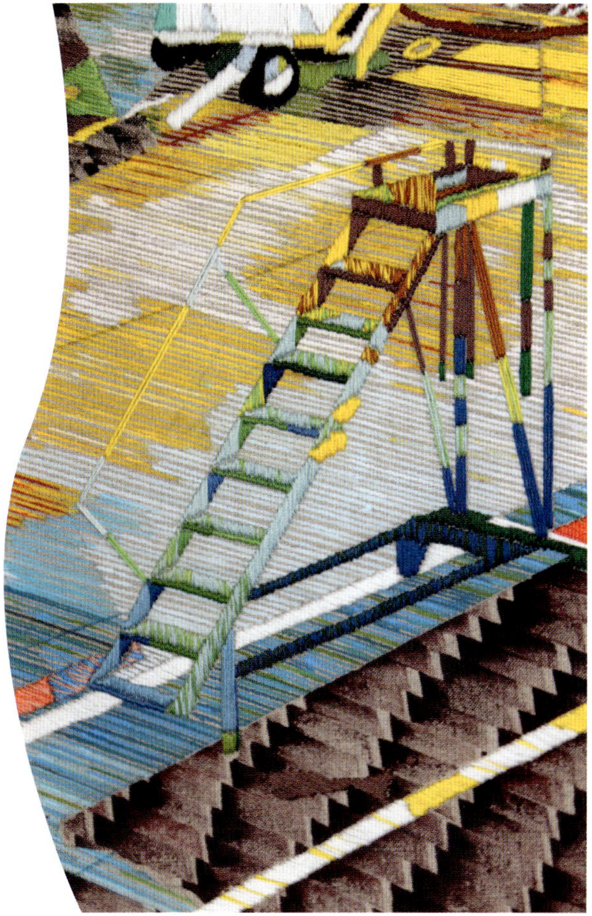

FastLandscape Airway. Acrylic and thread on untreated canvas. 59" × 39.4". 2015. | Detail

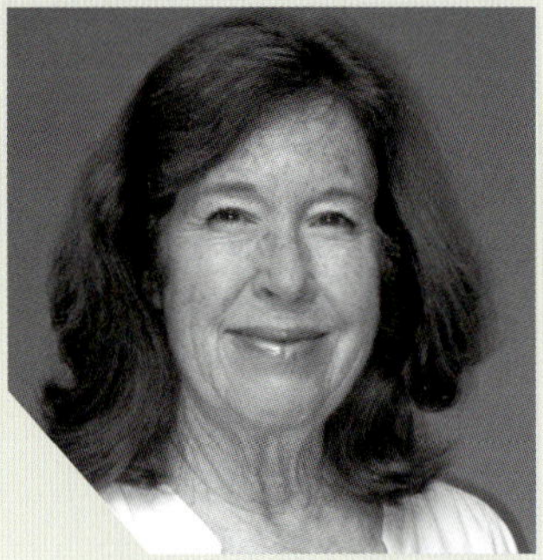

Courtesy of Ken Parker.

Sharron Parker

Wake Forest, North Carolina

The past and the uncertain future have been on my mind. I've been working with imagery of weathered, rusted surfaces (the past) and luminous, misty surfaces (the future?), using dyed, unspun wool and silk.

My technique comes from the past as well. Felting is believed to date to the Neolithic Age. Combing, layering, and working the fibers in hot water until they lock has an earthy, primal quality. Stitching felted pieces together and adding more yarns by hand is a quiet, meditative time. The process lets me respond to what I experience from the past and present, and from there create something new.

I hope felting becomes more widely known. To help, I try to exhibit my work and teach workshops in many different places, which gives me an excuse to travel too!

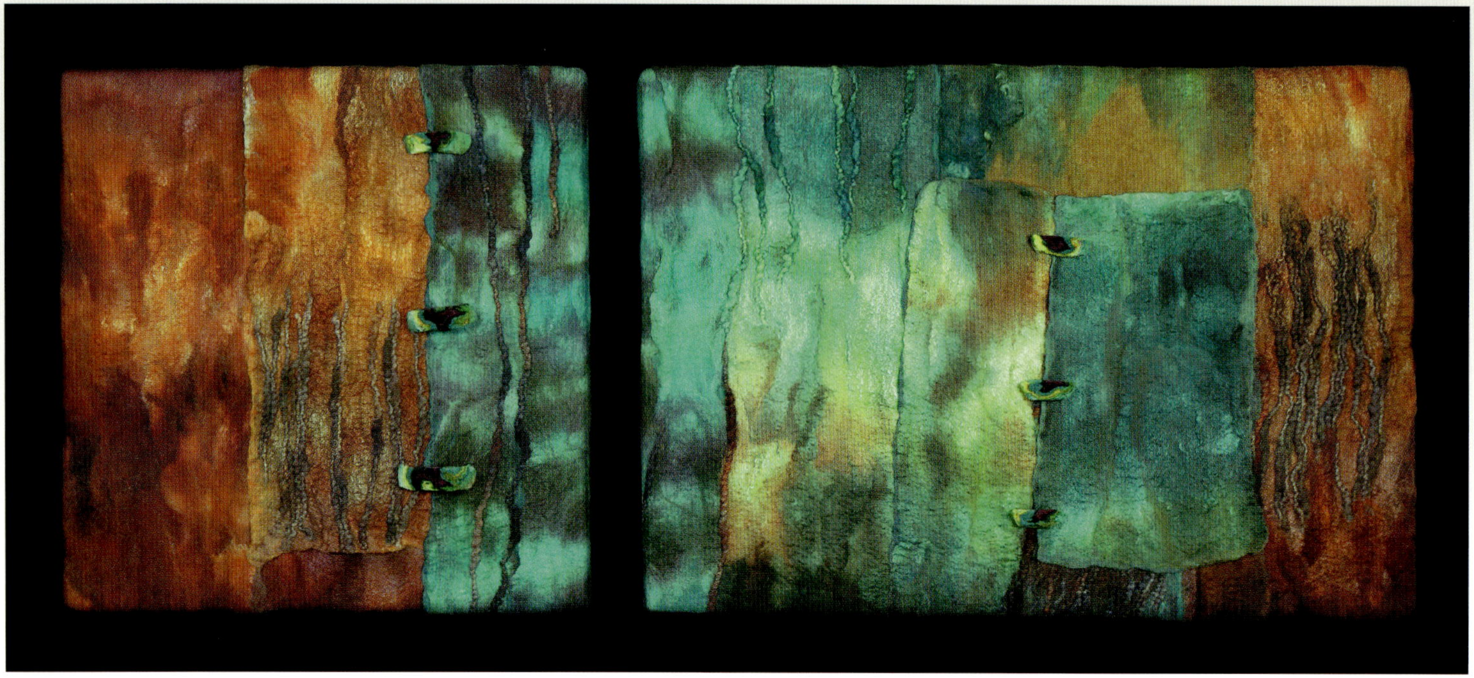

Prophecy (diptych). Unspun wool, silk, and yarns. 23" × 58". 2013.

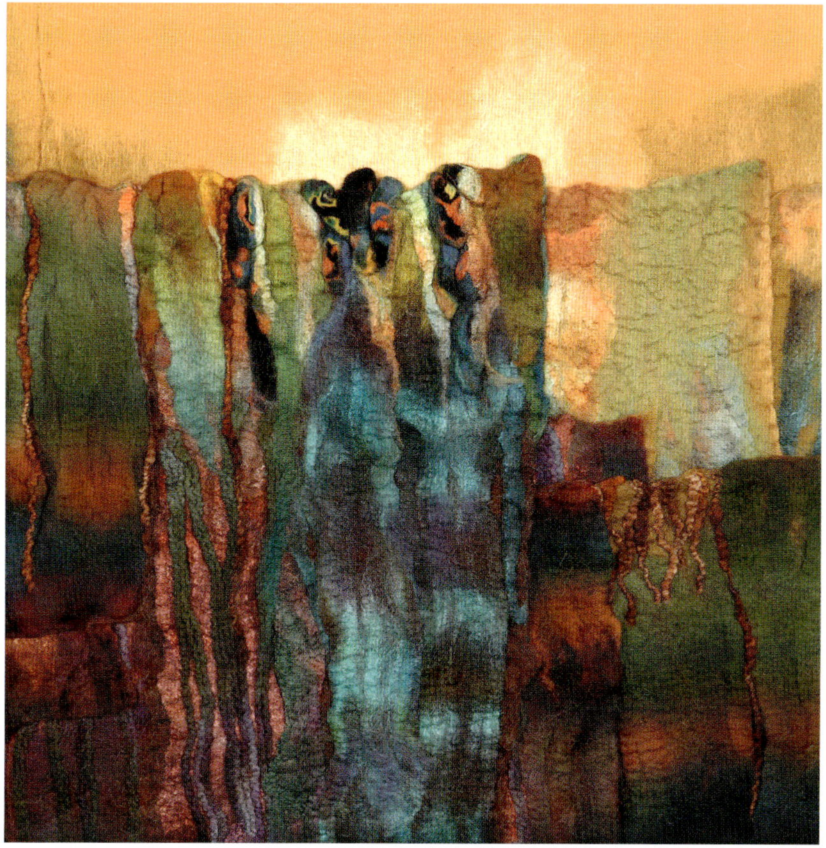

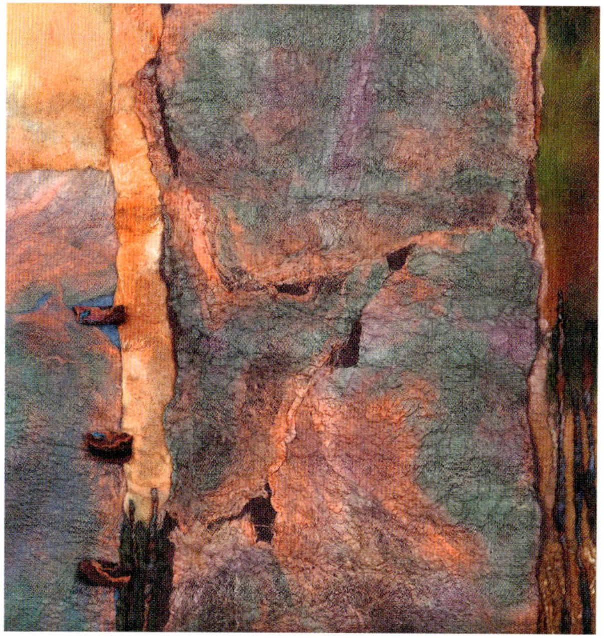

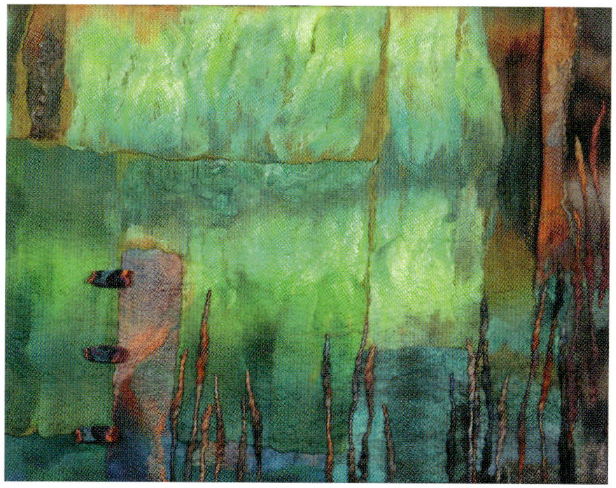

▲ *Prophecy III.* Unspun wool, silk, and yarns. 29" × 29". 2014.

◄ *Prophecy IV.* Unspun wool and silk. 23" × 24". 2014.

► *Prophecy II.* Unspun wool, silk, and yarns. 24" × 33". 2014.

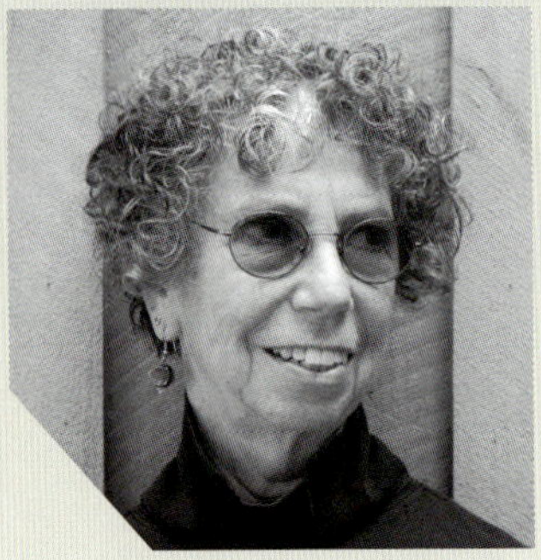

Judith Plotner

Gloversville, New York

This series is based on years of living and working in New York City. I don't live there now, so I am looking at it from a different perspective. I am intrigued by the need people have to make their mark, using blank walls as their canvas. Graffiti fascinates me. In this day and age, when handwriting is almost non-existent, scrawls on the wall abound. I walk around the city with my camera, taking photographs of construction, textures, and graffiti, which I then manipulate on my computer, and print, overprint, and monoprint to create my own artistic statement. I combine ideas and techniques on raw canvas, using color that speaks to me of rust, peeling paint, and crumbling walls.

My work has been included in many national exhibitions such as Quilt National and Visions, where I won awards, and Art Quilt Elements.

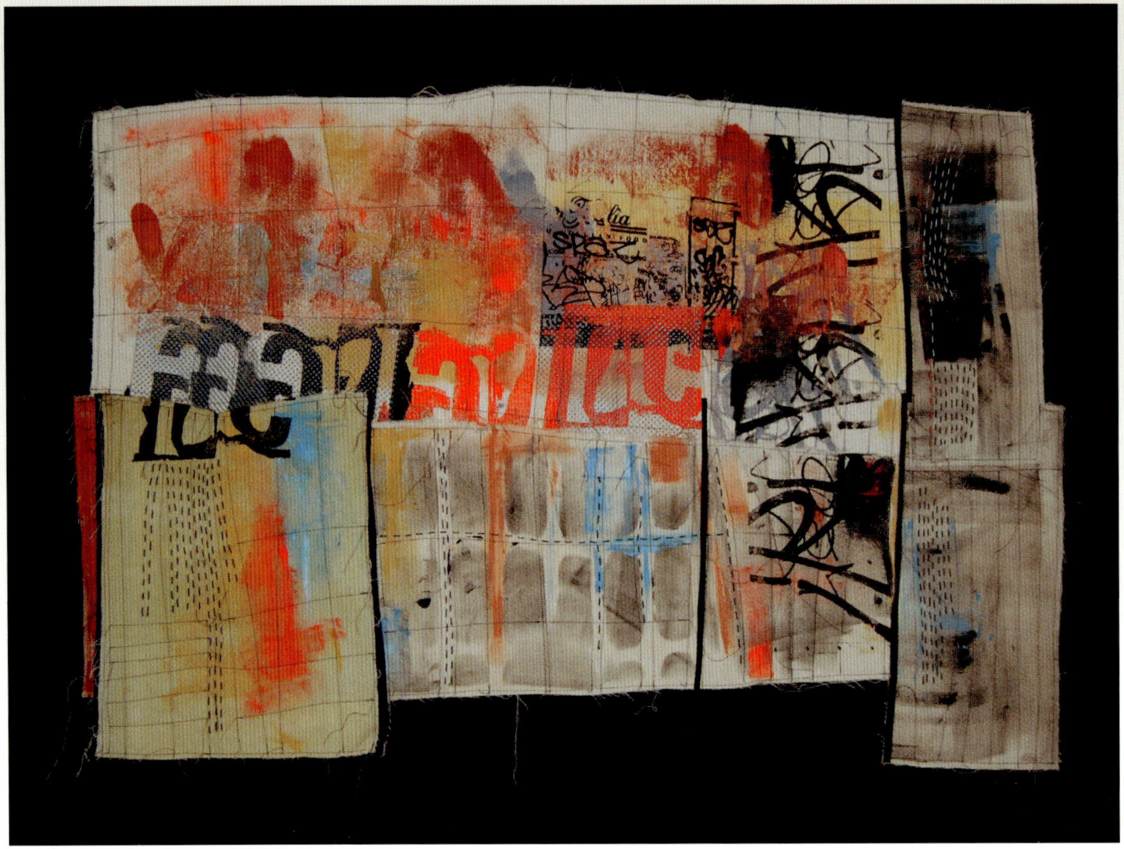

Letters from Broadway.
Canvas, paint, and thread.
29" × 44.5". 2014.

All images courtesy
of S. Plotner.

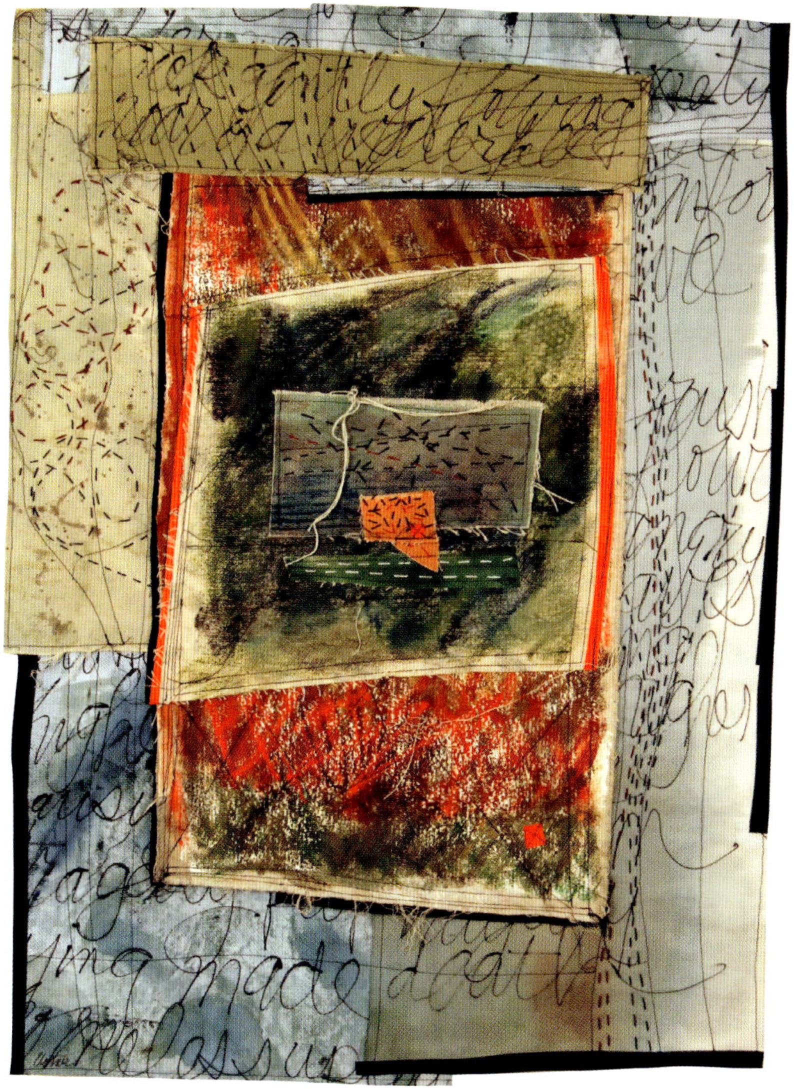

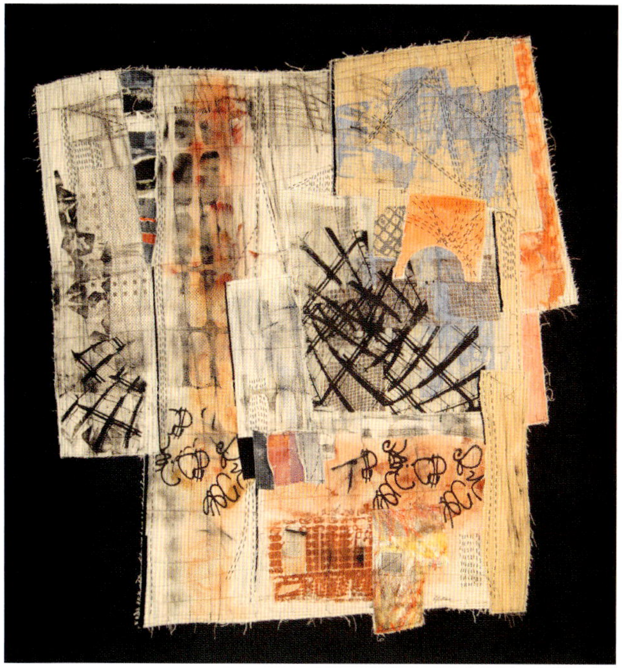

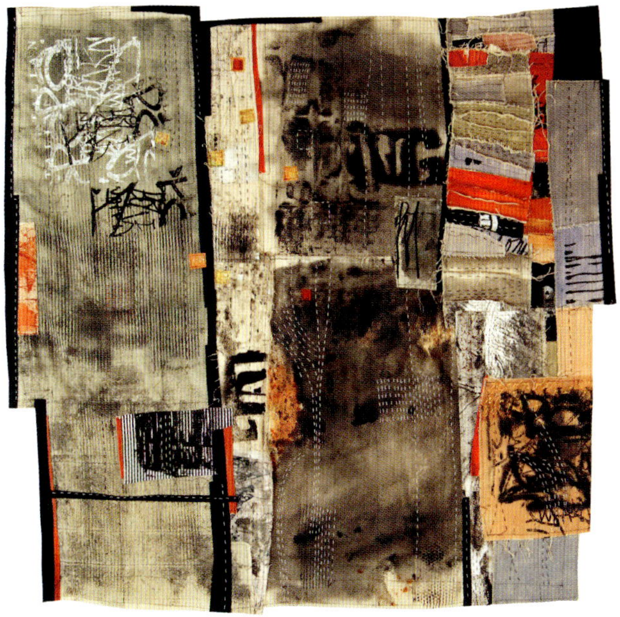

▲ *Aftermath.* Canvas, paint, and thread. 33" × 24". 2013.

◄ *Brooklyn Ensemble.* Canvas, paint, and thread. 46" × 41". 2015.

► *Urban Vibrations.* Canvas, paint, and thread. 43" × 29". 2014.

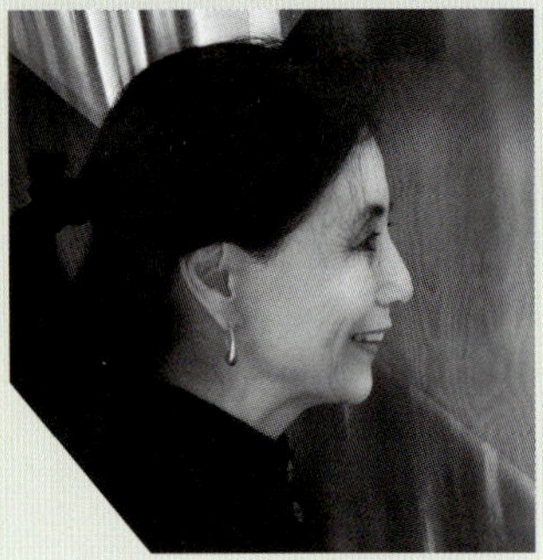

Junco Sato Pollack

Atlanta, Georgia

Having studied silk weaving and dyeing in Kyoto, Japan in the 1970s, I began hand-processing natural materials to achieve unique works of art. In the '80s while living in upstate New York, I raised silkworms to obtain sericin-rich reeled silk yarn with which to color and weave fabric and shaped it into three-dimensional sculpture while it was on the loom. Now, after forty years, I find myself returning to the pure craft practice of working with my hands and through nature. I harvest wild kudzu vines in the fields of the North Georgia mountains in order to naturally process fibers fine enough to weave, make paper, then create two- and three-dimensional art.

After receiving a MFA in textile design, I focused on working with iridescent and metallic silk and polyester organza, heat-compressing through an industrial heat-roller press and applying colors through digital imaging and printing processes known as dye-sublimation. The transparent and atmospheric dispersed colors imprinted by heat in the molecular structures of the fibers appear iridescent and luminous over the multi-layered, translucent, three-dimensional folds of fabrics.

My most recent series since 2006 involves hand-stitching as a metaphor for walking meditation, known as *kinhin* in Zen Buddhism. Over the layered and pieced together fragments, metallic threads that accumulated stitch by stitch as traces of internalized meditation walks over time create an expansive field of meditative awareness into a series of mandalas.

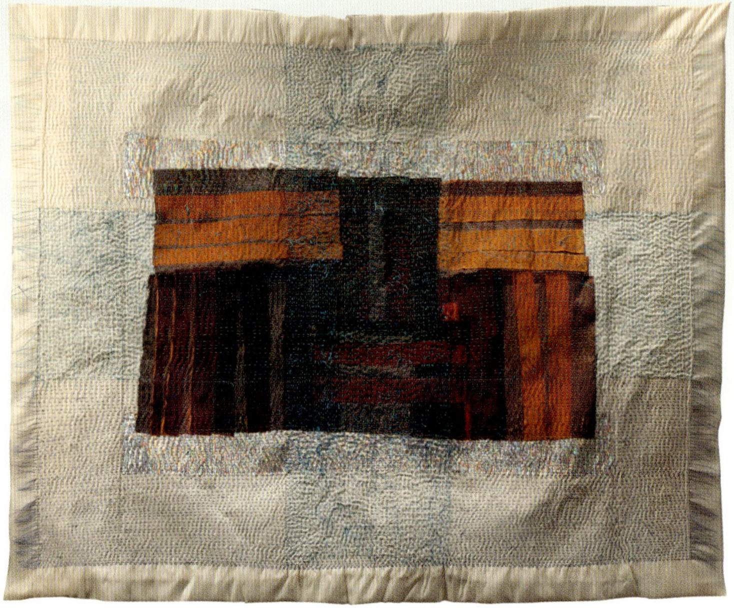

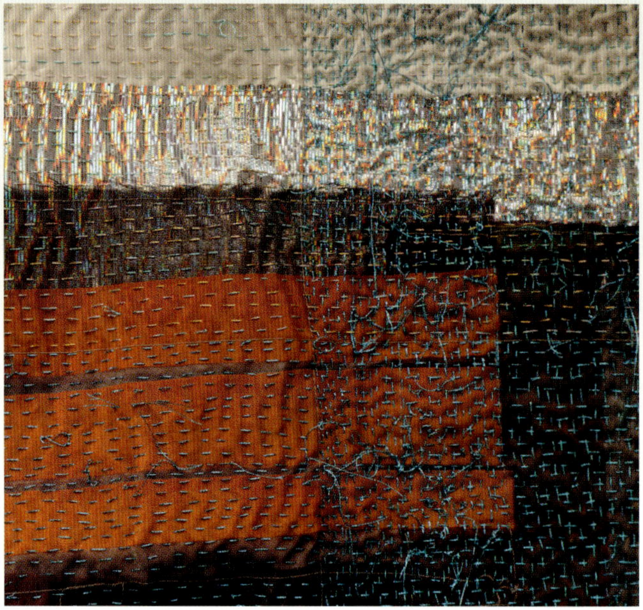

Kinhin6 Nirvana. Metallic threads stitched on layered polyester organza. 36" × 45". | Detail

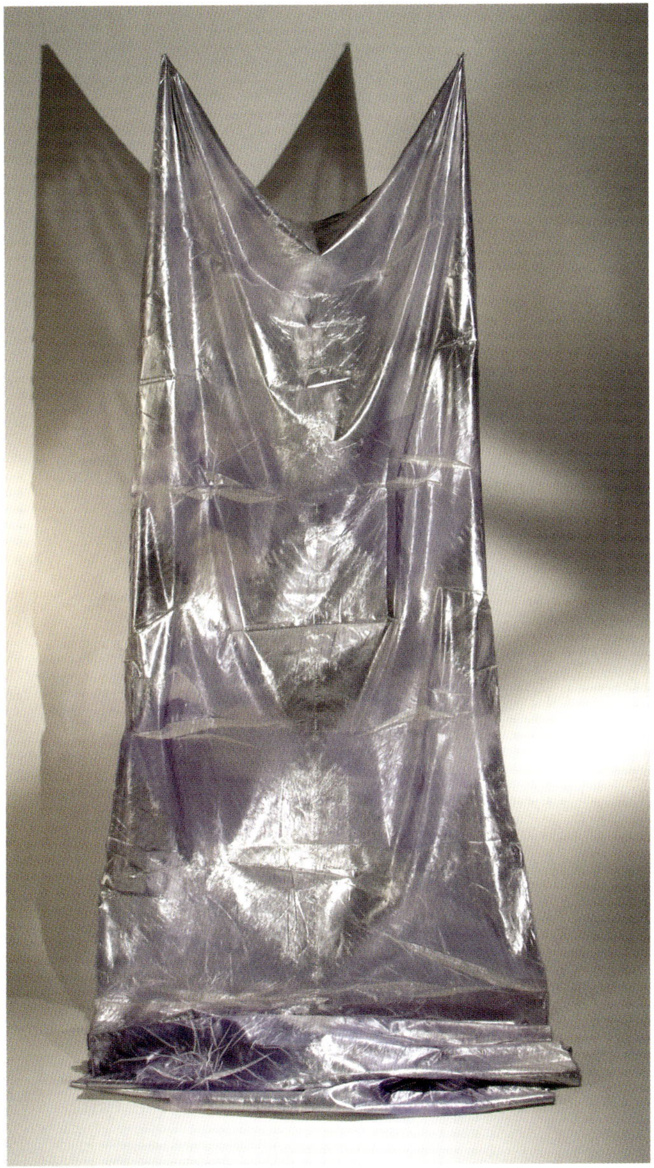

Sky-Clouds-Wind. Disperse dye printed on voided metallic polyester organza. 180" × 65" suspended.

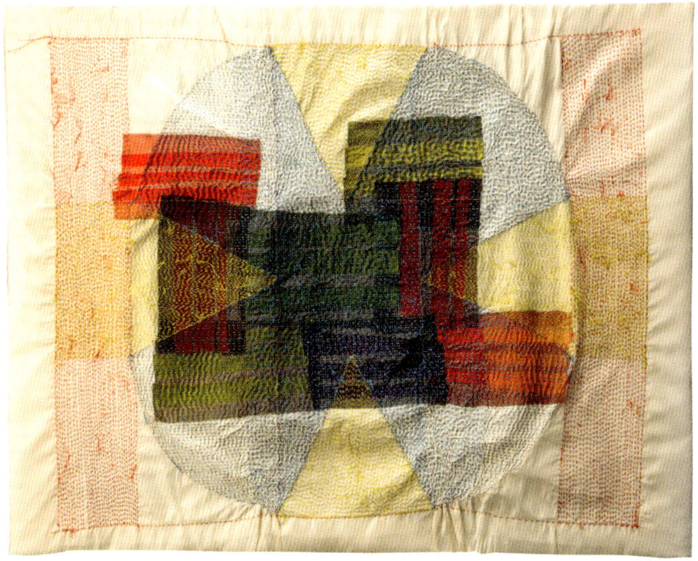

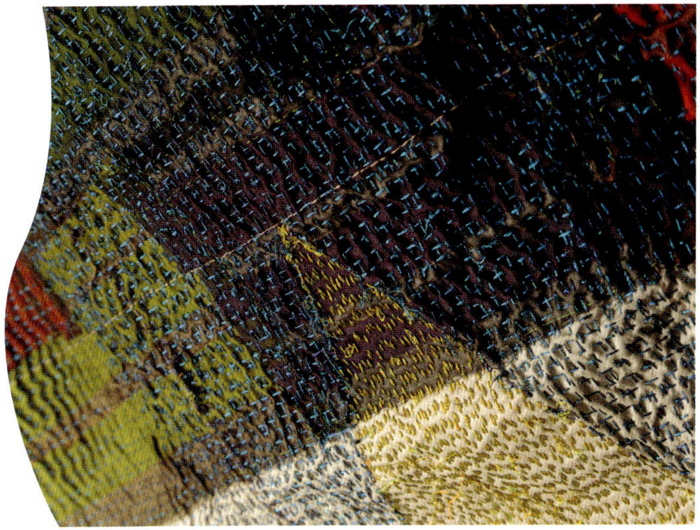

Kinhin5 Samadhi. Metallic threads stitched on layered polyester organza. 36" × 45". | Detail

All images are courtesy of Departure 2015.

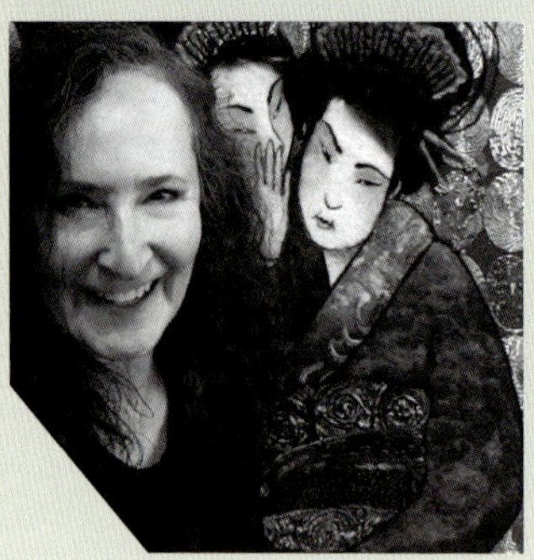

Stacy Polson

Portland, Oregon

My affair with needle-felting began the day I tried to re-create a seventeenth century Japanese woodcut using wool. I loved the clashing kimonos and cartoon-like faces and thought it might be fun to give them a modern twist. That was eight years and many "wool paintings" ago. These days every nook and cranny of my workroom is overflowing with rainbows of wool—every color and texture you can imagine.

A self-taught artist, I've used almost every medium there is, but I enjoy needle-felting for its versatility and texture. All of my pieces are felted by hand, sometimes gently poking with a single fragile needle and other times pounding the canvas with medieval-looking tools.

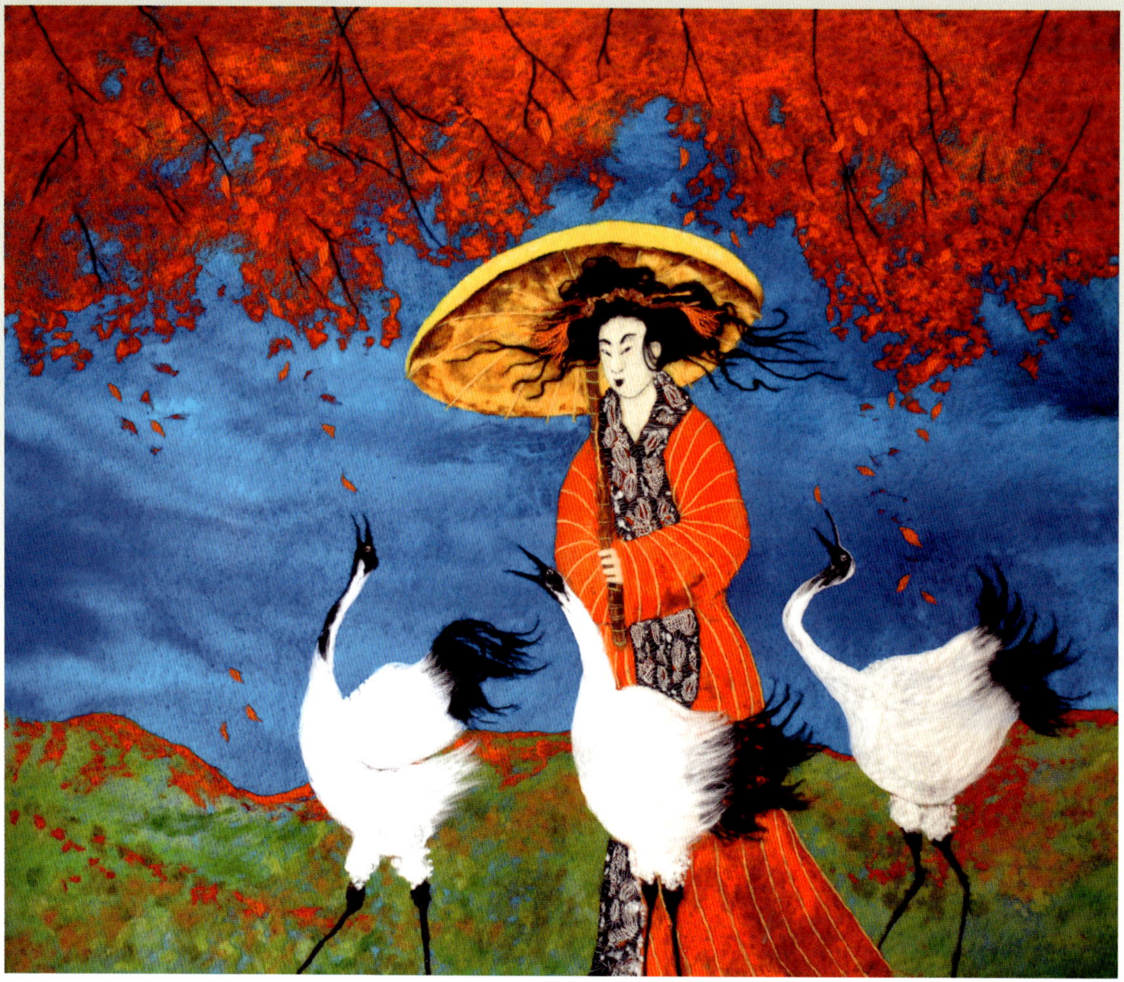

The Dancing Cranes.
Hand needle felted using wool, thread, and fabric. 50" × 46". 2015.

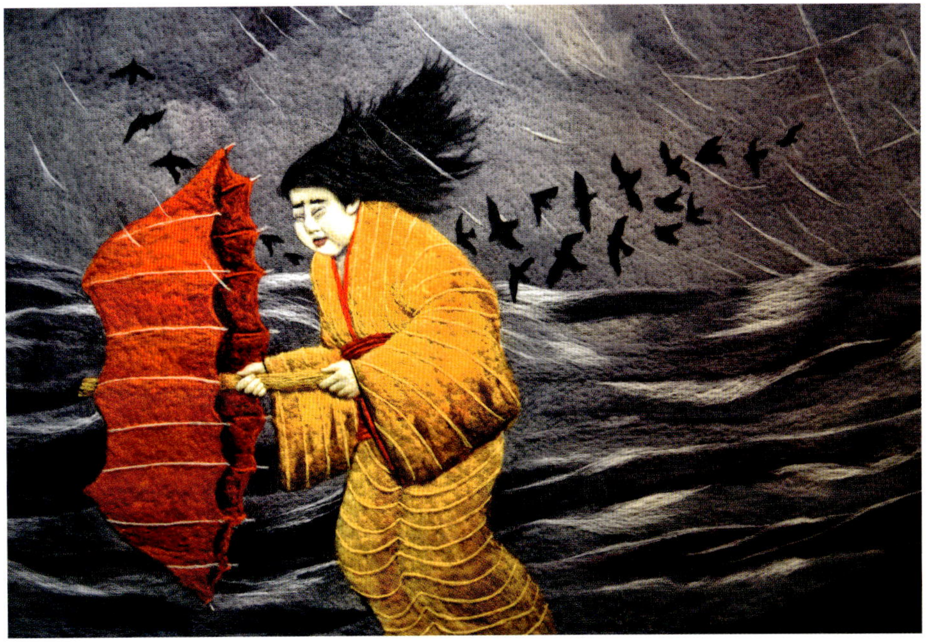

➤ *An Inconvenient Day.*
Hand needle felted using wool.
38" × 50". 2015.

▼ *The Three Aunts.*
Hand needle felted using wool, thread, and fabric. 38" × 50". 2014.

➤ *The Seagull.*
Hand needle felted using wool, thread, and fabric. 18" × 24". 2012.

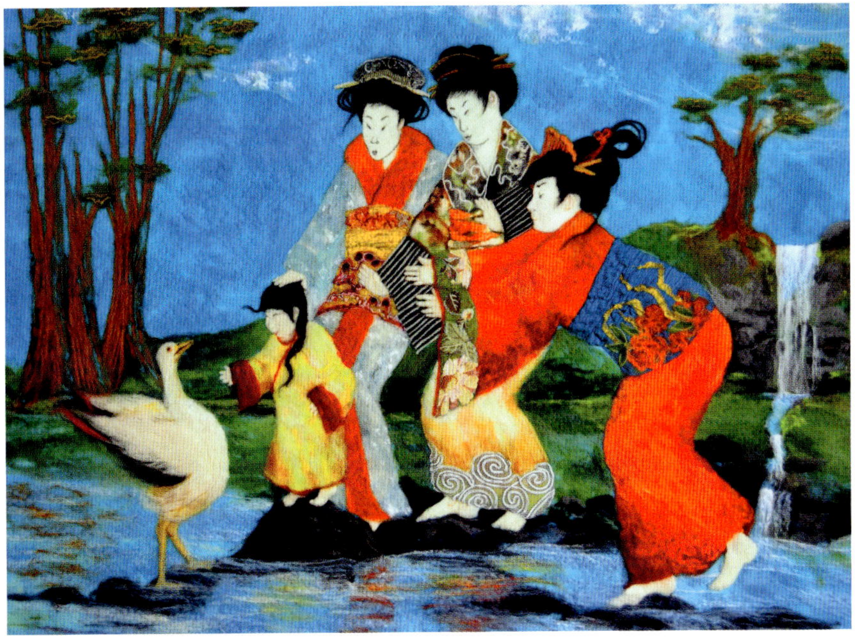

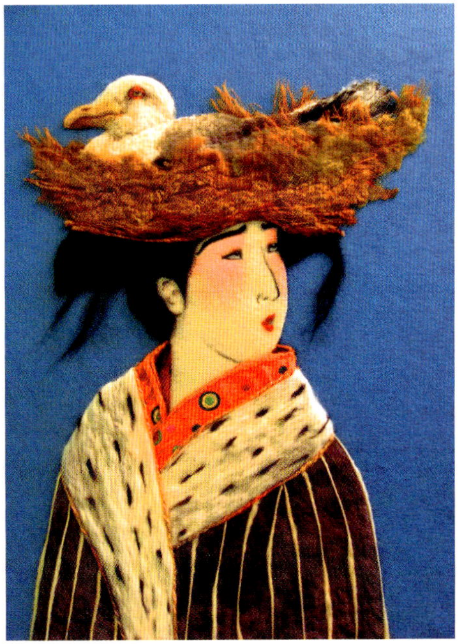

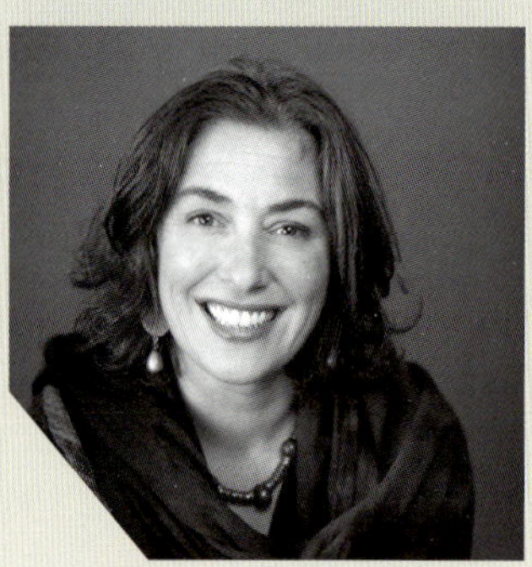

Courtesy of Camilla Canlan Photography.

Amy Putansu

Waynesville, North Carolina

I am a hand-weaver, an artist, and an educator. My passion for textiles has only deepened over time as I have had the opportunity to teach students, learn from my mentors, research, and develop my work. My focus has been making elegant cloth using traditional hand-weaving methods. Common threads stretch through all of my work, such as a reverence for material and a propensity for minimalist aesthetic. I find power in fields of subtlety and am interested in the challenge of restraint.

As I meditate on the geography of the northern seacoast, my place of origin, I recall scenes of great distance, often gray with clouds or fog, and rugged, spare beauty. The nature of that setting speaks to me as something that is authentic and true, and unadulterated. I reference this and related themes in my current work.

My technical focus is a weaving technique called ondulé. Threads are maneuvered out of the strict grid and into undulating waves on a traditional floor loom using specialized tools. One of the many reasons ondulé has captured my attention is the ever-present waves within the very interlacement of the cloth that represent my connection to the sea and the shore.

My work has been included in international juried exhibitions including the Surface Design Association's *Materialities: Contemporary Textile Arts* and *Contemporary Art of Shibori and Ikat* in Hangzhou, China. In 2015, The China National Silk Museum purchased my *Diptych* for its permanent collection.

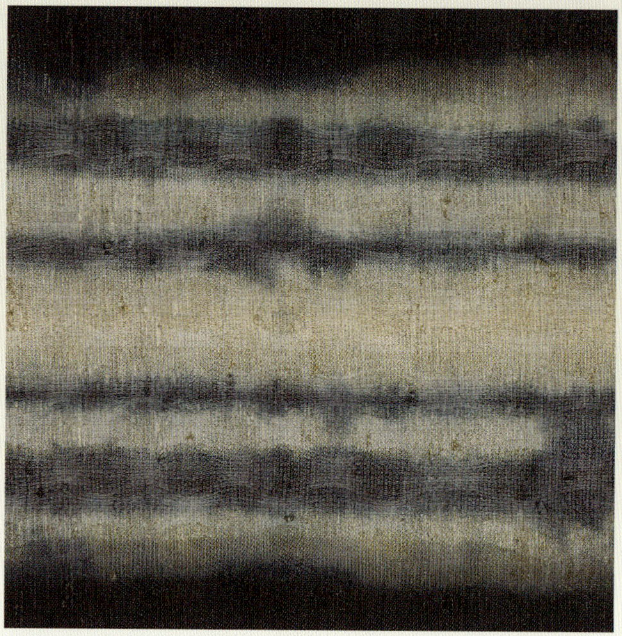

Beacon. Hand woven in ondulé technique, hand dyed and metallic "melt-off" using shibori resist techniques in linen, gold lame, and polyester. 28.75" × 29" × 1.5". 2015.

➤ *Horizon*. Hand woven in ondulé technique, with hand painted threads in cotton, rayon, and metallic. 35" × 35" × 1.5". 2014.

All art photographs by Steve Mann.

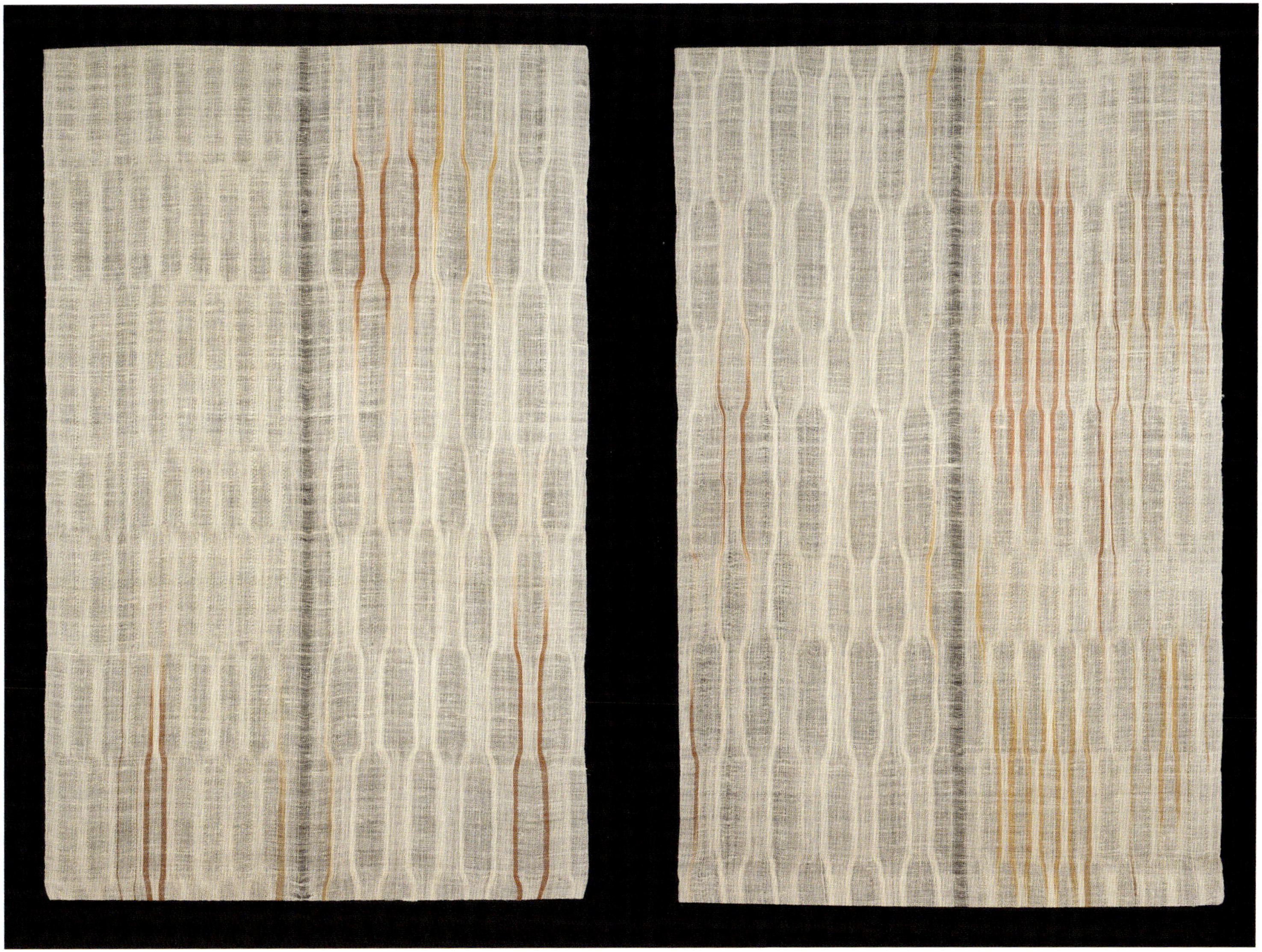

Diptych. Hand woven silk in ondulé technique, resist dyed with madder, black walnut, and Osage orange natural dyes. 58" × 80". 2009.

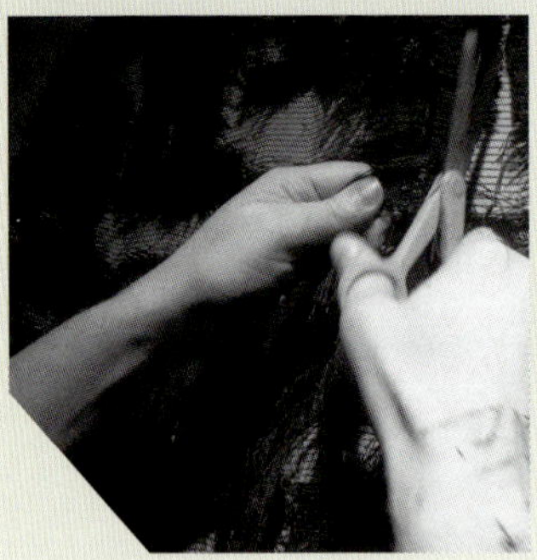

The making of woven cloth is at the core of my artistic practice. In the textiles I produce, there is a consistency of influences and a multilayered or mosaic-like approach to research. As I weave my body around the halls of museums, or my eyes around architectural references or my local surroundings, the layering of these influences starts to overlap and underlap, touch, and diverge. Weaving together a sort of atlas of influence and memory, my aim is to demonstrate the evocative power of images which occur/recur, to expose their impact and their nature, to explain how they function and how they infect one another.

I have taught, lectured, offered workshops, and held a number of fellowships and residencies. My work has earned numerous prizes and is in the permanent collection of the Cleveland Museum of Art.

Michael Radyk

Kutztown, Pennsylvania

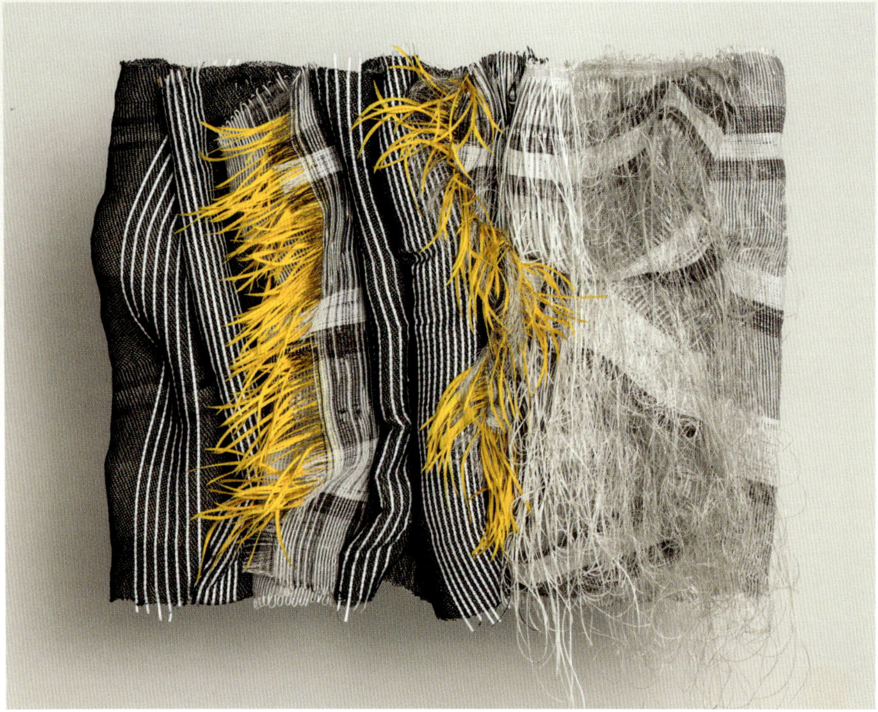

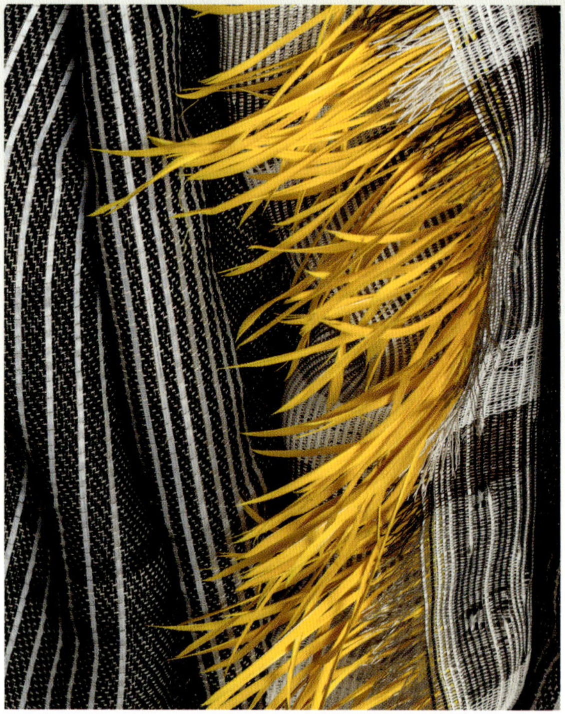

Corduroy #1. Vinyl-coated recycled polyester, repurposed plastic tape, feathers, glass fiber, and recycled polyester. 32" × 36" × 6". 2013. | Detail

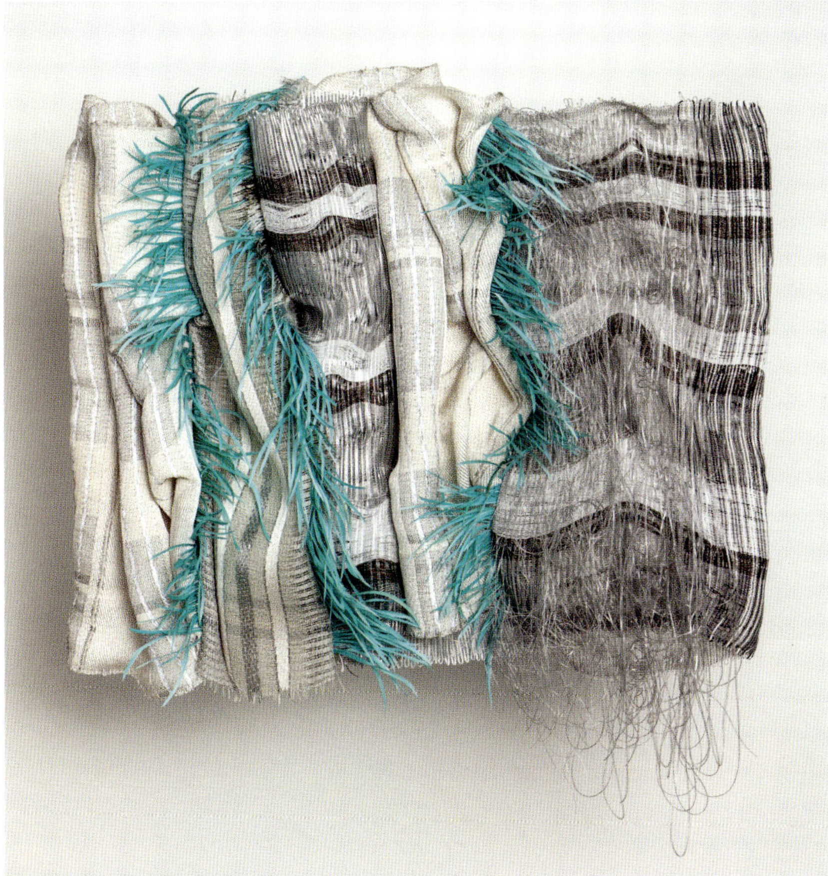

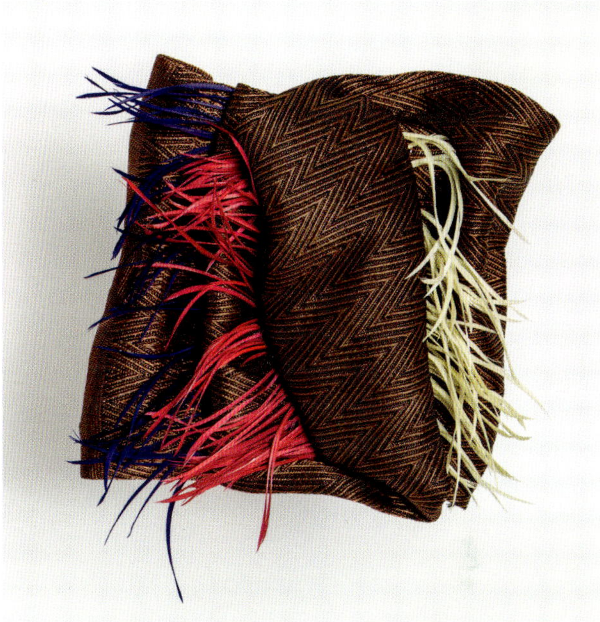

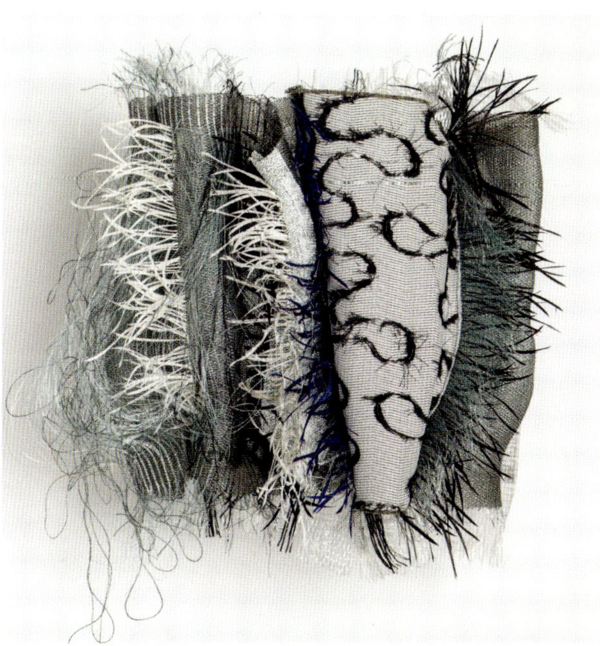

▲ *Corduroy #2.* Vinyl-coated recycled polyester, repurposed plastic tape, feathers, glass fiber, and recycled polyester. 32" × 36" × 6". 2013.

◄ *Drift.* Vinyl-coated recycled polyester, repurposed plastic tape, feathers, and recycled polyester. 12" × 12" × 6". 2014.

► *Sow Sow.* Vinyl-coated recycled polyester, repurposed plastic tape, feathers, glass fiber, recycled polyester, milk fiber, and fique. 28" × 30" × 10". 2015.

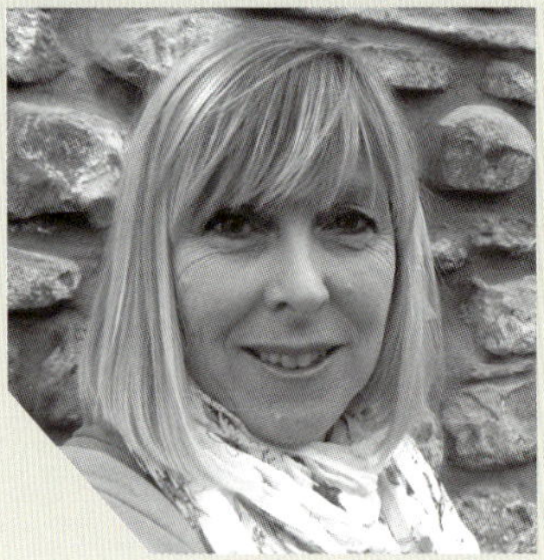

Shelley Rhodes

Burton in Kendal, Lancashire, England

My mixed media work combines paper, drawings, photographs, and prints with painted and dyed fabric. I am often drawn to surfaces that have been affected by aging, corrosion, and weathering. I particularly love the coast and have been recording, gathering, collecting, and drawing during my walks along the shoreline. Rock pools, reeds, grasses and pebbles, tide lines, and marks left in the sand are all sources of inspiration for mark making, drawing, and printmaking.

Fragmentation and reconstruction are central to my work. I usually work in layers by creating then obscuring, revealing then hiding, constantly adding and subtracting elements. Handling and manipulating the fabric and paper helps to soften the image and color and to break the surface down. I select, rearrange, and assemble small elements to make a new whole, which I may join using stitch, wire, tape, pins, tacks, nails, metal, or wax. Layers are scratched, rubbed, and distressed to reveal marks and colors beneath the surface.

I run workshops from my own studio and travel to teach throughout the United Kingdom and abroad.

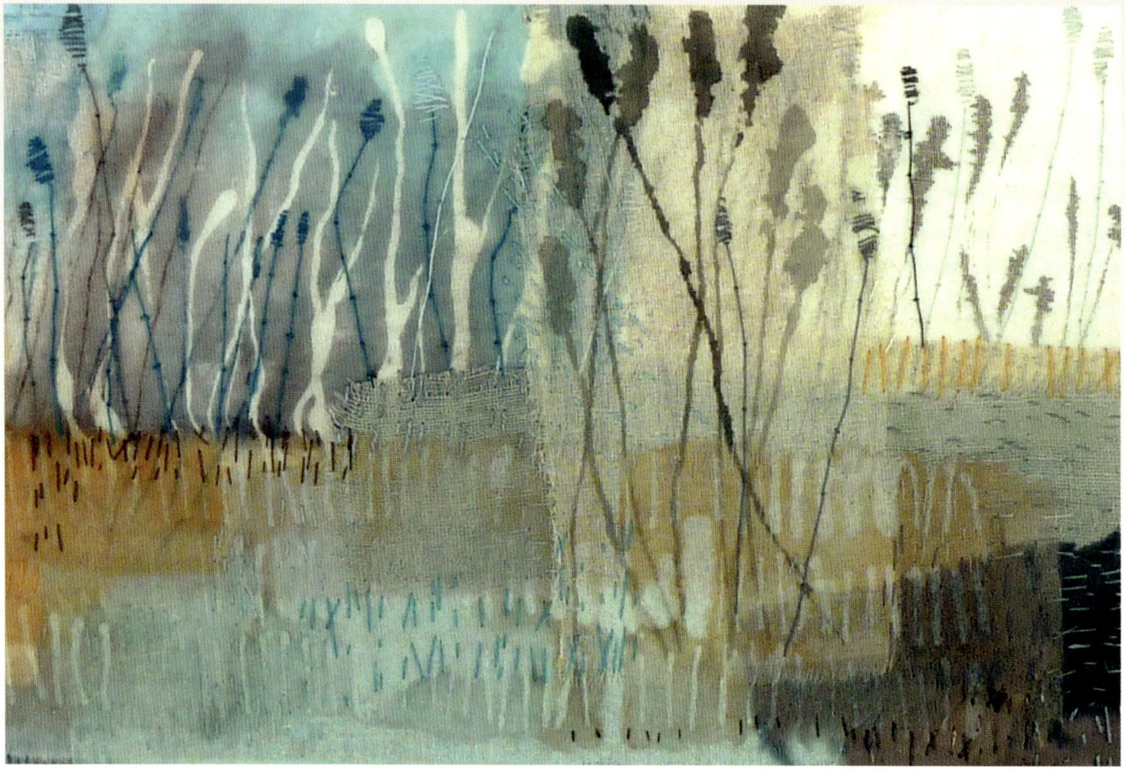

Shoreline Series (detail). Fabric and stitch. Four works, each 5.9" × 39.4". 2015.

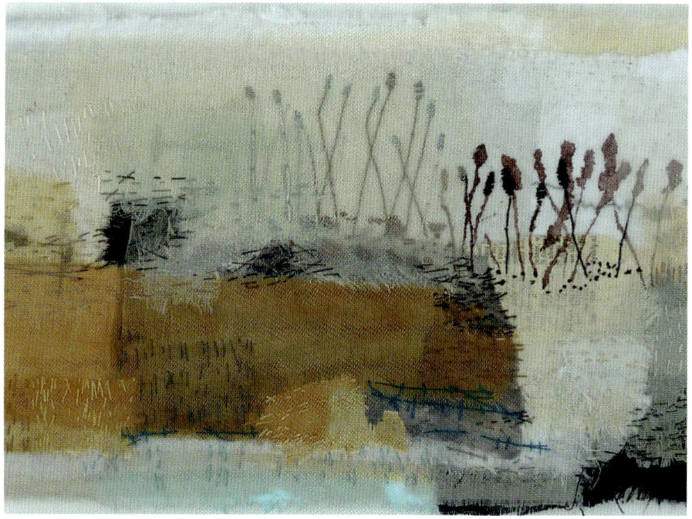

Shoreline Series 5.9" × 39.4". 2015.

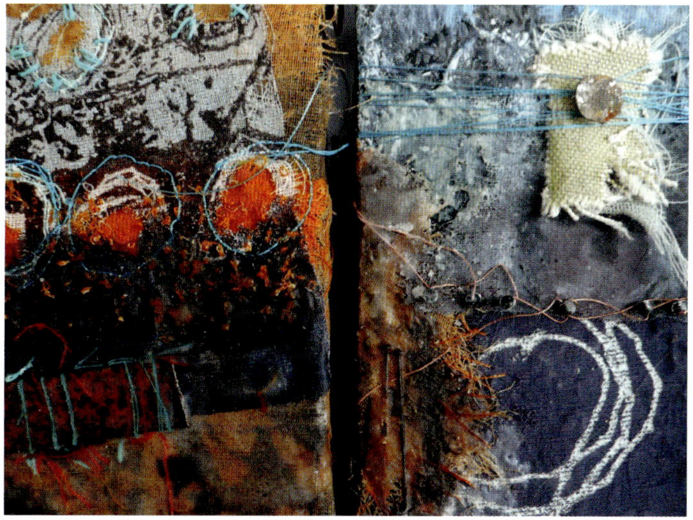

Found Series (detail). Fabric and stitch. 9.8" × 78.7". 2013.

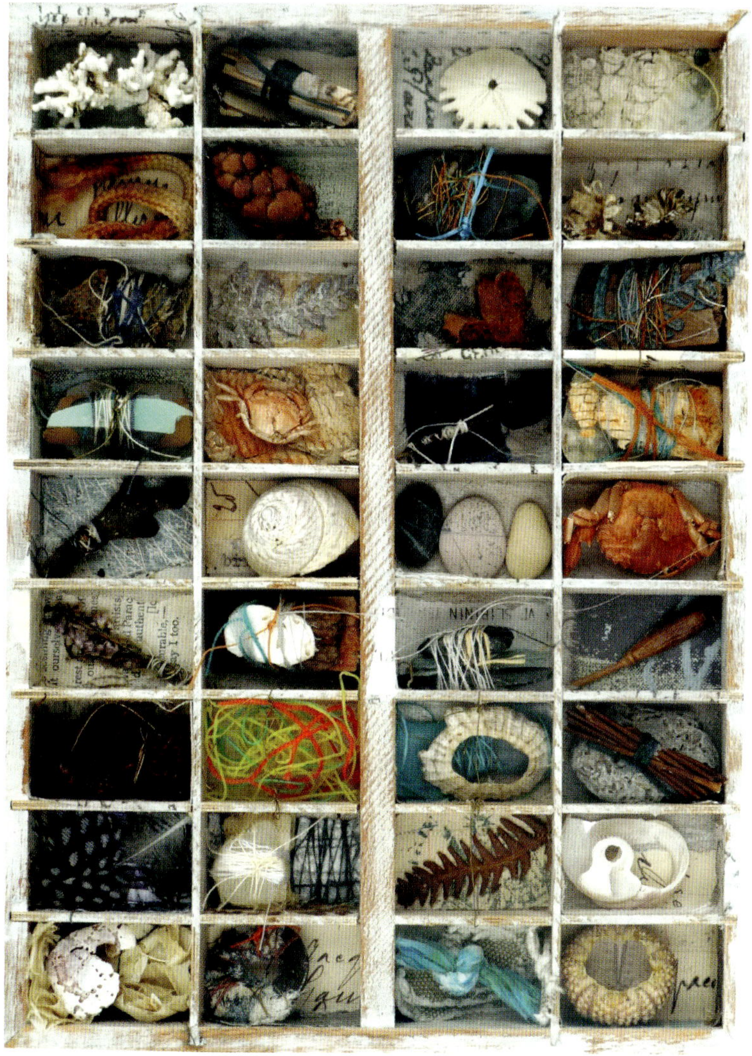

From Here to There. Fabric and stitch. 16.4' × 4.9'. 2015.

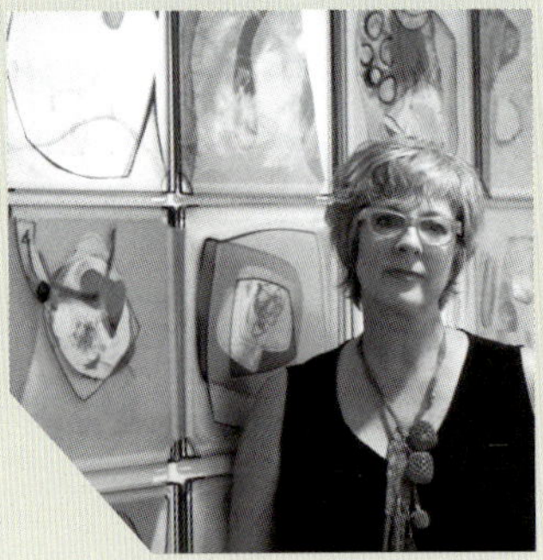

Leisa Rich

Atlanta, Georgia

Even when I create a two-dimensional artwork, I always include three-dimensional and unusual elements. I frequently employ the technique of Free Motion machine embroidery, a method that uses a sewing machine and thread to "paint" and build texture. Despite my MFA and BFA degrees in fiber art, I knew early on that I wasn't interested in making pretty art to hang on a wall as only a decorative element. I wanted to suck viewers in for a closer look.

Some of my wall-hung pieces facilitate viewer interaction. They can be played with via hook-and-loop tape, elements that cling, or metal frames that can be moved around on the wall. I seek to re-communicate with my audience in reaction to our disconnected society. Humans are active participants and become my collaborators as they change out the elements of the environment I have envisioned one way in a myriad of other ways. Creating art that invites play empowers viewers.

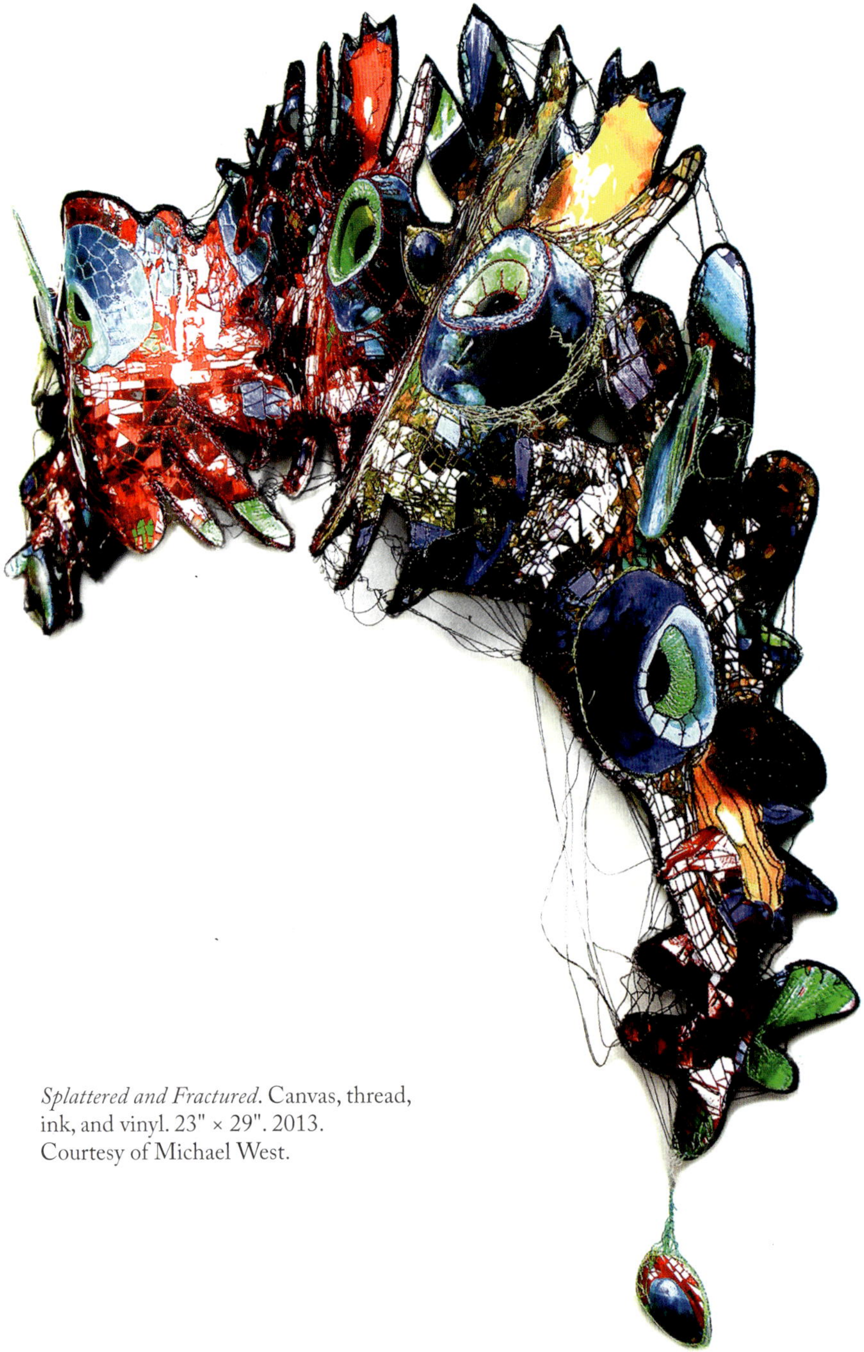

Splattered and Fractured. Canvas, thread, ink, and vinyl. 23" × 29". 2013. Courtesy of Michael West.

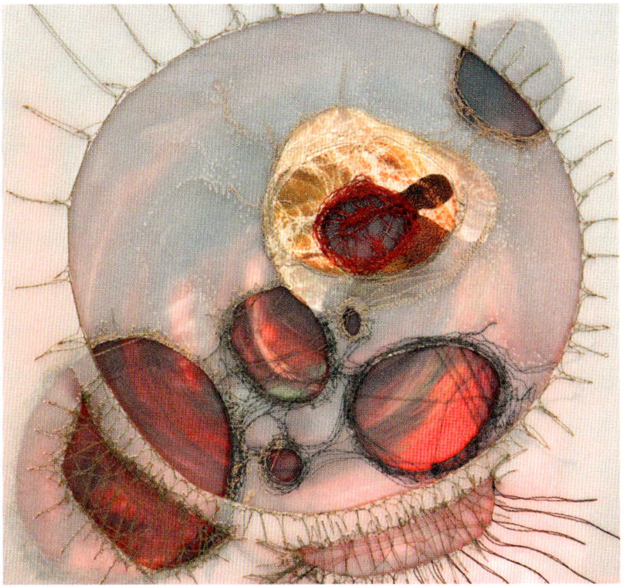

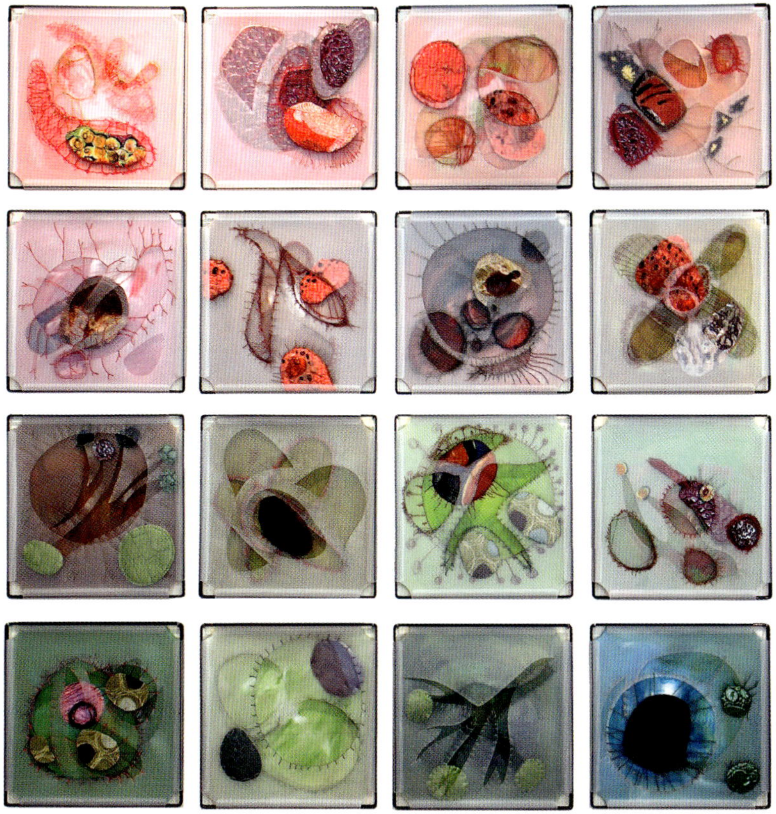

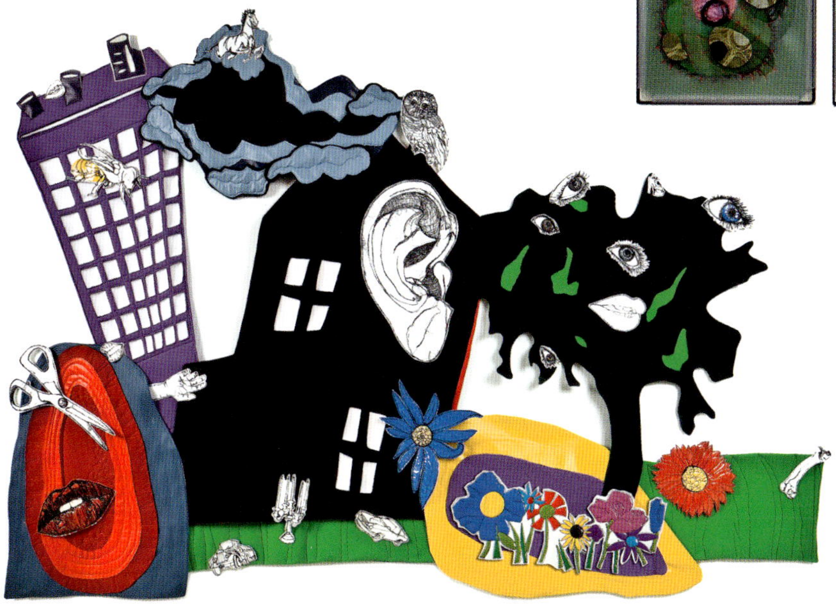

▲ *Architects in Flux*. Hook and loop tape, loop fabric, vinyl, and thread. 88" × 108". 2010. | Detail Courtesy of Michael West.

◄ *On Scarlet Wings in Verdant Fire*. Metal, plastic, thread, embroidery floss, and acrylic. 60" × 60". 2014.

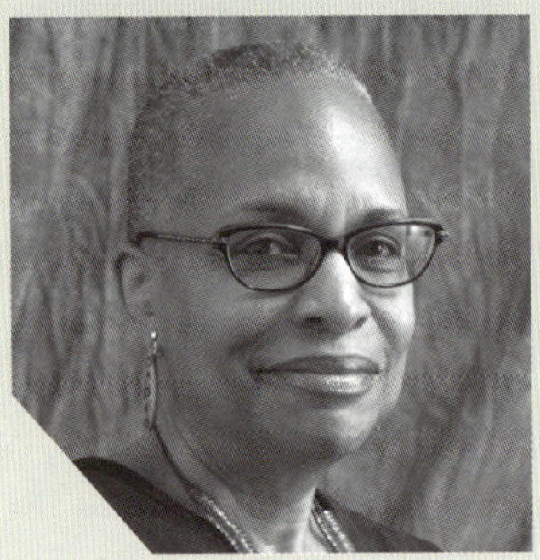

Glenda Richardson

Fort Washington, Maryland

My art quilts and collages tell a personal story whose themes have universal meaning. These themes include physical and spiritual healing, family and cultural heritage, memorializing loved ones, rites of passage as they relate to women, and the spiritual aspects of love and sensuality. I am also inspired by the poetry, proverbs, and truisms of varied cultures, African-American folkways, and the art of India and Africa.

I choose fabric as a medium because of its intrinsic ability to evoke a memory, an era, or an emotion. My compositions use found objects, buttons, beads, handmade papers, jewelry, lace, vintage linens, and repurposed clothing. The fact that many of these materials have been donated by members of my community of supporters imbues the work with a depth that otherwise would not be present.

Most recently, my work has been exhibited in *Conscience of the Human Spirit: The Life of Nelson Mandela* at the International Quilt Conference in Johannesburg, South Africa. I also have work in a seminal exhibit of African American quilts, *And Still We Rise*, which has traveled the United States.

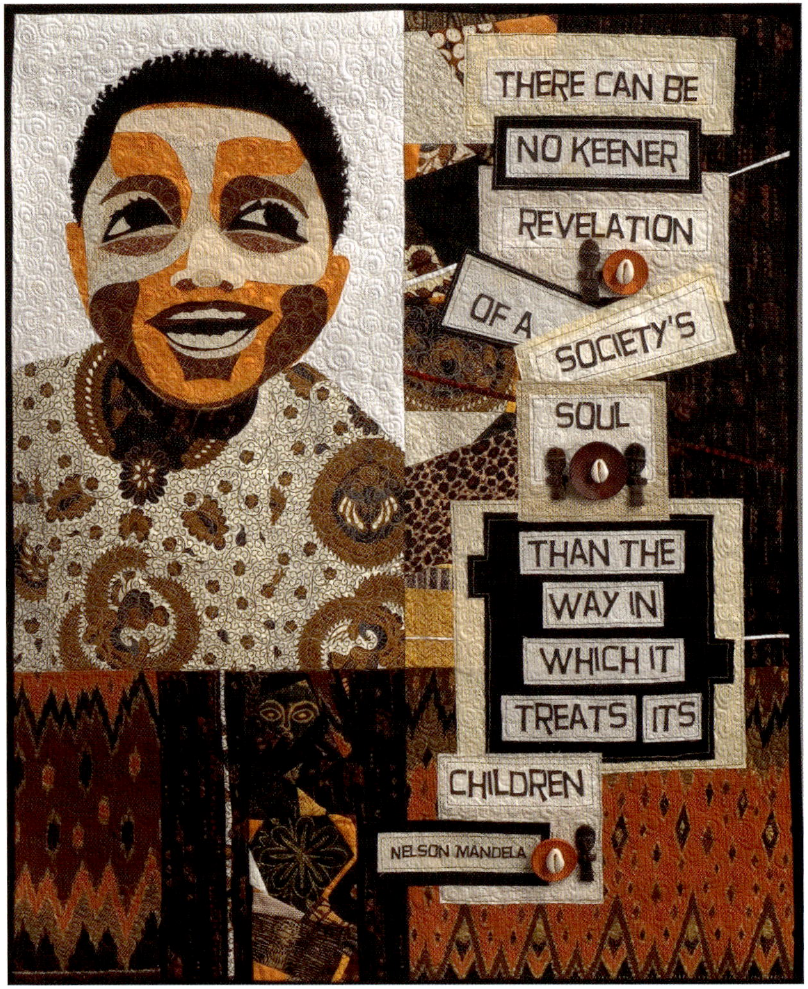

Mandela Quote #2. Indonesian and commercial cottons, found objects, photo transfer on cotton, buttons, and cowry shells. 38" × 31". 2012.

All images courtesy of John Woo.

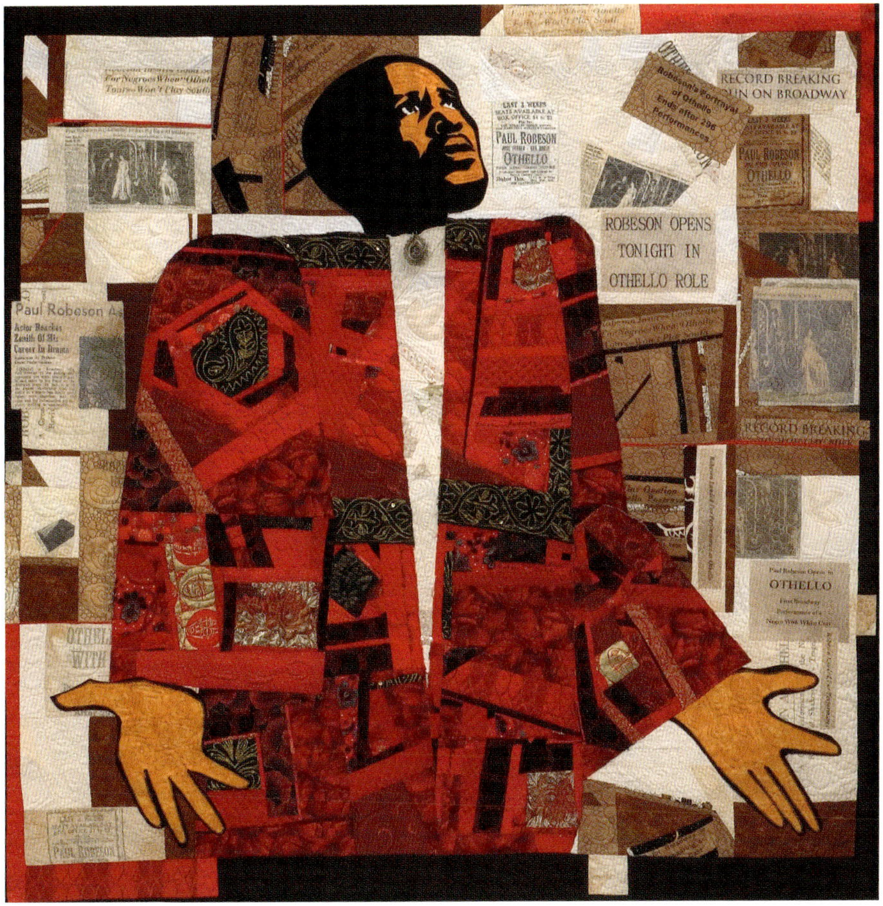

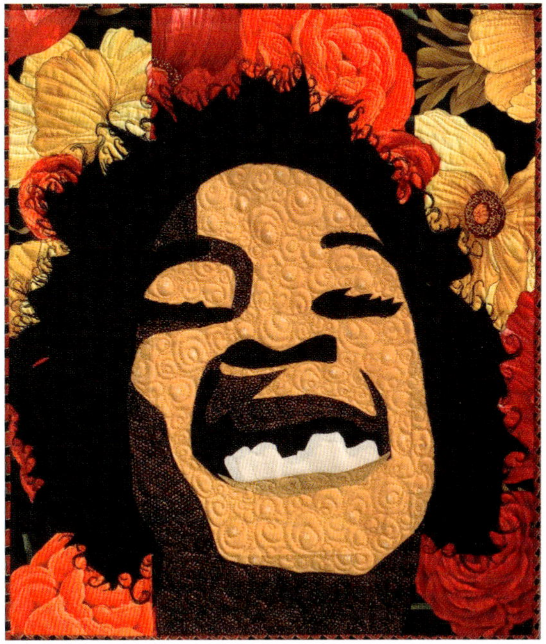

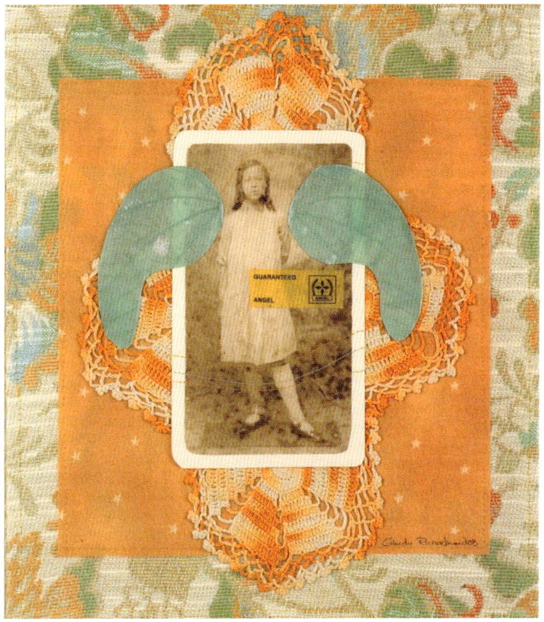

▲ *Paul Robeson as Othello*. Commercial cottons, found objects, velvet, satin, tea dyed vintage linens, and photo transfer on cotton. 50" × 50". 2012.

◄ *Windy*. Machine quilted commercial cottons. 18" × 16".

► *Guaranteed Angel*. Photo transfer on cotton, vintage doily, upholstery fabric, pressed leaves, commercial cottons, and watercolor paper. 14" × 14". 2011.

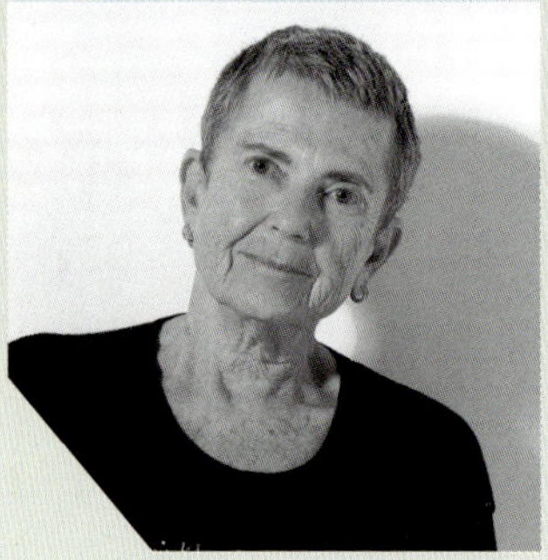

Roz Ritter

Berkeley, California

I am a fiber artist and visual storyteller, piecing together my life stories using hand embroidery, photo transfer, stitching, and appliqué. My work explores family relationships, personal transformation, and upheaval, challenging social mores, societal expectations, and class structures.

I call my generation "The Swing Generation." We are not baby boomers, nor do we remember World War II. Rather, we swing between the two on a wild ride through schizophrenic times. I don't want us to be forgotten.

I draw inspiration from my paternal grandmother, Julia, who was a seamstress in the summer palace of Franz Joseph during the Ottoman Empire, and my father Lew, who was a haberdasher to the stars in Beverly Hills. The Bayeux Tapestry, as well as historical American samplers, also influence my award-winning work.

Self Portrait (1962-1977). Circa 1962 deconstructed linen wedding dress (belonging to the artist) and photo transfer. 61" × 26". 2013. Courtesy of Dana Davis.

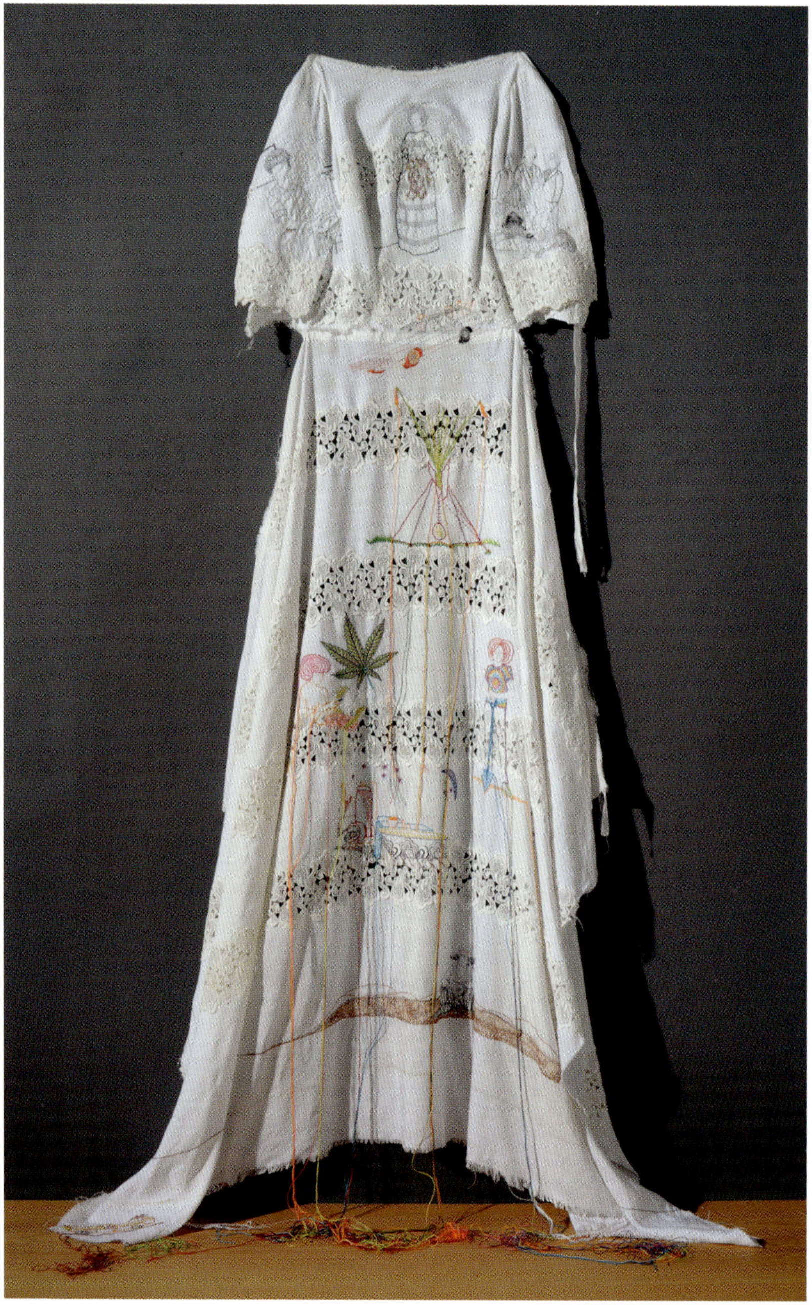

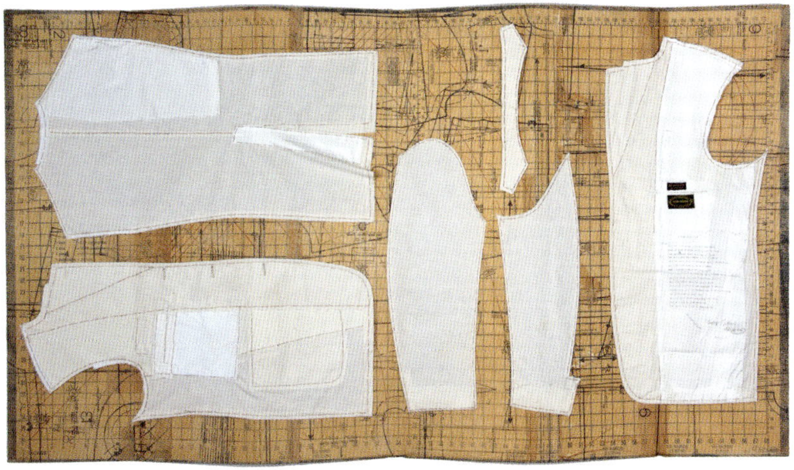

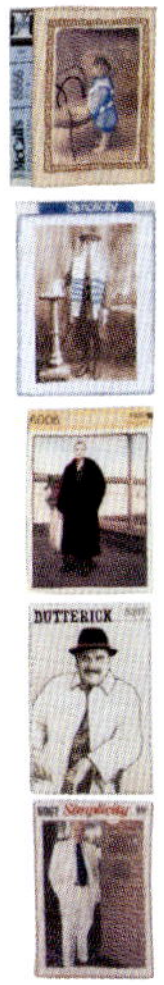

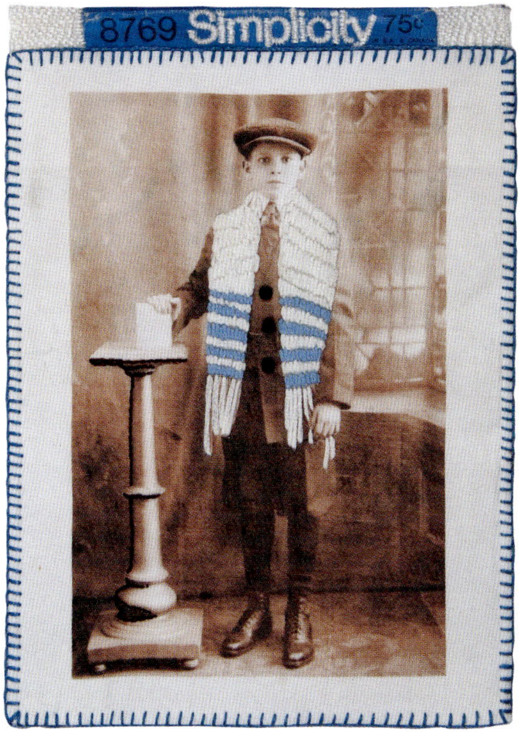

▲ *Lew the Clothesman*.
Photo transfer, suit belonging to the artist's father, vintage patterns, and pattern board. 40" × 72" × 12". 2011. | Detail. Courtesy of Cindy Pavlinac.

➤ *More Things to Do*. Circa 1949 Brownie dress, polyester fabric, and photo transfer from c. 1949 *Brownie Scout Handbook*. 68" × 24". 2011. Courtesy of Dana Davis.

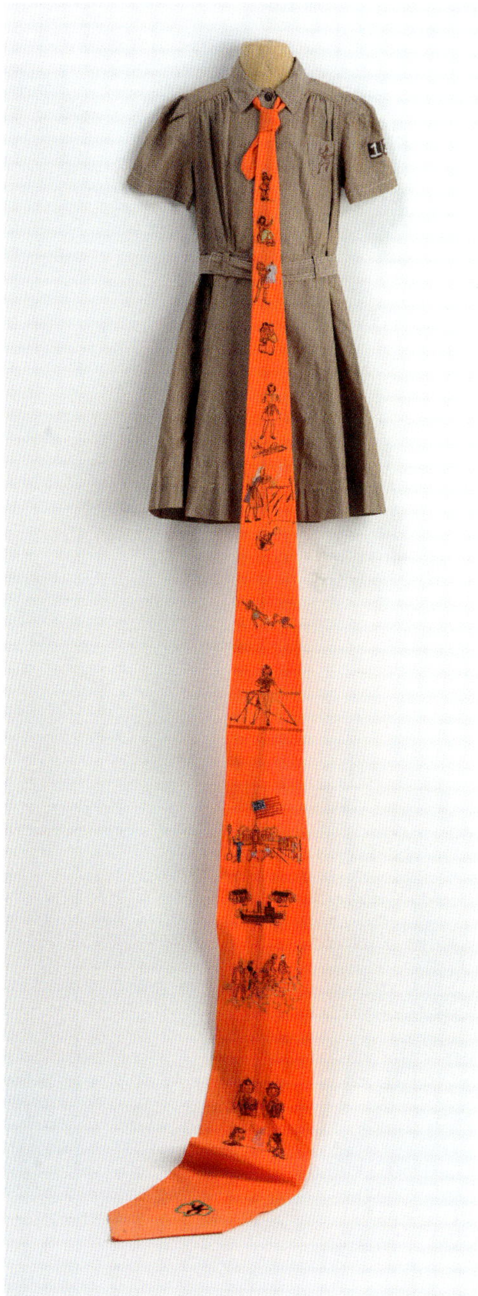

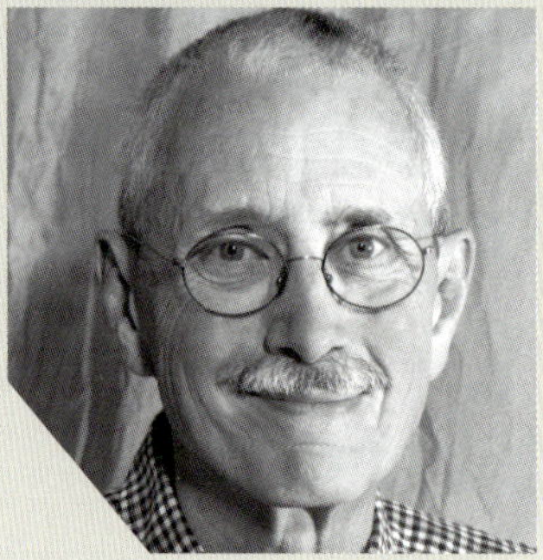

Courtesy of Barbara Pickles.

Michael F. Rohde

Westlake Village, California

My work is infused with the joy of creating the work: I start with undyed wool, silk, and alpaca yarns, to which I add traditional, lightfast natural dyes, mixing colors to give a palette of subtle shades. The medium is hand-woven tapestry, but with a modern sensibility. Imagery is most often abstract, but may hint at something recognizable: the texts of Tibetan prayers, references to ethnic textiles, and pixelated faces.

Though I often do variations on a theme, each piece is unique and takes about a month for me to weave.

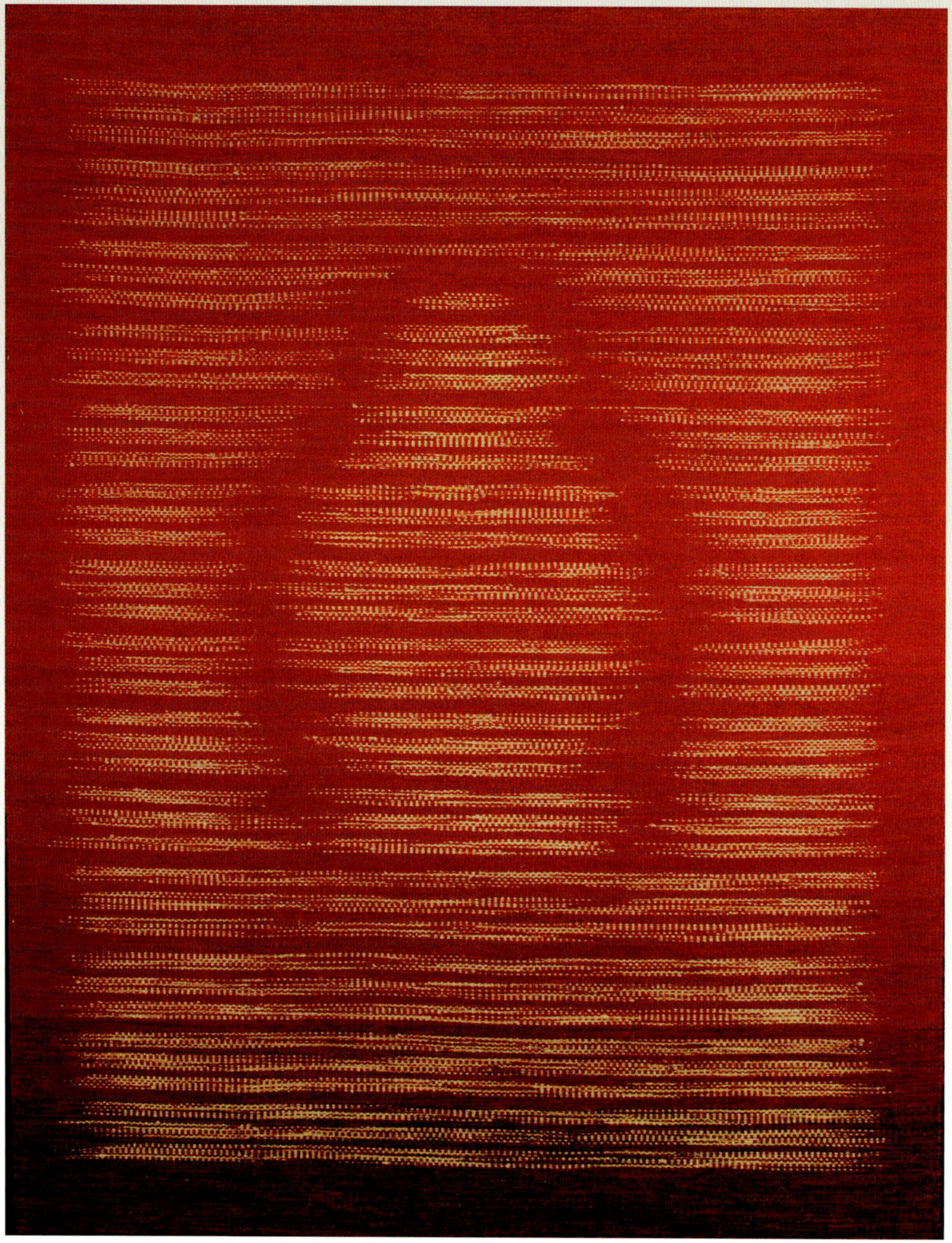

Golden. Wool and natural dyes.
47" × 36.5". 2014.

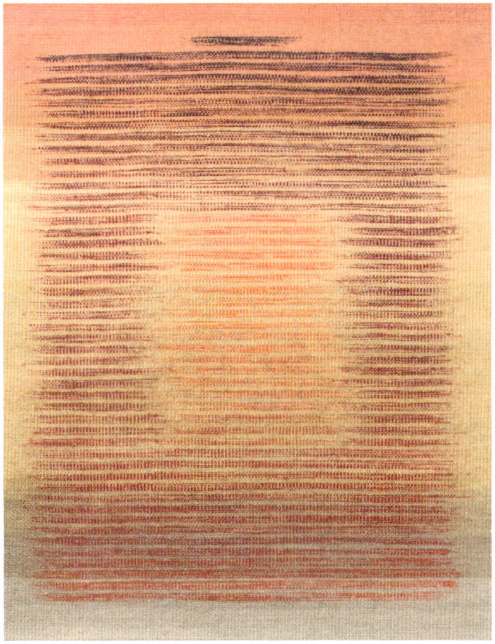

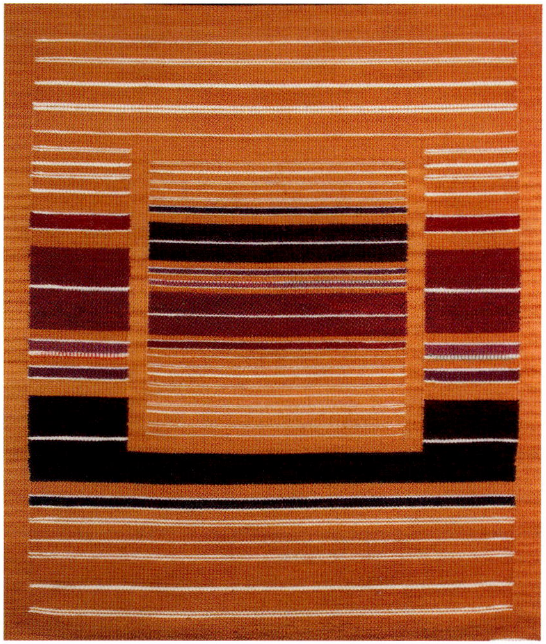

Tara. Wool and natural dyes.
45" × 36.5". 2011.

➤ *Inversion.* Wool silk and natural dyes. 42" × 37.5". 2014.

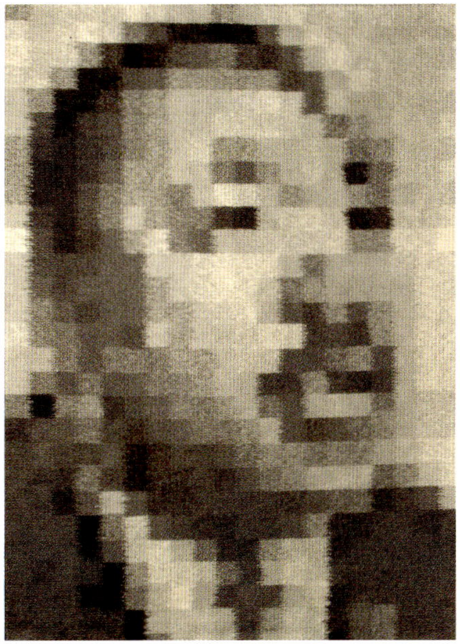

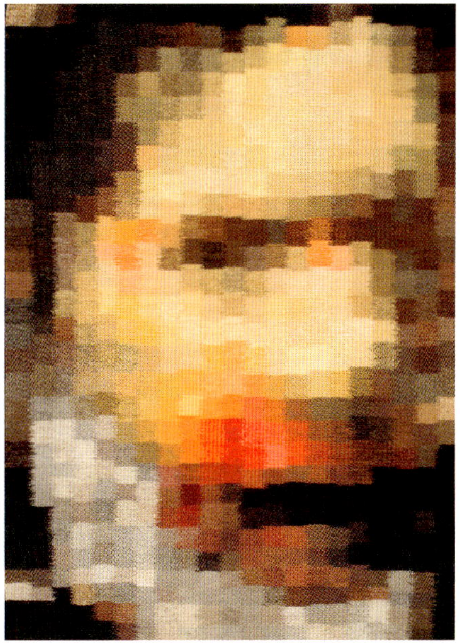

◄ *Dream.* Embroidery, and undyed alpaca.
43.5" × 41.5". 2014.

Huli. Wool and natural dyes.
42" × 32". 2012.

All art images courtesy of Andrew Neuhart.

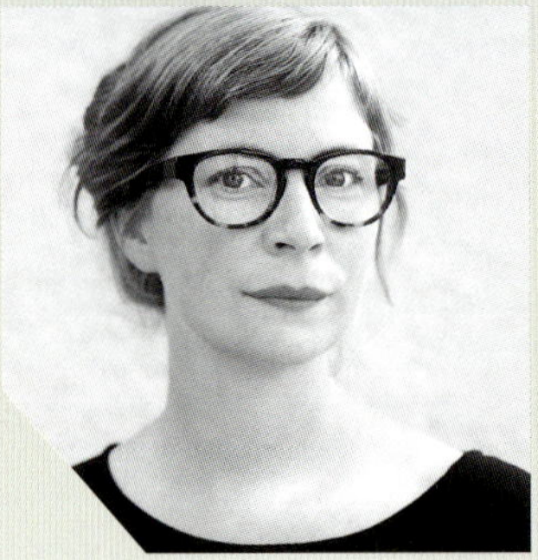

Photo: Magnus Rudolfsson.

Ida-Lovisa Rudolfsson

Göteborg, Sweden

With embroidery, I encapsulate time and attach my thoughts onto something definite. The seemingly mundane, and what can hide behind it, interests me. I am both frightened and fascinated by the difficulty of just existing. Fragments of memories along with the daily events and the derailed world around me become building blocks for my imagery. In my work, the embroidery is constant; the careful stitches are mixed with stains of color. The narrative is important, and it is with the thread I tell my stories. My artistic process is intuitive; I cut to pieces and join together again. The starting point can be a conversation at the dinner table, a facial expression on the tram, or a sentence I read in the newspaper.

I received my master's degree in textile arts at the School for Design and Craft in Gothenburg in 2010. Since then I have done several solo and group exhibitions and received a number of grants.

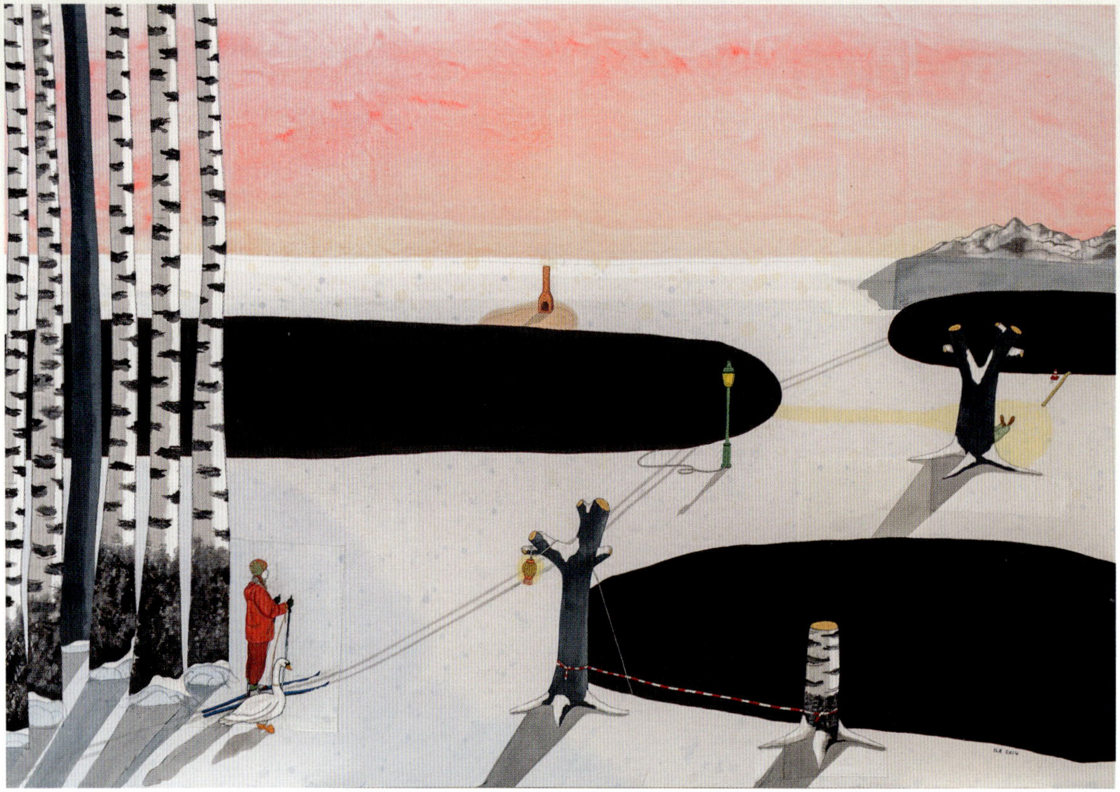

Spår. Cotton thread, cotton canvas, and acrylic paint. 47.2" × 70.9". 2014. Photo: Hendrik Zeitler.

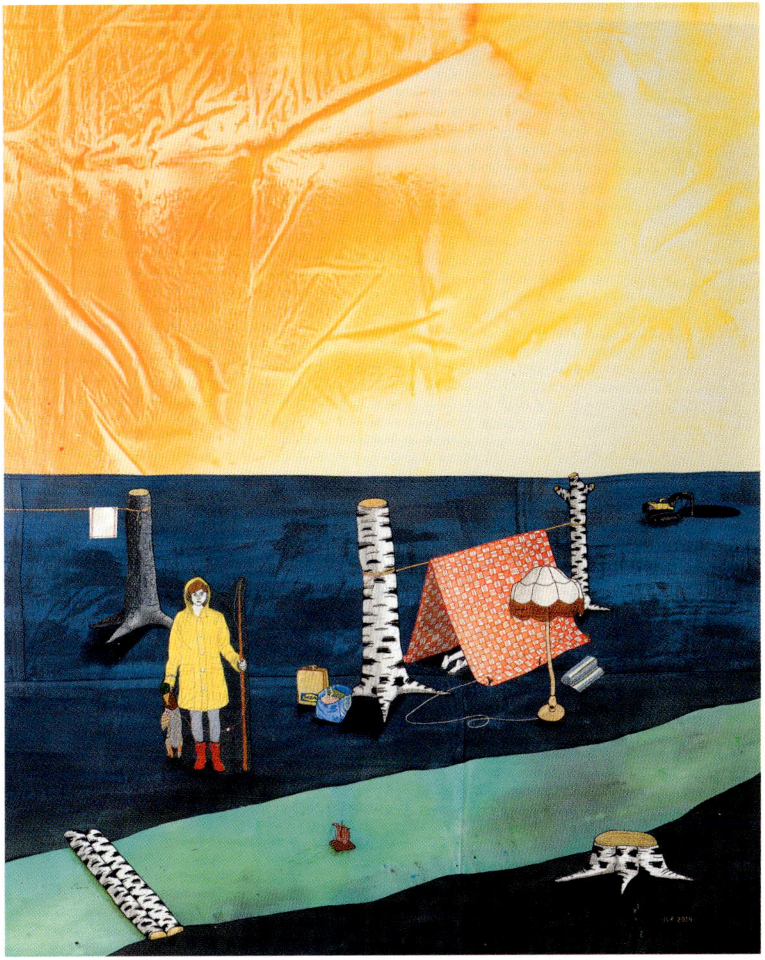

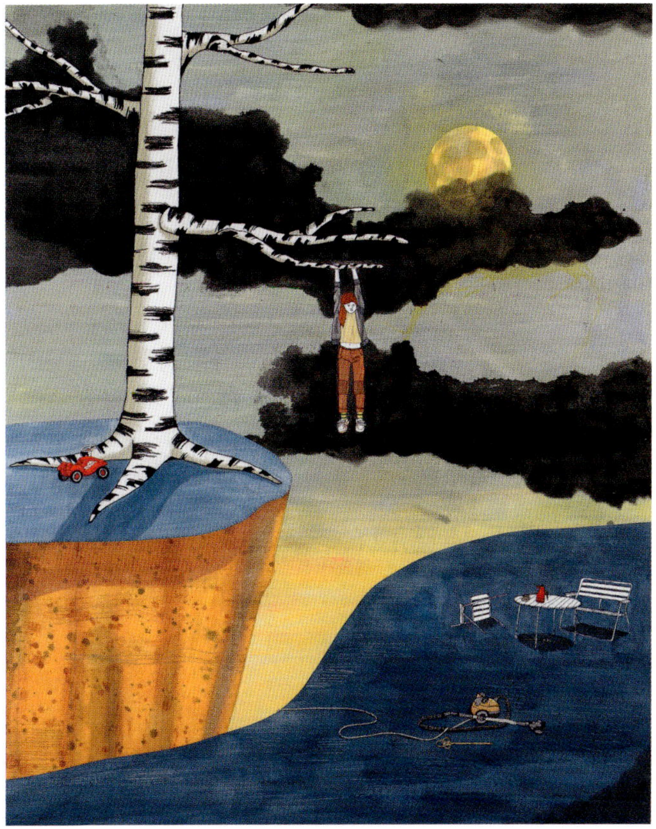

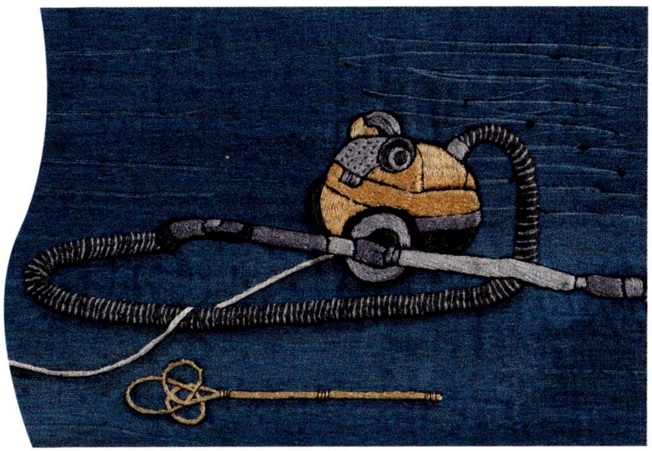

▲ *There Was Something about the Sky.* Cotton thread, cotton canvas, and acrylic paint. 51.2" × 39.4". 2014. Photo: Hendrik Zeitler.

➤ *Ergospace.* Cotton thread, cotton canvas, and acrylic paint. 51.2" × 39.4". 2015. | Detail. Photo: Hendrik Zeitler.

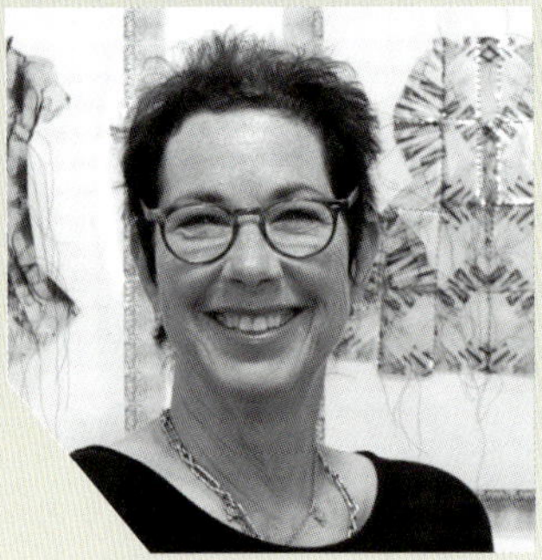

Courtesy of Hope Kahn.

Gwen Samuels

Santa Monica, California

My love of textiles began early and has continued as a life-long resource. As a naïve seventeen-year-old, I went off to Paris for a weekend as a *Mademoiselle* magazine college competition fashion winner. My interest in fashion continued to grow, and I began as a textile designer before becoming a full-time artist. The joy of pattern informed my vision from early on.

Fifteen years ago, I began using a camera in my travels, not realizing I was creating a context for my future work. Soon I began rearranging and cropping my photos and finally printing them on transparencies in repeat patterns made on the computer. The shapes of my early image composites took the form of large squares and dresses. Later, I pieced image fragments into fantastical things like insects and Greek vases arranged as installations on the wall.

My love of the handmade made the needle the natural tool to pull the pieces together, and I leave threads hanging as evidence of the process. I arrange my work slightly off the wall with straight pins to permit shadows to interact with the forms. From a distance my work appears as an abstract composition, but upon closer inspection segments carry recognizable imagery. My work is about craft, time, and intimacy.

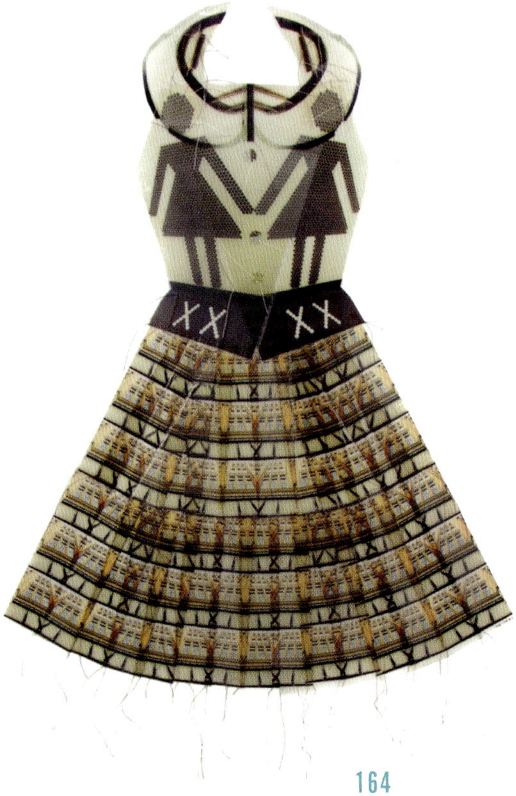

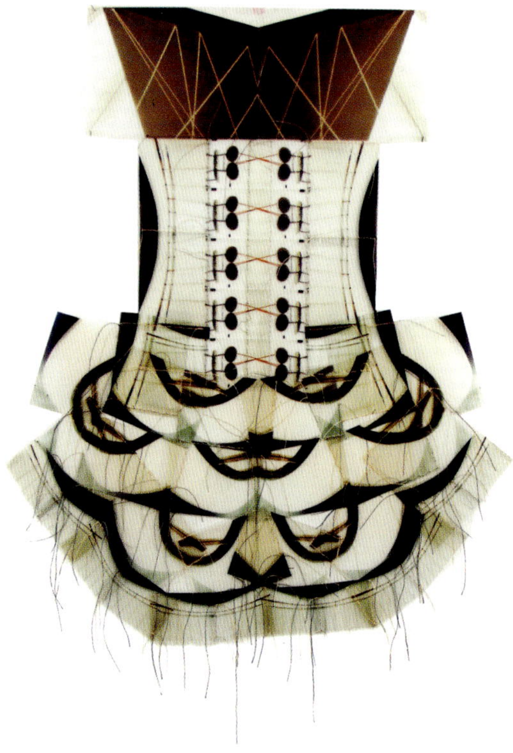

Well Supported. Digital images of architectural elements printed on transparency and hand stitched. 26" × 22". 2012. Courtesy of Brianna Lopez.

➤ *Vintage.* Digital images taken in Seattle, Washington, printed on transparency, and hand stitched. 32" × 25". 2012. Courtesy of Brianna Lopez.

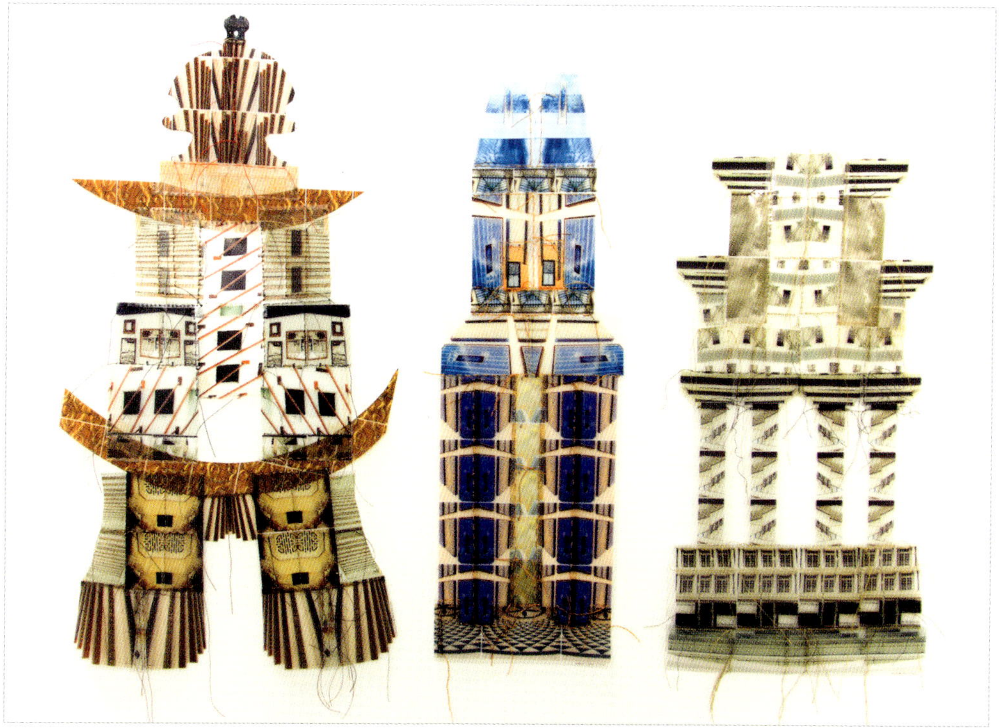

➤ 3 *Buildings:* From left to right: *Fortress Gate, Rhythm/Blues,* and *Classical.* Digital images of architectural elements printed on transparency, and hand stitched. 25" × 8.75", 29" × 14.5", and 21.75" × 11". 2012. Courtesy of Brianna Lopez.

▼ *Treasure Hunting.* Digital images, printed on transparency, and hand stitched. 18" × 48". 2009.

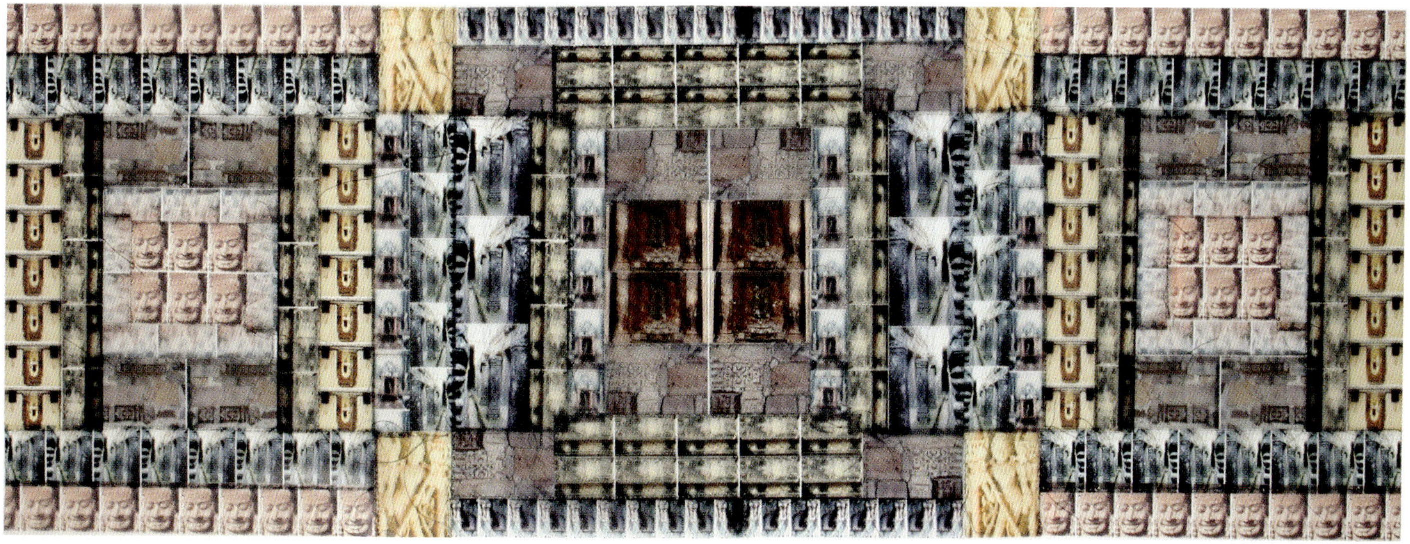

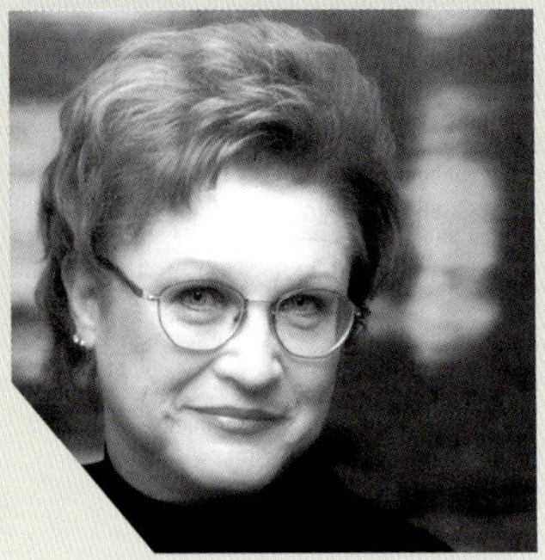

Louise Schiele

Sacramento, California

I use my sewing machine as my drawing tool, and I drive my sewing machine like I drive my car: hard and fast. I like to work in series because the idea I usually start with changes many times as I work it through, and the most wonderful and unusual pieces of work develop. I call myself a fiber collage artist. I like to use different techniques and materials in each piece, stretching to that out-of-the-box piece to top the series off. I've been working with old black-and-white photos for several years, printing the images to cotton, colorizing them, and placing them in new background settings, thus giving them new life. While creating these images for a local gallery, I'm also working on my latest wild animal series, changing to another technique, a new direction, moving forward—always moving forward.

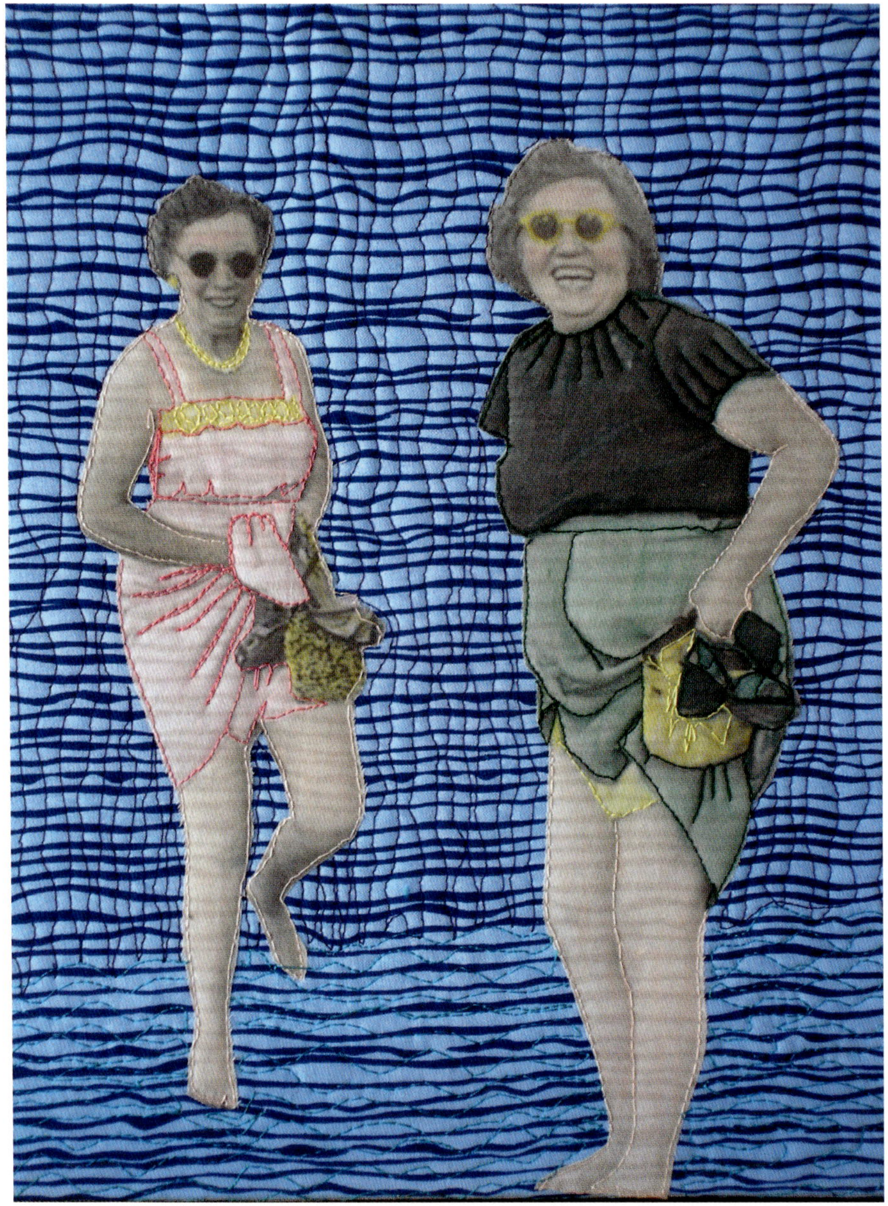

Toe Dippin' on the Jersey Shore. Photos printed on cotton. 12" × 10". 2012.

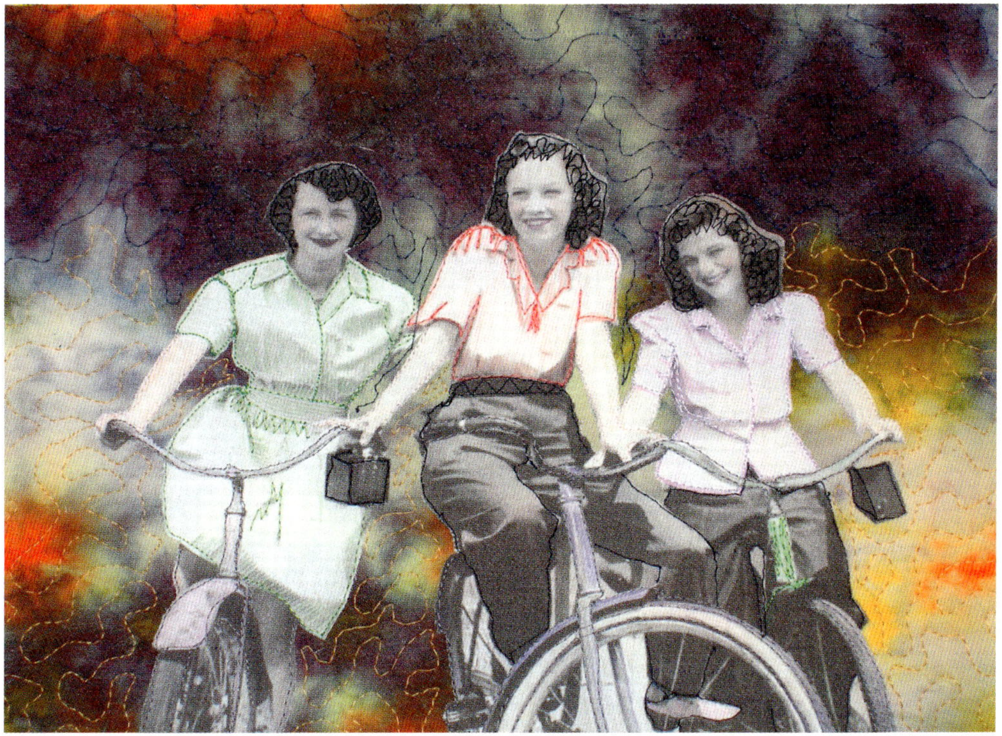

◄ *A Ride in the Park.* Photos printed on cotton. 14" × 16". 2014.

► *Time Traveler.* Photos printed on cotton and organza. 18" × 24". 2010.

▼ *Missouri Moon Light.* Photos printed on cotton. 16" × 14". 2014.

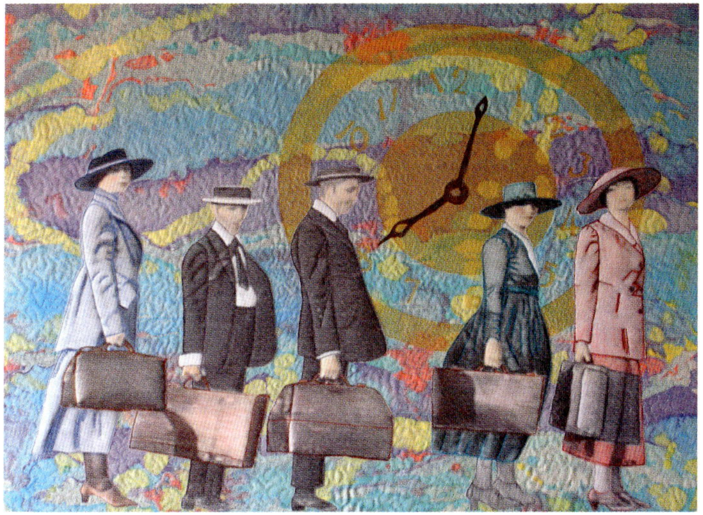

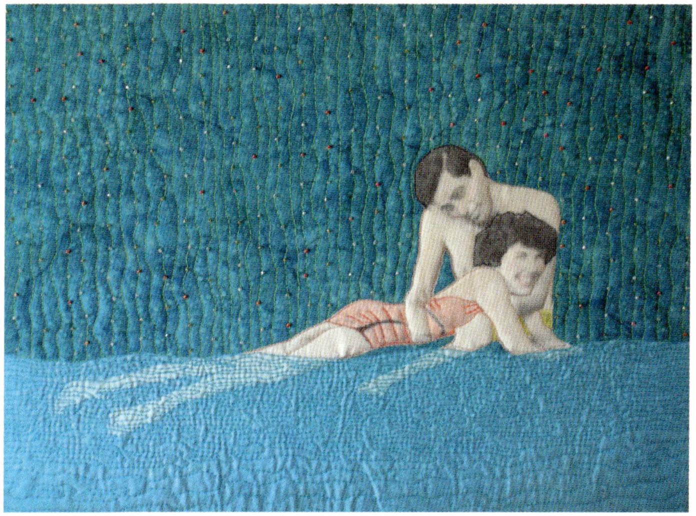

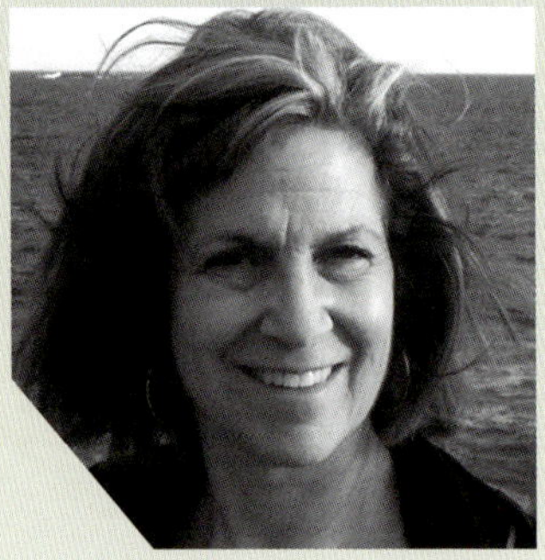

Rowen Schussheim-Anderson

Davenport, Iowa

Although I weave tapestries the same way they've been woven for hundreds of years, I introduce new elements and materials, pushing the boundaries of traditional tapestry. Texture and color are integral components. Traveling to Africa inspired some recent works; others are inspired by the organic latticework of butterflies, with their rich color and lively organic shapes. As artists, we pick and choose, collage, synthesize, and weave a tapestry revealing interplay of pattern, surface, and color.

I am chair of the Augustana (Illinois) College Art Department. Previously, I taught at Arizona State University, the Smithsonian, and the National Endowment for the Arts' Artists-in-Education program. My tapestries are in various permanent collections and have been published in several books and art journals. Recent juried exhibitions include *Fiberart International* and the *International Fiber Biennale: From Lausanne to Beijing*.

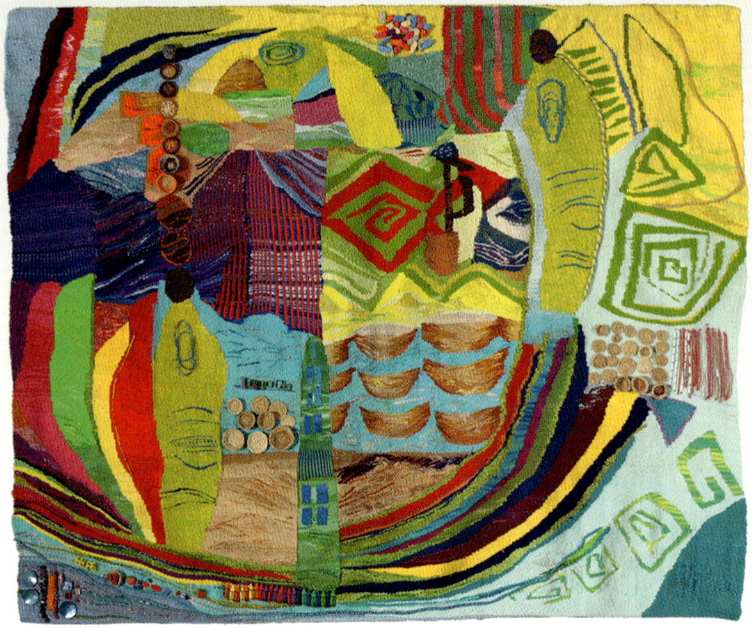

Thursday Market. Linen, wool, silk, rayon, cotton, raffia, beads, and buttons. 42" × 52". 2012.

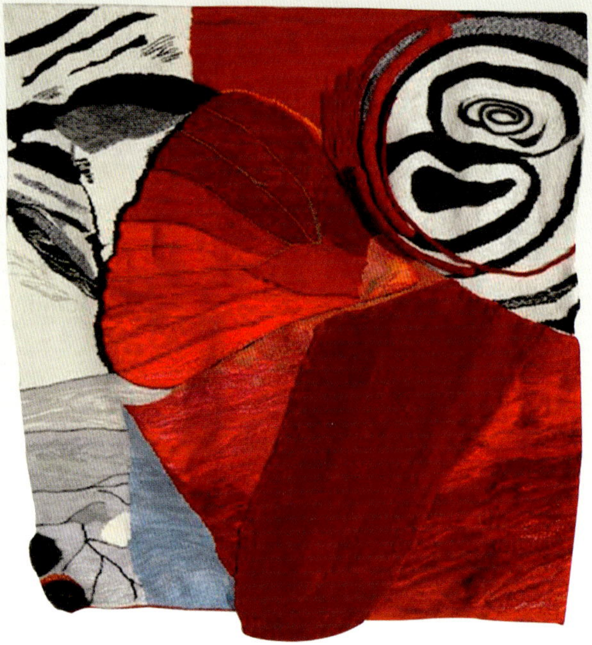

Crimson Prelude. Linen, cotton, wool, and rayon. 52" × 48". 2012.

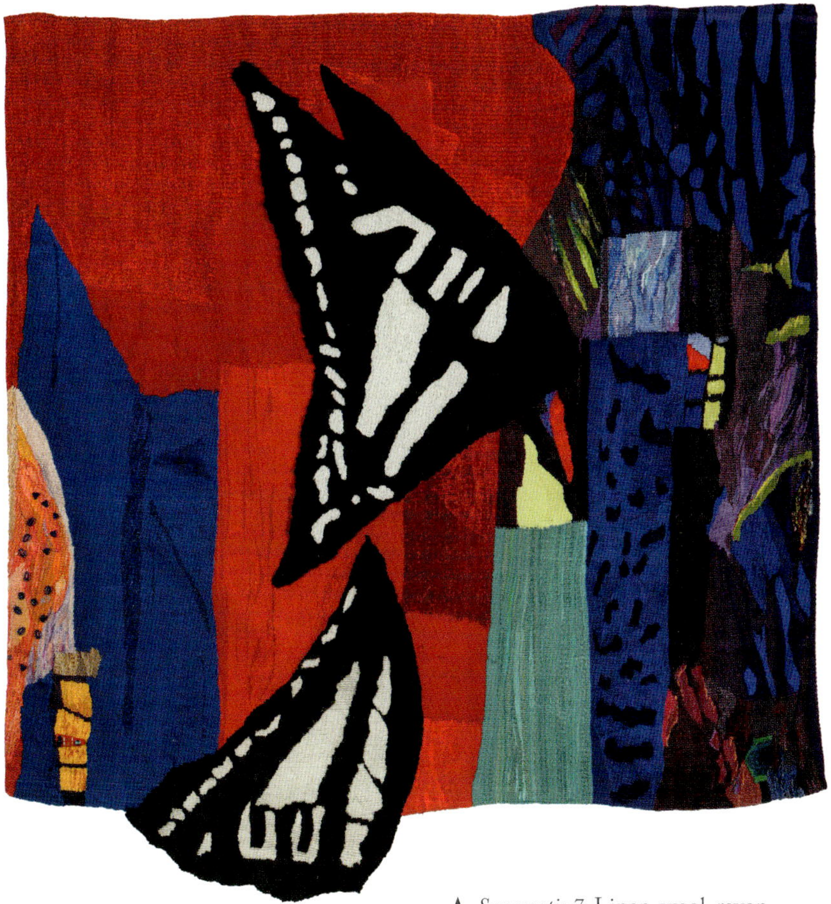

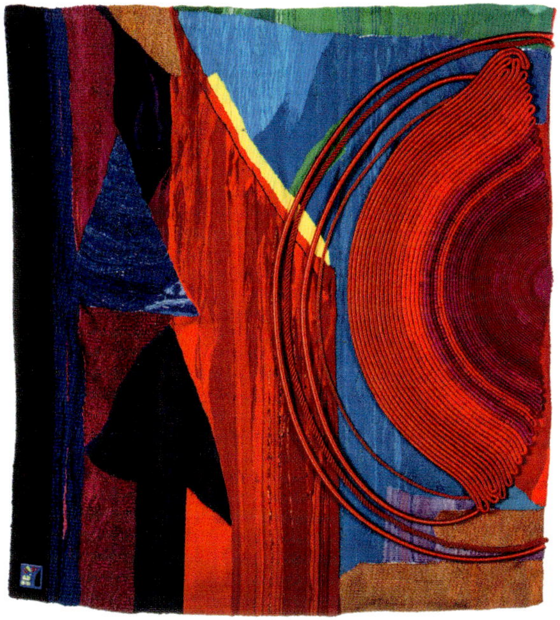

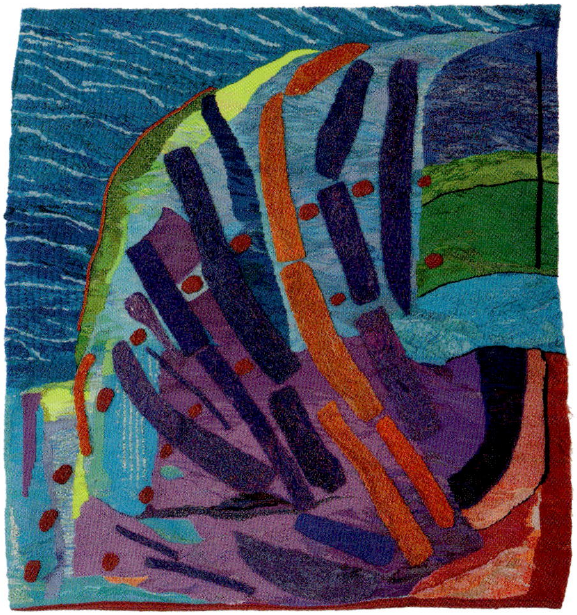

▲ *Synergetic 7.* Linen, wool, rayon, cotton, and beads. 56.5" × 61". 2014.

◄ *New Balance.* Linen, wool, cotton, rayon, silk, beads, and glass. 50" × 55". 2014.

► *Monarchy.* Wool, linen, cotton, rayon, and beads. 57" × 54". 2010.

All art images courtesy of Ogy Blazevic.

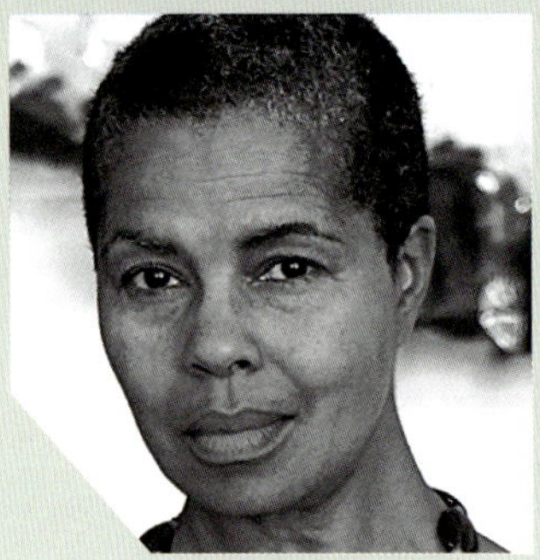

Margaret Scott

Saint-André-de-Roquepertuis, Gard, France

As a visual artist, my work is created from the particularity of who I am: a black woman, a feminist, a daughter, a mother, an activist, and a British textile artist. My textiles often explore the politics of representation and the tensions and contradictions of a Black European or Black British identity.

My digital photographic images are interpreted through the laborious, low-tech process of hand-felting, a soft medium for a hard subject . . . In 2013 the catalyst for my work was the phenomenon of Zwarte Piet, the black servant/slave who accompanies Saint Nicolas at Christmas in Holland. The earlier pieces, including a short film and sets of large felted portraits, are direct critiques of this quaint (and offensive) Dutch ritual.

In other work, I use images from my own life, growing up in Britain in the 1950s and '60s. Visual metaphors, memories, and symbols are used to illustrate some of the confusing mixed messages young black children received at school, on television, and in our homes.

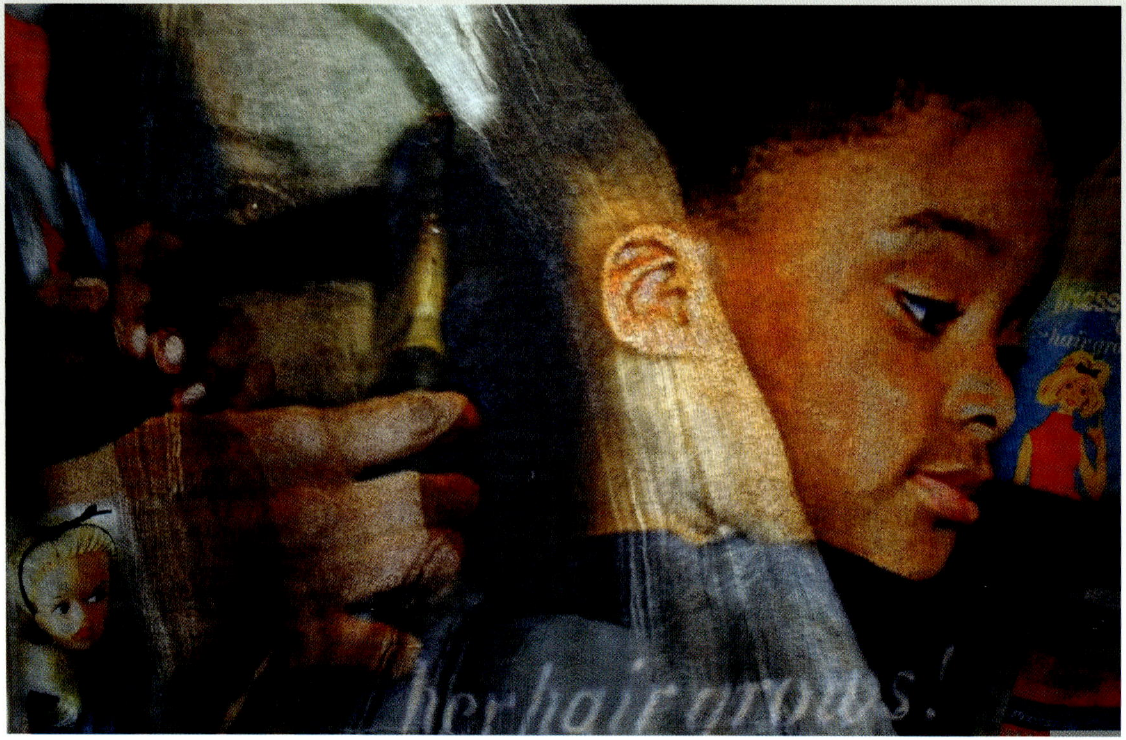

her hair grows.
Hand felted silk chiffon and merino wool. 46" × 75". 2011.

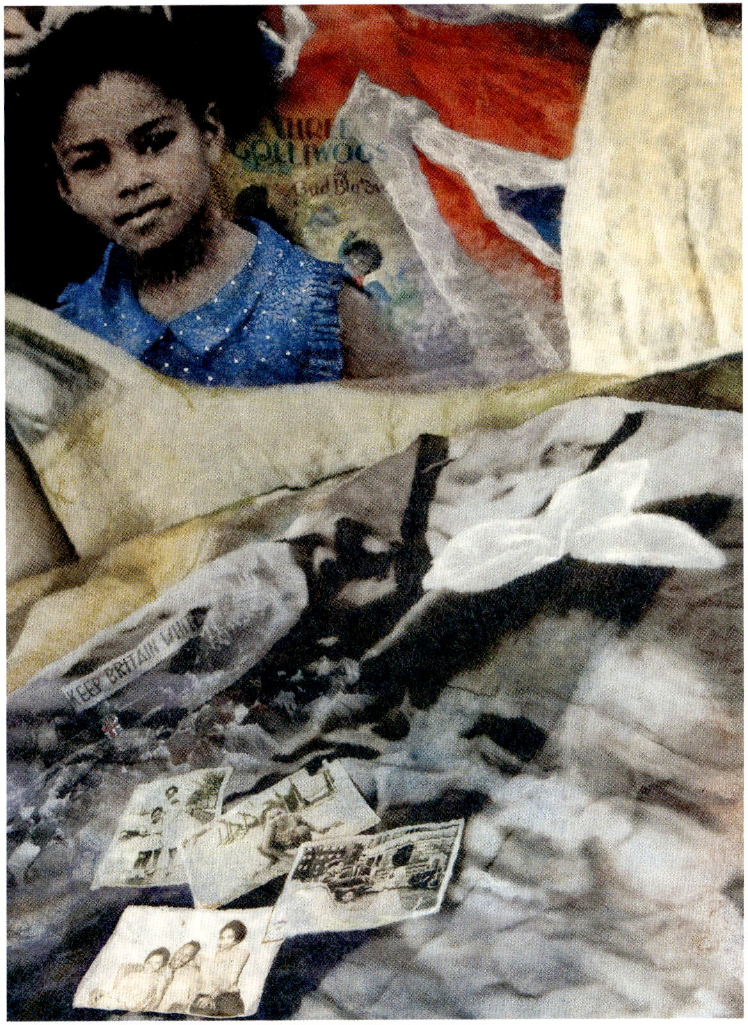

Mixed Messages: "Enid". Hand felted silk chiffon and merino wool. 44" × 33". 2011.

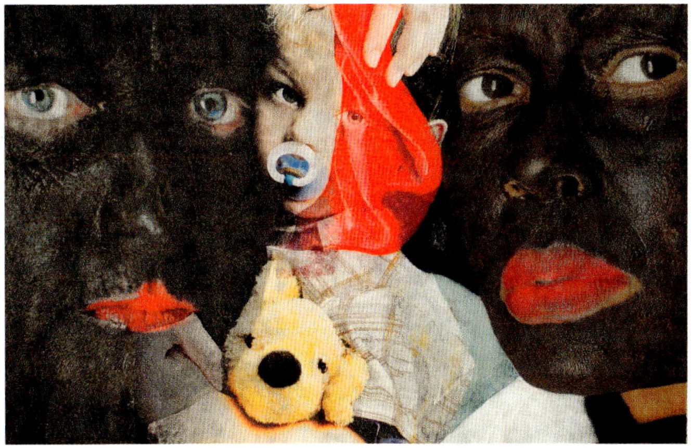

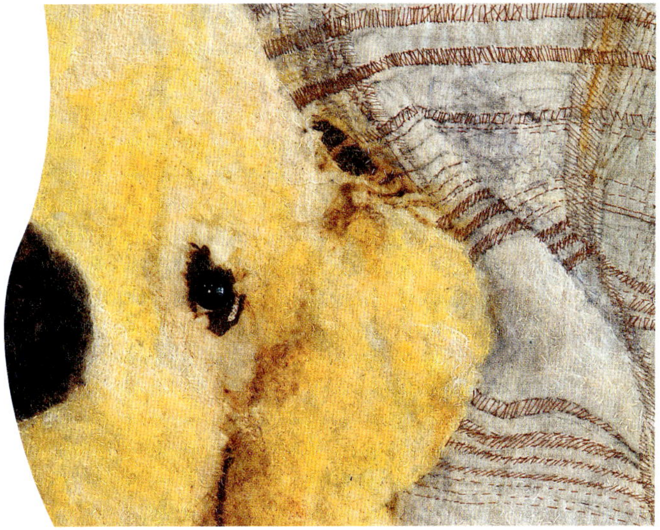

I see you Zwarte Piet. Hand felted silk chiffon and merino wool. 50" × 79". 2014. | Detail

All art images courtesy of Hans Poot photographer.

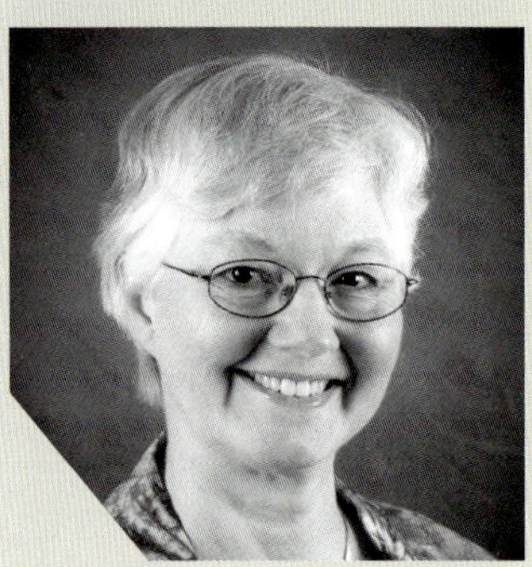

Sandra Sider

Bronx, New York

Since moving to New York City in 1979, I have worked mostly with photographic imagery via cyanotype photograms and prints, digital photo transfer, and screen printing. My work in textile and fiber art ranges from naturalistic representations of people, places, and objects, to symbolic interpretations of our universal experiences as human beings. I welcome serendipitous surprises that magically can appear in imagery of all types.

My pieces are owned by several public collections and are exhibited internationally in juried shows. As a teacher, I facilitate critique workshops based on principles of art and design, enjoying the process of mentoring other artists.

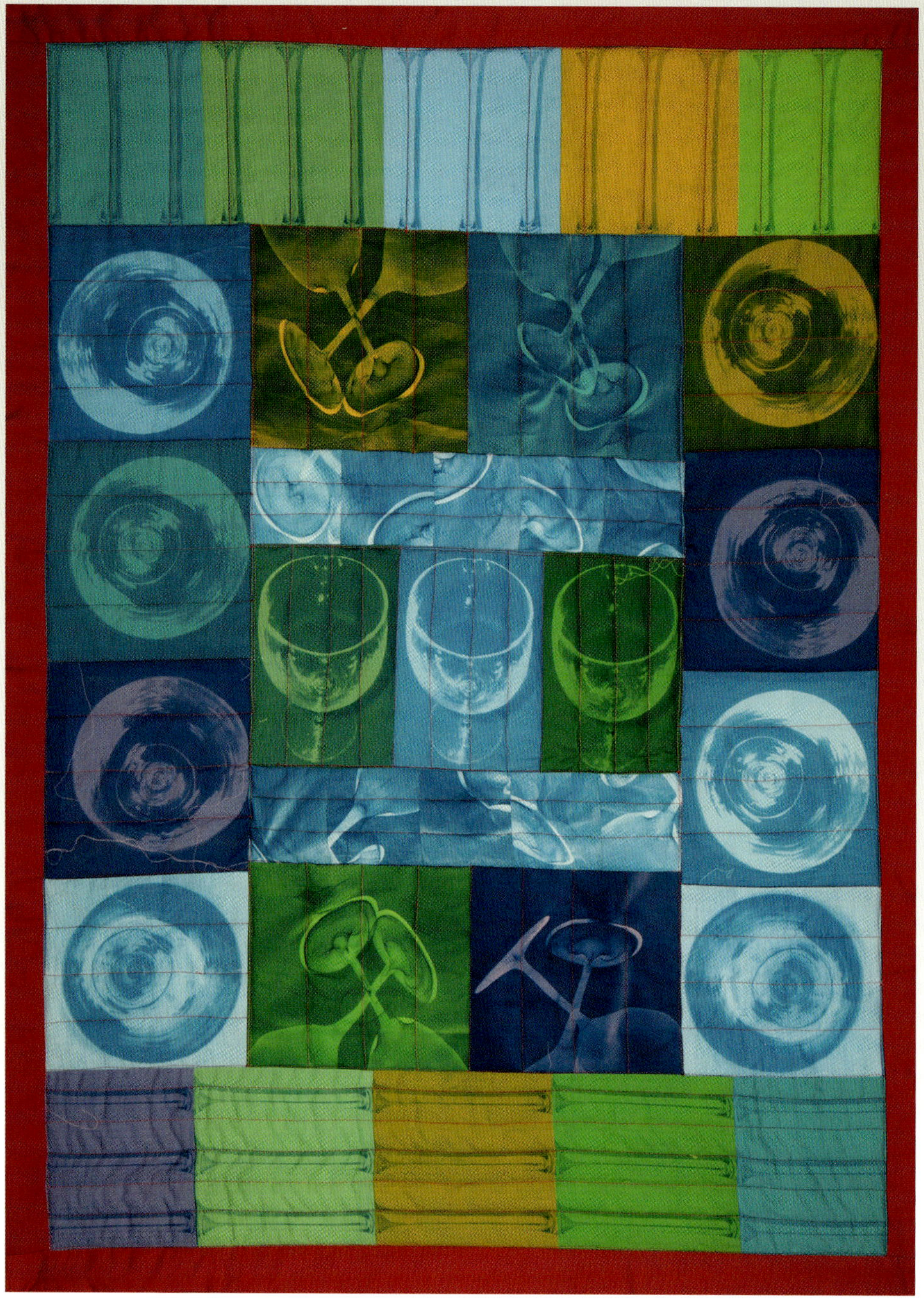

Bottoms Up! Cotton fabric and thread.
44" × 32". 2013.

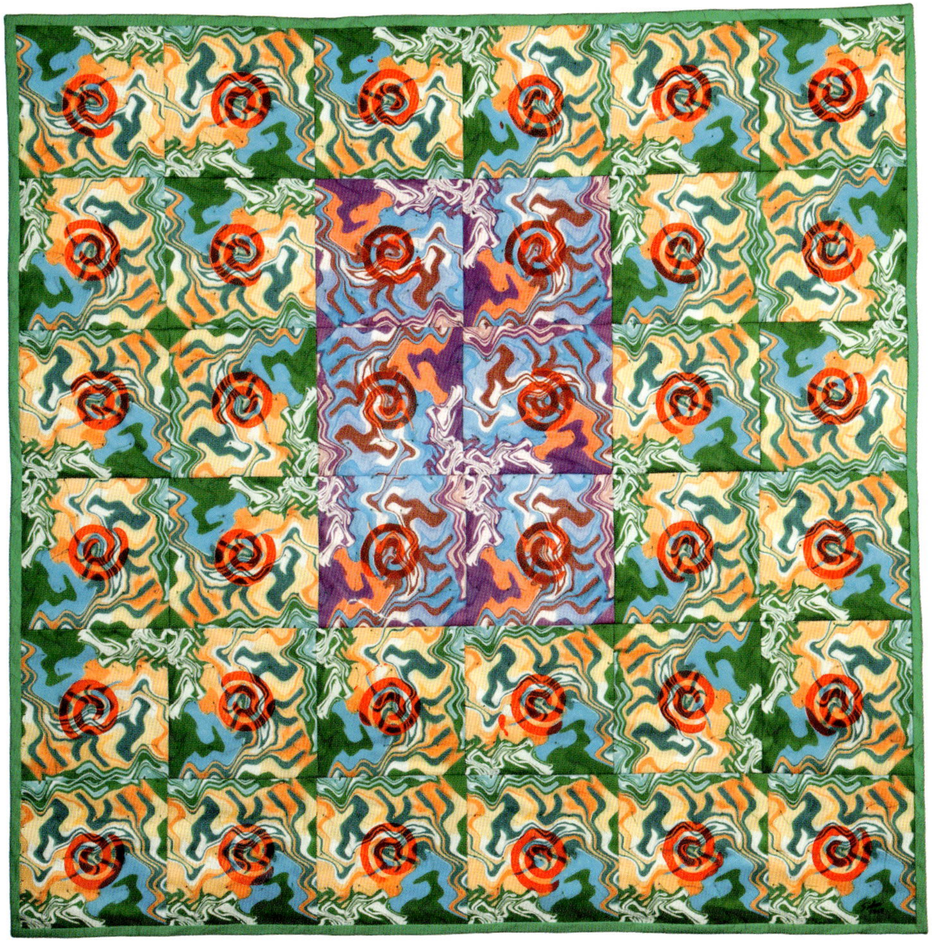

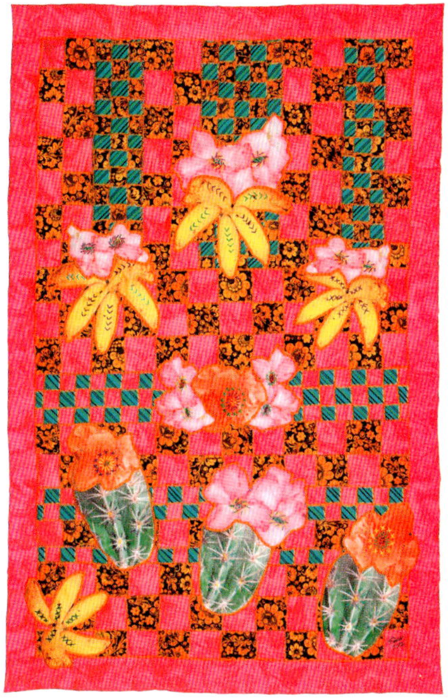

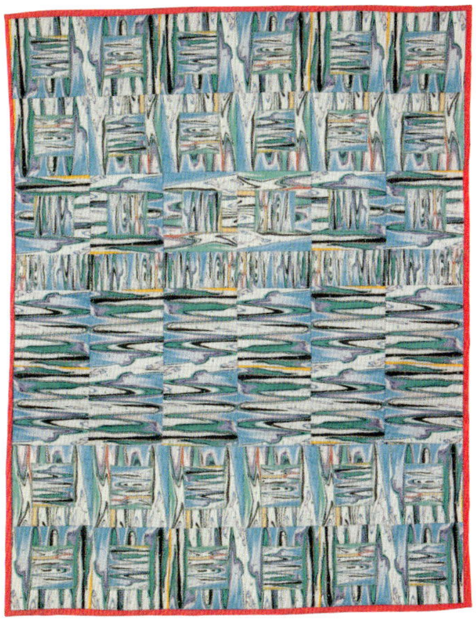

▲ *On the Road: Road Rage.* Cotton twill, thread, and acrylic paint. 40" × 41". 2010.

◄ *Garden Grid #5*. Cotton twill, commercially printed cotton fabric, and thread. 40" × 26". 2012.

► *Road Rage: Slippery When Wet*. Cotton twill and thread. 34" × 34". 2010.

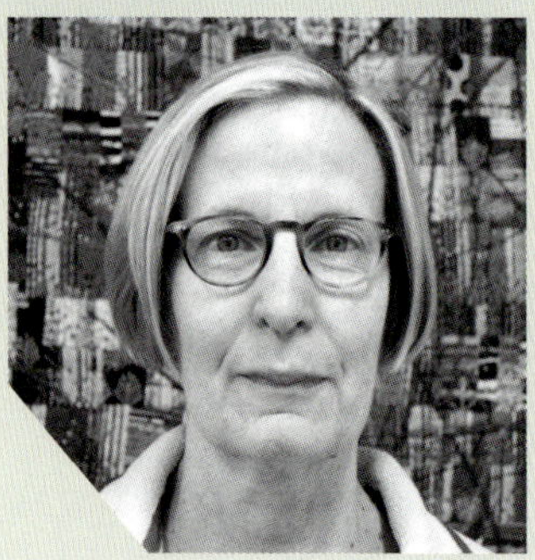

Diane Siebels

Charlottesville, Virginia

I have always loved textiles: quilts, fabrics, and linens. I began sewing as a child, making clothes, progressing to quilts and wall hangings. Over time, my work has become increasingly complex, utilizing thread more and more as the primary means of expression. I am continually learning and exploring the stitch mostly in an intuitive and organic way, one thing leading to another. Mostly by accident, I discovered how much I love the process of hand-stitching. I stitch with both hands so it becomes very rhythmic and meditative.

My work explores interiority, making structures from imagination, thought, and emotion generated by the entanglements of daily life. The plane that I am working on becomes like an environment, a structure that develops as the piece progresses and that begins to take on a life of its own.

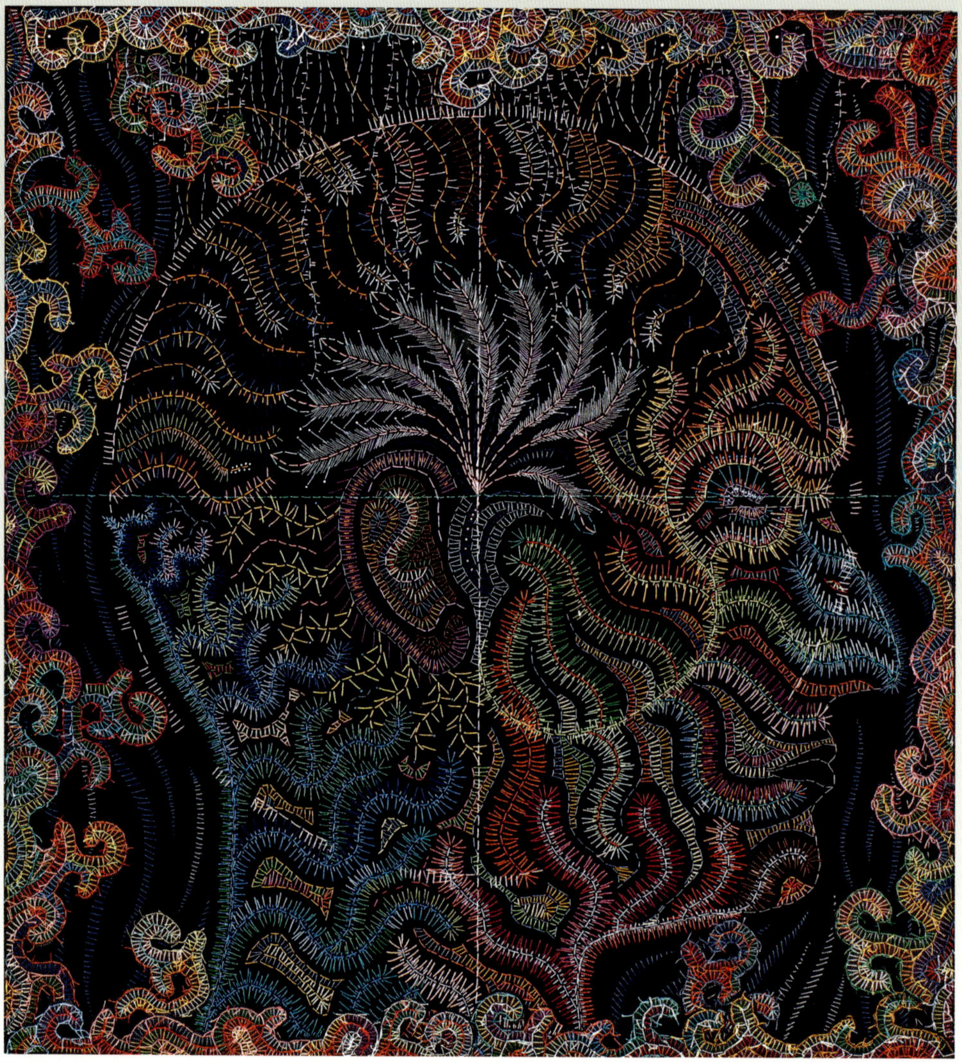

Head 3. Hand stitching on cotton fabrics with pearl cotton thread. 48" × 45". 2012.

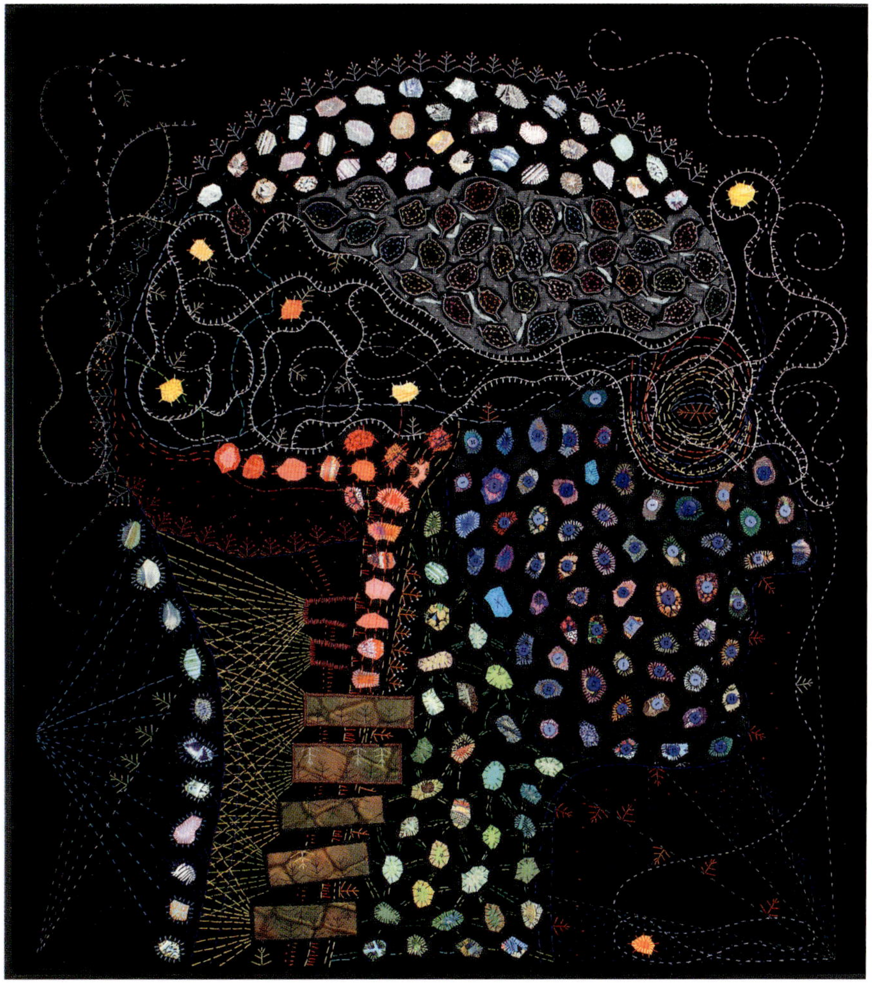

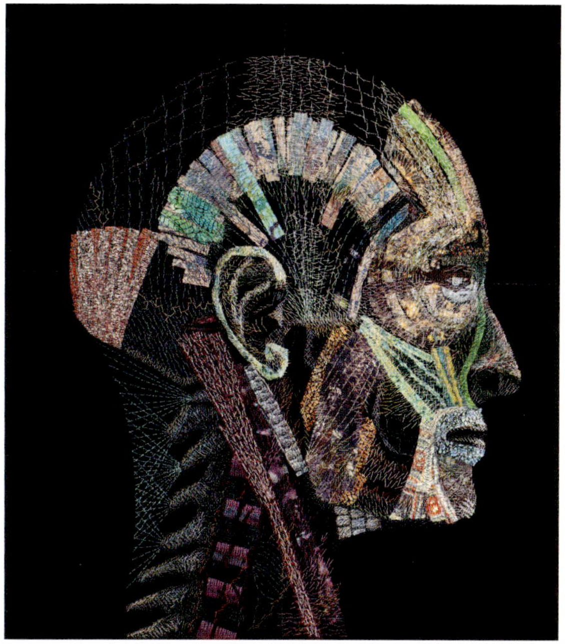

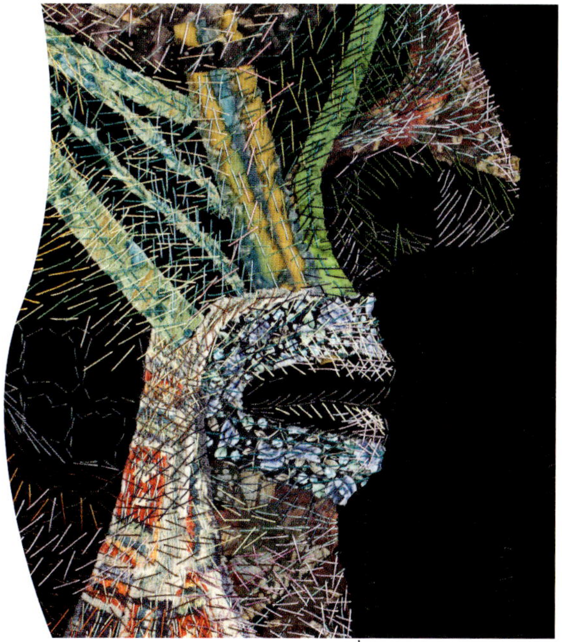

▲ *Head 4.* Machine and hand stitching on cotton fabrics with batting, wool felt, buttons, and pearl cotton thread. 48" × 45". 2012.

◄ *Head 2.* Hand stitching, raw edge appliqué on cotton fabrics with pearl cotton thread. 48" × 45". 2012. | Detail

All art images courtesy of Scott Smith.

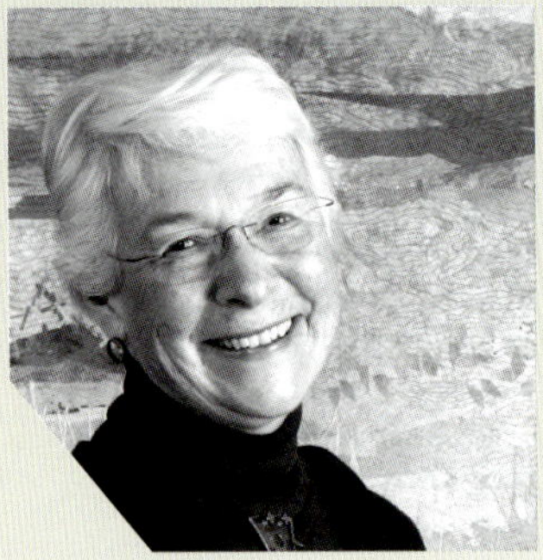

Barbara Lee Smith

Gig Harbor, Washington

I once saw a sign by a tip jar at a coffee shop that said, "If you fear change, leave it here." Many years ago I wrote a book titled *Celebrating the Stitch: Contemporary Embroidery of North America*. That book changed my life as I traveled the world with my book and the accompanying exhibition. I learned that I don't need to be from any place in particular, but can be in a place and absorb its essence and its influence. Change, while uncomfortable at times, is necessary to me.

Each day in my studio I experience change. For many years, I've lived in the Pacific Northwest and watched the sky, the light, and the shadows of this water-saturated environment. The sky sometimes looks exactly like the pearl-like interior of an oyster shell; it glows. Major change—moving and resettling in a new environment—encourages me to look beyond this peaceful place and think about transitions.

I make my work in three steps: First, I paint on a synthetic non-woven fabric with light-fast acrylics; next, I collage that surface with more of the same painted material; and finally, I bring it all together by drawing a topographical map on the surface with machine stitching. As I work through this process, the work changes, and so do I.

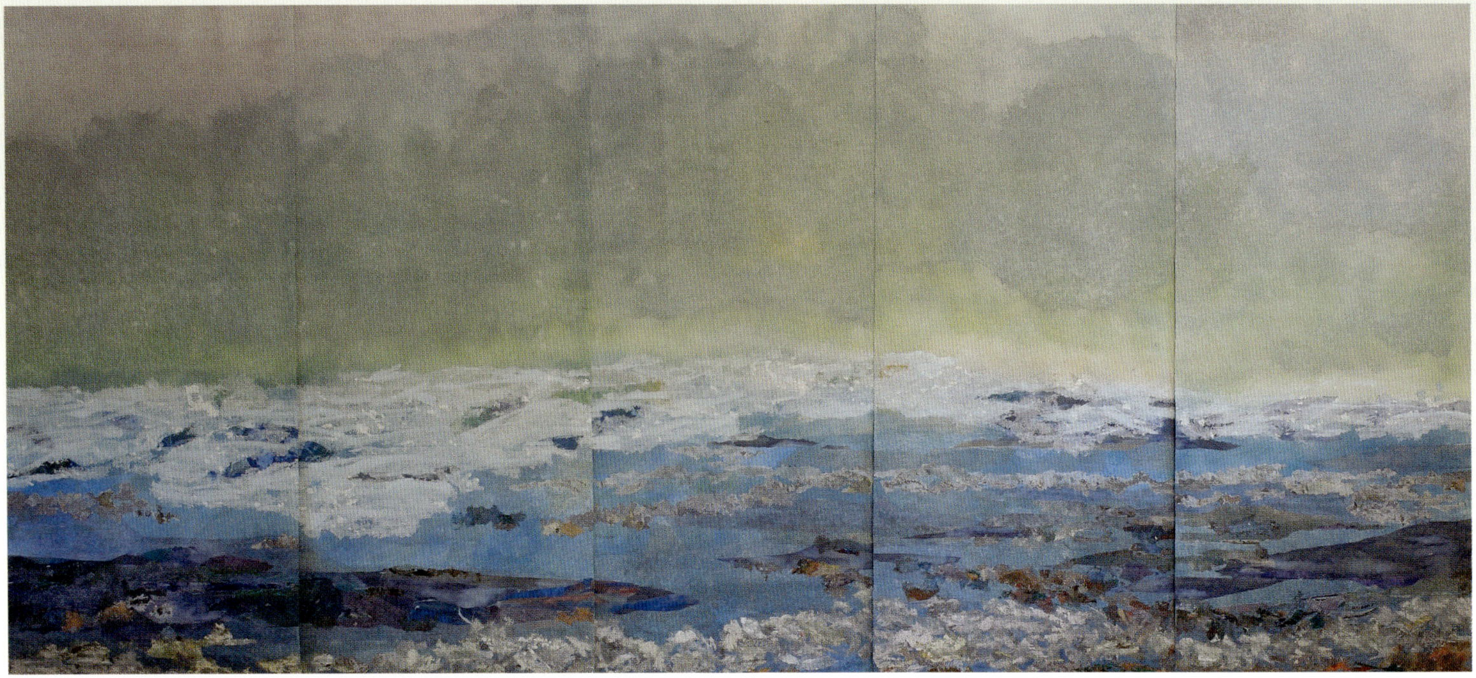

Oyster Light. Non-woven synthetic fabric. 84" × 180".

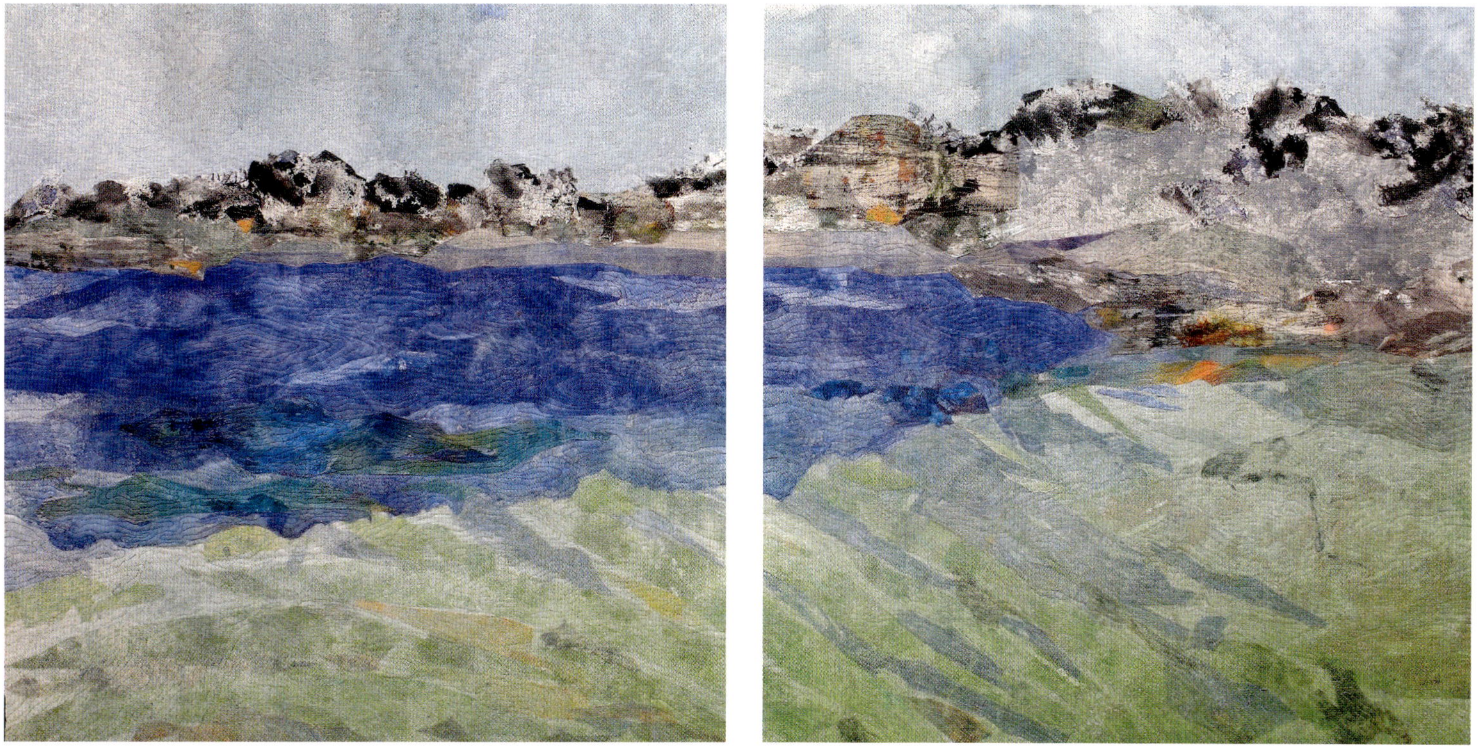

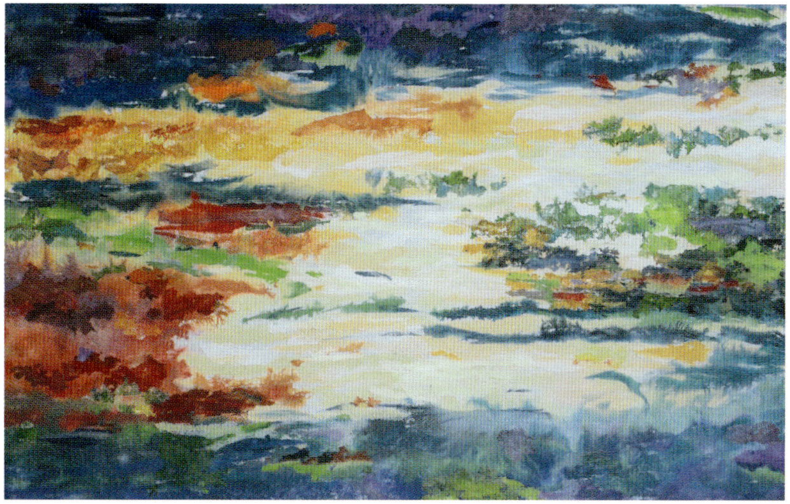

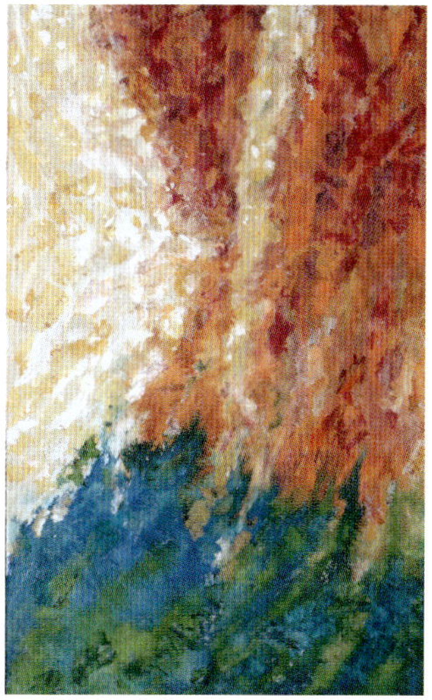

▲ *Reflections on the San Juans.*
Non-woven synthetic fabric.
32" × 65". 2015

◄ *Solstice Summer.*
Non-woven synthetic fabric.
50" × 79".

Transitions #2.
Non-woven synthetic fabric.
79" × 50". 2015.

All photos courtesy of
Tom Holt.

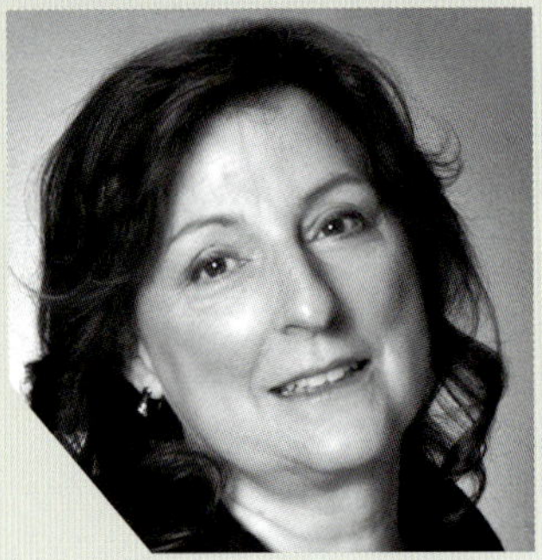

Bonnie Jo Smith

San Jose, California

In 1999, I had a work-related injury that required me to be completely off my feet for a while and to use a wheelchair. After I had been sitting and letting my body heal for months, doctors said I could start exercising, and I asked, "How about swimming?" One day my youngest daughter, Shara, purchased a pair of swim fins for me. Well, I must tell you I had my doubts; however, within about eight months, I had witnessed a remarkable change in my feet. Then I realized those fins were probably the best physical therapy I could do: they forced the feet to create and rebuild muscle. I knew I was on my way. Enjoying my swims, I began to imagine what an artwork of myself swimming would look like. Then I wondered whether I could really create one, and would viewers accept my minimalist creative style or reject my work? I then created *Swimming Upstream*, which received an award from Voters Injured at Work, in San Jose, for depicting how we can all prevail, and swim upstream. Three individual pieces of the installation have received NICHE Awards and/or recognition from *NICHE* magazine.

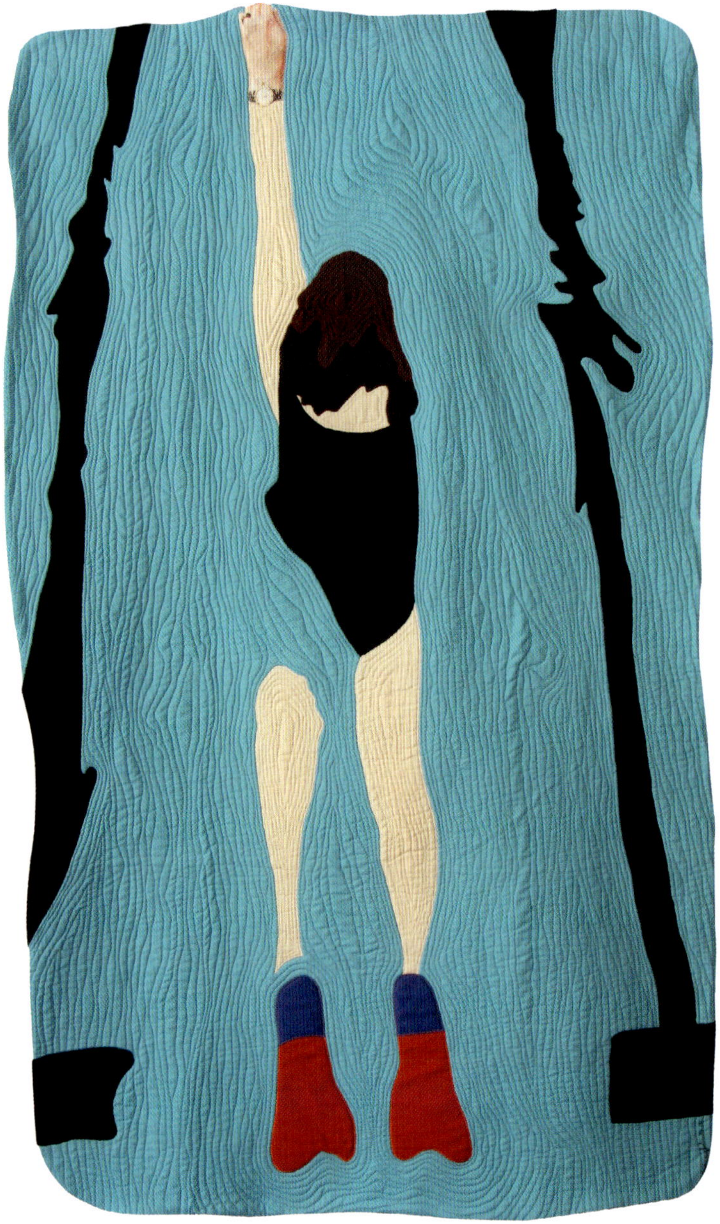

Swimming Upstream. Cotton fabrics, wool fabric, polyester batting, and polyester threads. 64" × 35". 2012.

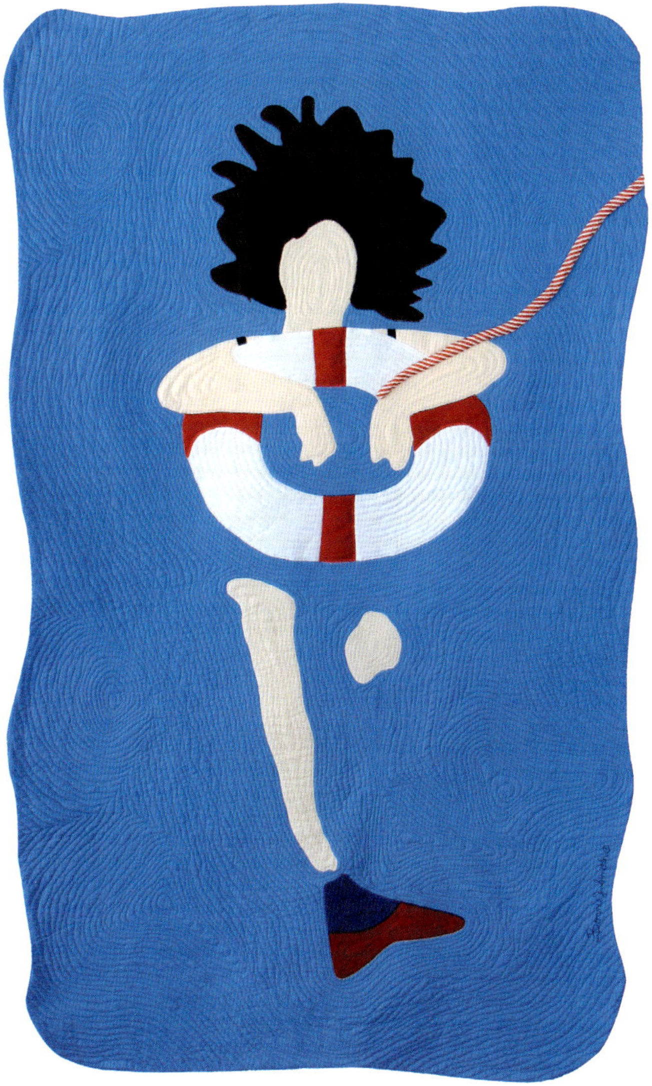

◄ *Tethered.* Cotton fabrics, wool fabric, polyester batting, and polyester threads. 65" × 35". 2013.

▼ *Companion.* Cotton fabrics and polyester batting. 65" × 35". 2013.

◄ *The Team.* Cotton fabrics, vintage fabrics, polyester batting, and machine appliqué. 65" × 35". 2013.

All art images courtesy of Luke Mulks.

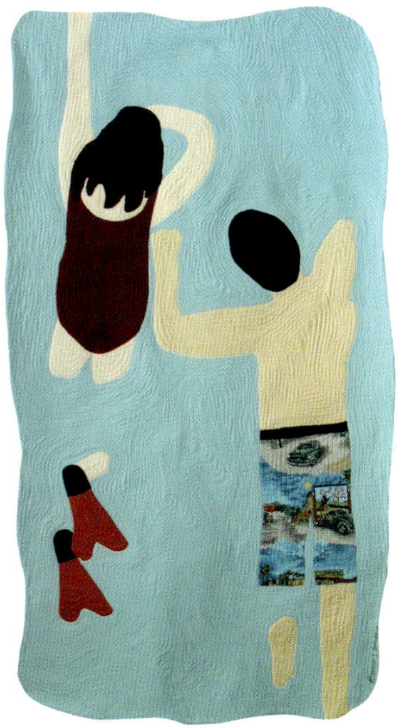

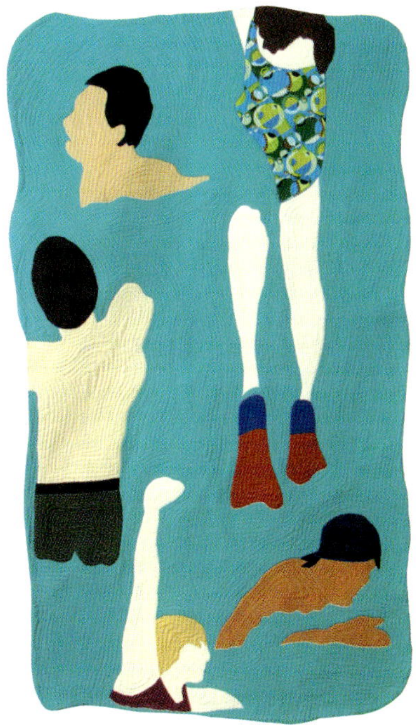

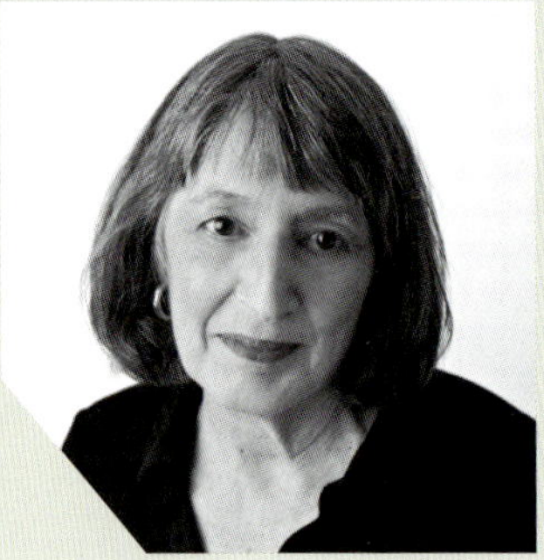

Catherine Whall Smith

Chaplin, Connecticut

In our highly complex information-sharing society, I feel the pressure to participate, which is why, at this stage in my life, my art is about being in and sharing a "moment in time." It only exists for that moment, and I attempt to capture that moment with my digital images. Enlarged hay images, for example, show fragmented lines, each one the stimulus for a quilt that explores how simple lines create visual space. Forms begin to take shape as haphazard slashing lines emerge during my design process.

Many of my construction techniques are rooted in my undergraduate and graduate studies in clothing and textiles. I intuitively understand the steps it takes to go from my one-of-a-kind designs to a finished product.

My final connection with each piece is to hand-stitch repetitive lines across the quilt's surface. Thousands of tiny stitches allow me once again to be "in the moment," as three layers merge into one, and my art transforms from a flat surface to one with texture, drape, and dimension.

My goal is to continue narrating the stories of my rural environment while developing the language of the line. I invite the viewer to consider and continue this dialogue.

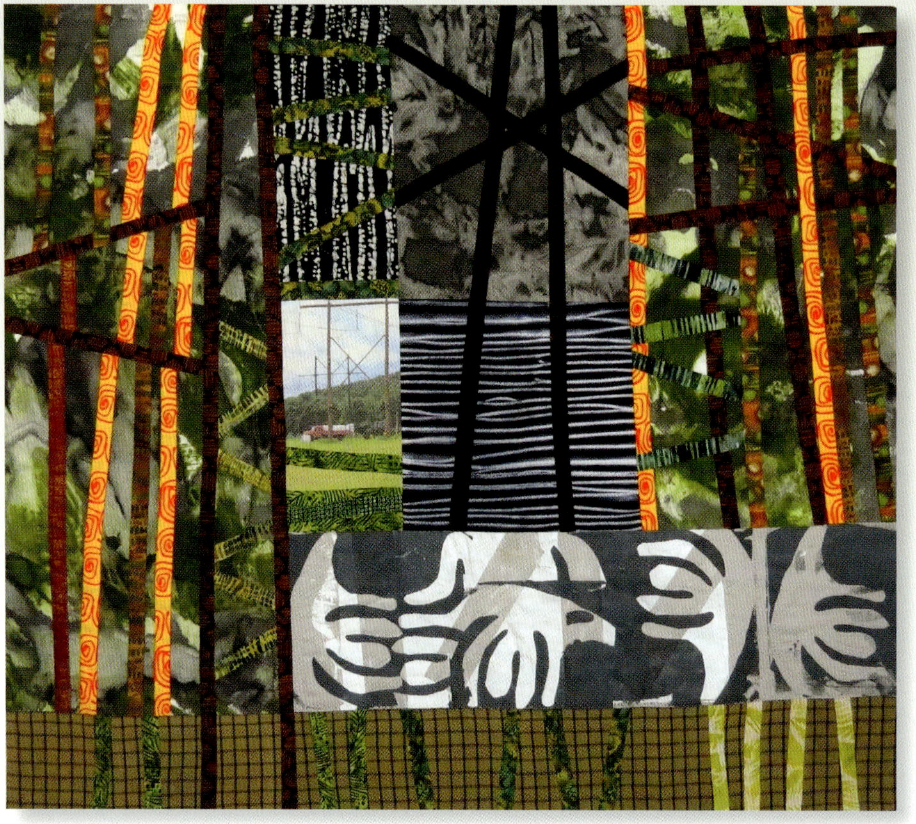

Grab and Go. Improvisational slashing. Artist's digital image applied to treated cotton materials, which include commercial, hand painted, and shabori dyed techniques. 35" × 40". 2015.

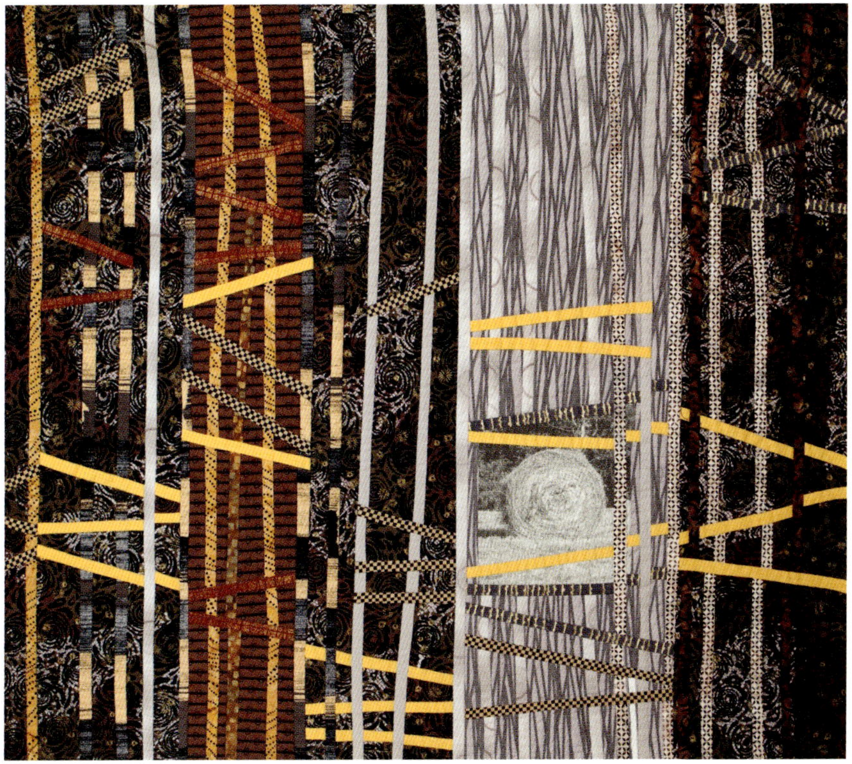

◄ *In the Hay Field Night.* Improvisational slashing. Artist's digital image applied to treated cotton. 39" × 44". 2014. Courtesy of Laurie Simonds.

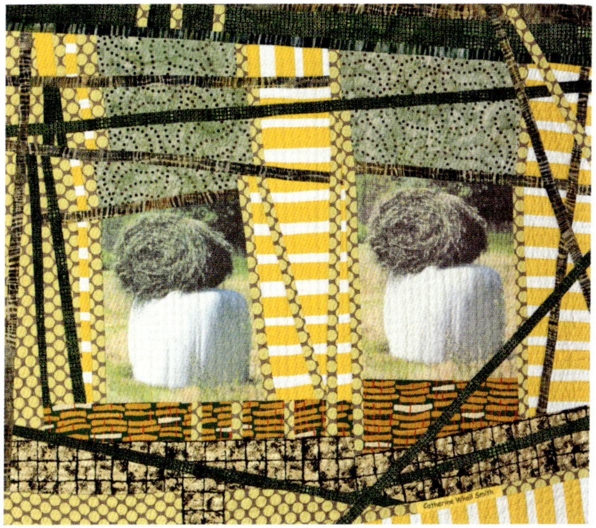

▲ *Twins with Matching Hats.* Improvisational slashing. Artist's digital images applied to treated cotton. 25" × 29". 2014. Courtesy of Laurie Simonds.

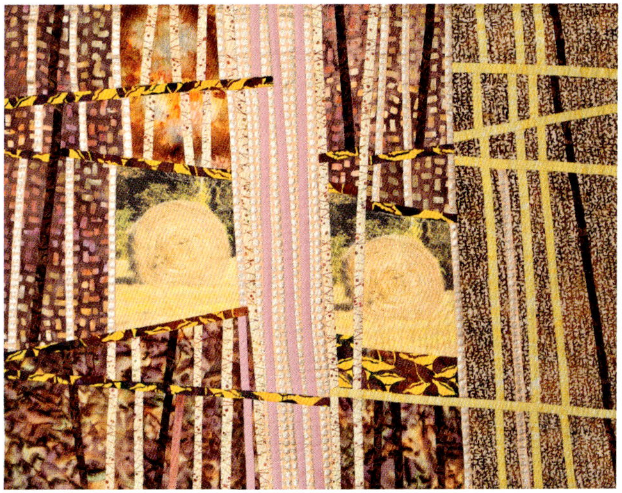

◄ *Rolled Hay.* Improvisational slashing. Artist's digital images applied to treated cotton. 30" × 34". 2014. Courtesy of Laurie Simonds.

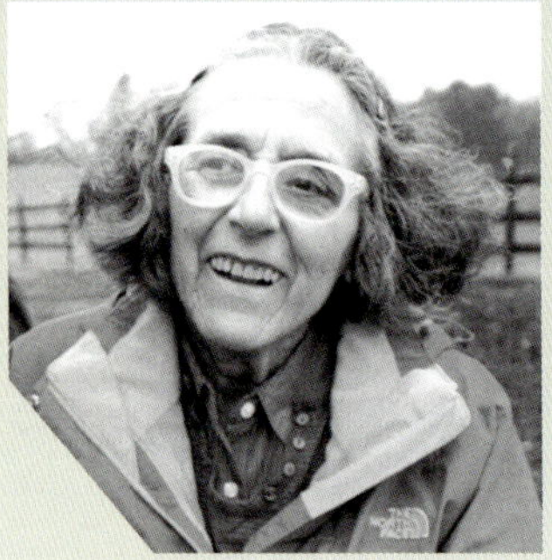

Courtesy of Talia Mayden.

Sherri Smith

Ann Arbor, Michigan

I teach fibers at the Stamps School of Art & Design at the University of Michigan and have also worked as a textile designer. I received a BA from Stanford and MFA from Cranbrook Academy of Art, and was elected a Fellow of the American Crafts Council in 2012.

I have been a fiber artist a long time and have exhibited my work widely in the United States and abroad. My current series of work is mostly images taken from astronomy, both current and historical. NASA works hard to obtain new images for me, so I'm not worried about running out of ideas. It is interesting to use one of the oldest forms of making to depict some of the newest discoveries and ideas.

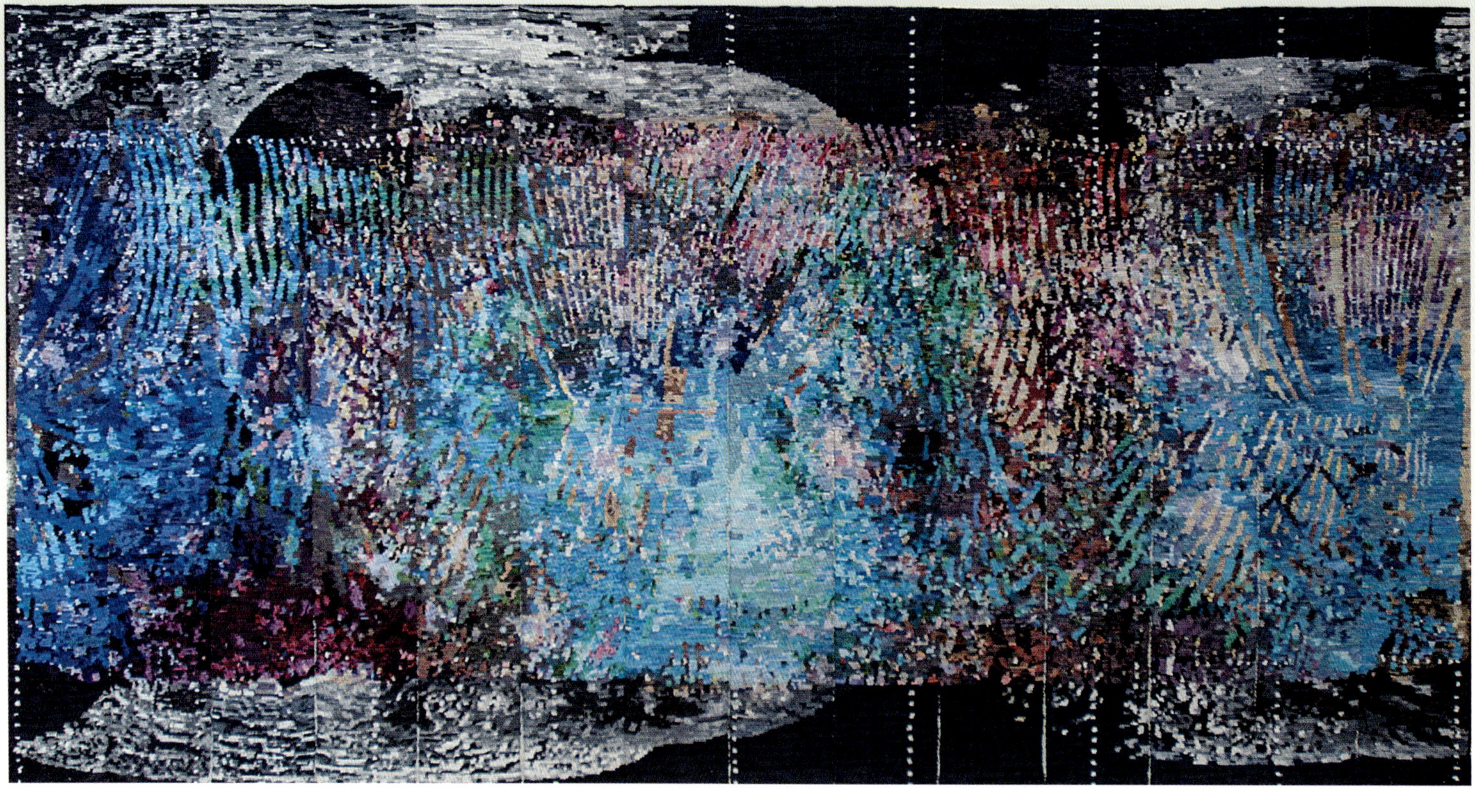

Mercury. Woven in strips of cotton fabric and cotton yarn. 54" × 108". 2015.

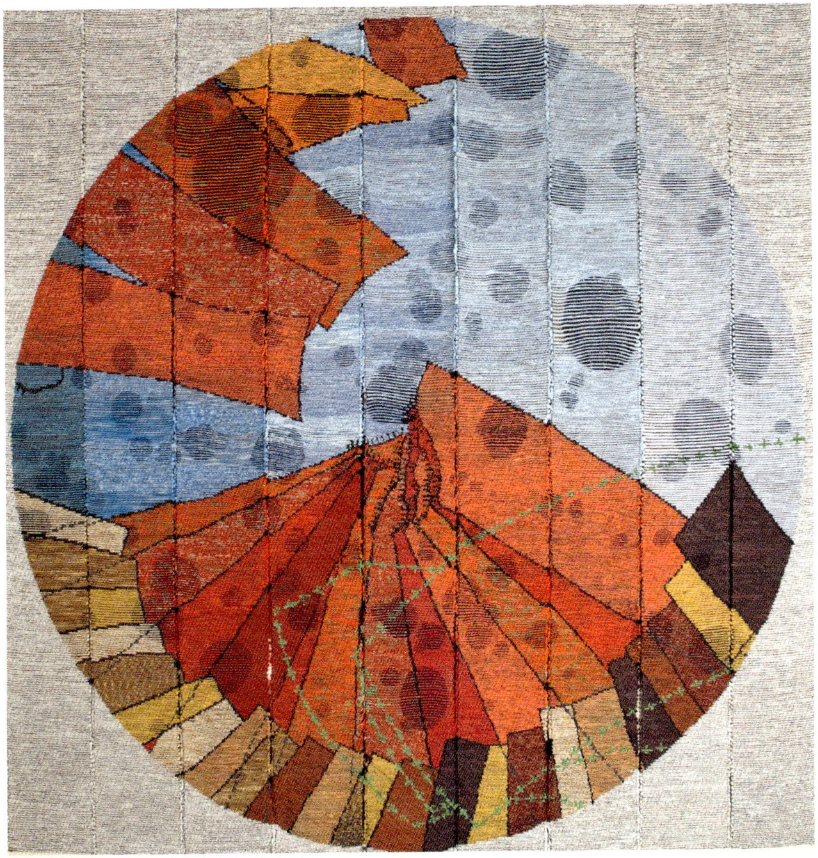

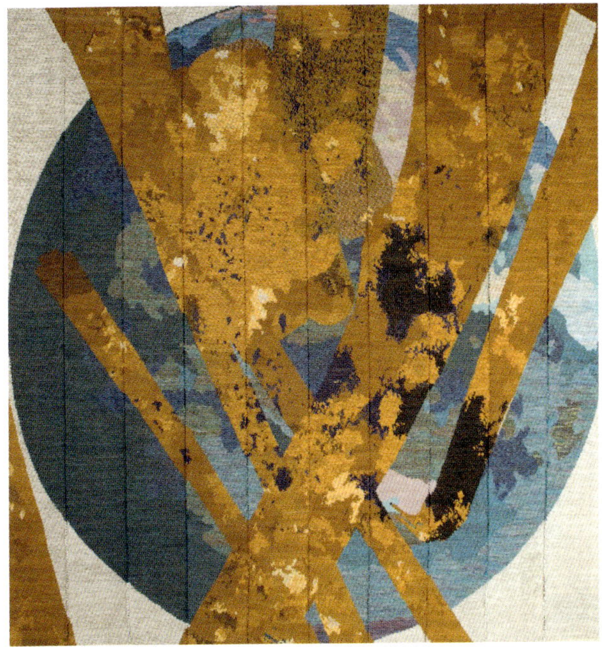

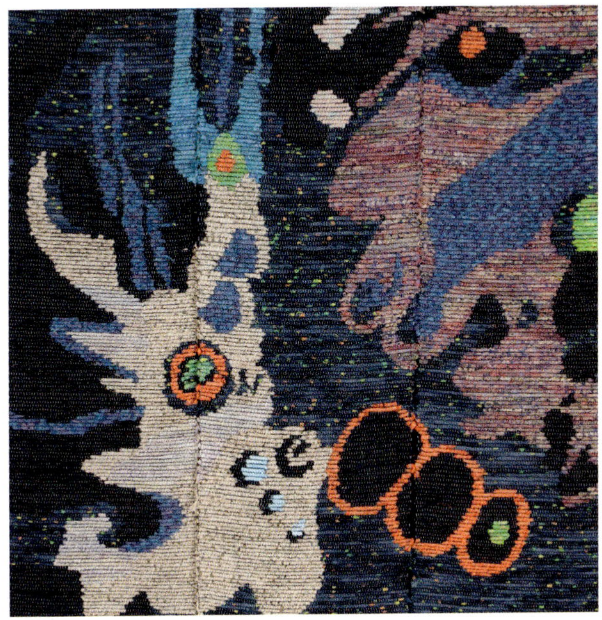

▲ *North Polar Region*. Woven in strips from cotton fabric and cotton yarn. 72" × 72". 2004.

◄ *Titan*. Woven in strips from cotton fabric and cotton yarn. 72" × 60". 2008.

► *Moon in 1747* (detail). Woven in strips from cotton fabric and cotton yarn. 84" × 60". 2008.

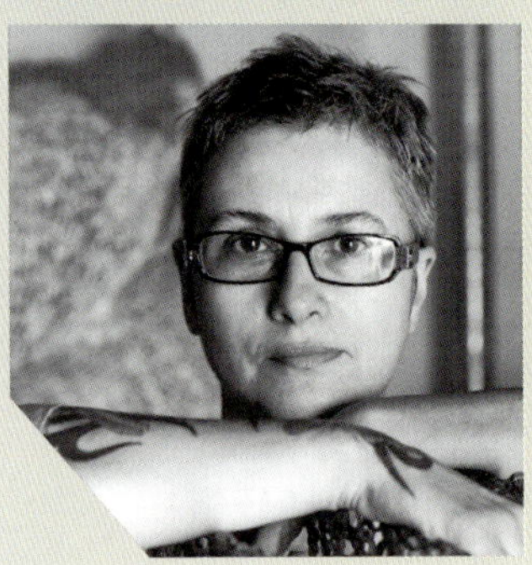

Photograph by Jim Newberry.

Yvette Kaiser Smith

Chicago, Illinois

My current practice of creating math-generated work and crocheting fiberglass began in 1992, when I started making sculpture that dealt with abstracting narratives of identity. Within this context, an exploration of fiberglass and resin led me to crocheting fiberglass roving. Years later, the same pursuit led me to start mapping patterns from math sequences by creating systems for visual articulation of mathematics as a way to generate random visual patterns through form and color distribution, utilizing the grid, Pascal's Triangle, and sequences from the infinite numbers pi and *e*.

I create systems for visual articulation of mathematics as a way to generate random visual patterns through form and color distribution. My signature process is crocheting continuous strands of fiberglass into flat geometric shapes. These are formed and hardened with the application of hard-finish polyester resin and the use of gravity, producing indoor, wall-based, geometric structures.

Born in Prague, Czechoslovakia in 1958, I now live and work in Chicago. A full-time artist since receiving my 1994 MFA from the University of Chicago, I have exhibited extensively at regional museums, art centers, and university galleries throughout the United States and alternative spaces abroad, working with art consulting firms, galleries, and individual clients to create site-specific, private, and public commissions since 2005.

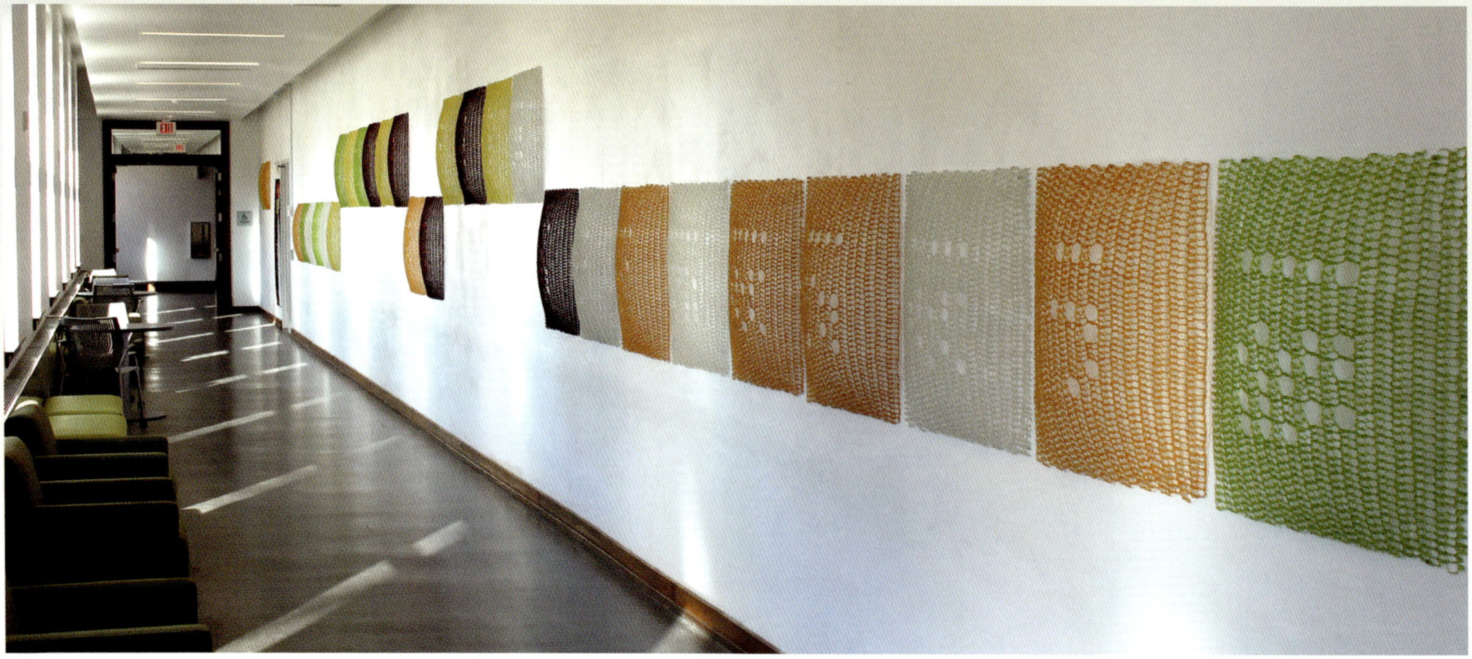

Lifesaver Movement in e. Crocheted fiberglass with polyester resin. 55" × 111' × 4". 2014.

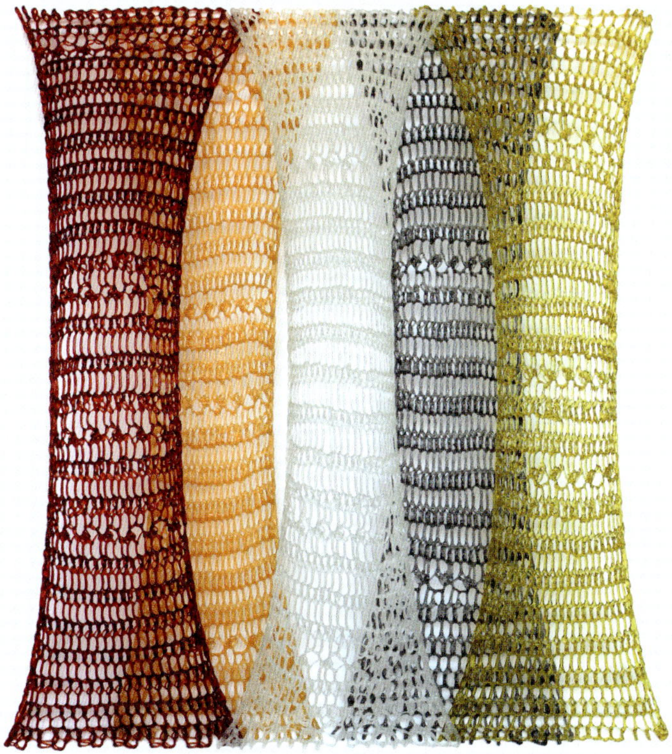

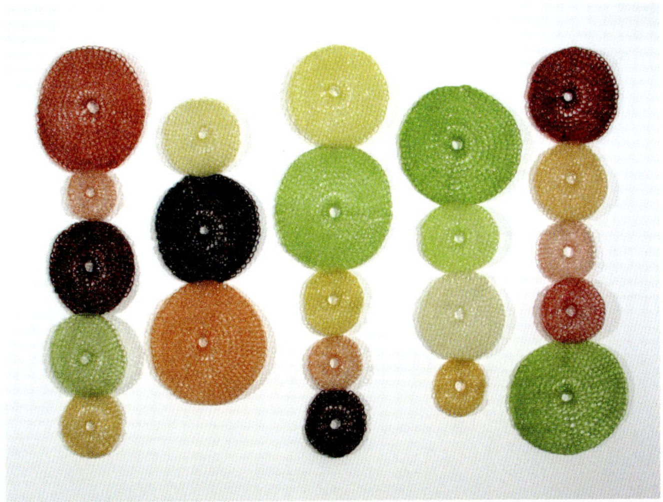

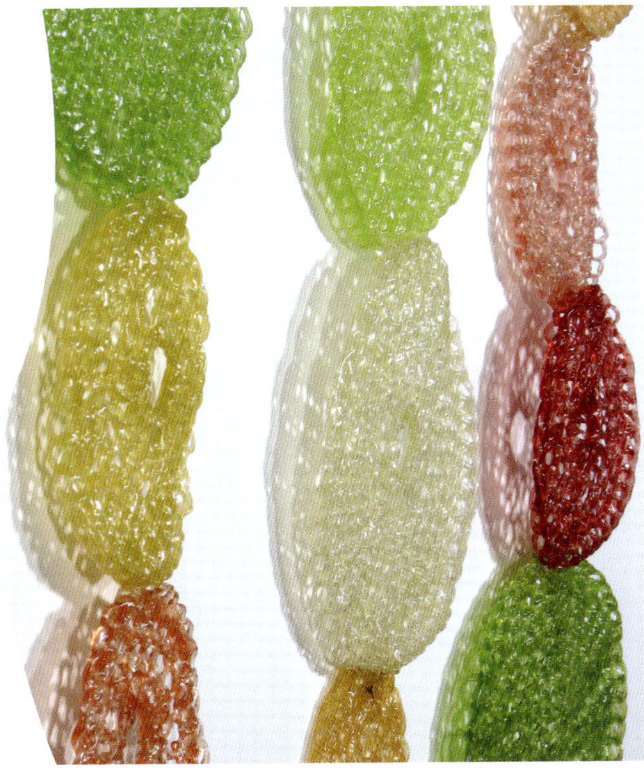

▲ *Etude from pi . . . 51413.* Crocheted fiberglass with polyester resin. 42" × 38" × 10". 2013.

◄ *Pi Line 22 in 5.* Crocheted fiberglass with polyester resin. 40" × 60" × 2". 2012. | Detail

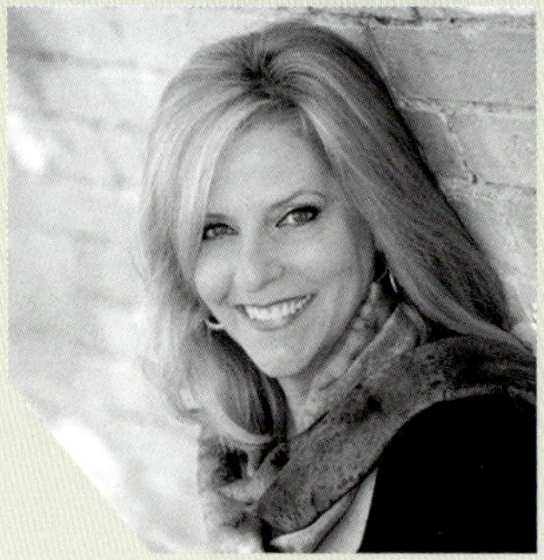

Courtesy of Marc Oxford.

Melissa Sobotka

Richardson, Texas

I was introduced to art quilts in 2007, and since then they have become my passion. Fiber adds a texture and richness to my work that I did not find in other mediums.

My two favorite things inspire my work: spirituality and travel. All of my quilts derive from my photographs. I spend several months transforming an idea into fiber, so I often choose my subject matter according to the intricacy of the image in order to engage and excite my creativity. I transform the photograph into an image by fusing numerous pieces of raw edge batik fabrics and then enhancing them with inks to soften the edges and add greater depth. I then quilt the piece on a long arm machine to permanently adhere the fabrics and give the feel of bas-relief sculpture.

My vision is to share with others a perspective through my eyes. My work has garnered many awards, including Best of Show at American Quilters Society, International Quilting Association, and Mancuso Quilt Shows.

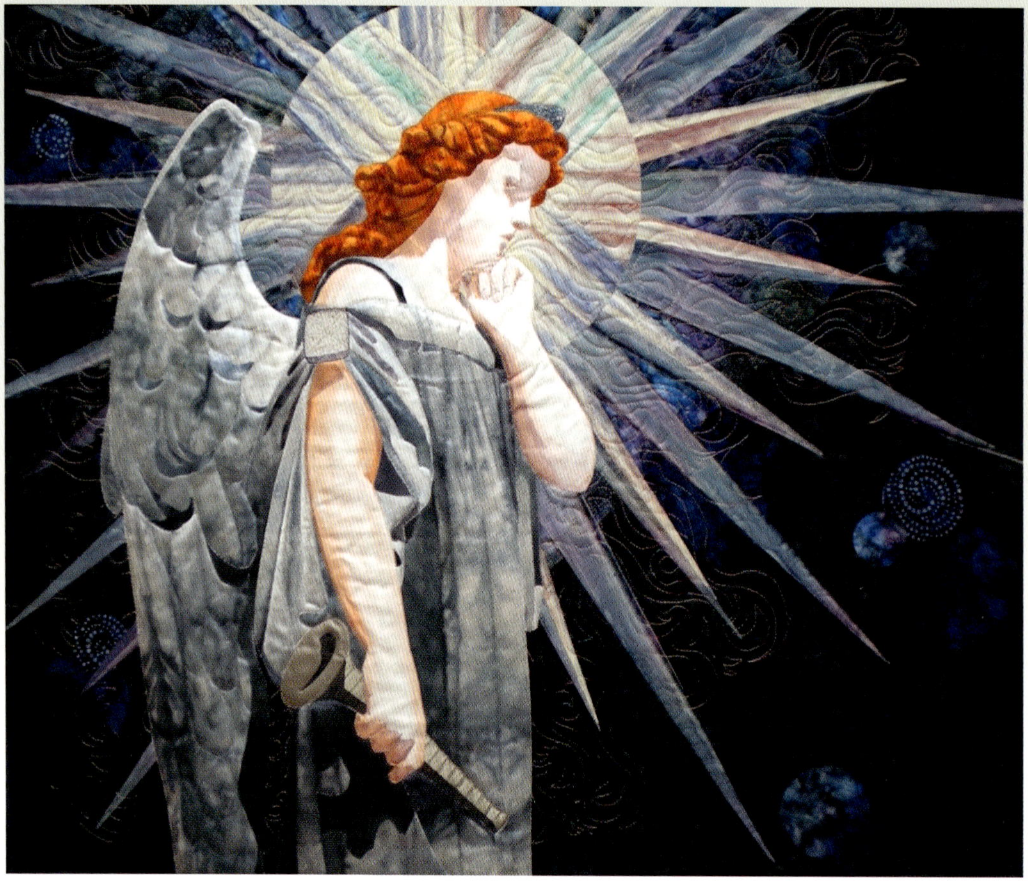

Archangel Haniel.
Raw edge, fused batiks, and satin. 43" × 36". 2009.

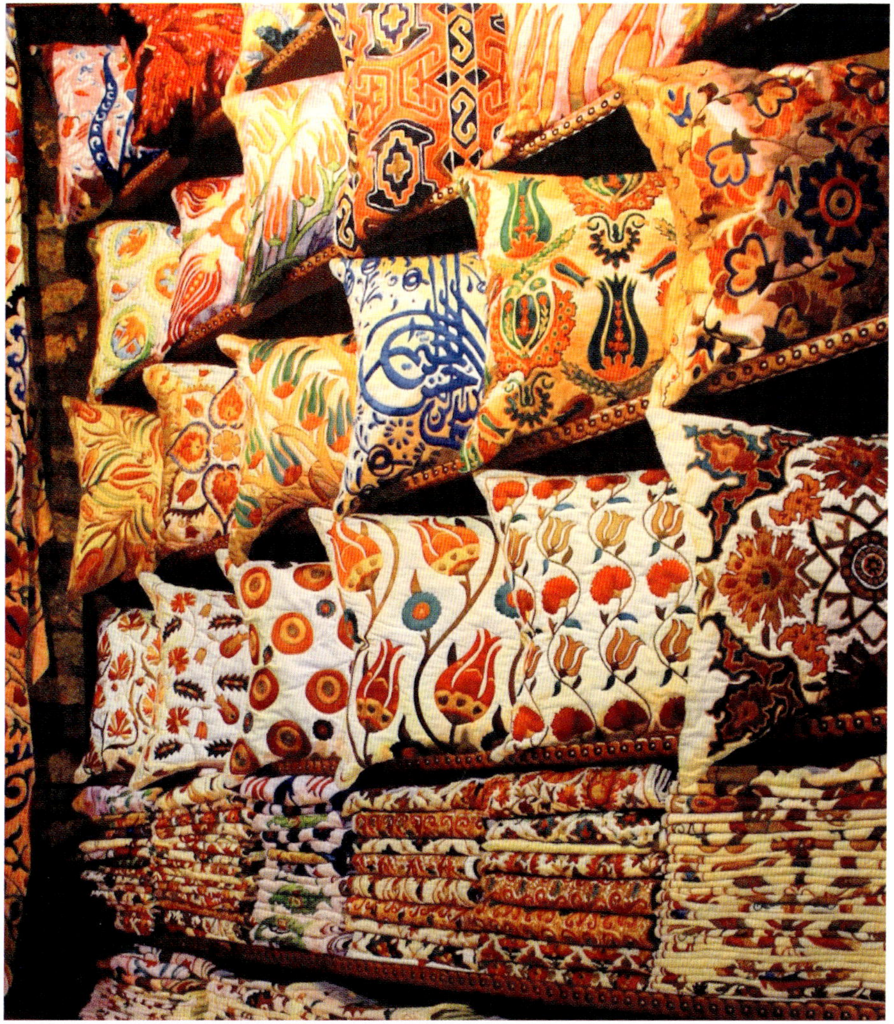

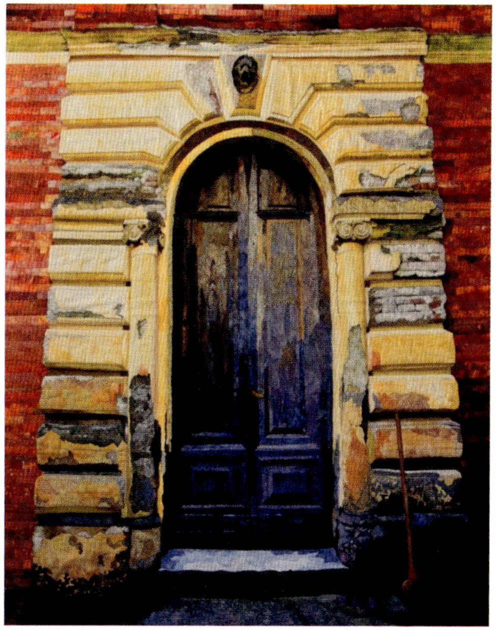

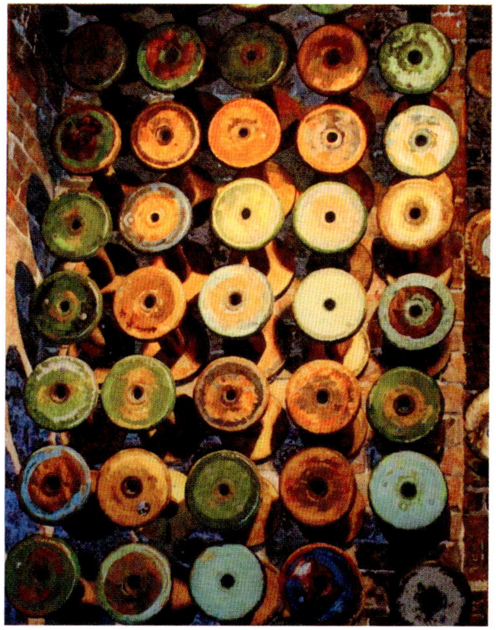

▲ *Silk Road Sampler*. Raw edge and fused batiks. 60" × 67". 2016.

◀ *Façade.* Raw edge and fused batiks. 42" × 52". 2010.

➤ *End of the Spin*. Raw edge and fused batiks. 43.5" × 57.5". 2014.

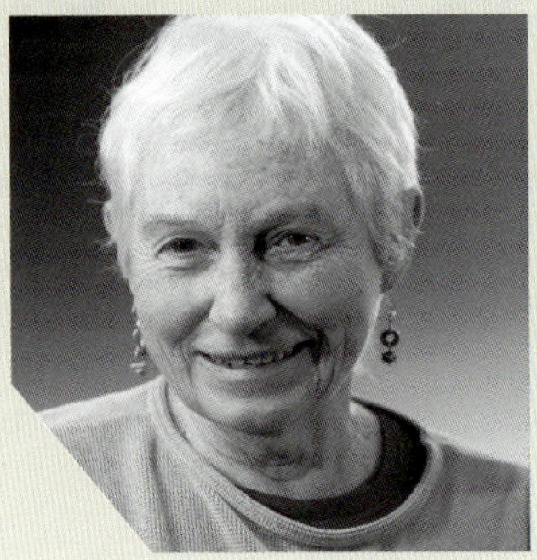

Courtesy of Tim Solar.

Frances Solar

Garibaldi Highlands, British Columbia, Canada

I love the challenge of playing with all the weird junk that I have collected or been given over the years, then reinventing new uses and forms for them. I have no idea why I am attracted to wire, bike cogs, industrial scrap, old keys, coins, and smashed bottle caps. I don't know how to weld or solder, so all the fastenings are textile based.

I like to doodle with ideas, colors, and materials. For a show titled *Snaps and Scraps*, I decided to design a wall hanging using only my leftovers. Weathered scrap copper panels, unused woven bits and pieces stashed in bags in my studio evolved into my *Steampunk* series. *Fest of Metal* was originally designed for a group show celebrating Gallileo's 400th anniversary. Somehow, when stitched onto stainless mesh panels, my huge collection of circular things—glass, metal, coins, bike cogs, wire—evoked Outer Space!

I have always been attracted to the clean geometry and colors of the traditional pieced quilt. The *Scrapyard Quilt* is my contemporary interpretation of this art form. Magical things happened with color when I wove long, narrow, flat, colorful panels of wire fabric and then shaped them with deep folds into a wall-mounted sculpture. The colors in *Rumpled* blend and shimmer into a richly textured surface. *Scrapyard Quilt* was a Winner of a 2016 NICHE Award and *Rumpled* was a Finalist.

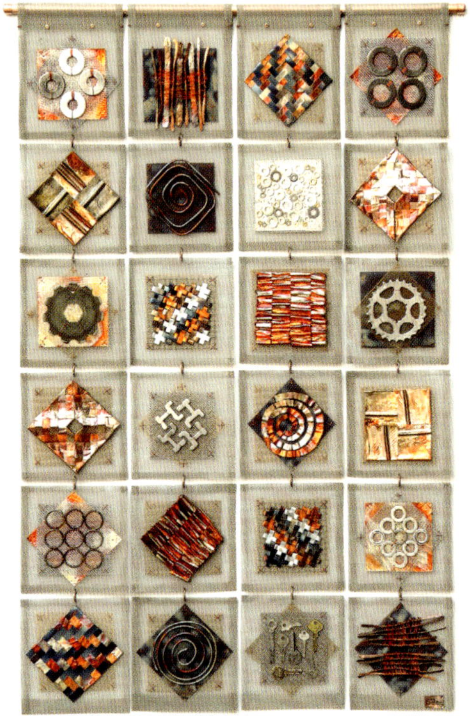

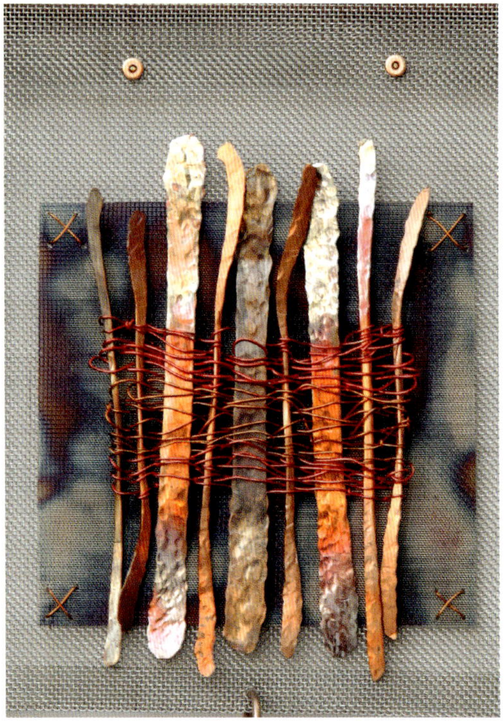

Scrapyard Quilt. Stainless steel mesh, copper wire, copper strip, brass, industrial scrap, bike cogs, keys, coins, and glass. 47" × 30". 2014. | Detail

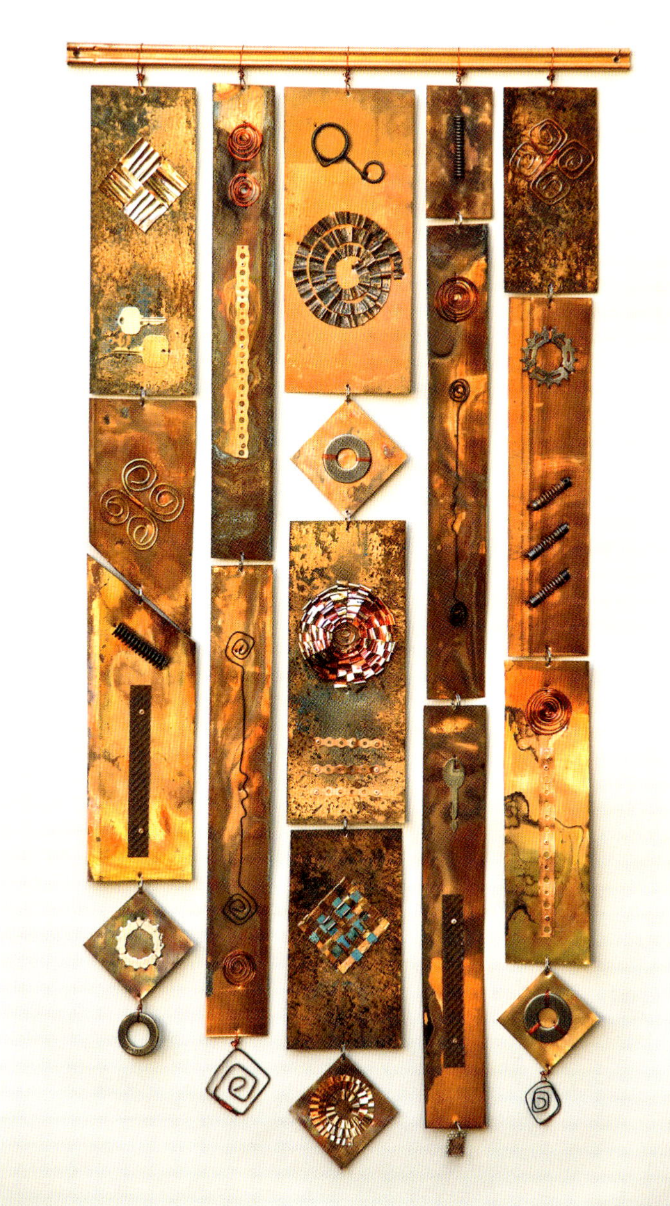

Steampunk. Sheet copper, copper wire, keys, springs, and industrial scrap. 46" × 23". 2011.

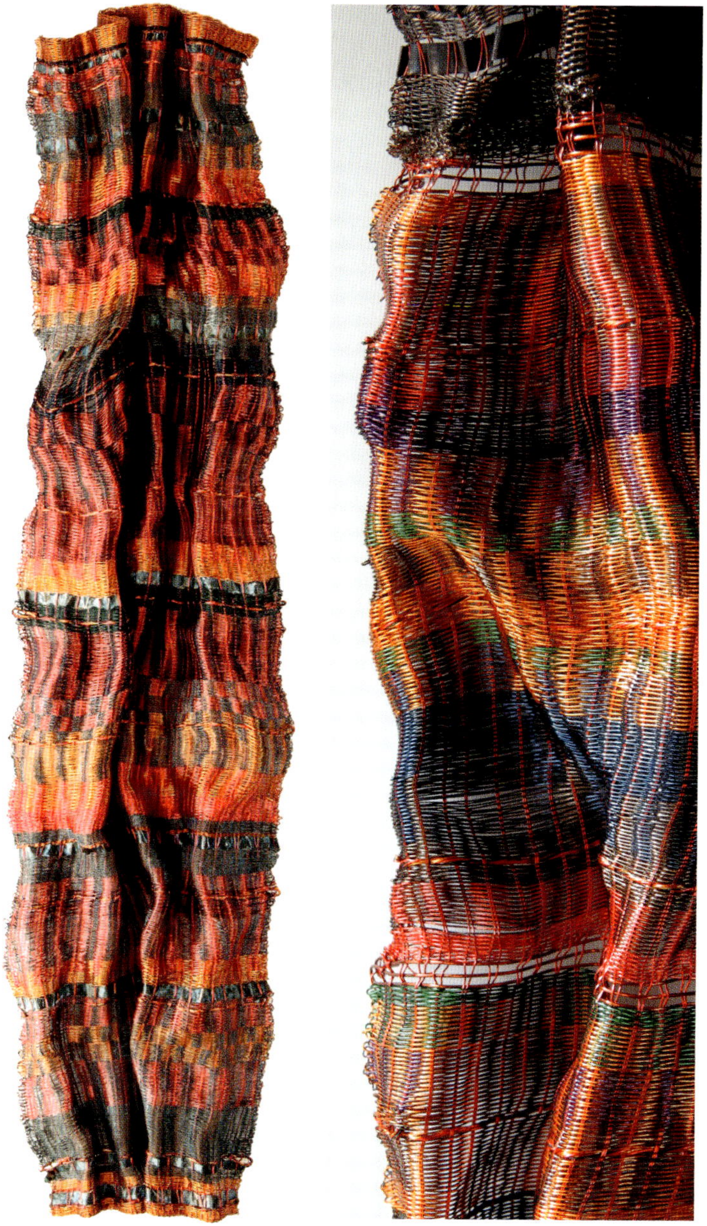

Rumpled. Copper wire, copper strip, and patina. 36" × 9". 2015. | Detail

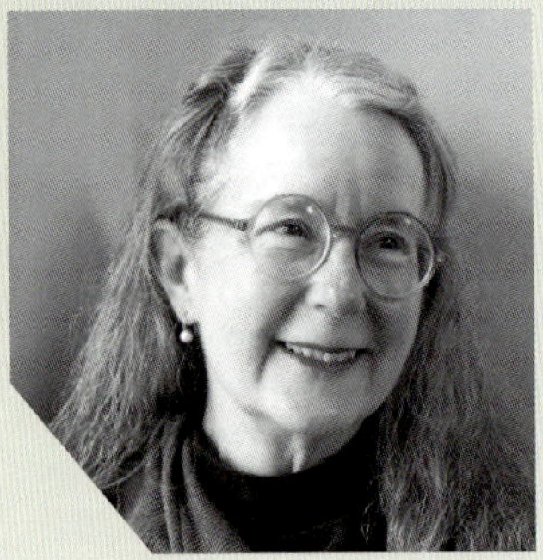

Courtesy of C. Douglas Payne.

Joy Stocksdale

Sebastopol, California

My main concern is design. Leaves, flowers, and geometric patterns, as well as parts of designs on historic ceramics, metal, and textiles, inspire me. Many designs emerge from small sketch notes in my imagination; the challenge is turning these sketches into designs that work within the format of a wall piece.

Another challenge is to find a process that allows a direct notation of design. As a result of studies at Goldsmith's College, University of London, I developed polychromatic screen printing, an innovative process that combines both painting and printing. It allows the same flexibility and spontaneity as painting on paper or fabric, with the added result of producing more than one print. I detail this unique process in my book, *Polychromatic Screen Printing*.

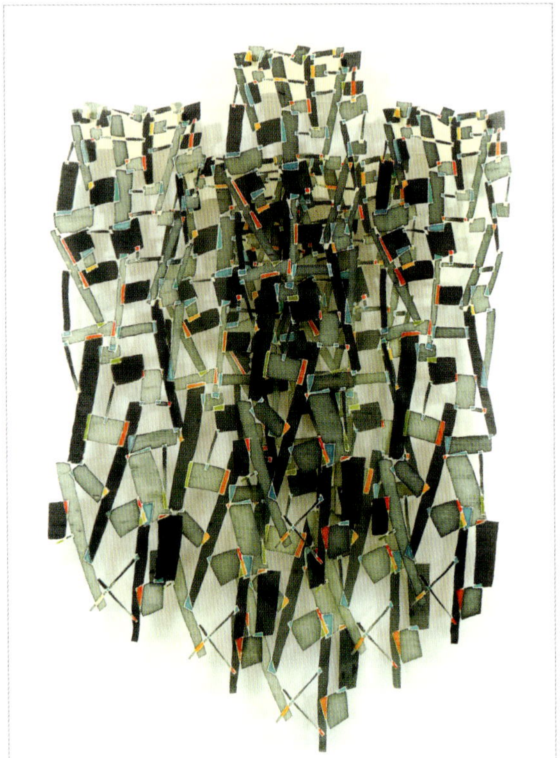

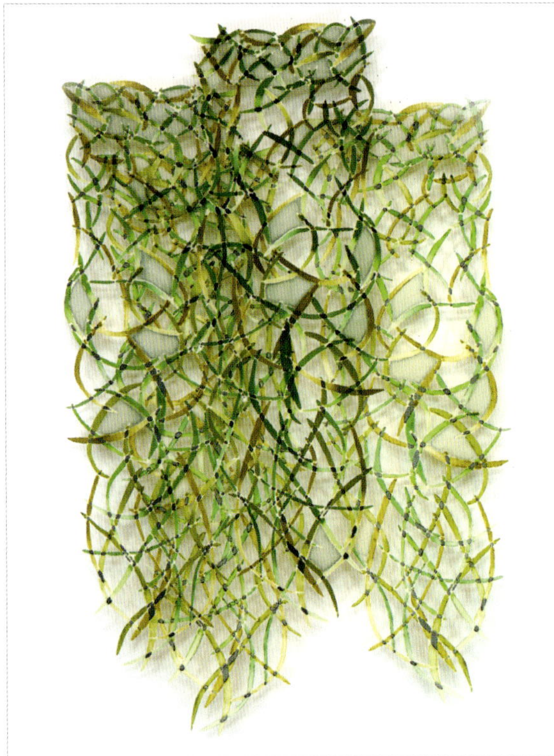

Black Rectangles. Cut silk hung from U-shaped acrylic mountings. 53" × 35". 2015.

➤ *Green Curved Leaves*. Cut silk hung from U-shaped acrylic mountings. 41" × 26". 2015.

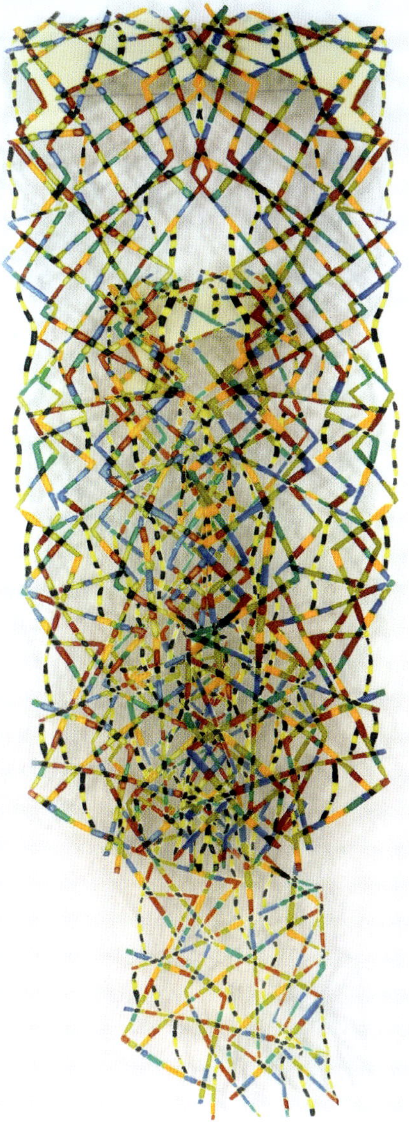

Sticks & Dots II. Cut silk hung from U-shaped acrylic mountings. 52" × 18". 2014.

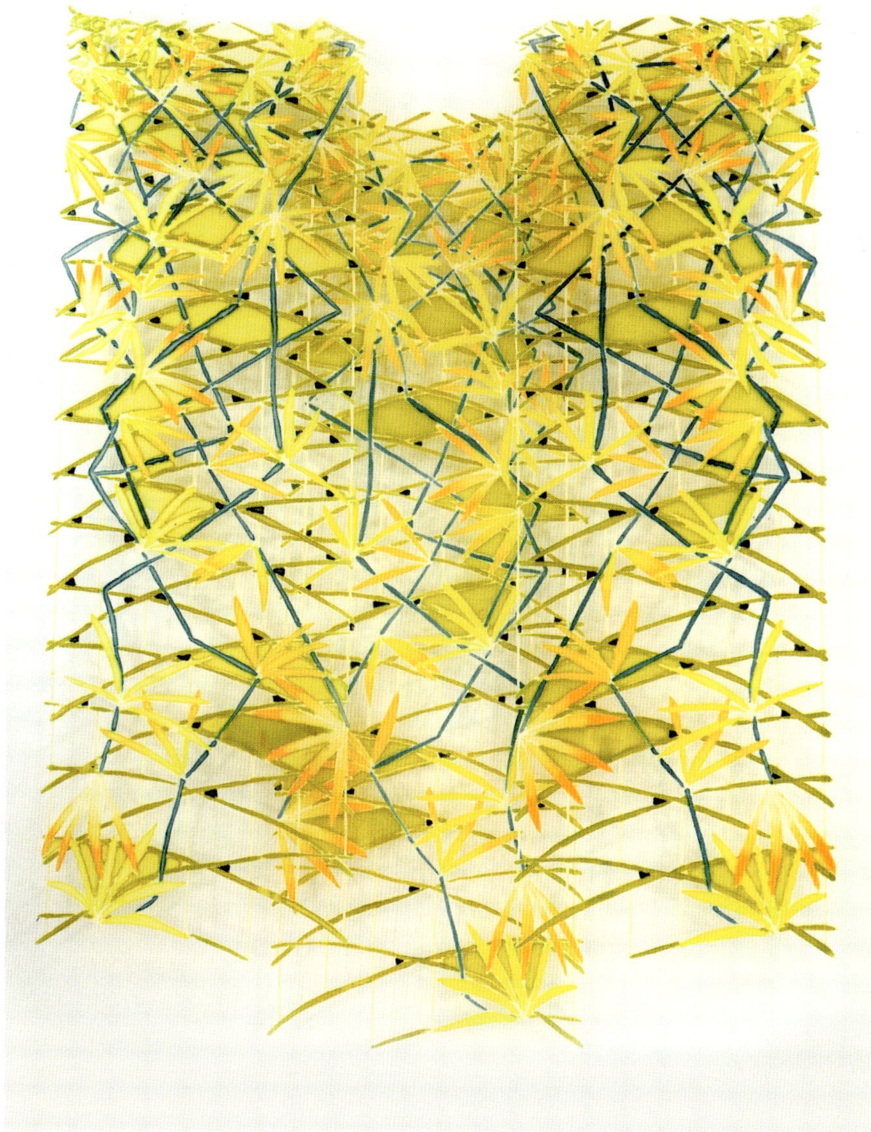

Net & Leaves. Cut silk hung from U-shaped acrylic mountings. 48" × 34". 2015.

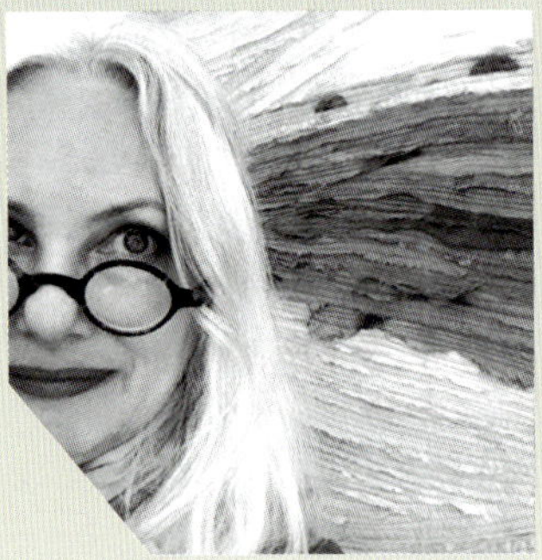

Elena Stokes

Clinton, New Jersey

I work with textiles in a quilt construct to form complex, texturally-rich quilted collages. Living in the Garden State, I find the light, space, and color of open sky vistas of rural west New Jersey are strong influences in my work. Horizon lines crafted in re-purposed materials are my primary visual elements, metaphors for transitions, transformation, and transcendence. Old clothing, once opulent silks now tattered and torn, transcend their functional beginnings and are transformed, reincarnated into a new body, a body of art. An interesting verse on reincarnation from the Hindu scripture of the Bhagavad Gita states, "Just as a person puts on new clothes and discards old and torn clothes, similarly, an embodied soul enters new material bodies, leaving the old bodies."

I'm a self-taught artist with extensive training in traditional patchwork quilt making. My work has been invited to and juried into numerous galleries, museums, and exhibitions, including Quilt National, and can be found in private collections throughout the United States and Europe.

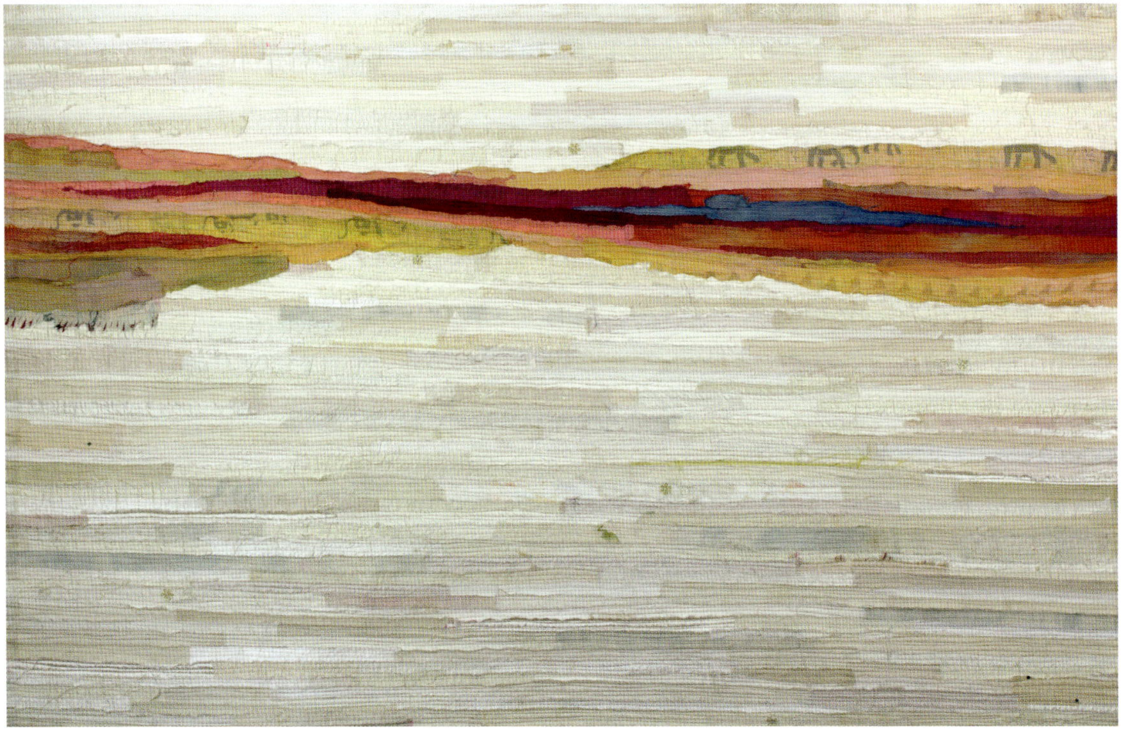

Infinity. Reclaimed sari silk and thread. 43" × 67". 2014.

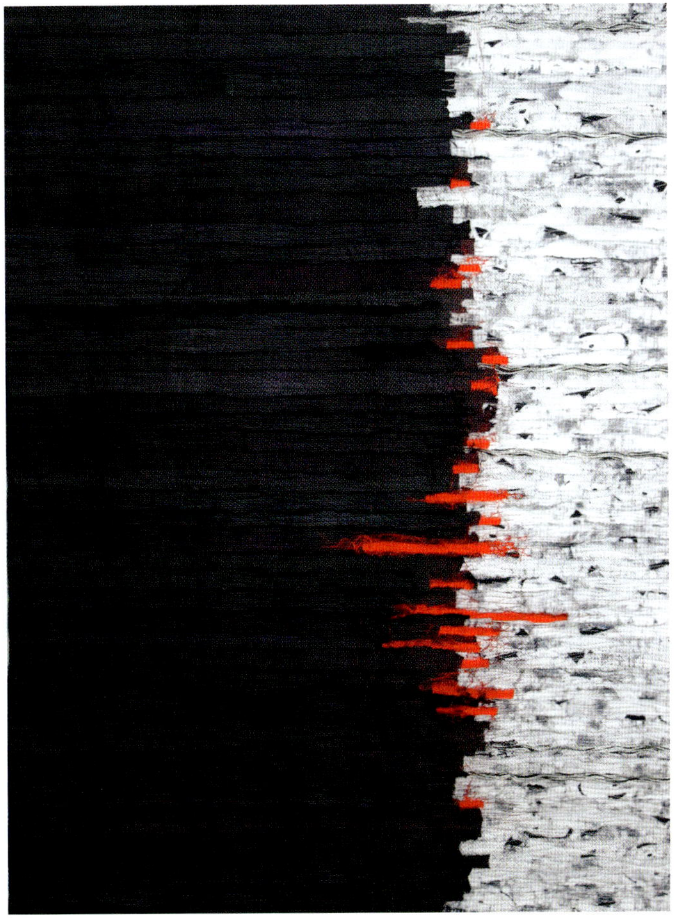

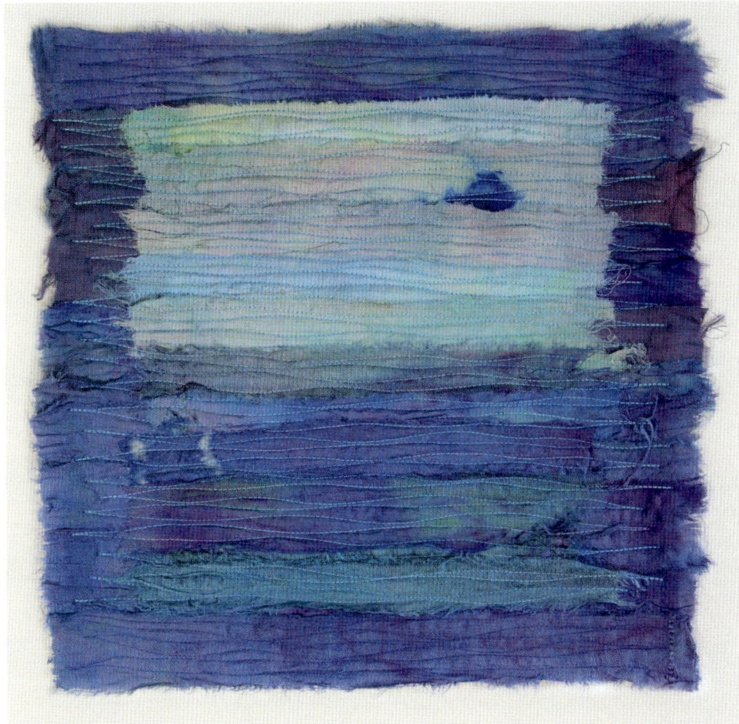

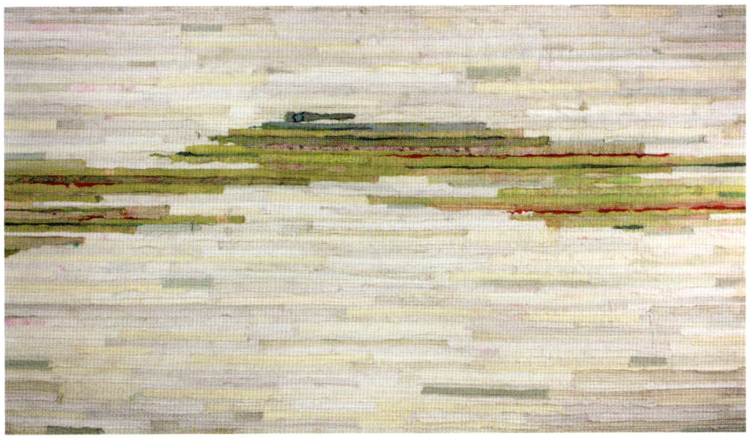

▲ *Tracking Passion.* Reclaimed sari silk and thread. 46.5" × 34.5". 2013.

◄ *Blue Lagoon.* Reclaimed sari silk and thread. 12" × 12". 2014.

► *Infinity VI—Lines and Layers.* Reclaimed sari silk and thread. 46" × 84". 2015.

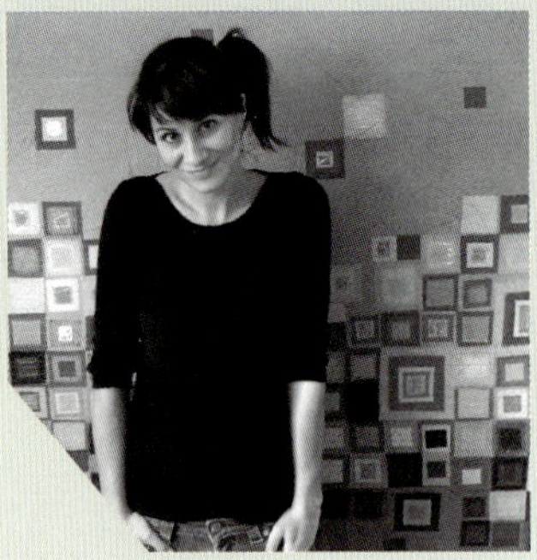

Sarah Symes

Vancouver, British Columbia, Canada

I aspire to recreate my internal experiences of places and people through my work. It represents an abstraction of real life, infused with memories and ideas evoked by the subject. I try to conjure emotion through color and manipulate composition to suggest familiar forms and landscapes.

My artwork has been exhibited in the United States, Canada, and Europe. I have been interviewed by a number of magazines and newspapers, and featured by some of the top influencers on the design scene. My work hangs in private collections worldwide.

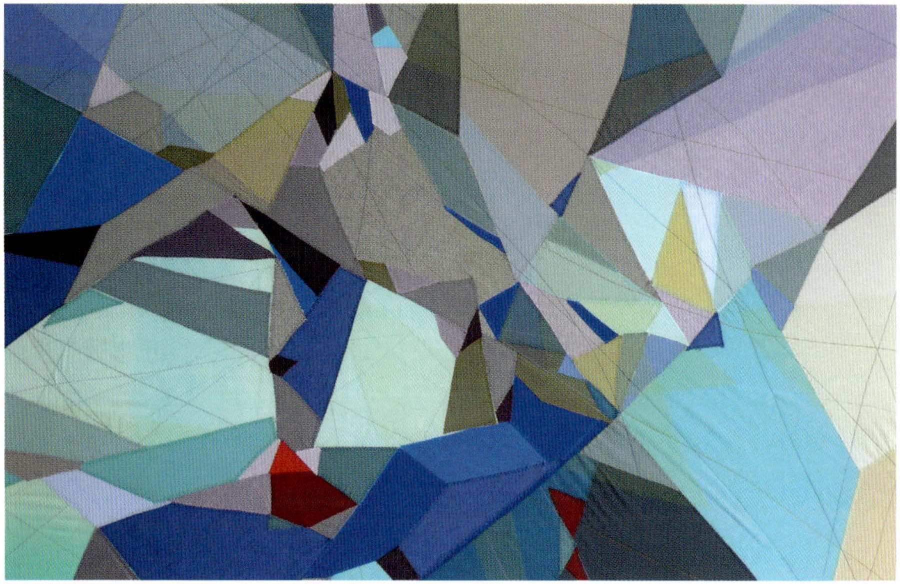

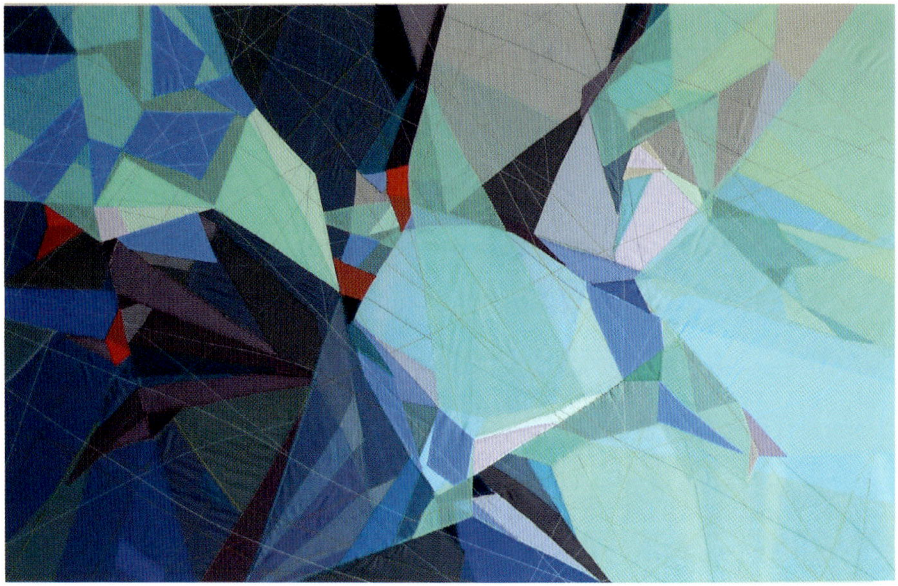

◄ *Abstract Mountain Landscape No. 2.*
Fabrics: cotton, tulle, mesh. 30" × 48". 2013.

► *Abstract Mountain Landscape No. 4.*
Fabrics: silk, cotton, satin, tulle, organza. 30" × 48". 2014.

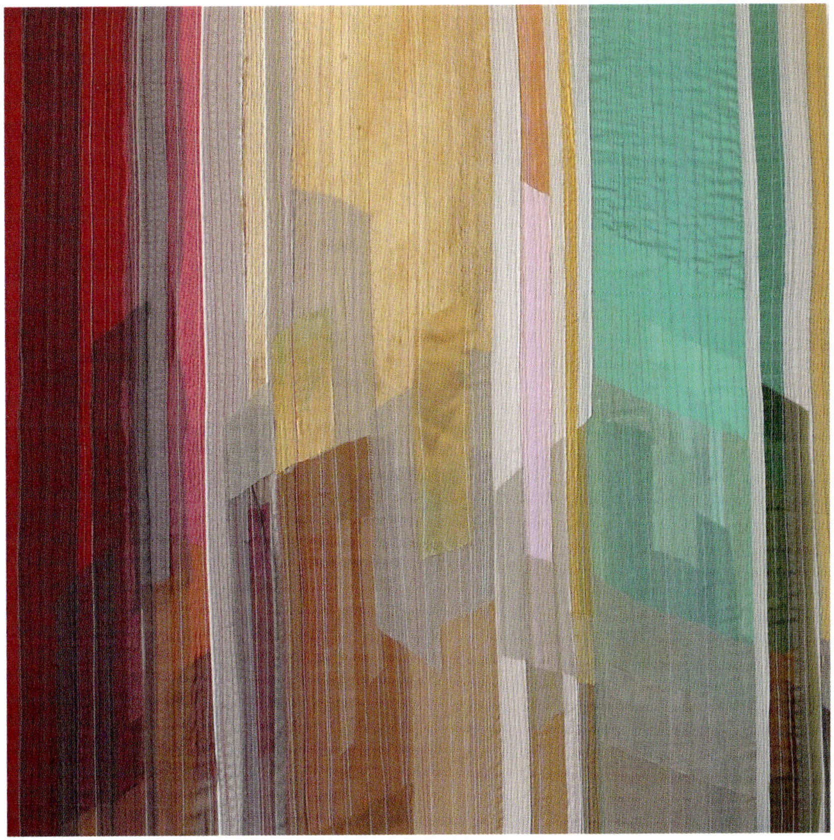

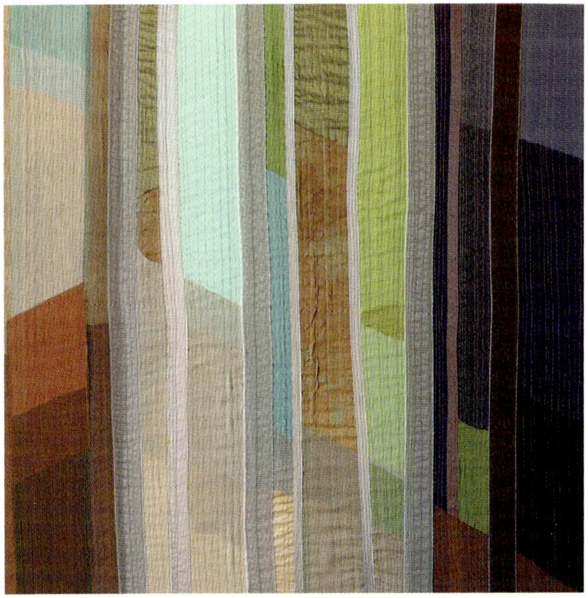

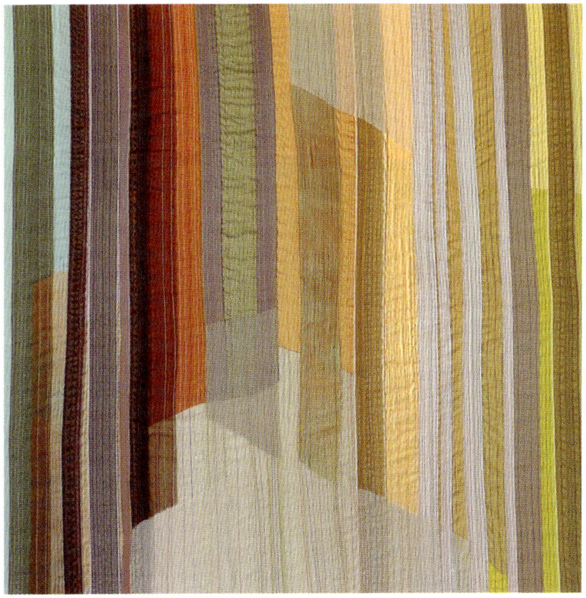

▲ *Havana Streetscape No. 1.* Fabrics: silk, cotton, satin, tulle, organza. 30" × 30". 2014.

◀ *Havana Streetscape No. 2.* Fabrics: silk, cotton, satin, tulle, organza. 30" × 30". 2014.

➤ *Havana Streetscape No. 3.* Fabrics: silk, cotton, satin, tulle, organza. 30" × 30". 2014.

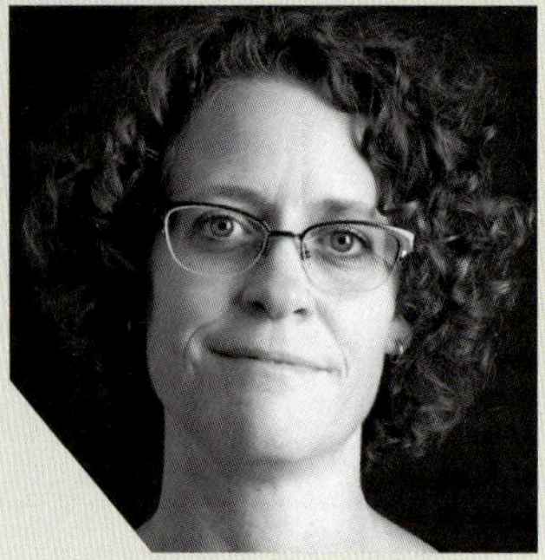

Susie Taylor

San Jose, California

My work combines origami and weaving to create a new woven form. This work originates on the loom where discontinuous pleats are engineered, woven, and incorporated into the ground cloth. When the fabric is taken off the loom, the pleats become the folded origami shapes that hover over the surface without using any cutting or sewing; only weaving and folding are used. Linen yarn is an obvious choice to weave with, as its natural characteristics produce and hold the folds nicely.

As an accomplished weaver, I push the limits of what can be produced on the traditional hand loom. I enjoy combining techniques that rely heavily on hand manipulation with loom-controlled structures. I am drawn to complex thought but strive to execute my work as simply as possible. My work celebrates the joy of producing basic cloth that transforms into perplexing, dimensional compositions.

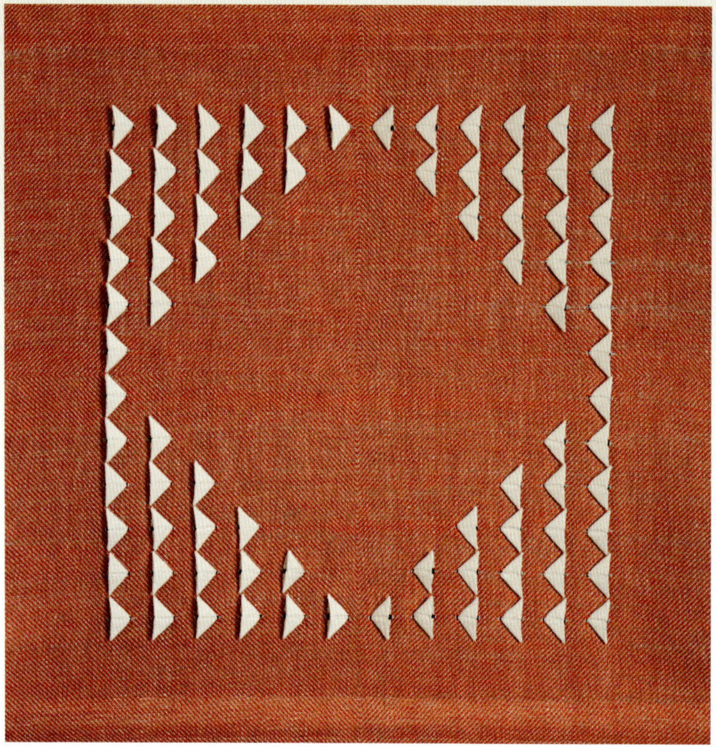

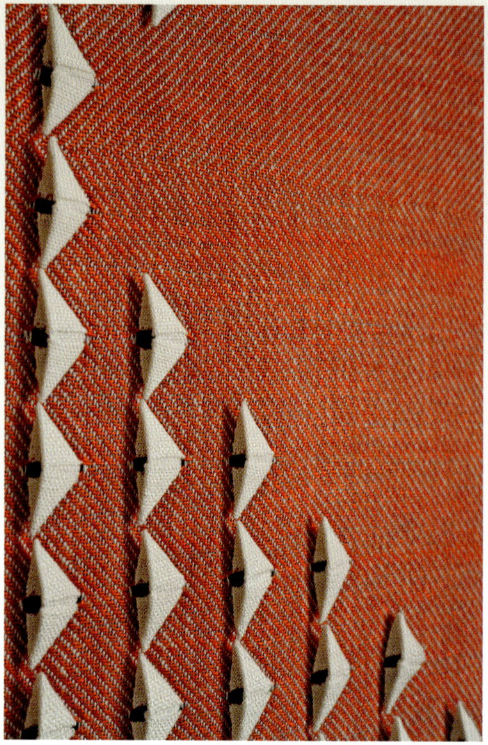

Twill Diamond Negative. Woven and folded linen. 24" × 24". 2015. | Detail

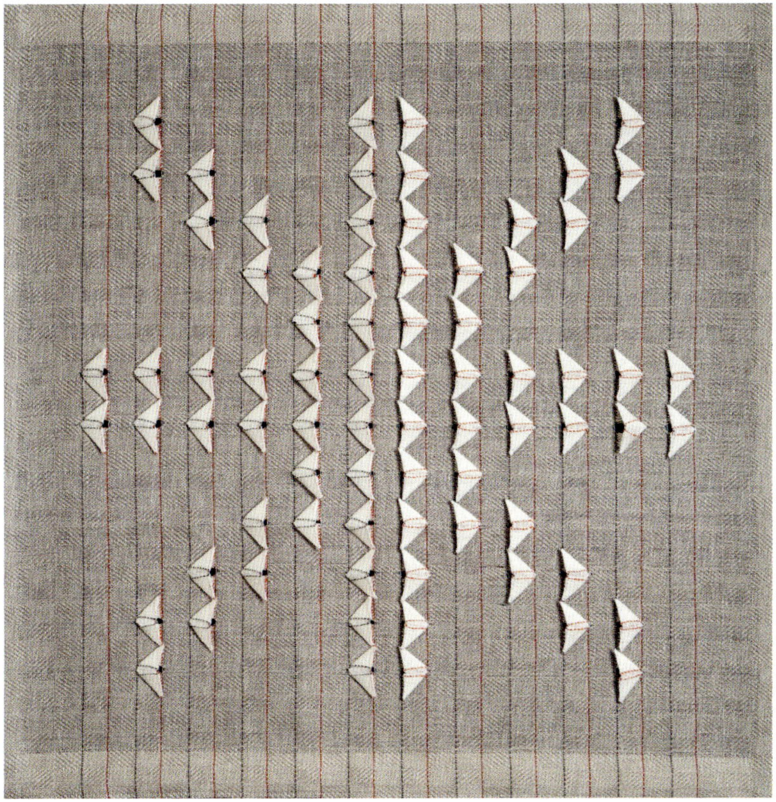

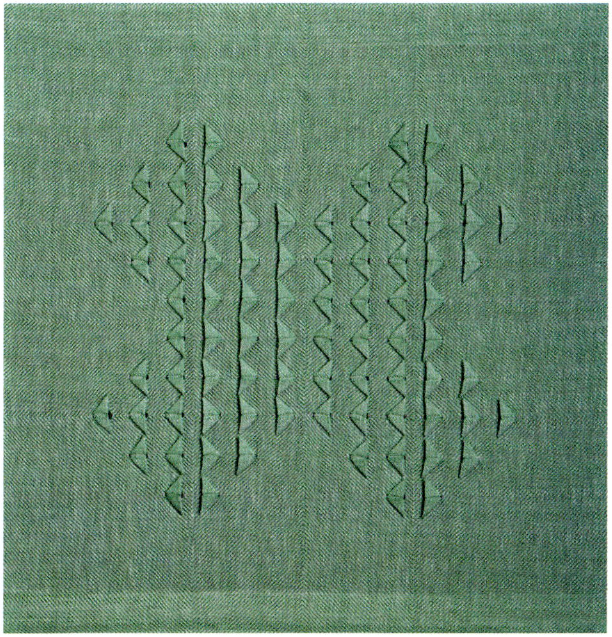

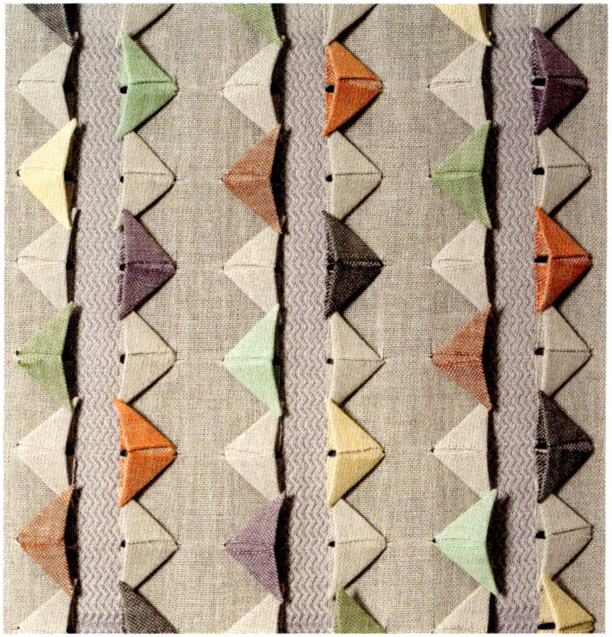

▲ *Twill X Positive*. Woven and folded linen. 24" × 24". 2015.

◄ *Square Two*. Woven and folded linen. 28" × 28". 2015.

► *Three Towers* (detail). Woven and folded linen and silk. 24" × 48". 2014.

All photographs courtesy of James Dewrance.

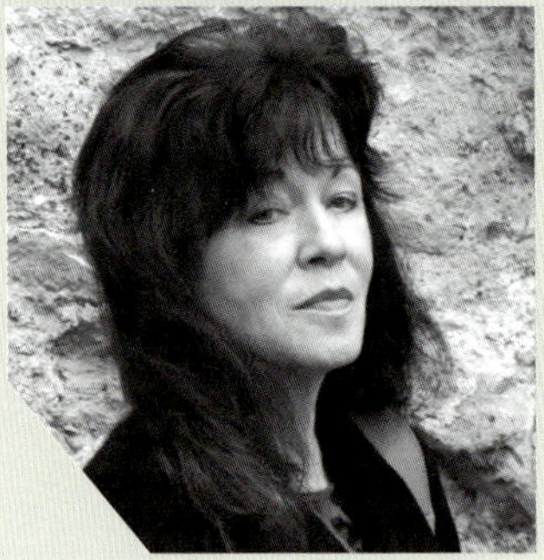

Lisa Van Herik

La Jolla, California

It all starts with a strand: a strand of copper wire, electrical wire, or a gorgeous strand of fiber. All that endless possibility in strands of things! Couple that with a real love of combining things in unexpected ways, and you'll understand why I'm compelled to make the art I do. On a personal note, my dad was an electrician; the first time he made me a quick copper wire bracelet, I was fascinated. Oh, and tools: I love tools and what they can do. Next, my grandmother taught me to crochet, and the wonder of making something solid from a simple strand has captured my attention for many a year. A simple strand is much like a line that you can draw. If you draw a line, how many ways can you make it change and move? That's how I see making my artwork.

As a metalsmith, I was immediately drawn to wire and wire-weaving. Having learned and experimented with many techniques, I realized that I could create my own unique methods of creating new looks with wire. My first book, *Make Wire Beads*, found forty-four different ways to make wire beads. My next book, *Fiber Wire Beads and Jewelry*, combined the gorgeous colors of lush, exotic fibers with wire: a great marriage of the two elements.

I also love moving from small to large artworks to see if the techniques translate. So, moving to large wall pieces was a great challenge and inspiration for me. Finding new ways of combining the incongruous elements of hard metal with the softness of fiber was my goal.

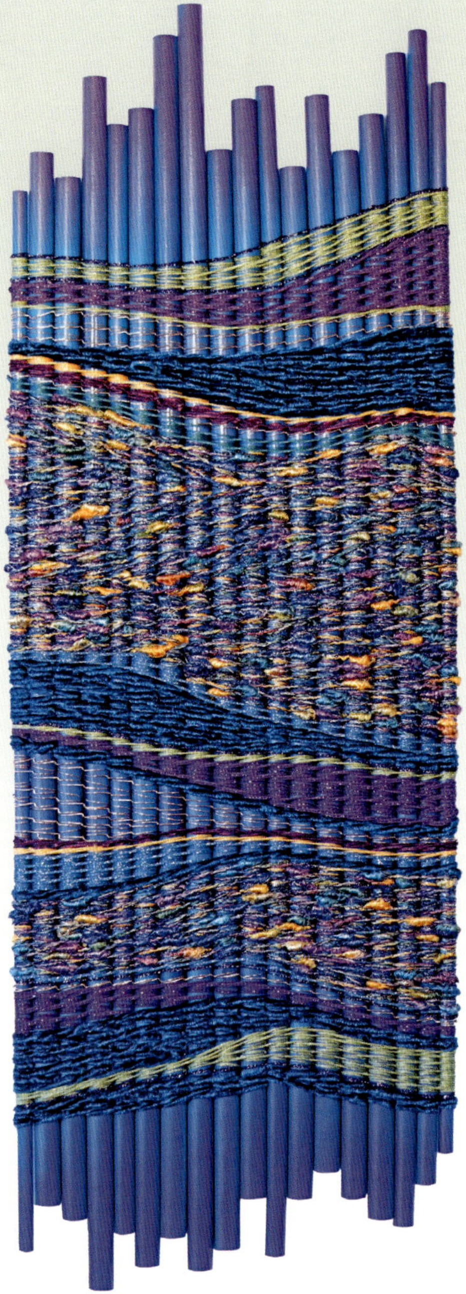

Blue Wave. Varied fibers, wire, acrylic paint, and industrial tubing. 36" × 27". 2014.

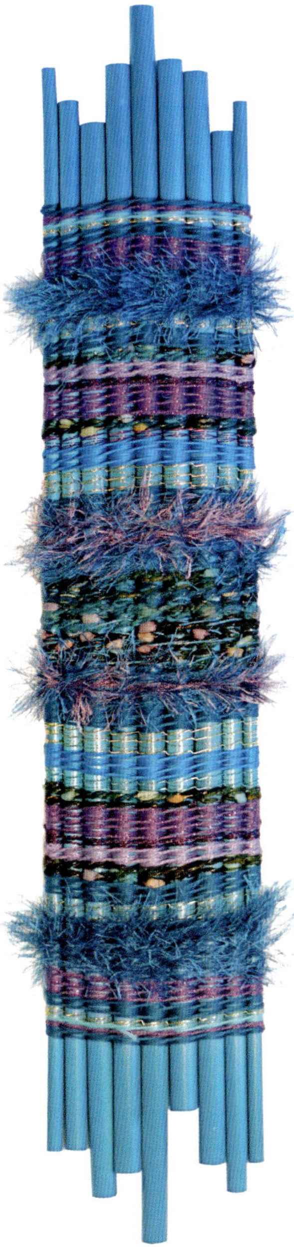

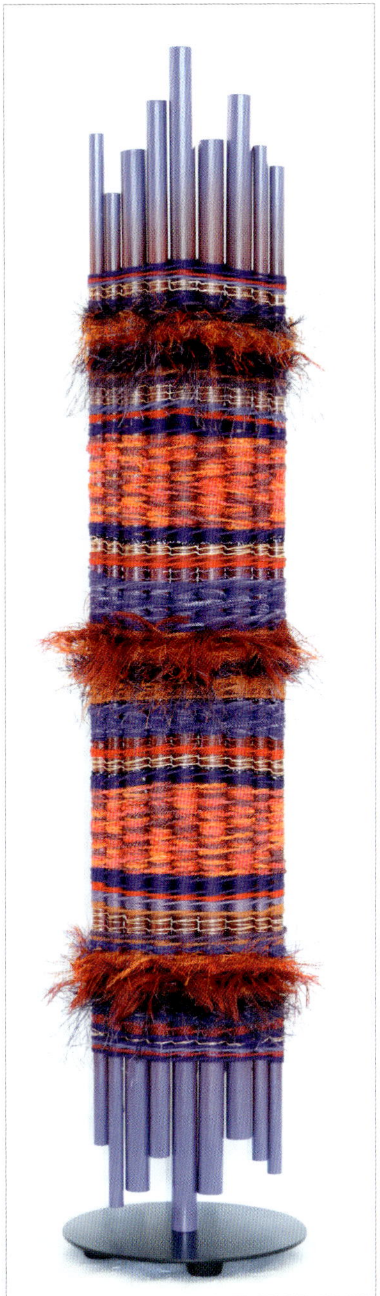

◄ *Aqua Totem*. Varied fibers, wire, acrylic paint, and industrial tubing. 36" × 9". 2014.

Ablaze Totem. Varied fibers, wire, acrylic paint, industrial tubing, and black steel stand. 30" × 9". 2014.

▼ *Deco Diptych*. Various fibers, wire, acrylic paint, industrial tubing, and canvas. 30" × 18" each. 2016.

All art images courtesy of Mark Goros.

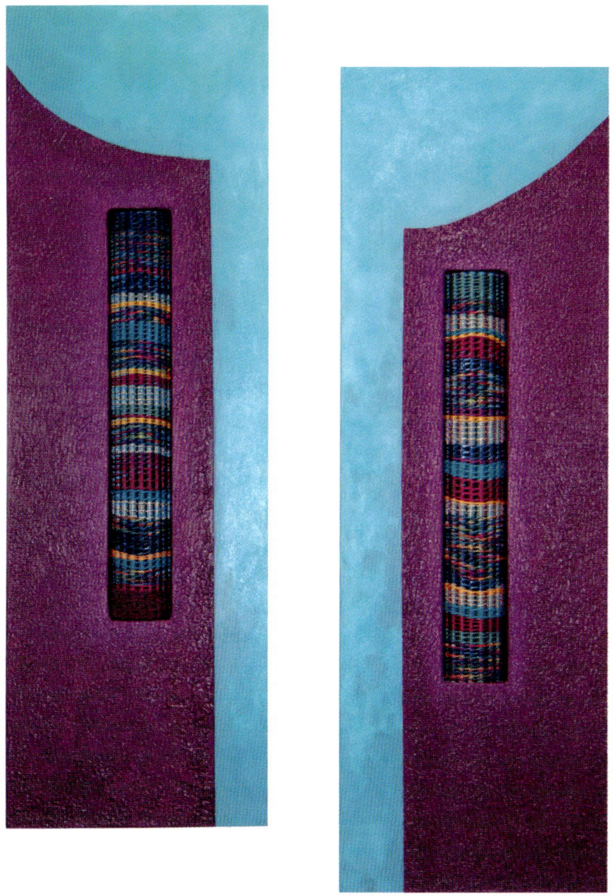

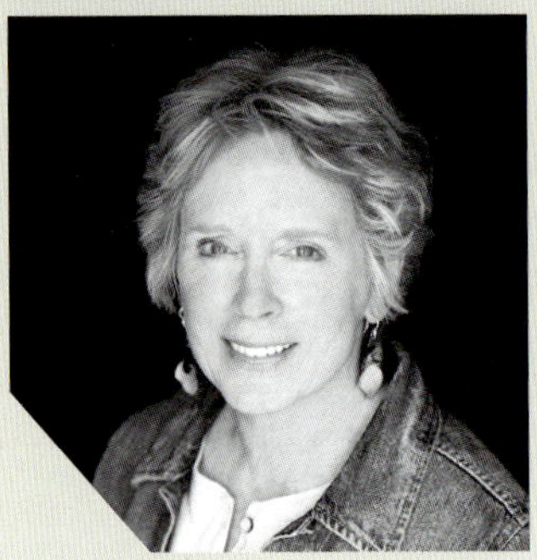

Photo: Daniel Nadelbach, Nadelbachphoto.com

Marti Waller

Santa Fe, New Mexico

I've always loved good historical fiction. If it is well done, it can create a strong connection to events and places long gone by. In my quilts, I attempt to do something that is very challenging: to evoke some sense and feeling for the historical past using geometric design. Many of the design bands are taken from the patterns sewn into clothing by the Seminoles in the 1920s, but they also have been found in the artifacts of most civilizations since the beginning of human time.

Most of the quilts incorporate a dozen or so fabrics; integrating them into a whole that captures the historical mood can take forty to sixty hours. The name that I give the finished quilt will, I hope, inspire the viewer to learn more about that particular time and place.

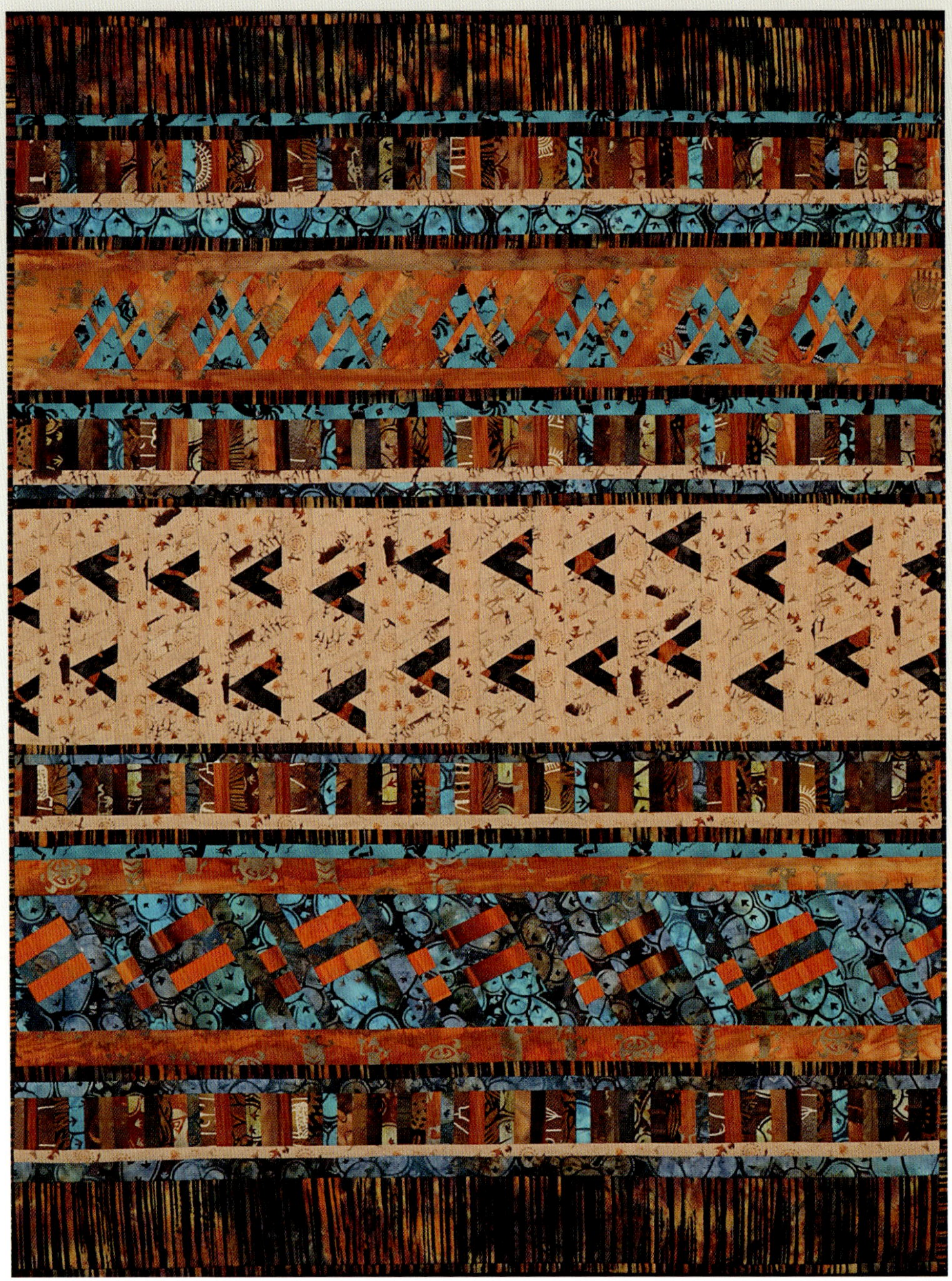

Yellowstone. Cotton fabric. 43" × 33". 2011.

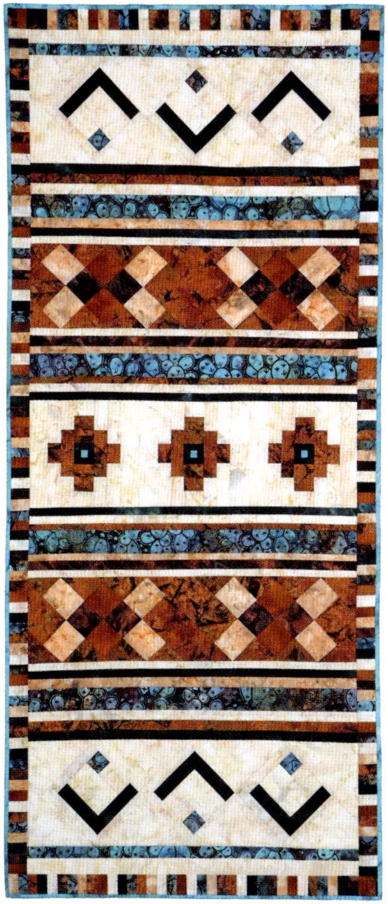

Turquoise Trail. Cotton fabric.
65" × 28". 2009.

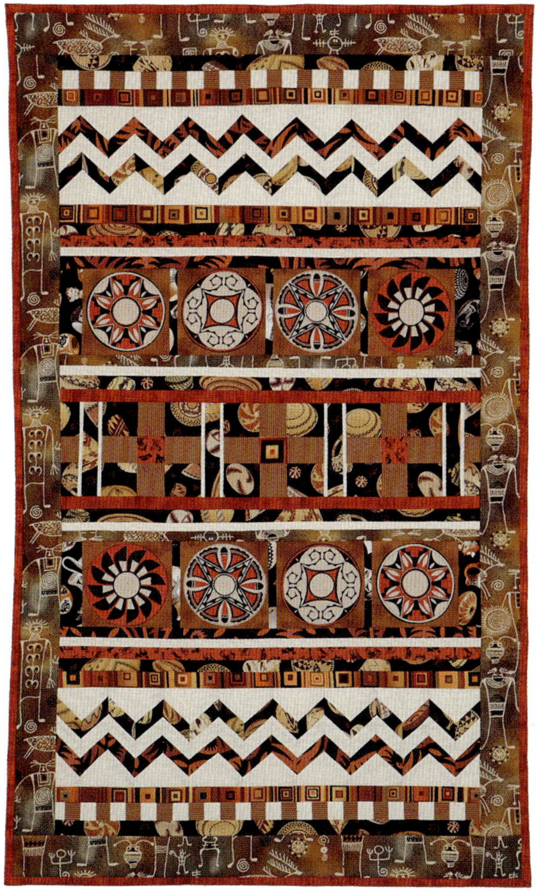

Caravan. Cotton fabric.
48" × 29". 2011.

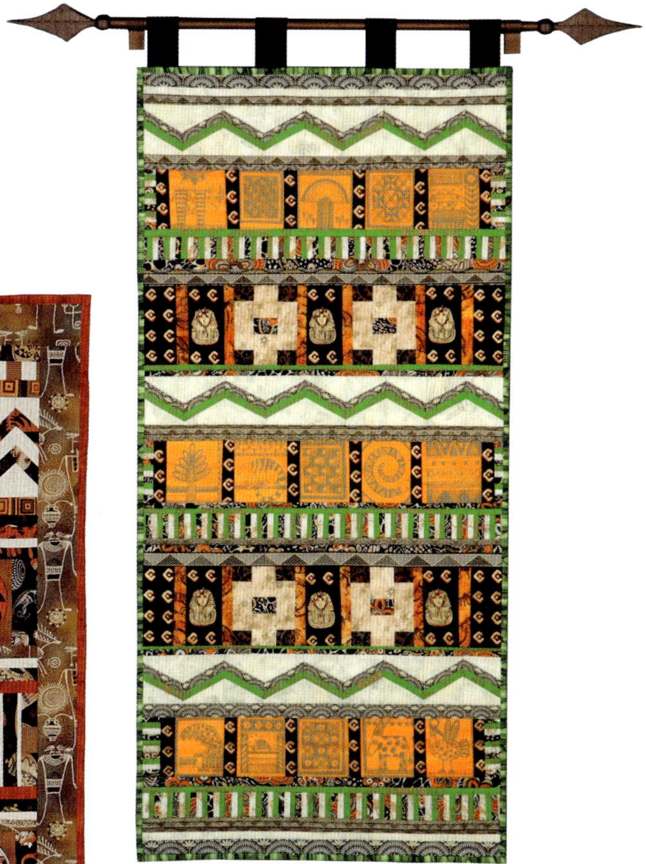

Life on The Nile. Cotton fabric.
48" × 23". 2012.

All art images courtesy of Carolyn Wright.

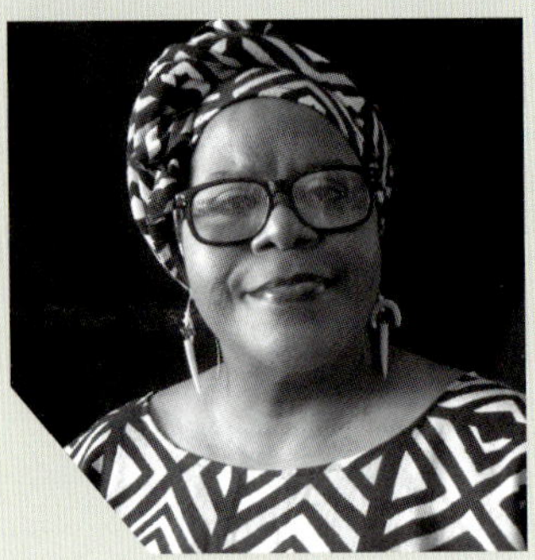

Trish Williams

Peoria, Illinois

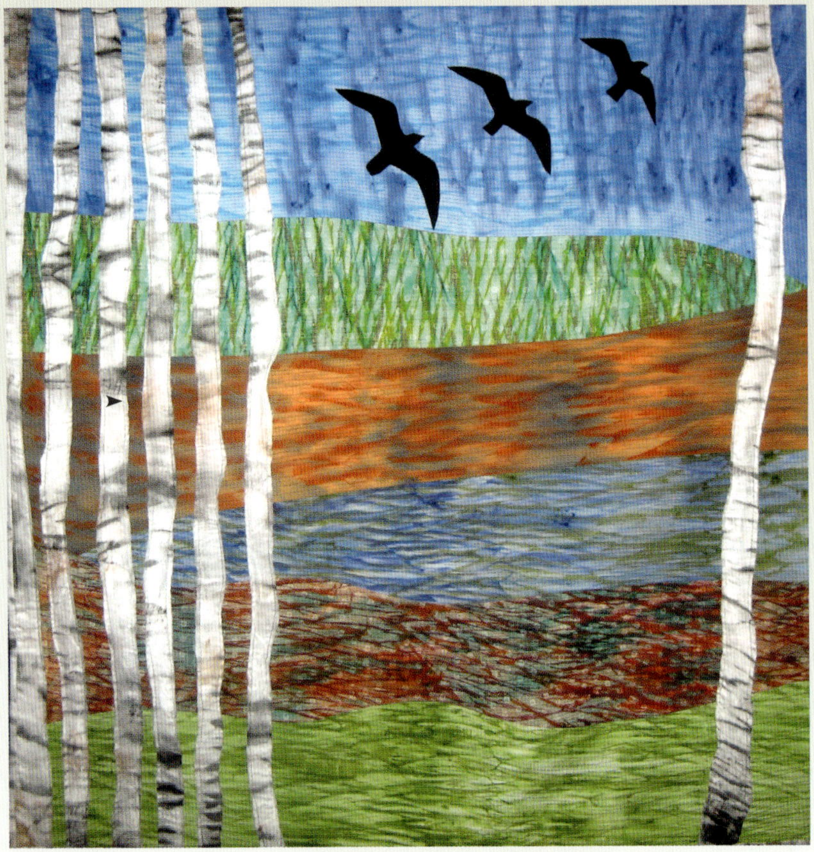

Having sewn all of my life, I became a self-taught artist in 1997, falling in love with quilting as my medium. Since I was familiar with working in fabric, transitioning to quilting seemed natural as a means to artistically express myself.

Quilting also allowed me to revisit my upbringing in the Midwest using an imaginative style of stitching and color that is inspired by my Midwestern and African roots. I find joy and inspiration in the bountiful ebb and flow of the rivers and lakes. My current works include some mixed-media aspects; incorporating paint, paper, plastic, metals, or other found objects has allowed me to explore new ideas and advance my quilting techniques.

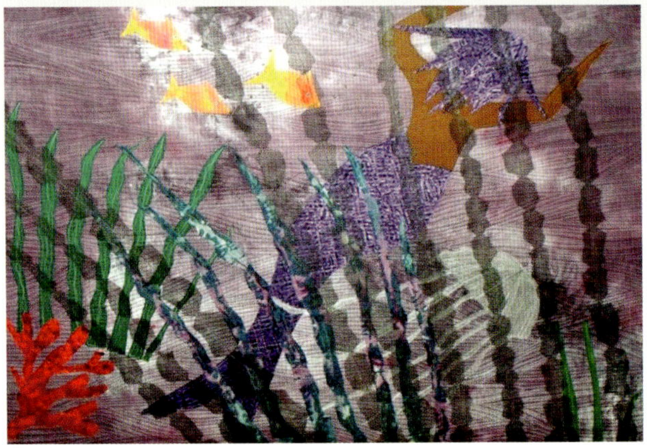

Through the Trees—Soar. Shibori-painted cottons and purchased fabric, machine pieced and quilted with raw-edge appliqués. 45.5" × 43.5". 2015.

➤ *Going to Meet a Man*. Hand-dyed, commercial, and hand-painted cotton, fiberglass window screen machine pieced and quilted, with glass bead embellishments. 33.5" × 44". 2010.

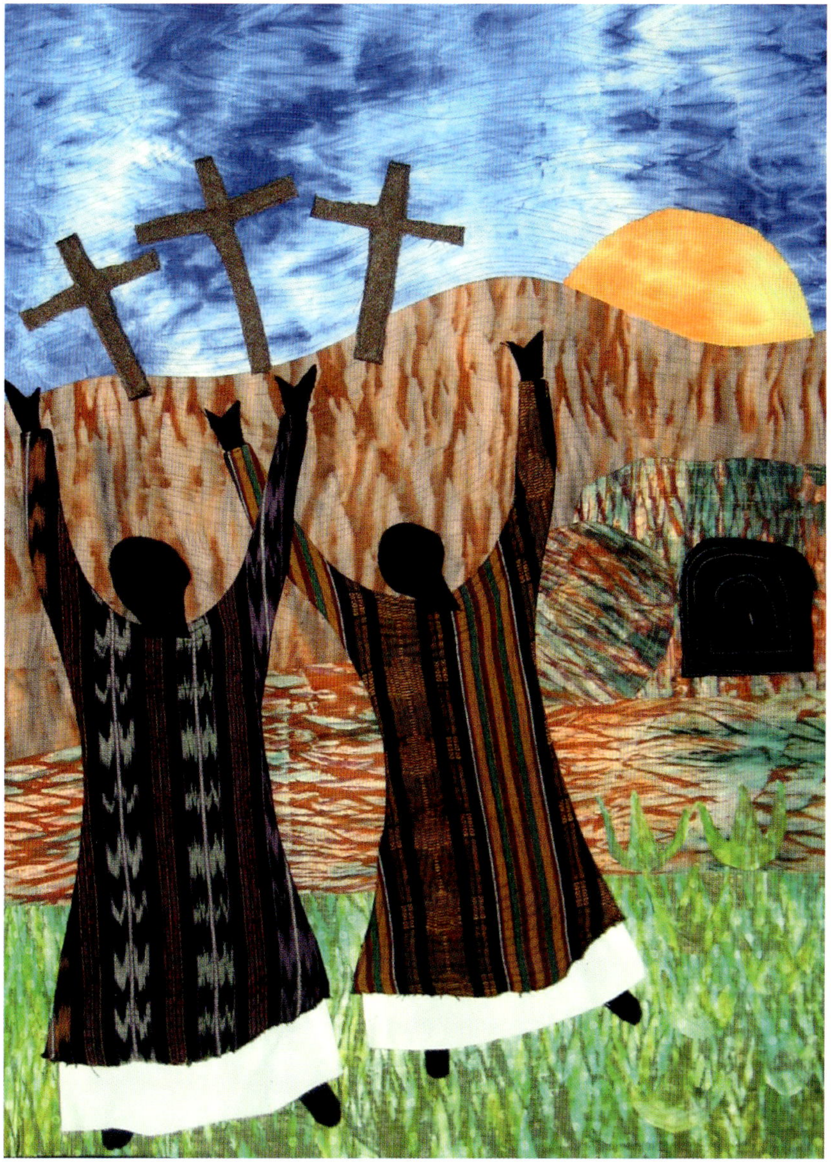

With Open Hearts. Artist shibori painted, vintage woven, and commercial cottons machine pieced and quilted. 48.5" × 33.5". 2015.

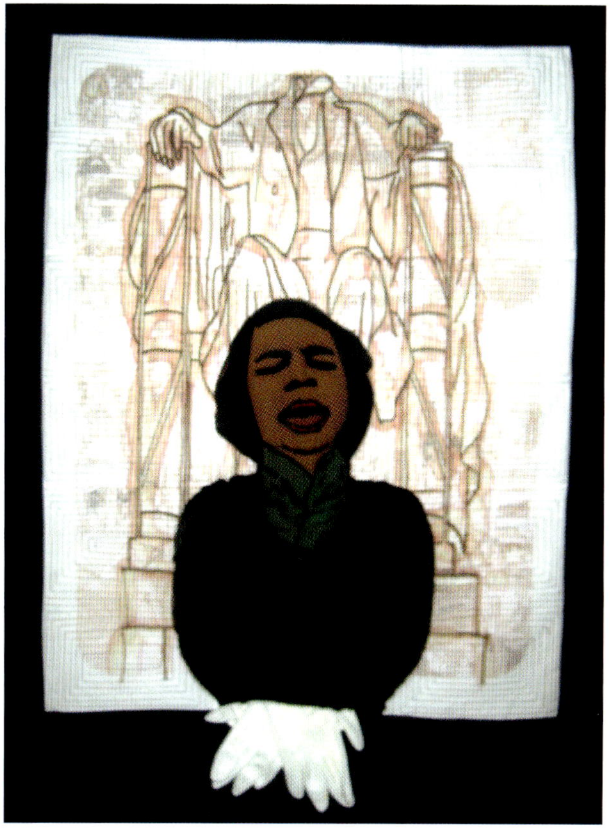

Marian Anderson. Photo collage using cottons, faux fur, and vintage gloves, printed onto paperback fabrics, pieced and machine quilted with appliqués. 40" × 33". 2015.

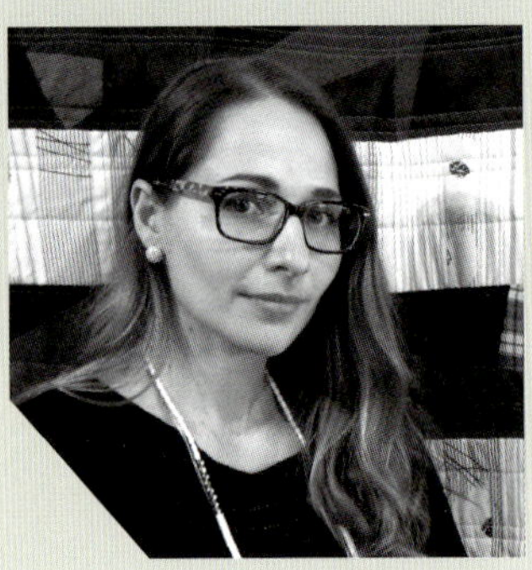

Jessica Wohl

Sewanee, Tennessee

I am especially drawn to the home and its residents and exploit the uncanny while subverting domestic representations of perfection and happiness. I use obsession, personification, and Gothic overtones to convey the idea that looks can be deceiving, and I use processes such as quilting and embroidery to subvert the notions of comfort and familiarity we often experience with domestic materials like family photographs and household fabrics.

I also think of the home as a living entity: aging, protecting, listening, witnessing, breathing, knowing, and retaining the energetic residue of those who live there, or once lived there. By working with domestic materials, I exploit the energies harnessed in used sheets, worn photographs, and other discarded household linens or previously worn clothes. In a climate of foreclosed homes, abandoned neighborhoods, broken families, and forgotten dreams, my work explores what remains in these domestic artifacts, and questions our society's obsession with, and definition of, the American Dream.

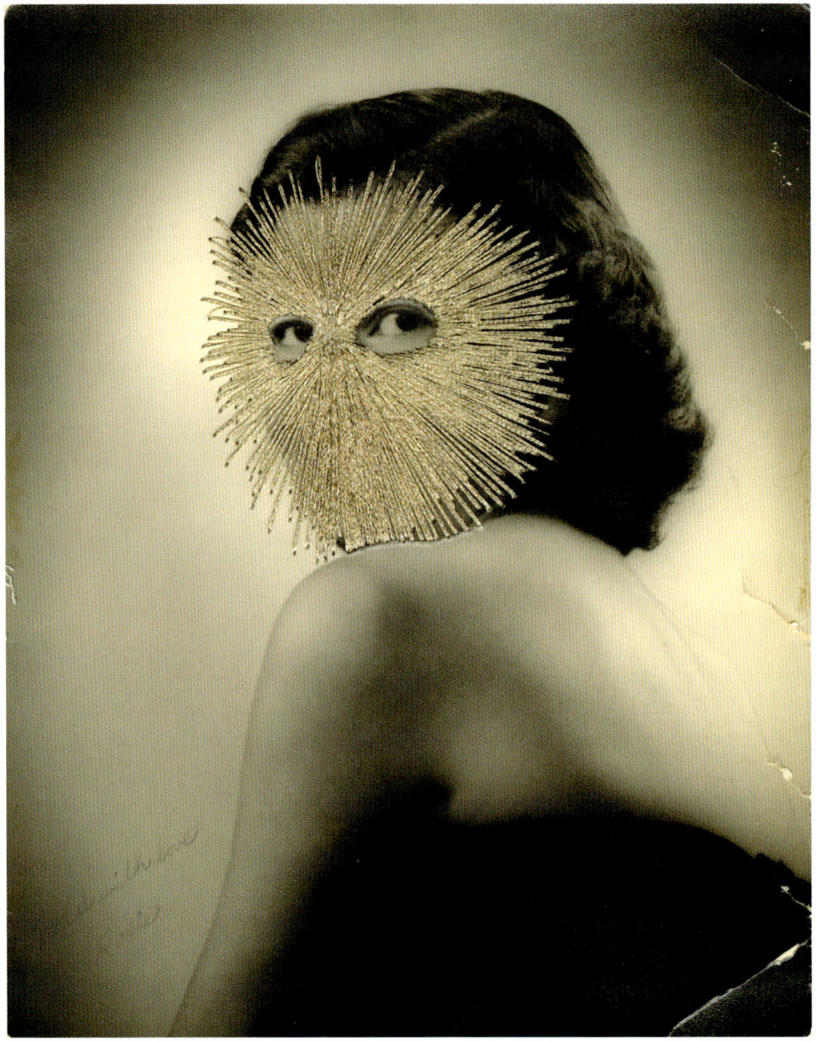

To Ed with Love, Rosie. Embroidery on found photograph. 10" × 8". 2012.

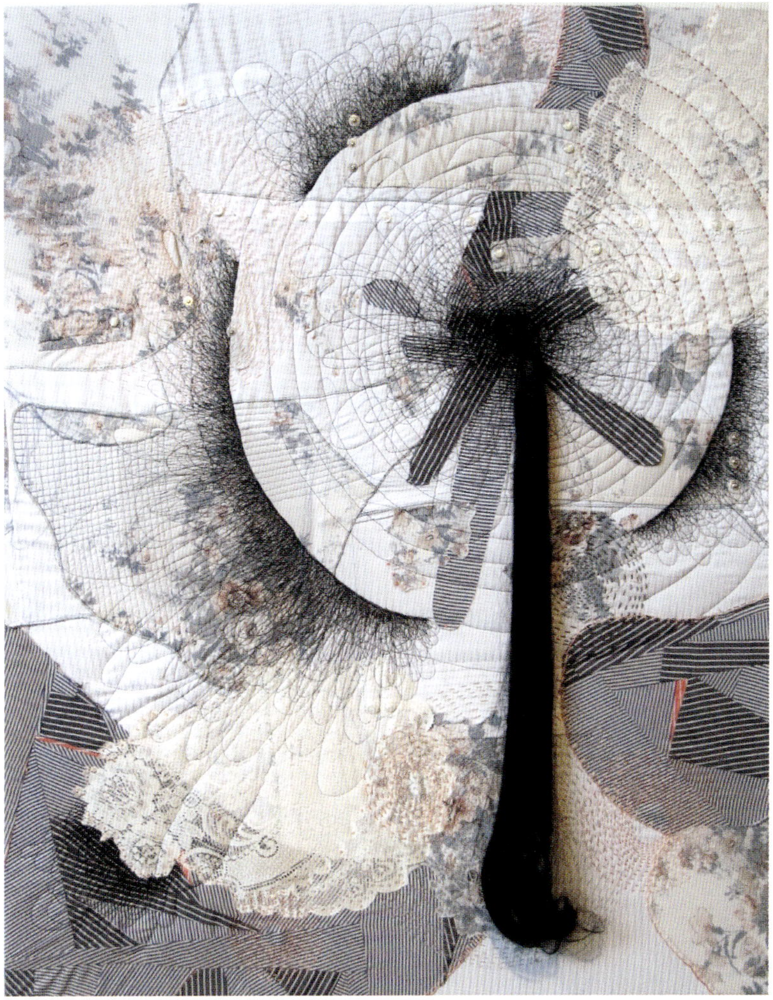

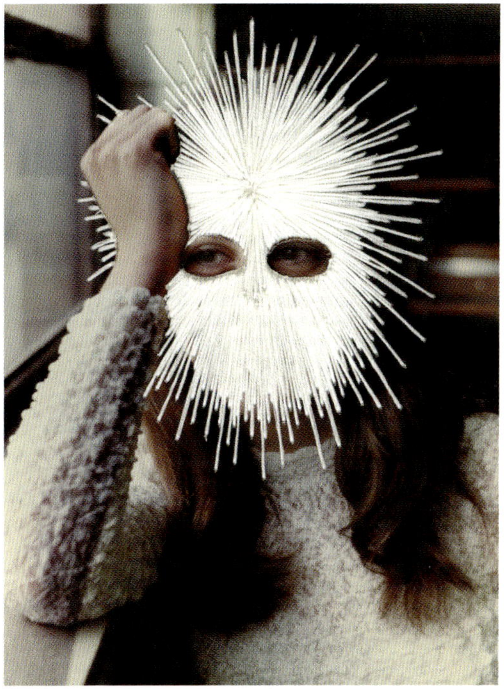

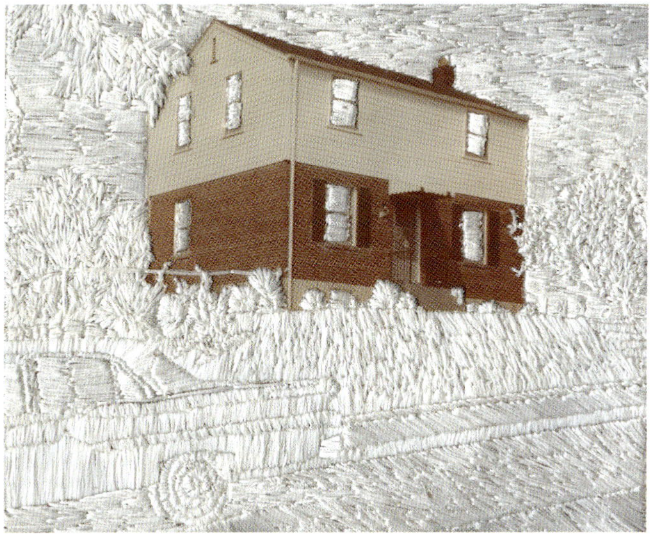

▲ *Black and Blue Burst*. Bed sheet, shirts, tablecloth, synthetic hair, and hair tie. 36" × 24" × 2".

➤ *White Mask*. Embroidery on found photograph. 10" × 8". 2012.

➤ *House on a Hill*. Embroidery on found photograph. 8" × 10". 2011.

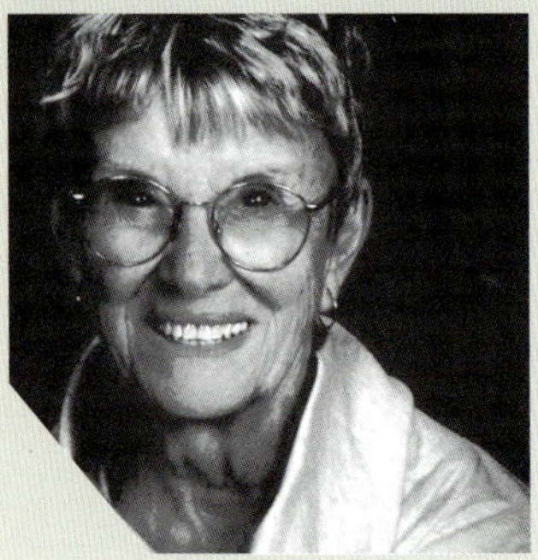

Joan Wolfer

Boulder, Colorado

Working with the combination of fabric, yarns, and threads gives me great pleasure. There are colors to use and mix, and threads and yarns to combine, giving texture to the work on the canvas background. I take a thought and use the various materials to tell a story that can make my idea visible. I enjoy the result; as I work, I wonder what the next story idea that I have will look like.

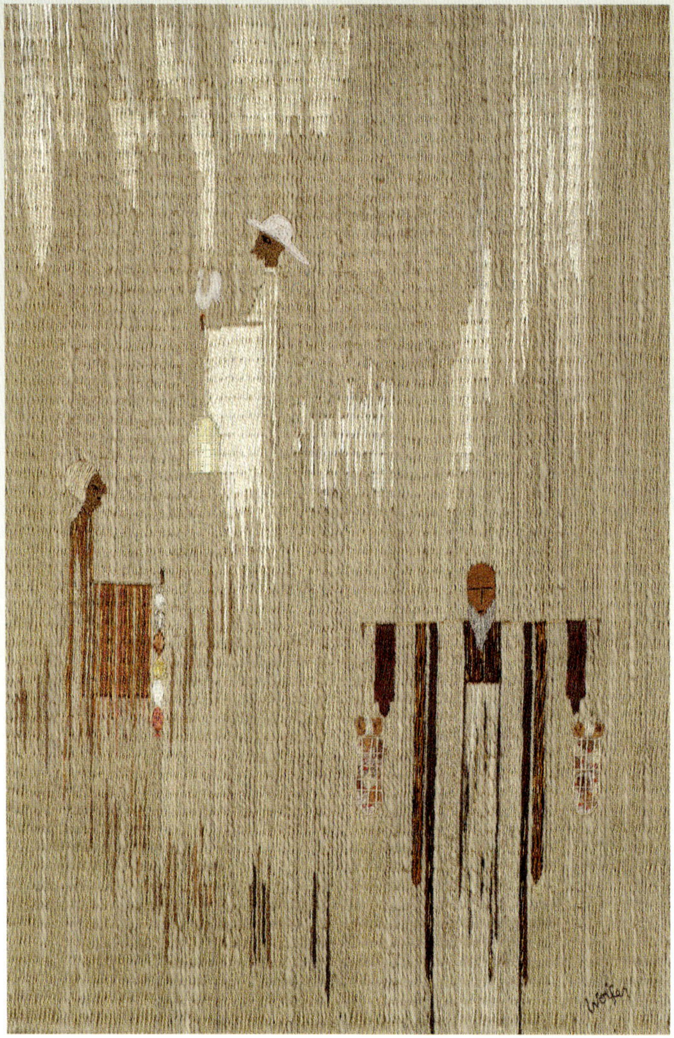

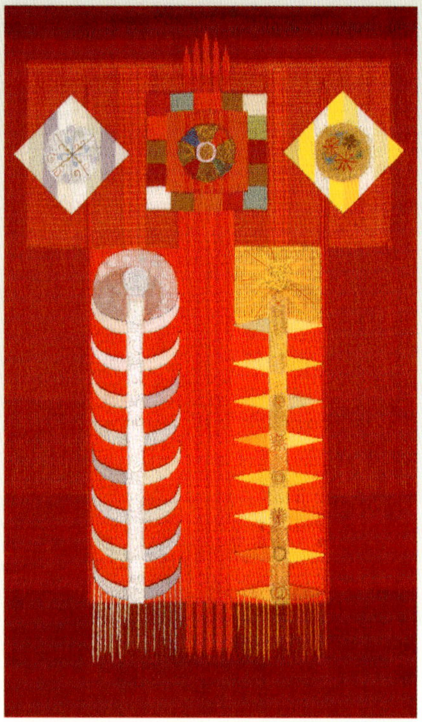

Three on the Path. Canvas work, wool yarn, silk, and cotton threads, free machine stitching, appliqué, and embroidery. 29" × 20". 2015.

➤ *Hot Day.* Canvas work, wool yarn, various threads, appliqué, free machine stitching, embroidery, and paint. 38" × 22". 2005.

All art images courtesy of Ken Sanville.

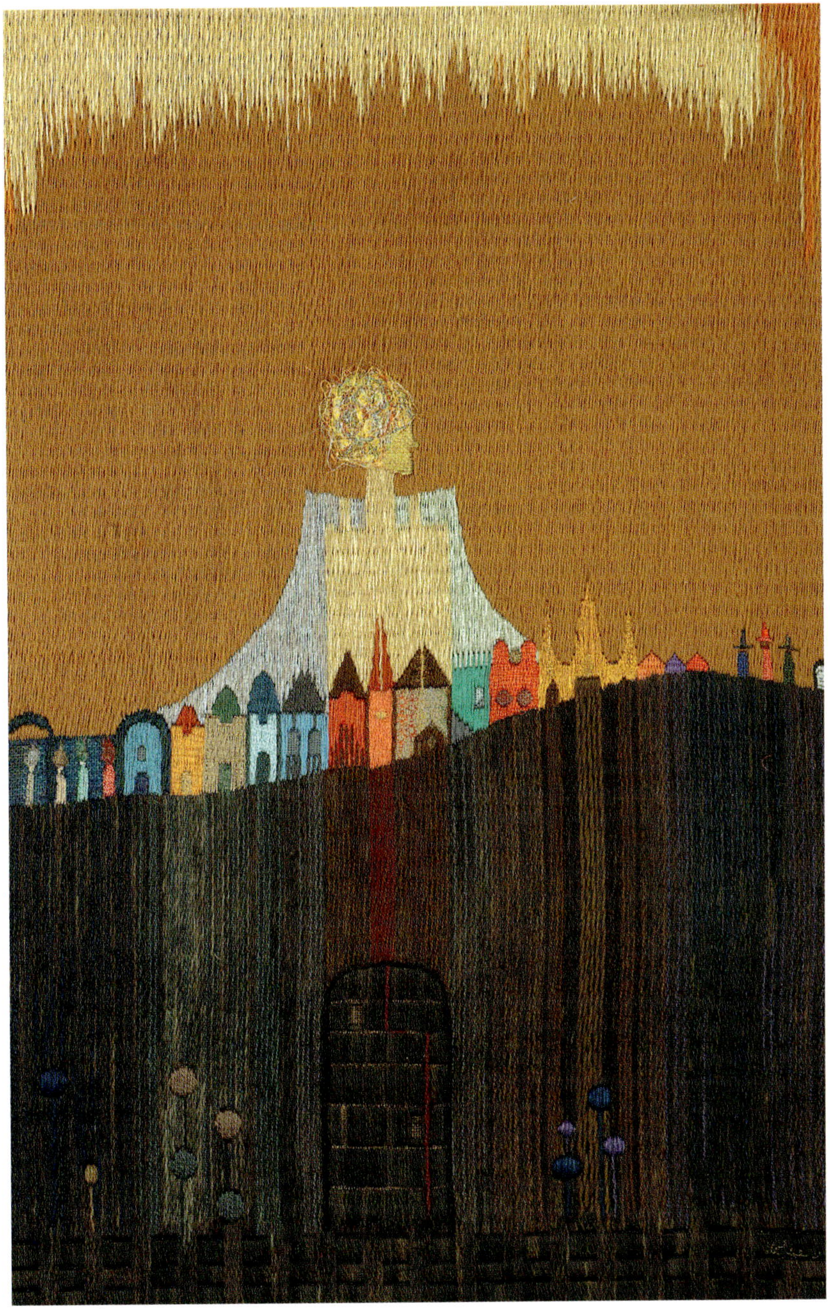

◄ *Time Line.* Canvas work, wool yarn, various threads, appliqué, free machine stitching, and embroidery. 33" × 21". 2009.

▼ *Amber Lights.* Canvas work, wool yarn, various threads, appliqué, free machine stitching, and embroidery. 38" × 24". 2005.

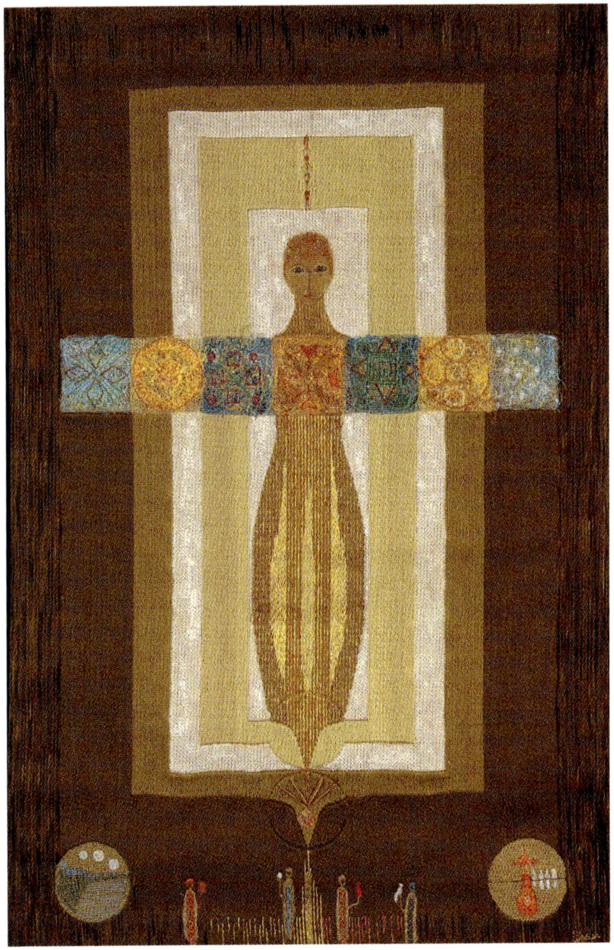

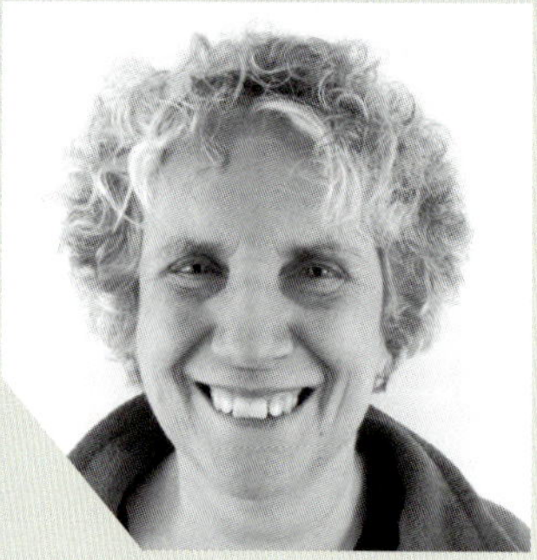

Peggy Wright

St. Paul, Minnesota

I am an award-winning artist, working in mixed media textiles, as well as a writer and teacher. Playing with color is my passion; to indulge that passion, I make art. I get lost in the surface of fabric, using hue, texture, and form to explore the world. I think the sense of touch is a lost sense in Western society, and through dyes, paints, fabric, and thread, I work to create a tactile surface that invites the viewer to look more closely.

While I have used other media, I have found that I need to work with materials that sustain my sense of touch. I need to see, feel, and manipulate fabric and thread to remain content. Painting, screen printing, dyeing, freehand machine stitching, and hand-stitching are my preferred techniques. My color palette is broad, from vibrant greens to peaceful blues to subdued purples.

Natural forms are my subject matter. When I observe nature, I find extravagant pattern and captivating detail. Interaction with the natural world provides refuge from the discordant notes in my daily life. A relationship with nature inherently incorporates the transformative experience, the touch of the metaphysical, and a vision of the possible. Whether I am creating my art about it or am walking in the woods, I need contact with nature to live.

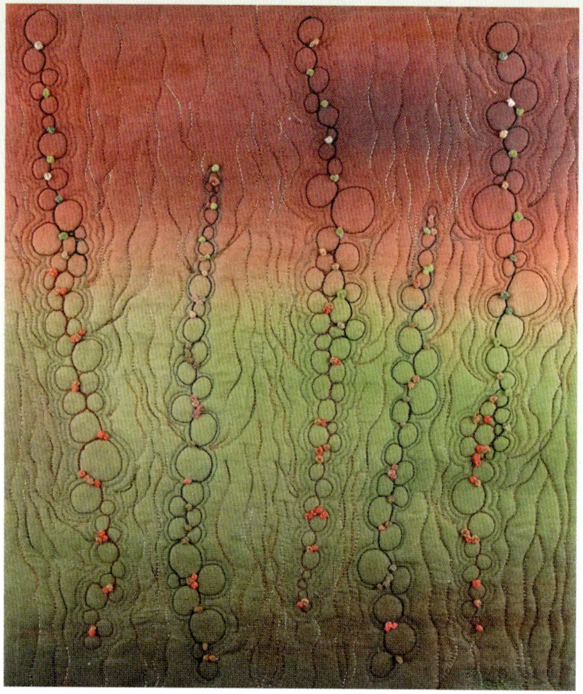

Seaweed. Fabric paint, cotton and polyester threads, cotton fabric, and felt stabilizer. 14" × 12". 2015.

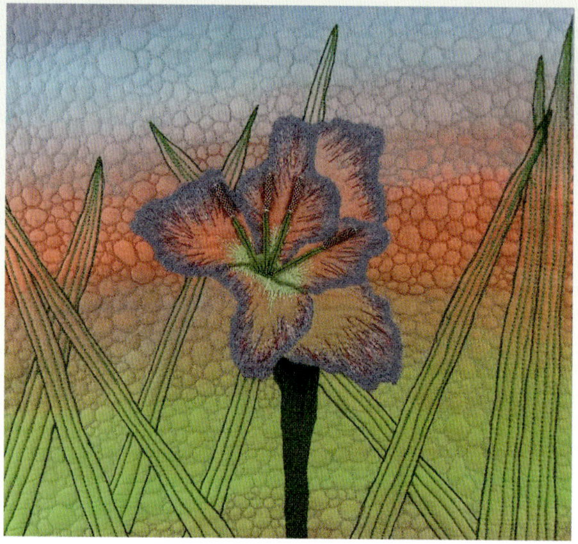

➤ *Gladiolus, Sword Lily.* Cotton fabric, fabric paint, cotton and polyester threads, glass seed and larger beads, and felt stabilizer. 14" × 15". 2014.

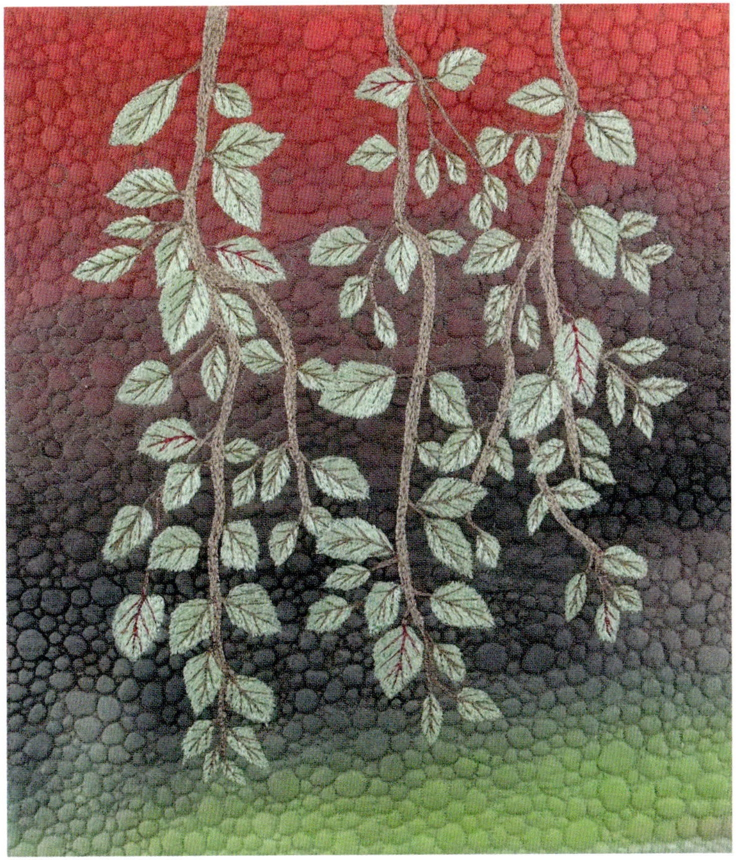

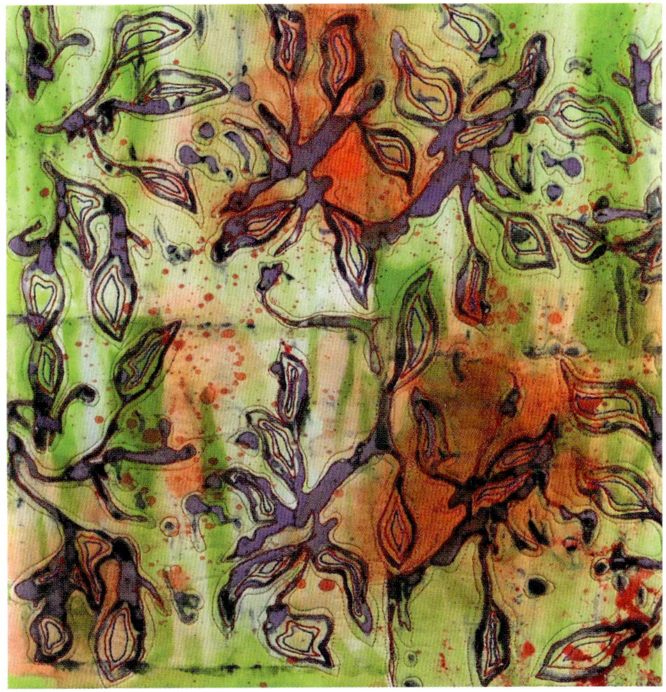

▲ *Branching.* Dyes, pigment inks, acrylic paints, polyester threads, cotton fabric, and felt stabilizer. 14" × 16". 2014.

▲ *Sheltered.* Fabric paint, cotton and polyester threads, cotton fabric, and felt stabilizer. 16" × 14". 2015.

➤ *Cellular.* Dyes, pigment inks, polyester threads, cotton fabric, and felt stabilizer. 10" × 20". 2015.

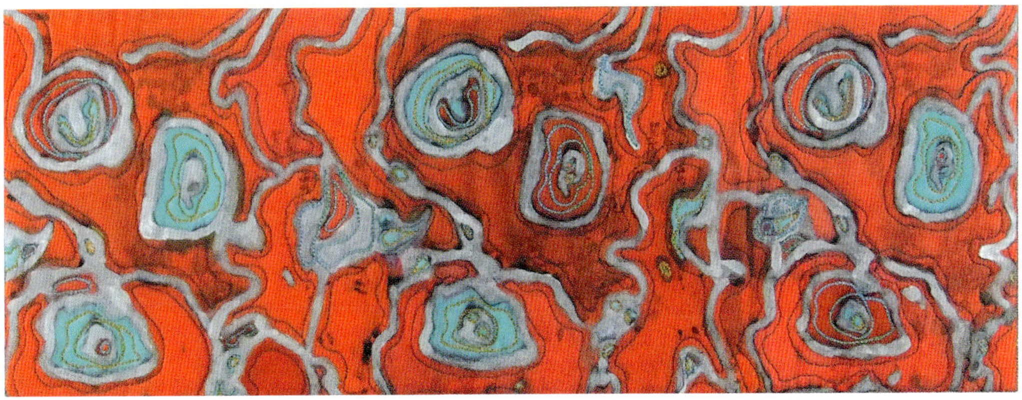

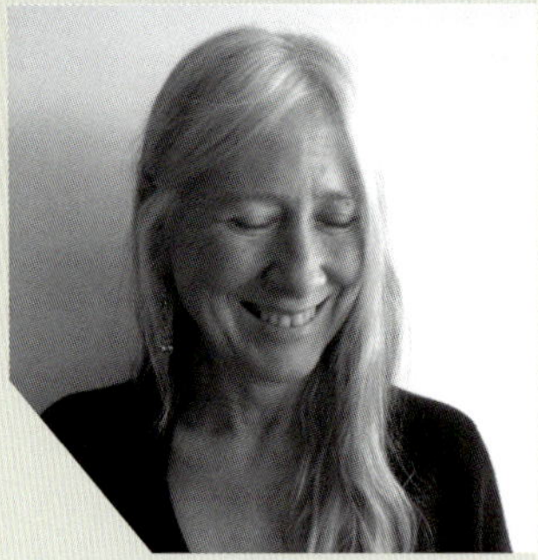

Carolina Yrarrázaval

Santiago, Chile

I have always lived in Santiago, between the Andes Mountains and the Pacific Ocean, which has influenced the contrasts and textures in my work. Throughout my entire artistic career, I have devoted myself to investigating traditional textile techniques from diverse cultures, especially pre-Columbian techniques, trying to adapt them to my creative needs. I am seeking for ways to speak of the beauty and dignity that we have lost through the decades.

I studied textile art at the Fine Arts University Chile. Since 1982 I have participated in many national and international exhibitions and teach textile techniques. My recent exhibition at the Museum of Contemporary Art in Santiago was selected as best national exhibition in the visual arts for 2013.

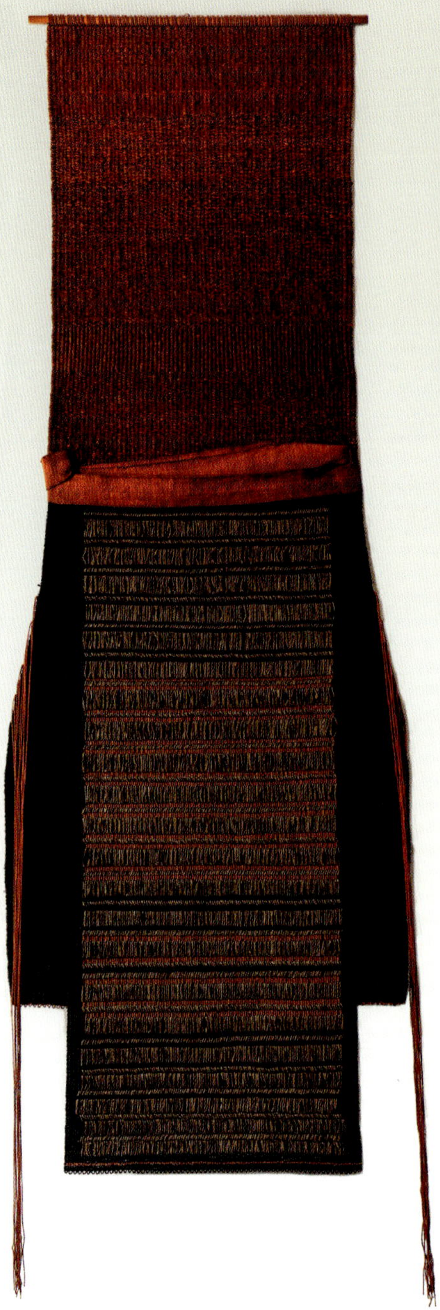

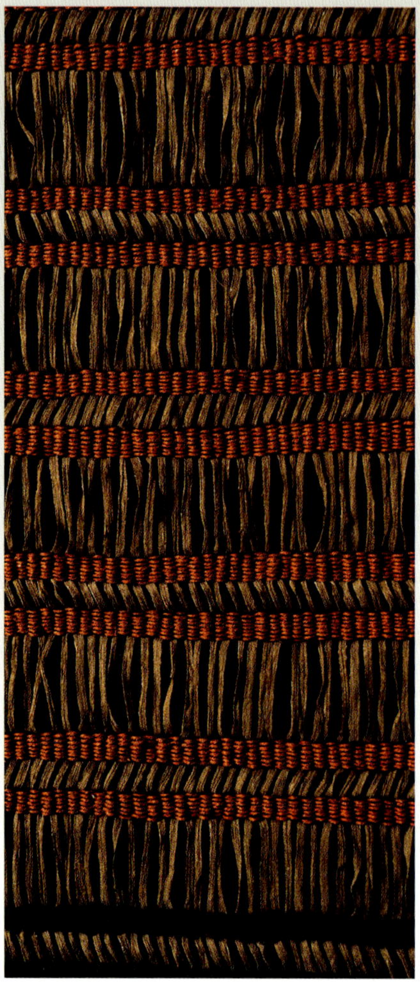

Un Lider (A Leader). Linen, jute, and Japanese paper. 86" × 31". 2013. | Detail

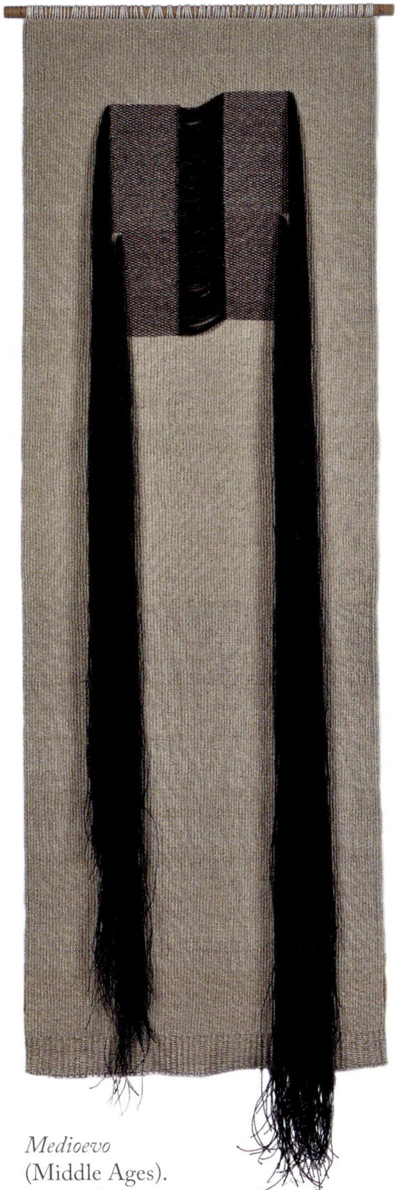

Medioevo (Middle Ages). Jute and linen. 78" × 19". 2011.

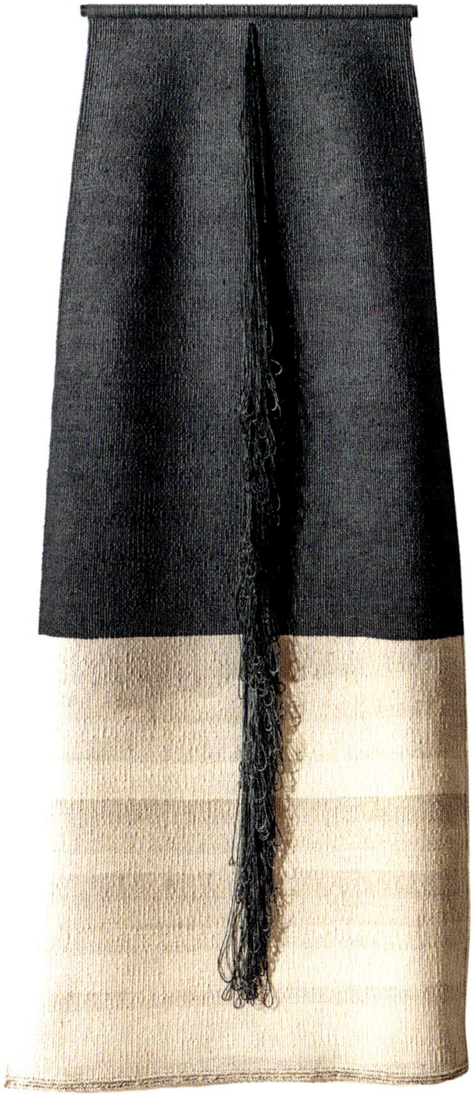

Mar y Arena (Sea and Sand). Silk and linen. 69" × 31". 2012.

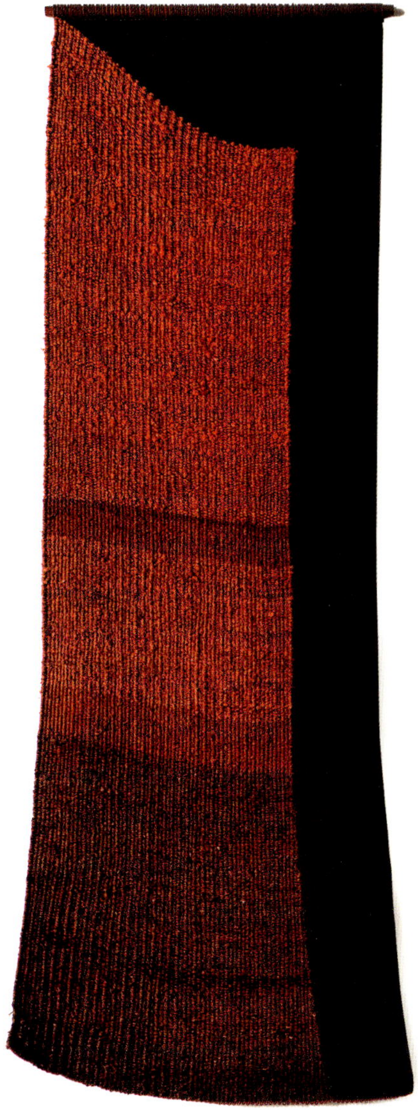

Forma (Form). Jute, cotton, and silk. 74" × 29". 2013.

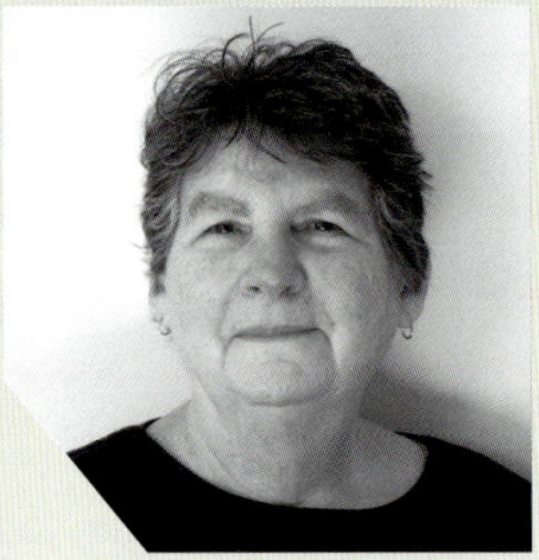

Courtesy of Mark Goodwin.

Bhakti Ziek

Randolph, Vermont

I place my work in the long lineage of narrative textiles, but my computerized looms places my work in the realm of contemporary digital art. Still I create the structures and images. I wind bobbins, and I throw the shuttles. At the loom, I feel like I have one foot in the past and one in the future—and my weaving is the present. At the intersection of warp and weft, there are only two choices—warp is over weft or weft is over warp. Today people understand pixels but think of weaving as an archaic process. They don't realize that the binary language of jacquard weaving gave birth to computer code. I hope my weavings, full of contemporary symbols like emoticons or handwritten notes about the process of weaving, both inform and tantalize—and introduce more people to the mystery and beauty of weaving.

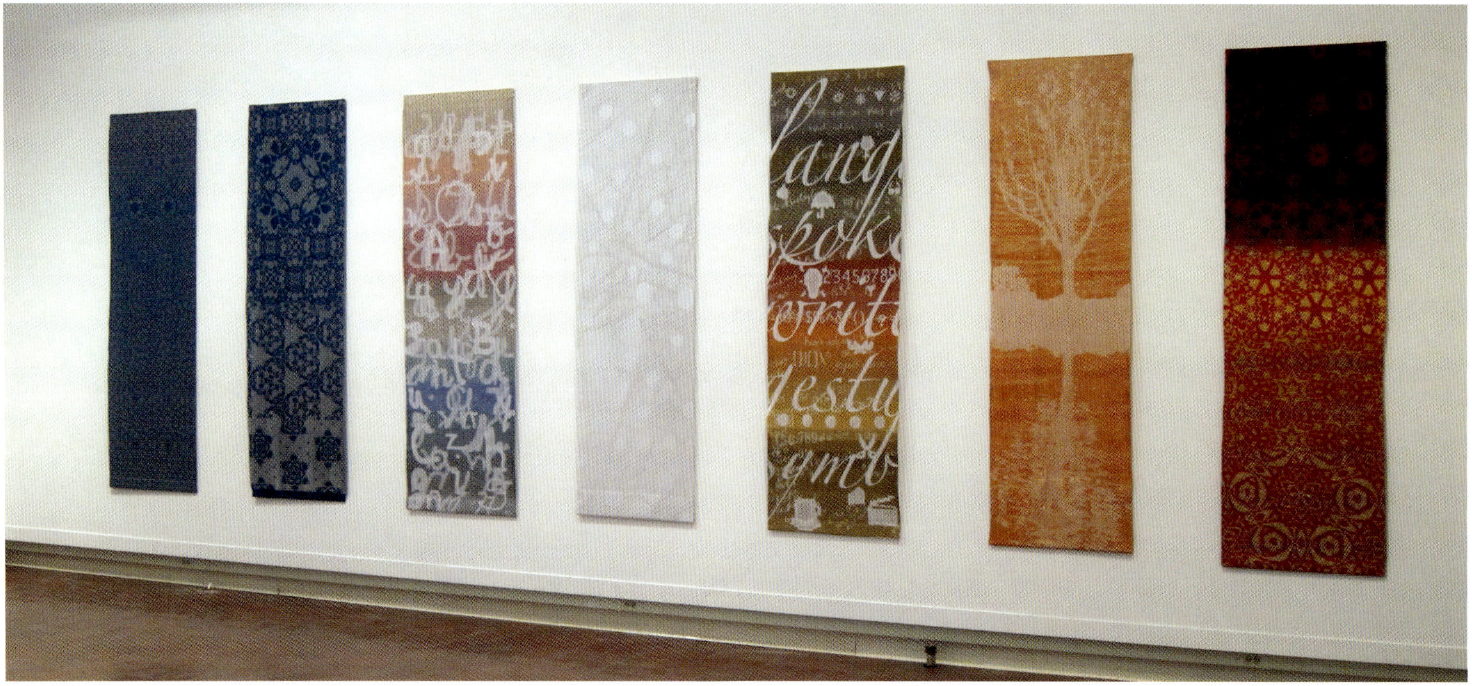

Sisyphus. Hand woven satin damask jacquard weaving; silk, cotton, and metallic yarns. Seven panels, each panel 88.5" × 28". 2015. | OPPOSITE (top left) Detail

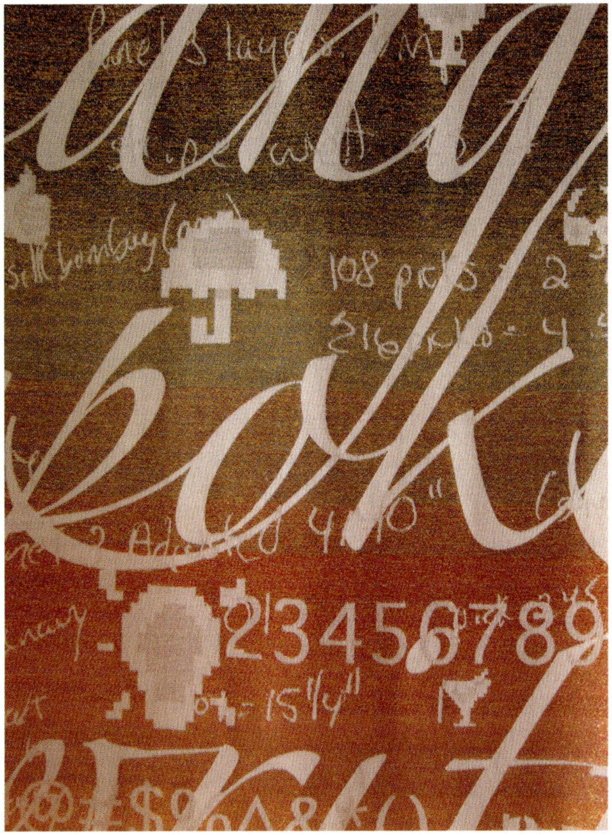

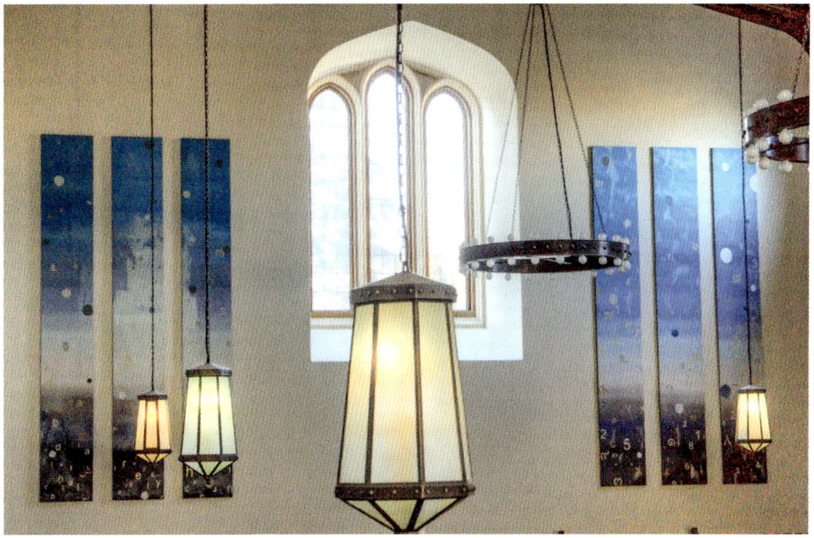

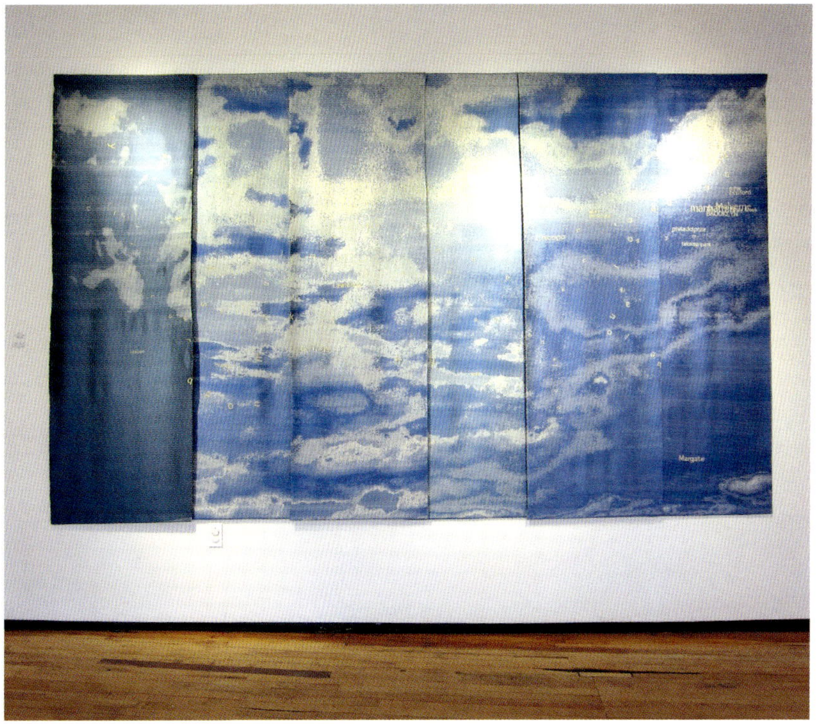

➤ *Stardust*. Hand woven weft-backed jacquard weaving; silk, Tencel, and metallic yarns. Six panels, each panel 16" × 28". Permanent installation at Whitman College, Princeton University, Princeton, New Jersey. 2014. Courtesy of Edward Wendell.

➤ *My Roof*. Dyed warp, hand woven weft-backed jacquard weaving; indigo dye, silk, Tencel, and silver gimp yarns. 82.5" × 144". 2012

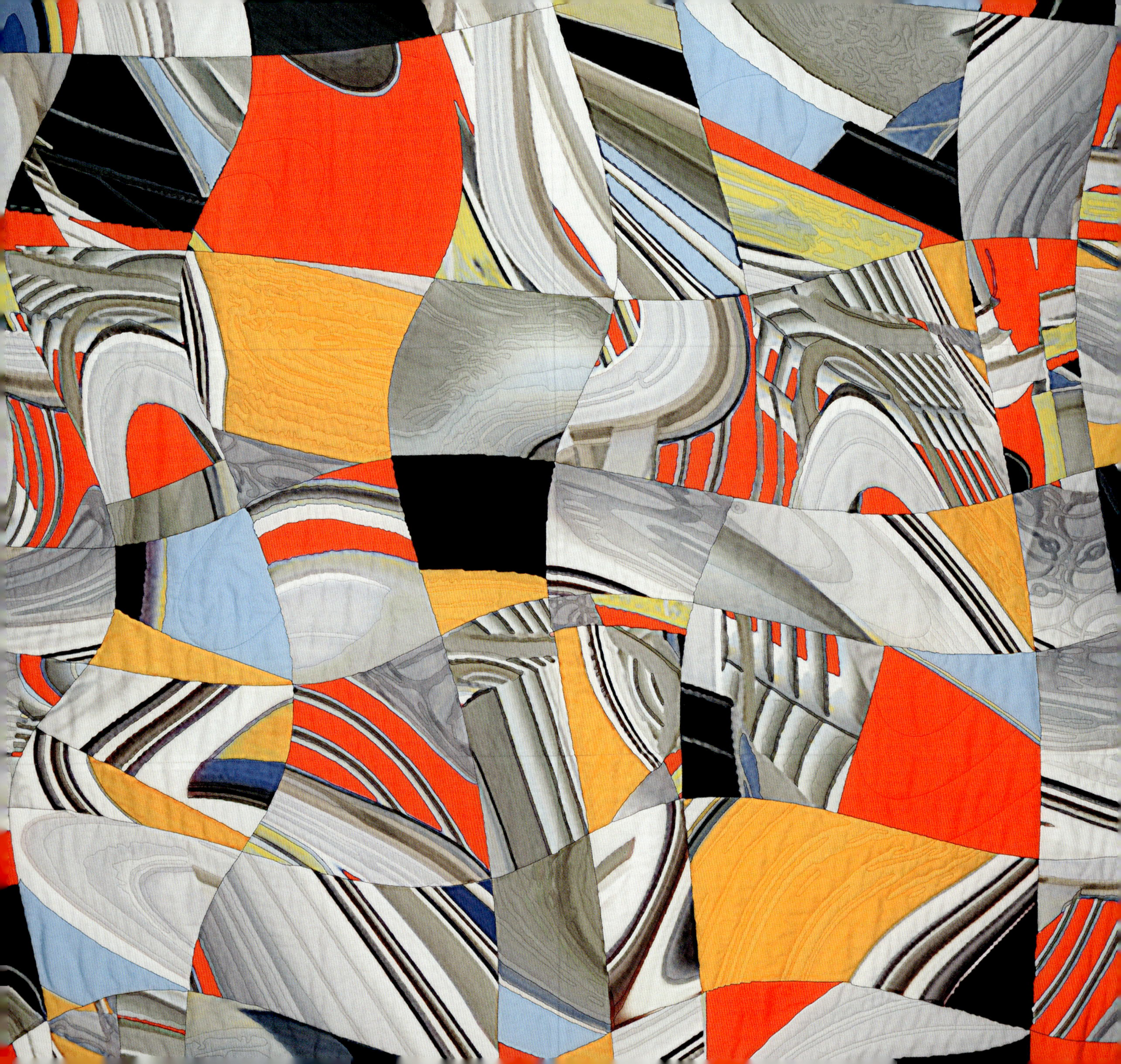

ARTISTS' WEBSITES AND CONTACT INFORMATION

Klaus Anselm
www.anselmtapestries.ne

Lucy Arai
www.lucyarai.com

Jim Arendt
www.jimarendt.com

Susan T. Avila
www.suta.com

Shelley Brenner Baird
www.shelleybrennerbaird.com

Pinky/MM Bass
www.colophon.com/gallery/pinkybass/

Alice Beasley
www.alicebeasley.com

Sue Benner
www.suebenner.com

Mary Bero
www.maryberoart.com

Chris Berry
ccberry2@gmail.com

Jerry Bleem
www.jerrybleem.com

George-Ann Bowers
www.gabowers.com

Terry M. Boyd
www.art.terrenceboyd.com

Michelle Browne
www.michellebrowne.info

Rosemary Campbell
www.textilestudygroup.co.uk

Ying Chew
www.yingchew.com.au

Chiachio & Giannone
www.chiachiogiannone.com

Jette Clover
www.jetteclover.com

Tarja Cockell
www.tarjacockell.com

Marion Coleman
www.marioncoleman.com

Merill Comeau
www.merillcomeau.com

Deborah Corsini
www.deborahcorsini.com

Helen Cowans
www.helencowans.co.uk

Candace Crockett
crockett@sfsu.edu

Jennifer Davies
www.jenniferdavieshmp.com

Eve Deisher
www.evedeisher.com

Susan Kathleen Doyle
www.susankathleendoyle.com

Candace Edgerley
www.candaceedgerley.com

Caryl Bryer Fallert-Gentry
www.bryerpatch.com

Liz Alpert Fay
www.lizalpertfay.com

Carson Fox
www.carsonfox.com

Kathryn Harmer Fox
kathryn.kathy@telkomsa.net

Alex Friedman
www.alexfriedmantapestry.com

Flore Gardner
www.floregardner.wixsite.com

Luisa F. Gil Fandino
www.fandindo.com

Meredith Re' Grimsley
mgrimsle@bloomu.edu

Louise Halsey
www.louisehalsey.com

Ann Harwell
www.quiltartisannharwell.com

Ulla Hein
www.ullahein.dk/engelsk

Ane Henriksen
www.anehenriksen.dk

Anna Hergert
www.annahergert.com

Susan Hersey
www.susanhersey.com

Pat Hickman
www.pathickman.com

Cas Holmes
www.casholmestextiles.co.uk

Sue Hotchkis
www.suehotchkis.com

Sara Impey
www.saraimpey.com

Terry Jarrard-Dimond
www.terryjarrarddimond.com

Patricia Kennedy-Zafred
www.pattykz.com

Toni Kersey
www.tonikersey.com

Alison King
www.textilestudygroup.co.uk

Susan Klebanoff
www.susanklebanoff.com

Sheila Klein
www.sheilaklein.com

Joan Konkel
www.joankonkel.com

Carol Larson
www.live2dye.com

Gaye S. Lasher
www.gayelasher.com

Susan Levi-Goerlich
www.susanlevi-goerlich.com

Susan Martin Maffei
www.susanmartinmaffei.com

Ruben Marroquin
www.rubenmarroquin.
squarespace.com

Fuyuko Matsubara
www.fmartworks.com

Jennie McMillen
www.jenniemcmillen.com

Kathy Miller
www.kathymiller-artist.com

Dominie Nash
www.dominienash.com

Pauline MM Nijenhuis
www.paulinemmnijenhuis.nl

Sharron Parker
www.sharronparker.com

Judith Plotner
www.judithplotner.com

Junco Sato Pollack
www.juncosatepollack.com

Stacy Polson
www.stacy-polson.squarespace.com

Amy Putansu
www.putansutextiles.com

Michael Radyk
www.michaelradyk.com

Shelley Rhodes
www.shelleyrhodes.co.uk

Leisa Rich
www.monaleisa.com

Glenda Richardson
www.glendarichardson.com

Roz Ritter
www.rozritter.com

Michael F. Rohde
www.michaelrohde.com

Ida-Lovisa Rudolfsson
www.idalovisa.se

Gwen Samuels
www.gwensamuels.com

Louise Schiele
www.louiseschiele.com

Rowen Schussheim-Anderson
www.tapestryart.com

Margaret Scott
www.mscottonline.com

Sandra Sider
www.sandrasider.com

Diane Siebels
www.dianesiebelsfiberart.com

Barbara Lee Smith
www.barbaraleesmith.com

Bonnie Jo Smith
www.bonniejofiberarts.com

Catherine Whall Smith
www.catherinewhallsmith.com

Sherri Smith
www.sherrismithfiber.net

Yvette Kaiser Smith
www.yvettekaisersmith.com

Melissa Sobotka
www.msfiberart.com

Frances Solar
www.francessolar.comolar

Joy Stocksdale
www.joystocksdale.com

Elena Stokes
www.elenastokes.com

Sarah Symes
www.sarahsymes.com

Susie Taylor
www.SusieTaylorArt.com

Lisa Van Herik
www.studiovanherik.com

Marti Waller
www.santafeartquilts.com

Trish Williams
www.handworksbytrish.com

Jessica Wohl
www.jessicawohl.com

Joan Wolfer
www.fiberartbywolfer

Peggy Wright
www.rubywings.com

Carolina Yrarrázaval
www.yrarrazaval.com

Bhakti Ziek
www.bhaktiziek.com

GALLERIES AND EXHIBITION SPACES

The artists featured in this book have noted the following galleries and spaces where their work has been exhibited.

NEW ENGLAND

Browngrotta Arts
Wilton, CT 06897
www.browngrotta.com

Center for Contemporary Printmaking
Norwalk, CT 06850
www.contemprints.org

City Gallery
New Haven, CT 06511
www.city-gallery.org

Danforth Art Museum and School
Framingham, MA 01702
www.danforthart.org

Fruitlands Museum
Harvard, MA 01451
www.fruitlands.org

Fuller Craft Museum
Brockton, MA 02301
www.fullercraft.org

The Loading Dock Gallery
Lowell, MA 01851
www.theloadingdockgallery.com

Mobilia Gallery
Cambridge, MA 02138
www.mobilia-gallery.com

New Canaan Library
New Canaan, CT 06511
www.newcanaanlibrary.org

NH Craftsmen League Galleries
Hanover, NH 03755
Littleton, NH 03561
Meredith, NH 03253
Nashua, NH 03060
www.nhcrafts.org

Nikki Sedacca Gallery
Edgartown, MA 02539
www.nikkisedaccagallery.com

Small Wonder Gallery
Camden, ME 04843
www.smallwondergallery.com

Soprafina Gallery
Boston, MA 02118
www.soprafina.com

Studio Art Quilt Associates
Storrs, CT 06268
www.saqa.com

Worcester Center for Crafts
Worcester, MA 01605
www.worcestercraftcenter.org

Yes Gallery + Studio
Warren, RI 02885
www.yesgalleryandstudio.com

THE MID-ATLANTIC

Art Quilt Gallery at The City Quilter
New York, NY 10001
www.artquiltgallerynyc.com

Christine Frechard Gallery
Pittsburgh, PA 15217
www.christinefrechardgallery.com

Fiberart International
Fiberarts Guild of Pittsburgh
Pittsburgh, PA 15206
www.fiberartspgh.org

Gravers Lane Gallery
Philadelphia, PA 19118
www.graverslanegallery.com

Long View Gallery
Washington, DC 20001
www.longviewgallerydc.com

Pittsburgh Center for the Arts
Pittsburgh, PA 15232
www.center.pfpca.org

Revision Space Gallery
Pittsburgh, PA 15201
www.revisionspace.com

Signature Designs
Moorestown, NJ 08057
www.signaturedesignsnj.com

Snyderman-Works Galleries
Philadelphia, PA 19106
www.snyderman-works.com

Wexler Gallery
Philadelphia, PA 19106
www.wexlergallery.com

Zenith Gallery
Washington, DC 20012
www.zenithgallery.com

THE SOUTH

530 Burns Gallery
Sarasota, FL 34236
www.530burnsgallery.com

Artspace, Inc.
Raleigh, NC 27601
www.artspacenc.org

Atlanta MADE
Atlanta, GA 30318
www.atlantamade.us

Fiberworks Studio
Alexandria, VA 22314
www.torpedofactory.org

Frank Gallery
Chapel Hill, NC 27514
www.frankisart.com

Heartwood Gallery
Saluda, NC 28773
www.heartwoodsaluda.com

Lark and Key Gallery
Charlotte, NC 28203
www.larkandkey.com

Michele Tuegel Contemporary
Art Gallery
St. Petersburg, FL 33701
www.mtcontempo.com

Piedmont Craftsmen Gallery
Winston-Salem, NC 27101
www.PiedmontCraftsmen.org

River Gallery
Chattanooga, TN 37403
www.river-gallery.com

Signature Gallery and Shop
Atlanta, GA 30305
www.thesignatureshop.com

Yeiser Art Center
Paducah, KY 42001
www.facebook.com/yeiserartcenter

Zeitgeist Gallery
Nashville, TN 37203
www.zeitgeist-art.com

THE MIDWEST

Begley Art Source
Evansville, IN 47708
www.begleyartsource.com

Brown County Art Guild Gallery
Nashville, IN 47448
www.browncountyartguild.org

Dairy Barn Gallery Shop
Athens, OH 45701
www.dairybarn.org

Editions Limited
Indianapolis, IN 46220
www.editionsltd.com

Fine Line Designs
North Ephraim, WI 54211
www.finelinedesignsgallery.com

Katie Gingrass Gallery
Milwaukee, WI 53202
www.gingrassgallery.com

Marta Hewett Gallery
Cincinnati, OH 45202
www.martahewett.com

Orchard Gallery
Fort Wayne, IN 46804
www.TheOrchardGallery.com

SOFA Chicago
Chicago, IL 60611
www.sofaexpo.com

Springfield Art Association
Springfield, IL 62702
www.springfieldart.org

Tory Folliard Gallery
Milwaukee, WI 53202
www.toryfolliard.com

THE WEST

Hockaday Museum of Art
Kalispell, MT 59901
www.hockadaymuseum.org

Houston Center for
Contemporary Craft
Houston, TX 77002
www.crafthouston.org

Surface Design Association
Albuquerque, NM 87154
www.surfacedesign.org

THE PACIFIC WEST

Applegate Gallery
Santa Monica, CA 90405
www.applegategallery.com

Avenue 9 Gallery
Chico, CA 95926
www.facebook.com/Avenue9Gallery

Bakersfield Museum of Art
Bakersfield, CA 93301
www.bmoa.org

Childhood's End Gallery
Olympia, WA 98501
www.childhoods-end-gallery.com

Cotsen Collection
Los Angeles, CA 90025
www.cotsen.org

Front Porch Gallery
Carlsbad, CA 92008
www.frontporchgallery.org

Gallery 825
West Hollywood, CA 90069
www.gallery825.com

Gallery Fine Art
Palm Desert, CA 92260
www.agalleryfineart.com

Hayward Area Historical Society
Hayward, CA 94541
www.haywardareahistory.org

Joyce Gordon Gallery
Oakland, CA 94612
www.joycegordongallery.com

Natoma 48 Gallery
Folsom, CA 95630
www.facebook.com/
TheGalleryat48Natoma

Orientations
Monterey, CA 93940
www.orientations.com

Pence Gallery
Davis, CA 95616
www.pencegallery.org

Ren Brown Collection
Bodega Bay, CA 94923
www.renbrown.com

RiverSea Gallery
Astoria, OR 97103
www.riverseagallery.squarespace.com

Studio 74
Fresno, CA 93711
www.studio-74.org

Visions Art Quilt Gallery
San Diego, CA 92106
www.visionsartmuseum.org

INTERNATIONAL

ARTexhibition Link – Gallery Uno
Projektraum
12049 Berlin, Germany
www.artexhibitionlink.com

Cat Street Gallery
Sheung Wan, Hong Kong
www.thecatstreetgallery.com

MacKenzie Art Gallery
Saskatchewan, Canada
www.mackenzieartgallery.ca

McManus Galleries
Dundee, Scotland
www.mcmanus.co.uk

Mountain Galleries at the Fairmont
Banff, Whistler, Canada
www.mountaingalleries.com

Orange Art Gallery
Ottawa, Canada
www.orangeartgallery.ca

Park Gallery
Falkirk, Scotland
www.falkirkcommunitytrust.org/venues/park-gallery

Quilters' Guild
York, England
www.quiltersguild.org.uk

Ruth Benzacar Galería de Arte
Buenos Aires, Argentina
www.ruthbenzacar.com

Salisbury Arts Centre
Salisbury, England
www.salisburyartscentre.co.uk

Saskatchewan Craft Council Gallery
Saskatoon, Saskatchewan, Canada
www.saskcraftcouncil.org

School Gallery
Paris, France
www.schoolgallery.fr

Shipley Art Gallery
Tyne & Wear, England
www.shipleyartgallery.org.uk
www.artexhibitionlink.com

Yael Rosenblut Gallery
Santiago, Chile
www.yaelrosenblut.com

MUSEUMS

The artists featured in this book are in the following permanent collections.

American University Museum
Washington, DC 20016
www.american.edu/cas/museum

Arkansas Arts Center
Little Rock, AR 72202
www.arkansasarts.org

Athenaeum Music and Art Library
La Jolla, CA 92037
www.ljathenaeum.org

Boston Museum of Fine Arts
Boston, MA 02115
www.mfa.org

Chicago Art Institute
Chicago, IL 60603
www.artic.edu

Cincinnati Art Museum
Cincinnati, OH 45202
www.cincinnatiartmuseum.org

The Cleveland Museum of Art
Cleveland, OH 44106
www.clevelandart.org

Craft and Folk Art Museum
Los Angeles, CA 90036
www.cafam.org

Dallas Museum of Art
Dallas, TX 75201
www.dma.org

Denver Art Museum
Denver, CO 80204
www.denverartmuseum.org

East-West Center
Honolulu, HI 96848
www.eastwestcenter.org

Erie Art Museum
Erie, PA 16501
www.erieartmuseum.org

Figge Art Museum
Davenport, IA 52801
www.figgeartmuseum.org

The George Washington University Museum
Washington, DC 20052
www.museum.gwu.edu

Hawaii State Art Museum
Honolulu, HI 96813
www.sfca.hawaii.gov

Hunterdon Art Museum
Clinton, NJ 08809
www.hunterdonartmuseum.org

International Quilt Study Center and Museum
Lincoln, NE 68503
www.quiltstudy.org

Madison Museum of Contemporary Art
Madison, WI 53703
www.mmoca.org

Michigan State University Museum
East Lansing, MI 48824
www.museum.msu.edu

Milwaukee Art Museum
Milwaukee, WI 53202
www.mam.org

Mingei International Museum
San Diego, CA 92101
www.mingei.org

Museum of Arts and Design
New York, NY 10019
www.madmuseum.org

Museum of Craft and Design
San Francisco, CA 94107
www.sfmcd.org

Museum of Geometric and MADI Art
Dallas, TX 75204
www.geometricmadimuseum.org

Museum of Modern Art
New York, NY 10019
www.moma.org

Museum of Northwest Art
La Conner, WA 98257
www.monamuseum.org

National Museum of Women in the Arts
Washington, DC 20005
www.nmwa.org

National Quilt Museum
Paducah, KY 42001
www.quiltmuseum.org

Neville Public Museum
Green Bay, WI 54303
www.nevillepublicmuseum.org

New England Quilt Museum
Lowell, MA 01852
www.nequiltmuseum.org

North Carolina Museum of Art
Raleigh, NC 27607
www.ncartmuseum.org

The Oakland Museum
Oakland, CA 94607
www.museumca.org

Philadelphia Museum of Art
Philadelphia, PA 19130
www.philamuseum.org

Racine Art Museum
Racine, WI 53403
www.ramart.org

Smithsonian Institution
Washington, DC 20006
www.renwick.americanart.si.edu

San Jose Quilt Museum
San Jose, CA 95113
www.sjquiltmuseum.org

Suffolk Museum
Suffolk, VA 23434
www.suffolkmuseumva.com

Texas Quilt Museum
LaGrange, TX 78945
www.texasquiltmuseum.org

The Textile Museum
Washington, DC 20037
www.museum.gwu.edu

University of Iowa Museum of Art
Iowa City, IA 52246
www.uima.uiowa.edu

Visions Quilt Museum
San Diego, CA 92106
www.visionsartmuseum.org

The Wadsworth Athenaeum
Hartford, CT 06103
www.thewadsworth.org

INTERNATIONAL

Braintree District Museum
Braintree, England
www.braintreemuseum.co.uk

City Art Centre – Edinburgh Museums
Edinburgh, Scotland
www.edinburghmuseums.org

Dalarnas Museum
Falun, Sweden
www.dalarnasmuseum.se

Kelvingrove Art Gallery and Museum
Glasgow, Scotland
www.glasgowlife.org.uk/museums

Museum of Art and History
Belfort, France
www.france-voyage.com

National Arts Centre
Ottawa, Canada
www.nac-cna.ca

National Centre for Craft and Design
Sleaford, England
www.nationalcraftanddesign.org.uk

National Museum of Scotland
Edinburgh, Scotland
www.nms.ac.uk/national-museum-of-scotland

Norfolk Museums & Archaeology Service
Norwich, England
www.museums.norfolk.gov.uk

Pierre Pauli Foundation
Lausanne, Switzerland
www.toms-pauli.ch

Savaria Museum
Szombathely, Hungary
www.savariamuseum.hu

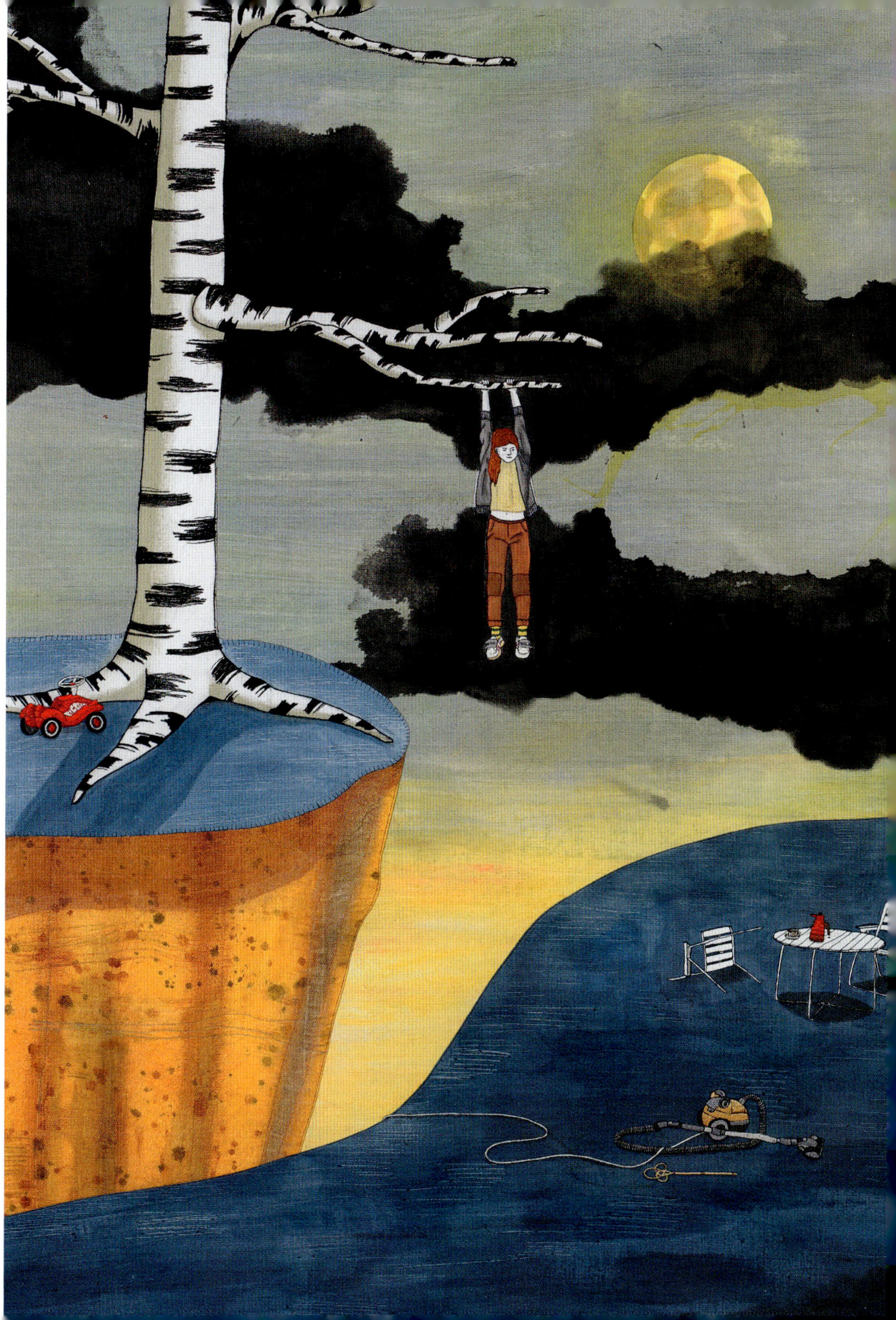

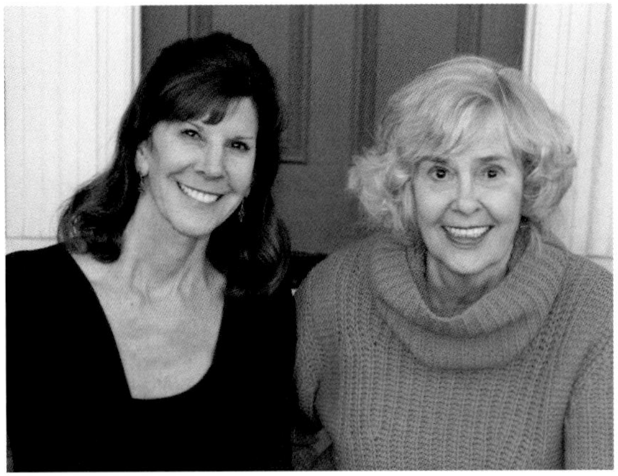

ANNE LEE
E. ASHLEY ROONEY

As coauthors, Anne Lee and E. Ashley Rooney balance each other and offer different experiences and perspectives: Rooney is the author of over fifty books, specializing in contemporary art and architecture; and Lee has researched, curated, and written about exhibitions at Vose Galleries in Boston. Exploring fiber art together has been a fascinating and fruitful journey they are eager to share. They have also coedited *Encaustic Art in the Twenty-First Century* (Schiffer).

MARCIA YOUNG

Marcia brings twenty years of publishing experience and a love of fiber arts and textiles to her work as founder and editor-in-chief of *Fiber Art Now,* an organization with a magazine at its center and a mission to inspire and connect the fiber arts and textiles community. She has juried several exhibitions and serves on the board of SAQA (Studio Art Quilt Associates) and on the collections committee at the Fuller Craft Museum, Brockton, Massachusetts.

MEREDITH RE' GRIMSLEY

Meredith received her MFA in 2002 and her BFA in 1999 in fabric design from the University of Georgia in Athens, Georgia. Today, this dislocated southerner is living the dream in the rolling hills of rural Pennsylvania with two amazing boys, an excellent husband, and their dog, Jefferson. She is a professor of fabric design at Bloomsburg University of Pennsylvania. Her work, including wearable art, installation, performance, and two- and three-dimensional forms, has been shown in numerous national and international venues in solo and group exhibitions.